NEO-CLASSIC DRAMA IN SPAIN

Neo-classic Drama
in Spain

THEORY AND PRACTICE

JOHN A. COOK

SOUTHERN METHODIST UNIVERSITY PRESS, DALLAS

1959

© COPYRIGHT 1959 BY SOUTHERN METHODIST UNIVERSITY PRESS

L. C. CARD 59-5737

PRINTED IN THE UNITED STATES OF AMERICA

To my wife
DAPHNE
and my daughter
DIANE

Preface

IN LITERARY BOOKKEEPING it has been the practice among critics of Spanish literature to write off the eighteenth century and the first third of the nineteenth as an almost complete loss, and to attribute the barrenness of Spanish literary production during that time to the hampering restrictions of neo-classicism. As a result research into the activities of this period has been limited almost entirely to an effort to prove that, even in the darkest moments of Spain's literary decadence, a considerable portion of Spanish writers resisted the doctrines of "pseudo-classicism" and championed the cause of literary freedom. Critics have left no stone unturned in their search for evidence of the persistence of that vein of native romanticism which produced the masterpieces of Golden Age literature and raised Spanish drama to a dominant position in Europe during the first half of the seventeenth century. An intense nationalism has in many cases prompted Spanish critics to explain the low quality of eighteenth-century drama in Spain as the result of literary subservience to France and Italy and to ignore the obvious truth that Spain had reached literary impotence and had produced no works of merit for almost a century before the introduction of neo-classic doctrines.

The author of this study feels that neo-classicism represented a natural and inevitable reaction against the affected style, bad taste, and irregularity into which Golden Age drama had degenerated. Although unproductive of literary masterpieces, the eighteenth century was a century of intellectual ferment. Spaniards were struggling to emerge from the ignorance and mental indolence that had accompanied their country's loss of political and economic supremacy and her steady decline in prestige among the nations of Europe. The truly dark age of Spanish drama lasted approximately from 1650 to 1750. This was followed by a half-century of twilight during which those Spanish intellectuals who envisioned a new and progressive

Spain were locked in combat with the forces of tradition. Neither political nor social conditions were favorable to a flowering of Spanish genius, and literary activity resolved itself largely into polemics between neo-classicists and nationalists. But during the entire time Spain was becoming increasingly aware of the intellectual activity that was taking place beyond her borders and was seeking new formulas to replace the old in social customs, sciences, and the arts. The eighteenth century and the early part of the nineteenth should not be written off by the student of Spanish literary history. It was a period of transition from the old to the new and as such deserves careful and sympathetic consideration.

It is recognized that this study represents a departure from standard practice in that all citations from foreign languages and the titles of all plays and critical works have been translated into English. This has been done, of course, to bring the work within the reach of a wider circle of readers.

In making these translations, the author has been well aware of the dangers involved. He knows that it is often impossible to find in English accurate and satisfactory equivalents for titles of foreign plays. Particularly is this true in the case of Spanish Golden Age comedies where clever and somewhat enigmatic wording was sometimes chosen to excite the curiosity of the public. To facilitate comparison both the translated and the original titles are given in an index.

Passages from plays and citations from critical works in verse have in all cases been translated into English prose, although for the sake of appearance the length of the original lines has usually been approximated. It is obvious that, even though the result may come reasonably close in thought content, in no case can these translations give an adequate idea of the dramatic effect of the passages or the style of the author.

While frequent reference has been made to the works of Menéndez y Pelayo, Cotarelo y Mori, Cueto, and other nineteenth-century critics, and material has been drawn freely from these sources, the conclusions of these writers with reference to the merits and contributions of neo-classicism have in many cases been rejected. Inasmuch as the studies that have been made of this period, with the exception of a short work by Robert E. Pellissier entitled *The Neo-Classic Movement in Spain During the XVIII Century*, have had as their primary purpose the exaltation of romanticism and have revealed a bias against neo-classicism, it has been considered advisable to examine carefully all plays and critical works cited and to give particular attention to authors' prefaces and notes and to contemporary comment in periodicals wherever they were available, rather than to rely upon later interpretations and evaluations.

The lists of play performances given in Cotarelo y Mori's works have been utilized, but these have been carefully checked against the record in the *Diario de Madrid*, since Cotarelo usually indicates only opening dates and gives receipts only in a few cases. For the lists of performances after 1818 it has been necessary to rely entirely upon the *Diario de Madrid* and the *Diario de Avisos de Madrid*, almost complete files of which are to be found in the Princeton University and University of Texas libraries.

The author wishes to express his sincere appreciation to these two institutions, and to the Boston Public Library, the New York Public Library, and the Library of Congress, as well as to the University of California, Cornell University, Dartmouth College, Harvard University, the University of North Carolina, Ohio State University, the University of Toronto, and Yale University, for the kindness and co-operation of their staffs while he was engaged in research in their libraries and for making many rare books and periodicals available to him as inter-library loans or in the form of microfilms and photostats. These works, supplemented by the author's private library of plays, books, and periodicals, assembled through a period of more than twenty years, have furnished the material for this study.

The author wishes also to acknowledge his indebtedness to Mrs. Margaret L. Hartley of the Southern Methodist University Press for her patient and efficient work in preparing the manuscript for publication.

JOHN A. COOK

Dallas, Texas
April 27, 1959

Contents

into comedies ridiculed. Violent disapproval of *graciosos*. Definitions of tragedy and comedy. Duty of government to promote regular theater as part of public education. Sensitiveness to foreign criticism. Sermon against immorality of Golden Age and contemporary plays. Campaign against *Autos Sacramentales*.

NEO-CLASSIC DRAMA IN SPAIN

I

The Beginning of Neo-classicism
In the Eighteenth Century

Historical, Political, and Cultural Background

THE CAUSES of Spain's decline, which reached its lowest point in the reign of Carlos II, can be traced to the period in which she attained the peak of her political power and cultural ascendancy. As a result of the policy of territorial expansion conceived and initiated by Fernando the Catholic, Spain was embroiled throughout the sixteenth and seventeenth centuries in almost uninterrupted wars with France, England, Italy, or the Netherlands. The attempt to control and administer her distant possessions exhausted her resources of men and materiel. She had performed miracles, but the very magnitude of the task she had assumed rendered its accomplishment impossible. Although catastrophes followed each other in rapid succession, Spain refused to accept or even to recognize the fact that she was not still the most powerful force in Europe. Like Don Diego in Eduardo Marquina's drama, *The Sun Has Set in Flanders,* she might well have said:

But, as I was once the master of two worlds and today when I tread a path I must ask permission from its owner, I cannot reconcile myself to being so little after having been so much; I try to cover with words the void in which I find myself; to conceal the fact that my sword is gone, I enlarge my cape; my attitude I need not change; for, though the world that I held in my hand has fallen, I still hold my hand aloft.[1]

The defeat of the Invincible Armada had been the turning point. Although the nation maintained an outward appearance of grandeur throughout the reign of Felipe II, the forces of decay were already at work. Ortega y Gasset, in his analysis of the reasons underlying the rise and fall of the Spanish empire, remarks:

But as we approach the Spain of Felipe III, we notice a terrible transformation. At first sight nothing seems to have changed, but in reality

3

everything is now made of cardboard and sounds hollow. The vigorous words of the past are still being repeated, but they no longer affect the heart. Exciting ideas have become mere topics for conversation. Nothing new is started in the field of politics, science, or morals. All the activity that is left is employed "in doing absolutely nothing new," in conserving the past—both in institutions and dogma—in smothering all initiative, all creative ferment.[2]

An overambitious foreign policy, the complete ineptitude of her rulers, and corruption in all aspects of Spanish life brought the nation at the close of the seventeenth century to such a desperate plight that any change of administration was welcome to the people as a whole. The extent of this degradation has been forcefully stated by Cueto:

> Perhaps there is no example in the history of the decay of nations of a more wretched picture than that presented by Spain in the last years of the seventeenth century and the first years of the eighteenth. No nation has expiated so severely and quickly the vanity of its people and the errors of its rulers. In all of the seventeenth century and particularly in the reign of Carlos II, Spanish society was slowly disintegrating and the magnificent structure that had been built during the glorious sixteenth century was collapsing stone by stone. God, the King, Honor, the three powerful levers that had moved and lifted spirits in that nation of soldiers, of gentlemen, and of poets, lost their strength or saw their influence twisted and perverted.[3]

The will of Carlos II, which left the throne of Spain to Philip of Anjou (Felipe V), grandson of Louis XIV, immediately subjected the nation to the full impact of the influence of French culture and involved it in the long Wars of the Spanish Succession. Spain thus became the pawn of France in her international intrigues. The French monarch is said to have presented his grandson to an assembly of nobles in the palace of Versailles with these words: "Gentlemen, behold the king of Spain. His birth has called him to that throne; the Spanish nation wanted and eagerly asked for him; I yield him to Spain in obedience to the decrees of Providence." The advice Louis XIV then gave to Felipe is an evidence of his cunning as well as of his determination to link the destinies of the two nations: "Be a good Spaniard; that is your first duty from this moment; but remember that you are a Frenchman by birth and maintain the union of both nations as a means of making them happy and of preserving the peace of Europe." The scene had been prepared so well beforehand that the Spanish ambassador exclaimed at this point, "What a wonderful thing! The Pyrenees have ceased to exist! They have disappeared into the earth, and from now on our two nations are one!"[4]

The accession of Felipe V to the throne of Spain in 1700 received, for the reasons we have given, the general approval of all classes, with the exception, of course, of an element of the nobility that espoused the cause of Carlos III of Austria and wished to see the continuation of the system that had so favored their interests during the reigns of the Spanish Hapsburgs. This did not mean, however, that the masses of the people were turning their backs on past tradition and were prepared to accept French culture as they had accepted a French monarch. The fame of the prosperity that had come to France during the reign of Louis XIV had spread beyond the Pyrenees, and the people fondly hoped that the new administration would put an end to the starvation and misery that had resulted from the maladministration and corruption of the preceding regime.

The reforms that were instituted by the newcomers, however, failed to satisfy either the masses or the nobility. The former, particularly, looked with increasing disfavor at the great number of Frenchmen who had transplanted themselves in Spain and who showed such contempt for her cultural and economic backwardness. Louis XIV, in his prophecy that the two nations would be welded into one, failed to take into consideration the character of the Spanish people. The fierce nationalism that had resulted from seven centuries of struggle against the Moors, and which had inspired the nation to colonize a new world and to dominate such a large part of Europe and Africa, was antagonistic to any reforms, no matter how beneficial and necessary they might be, that could be traced to a foreign source.

Any noticeable influence upon Spanish life was limited, at least for half a century, to the upper class, and particularly to the intellectuals. This group had become aware of the immense strides that France had made in the field of science and letters during the reign of Louis XIV and was certain that a goodly part of this progress had been due to the direct interest of the monarch and his ministers. The intellectual leaders of Spain must have envisioned something similar for their country. Every attempt, therefore, was made to flatter the egotism of the new king and to make him feel that through his sponsorship of the sciences and the arts he might equal in Spain

what had been accomplished in France and, in doing so, prove himself worthy of his illustrious grandfather. The erudite class felt
keenly the stigma that had been placed upon Spain by foreign countries because of her intellectual impotency and became increasingly
aware that drastic reforms must be made in all walks of life. The
Wars of the Spanish Succession occupied the attention of the king
so completely that for a decade at least he could take no part in
such reforms.

With the victory of Villaviciosa and the treaties of Utrecht and
Rastady, by which Spain relinquished her claims to European terri-
tory beyond the Pyrenees, Felipe was allowed the peaceful possession
of his throne on the peninsula, and it was now possible for him to
give some attention to economic and cultural improvements in his
kingdom. The morose and retiring nature of the king, however,
restricted the extent of his interest and participation in these
improvements. The few innovations that were made were due, not
to the initiative of the king, but to the influence of his court and of
members of the Spanish nobility like the Marqués de Villena.
In 1713, through the efforts of the latter, a Royal Academy was established in Madrid patterned closely upon the one that existed in Paris.
In his memorial to the king, the Marqués offered his house and his
person to this undertaking and solicited the approval and sponsorship of the sovereign:

> As this is a matter that affects the public good, the glory of the king-
> dom of your Highness, and the honor of the nation, it is not proper that
> it should come from any other hand than the one in which God has
> placed the defense of our liberty and from which we expect our com-
> plete restoration.[5]

The constitution of the Academy explains adequately the purpose
of its formation, the program it expected to follow, and the abuses it
hoped to correct:

> The principal purpose of this Academy being to cultivate and to fix
> the purity and elegance of the Castilian language, freeing it of all the
> errors introduced in it by ignorance, vain affectation, carelessness, and
> excessive freedom of innovation, its task will be to distinguish foreign
> words, expressions, or constructions from the native, the archaic from
> the modern, the low and uncouth from the courtly and lofty, the burlesque
> from the serious, and finally the appropriate from the rhetorical. With
> this end in mind, it is considered fitting to make a start immediately
> with the formation of a Dictionary of the Language, the most complete

that can be made, in which attention will be called to those words and phrases that are in good usage and those that are archaic . . .

After the Dictionary has been completed, the next tasks will be a Spanish Grammar and Poetics, and a History of the Language, in view of the need for such works in Spain . . .

And since creations of pure intellect are regularly within the jurisdiction of eloquence, which is concerned, not only with words, but also with concepts, the Academy will assume the task of examining some works in prose and in verse in order to propose in its criticism of them the rules that seem most appropriate for good taste both in thought and in writing.[6]

The so-called neo-classic movement in Spain in the eighteenth century was the embodiment of all the principles of restraint and regularity that had grown out of the efforts of Italian and French commentators to establish the *Poetics* of Aristotle and Horace as a guide to literary excellence. Those who were seeking to create a new Spain upon the ashes of the old could ill afford to neglect such basic manifestations of the Spanish spirit as lyric, epic, and dramatic poetry. Indeed, the neo-classic program was broadened to include almost every phase of human culture.

During the first half of the eighteenth century there was little apparent change in intellectual conditions or cultural institutions in Spain. Three works appeared, however, before 1740 that may be considered milestones in the development of a neo-classic program: the *Critical Theater* and the *Erudite Letters* of Father Feijóo; a periodical, the *Diario de los Literatos;* and Luzán's *Poetics.*

Feijóo

Although the middle and lower classes were opposed to the infiltration of new ideas and customs, it is evident that by the close of the first quarter of the eighteenth century considerable progress had been made in some quarters in introducing not only French ideas but also French habits of dress and speech. The greatest single force in preparing the intellectual class to accept reforms that affected every phase of their lives was the Benedictine monk, Father Feijóo. Though his works are usually cited to prove that long before romanticism appeared in Europe as a definite literary movement certain Spanish writers gave clear expression to its basic creed, his *Critical Theater,* published in eight volumes from 1726 to 1739, and his *Erudite Letters,* which appeared in five volumes from 1742 to 1760, probably more than any other works cleared the ground for

whatever success the neo-classic movement was to have in Spain.
In the second volume of his *Critical Theater* he attempts to analyze
the causes of the apparent antipathy that exists between Spaniards
and Frenchmen and concludes that this antipathy has arisen primarily from wars and political rivalry between the two nations,
rather than from innate differences of temperament. He feels that
the salvation of Spain as well as the peace of Europe depends upon
the friendly collaboration of the two countries:

> But coming back to the subject of the antipathy between Spaniards
> and Frenchmen, a fact which proves conclusively that their opposition,
> when it exists, is voluntary and not natural, is the friendship and good
> relations which exist between them today. We should all repeat our
> prayers to heaven that this friendship not be broken. Today upon the
> friendly union of the two kingdoms depends the successful outcome for
> Spain of the present negotiations on the peace of Europe, and our repose
> and tranquillity will always depend upon the same principle.[7]

His next statement shows that he is favorable, rather than opposed,
to the introduction of French culture and habits of industry:

> If one considers the intrinsic value of the French nation, he must admit
> that there is none more glorious no matter how it is regarded. Letters,
> arms, the arts, everything flourishes in that most opulent kingdom. It has
> given a great number of saints to Heaven, innumerable heroes to military
> campaigns, infinite wise men to schools. The valor and vivacity of the
> French makes them shine wherever they are found. Their industry should
> rather excite our admiration than our envy. It is true that this industry
> among the common people is so officious that it seems avaricious; but this
> industry is fitting to their position, because the humble are like ants to a
> state. From their mechanical activity the greatest empires draw all
> their splendor.[8]

Feijóo seeks to steer a middle course, condemning at the same
time the narrow nationalism of one group of Spaniards and the haste
with which those who have traveled in other lands or who have been
exposed at home to the influence of foreign culture turn against their
own customs:

> I notice in our Spaniards two extremes, equally reprehensible, in their
> evaluation of national things. Some exalt them to the skies; others beat
> them down to the abyss. Those who have not, either from association
> with foreigners or from reading books, extended their spirits beyond
> the confines of their fatherland, consider that everything good in the
> world is contained in their own country. From this arises that barbarous
> disdain with which they regard other nations, loathe their language, abom-

inate their customs, refuse to listen, or listen with scorn to their progress in the arts and sciences. It is enough for them to see another Spaniard with an Italian or a French book in his hand to condemn him as extravagant or ridiculous. They say that all that is good and worth reading is written in the Latin and Castilian languages; that foreign books, especially French, carry nothing new except trivialities.[9]

His remarks about the other group show that even in the university city of Oviedo in the north of Spain, French influence was becoming an important factor. Its influence must have been much more noticeable in the capital city of Madrid. Feijóo looks with contemptuous amusement upon Spaniards who disdain their native customs and manners and are too ready to accept those of other nations:

In their opinion, only in France can delicacy, order, and good taste be found; here everything is crude and barbarous. It is amusing to see some of these natives (whom I consider antinational) do violence to all their members in order to imitate foreigners in expression, movements, and mannerisms, striving to walk as they walk, sit as they sit, laugh as they laugh, curtsy as they curtsy, and imitate them in all they do. They do everything possible to denaturalize themselves, and I should be glad if they succeeded completely so that our nation might be rid of such figures.[10]

The conception of Feijóo as a precursor of romanticism has to a considerable extent been based upon an essay written in 1734, entitled "The I Do Not Know What." This is the essay that Menéndez y Pelayo calls a "true manifesto of romanticism,"[11] superior to everything that was known at that time in aesthetics. Critics who credit Feijóo with such originality have overlooked an essay written in Paris around the middle of the seventeenth century by the Jesuit priest, Father Bouhours. This essay also bears the title "The I Do Not Know What." There is no difference between the two works in the fundamental idea of the existence of an unexplainable something that gives charm to artistic creations independent of and superior to rules. We may compare the expressions of the two writers. Father Bouhours says:

The *I do not know what* pertains to art as well as to nature.... What charms us in paintings and statues is an unexplainable *I do not know what*. So those great masters, who have discovered that nothing is more pleasing in nature than that which pleases without one's knowing exactly why, have always endeavored to make their works agreeable by hiding their art with great care and skill. Delicate works in prose and in verse have an *I do not know what* of polish and refinement which gives them almost their entire value. . . . If one considers the things in this world we admire most, he will see that what makes us admire them is an *I do not know what* that surprises, dazzles, and charms us.[12]

Although the language is different, the following extract from Feijóo's essay is too close in thought to be a mere coincidence:

In many productions not only in nature but also in art, and even more in art than in nature, one finds, besides those perfections subject to rational comprehension, another kind of mysterious beauty which, flattering the taste, torments the understanding. Our senses feel it, but our reason cannot decipher it; and so, when we attempt an explanation, we can find no words or concepts that fit, and we get out of our difficulty by saying that there is an *I do not know what* that pleases, enamors, and charms us.[13]

There is nothing either in Feijóo's *Critical Theater* or in his *Erudite Letters* that shows any acquaintance with, or interest in, the poetry or drama of his day. In his discourse entitled "Glories of Spain," published in 1730, he discusses at considerable length Spain's contribution to the literature of the Roman empire but does not mention writers of the sixteenth or seventeenth centuries. He conveniently excuses himself from the necessity of dealing with literary works written by his countrymen in their native language by saying: "I have decided to end my discourse here because, although the last two centuries are as filled with illustrious accomplishments as all the preceding, their closeness to our time makes them so well known that it would be a waste of time to discuss them."[14] One important exception to the above statement occurs in his brief discussion of the influence of Spanish comedy upon the French theater. He has read some of the works of the French critic Saint-Evremond, and finds satisfaction in the latter's admission of the important role Spain has played in the development of European drama:

It would not be just to omit here the statement that modern dramatic poetry owes its origin almost entirely to Spain, since although the theater was developed first in Italy, the plays performed in it were rather an aggregate of amorous concepts than true comedy and remained in that condition until the renowned Lope de Vega gave them form and design. And though our dramatists have not conformed to the laws of ancient comedy, incurring for that reason the severe criticism of the French, the latter do not deny us the advantage we have over them in inventiveness and admit that their best authors have copied many of our plays. Let us hear this confession from one of the most discreet writers in prose and in verse that France has had in recent years, Saint-Evremond. "Let us confess," he says, "that the writers of Madrid are more fertile in invention than ours and this has been the main cause for our having taken from them most of the subjects of our comedies, giving them, however, more regularity and verisimilitude."[15]

Feijóo is not in complete agreement with the French critic in the last part of his statement and cites *The Princess of Elide* by Molière, which he calls "an unmistakable and clear adaptation of *Disdain Conquered by Disdain* by Moreto." There is, he says no more regularity in the French work than in the Spanish and, in fact, no noticeable irregularity in the Spanish original.

It should be remembered at this point that Feijóo is listing the glorious accomplishments of his countrymen and probably availed himself of the one bit of information he possessed about the relative merits of the French and Spanish theaters. It is hard to believe that, had he been familiar with the theaters of the two countries, he would have failed to call attention to *The Cid*, by Corneille, as the most important example of French indebtedness to the Spanish theater. Since this is Feijóo's only comment on Spanish drama, it is significant to note that he makes no defense of the irregularity of Spanish plays and takes the same basic position that we shall see adopted by subsequent advocates of neo-classicism, who insisted upon the contribution of the Spanish theater to the French in the seventeenth century and called attention to a number of Spanish plays that could be made regular with a few minor changes. The comedy cited by Feijóo was, in fact, one of the most regular plays that had been produced in Spain and was the one most frequently praised by neo-classicists. We shall see how Luzán uses it in his *Poetics* to illustrate correct dramatic technique.

Some Spaniards, Feijóo says, carry their admiration for French culture to such an extreme that they prefer the French language to their own and, even when they speak Spanish, include a liberal sprinkling of Gallic words. It has become fashionable to regard those who speak pure Spanish almost as barbarians. Feijóo hastens to disclaim any desire to discourage the study of foreign languages. He considers a knowledge of French absolutely essential in every field of erudition, since works have been composed in that language for which there are no substitutes in either Latin or Spanish. In experimental physics, which Feijóo seems to consider the most significant contribution of modern science, France has led the way and much information on this subject can be found only in French works. The same, he says, is true in history and geography. Feijóo's concern over the lack of progress of his nation in the field of science was amply justified. So backward, indeed, was scientific education in Spain even as late as 1752 that the Marqués de la Ensenada, in a report to Fernando VI, called attention to the fact that there was not a single chair of experimental physics, of anatomy, or of botany in any university in the country.

When he published the first volume of his *Critical Theater* in 1726, Feijóo believed that, with the exception of a few scientific terms, the introduction of foreign words into the Spanish language was entirely unnecessary; but by 1742, when he began to publish his *Erudite Letters,* he was moved to write a heated defense of the neologisms he had been compelled to use in his own writings. It would appear that criticism had come from some exponent of neo-classicism, for Feijóo goes off on a complete tangent and berates those who tie themselves servilely to rules. This is one of the passages so often quoted to show Feijóo's essentially romantic creed. The following passage will enable the reader to judge for himself the appropriateness of his remarks:

My Dear Sir:
    The tone in which you inform me that many people are reproving my introduction of new words into our language clearly indicates that you are one of that group. The notice does not frighten me or take me unawares, for I had foreseen that many would accuse me of doing so. The worst thing is that those who regard the use of foreign words as a literary sin place themselves in the class of supreme critics of style, although I would place them in the lowest class.
    It can be affirmed that those who tie themselves scrupulously to ordinary rules do not reach even a reasonable mediocrity. Man has never formed, nor can he ever form, a sufficiently comprehensive body of rules for any art. . . . I would agree quite readily with those who tie themselves servilely to rules, provided they did not try to subject everyone to the same yoke. They are justified in doing so because their lack of talent forces them to that servitude. Men of slight genius are like children in school who, if they attempt to write without guide lines, waste all their ink in blotches and scrawls. On the contrary, sublime spirits achieve their happiest strokes when they freely depart from ordinary rules. Let those who do not have strength to reach the summit remain on the slope, but let them not try to make dulness pass for mastery or brand boldness of inspiration as ignorance.

But to return to my subject. I will grant that the introduction of new or foreign words into a language is usually a vice. But, why? Because there are few who have the necessary skill to make that mixture. To do so one must have a subtle touch, a delicate judgment. I am assuming that there will be no affectation, or excess. I maintain that the use of a foreign word is permissible when there is no equivalent in one's own language, and also that, even though the same thing can be explained by a combination of two or more native words, it is better to use a single word, no matter what its source may be. For this reason, in less than a century, more than a thousand Latin words have been added to the French language and as many, or more, Latin and French words have been added to the Spanish. . . . There is no language that does not need the aid of others, because no language has words for everything.[16]

If we remove from the above passage that part which seems to have been inspired by personal resentment, we must admit that Feijóo's position is well taken and that he is entirely right in his insistence upon the constant necessity of enriching vocabulary to keep pace with human progress. There is no question of Feijóo's attitude toward all types of affectation in manners, speech, or literary expression. In this respect his affiliation with neo-classicism is clear.

Propriety of language must be distinguished from propriety of style, because the latter, within the same language, admits variation according to the ability and genius of the one who speaks or writes. Propriety of style consists in using expressions that are most natural and representative. In this regard, if one compares modern writers, he cannot deny that the French have the advantage over the Spanish. In the former one finds more naturalness; in the latter more affectation. Even in those French writers who cultivated the most lofty style, like the Archbishop of Cambray and Magdalene Scudery, one sees art pleasantly joined to nature. . . . Their writings are like gardens where flowers grow spontaneously; not like canvases where they are studiously painted. Spanish writing has been characterized for a long time by a childish affectation of rhetorical figures, a multitude of synonymous epithets, a violent arrangement of pompous words that make style not gloriously majestic but loathsomely bombastic. . . . Certainly in Spain there are few who distinguish sublime from affected style and many who confuse them.[17]

This condemnation of gongoristic style is particularly significant in that it constitutes one of the first attacks upon the literary taste that had prevailed in Spain for almost a century. Although Feijóo opposes a blind acceptance of foreign ideas and culture, there appears to be very little that he approves and believes should be perpetuated in the Spain of his day. It would, therefore, be a mistake to align him in any way with the forces of chauvinism. Probably no one of his time was more active in dispelling the errors that had characterized Spanish intellectual processes. He devoted his life to an attempt to lead his nation into the current of European ideology, combating all forms of superstition and intellectual intolerance. His ideas on scientific methods and philosophical concepts were far in advance of those held by his contemporaries. Vicente de la Fuente explains that Feijóo's membership in the Benedictine order and his salary as a teacher enabled him to buy books and to subscribe to journals that were entirely unknown to the vast majority of his countrymen.[18] Sempere y Guarinos has correctly evaluated the accomplishment of the Benedictine monk:

> The works of this scholar produced a useful fermentation; they made people begin to question; they directed attention to books that were very different from those found in Spain; they excited curiosity; and, in short, they opened the door to reason, which had been closed by indolence and false learning.[19]

The Diario de los Literatos

Closer association with France and an increasing awareness of the cultural accomplishments of that country slowly awakened the erudite class in Spain to a realization that, if their country was to take its place again among the progressive nations of Europe, some definite program of propaganda must be initiated. It was to meet this need that the *Diario de los Literatos* made its appearance in 1737. Increasing familiarity with the journalistic activity that had become such an important factor in the intellectual life of France quite naturally suggested that a similar medium might be effective in Spain. The editors, Francisco Manuel de Huerta, Juan Martínez Salafranca, and Leopoldo Jerónimo Puig, in a very flattering dedication to Felipe V, made a strong bid for his support by insisting that under his sponsorship the *Diario* might well deserve to take its place among the other outstanding accomplishments of his reign, such as the erection of the School for Noblemen's Sons, the formation of the Royal Library, the restoration of the Medical Society of Seville, and the establishment of the Royal Academy and the University of Cervera. In this same dedication the *Diario* admits that it expects a hostile reception from some quarters:

> The novelty of the idea and the criticism which must be made in

carrying out the purposes of this *Diario* warn us of the attacks it will suffer, a sufficient reason in itself to make us turn back; but encouraged by the favor of your Majesty upon which we are counting, we live with the conviction that under the shadow of your Majesty we shall be able to overcome the invectives and slander that come from envy and ignorance.[20]

In the introduction to the first volume the *Diario* announced its intention to pass impartially upon all new books published in Spain and declared that it would take as its guide the *Journal de Trévoux,* a French periodical, which had been characterized by fairness and moderation in its reviews of French and foreign literature. It was clear from the start, however, that the *Diario* had no intention of compromising with the extravagance and bad taste that pervaded the literature of the day. Indeed, it stated at the outset that it proposed to attack those books which, because of their chivalrous spirit and extravagant treatment, tended to foster the very defects that had been typical of the race. Among these defects the *Diario* cites "... the ridiculous customs in love-making which are still kept in our Spain and which are the consequence of the frequent perusal of books of chivalry, novels, and love comedies that, because of their arduous and spectacular nature, were the delight of past centuries."[21]

The *Diario* makes no concerted attack upon Spanish drama, although in its reviews of *Cruelty for Honor's Sake,* by Ruiz de Alarcón, and *The Tutoress of the Church,* by Tomás de Añorbe y Corregel, it gives clear evidence of neo-classic taste. It is true that it calls Alarcón one of "the first masters of dramatic art" and praises his comedy for "its pure and elegant style, its profound maxims and thoughts, its ingenious arrangement of incidents, and its sharp and spicy wit." The *Diario,* however, adds that these incidents are suited to the taste of a nation which is more diverted by the unusual than by the probable and that the subject is more appropriate for a tragedy than for a comedy. Its criticism of *The Tutoress of the Church* is almost entirely condemnatory. The subject cannot possibly be made to conform to the three unities without running counter to the tenets of the church, and the action is so extravagant that adequate staging would require an impossible assembly of machinery and of decoration.

Although no other reviews of plays are to be found in the *Diario,* it made, as we shall see later, a major contribution to the spread of neo-classic doctrines through the publication in its first year of a lengthy review of Luzán's *Poetics,* accompanied by a commentary of almost equal length.

Convinced of the justice of their cause and the necessity for reform in all phases of Spanish intellectual life, the editors reviewed works as they were published in philosophy, science, philology, history, church oratory, and literature. Although they made a sincere effort to be fair and moderate in their judgments, the books reviewed were of such low quality that praise was seldom warranted. Their unwillingness to compromise with ignorance, ineptness, and dishonesty in literary and scientific production brought upon the editors the wrath of writers who had become accustomed to complete freedom from censure. So much opposition was aroused from those Spaniards who were steeped in tradition and backward in intellectual development that the *Diario* was not able to adhere to its avowed policy of moderation. The tone of its criticism became progressively sharper as it found itself the target for the insults, slander, and threats of its opponents. The attacks so hampered the effectiveness of their program that the editors declared in February, 1742, "We labor as hard in defense as on the work itself. We began our task and continue like the builders of the walls of Jerusalem with sword in one hand and tools in the other."[22]

The only articles in the *Diario* that have literary merit in themselves and that show a highly developed critical judgment were written not by the editors but by two collaborators, Juan de Iriarte and José Gerardo de Hervás. The best-known essay of the latter, who wrote under the pseudonyms of "Jorge Pitillos" and "Don Hugo Herrera de Jaspedós," is his satire entitled "Against the Bad Writers of His Time," which, according to Cueto, reveals a complete assimilation of the ideas of Boileau.

The reasons underlying the founding of the *Diario de los Literatos* come to light in the prologues to the last volumes of that periodical. The editors declare that the inadequate and narrow type of instruction given to the youth of Spain had inspired in them during their early years a contempt for everything foreign, but that when intellectual curiosity had moved them to delve more deeply into the study of the arts and sciences and to study foreign languages they became convinced that the type of training they had received was responsible for the inferiority of contemporary Spanish culture, and "as a result of this knowledge and grieved at the harm that had been done to ourselves and to others, we proposed to apply our energy to disillusion our fellow countrymen by means of this invention."[23]

Nettled by the attacks of its opponents, the tone of the *Diario* became so sharp that some friends of the editors were moved to remind them of their declared intention to emulate the *Journal de Trévoux* in its courtesy and moderation. The *Diario* replied to the remonstrances in the prologue to the fifth volume:

... And if anyone wishes to object that in other countries the *Diarios* are written with more moderation, we reply that he has neither reflected upon the quality of foreign books nor upon the value and reputation of ours. Foreigners, as a rule, are well versed in the Latin and Greek languages, in ancient and modern erudition, avoid the most visible defects of style and method, and try to reason with some originality or to treat a subject with a new effectiveness. Therefore, the editors do not need to censure so harshly as we, who find many books written without style, without method, without originality, without erudition except that which is copied from the most ordinary writers ... and without proper regard for truth, ... and so we now admit that those who say that we should not censure them are right, because it is enough to say that they do not deserve to be called books but literary abortions, formless, and useless because of their lack of intellectual activity.[24]

Repeated attacks by its enemies brought about the suspension of the *Diario* for a short time in 1739 and its final downfall in 1742. Although the editors had fought a good battle, the forces of inertia, ignorance, and chauvinism had won a decisive victory. Both the writers and the public were satisfied with things as they were and would tolerate no interference, especially if it seemed to be based upon a desire to rebuild Spanish culture after a French pattern. As a result of the suspension of the *Diario de los Literatos,* Spain remained for nearly half a century with no literary or scientific journal worthy of the name. The few so-called periodicals that appeared during this time and that lasted as a rule not more than a year reflected the ideas of a single editor and were designed, as in the case of *El diario extranjero* and other periodicals by Nipho, and *El Pensador* by Clavijo y Fajardo, to cover a limited field or to figure in a literary polemic.

1. Eduardo Marquina, *En Flandes se ha puesto el Sol* (Madrid, 1910), Act IV.
2. José Ortega y Gasset, *España invertebrada (Obras,* segunda edición, Madrid, 1936), II, 782.

3. Leopoldo Augusto de Cueto, *Poetas líricos del siglo XVIII (Biblioteca de Autores Españoles,* LXI, 5). The initials B.A.E. will be used in future references to this collection.

4. Antonio Ballesteros y Baretta, *Historia de España y su influencia en la historia universal* (Barcelona, 1929), V, 8.

5. Juan Sempere y Guarinos, *Ensayo de una Biblioteca Española de los Mejores Escritores del Reinado de Carlos III* (Madrid, 1785), I, 59.

6. *Ibid.*, pp. 59-60.

7. Jerónimo Feijóo y Montenegro, "Antipatía de franceses y españoles," *Teatro Crítico*, Tomo II, discurso 9 *(Clásicos Castellanos*, XLVIII, 334).

8. *Ibid.*

9. Feijóo, "Paralelo de las lenguas castellana y francesa," *Teatro Crítico*, Tomo II, discurso 15 *(Clásicos Castellanos*, XLVIII, 256-57).

10. *Ibid.*, p. 257.

11. Feijóo, "El no sé qué," *Teatro Crítico*, Tomo VI, discurso 11.

12. Père Bouhours, *Entretiens d'Ariste et d'Eugène*, Dernière Edition (A Amsterdam, 1671), Sur la Copie imprimée a Paris, pp. 272-74.

13. *Ibid.*

14. Feijóo, "Glorias de España," *Teatro Crítico*, Tomo IV, discurso 14 *(Clásicos Castellanos*, LIII, 199).

15. *Ibid.*, p. 249.

16. Feijóo, "Introducción de voces nuevas," *Cartas Eruditas*, Tomo I, carta 33 *(Clásicos Castellanos*, LXXXV, 31-34).

17. Feijóo, "Paralelo de las lenguas castellana y francesa," *Teatro Crítico*, Tomo II, discurso 15 *(Clásicos Castellanos*, XLVIII, 264).

18. Feijóo, *Obras escogidas*, con una noticia de su vida y juicio crítico de sus escritos por Don Vicente de la Fuente *(B.A.E.*, LVI, xxvi-xxvii).

19. Sempere y Guarinos, *op. cit.*, III, 25.

20. *Diario de los Literatos de España; en que se reducen a Compendio los Escritos de los Autores Españoles y se hace juicio de sus obras desde el año 1737-1741*. 7 vols.

21. *Diario*, "Introducción," Vol. I.

22. *Diario*, "Prólogo," Vol. VII.

23. *Diario*, "Prólogo," Vol. VI.

24. *Diario*, Vol. V.

II

Luzán and His Age

Poetics of 1737

THE THIRD and most important stimulus to the development of the neo-classic movement in Spain was the appearance in 1737 of an *Arte Poética* to fill a vacuum that had existed in literary criticism in that country since the early years of the preceding century. It was only natural that such a work should come from someone who had received his education beyond the borders of Spain, because no training he could have received in that country would have enabled him to compose such a work. It was indeed fortunate for neo-classicism that a young Spaniard should have spent his formative years in Italy, where he had the opportunity to study the humanities and to acquaint himself with the Aristotelian rules of literary expression. This young man, Ignacio de Luzán, upon his return to Spain was shocked at the conditions that prevailed in the literature of his native land and particularly in the drama. He soon became convinced that the only remedy for the prevailing bad taste was the introduction of the classic precepts. To this end he published his famous *Arte Poética,* which was destined to become the code of the neo-classicists. Since this *Poetics* is the basis for nearly all subsequent statements of the rules by Spanish neo-classic critics, it may be well to examine in detail those sections that deal with tragedy and comedy, as well as the evaluation the author makes of the Golden Age theater.

Luzán was eminently qualified for the task he had assumed. From his long residence in Italy and his association with an erudite group in that country he had become convinced of the merits of classicism and, we are told by his son, in preparation for the composition of his *Poetics* he

... studied thoroughly the poetics of Aristotle and of Horace in their originals and the works of their commentators, in addition to the best treatises that had been written on the subject. He read carefully the most famous poets, both Spanish and foreign, ancient and modern; he took notes from them and made extracts and critical estimates from all of their works.[1]

In 1728 he presented to the Academy of Pantó the results of his labor in the form of six discourses which he entitled *Reasoning upon Poetry* and which formed the basis of the complete *Poetics* published at Zaragoza in 1737 after his return to Spain.[2] A second edition of this work, published in 1789,[3] contains certain suppressions and a number of additions. Luzán's son tells us that shortly after the publication of the first edition his father "began to rework several things in his *Poetics* and to add others which were rather essential, without ceasing to continue at the same time his offerings to the Muses, composing many Castilian and Latin poems."[4] Around the year 1751, after a residence in Paris, he was still working on these revisions. According to his son,

... His continuous association in Paris, not only with the best poets and the most distinguished scholars of France, but also with those of other nations, and at the same time the reading of many works he had not been able to examine before, refined his taste and broadened his perspective, so that he considered it necessary to look over his work again carefully, to revise it where necessary, and to add what was lacking.[5]

The editor of the second edition, D. Antonio de Sancha, explains the reasons for the republication of the *Poetics* and the changes that were made:

The first edition, which was pubished in Zaragoza in folio in 1737, does not correspond to the merit of the work, but to what could be done at the time in that city and to the facilities of its author. Having proposed to reprint it in the best form and in a practicable size, I had made three or four *pliegos*, when an erudite gentleman informed me that several additions and corrections which Luzán himself had made were in the possession of Don Eugenio de Llaguno. I wrote to Llaguno, who was at the Escorial, asking him whether it was true, and he answered that, in fact, Luzán, in his last years, at the request of his friends, undertook to revise his *Poética* in the time which his occupations and his delicate health permitted; that when he died he had made considerable progress, and that his widow delivered to Agustín Montiano, an intimate friend of the deceased, the printed copy, with what had been added and corrected both on the copy itself and on loose sheets; that at the death of Montiano he, Llaguno, gathered it all up and kept it in his possession until he delivered it to Juan Ignacio de Luzán, Canon of the Holy Church of Segovia, because the latter had assured him that he and his older brother intended to make a new edition of the *Poética*, adding other works of their father; that since the Luzáns still had not carried out their intention, he would ask them for the aforesaid copy and additions, not doubting that they would surrender them, because of the honor which would result to the memory of their father from the revised edition of a work that had brought him so much credit both in Spain and in foreign countries; and that if all the additions and corrections were not prepared for printing, he himself would assume the task of arranging them, manifesting in this manner his gratitude to Luzán for the excellent advice which he had received from him as a youth and which had been very useful. In fact, the Canon not only returned to Llaguno the printed copy and the manuscripts in the same condition in which they had been delivered to him, but afterward offered to write some memoirs of the life of his father to accompany this edition.

Both of these gentlemen fulfilled their offers, the first by arranging in their places the additions and corrections and especially the chapters which Luzán had enlarged but not completed, correcting them where necessary in that part which pertained to the history of Spanish versification and dramatic poetry . . . and the second by sending the memoirs of the life of his father.[6]

Menéndez y Pelayo, although admitting that "generally speaking, the additions and corrections improve the text and usually refer to books that Luzán had not read before . . . or to historical notices about our ancient poetry and versification," notes some suppressions which he considers very suspicious. He suggests that Llaguno, who prepared the work for publication, "may have had the audacity to alter the text in support of his opinions, which were more radically neo-classic than those of Luzán."[7] As we shall see, however, these omissions in no way affect the tone of Luzán's evaluation of the Spanish *comedia*.* Indeed, the praise of Golden Age dramatists omitted in the second edition is more than equaled by new expressions of admiration for the genius of these writers. In the section which deals with the theater, the only significant change is in the addition of two chapters at the beginning of Book III of the 1789 edition: Chapter I, which is entitled "Spanish Dramatic Poetry, its Beginnings, Progress, and Present State"; and Chapter II, which is called "On the Rules Which Are Supposed to Govern Our Dramatic Poetry."

Menéndez y Pelayo, after saying that the first edition "is the only

*The term *comedia* will frequently be used in this volume to refer to all Golden Age plays, inasmuch as no distinction was made in Spain at that time between tragedy and comedy, all full-length theatrical productions being called "comedies."

one that Luzán directed himself, and so we may believe reflects his ideas more exactly," proceeds to make a compendium, presumably of the 1737 edition, without indicating that he is, in fact, drawing material from the second edition which is not found in the first. Indeed, from the new material in the second edition, the complete reliability of which Menéndez y Pelayo questions, comes one of the principal passages he cites as evidence of Luzán's admiration for Golden Age dramatists.[8]

In spite of the fact that since the opening years of the eighteenth century Spain had been subjected to the influence of French culture in court circles, and although the numerous Frenchmen who were attached to the court of Felipe V had found many imitators among those Spaniards who were sympathetic to foreign rule and who aped the customs and dress of the foreigners, the national spirit had remained largely unaffected among the middle and lower classes. Luzán must have realized that his *Poetics* would be received as a bombshell and sought in every way possible, without surrendering his literary principles, to soften the shock. We find, therefore, that his entire *Poetics* has a persuasive tone and is calculated to appease the resentment which his countrymen might feel upon seeing the literary precepts of their idols attacked. Fr. Miguel Navarro, in his "Approbation,"[9] begs the readers to withhold judgment until they have read the praise Luzán gives to dramatists of the Golden Age. He lists the pages where this praise may be found and adds: "In these and other pages they will see clearly the high esteem in which he holds our dramatists wherever they gave evidence of skill by conforming to art and will not take amiss his censure of some substantial errors."[10]

Fr. Manuel Gallinero, in his "Censure," prefaces his remarks with a recognition of his own limitations, but welcomes the opportunity to criticize the work, because he finds that it follows so admirably Horace's precept of blending the delightful and the useful. He comes strongly to the defense of Lope, Solís, and Calderón against foreign critics:

Although our Spanish poets have fulfilled in practice all the perfection to which the rules of theory conduce, other nations condemn their works as little adjusted to art, their censure being so severe, especially against comedies, which they treat as the despicable object of their criticism and laughter, without pardoning in their unjust severity Lope de Vega, Solís, or the inimitable Calderón. In regard to the first, their censure might be more tolerable if their laughter and scorn were not entirely unfair, because this author, compromising with the ignorance of the masses, was forced to write in a different manner, deviating at times from the precepts of art, in order to accommodate himself to the taste of the untutored, as he himself says in his *New Art of Writing Comedies*.[11]

This reason, Gallinero says, was noted by the author of the annotations of Boileau's *Poetic Art* "to moderate the harshness with which Boileau treated that great genius in his censure, but the evaluation foreigners make of Calderón and of Solís can never be justified before the tribunal of discretion, since their defects are so few and so slight that they might easily be pardoned."[12]

Gallinero is unwilling to admit that ancient art cannot be improved. His ideas are quite similar to those expressed by the Golden Age dramatist, Tirso de Molina, in his *Orchards of Toledo* and anticipate the arguments of romanticists of the nineteenth century:

I hold that this excessive severity proceeds from the fact that our poets having achieved in their poems an excellence of art, which the ancient teachers could not attain (since in the time of Aristotle comic poetry did not have all its perfection and beauty), these critics condemn the improvements themselves as disordered departures from the rules, without considering that these same rules may be improved with the skilful addition of excellencies. Greater defects than are noted in the comedies of Calderón, Solís, and other authors were reproved by some critics of Paris in the comedy *The School for Wives*, composed by Molière for . . . the theater in 1662, which obliged the author, one of the most famous in France, to write a *Critique* in defense of his work; and to the objection that it did not observe the rules of art, he answered, in my opinion discreetly, that "these scrupulous critics confuse the ignorant with their rules, bewildering them every day, in such a manner that it seems to one who hears them speak about this matter that these rules are the greatest mysteries in the world, and nevertheless they are nothing but some convenient observations, which have been made by common sense, upon those things that can mar the pleasure which results from this kind of poetry, and the same common sense which made these observations at an earlier time makes them now every day without the help of Aristotle or of Horace. I should like to know whether the great rule of all rules is not to please, and whether a theatrical work which has achieved this end has not followed a good road. Do they claim the whole public is deceived about this and is not a competent judge of what pleases it?" (Molière, *Critique de l'Ecole des femmes*.)[13]

Gallinero believes that Luzán has shown due moderation in his

Poetics because he has tempered the severity of his criticism with
words of praise, applauding Spanish dramatists in the main, but reproving "with zealous indignation" these same writers whenever he
considers that their negligence has disfigured the beauty of their
creations. Gallinero leaves no doubt about his own position and his
admiration for Golden Age drama. One has the feeling that, had he
realized that Luzán's *Poetics* would be the signal for a concerted
attack against the *comedia*, he would have refused to allow his
"censure" to accompany the work.

Luzán himself, in his "Word to the Reader," goes to the extreme
in denying any desire to detract from the credit due to Spanish
dramatists of the Golden Age. He has heard, even before his work
has come from the press, that some are imputing to him ideas which
he does not hold or twisting his words so that he himself does not
recognize them. The mere mention of rules seems to have alarmed
many and caused them to fear that he is recommending something
entirely new in dramatic technique. He hastens to say, therefore:

> First of all, I say, do not condemn the rules and opinions in this work,
> because, although they may seem new to you in that they are different
> from what the masses have been accustomed to up until now, I assure you
> that they are far from being new, since two thousand years ago these
> same rules (or, at least, all that is substantial in them) had already been
> written by Aristotle and afterward have been successively epilogued by
> Horace, commented upon by many scholars, spread through all the cul-
> tured nations, and generally approved and followed.[14]

Luzán insists that all he says in his work is based upon reason and
on the venerable authority of the wisest and most famous scholars.*
If some expression or censure, especially of the comedies of Calderón
and of Solís, seems to the readers too severe, he wishes them to bear
in mind that he is only repeating what others have said, or only
following the example of an officer who, to quell a popular uprising,

---

*Cano, in his careful study of the sources of Luzán's *Poetics*, finds that some-
where in the work Luzán finds an opportunity to cite all of the following French
critics: Lamy, Boileau, Rapin, Dacier, Madame Dacier, Le Bossu, Corneille, Crousaz,
Conti, Voisin, Racine, and Fontanelle; and the following Italian commentators:
Muratori, Vettore, Benio, Minturno, Gravina, Monsignani, Orsi, Crescimbeni, Quara-
drio, Trissino, Tasso, Robortello, Paccio, Piccolomini, Pallavicino, Mazzonio, Maggio,
Bonamici, and Castelvetro. Of the Spanish he cites only González de Salas and
Cascales. (Juan Cano, *La Poética de Luzán* [Toronto, 1825], pp. 8-10). The princi-
pal sources for his chapters on tragedy and comedy are, however, the Italians:
Muratori, Benio, Minturno, Robortello, and Donato; and the French: Le Bossu,
Corneille, Boileau, and Dacier.

lays hand on the first one he meets even though that one may not be the most guilty. Certainly, he says, Calderón and Solís are not the most culpable and "the scorn with which some speak of our comedies should, with greater reason, be applied to writers of lesser rank and of a different class." He believes that this frank declaration is due the merit of these two poets, "to whose genius and success I pay special tribute, as will be seen in several places in this book."

As one reads the "Approbation" by Navarro, the "Censure" by Gallinero, and Luzán's own prefatory remarks, he is made aware of the trepidation with which all of these men approached anything that might appear to be a condemnation of the Spanish *comedia.*

As justification for writing a *Poetics* Luzán says that Aristotle's work has undergone mutilation since it was originally written, and that, in spite of various commentators, obscurities still exist. Scholars in Italy and in France have written treatises on poetics in which the most intricate points of art have been clarified. Only in Spain has this type of scholarship been neglected, with the result that not a single complete and perfect treatise on poetry exists in that country. To this supposed lack of instruction on the principles of art Luzán attributes the corruption of poetry during the preceding century, particularly in the field of drama. He is unwilling to concede that the absence of such works is due to lack of talent and insists that if Spaniards had devoted a part of the time they gave to writing poetry to an explanation of the rules of their art, Spain would have a plentiful number of perfect treatises with which to discipline her poets. He says further that if Lope de Vega, Calderón de la Barca, Solís, and others had combined study and art with their natural lofty talent, Spain would have such well-written comedies that they would be the envy and admiration of other nations, instead of being the object of their criticism and laughter; "but with regrettable loss, we see such unusual qualities with which nature endowed them, misused for the simple reason that, deceived by a common error, they thought their genius alone was enough to enable them to succeed."[15]

Luzán has read the *Illustration, or Commentary on the Poetics of Aristotle* by the Spanish scholar Joseph Antonio González de Salas, and sharply disagrees with him when, after censuring the affected obscurity of lyric poets of his day, he flatters the writers of comedy as being relatively free from that fault. Luzán seems to know nothing of the *Philosophia Antigua Poética* by Pinciano and says that he has seen no Spanish treatise on poetics except González de Salas' work and the *Poetical Tables* by Francisco Cascales. These scholars, he admits, have written with some authority on poetic precepts and on tragedy, following and commenting upon the *Poetics* of Aristotle; but he neither censures nor praises their efforts, evidently considering their works incomplete or inaccurate in their treatment of the rules. The *New Art of Writing Comedies* by Lope de Vega he considers unworthy of serious consideration. The lack of treatises on poetry "could scarcely be filled by a work whose fundamental ideas and principles are directly opposed to reason and to the rules of Aristotle, which have always been the most venerated by all good poets."[16]

After dealing with poetry in general, Luzán discusses in Book III the origin, progress, and definitions of tragedy. It is only natural that he should follow the practice of Aristotle and later scholars in discussing tragedy before comedy. In due deference to the master he starts with Aristotle's own definition:

> Tragedy is an imitation of a serious action or (as some wish) illustrious, and good; complete and of proper magnitude, with verse, harmony, and dance (each of these being done separately), and which, not by means of narration, but by means of compassion and terror, purges the heart of this and other passions.[17]

Inasmuch as all commentators are not in agreement on some points in Aristotle's definition, Luzán proposes one that he considers clearer, more intelligible, and better adapted to modern drama:

> Tragedy is a dramatic representation of a great change of fortune which befalls kings, princes, and personages of high rank and dignity, whose falls, deaths, misfortunes, and dangers excite terror and compassion in the hearts of the spectators and cure and purge them of these and other passions, serving as an example and warning to all, but especially to kings and persons of the highest rank and power.[18]

Luzán approves Le Bossu's doctrine, which he says is based directly upon Aristotle, with reference to the construction of the plot:

> First it is necessary to begin with the moral instruction which one wishes to teach and conceal under the allegory of the plot. . . . Having found the moral that is to serve as a basis and foundation for the plot, it is necessary to reduce it to an action which is general and imitated from

real actions of men and which will contain in allegorical form the aforesaid maxim.[19]

According to Le Bossu, if one wished to construct a "rational plot"
he would use names of his own invention. A plot, however, which
dealt with pretended names and private families, being of no
importance to the public, would not be suitable for tragedy and
could only serve for comedy. Le Bossu added that a plot could be
covered with historical truth in such a manner that the fiction
would scarcely be noticed. This might be achieved by seeking in
history the names of those persons to whom an action had happened
similar to the one chosen for the plot.

Le Bossu's plan seems to Luzán very practicable for comedy;
but for tragedy, the themes of which are taken from history, he prefers to follow Benio and believes that it would be easier and more
natural for the poet, since he already knows that the moral purpose
of tragedy is to correct and purge the passions and to inspire compassion and fear, to go first to history and to seek in it a case adapted
to tragedy—that is, a change of fortune, or a grave danger to some
king or some other illustrious person—and, having found this historical plot, to form from it the complete tragedy with names, episodes, and circumstances in keeping with the rules of that genre.
Luzán shows, however, his respect for Le Bossu's opinion by adding
that he does not wish to contradict an author of such merit and
only wishes to make the composition of plots easier for poets by proposing to them another method which, in his opinion, is more practicable. He says, moreover, that even Le Bossu has admitted that this
plan may be used at times.

Luzán agrees with Aristotle that the plot must be complete; that
is, it must have a beginning, middle, and end. The beginning is that
which of necessity must precede everything else; the end must follow something but leaves nothing to follow it. The middle is that
which has something before and after it. Luzán cites *Disdain Conquered by Disdain* by Moreto as an example of a play with a properly
constructed plot:

In the comedy, *Disdain Conquered by Disdain*, the plot is as follows:
Carlos, Count of Urgel, in love with Diana, a princess who is extremely
cold and opposed to love and marriage, believing it an impossible task
to conquer her coldness by the regular means of love and courtship,
chooses to pretend indifference and disdain; and by this strategy he
achieves his purpose, since Diana, overcome by the pretended disdain

of Carlos, gives him her hand. In this action the *beginning* is this: Carlos,
in love with Diana, and despairing of conquering her coldness by any
other means, upon the advice of an astute servant, chooses to pretend that
he is indifferent and opposed to love. It is obvious that this precedes all of
the rest of the action and that it leaves dependencies to follow, since the
action remains imperfect and in suspense, if one does not know how
Carlos' plan is put into execution and how it turns out. The *middle* of
this plot, or action, is all that which Carlos does to carry out his plan
to convince Diana of his pretended disdain, and all that which Diana
does to overcome his coolness. It is evident that this requires something
antecedent, that is, the coldness of Diana, the passion of Carlos, and his
determination to affect indifference and disdain. This *middle* leaves
something which must follow, because the action is unfinished and the
audience is in suspense, desiring to know the end of this strategy and the
outcome of Carlos' plan. The *end* is this: Diana, overcome by Carlos'
disdain, ... chooses him for her husband; Carlos, therefore, sees his
strategy successful and his love rewarded. It is clear that this last part of
the action is the consequence of the preceding *beginning* and *middle* and
that it leaves nothing to follow, since the curiosity of the spectators is
entirely satisfied.[20]

According to Luzán, it is not so important to know that a plot
must be complete, with a beginning, middle, and end, as to know
where to begin and where to end the action. Horace, he says, did
not censure those poets who started the story of the return of Dio-
medes with the death of Meleager and the Trojan War with the par-
turition of Leda because their plots did not have a beginning, middle,
and end, but because they chose an improper point as a beginning.
The proper time and place to end the action, in Luzán's opinion, presents no difficulty, for Aristotle has made it clear that actions should
"end when things have changed from felicity to infelicity or the
contrary."[21]

It is much more difficult to determine where to start the action.
Upon this subject Aristotle has said nothing specific, and Luzán
is forced to attempt a clarification of the problem. As a starting point
he insists upon the difference in duration of tragedy and comedy as
compared with the epic. The action of tragedy and comedy is
limited to a few hours, while the epic has no definite duration. The
poet will choose as the starting point for his tragedy or comedy "that
part of the action, which, from beginning to end, will require no
more time than that covered by the plot, if he wishes to form it according to the rules of art."[22] Luzán realizes that it would be practically impossible to compose a tragedy or comedy if the whole plot

were restricted to the material time which the action lasts on the stage. He provides, therefore, for the narration of that portion of the plot which precedes the opening of the action of the play. He cites as an example the comedy *Disdain Conquered by Disdain*, in which Carlos tells his servant Polillo the beginning of his love and thus indirectly informs the audience through narration of the nature and disposition of Diana, and of the reasons that move him to the decision he has made; all of these things having preceded the opening of the play.

Another requirement of the plot, prescribed by Aristotle, is that it be of proper and perfect magnitude. Luzán interprets this to mean that the plot should not be so charged with incidents that it is tiresome and cannot be followed easily, or so thin that it makes no impression on the memory. The poet should endeavor to give variety to his plot, which he will be able to do by varying the character and inclinations of the persons and their language. If all the characters in a play are uniform, all good or all bad, all valiant or all cowardly, the result will be disagreeable and tiresome. Luzán maintains that Solís sinned in this respect in his comedy, *The Castle with the Secret*, by giving to the four principal persons the same character and disposition.

A plot should combine the marvelous and the probable. Luzán realizes that these two conditions seem contradictory "because the marvelous and extraordinary almost always border on the improbable and incredible."[23] He resolves the difficulty by saying that Aristotle preferred the marvelous for the epic and the probable for dramatic poetry. Luzán cites Madame Dacier as his authority for saying that in the epic the marvelous should occupy first place. A plot may be made marvelous provided it not be at the expense of probability. Luzán agrees with Aristotle in preferring a convincing impossibility to an unconvincing probability. This applies, he says, to historical truths which at times are incredible. In this case the poet will do well not to use dramatic plots which are improbable even though they may be supported by history, and to use instead an invented probability.

With regard to whether tragic plots should be taken from history or invented, Luzán is persuaded by reason and by the authority of Aristotle that both types are admissible. He chooses, however, to follow Benio and Muratori in giving preference to plots derived from history and accepts the latter's recommendation that plots not

be taken from recent history, since the details may be so well known
to the audience as to make it difficult for the author to vary the circumstances and the names and to adapt the subject to the theater.
He does not object, however, to Racine's contention that plots may
be taken from recent history provided the scene is in distant countries, because "to the public a thousand leagues in distance is the
same as a thousand years in time."[24] In the plot of comedies this
problem does not arise, because a comedy is neither better nor worse
because its plot is true or invented. The reason for this is that the
actions of private individuals are not known beyond the district
where they happen, nor is the memory of them preserved in
history. Even though it may seem that the freedom of the poet is
very much limited by a restriction that prevents him from deviating
openly from history which is well known to all, Luzán does not consider this objection a serious one. If the subject is such that it cannot be adjusted to probability and to the rules of the theater, it
should be abandoned. If the events admit some variation and can be
handled according to the rules, the poet can then use his privilege
and liberty, taking away and supplying what he deems best.
Although he cannot alter the basic story, he may change the circumstances and the minor personages. This license is based upon the
assumption that the audience has only a scant knowledge even of
notorious historical events.[25]

Luzán considers unity of plot "a quality that is indispensable and
necessary for perfection."[26] Under unity of plot he includes not only
action, but also time and place. All of the various parts of the plot
must be directed to the same end and to the same conclusion.
"They must be so coherent, so linked to each other, that if any one
is taken away, the plot will remain imperfect and mutilated."[27]

Aristotle condemned certain writers who narrated in verse all the
deeds of Hercules or of Theseus, believing that their plots had sufficient unity because they dealt with only one individual. Luzán condemns, in his turn, *The Daughter of the Air* by Calderón and other
similar Spanish comedies which, he says, should be called histories
in verse rather than comedies.

No less necessary, in Luzán's opinion, is the unity of time, which
he defines as follows: "Unity of time, in my opinion, means that the
duration of the action of the play should be identical with the time
required for the performance on the stage."[28] He is well aware that
authors of poetics have differed widely in their interpretation of this

unity, allowing twelve, twenty-four, thirty, and even forty-eight hours. He is unable to agree with any of these interpretations and asks: "What unity can there be in two periods of time so divergent as the space of three hours, which is the time of performance, and the space of twelve, twenty-four, or forty-eight hours, which is supposed to be the duration of the plot?"[29]

Many, Luzán realizes, will say that it is impracticable to restrict the plot of a tragedy or comedy to three or four hours; that it is hard enough to limit the action to one or two days. He answers that the fact that it is difficult proves nothing. He is willing to grant that it is difficult to conform perfectly to the unity of time and that few authors have succeeded in doing so. For this reason good writers have composed very few dramatic works and have contented themselves with very simple plots in order not to violate verisimilitude. On the contrary, bad and ignorant poets, "free from this yoke and from others which the observance of the rules imposes, have written with great ease hundreds of comedies for the theater." Although Luzán does not mention Lope de Vega, Tirso de Molina, and Calderón at this point, he must have been thinking of their fecundity. He is convinced that Aristotle intended to fix one period of the sun as the extreme limit of the action of a play and did not mean to exclude actions of shorter duration. He places reason, however, even above the authority of the master and says that this authority is not binding if it contradicts reason.*

Luzán is willing to concede that, inasmuch as the audience does not measure time exactly, the dramatist may extend the action one or two hours more. Since the doctrine of the unities is based upon the principle of verisimilitude, he approves Corneille's recommendation that the poet leave out of his play all allusions to time, whether oral or visual. In this manner the spectator will be more ready to accept slight infractions of the unity of time. If, however, in the same comedy a woman conceives and gives birth, or one who at the beginning was a child appears later as a man, the audience will realize that the action lasts many months or many years. Luzán modifies his severity somewhat at the close of his discussion and

*The rigid interpretation of the unity of time dates from 1550 when Maggi sought a logical basis for this unity. In 1561 Scaliger based it entirely upon the principle of dramatic illusion, saying that, "since the whole play is presented on the stage in six or eight hours, it is not in accordance with the exact appearance of truth that within that brief space of time a tempest should arise and a shipwreck occur, out of sight of land" (J. E. Spingarn, *A History of Literary Criticism in the Renaissance* [New York, 1925], p. 96).

says: "Finally, if the poet cannot limit the plot of his tragedy or comedy to so short a space and wishes to follow the opinions already mentioned, allowing twelve hours, twenty-four hours, or two days, his plot will not be as exact as it should be, but it can be tolerated."[30]

Luzán finds the unity of place "a difficult and rough problem." Aristotle made no mention of this requirement and Luzán is forced to conclude that, since it is a natural consequence of the unity of time, the Greek scholar must have considered such mention superfluous. So thoroughly does Luzán believe in the doctrine of "illusion of reality" that he considers it ridiculous to assume that the actors can travel to distant places while the spectators remain seated in one spot. He applies the doctrine of verisimilitude rigidly and defines the unity of place in the following terms:

> This unity consists, then, in having the place where the characters are supposed to be and to speak the same from the beginning to the end of the drama.... Let us suppose that in a comedy the scene represents a street in Zaragoza. I say that the scene must be the same street throughout the entire comedy.[31]

In spite of the dogmatism of his original statement, Luzán later concedes that it is a "slight and pardonable error" to place one act in the Street of the Cosso and another in the Plaza del Pilar. But if the scene shifts from the Cosso to the Arenal of Seville, or to a palace on the Island of Cyprus or Mount Atlantis in Africa, no one will be able to endure such an absurdity. He is well aware that other critics do not define the unity of place so rigorously and allow the scene to represent an entire city and some leagues around it. Corneille, he says, considered this license excessive and preferred that the scene be limited to two or three parts of the same city. After struggling with his conscience, Luzán is forced to confess that even the latter concession appears to him a serious violation of verisimilitude. It requires, he says, a great strain on the imagination of the audience to accept that a place which shortly before was supposed to be an antechamber of a palace has become, without any actual change in the scene, an open field outside of the city and that it should then become a ladies' drawing room. He believes that to avoid this difficulty there have been introduced in the Italian operas and in the comedies which are called *de teatro* in Spain, the practice of changing scenes, making disappear as by magic what was a hall, and appear in its place a garden, and then transforming the garden into a bedroom, and this into a beach where the sea and a naval armada can be seen.[32] Luzán considers that all of these metamorphoses are extravagant and do violence to the intelligence of the spectators. He recognizes at the same time that it is not reasonable to suppose that the characters will always assemble in one place to talk and to act, inasmuch as they will be of different dispositions and have different aims. He admits also that it seems incongruous to represent all the various episodes as occurring in one place.

But as on the other hand it is highly improbable, incompatible, and against all reason, that in the same invariable place, for example, in the same room, there should come for the purpose of speech or action the persons of the comedy or tragedy, who are supposed to be of different dispositions and with different aims, and perhaps with enmity toward each other; and that all the intrigue and incidents should happen in that place, that there two rivals should quarrel, ladies should visit, lovers should meet, letters should be written, strolls be taken, songs sung, secrets entrusted, and similar things which no man of sane judgment will concede to be probable in the same place; the result of all this is that it is extremely difficult and almost impossible for a poet, no matter how much he works and sweats, to give perfect unity of place to his plot.[33]

Luzán suggests as a solution of this difficulty the expedient proposed by the Italian scholar Geronimo Baruffaldi. This plan would provide for a stage divided horizontally into as many sections as the performance of the play requires. In this manner, one scene might represent, for example, a room, another a street, and another a garden. Luzán agrees with Baruffaldi that the ancients must have used such divisions, because without such an expedient their plays would have lacked verisimilitude. He grows more enthusiastic about his proposal as he proceeds. This new invention, he says, would avoid much inconvenience in trying to conform to the unity of place,

. . . which in this manner would be observed perfectly, the scene not changing throughout the drama and the place of performance being the same, although divided into parts which would be contiguous; the persons would speak and act where it suited them according to their purposes and natures; they would take their strolls in the street and not in a bedroom, visits would be received in a drawing room and not in a public square; there would be a garden where an enamored lady might indulge in soliloquies; and finally the poet could more easily delight the audience with new and strange incidents, without having an improper scene make these things incredible.[34]

It is obvious that even in the time of Luzán stage settings in the public theaters had progressed little beyond those used during the Golden Age, except in the performance of the *comedias de teatro,* which occurred very infrequently because of the expense entailed. Since no attempt was apparently made in the usual performances to produce any illusion of reality, it is curious that Luzán and later neo-classic critics should have been so insistent that the unities of time and place be observed lest the public be made conscious that what it was witnessing was a mere play and not reality.

The divided stage which Luzán proposes as an innovation is only a modification of the simultaneous setting used on the medieval stage. He would merely partition the stage to represent a variety of scenes, instead of having one large stage spotted with decorations to depict these same scenes. In spite of his apparent acceptance of the extreme interpretation of the unity of place, he cannot quite bring himself to endorse the French practice of limiting the action to a street, a palace, or one room in a house. In his dilemma he naïvely advocates a stage setting the effect of which could only bewilder the spectators and could not conceivably contribute to any illusion of reality. He realizes that this type of stage would need to be tested carefully to determine whether the audience could see and hear well what was being performed. By experience, he says, it could be determined whether preference should be given to horizontal or to perpendicular divisions. In the event neither should prove practicable he is definitely of the opinion that changes and drop curtains are much preferable to the use of "four cloths or fixed curtains" which served at that time in Spain to represent all manner of places. Luzán does not mention the possibility of lowering a front curtain while changes of scenery are being made. It seems quite probable that this curtain had not made its appearance yet in the Spanish theater, and that the practice of changing scenes by means of backdrops was still in use.

Luzán says that plots are divided according to Aristotle into *simple* and *involved,* simple plots being those in which changes of fortune or passage from felicity to infelicity occur without *peripety* or *agnición;* and involved plots being those in which changes of fortune are brought about with *peripety* or *agnición,* or with a combination of both. Aristotle has indicated his preference for involved plots and later has appeared to contradict himself by saying that simple plots are preferable to double plots. Luzán prefers to attempt to reconcile these statements, not by recourse to the commentators on Aristotle, but by a close examination of the text itself and by a definition of terms:

Peripety is a change of fortune contrary to what the incidents of the action may have promised up until that point; not just any change, but a sudden and completely unexpected change. *Agnición,* or recognition, as the name implies, is the sudden transition from ignorance to the knowledge of the identity of a person, or of some special quality of his, or of some deed, which gives rise to friendship or enmity between the persons who are destined to be happy or unhappy in the drama.[35]

Peripety and recognition must be prepared with art and must concern the principal characters. Luzán agrees with Aristotle that, in the light of the above explanation of terms, involved plots are preferable to simple plots, because they are "more marvelous, more intricate and, consequently, more pleasing, and more likely to move the emotions of the spectators by the unexpectedness of their incidents."[36] The apparent contradiction noted above is due, according to Luzán, to the fact that Aristotle uses the term *simple* in two different senses. This term, he says, was used at that time to refer to plots with a single transition from felicity to infelicity and the term *double* to refer to plots with two transitions, one in which some persons fell from felicity to infelicity and another in which other persons passed from infelicity to felicity. He is convinced that only in this sense does Aristotle say that simple plots are preferable. Luzán cites *The Force of Nature* by Moreto as an example of a plot which is both double and involved, with peripety and recognition.

The principal characters are divided by Aristotle into two categories: those that are *better* and those that are *worse,* the former being suitable for tragedy and the latter for comedy. Luzán says that Aristotle clearly means here by the term *better* those who are superior in fortune, power, wealth, and fame; and by *worse* the common people and private individuals. The former alone, he says, are suitable for tragedy. He is particularly concerned with the ethical function of this genre and adds a reflection which, in his opinion, confirms the usefulness of tragedies that have an unhappy ending:

Changes of fortune, falls, and deaths of princes and nobles make the audience leave the theater with an internal sadness, with a bitter and unpleasant taste, which for a time keeps their minds in melancholy and thoughtful silence.... This bitter taste produces a great part of the usefulness of tragedy, being as beneficial to the mind as the taste of bitter medicine usually is for the body. There is no doubt that too great joy, too much consideration of external objects, and various desires distract the mind and remove it from self-contemplation.[37]

So convinced is Luzán of the public utility which can result from the performance of good tragedies, in which people may learn to moderate their passions, that he expresses deep regret that Spaniards have not followed the example of Italy, France, and England in cultivating this genre. Although he has allowed himself up until this point in his discussion to be influenced by the commentators whose works he has read so carefully, and has given the twofold function of pleasing and teaching both to comedy and to tragedy, he now reveals his real attitude toward the didactic purpose of tragedy:

> From this observation and from those of various authors whom we have cited, one can recognize the great benefit which could result to the public from the performance of good tragedies, in which all manner of people might learn insensibly the moderation of their passions and desires, finding in the theater a hidden teaching and a delightful school of morals.[38]

Throughout the neo-classic period the didactic purpose of drama was paramount and the terms "a school of morals" and "a school of manners" recur with monotonous frequency in discussions of the theater.

Almost all of the commentators on Aristotle, including Minturno, Riccobono, Maggio, and Victorio, denied the appropriateness of deaths on the stage and maintained that the audience must be informed by narration of these events. Luzán finds Aristotle's text clear on this point:

> But Aristotle's text seems clear to me, and the interpretation which these authors wish to give it seems very violent and forced. Furthermore, the reason for admitting public and manifest deaths in the theater is evident; because the use of narration will move the mind lukewarmly and no matter how the poet may exert himself, the tragedy will always be cold and uninteresting.[39]

The ancients used both methods, sometimes executing the deaths in public and sometimes having a messenger or one of the actors narrate the event. Luzán prefers to follow the opinion of Benio, who said:

There is no doubt whatever that Aristotle admits deaths on the stage; but it is to be understood that this applies to those deaths, the execution of which is neither barbarous nor cruel; so deaths brought about with poison, swords, or daggers can be offered to the view of the audience; but when the manner of death is entirely inhuman and barbarous, then it should be pretended that they occur behind the scene and the audience should be informed of them by means of narration.[40]

Luzán discusses at length the four conditions which Aristotle prescribes for character: goodness, appropriateness, resemblance, and consistency. The first condition he finds subject to many difficulties but concludes that what Aristotle has in mind is poetic goodness. This interpretation is essentially that of Corneille, who said that goodness of character did not mean extreme goodness "but an outstanding and high character, with some good or bad habit, in keeping with the person portrayed."[41]

Luzán believes Corneille meant that if a lover is introduced, for example, he should be painted as an ideal lover; if a miser is portrayed he should be represented as having all the qualities commonly attributed to such a person. The poet should perfect nature and paint characters which are excellent in their kind, whether good or bad.

To be able to observe properly the second requirement of appropriateness, or decorum, the poet must know what is fitting to people differing in age, sex, nationality, position, and dignity; he should know the "obligations of a king, of a general, of a counselor, or of a friend."

The third condition is resemblance, which, Luzán says, applies only to historical subjects. In this case the character ascribed to the person should conform to his historical reputation. It would be improper, therefore, to represent Alexander the Great as cowardly or miserly.

The fourth condition, consistency, requires that a person sustain the same character or disposition throughout the drama. According to Luzán, this does not mean that the personages must persevere obstinately in their opinions. Since the purpose of drama is to teach and to correct, he sees no objection to a change in a character provided such a change is sufficiently motivated, and provided the change comes only at the end of the play. In support of his position he cites the case of old Demea in the *Adelphi* by Terence and that of Diana in Moreto's *Disdain Conquered by Disdain*, in both of which plays he finds sufficient reason for a change.

Aristotle gave first emphasis in a play to the plot, relegating character to a secondary role. Luzán signifies his general agreement with this evaluation but clearly indicates that he places character not far below plot. He has repeatedly paid tribute to the ability of Spanish dramatists in plot structure, but says now that they have usually been neglectful of character and the other qualities which contribute to a perfect plot.

All the gallants of our comedies must of necessity be in love and valiant; for the first a portrait suffices to lead them into passionate and blind extremes; and for the second a word or the slightest happening makes them undertake a task worthy of a knight errant; and ladies, in order to show themselves worthy of the name on the stage, must forget their modesty completely and throw themselves unhesitatingly into all of those adventures which involve papers, windows, and gardens, going in disguise to see their gallants or hiding them in their own rooms in order to evade the vigilance of a father or a brother. I leave it to the judgment of wise and prudent men whether it is advisable to hold always before the people as so beautiful the idea of a false valor and as so desirable the ravishment of a disordered passion; and I only say that, in my opinion, to inspire continually in the audience such mistaken moral maxims cannot fail to cause notable damage to character.[42]

Luzán is generalizing here about Golden Age drama, but he immediately cites as an illustration *The Perfect Prince* by Lope de Vega. He can conceive of no prince lower and more unworthy of the title than Prince Juan, who, in this comedy, initiates his so-called perfections and deeds with a murder which he commits on a nocturnal stroll and who not only plays the role of an ordinary assassin, but acts as a go-between and accomplice in the love affair of one of his servants. Equally reprehensible are the plays *The Beach of Seville*, *A Friend Until Death*, and *The Steel of Madrid*, by the same author. Moreto's *Pranks of Pantoja* he considers a "school of cruelty, of vengeance, and of false valor." He does not deny that Calderón was more circumspect than others, "but nevertheless most of his comedies contain no other themes than love affairs and duels."[43]

Luzán cannot bring himself to condemn unconditionally the use of love affairs in comedy. He does say, however:

The appearance of modesty in comedies makes them much more harmful and dangerous. The most circumspect women, whose modesty would flee from comedies which were manifestly impure, do not hesitate to attend others whose poison is equally harmful although more concealed.

If this statement seems insufficient, consider whether there is any father or husband who would be content that his wife or his daughter lead the same life as the most virtuous princess or the most circumspect lady in these comedies. If a test were made these false virtues would be revealed as true vices.[44]

Boileau not only defended the love element but considered it the richest adornment of the theater, and Pedro Corneille admitted this passion even in tragedies—relegating it to second place, however, and preferring that the principal intrigue be based on more manly passions like ambition and vengeance. Luzán goes beyond Corneille and approves love affairs provided they are treated with proper modesty and decorum. The church fathers and the councils at times condemned all drama as licentious and harmful. Although Luzán admits that some poets have misused an art which is in itself useful, he does not believe this abuse justifies an absolute condemnation of the *comedia*.

Let bad poets be censured and bad comedies reproved; but allow to remain intact the esteem due to good poets and to dramas written with judgment, with good taste, and according to the rules of perfect poetry; for, provided they are subordinated to morals and public interest, not only will they not vitiate character, but they will by entertaining and teaching at the same time, with an insensible and gentle attraction, contribute very much to the correction of vices and defects, and to the practice of virtue.[45]

This emphasis on the moral office of tragedy and comedy is the keynote of subsequent neo-classic criticism in Spain, whether because of an inward conviction on the part of the champions of this school or through a desire to win to their cause both political and ecclesiastical support. According to Luzán, in judging the *comedia* it is necessary to find a middle ground "between the severity of some and the liberty of others." Luzán naïvely justifies comedy on the grounds that since idleness breeds vice, and since comedies are the most popular public diversion, "by their performance better than by any other means can the idleness of the people be held occupied and charmed."[46]

Comedies are divided into three classes: those completely bad, those perfectly good, and those defective in part. In the first class are included those in which vice is rewarded and virtue is disregarded, in which the passions of love and vengeance are aroused, and which teach maxims contrary to religion. Such comedies should be banned from the stage and from the press. On the contrary, those comedies that are perfectly good, that is, "those that are careful in the correction of defects and in censuring vices by painting them as horrible and pernicious" not only should not be banned from the theater but should meet with universal approval and their authors should receive applause and rewards. In regard to comedies which are not entirely bad but only in part defective, in which "love is treated with modesty, duels with moderation, virtue, although mixed with some common defects, is rewarded and triumphant, and a vice or defect, even though it not be of the major kind, receives its punishment,"[47] Luzán believes that for want of better ones, they may be tolerated for the diversion of the idle public because in such comedies "the usefulness outweighs the harm."[48]

In regard to dramas which may be written in the future, however, Luzán earnestly advises the writers

> ... to devote all care and study to arranging the action according to the above-mentioned rules, and with all the conditions and qualities necessary for complete perfection, and to give particular attention to character, from the good or bad portrayal of which great advantage or serious harm may result to the public.[49]

The poet is privileged to introduce and paint the character of a lover or of a *duelista guapetón* as he might any other kind of character, provided he "not make passion pass for glory, virtue for vice, or defects for laudable qualities, since the harmfulness of such pictures consists especially in this distortion."[50] Luzán wishes, however, to banish from the minds of dramatists the idea that no comedy can be successful "unless its principal plot and theme is love intrigue, duels, ostentatious bravery, and quarrels." Let them portray a *braggart soldier,* like the *Pirgopolinices* of Plautus, or like the *Thrasón* of Terence, a *Miser* like that of Molière or of Plautus, a *ridiculous clergyman* like the *Don Claudio* of Zamora, and their success on the stage will prove conclusively that love affairs and duels are not necessary to amuse the public.

Luzán believes it would be a very wise policy for the magistrates of the cities to designate certain scholarly individuals well versed in poetics, whose duty it would be to examine carefully all comedies before they are published or performed. These censors should also be empowered to examine and to order burned all plays which, in their opinion, are entirely bad and to allow the performance only of those which are good or those whose usefulness outweighs their harm. Such a censorship, Luzán says, has already been advised by the Spanish historian Mariana and is in line with the precaution which Plato advised for his ideal republic.

In regard to the choice between verse and prose in drama Luzán is not so dogmatic as he is on other points. It is so commonly accepted that tragedies should be written in verse that he knows no authors, good or bad, who approve prose for this genre. There are several good comedies, however, which have been written in this medium. All those by the Italians Nicola Amenta, Octavio Disa, and Juan Bautista La Porta, as well as many by the French dramatist, Molière, are in prose. Among the Spanish dramatists who used prose for comedies he cites Lope de Rueda and the *Dorotea* by Lope de Vega. This latter work, however, was called by its author a *novel in prose* and is, in fact, a dialogued novel in the *Celestina* manner. Inasmuch as comedy requires a natural style, and verse, because of its harmony and poetic license, is always characterized by loftiness and elegance rather than naturalness, it seems to Luzán that preference should be given to prose, which is easier to reduce to comic simplicity. He recognizes, nevertheless, that verse has always been considered necessary to poetry, and that a good poet can make his verse as clear and natural as the purest prose. Luzán concludes his rather confused discussion of this question by saying: "There being, then, examples and reasons on both sides, it is unjust to condemn either of these opinions absolutely, and a poet is at liberty to write his comedies in prose or in verse as he chooses."[51]

Nor does Luzán go to the extreme of some later critics in barring rhyme from drama:

There is another question concerning pure rhyme in tragedies or comedies. Some consider it untrue to life; others do not hesitate to use it. I believe that, although it is well not to use rhyme, those who do so with judgment and moderation will commit no error, especially in tragedies.[52]

There was a sharp divergence of opinion in Luzán's time on this point, and the Spanish critic chooses to steer a middle course, evidently considering this of minor importance. Luzán gives Trissino, the author of the Italian tragedy *Sophinisba*, credit for being the first to attempt to free tragedy from the slavery of pure rhyme. He cannot, however, approve the use Trissino makes of rhyme in some parts of his *Sophinisba* where the effect is that of a lyrical composition. He considers even more to be censured the practice of the Spanish dramatist Christóbal de Mesa in his tragedy *Pompeii*. In this work there is a mixture of *canciones, tercets, octaves, couplets, décimas,* and other forms of rhyme which Luzán considers directly opposed to verisimilitude. He believes that verses of eleven and seven syllables are not only the most frequent but the most suitable for drama in general. Spanish comedies, however, are usually composed in short verses, that is, in *quartillas, quintillas, décimas,* and ballad meter. Luzán is comforted somewhat for the Spanish practice by the fact that Gravina and Corneille occasionally used such forms. Unquestionably he has a marked preference for ballad meter, but cannot bring himself to condemn completely the Spanish practice of metrical variety:

And in regard to ballad meter in assonance, it seems to me that it is very suitable for comedy because of its resemblance to prose; but with respect to the *décimas, quintillas,* and *redondillas,* even though their rhyme is too regular and artificial, and for that reason not very natural in one who speaks in a sudden outburst, it does not seem to me that there is sufficient reason to deprive them of the peaceful possession of the theater which they have enjoyed for so many years.[53]

Although later neo-classicists usually recommended ballad meter for comedy and hendecasyllabic assonance for tragedy, this question was never definitely settled and continued to be a subject for controversy throughout the neo-classic period. It will be noted that the various critical writings of the neo-classic school almost never condemn the use of consonantal rhyme.

Under the general heading of *apparatus* Luzán includes the disposition and the adornment of the stage setting, the persons of the actors, and their dress. Although he says that, strictly speaking, this is outside the field of the poet, he admits that to a certain extent it may contribute to the perfection of a performance. Architecture and painting, with proper attention to perspective, can be used in such a manner that an appeal will be made to the eye as well as to the ear. Luzán cites a statement made by González de Salas that the illusion was so perfect in the Roman theater that crows were seen trying to alight on tile painted on the scenery.

Luzán touches very lightly on histrionics in his *Poetics.* But this is a problem which appears to have been uppermost in his mind, at least after his stay in Paris, for in his *Memoirs of Paris* he discusses in detail the rules for acting. In his *Poetics* he says only that effort should be made to suit the actor to the role, according to his disposition, his ability, his stature, and his age. He believes that if care is taken in choosing actors with some capacity and intelligence, or, at least, those who have some education, the quality of acting will be vastly improved. Dress, he says, should be in keeping with the nationality, dignity, and social position of the characters represented. He does not believe, however, that realism in dress should be carried to the extent of having peasant girls appear as ragged and unkempt as they are accustomed to be in real life; it is sufficient that they appear in the dress which they wear on festival occasions. Nature, Luzán says, should not be slavishly imitated, but improved and ennobled.

Luzán accepts Horace's precept that no more than three persons should have speaking parts in a scene. He considers it a serious mistake to load a play with so many characters that the spectator has difficulty in remembering their names and characteristics, and he finds that Lope's plays usually have an excessive number of characters.

Leaving aside those that have only twenty-four or thirty, the comedy *The Baptism of the Prince of Fez, and Death of King Sebastian* has sixty persons with a procession in addition, a number sufficient to replace the losses suffered by a regiment badly defeated in battle. A poet should reduce the number of actors to the minimum necessary for the performance of a play; otherwise it would be necessary to draft actors like soldiers.[54]

Luzán believes that eight or ten characters are sufficient and that any excess will result in confusion.

He is more liberal in his interpretation of the rules where mere mechanical features are involved. It makes no difference, he says, whether a play is divided into three or five acts; let each nation follow its own preference; nor is it necessary that an act have a fixed number of scenes, even though some critics have wished to set seven or ten as the desirable number. He explains that he means by scenes the entrances and exits of the actors, or the increase or decrease of the number on the stage, so that whenever either change occurs, it is considered that there is a new scene. In Spain, he says, it is not the practice to call these entrances and exits scenes as is done in other countries. Luzán finds much more important the rule that the scenes should be so linked that the stage will never be vacant for a single moment. This, he admits, is difficult; but he considers it of such importance for dramatic perfection that the poet should make every effort to observe it. Luzán believes that a strict observance of this rule is necessary in order to hold the spectators' attention. He is afraid that if the stage is left vacant their minds will wander and they will lose the thread of the story.

Luzán divides prologues into two classes: those which he calls "manifest and separate prologues" and those which he designates as "prologues hidden and united with the drama." The latter type he considers much more desirable. Since one of the most frequent criticisms of the *comedia* was directed against the lack of verisimilitude in the exposition, it is not surprising that Luzán should be very explicit on this point. He explains his preference for "hidden prologues":

> In my opinion, they are the best and most artistic, their artifice consisting in having the characters of the drama, in their first appearance and in the course of their conversation, relate the origin and principles of the entire play, informing the audience indirectly of all the antecedent circumstances and of the disposition and particular purpose of the principal roles. But this must be done with such art and with such ingeniousness that the purpose of the poet to inform the audience will not be apparent.[55]

Although some Spanish dramatists have given evidence of ingenuity in this respect, others have not been so successful. Luzán censures the long narration in which one friend informs another, or a servant informs his master, of antecedent events, although they are already well known to the one who hears them. To be condemned also are the long soliloquies by means of which some authors try to reveal the hidden thoughts of the characters. To achieve verisimilitude in such speeches requires all the skill and ingenuity of the poet.

Luzán is thoroughly convinced that dramatic poetry must produce an illusion of reality:

> This is the purpose of all the rules that are urged upon poets with reference to the verisimilitude of the action, of manners, of constructions and language; and this is also the purpose of all that has been said about the prologue and of the manner of informing the audience of what is supposed to be happening on the stage and of the thoughts and intentions of the actors. So if verisimilitude is in any way violated and the spectator

through the conversations or through the soliloquies recognizes the deception, seeing that they are not true to life, and that they only serve to apprise him of some fact; then coming back to himself and disillusioned, he recognizes the trick of the poet and realizes that all is mere pretense.[56]

This idea of *dramatic illusion,* as we shall see, was soon to be called into question and was to serve as a target for opponents of neoclassicism.

In order to heighten the illusion, Luzán finds perfectly legitimate and even laudable the practice of some authors, who "speak of comedy in the comedy itself as of something foreign and distinct from what is taking place on the stage . . . saying that such an incident seems fitting for comedy."[57]

After giving the rules pertaining to tragedy, Luzán finds that little remains to be said about comedy, since almost all of the rules already given are equally applicable to both genres. He defines comedy as

. . . a dramatic representation of a private action and of a plot of little importance to the public, which action or plot is supposed to occur between private or plebeian persons and to have a happy and merry purpose. Everything must be directed toward the profit and entertainment of the audience, inspiring insensibly love for virtue and aversion for vice, by making the former pleasing and happy and the latter ridiculous and unhappy.[58]

Tragedy and comedy differ in the events which form the basis of the action. Tragedy represents "an illustrious and great event" in which a whole state or kingdom is affected; comedy limits itself to "a private event," the effect of which rarely extends beyond the district in which the action takes place. Tragedy deals with illustrious personages such as kings, heroes, captains, etc., while comedy only admits "ladies, gentlemen, and private individuals." This distinction leads Luzán to condemn the prevalent practice in Spain of introducing princes, kings, and other persons of high rank in the *comedia.* He agrees with Cascales that such comedies "are not comedies, nor their shadow; they are hermaphrodites, monsters of poetry." Although Corneille admits a mixture of characters, saying that such comedies may be called *heroic* to distinguish them from the regular type, Luzán can find no doctrine or example to justify such liberty. In the Spanish theater, he says, most of the incidents which are supposed to happen to kings are completely improbable. He cites the

comedy *Deeds Prove Love* as a flagrant violation of the principle of
propriety: "In the comedy, *Deeds Prove Love*, by Lope de Vega it is
laughable to see the King of Hungary admit to his presence the
squire and even the coachman of a lady not of noble birth, and to
engage in a very familiar conversation with them."[59]

Although Plautus in the prologue of the *Amphitryon* called his
work a tragi-comedy, Luzán is certain that he did so with the intention of causing the audience to laugh at the newly invented term.
Jupiter and Mercury appear in Plautus' comedy not with the seriousness and loftiness which befit these deities but with a ridiculous and
comic character. Only in this manner does Luzán believe that such
beings can have a role in comedy. In a later chapter Luzán goes
into detail in his criticism of the *tragi-comedy*, which he calls "a new
monster not known by the ancients." To mix kings and princes with
ordinary men and "sad happenings with jocose mockery, the tragic
and the comic, is to spoil both."[60] Luzán admits that many dramatists
call their plays *tragi-comedies* and that some believe "that all of
those dramas should be so called which partake of the nature of
tragedy and comedy either because of the mixture of serious and
happy events, or of illustrious and plebeian characters."[61] In this
sense, Luzán says, the greater part of Spanish plays would be classed
as tragi-comedies. It seems evident that Luzán in his sweeping condemnation of this genre as something characteristic and peculiar to
the Spanish theater was not aware that the majority of Hardy's plays
in France at the turn of the seventeenth century and a large proportion of the plays which were performed in that country during the
period of Corneille and Molière were called tragi-comedies, and,
indeed, fell within the definition he had just given for this illegitimate genre. By his condemnation of tragi-comedy, Luzán opened
a controversy which was to rage for over a hundred years and
was to figure prominently in the polemics between romanticists
and neo-classicists at the end of that period.

Tragedy and comedy differ also in the solution of the plot. Luzán
follows Aristotle in recommending an unhappy ending for tragedy
and is certain, although Aristotle says nothing directly on this point,
that comedy should have a "happy and merry ending."[62]

For tragedy, Luzán recommends "the simple action," that is,
"with a single change," and for comedy "the double, or with two
changes." Comedy, therefore, admits more intrigue and complication of plot. When some of the later neo-classic dramatists like

Moratín simplified the plot of their comedies to the point that the element of suspense was no longer operative, the fault cannot be attributed to a rigid adherence to the precepts of Luzán, but to a mistaken desire to achieve simplicity in order that the moral lesson might be made more effective. The emphasis of the French theater of the seventeenth century on character rather than intrigue is also a direct departure from the doctrine of Aristotle, who, as we have seen, gave first emphasis to plot and relegated character to a secondary role.

Finally, Luzán says, tragedy and comedy are to be distinguished by their style. Since the subject matter of tragedy is lofty, the passions violent, and the characters illustrious, a lofty style is required with rhetorical figures, which are the proper language of passion. Inasmuch as comedy admits only characters of the middle class, in whom lofty thoughts, elegant style, and violent passions are out of place, it should have "a simple, pure, natural, and easy style." Luzán cautions against the idea that it is easier to write comedy than tragedy: "Anyone may think he can write one with great ease; but when he tries to do so, he finds that he has fooled himself and that it is extremely difficult."* Luzán backs up this point with a citation from Horace to the effect that success and excellence in the production of comedies requires all the more pains and effort inasmuch as faults in this genre are more easily detected by the public and are, therefore, more subject to censure.

According to Luzán not only the manner of speech in comedy, but also flights of the imagination, daring rhetorical figures, and all excessive and affected adornment should be modified. This does not mean that comedy cannot raise its voice upon occasion so long as this does not entail affectation. (There is hardly a commentator on the rules who does not, like Luzán, avail himself of this license

---

*Luzán's recognition of the difficulties attendant upon the composition of comedies brings to mind Molière's statement in his *Critique de l'Ecole des femmes* where Dorante says: "Certainly Madame, and if in the matter of difficulty you should lean a little toward comedy, perhaps you would not make a mistake, because, indeed, I find that it is much easier to let oneself go in lofty sentiments, to rage against Fortune, to accuse Destiny, and to insult the Gods, than to enter as one should into the ridiculous side of mankind. When you paint heroes, you do whatever you like. These are portraits designed to please where one expects no resemblance; and you have only to follow an unbridled imagination which often leaves the true to catch the marvelous. But when you paint man it is necessary to paint him according to nature. It is necessary that these portraits be faithful and you have failed if you do not make the people of your age recognizable." (Molière, *La Critique de l'Ecole des femmes*, Sc. VI.)

granted by Horace.) Under the stress of emotion a character may speak with more force than normally, but he must not fall into far-fetched conceits and metaphors. Luzán commends Terence for the moderation and circumspection which he uses in his comedies. The style of this writer, he says, may be taken as a pattern of the naturalness required in the comic genre.

The technical requirements of tragedy and comedy are the same: "Comedy is, in short, a parallel to tragedy; the latter excites tears; the former, laughter. The extreme misfortunes of kings, etc., move to pity and terror in tragedy, and the excess of vices and defects of private individuals excites laughter and joy in comedy."[63] In spite of the difference in the emotions aroused in tragedy and comedy, both are directed to the same end, that is, the profit and instruction of the audience. With Luzán and with the entire neo-classic school in Spain the didactic note prevailed. To this pedagogical attitude even more than to an overemphasis upon rules are the coldness and lack of interest of most of their plays to be attributed. Both tragedy and comedy are conceived as moral instruments to be used in cor-recting vice and exalting virtue. According to Aristotle, the sole end of dramatic poetry was to please the audience. Those critics who chose to assign to it a moral purpose were fond of citing the Horacian precept: *omne tulit punctum qui miscuit utile dulci*. This didactic emphasis gained ground throughout Europe until it threatened to destroy dramatic interest.

Luzán holds that in tragedy and in comedy the emotions that are aroused are directed to the same end because "great changes of fortune as well as ridicule and punishment of vices have as their purpose the benefit of the spectators, making them either more con-stant and patient in their tribulations, or wiser and more prudent in their defects."[64] Just as in tragedy the change of fortune must fall upon the principal character, so in comedy the principal roles should be the ones that provoke laughter with their well-portrayed defects and extravagant natures. Luzán praises Cañizares for the consistency with which he observed this precept, but finds reprehensible "the practice of other Spanish writers of comedies who ordinarily make serious and at times tragic the entire principal theme of their come-dies and entrust the comic element to servants and buffoons to whom they give the name of *graciosos*."[65]

In discussing the technical requirements of drama, Luzán uses the stock language of neo-classic criticism. He defines and discusses the terms *recognition (agnición), peripety, protasis, epitasis,* and *catastrophe.* The pedantry which made use of these terms as talismans in dramatic criticism had been vigorously satirized by Molière in the *Critique de l'Ecole des femmes:*

LYSIDAS. What, Monsieur? The protase, the epitase, and the peripetie ...

DORANTE. Ah! Monsieur Lysidas, you overwhelm us with your big words. Do not appear so erudite, please. Humanize your speech, and speak so that you will be understood. Do you think that a Greek word gives more weight to your reasons? And don't you think that it would be just as well to say the *exposition* of the subject, instead of the *protasis;* the *climax,* instead of the *epitasis;* and the *solution* instead of the *peripety?*

Luzán does not cite Molière in his *Poetics* and may have been entirely unfamiliar with his works. But even if he had been acquainted with them, he would not have been deterred from his purpose, to give a learned exposition of the rules, by any amount of satire to which they might have been subjected by such a recalcitrant. Some neo-classicists in Spain took all of these learned terms fondly to their bosom and made an ostentatious show of their superficial erudition. The shallowness of knowledge of the real essentials of drama on the part of many pseudo-critics awakened the ire of the leaders of neo-classicism itself. As we shall see, Leandro Fernández de Moratín, in *The New Comedy,* directed the shafts of his satire at the pedant, Don Hermógenes, for using the same terms which had been ridiculed by Molière and defined so carefully by Luzán.

Luzán gives his complete approval to Aristotle's recommendation that the dramatist work out a sketch of the whole tragedy or comedy, "with its beginning, its plot, solution, and end." In this sketch the author should indicate and outline clearly "the qualities of each person, the characters, the dispositions, the purposes, the scenes, that is, the entrances and exits," and give "a résumé of what each of the actors is to say and do in each scene and act."[66]

After expounding the theories which, in his opinion, should govern dramatic composition, Luzán proceeds to show how far short the Spanish *comedia* has fallen in the observance of these precepts. This he does "in order to give greater clarity to the rules themselves and to bring them within the comprehension of the most untutored."[67] By numerous examples he wishes to make clear "on how many shoals ignorance of art may run aground," and that

genius alone is not sufficient to produce a perfect poet. He is impelled to make use of examples taken from Spanish poets by the
fact that

... our comedies are books which are in the hands of everyone; for that
reason the examples will be more intelligible and more profitable. In addition, if we correct our own errors we will anticipate criticism and in a
certain measure make less painful and less ignominious the reproaches
of foreigners.[68]

Inasmuch as Spanish poets were not perfect but susceptible to
error, Luzán believes it is time that the truth be told and popular mis-
conceptions corrected. He declares that he is wronging no one,
because in calling attention to occasional falls he does not deny the
merit of lofty flights. The unbiased critic, he says, must be equally
alert in discovering and pointing out excellencies and defects.

The passage which Menéndez y Pelayo cites as an example of
the "notable concessions" which Luzán makes to the Spanish theater
in the first edition, and which was omitted in the second, is more
intelligible when it is considered in its complete context. Menéndez
y Pelayo says that these concessions were made by Luzán "either
because they represented his convictions, or in order to avoid a
direct attack upon prevailing opinion." The entire section in which
Luzán expresses his admiration for certain qualities in Golden Age
drama is of sufficient importance to warrant quotation. It is as though
Luzán wished to give vent in wholesale fashion to all the good he
could conscientiously say about this theater, in order that he might
feel free thereafter to censure it to his heart's content.

And as evidence that I am not lacking in fairness, not being able here
to enumerate separately and in detailed manner all of the excellencies of
our dramatists, because to do so would require a large volume, I shall
content myself with the general and inclusive statement that in all of them
I find as a rule rare ingeniousness, singular acuteness, and discretion,
qualities which are very essential to the formation of great poets worthy
of admiration; and I add that in particular I shall always praise in Lope
de Vega the natural facility of his style and the supreme dexterity with
which he paints in many of his comedies the manners and the character
of some personages; in Calderón I admire the nobility of his language,
which without ever being obscure, or affected, is always elegant; and I
consider especially worthy of praise the ingenious manner and technique
with which this author, always holding his audience in suspense, has been

able to entangle the plots of his comedies, and particularly of those we call "cloak and sword" plays, some of which offer critics very little or nothing to censure and much to admire and praise. Of such a type are the comedies: *I Am First, To Give Time to Time, Fortune and Misfortune of a Name, Which Is the Greater Perfection? Two Effects from One Cause, There Is No Joking with Love, The Pawns of Chance,* and others. Solís is not inferior to Calderón in natural elegance and nobility of style; he has written some comedies which are worthy products of such an elevated and cultured genius, such as the *Little Gypsy Girl of Madrid, The Castle with the Secret,* and *One Fool Makes a Hundred.* Some comedies of Moreto also merit applause, especially *Disdain Conquered by Disdain;* because good criticism (as Horace teaches) should not proceed with such severity or such scrupulous inclusiveness that it will single out some slight faults when all the rest of the work is good. . . . *Bewitched by Force* by Don Antonio Zamora is a comedy written with singular skill and conforms very closely to the rules of dramatic poetry; almost equally commendable in this respect is *The Punishment of Avarice* by the same author. [Luzán in the second edition correctly credits this comedy to Juan de Hoz.] Don Francisco Candamo also deserves the praise and the favor with which the public has received his works because of his wit, his elegant style, his rather broad information, and the great care which he gives to verisimilitude, decorum, and propriety in incidents and characters. Finally Don Joseph Cañizares, following with prudence a course more suitable for comic poetry than that followed by others, has written many comedies which are worthy of exceptional praise. In *Dómine Lucas,* in *A Musician for the Sake of Love,* and in others I have seen with particular pleasure characters well painted and consistent throughout, themes and style appropriate for comedy, humor in the action itself and in the principal personages, and not (as is usually the case in comedies by other authors) in the speeches of a servant, qualities all of which are very appreciable, and which I have sought in vain in other writers of comedies.[69]

It is noteworthy that in the tribute which he pays to the Golden Age theater Luzán is as lavish in his praise of inferior dramatists like Solís, Zamora, Candamo, and Cañizares as of Lope de Vega and Calderón. With the feeling that he has discharged his patriotic duty by recognizing certain meritorious qualities in the *comedia,* he now feels justified in pointing out some of the serious errors committed by Spanish dramatists because of their ignorance or neglect of the rules. He does not believe that the ardent partisans of the writers whom he has just mentioned have any reason to become offended if he indicates these errors "for the instruction of those who will write in the future." Some of the errors into which poets fall, he says, concern poetry. Among the errors which belong to this class are disproportionate images, extravagant metaphors, bombastic style, coarseness, coldness, and excessive subtlety. These defects, which mar any type of poetry, are especially unpardonable in tragedy and comedy, the goal of which should be verisimilitude. Luzán believes that even the most moderate critic will find cold the speech of Medusa in *The Fortunes of Andromeda and Perseus,* by Calderón, which, he says, is only fitting for a child who is studying syntax. Nor can he tolerate the extravagant metaphors used by Julia in the comedy *A Friend Until Death,* by Lope de Vega.

The errors which are peculiar to dramatic poetry are easy to recognize, Luzán says, if one knows the rules. These errors are: "for the story not to be true to life, not to observe the unities of action, time and place; for customs to be harmful to the audience or painted contrary to nature and verisimilitude; to make the characters speak with improper conceits and with affected langauge."[70] In his desire to be brief he will cite only a few of the defects which are to be found in the *comedia.* He finds the plot of *The Gardener's Dog* by Lope de Vega improbable. In this play a lady falls in love with a servant and is so imprudent and immodest in her passion that she publicizes her feelings. In *The Bouquets of Madrid,* also by Lope, a well-known gentleman dares to disguise himself as a gardener in order to serve a lady of high rank. In *Love Is All Confusion,* by Moreto, although Doña Elena could very easily arrange her marriage with Don Felix, with whom she is in love, since there is no one to prevent her from doing so, she chooses to leave home, disguise herself as a student, and go to Salamanca for the sole purpose of finding out whether Don Felix is as wild as he is reported to be. In Salamanca she plays the role of Don Lope when she is with Felix, and the role of the servant girl, Damiana, when she is with Doña Manuela; with others she plays the role of a lady. After citing *The Lady President, The Lady Magistrate,* and *To Serve a Discreet Master,* the authors of which he does not mention, Luzán asks: "In which of these cases can one find a trace of verisimilitude? Which of them can be a mirror of human life?" These things, he says, seem to belong to another world because in Spain such adventures never happen and can only be the product of the imagination of the poet; they can serve neither for instruction nor as an example of happenings in real life. Luzán chooses to forget that the assumption of male disguise by girls was used by both Plautus and Terence as a means of complicating the plot and was a commonplace in the theater of the Italian imitators of the classics. From the comedy *I Suppositi* by

Ariosto the device passed to all of the theaters of Europe. In many cases Luzán leaves the impression that the errors he is censuring are peculiar to the Spanish stage when, in fact, they were just as prevalent in the French, Italian, and English theaters.

Luzán condemns the use of pagan legends in such comedies as *Euridice and Orpheus, There Is Love Also in the Abyss, The Statue of Prometheus,* and *Even Love Cannot Free Itself from Love.* Although these legends may have been believed by the common people in earlier times, and although they may have been used by scholars to teach indirectly some mystery or some truth, Luzán does not believe that they can be considered verisimilar and suitable for comedy in this time. If he has not approved these themes in comedy because of their irreverence and their harmful effect, no more can he bring himself to sanction the *Comedies of Saints* which are so popular in Spain. The benefit to be derived from such comedies is far outweighed by their harmful effects.

By no means the least of these is the profanation of things so sacred with love affairs, with vanity, and indecent jests. In addition to this, how many false miracles, how many apocryphal stories are spread in this fashion among the ignorant masses, who believe them as truths of religion and as dogmas of faith, when they have no other authority than the imagination or ignorance of the poet![71]

Luzán brands as entirely incredible the account given by Sigismundo in *The Castle with the Secret* of how he used his shield as a boat in order to cross from the coast of Epirus to the island of Cyprus. Luzán says that "anyone who knows how many leagues there are between Epirus and Cyprus will find it hard to believe that such a thing could happen without a miracle."[72] Nor does he believe that so many *galanes* can hide in glass closets or behind curtains without being found or seen. He condemns also the frequency with which the *comedia* has recourse to papers and portraits to complicate the plot. If such devices must be used, Luzán recommends that the poet exercise all his ingenuity to make them seem probable.

Luzán condemns the synchronization of a song with the performance in such a manner that the very verse being sung is the one with which the actor must conclude some *décimas* or couplets. He finds also completely improbable the oracular voice which from behind the curtain interrupts the performance and foretells what the actor is going to say. He considers equally improper the use of echoes and words said in a dream at such a timely moment as in the comedy *Apeles and Campaspe* by Calderón. Just as improbable and as improper, in Luzán's opinion, is the emergence of two persons from opposite sides of the stage who have studied their roles so perfectly that one says not a syllable more than the other, and each, believing that he is alone, speaks to himself in such a fashion that his speeches alternate perfectly with the speeches of the other. Luzán cites the comedy, *Weep, Lady, and You Will Win*, by Calderón as an example of such impropriety. In this comedy Federico and Enrique come out, each practically duplicating what the other is saying, and each unaware of the presence of the other:

FED.	Guided by this music,
ENR.	Called by these accents,
FED.	I come in spite of the anger
ENR.	I return in spite of the wrath
FED.	Of my Lady because I judge
ENR.	Of my Lady because I think
FED.	That when the risk is so noble The risk is to be desired.
ENR.	That when the danger is such The danger itself is the remedy.
FED.	But here she is and I indeed hesitate
ENR.	But here she is and I indeed fear
FED.	To see her face again.
ENR.	To see her frown again.
FED.	She has already seen me; I await her disdain.
ENR.	She has already seen me; I await her scorn.

All this, Luzán says, is more like praying in chorus than acting roles in a comedy.*

Luzán finds that the Spanish *comedia* has committed many sins against the unities of action, time, and place. *Madness for Honor's Sake*, by Lope, he says, has three actions, so loosely connected that each could form a separate comedy. He admits that this unity is not so frequently violated, however, as the unities of time and place. He reveals his sensitiveness to the criticism by Boileau, which he cites in a note, that Lope de Vega crowded the action of years into the space of one day, introducing the hero as a child in the first act and as a bearded man in the last.

The comedies of *Bernardo del Carpio, The Count of Saldaña,* and

*This is no isolated case, but a favorite device in Calderón's plays. It even occurs in his most famous work, *Life Is a Dream* (Act I, Sc. VI).

others like them have served as the subject of scorn and mockery for a
French critic; and not without sufficient reason; for it is intolerably absurd
that at the beginning Bernado del Carpio should come out as a child and
that before the comedy is over he should be a full-grown man and should
perform prodigious feats against the Moors. In the comedy, *The Steward
of the Duchess of Amalfi,* by Lope de Vega, nine years pass; in the
Genízaro of Hungary more than twenty; an equal number in *The Seven
Princes of Lara* and in *Vengeance in the Sudden Fall,* both by Juan Matos
Fragoso; and finally in the comedy, *The Seven Sleepers,* not less than two
hundred years pass; an equal time transpires in the comedy *San Amara,*
and in others which were rightly ridiculed by Francisco Cascales; there
are many which last two or three years, others less; but it would be an
endless task to attempt to mention all those that sin much or little against
the unity of time.[73]

    The errors committed by the *comedia* against the unity of place
are no less notable and frequent:

In *A Friend Until Death,* by Lope, the scene, or rather the place of
performance, is now in Tetuan, now in Seville, now in Cádiz, now in
Gibraltar. In the comedy, *To Conquer Love One Must Wish to Conquer It,* by Calderón, a part of the performance is in the Esquizaros, and a
part in Ferrara; in *Fortune and Misfortune in a Name* a part is in Parma
and a part in Milán; in the *Fortunes of Andromeda and Perseus* the persons pass from Achaya to Trinacria, and from Trinacria to Mount Atlantis
in Africa; in the comedy *To Serve a Discreet Master* the action is in
Seville, Madrid, and Córdoba. These examples will suffice to make one
conscious of similar defects in many other comedies, where the characters,
in the brief space of three or four hours which the performance lasts,
fly as if they had wings from one part of the world to another, traveling
with great frequency and without weariness hundreds of leagues.[74]

    Luzán finds in the *comedia* frequent violations of the principle of
verisimilitude in the portrayal of character. Inasmuch as each nation,
each age, and each sex has its own peculiar characteristics, the characters should be copied from nature. It has surprised him to see the
manners and dress of Madrid transferred to Vienna, to Hungary,
and even to Asia in the comedies *It Is Better Than It Was, The Gardener's Dog,* and *The Marvelous Magician.* In the comedy *Euridice
and Orpheus,* by Antonio de Solís, Aristeo and Felisardo, in their
familiarity with the laws against dueling, "seem rather Spaniards of
our time than persons of such a different nation and of such remote
centuries."[75] Luzán cannot refrain from saying that "women in
our comedies speak with more erudition and elegance than is nat-

ural and proper to their sex and capacity."[76] He admits that Spanish women through special favor of Heaven or of the Spanish climate are born endowed with unusual cleverness and wit along with their beauty, but he believes that Spanish poets have carried these qualities to the point of exaggeration. The male characters are equally prone to exceed the bounds of reason in their erudition and in the elegance of their language:

> Heraclius and Leonidas in the comedy, *In This Life All Is True and All Is False* by Calderón, having been reared in a desert among wild animals, without human contacts, would naturally be expected to be unpolished and coarse; nevertheless, the poet makes them use repartee and concepts which would only fit the most discreet courtier.[77]

The most frequent errors of Spanish comedies are against history, chronology, and geography:

> For example, in the comedy above, *In This Life All Is True and All Is False,* one of the characters is Cinthia, Queen of Trinacria; but neither in the time of Phocas nor afterward has a Cinthia ever reigned in Sicily. Two other comedies by Calderón, *The Arms of Beauty* and *Pains of Love and Loyalty,* are manifestly contrary to history. And although in the case of private persons the poet may invent names and happenings because such persons are not mentioned in history, in the case of emperors and kings whose names and deeds are definitely recorded in annals, the poet does not have the authority to invent names and events contrary to history. In the comedy, *Count Lucanor,* by Calderón, there are Ptolemies who are represented to be sultans of Egypt and there are dukes in Tuscany; although at the time of the Ptolemies there were no sultans in Egypt or dukes in Tuscany.[78]

Spanish writers have been equally careless in geography. Luzán cites a number of such errors as a warning to those writers who may in the future wish to construct their plays with due regard to historical accuracy:

> In the comedy, *It Is Better Than It Was,* Vienna is made the capital of Bohemia; in *Perico Urdemalas,* Capua is a seaport, and in *With Whom I Come, I Come* and others, Verona and Paris are located also on the coast; in *Emotions of Hatred and Love,* the armies of Russia and of Sweden camp on the banks of the Danube, although that river passes through neither of those countries. This river is still more distant from Palestine and, nevertheless, Calderón was careless enough in the comedy, *The Great Queen of Saba,* to name it along with the Tigris and the Euphrates in connection with the deeds of Joab.[79]

Although later neo-classicists were to wage a determined battle against the *Autos Sacramentales*, Luzán omits discussion of this genre until the final paragraph of his section on the drama, considering that because of its peculiar nature it is not subject to the rules which he has so carefully expounded:

> The *Autos Sacramentales* are a specie of dramatic poetry known only in Spain; and their artifice is reduced to forming an allegorical representation in honor of the sacred mystery of the Eucharist. Because of their purely allegorical nature they are free from most of the rules of tragedy. The happy wit of Pedro Calderón de la Barca exercised its talent in this new type of poetry with general applause.[80]

Second Edition of Luzán's Poetics

In the two chapters added at the beginning of the 1789 edition of Luzán's *Poetics,* we find no substantial difference in attitude toward the old theater, praise being mixed with censure in about the same ratio as in the earlier edition. As we shall see, the new praise offsets the passage, the omission of which was noted by Menéndez y Pelayo. As in the first edition, Luzán seems to realize that in criticizing Lope and Calderón he must proceed cautiously. He is willing to concede that in such intangible matters as imagination and charm of style many of their plays are admirable, but that is as far as he is willing to go. He finds both dramatists woefully lacking in verisimilitude and in the adherence to certain rules which he believes to be the natural consequence of this general principle. He praises Lope particularly for the "scope, variety, and amenity of his genius"[81] and for the facility with which he produced works of such a diverse nature. These qualities, he says, place him in the class of extraordinary men; but he adds that

> ... it was unfortunate that he came at a time when no great progress had been made in good criticism, that is, in the art of judging correctly the works of the intellect and of the imagination; and so a man who was born for the glory of Spain, by abusing his superior qualities, far from fulfilling his destiny, contributed infinitely to preventing other great geniuses who came later and who tried to imitate him from fulfilling theirs; because Lope is not a model for imitation, but an immense storehouse from which one who enters to choose with discernment and taste comes out rich in poetic goods.[82]

Luzán finds a facile explanation for Lope's fecundity, which, he says, was made possible by

... not stopping to choose subjects appropriate for imitation on the stage; taking at times as a theme the life of a man, and the whole universe as the stage; changing and misrepresenting history, without respect for the most notorious facts and with a mixture of absurd plots; and by attributing to kings, princes, heroes, and illustrious ladies shameful or ridiculous characters, manners, and actions; making the interlocutors use any language which occurred to him; making ordinary women, servants, and rustics speak like learned philosophers, pouring out trivial erudition and commonplace remarks, a defect which is found in all of his works; and making kings and important personages speak like people on the street, without dignity or decorum.[83]

Feeling perhaps that this severe indictment may offend Lope's partisans too much unless it is tempered with a measure of praise, Luzán hastens to add: "Nevertheless, one finds in many of his dramas scenes of great interest which could serve as a model of naturalness and good style."[84] He believes that a play mentioned without name in *Dialogue IV on Painting* by Vicencio Carducho must have been of this type; for such was the vivid impression produced upon the spectators, according to Carducho, that "one of the audience, carried away by his anger and pity, stood up in fury, shouting against the cruel murderer who was apparently cutting the throat of an innocent lady."[85] But even though some of Lope's scenes may be realistic, Luzán declares that he has been unable to find in Lope's theater a complete drama which is even passably regular and does not believe such a drama can be found among all of his plays. No one, he says, has ever been able to find the six which Lope claimed to have written "in accordance with the rules of art."[86] According to Luzán, Lope was subjected to criticism by his contemporaries—who, however, being afraid to attack too openly the "public idol," usually refrained from calling him by name. Lope pretended to disregard this criticism, attributing it to envy; but Luzán says it is evident that he was worried and that, in attempting to justify his practice, he was guilty of numerous contradictions. As evidence of the confused state of Lope's mind, Luzán cites Lope's statement in the prologue to the comedy, *The Certain for the Doubtful*, that "in Spain comedies have no precepts," and in the novel, *The Misfortunes of Honor*, his belief that "novels have the same precepts as comedies, the purpose of which the authors conceive to be the pleasure and contentment of the masses, even though art be hanged."[87] At other times, Luzán says, Lope attempted to place the blame for the irregularity of his theater upon public taste, as in his *New Art of Writing Comedies.* Luzán denies emphatically at this point that the public as a whole is incapable of appreciating good plays and accuses Lope and his contemporaries of responsibility for the so-called "bad taste" of the public.

In Chapter I of the 1789 edition Luzán traces briefly the history of Spanish drama from its humble beginnings in the fourteenth-century dialogues to the advent of Lope de Vega at the beginning of the seventeenth century and to the peak of the Spanish *comedia,* which he says was reached with Calderón. He mentions some early attempts by scholars to imitate the ancients and to observe rules of art, but concludes that these attempts were without influence upon the development of the theater in Spain. Spanish drama, he says, has been irregular from the beginning:

Reflecting now without prejudice upon the beginning, progress, and present condition of dramatic poetry among us, and upon the two classes which I distinguish as the old and the modern, it will be seen that the old is the only one that has ever had a following in Spain; and that the modern, that is, the one based upon the rules which Aristotle and Horace left us, has not been received or practiced in our theaters, even though some Spaniards have written upon its rules, suggested or approved some of its precepts, written some tragedies or comedies with the intention of observing them, and made judicious criticism or satires upon the general irregularity. Four or five tragedies which were never performed, even though they were perfect, and many others which are tragedies only in name, are not enough for us to consider this class of poetry naturalized among us at any time.[88]

Luzán does not believe that the testimony of Pinciano that tragedies were performed in the theaters during his time is at all conclusive, and he is confident that the plays to which he had reference did not deserve to be called tragedies. If tragedies had been as common as some people claim they were, surely some would still be extant either in printed or in manuscript form. Luzán has more confidence in the testimony of Cascales in his *Tablas Poéticas* printed in 1617: "Now it occurs to me to wonder ... why tragedies are not performed in Spain. Is it by chance because they deal with sad things, and we are inclined by nature to prefer happy things?"[89] Luzán considers that this question implies a positive negation that tragedies were performed either in Cascales' time or at any earlier period.

In Chapter II, "Upon the Rules Which Are Supposed to Govern Our Dramatic Poetry," Luzán reaffirms his statement that Spanish dramatic poetry never had rules or fixed principles worthy of the name. He is aware that many disagree with him, considering it an offense against the nation to accuse Spanish poets of having written without art. Others say that poetry does not need art, that genius alone is enough. Others, apparently more moderate, say that the rules of Aristotle were made for the Greeks, and those of Horace for the Romans, and that the Italians, French, and other nations may follow them if they wish, but the Spaniards have no obligation to conform to these rules, inasmuch as they have rules of their own which are much more suitable and much more in keeping with their national spirit and manners. Granting for the sake of argument that the Spaniards have such a body of rules, Luzán examines *The New Art of Writing Comedies* by Lope, which he says is the only work known to him that purports to expound these new precepts. Inasmuch as this work is little known and has become very rare, he reprints it in its entirety, and then asks: "How could Lope have spoken more clearly in favor of the rules of Aristotle and against the defects which characterize our dramas?"[90] Luzán wishes to rectify a statement he made in the earlier edition to the effect that Lope was the "corruptor of our theater." After careful investigation he is now convinced that the Spanish theater never had any rules or works which could be called regular. Spanish comedies, he says, were born and grew without art, and Lope did no more than follow and help to perpetuate by his example a disorder which already existed. Luzán goes into considerable detail in his analysis and criticism of Lope's *New Art,* and then disclaims any intention of writing a *Poética* in conformity with such a system. His work will follow the rules given by Aristotle and Horace and observed by all cultured nations in theory and in practice. Spanish poets are at liberty to choose the system which suits their caprice and the taste of the public, "but at all times there will be people who are intelligent and superior to the common herd, who will do justice to what is based upon reason, and will not confuse it with what merits scorn."[91] Luzán recognizes in Calderón a dramatist superior to Lope, but here again censure outweighs praise. Calderón, he says, came upon the scene at a propitious time when Felipe IV was actively encouraging dramatic production. If Spanish poets had had any knowledge of the rules of art and had had better taste, the wealth of native talent might have carried Spanish drama to a pinnacle of perfection. Calderón, he says, was the outstanding dramatist of his time. As a

result of his education and constant association with the elite of the
court, his language was "so urbane, so pleasing, and so seductive,
that in this respect he had no competitor."[92] Luzán divides Calderón's plays into three classes: those which are called "de teatro,"
that is, those "which are performed with decorations, stage machinery, and change of scenery"; others called "heroic," the personages of which are from the nobility; and others, commonly called
"cloak and sword plays," which deal with gentlemen and ladies and
the lower classes, and which are performed without decorations or
change of scenery. Luzán says that in the first two classes Calderón
followed, as did all of his contemporaries, the pattern set by Lope,
although with somewhat more attention to regularity. In the "cloak
and sword plays," however, Luzán says he does not believe that
Calderón had a model:

... The invention, formation, and solution of extremely complicated plots;
the subtleties, repartee, gallantry, sudden love affairs, nocturnal strolls in
front of a lady's house, clandestine entrances, and scaling the walls of
houses; the point of honor, swords in hand, duels for the slightest cause,
killing a man for the very offense of which the killer is guilty; ladies
proud and at the same time wanton and clever in evading the vigilance
of their fathers or brothers and hiding their lovers in their own bedrooms;
nocturnal dates at the windows or in the gardens; rascally menservants;
maidservants schooled in all kinds of procurement, by reason of which
they always play an important role in the play; and in short the exaggerated picture of love-making and incidents of those times, all this was
characteristically his.[93]

In thus enumerating the exaggerations that characterize the
theater of Calderón, Luzán sets a precedent which was followed by
most of the subsequent critics of the *comedia*. Luzán finds Calderón's theater a deplorable school of character, but aside from
the moral element, he admits that

... as far as art is concerned, one can say that, although Calderón did
not subject himself to the just rules of the ancients, there is in some of his
comedies the first essential of art, which is to interest the spectators, and
to carry them from scene to scene, not only without boredom, but with a
keen desire to see the end; a most essential quality of which many poets
of other nations who are scrupulous observers of the rules cannot boast.[94]

The above passage, which does not appear in the 1737 edition, is
certainly as important a concession to the genius of Calderón as the

passage cited by Menéndez y Pelayo, the omission of which in the later edition this critic attributes to a change of heart on Luzán's part or to alteration by later neo-classicists in support of their theories. Luzán concludes his initial discussion of the theater of Calderón with the following remarks, which are no less encomiastic:

> Some accuse him of having little variety in his themes and characters, saying that one who has seen what Don Pedro and Doña Juana do and say in one *comedia*, can imagine what Don Enrique and Doña Elvira will do and say in another. This criticism is not without foundation; but the superior qualities of Calderón, and the charm of his style, make up for many defects and will be considered marks of excellence until another comes, who equaling him in virtues, lacks his vices. Since such a dramatist has not yet appeared among us, Calderón maintains almost all of his original popularity; he served and still serves as a model; and his *comedias* are the richest source of plays for our theater.[95]

Upon careful consideration it becomes apparent, however, that this praise is only relative, since it recognizes the absolute dearth of contemporary dramatic talent.

In the theater of such contemporaries of Calderón as Moreto and Francisco de Rojas, Luzán finds much that is worthy of praise, particularly in the *comedies of character*. About Moreto he says:

> Moreto was a man of clear judgment, and of vivid and rich imagination. In his works there is a little of everything; but it is evident that when in his natural style and laying affectation aside, he tried to follow the course of true comedy, he knew how to choose subjects, weave plots with clarity, adorn them with unexpected incidents, vary the characters and emotions, and portray them expressively, as he did in *Disdain Conquered by Disdain, The Aunt and the Niece,* and others.[96]

He also praises Moreto for his ability to choose what was good in the "old farces" and to take from them the idea and the scheme of certain scenes. He believes that contemporary dramatists would do well to emulate Moreto in this respect, "availing themselves of the excellent qualities which they will find mixed with the chaff of our innumerable comedies."[97] Luzán does not recommend the complete abandonment of the *comedia,* but believes that much can be salvaged. In this recommendation he anticipates the *refundiciones,* which, starting with Sebastian y Latre in 1772, ran through the entire eighteenth century and well into the nineteenth.

Francisco de Rojas resembled Moreto in his *cloak and sword* plays and in comedies of character like *Open Your Eye* and *The Game Is Between Fools,* and at times probably surpassed him in language; but in his *heroic comedies* bad taste reaches the height of depravity. Luzán doubts that there is a poet of that time "who does not participate in this delirious jargon, which is much less tolerable in dramas than in any other class of composition."[98] According to Luzán, Juan de Matos Fragoso had a clear claim to the prize in this respect, because a natural expression never slipped from his pen, all of his plays abounding in adjectives, hyperboles, and extravagant comparisons.

In the comedy after Calderón, Luzán finds almost nothing worthy of praise, except in the *comedia de figurón;* he does, however, note the increased popularity of plays of this type which he says may properly be called comedies, since they ridicule the vices and folly of some extravagant character. Moreto in *The Aunt and the Niece* and Rojas in *Don Lucas del Cigarral* had already set the pattern. Among later plays which Luzán thinks most closely approximate true comedy he mentions *The Punishment of Avarice,* by Juan de la Hoz, *One Fool Makes a Hundred,* by Solís, *Bewitched by Force,* by Zamora, and among those which were relatively contemporary, *El Dómine Lucas,* by Cañizares. While these comedies are by no means perfect, Luzán believes they point the way which should be followed by contemporary dramatists, and cites their continued popularity as an adequate answer to Lope's maxim:

> The stupid rabble pays and in fair measure
> The Poets must speak as fools to give it pleasure.[99]

Menéndez y Pelayo admits that "in what we might call negative criticism, that is to say, in the censure of the most common and palpable defects of our old comedies, Luzán hits the mark, and one can admit that he is almost always right."[100] It is hard to agree with this critic, however, when he says that this censure on the part of Luzán implies nothing for or against the Spanish theater "because this criticism by Luzán is so minute and so detailed and leaves so untouched the spirit of the works he analyzes, that the real evaluation remains to be made after these mechanical observations."[101]

The points criticized by Luzán are precisely those which furnished materials for debate during the entire neo-classic controversy, and which made necessary the reworking of the old plays before they could be performed upon a modern stage. Luzán does not minimize the value of imagination, but insists that imagination must be subjected to certain restraints in the interest of verisimilitude. It must be borne in mind that the efforts of the neo-classicists were not directed merely toward the observance of the unities, but principally in the direction of the broad principle of verisimilitude, which includes not only the much buffeted unities, but also the avoidance of the extravagances of style and subject matter which marred the *comedia* of the Golden Age and the plays of Comella and his school in the latter part of the eighteenth century.

There has been a sharp difference of opinion on the part of critics concerning the immediate and the lasting influence of Luzán's *Poetics*. Quintana says that it was "little read then and that for the time being its influence upon the progress and improvement of art was slight, or rather null."[102] Gil y Zárate is nearer the truth in saying that at first it produced no sensation whatsoever, but that later it became "the literary code of the best writers."[103] Tichnor is convinced that its effect "was immediate and great" and that it "exercised from its first appearance a controlling authority over opinions at the court of Spain, and over the few writers of reputation then to be found in the country."[104] We shall see that from the date of its publication Luzán's *Poetics* became the manifesto of the neo-classic movement and that at no time during the eighteenth century was its authority seriously questioned by neo-classicists.

Criticism by the Diario de los Literatos

Almost immediately the *Diario de los Literatos* took cognizance of the *Poetics*, publishing in the same year a detailed résumé and a criticism of the work.[105] The first sixty-two pages of the résumé were written by Juan Martínez Salafranca and the remainder of the article by Juan de Iriarte. While the *Diario* feels that Luzán has done his country a genuine service and that "no writing was more needed in our Spain than a complete and authoritative *Poetics*," it does not admit that Spain has been entirely negligent in this field and mentions Pinciano, Lope de Vega, Cascales, Carvallo, Pellicer, and Salas among early "legislators." It is interesting to note that no distinction is made between Lope and such avowed classicists as Pinciano, Cascales, and Salas. The *Diario* admits that all previous writers on poetics have been too lenient with existing abuses or have treated the subject inadequately. Luzán's *Poetics*, therefore, fills a long felt need in Spain for a work which would be "a kind of poetic code."

In his comments and criticism, Iriarte finds much to praise in Luzán's work, but he is not entirely content with his evaluation of Golden Age comedy: "Among the flowery eulogies with which Don Ignacio crowns our celebrated poets, he is wont at times to weave the thorns of a severe and somewhat impassioned criticism directed principally against Lope de Vega and Luis de Góngora."[106] Nor can he bring himself to concur in Luzán's condemnation of Lope's *New Art of Writing Comedies*. He objects to the statement that Lope wrote his *New Art* to defend and to support the novelty of his comedies, and that his work is "a book, the fundamentals and the principles of which are directly opposed to reason and to the rules of Aristotle."[107] Iriarte insists that if Lope had intended to defend the irregular theater he would have had to assume the position of discrediting the laws established by the ancients. On the contrary, we find that he pays marked tribute to the ancient laws and evinces scorn for the modern innovations. He takes at its face value Lope's justification of irregularity of his theater on the grounds that the public demanded extravagance and dwells at length upon the despotic power wielded by the uncultured spectators during the seventeenth century. So far is Lope from giving his approval to the irregularity which has been introduced into the theater that, if his statements are examined and interpreted properly, it will be seen that "his work in reality is more a *new art* of criticizing comedies than of composing them."[108]

Iriarte does not defend Lope's irregularities but seeks to explain and to excuse them. Indeed, he considers Lope as much an admirer and an exponent of true poetics as Pinciano, Cascales, Salas, or Luzán himself. He even censures the latter for having neglected to take his illustrations from the six comedies which Lope declared he had written according to rules of art and is certain that these comedies would have revealed that Lope was not only well acquainted with the Aristotelian rules, but also capable of putting them into practice. Lope, then, would have been completely exonerated from the accusation of being ignorant of true art.

Iriarte feels impelled to defend tragi-comedy on the ground that, since life is itself a mingling of the tragic and the comic, this genre does not violate the principle of verisimilitude. Luzán has said that tragi-comedy is "a new monster unknown to the ancients." Without going into the question of whether Plautus called his *Amphitryon* a

tragi-comedy seriously or in jest, Iriarte declares "it is certain that
the ancients recognized a type of drama which partakes of tragedy
and comedy and which admits the mixture of the serious and the
jocose."[109] He points out that not only Plautus, but also Euripides,
Aeschylus, Sophocles, and especially Pratinas, mixed serious and
comic roles and asks: "If in the theater of human life true tragi-
comedies happen, why should they not be represented in the
theater, provided they observe the conditions and laws of decorum
and propriety?"[110] Iriarte believes that it would be unreasonable to
add to the three unities to which comedy is already subject a fourth
"unity of species," when the Romans themselves recognized so many
different kinds of comedies: *pretextatas, togatas, atelanas,* and *tab-
ernarias,* depending upon the nature of the themes and the characters. He does not admit the validity of the objection that comic scenes
interrupt and destroy the effect of tragic emotions "because the same
thing happens in a tragedy or comedy, where the emotions of pity,
tenderness, and love destroy those of anger, fury, and hate."[111]
This train of thought leads him to assert that "it could be demonstrated that many of the maxims that critics establish as general laws
of dramatics are only particular laws applicable to the genius and
taste of each century and of each nation, as is evidenced by the
history of the ancient and the modern theaters."[112]

After citing the above words of Iriarte, Menéndez y Pelayo cannot restrain his enthusiasm and exclaims: "This is a truly sensible and
admirable page of criticism, but not the only one written in the
same vein by the apologists of the national tradition, which was
never killed or smothered in the eighteenth century."[113] In view of
the greater liberalism of criterion which Menéndez y Pelayo notes in
Iriarte's attitude toward the rules, he finds it only natural that this
critic should oppose the narrowness of Luzán's interpretation of the
unity of time:

> It is obvious that Iriarte, thinking in such a free and rational manner,
> could not help disagreeing with Luzán's interpretation of the unity of time.
> He not only calls arbitrary the rule of four hours, but affirms roundly that
> to narrow the limits of the action only serves to suffocate and to oppress
> genius and to cut off the flight of the poet's pen, thus spoiling the most
> substantial part of drama, which is the artifice of the plot.[114]

What Iriarte actually says, however, is that "it seems greatly excessive to limit to three or four hours that which the most wise master

fixed as twenty-four and a fraction." He says nothing about any extension of time beyond that advocated by Aristotle and is far from advocating the freedom in regard to the duration of the action which characterized the Golden Age plays. He contents himself with the statement that "the more the limits of the action are restricted, the more genius is oppressed and smothered; and in proportion as the flight of time is curtailed, the pen of the poet is clipped to the detriment of the substantial part of drama, which is the artifice of the plot."[115]

Although this criticism of the *Poetics* by the *Diario* was accompanied by lavish praise for the work as a whole, Luzán felt moved some two or three years later to answer the objections which had been raised. In a pamphlet published under the imperfect anagram of Don Iñigo de Lanuza, Luzán reaffirms his position and cites more authorities, but contributes nothing new to the basic statement of his doctrine. Menéndez y Pelayo says that Luzán answered "in a discourteous tone,"[116] and Cueto asserts that Luzán defended his *Poetics* against Iriarte's criticism "with the harsh tone of invective."[117] Pellissier, however, declares that "what is noticeable is the tone of perfect affability which rules the style of this little discussion,"[118] and cites as a proof of the friendly spirit which existed between the participants the words of Luzán:

> The objections of the editors of the *Diario* to the *Poetics*, although they do not, as I have said, strike at any essential part, are so adorned with urbanity and modesty (circumstances which stand out singularly not only in this censure but in all of those contained in the *Diario*) that they justly deserve that my appreciation be made as public as their moderation has been.[119]

Indeed, the discussion between Luzán and the editors of the *Diario* is characterized by a moderation which is unfortunately absent from the polemics that raged throughout the remainder of the century, and even from those carried on by the same periodical with its opponents. It is true that this was a controversy between friends with ideas which were not, on the whole, widely divergent.

Although Luzán had given in his *Poetics* strict rules for the composition of tragedies, his first and apparently only attempt to follow these rules in an original play resulted in concessions to popular taste. In 1742 he composed a comedy, *Virtue Crowned*, for performance in the city hall by a group of ladies and gentlemen of

Monzón. Our only information about this play, which was apparently composed only for a particular occasion with no intention of publication, is furnished by his son:

> In this comedy, doubtless in order to condescend to the taste of the actors, he did not observe the rules of art with that exactitude which was to be expected from one who had taught and defended them with such intelligence and constancy. Nevertheless, the play has well-sustained characters, excellent morals, good subject and plot, and a solution which is natural, although, as I believe, imitated; the versification is fluent, easy, and free from all affectation . . .[120]

At the time of the publication of his *Poetics* Luzán had had no direct contact with the French theater and could judge it only by the limited number of plays and criticisms he had read. His residence in Paris from 1747 to 1750, however, enabled him to make a comparison between the Spanish and the French theaters. He must have been surprised to find the extent of the reaction in France against classical tragedy and comedy and to find that even the comedies of Molière and the tragedies of Corneille and Racine no longer interested the public. As early as 1739, Voltaire had commented upon the almost complete cessation of Molière's popularity: "The theater is deserted when those comedies are played and almost no one attends the performance of that same *Tartuffe* which formerly attracted all of Paris."[121] And only the year before Luzán's arrival the Duke of Aumont had forbidden the further performance of Molière's plays at the *Comédie Française* because they were "now entirely abandoned by the public."[122] In 1754 the French dramatist, Palissot, lamented the decline of a genre formerly perfected by the great masters and productive of useful pleasure, which "for a long time has suffered a kind of proscription on our stage."[123]

No dramatist remotely approaching the stature of Molière had appeared to carry on his work and, according to Palissot, "A childish jargon, indicative neither of study nor knowledge of the world, a cold metaphysics based upon improbable events, a moral devoid of action had taken the place of that genre which Molière raised among us to such a high level."[124] The reputation of such writers as Regnard had been made, he says, from the debris left by Molière. Pallisot believed that the very superiority of the models had produced discouragement among their would-be followers and agreed with La Bruyère that "everything has been said; one comes too late after more than

seven thousand years that men have been thinking. In the treatment
of manners the best has been used; one only gleans after the ancients
and clothes their works with modern dress."[125]

Memorias Literarias de París

In his *Memorias Literarias de París*,[126] published in 1751 after
his return to Spain, Luzán is enthusiastic in his praise of France's
scientific and cultural progress but rather critical of contemporary
dramatic trends. It is evident that the French theater itself did not
measure up to the rigid standards he had set in his *Poetics:*

> Generally I have seen the principal rules of the theater well observed,
> both in tragedy and in comedy: the three unities of action, time, and place;
> character and the linking of scenes to the end of each act. Nevertheless,
> in some plays something might be said about the unity of action; in others
> about the lack of proportion between action and time; and in others the
> characters have seemed to me to be so unnatural that the illusion of the
> audience is destroyed.[127]

Luzán is especially critical of contemporary French tragedy.
In their attempt to make this genre very sententious and tragic the
French, in his opinion, make it affected and bombastic. He warns
that "if this abuse and this false sublimity continue to increase, the
natural will be lost sight of and true eloquence will be corrupted
in France."[128] He finds the style of comedies generally free from this
defect. Pallisot, however is equally critical of French comedy and
tragedy of the period:

> It is necessary to count . . . among the causes of our loss the almost
> general abandonment in our comedies of the use of dialogue. That tissue
> of perpetual epigrams which abounds in most of our plays is as out of
> place in comedy, which should imitate especially the natural tone of
> conversation, as that mass of antitheses and of maxims which crushes
> our tragedies today and which with us has almost destroyed the art
> of acting.[129]

Luzán condemns French tragedy for lack of originality in themes
and for slavish imitation of the ancients. In their attempt to imitate
and even to surpass the fame of the Greeks, the French have brought
forth a new crop of Phedras, Electras, Oedipuses, Iphigenias, Ores-
teses, etc., without realizing that subjects which were considered

plausible by the ancients are now completely incredible. The people, he says, "no longer believe in Oracles or in false Gods."[130]

He approves wholeheartedly the French practice of giving all five acts of a tragedy or comedy in succession without the interpolation of *interludes* and recommends its imitation on the Spanish stage,

...because...the interposition and mixture of a different and opposite subject cannot fail to confuse the imagination of the spectator and to interfere with the understanding of the play, dispelling or lessening the illusion, the theatrical deception, and the emotions which are in the process of being aroused.[131]

He approves also the use of music during the intermissions while preparations are being made behind the curtain for the next act and while the audience is being allowed to rest. He has only praise for the manner of staging French plays. Although he makes no comparison with the Spanish stage of the time, his dissatisfaction with conditions in his own country may be sensed from his praise of the French: "The staging is very good in the beautiful and well-executed mutations and in the good taste of the actor's dress, in the illumination and in the variety and perfection of the dances."[132]

In his *Poetics*, Luzán had revealed a certain dissatisfaction with a fixed stage. After seeing its use by the French he does not hesitate to accept it. His description of the French theater serves to show the difference between that stage and the simple, unadorned stage with its four curtains or the stage with the crude mutations produced by backdrops which still prevailed in the Spanish theater:

The scene is fixed and stable, representing the same place from the beginning to the end of the comedy or tragedy. Although the scene is fixed, the perspective does not fail to represent several contiguous places which open upon a common hall or courtyard where the entire action of the play occurs. In the tragedy *Semiramis* by Voltaire, the scene represented a magnificent temple courtyard; at one side was the mouth or entrance to the Sepulchre of the Child. In other tragedies the scene represents a palace hall or other place according to the requirements of the plot. In comedies the scene usually represents an antechamber, or room, where all the interlocutors converse. The stable and fixed scene is more appropriate, more verisimilar and more in keeping with the unity of place interpreted in its strictest sense. To change scenes and to see what was a hall disappear to be replaced as if by magic by an open country or a prison cannot fail to do violence to the imagination of the audience and to dispel the deception or theatrical illusion, making it apparent that what is being performed is fiction and not reality. It is true that the fixed scene requires that the poet exert greater effort to conciliate the verisimilitude of the plot with stability of place, but that is as it should be.[133]

It is curious that Luzán makes no mention of the peculiar custom in the French theater, which dates from the middle of the seventeenth century, of allowing a certain number of spectators on the stage itself. This unusual practice, which lasted until 1759, made impossible any change of scene, hampered the actor's movements, and was instrumental in reducing French plays to conversations with a minimum of action. Tallemant, writing somewhere around 1657, tells us:

There is at this time a frightful inconvenience to the staging of comedy, and it is that the two sides of the theater are completely filled with young men seated in straw chairs.... The loges are very expensive and it is necessary to apply early for tickets. For an ecu or a demi-louis, one can have a place on the stage itself; but this spoils everything, for one insolent spectator suffices to throw everything into disorder.[134]

A gravure by Coypel, printed in 1726, shows the presence of spectators on the stage. The play is about to start, but the front curtain is still lowered. The stage itself is very small, not more than fifteen feet wide. Some spectators are standing behind the curtain and, impelled by their curiosity, are pulling it aside to see what is going on in the hall.

They are enclosed in a double balustrade which, starting at the angle of the theater where the curtain descends, describes a quarter of a circle to the rear. One can see that this arrangement absolutely suppresses the first wings. The actors can only come from the rear of the stage, and one can see that the decoration is almost entirely restricted to the back curtain. ... It is obvious that this arrangement prevented any action on the stage: everything had to be restricted to a more or less animated conversation under the two lights.[135]

Nine years after Luzán left Paris, the *Mercure de France* pointed out the inconvenience of the practice. No realistic staging was possible. When the curtain was raised the audience saw a stage hemmed in by the young gallants with the actors so close at times that the spectators could almost touch them. Commenting upon the performance of Molière's *Tartuffe*, the *Mercure* says: "Auguste is deliberating in the midst of the young dandies, and while Tartuffe is making a careful examination to see that no one can surprise him while he is making love to his benefactor's wife, he has around him a hundred witnesses to his tête-à-tête with her."[136]

The pernicious effect of such an abuse upon the performance of plays on the Paris stage may be further judged from the following account of the performance of Voltaire's *Semiramis:*

> The great obstacle to the effectiveness of the performance was the crowding of the spectators upon the stage. The first evening there was such a crowd that the actors could not move around. In the scene of the tomb of the child, the sentinel posted on the stage, seeing that there was not even room for the phantom to enter, cried out in a loud voice: "Make way for the Ghost!" The Ghost became entangled in the legs of the young gallants and almost fell.[137]

Voltaire himself, in his "Dissertation upon Ancient and Modern Tragedy," vigorously condemns the practice, which, he says, has hampered the proper development of tragedy in France and has forced this genre to limit itself to conversation:

> One of the greatest obstacles in our theater to the representation of any great and pathetic action is the crowd of spectators confused on the stage with the actors. This impropriety was particularly noticeable at the first performance of *Semiramis.* . . . One must make no mistake about it: such an inconvenience alone has been sufficient to deprive France of many masterpieces, which dramatists would have dared to write if there had been a theater free and suitable for action such as that found in all the other nations of Europe. . . . All the spectators should be able to see and hear equally no matter where they may be. How can this be accomplished on a narrow stage, in the midst of a crowd of young men who scarcely leave ten feet of acting room? This condition is responsible for the fact that the majority of our plays are nothing but long conversations; all theatrical action is cramped and ridiculous.[138]

Luzán had certainly witnessed the performance of *Semiramis;* yet, in spite of the evidence of his own eyes, he reports that he found the staging, the manner of performance, and all that is included under the term theatrical art well done on the French stage. It seems incredible that, after seeing such things in the French theater, he could still write that any change of scene did violence to the imagination of the audience and dispelled the deception or theatrical illusion, making it apparent that what was being performed was fiction and not reality. Certainly no French audience was for a moment under any illusion or suffering any deception when it could see at all times these young dandies only a few feet removed from the actors. Luzán was particularly impressed by the fact that the actors knew their roles and rarely needed the aid of the prompter. He also found the pronunciation of the actors clear and distinct, their expression appropriate, and their action lively, free, and artistic. He confesses, however, that at times the performance in French tragedies seemed to him "somewhat affected and declamatory."[139] Feeling that the Spanish stage was suffering from ignorance not only of the rules that should govern the composition of plays, but also of the rules of acting, Luzán translates in his *Memorias* a part of the *Art of the Theater* by the Italian actor and critic, Francesco Riccoboni. This section gives careful directions on the proper manner of gesticulation.

The activities of the neo-classicists during the eighteenth century were directed not only toward the regularization of the plays themselves but also toward the achievement of an illusion of reality in stage performances and setting. Indeed, their insistence that the scene remain fixed, or at least that it not change during the acts, constituted an attack in itself against the Golden Age theater with its practice of allowing the scene to shift from one place to another within a city or even to remote regions while the actors remained on the stage, such a change being effected merely by having the actors cross the stage and indicate by their speeches that they were in a new location. As most Golden Age plays were written it would have been impossible to present them on the stage advocated by Luzán and later neo-classicists. As long as the audience was satisfied with four curtains as the only stage adornment it was possible for novels in action to be performed with even greater ease than in modern talking pictures and with infinitely less effort and expense on the part of the producers. The matter of composition and staging was inevitably joined in all of the neo-classicists' conception of a regular theater.

The *Memorias de París* circulated among the same group which had found interest in Luzán's *Poetics* and served to round out his theories about the drama with observations based upon direct contact with a theater which at that time was the principal example of so-called dramatic regularity. We shall see that Montiano in his second discourse on the theater cites the *Memorias* respectfully.

Luzán and the Tearful Comedy

Menéndez y Pelayo sees evidence of a change of attitude on

Luzán's part toward the purity of the genres as a result of his residence in Paris:

> Luzán had defended with extraordinary warmth in his *Poetics* the theory of pure genres, but in Paris he changed his mind in view of the works of La Chaussée and Diderot, became an enthusiastic partisan of the sentimental or tearful comedy, and the year after his return from Paris published ... a translation of *Le préjugé à la mode* by La Chaussée with the title *Reason Against Fashion,* accompanied by an enthusiastic prologue.[140]

Menéndez y Pelayo says also that in condemning the sententious style of French tragedy Luzán was following in the steps of Diderot. The latter's plays and the definite crystallization of his dramatic principles, however, did not appear until some seven or eight years after Luzán's return to Spain. It is true that in 1748, only three years before the publication of Luzán's *Memorias* and of his translation of *Le préjugé à la mode,* Diderot had written the *Bijoux indiscrets* (1748), in which he seems to attack the tyranny of the rules:

> I do not understand the rules at all and even less do I understand the learned words in which they are expressed. But I do know that only what is true pleases and moves. I know also that the perfection of a play consists in an imitation of nature so exact that the spectator, constantly deceived, imagines that he is present at the action itself. Is there anything which resembles this in those tragedies of which you boast?[141]

Among the sins committed by French tragedy Diderot cites the complication of the plot and the accumulation of events within the space of twenty-four hours. The dialogue of tragedy seems to him completely unnatural: "The emphasis, the spirit, and the dazzle which reign there are a thousand miles from nature. The author seeks in vain to conceal himself; my eyes penetrate the deception and I see him always behind his characters. Cinna, Sertorius, Maxime, Emilie are at all times the speaking tubes of Corneille."[142]

Diderot severely censures the stereotyped denouements and the bearing and manner of speech of princes and kings:

> With regard to denouements there are a hundred bad ones for every good one. One denouement is not warranted, another is miraculous. When an author becomes weary of dragging a character from scene to scene for five acts he gets rid of him by a dagger thrust; everyone begins to weep, and I laugh like a fool. And again, has anyone ever spoken as we declaim?

Do queens and kings walk any differently from other normal human beings? Have they ever gesticulated like people possessed or like madmen?[143]

Lest we be led to think that Diderot's dissatisfaction with the theater of the time caused him to advise a mixture of genres and an abandonment of the rules, it would be well to compare his early statements with the dramatic criticism which accompanied his play, *The Natural Son* (1775), where he places his stamp of approval upon the three unities, saying: "The laws of the three unities are difficult to observe, but they are sensible." He is in favor of simplicity of action and strongly opposes any confusion of genres:

Will you be convinced of the danger which exists of crossing the barrier which nature has placed between the genres? Carry things to excess, bring together two genres as far apart as tragedy and burlesque, and you will see in turn a grave senator play at the feet of a courtesan the most debauched role and factionists plot the ruin of a republic.... Tragi-comedy can only be bad since it confuses two genres which are separated by a natural barrier.[144]

During the years that Luzán spent in Paris the *tearful comedy*, initiated by La Chaussée, was the main topic of conversation among the literati. Extreme neo-classicists like Piron and Collé insisted that there was no precedent for such a genre among the ancients, that no one had the right to change the nature of comedy, and that the new genre was destined to fail. Freron and l'Abbé Desfontaines came to La Chaussée's defense, while others like d'Alembert, La Harpe, and Grimm gave a qualified endorsement to the new genre in view of the impossibility of equaling the great masters, the exhaustion of comic types, and the necessity of reviving interest in drama by new combinations. *Le préjugé à la mode* was the outstanding theatrical success of the first half of the eighteenth century in France, being given twenty performances at its first playing and being repeated every year from 1735 until 1752. In view of La Chaussée's sustained popularity it is not surprising that Luzán should have caught some of the general enthusiasm. It is entirely possible that he saw no significant violation of neo-classic precepts, as he interpreted them, in La Chaussée's plays. The moral function of drama was always uppermost in Luzán's mind, and he could certainly find no fault with the new genre on that score. All of La Chaussée's plays fitted well into the general pattern of neo-classic precepts, and Luzán seemed quite

willing to admit a mixture of the comic and the sentimental so long
as the latter did not verge too closely upon the tragic and so long as
there was no undue mixture of princes and commoners. The change
which Menéndez y Pelayo hails with such evident satisfaction in
Luzán's attitude toward the purity of the genres is indeed more
apparent than real. Both Nivelle de la Chaussée and Diderot were
staunch supporters of the unities and of the didactic purpose of
drama. The type of *sentimental comedy*, which meets the approval
of Luzán and of many of the Spanish neo-classicists, is by no means
the same as the Spanish tragi-comedy with its mixture of princes and
commoners, tragedy and farce. It is really a *serious comedy* in which
sentiment replaces ridicule. The ending is usually happy and there
is no attempt to purge through terror. It will be observed that even
some of the most rigid neo-classicists, like Jovellanos, were not opposed to this type of comedy even though it was lacking in comic
force and did not correct through ridicule. It is significant that
Luzán's translation was dedicated to the Marquesa de Sarria, in
whose house assembled the famous Academy of Good Taste. The frequent inclusion by later neo-classic dramatists of sentimental scenes
in their comedies is but a reflection of what was a fashion in France
during the same period. In both countries the theater became more
and more a pulpit from which the dramatists launched their sermons
against vice. Spanish critics throughout the neo-classic period found
themselves in somewhat of a dilemma when they came to deal with
sentimental comedy. The criterion of judgment seemed to be the
extent to which tragic and comic elements were mixed. If a tragedy
was merely threatened and the solution was happy; if there was a
definite moral teaching; if the language was free from affectation and
the unities were observed, it was considered a *regular comedy* and
the critics were inclined to be liberal and even at times, as in the case
of Jovellanos' *The Honorable Culprit*, encomiastic. It will be seen
that the sentimental note found increasing favor with Spanish
audiences.

The Academy of Good Taste

From the inception of the movement the neo-classicists assumed
a superior attitude and considered themselves the champions of
good taste. To have this quality was the *sine qua non* of all literary
production. The standards set were, of course, the neo-classic precepts. It was only natural that those who held to these principles

should feel the necessity of banding together in a country where the majority of the people were violently opposed to any innovations in their cherished institutions. The year 1749, which saw the establishment of the Academy of Good Taste, may be considered as the beginning of a concerted effort to introduce neo-classicism into Spain. Menéndez y Pelayo says that this Academy was "without doubt, the outstanding literary phenomenon of the reign of Fernando VI."[145] The Academy of Good Taste, which was distinctly of an aristocratic character, met in the house of the Marquesa de Sarria and combined the qualities of the *salons* of France like the Hotel de Rambouillet with the literary academies which had long been in vogue in Italy and Spain. The name of the academy itself and the extravagant pseudonyms of its members were patterned after Italian practice. According to Cueto, even the name Academy of Good Taste had already been used by a group in Palermo.[146]

During the last years of the reign of Felipe V a Poetic Academy of Madrid was established, the members of which, like the dramatist Cañizares, were entirely satisfied with the prevailing literary taste and were proud to imitate the style of Góngora. The vogue of academies, however, had passed and the group, lacking enthusiasm and any definite crusading objective, soon broke up of its own accord. The Academy of Good Taste, on the contrary, was established under the most favorable auspices. As the name of the academy implies, the members were dedicated to reforming Spanish literary taste, although it is true that they did not always agree as to what constituted good taste or what past practices needed correction. The aristocracy of blood was already inclined to French tastes and was, for the most part, ashamed of Spain's relative position in the literary and cultural world. This group was joined by what might be called the literary aristocracy. The founders themselves, with the exception of Augustín de Montiano, were all of the aristocracy of blood. The membership was soon increased to include such leaders of the incipient neo-classic movement as Luzán, Nasarre, and Velázquez, who were dogmatic in their attitude toward past abuses and the necessity for reform.

As Menéndez y Pelayo points out, the Academy was not a solid body of neo-classicists, since it contained some members who, while paying lip service to neo-classic precepts, did not always choose to follow them in their own works and at times expressed ideas directly opposed to neo-classicism. The minutes of the Academy, which were kept by Montiano, contain many poems written by members who seemed to have no conception of the new rules or who wilfully followed the old school. Menéndez y Pelayo explains the lack of complete harmony among the members of the Academy of Good Taste as the result of the incorporation of elements from the Academy of the Tripode, which had lasted for some ten years in Granada. The Count of Torre-Palma, founder of the Granadine academy, and his friend, Porcel, had already revealed in their poetry definite Gongoristic traits combined with flights of imagination which were characteristic of the national school. Porcel himself confesses at the beginnin of his *Adonis,* a collection of hunting eclogues, that he attempted to imitate the best Spanish and Latin poets; and among these he names Garcilaso de la Vega and "the incomparable D. Luis de Góngora." Of the two poets cited, Garcilaso was a consistent favorite among neo-classicists, while Góngora never failed to excite their wrath. It is evident that ten years after the publication of Luzán's *Poetics* Góngora had by no means lost his hold on Spanish poets; indeed, he was still the literary idol of many. We have noticed that Iriarte, although he was willing to sanction most of the reforms proposed by Luzán, had opposed too rigid an interpretation of certain rules and had even defended a sonnet by Góngora.

It seems that Porcel found some comfort for his restlessness under classical restraint in the recently published volumes of the *Teatro Crítico* by Feijóo. There is a striking similarity in the ideas expressed by the two writers. In the first volume of his *Critical Theater,* published in 1726, Feijóo had accused the French poets of lack of warmth in their works because of a too servile adherence to rules. "One sees that in order to appear very regular in their thoughts the French poets leave their compositions very languid, clip the wings of the Muses, or with the weight of reason beat their feathers to the ground."[147] Porcel rephrases Feijóo's statement, combining it with the latter's well-known phrase, "an I do not know what." "Although their poems conform to all the rigor of art, they are accustomed to lack an 'I do not know what,' unless it be poetic warmth; for, with too much tempering their verses remain languid and their thoughts cold."[148]

Porcel, like Feijóo, could not take docilely the abuse that the French critics had heaped upon Spanish literature from the time of Boileau. Although he had translated Boileau's *Lutrin,* he resented the French critic's evaluation of Spanish literature and disagreed sharply with him in his *Juicio lunático.* Porcel and Feijóo thus initi-

ated the custom of attributing coldness and lack of life to French
literature as an answer to the French claim that Spanish literature was characterized by excessive imagination, bad taste, and
irregularity.

It was too much to expect Spaniards to turn their backs upon all
of their past training. We find, therefore, that many, like Porcel,
found themselves mentally convinced of the extravagance of Spanish poetry but at heart reluctant to abandon even the grandiloquence
and affectation of Gongorism. They could not bring themselves to
accept rules which they instinctively felt hampered the imagination.
So we find Porcel at one time ridiculing the bad taste of his own
poetry and at others expressing romantic ideas which might well
have been taken from Tirso de Molina's *Orchards of Toledo* and
which anticipated by almost a century Victor Hugo's outburst
against classical restraint. At one of the meetings of the Academy of
Good Taste Porcel did not hesitate to express in the presence of
Luzán, Velázquez, and Montiano his rebellion at the narrowness of
the rules fixed by Boileau. Putting his ideas into the mouth of Garcilaso de la Vega, he represents this Golden Age poet as saying:

> I confirm the judgment which I made among mortals that poetics are
> only opinions. Poetry is the product of genius and, with the exception of
> some general rules and of the universal discretion which every sensible
> man has, the poet should adopt no other law than that of his genius. The
> spirit of a poet should rush in freely; it is for that reason that Pegasus is
> painted with wings and not with a bridle. For that reason it is folly to
> bridle him as the French Parnassus has recently attempted to do. . . .
> In vain do the masters of art tire themselves pointing out these or other
> rules, because this only tyrannizes over man's free thought, which varies in
> each individual according to the force of his genius, the value of his
> language, the doctrine imposed upon him during his formative years, the
> passions which dominate him, and many other things.[149]

Although Porcel appears to have been torn between an emotional
admiration for the old school and an intellectual appreciation of the
benefit to be derived from the classical rules, his heresies were not
sufficient to make his presence incongruous in the Academy of Good
Taste. One member, Villaroel, however, was distinctly out of place.
Affected by the perverted taste which had characterized recent
Spanish poetry, he was content to imitate Calderón in his vices rather
than in his virtues. He was frankly and brazenly unashamed of his
nationalistic taste, and probably maintained his position in the group

by his native wit and agreeableness and because of the tolerance of
the Academy as a whole. His patriotism was unquestionable and may
have contributed to the affection evinced toward him by Luzán,
Nasarre, Montiano, and Velázquez—who, for all their criticism of the
prevailing taste, never failed to take up arms against French attacks
when they seemed to be directed against all of Spanish literature.
Luzán himself had upon one occasion heatedly defended Spanish
literature against some derogatory remarks which he had read in
the *Memoirs de Trevoux*. Luzán's son gives the following account of
the incident:

> In the following year, 1742, while he was in Madrid, there fell into
> his hands a volume of the *Memoirs de Trevoux* corresponding to March
> of that year and in article 22, page 474 of José de Torres' translation he
> found some passages which offended him in the most susceptible part
> of his heart, which was his patriotism, and caused him to write, as
> soon as he reached Zaragoza, a letter in Latin to the editors of that
> journal.... I shall not pass upon the merit of either work; but I shall
> vouch for the truth of the fact that the Fathers of Trevoux, to whose
> hands it seems the letter did not come until July of the year 1747,
> acknowledged it in flattering terms in the next issue of their journal, and
> from that time changed entirely the tone of their language about Spanish
> literature, and began to make extracts of several of our works.[150]

Villaroel saw in the spread of French customs and taste a definite
threat to Spanish nationalism and warned his countrymen against the
danger:

> My muse is Castilian, though it would be much better received were
> it French. For they say that nothing is good unless it comes from Paris,
> and even heresy itself will be accepted if it comes from there. When,
> unsuspecting Spain, will you come to understand that they are whetting
> their swords on your own stones? When will you realize that France is
> astutely introducing her manners among you in order to put you in
> bondage?[151]

It was Villaroel who good-naturedly chided Luzán, upon the latter's
entrance into the Academy of Good Taste in 1750, for his French
leanings in a ballad composed for the occasion in which he ironically
said that the subtle intellect of Luzán was capable of selling France
to the Parisians themselves.[152]

Du Perron's Criticism

At various stages in the neo-classic controversy in Spain there appeared works in France and Italy which served to aggravate the situation by their unreasonable censure of Spanish literature. One of the most provocative of these appeared one year after the publication of Luzán's *Poetics*, with the title *Extracts of Several Plays from the Spanish Theater with Some Comments and Translations of the Most Remarkable Passages*. Although it seems that the author, Du Perron de Castera, had no particular intention to offend Spanish pride, his remarks reveal clearly a condescending attitude toward the plays he treats. French drama was definitely in the doldrums and Du Perron evidently felt that he was doing his countrymen a service in making available to them certain extracts from the Spanish theater and in recommending the utilization of Spanish subjects. He seems to have been ignorant of the extent to which Pedro Corneille, Thomas Corneille, Scarron, Rotrou, Molière, Quinault, and others had anticipated his advice during the preceding century.

Thus the knowledge of the Spanish theater is by no means a matter of indifference to the Belles-Lettres, for from it one can derive excellent subjects which will have for us all the grace of novelty. It is only necessary to adopt the invention, simplify the material, curtail the adventures, quicken the movement, and at times accentuate the comic element. This type of imitation, practiced with taste, could furnish us with copies as valuable as originals.[153]

Du Perron must have been aware of Lesage's *The Spanish Theater, or the Best Comedies of the Most Famous Spanish Authors* (1700), in which the author proposed to make a collection of Spanish plays in French translations. Only one volume of this work was published, containing free translations of Lope de Vega's *To Guard and to Guard One's Self*, and Rojas Zorilla's *Treachery Invites Punishment*, presumably made by the author himself;[154] but, in addition to these two plays, Lesage had adapted Rojas Zorilla's *There Is No Friend for a Friend*, with the title *The Point of Honor*, and Calderón's *It Is Worse Than It Was*, with the title *Don César Ursini*. After admitting the indebtedness of the last two plays to their Spanish sources, the French critic, Lenient, says that they were complete failures on the French stage and that Lesage finally realized that the French public was little interested in tracings of foreign models and began to draw his characters from French soil.[155] He then cites the first two successes of Lesage, *Crispín the Rival of His Master* in the theater and *The Limping Devil* in the novel, without calling attention to the fact that *The Limping Devil* is a reworking of a novel with the same title by the Spanish author, Vélez de Guevara, and *Crispín the Rival of His Master* derives in part at least from Scarron's *Le Valet Maître,* which was in turn based upon Rojas Zorrilla's *Where There Are Wrongs There Is No Jealousy.* Lenient does say that Crispín seems to come from the cave "where Gil Blas, at the end of his voyage, meets a band of robbers," and that although the play is Spanish in its novelesque plot, it is typically French in style. He also recognizes the fusion of Spanish and French elements in Lesage's genius.

Under the influence of Spanish Golden Age drama, Lesage rebelled at the narrowness of neo-classic precepts and was convinced that nonobservance of the unity of place by the Spaniards had contributed greatly to the beauty of their plays:

> As long as an author observes the unity of place, he will offer us only very mediocre plots; and I believe he will please the audience less by the merit of that servitude which he shall have imposed upon himself than he would please it by the representation of a great number of incidents which the inconvenient and troublesome unity of place will have made him suppress. And by such suppressions he will deprive his plays of more beauties than he will be able to give them in other ways.[156]

Lesage had anticipated Du Perron by some forty years in recognizing the necessity of remedying the lack of inventiveness on the part of his countrymen; and he goes beyond the latter in admitting the lack of plot interest in French plays and in his enthusiastic praise of the Spanish theater for its clever handling of intrigue:

> ... I do not understand why with all the delicacy and good taste which we have, our authors, even the best of them, have neglected what should unquestionably be considered the soul and foundation of every dramatic action. I shall not hesitate to say that the Spaniards have judged more wisely than we and that they are masters in inventing and handling an intrigue.[157]

Du Perron did not share Lesage's admiration for the Spanish theater and believed that since that theater violated the three unities "it could not fail to form a spectacle which is monstrous in comparison with ours."[158]

The condescending praise which Du Perron mixed with his censure was as offensive to Spaniards as Boileau's unqualified condemnation had been. Du Perron recognizes the very qualities that Lesage had extolled in Spanish drama, but spoils the effect of his praise by a negative approach. After contrasting the Spanish and French theaters he concludes:

All of these contrasts of spirit, these prodigious differences between our stage and the Spanish theater, should not make us imagine that their plays have no merit. One finds there a great deal of invention, some sentiments that are noble and full of delicacy, some characters drawn with force and sustained with dignity, some happy situations, some well-managed surprises, a great fund of humor, and a fire of interest that holds the spectator's attention.[159]

Probably the remark made by Du Perron which most offended the Spanish intellectuals was that tragedy was unknown in Spain: "As for tragedy, the Spaniards have written none, because one could not properly give that name to the few of their works which bear it undeservedly; such are the *Celestina* and the *Ingenious Helen*, which can only be called novels in dialogue."[160]

For some reason Du Perron's criticism remained unanswered for more than ten years. It is evident that during this time certain changes had taken place within the ranks of the neo-classicists. Even though an inferiority complex had developed with reference to contemporary Spanish literature, national pride began to prompt a desire to find extenuating circumstances, or to prove that there were and always had been a considerable number of Spaniards capable of appreciating good literature and cognizant of its rules. For the term *uncultured* to be applied indiscriminately to all Spaniards was extremely distasteful to these intellectuals. It did not occur to them at this time to defend Golden Age drama by showing that it was no more irregular and characterized by no worse taste than the French theater before Corneille. They apparently knew little or nothing of the early French farces or of the irregular tragedies, tragi-comedies, and pastorals of Hardy. They seem to have been equally unaware of the sustained popularity of the tragi-comedy in France long after Corneille's *Cid*. In fact, they did not choose to defend Golden Age plays at all, but were willing to admit that these plays deserved the censure to which they had been subjected. How to convince foreigners in the face of this admitted evidence that Spain was not inherently barbarous, was the problem which confronted them. Both Nasarre and Montiano believed that they had found the answer.

1. Juan Ignacio de Luzán, *Memorias de la vida de Don Ignacio de Luzán,* escritas por su hijo Don Juan Ignacio de Luzán (*B.A.E.,* LXI, 100).
2. Ignacio de Luzán, *La Poética, o reglas de la poesía en general* (Zaragoza, 1737).
3. Ignacio de Luzán, *La Poética, o reglas de la poesía en general, corregida y aumentada por su mismo autor* (Madrid, 1789).
4. Juan Ignacio de Luzán, *op. cit.,* p. 103.
5. *Ibid.,* p. 104.
6. Luzán, *Poética* (Madrid, 1789), "Prologue" by the editor.
7. Marcelino Menéndez y Pelayo, *Historia de las Ideas Estéticas en España* (Madrid, 1940), III, 220.
8. *Ibid.,* p. 227.
9. Luzán, *Poética,* 1737.
10. *Ibid.*
11. *Ibid.*
12. *Ibid.*
13. *Ibid.*
14. *Ibid.,* "Al lector."
15. *Ibid.,* p. 5.
16. *Ibid.,* p. 7.
17. *Ibid.,* p. 277.
18. *Ibid.*
19. *Ibid.,* pp. 286-87.
20. *Ibid.,* pp. 293-94.
21. *Ibid.,* p. 294.
22. *Ibid.,* p. 295.
23. *Ibid.,* p. 300.
24. *Ibid.,* p. 306.
25. *Ibid.*
26. *Ibid.,* p. 307.
27. *Ibid.,* p. 308.
28. *Ibid.,* p. 311.
29. *Ibid.,* p. 312.
30. *Ibid.,* p. 318.
31. *Ibid.,* p. 319.
32. *Ibid.,* p. 320.
33. *Ibid.*
34. *Ibid.,* p. 322.
35. *Ibid.,* p. 324.
36. *Ibid.,* p. 325.
37. *Ibid.,* p. 354.
38. *Ibid.,* p. 355.
39. *Ibid.,* p. 356.
40. *Ibid.,* p. 357.
41. *Ibid.,* p. 360.
42. *Ibid.,* p. 366.
43. *Ibid.,* p. 367.
44. *Ibid.,* pp. 367-68.
45. *Ibid.,* p. 373.
46. *Ibid.*
47. *Ibid.*
48. *Ibid.,* p. 375.
49. *Ibid.*
50. *Ibid.*
51. *Ibid.,* p. 381.
52. *Ibid.,* p. 380.
53. *Ibid.,* p. 381.
54. *Ibid.,* p. 384.
55. *Ibid.,* pp. 392-93.
56. *Ibid.,* p. 395.
57. *Ibid.,* pp. 396-97.
58. *Ibid.,* pp. 399-400.
59. *Ibid.,* p. 401.
60. *Ibid.,* p. 424.
61. *Ibid.*
62. *Ibid.,* p. 401.
63. *Ibid.,* p. 406.
64. *Ibid.,* pp. 406-7.
65. *Ibid.,* p. 407.
66. *Ibid.,* p. 408.
67. *Ibid.,* p. 409.
68. *Ibid.,* p. 410.
69. *Ibid.,* pp. 411-12.
70. *Ibid.,* p. 414.
71. *Ibid.,* p. 416.
72. *Ibid.,* p. 417.
73. *Ibid.,* pp. 419-20.
74. *Ibid.,* p. 420.
75. *Ibid.,* p. 421.
76. *Ibid.*
77. *Ibid.,* pp. 421-22.
78. *Ibid.,* p. 422.
79. *Ibid.,* p. 423.
80. *Ibid.,* p. 430.
81. Luzán, *La Poética,* 1789, p. 20.
82. *Ibid.,* p. 21.
83. *Ibid.,* pp. 23-24.
84. *Ibid.,* p. 24.
85. *Ibid.*
86. *Ibid.,* p. 25.
87. *Ibid.*
88. *Ibid.,* p. 44.
89. *Ibid.*
90. *Ibid.,* p. 63.
91. *Ibid.,* p. 69.
92. *Ibid.,* p. 28.
93. *Ibid.*
94. *Ibid.*
95. *Ibid.*
96. *Ibid.,* p. 30.
97. *Ibid.*
98. *Ibid.,* p. 32.
99. *Ibid.,* p. 35.
100. Menéndez y Pelayo, *Ideas Estéticas,* V, 186.
101. *Ibid.*
102. Manuel José Quintana, *Introduc-*

ción a la poesía castellana del siglo XVIII (B.A.E., XIX, 117).

103. Antonio Gil y Zárate, "Resumen histórico," Manual de Literatura (Madrid, 1844), p. 310.

104. George Tichnor, History of Spanish Literature (Boston, 1863), Fourth American Edition, III, 313.

105. Diario de los Literatos, Año 1737, Tomo IV.

106. Ibid., p. 79.

107. Ibid., p. 80.

108. Ibid., p. 85.

109. Ibid., p. 103.

110. Ibid., p. 106.

111. Ibid., p. 107.

112. Ibid.

113. Menéndez y Pelayo, op cit., III, 237.

114. Ibid

115. Diario de los Literatos, IV, 109.

116. Menéndez y Pelayo, op. cit., p. 237.

117. Cueto, op. cit., p. lxiii.

118. Robert E. Pellissier, The Neo-Classic Movement in Spain During the XVIII Century (Palo Alto: Stanford University Press, 1918), p. 43.

119. Discurso apologético de Don Iñigo de Lanuza. Donde procura satisfacer los reparos de los señores diaristas sobre la Poética de Don Ignacio de Luzán, En Pamplona, n.d., p. 6.

120. Luzán, op. cit., p. 102.

121. See F. Gaiffe, Le Drame en France au XVIII Siècle (Paris, 1910), p. 23.

122. Ibid., p. 22.

123. Pallisot, Oeuvres de Palissot (Liège, 1777), Vol. I, "Discours préliminaire de l'Edition de 1754." Precedes the comedy, Les Tuteurs, by Pallisot, p. 72.

124. Ibid.

125. Ibid., p. 75.

126. Ignacio de Luzán, Memorias Literarias de París, actual estado y méthodo de sus estudios (Madrid, 1751).

127. Ibid., p. 84.

128. Ibid., p. 85.

129. Palissot, op. cit., p. 87.

130. Memorias Literarias, p. 86.

131. Ibid., p. 87.

132. Ibid., p. 107.

133. Ibid., p. 116.

134. See Eugene Despois, Le Théâtre

Francais sous Louis XIV (Paris, 1874), p. 116.

135. Ibid., p. 129

136. Mercure de France, May 23, 1759. See Despois, op. cit., p. 129.

137. F. Arouet de Voltaire, "Advertissement to Semiramis," Oeuvres Complètes de Voltaire (Paris, 1880), IV, 481.

138. Voltaire, "Dissertation sur la Tragédie Ancienne et Moderne," Oeuvres Complètes, IV, 499.

139. Memorias Literarias, p. 116.

140. Menéndez y Pelayo, op. cit., p. 240.

141. Denis Diderot, Les Bijoux indiscrets, XXXVIII. See Lenient, La Comédie en France au XVIII Siecle, I, 323.

142. Ibid.

143. Ibid.

144. Diderot, "Troisième entretien sur le Fils naturel." See Lenient, op. cit., p. 325.

145. Menéndez y Pelayo, op. cit., p. 263.

146. Cueto, op. cit., p. lxxxix.

147. Feijóo, "Paralelo de las lenguas castellana y francesa," Teatro Crítico, Tomo I.

148. José Antonio Porcel, Juicio lunático del Fiscal de la Academia, from the Actas de la Academia del Buen Gusto. See I. L. McClelland, The Origins of the Romantic Movement in Spain (Liverpool, 1937), p. 47

149. Cueto, op. cit., p. ci.

150. Memorias de la Vida de Don Ignacio de Luzán, p. 101.

151. See Cueto, op. cit., p. xciv.

152. Ibid., p. lxiv.

153. Du Perron de Castera, Extraits de plusieurs pièces du théâtre espagnol avec des réflexions, et la traduction des endroits les plus remarquables (Paris, 1738), pp. 9-10.

154. A. R. Lesage, Le théâtre espagnol, ou les meilleures comédies des plus fameux auteurs espagnols, 1700. See McClelland, op. cit., p. 9.

155. C. Lenient, La comédie en France au XVIIIe Siècle (Paris, 1888), p. 129.

156. Lesage, "Préface," Le Théâtre espagnol.

157. Ibid.

158. Du Perron, op. cit., p. 2.

159. Ibid., pp. 8-9.

160. Ibid., p. 4.

III

Defenders of Spanish Culture

Nasarre

WHILE READY to confess that the authors criticized by Du Perron deserved all the censure which could be heaped upon them, Nasarre and Montiano refused to believe that all Spanish drama was irregular. Nasarre, who was the first to take up arms against the French writer, hit upon what appeared to be a very plausible answer. The famous forty-eighth chapter of the first part of Cervantes' *Don Quijote* was well known not only in Spain, but throughout Europe. In this chapter Cervantes expressed his opposition to irregularities in the Spanish theater in as clear a manner as could be desired. The only fly in the ointment was that Cervantes did not observe regularity in his own comedies and tragedies—at least, not in those which had been published under the title *Eight Comedies and Eight New Entremeses* (1615). If this contradiction could be explained away, the great Cervantes could be made to appear, both in theory and in practice, as a champion of good taste and as an exponent of the rules. This Nasarre sought to do in a long prologue to an edition of Cervantes' comedies and *entremeses*, which he published in 1749, and in which he clearly stated that his purpose was, in part at least, to answer the attack on the Spanish theater by a French author.[1]

Of the three plays, *Life in Algiers, Numancia,* and *The Naval Battle,* which Cervantes mentions in the prologue to the edition of his comedies and *entremeses* and which he claims to have written during his first period of dramatic activity, not one was extant at the time of Nasarre, and only the first two have subsequently been discovered. Inasmuch as this discovery was not made until 1782 and these plays were not published until 1784, all estimates of Cervantes as a dramatist were necessarily limited prior to that time to what could be gleaned from his other writings and from an examination of the eight comedies published in 1615. In the "Prologue," Cervantes had boasted that, in addition to the three plays cited above, he had composed "at that time some twenty or thirty comedies" and that all of these plays were performed "without receiving any offering of cucumbers or other projectiles" and that "they ran their course without hisses, outcries, or noisy demonstrations." In the "Addition" to his *Trip to Parnassus* (1614), he gives the titles of seven of his early comedies: *The Great Turkish Lady, The Naval Battle, Jerusalem, Amaranta, The Forest of Love, Arsinda,* and *The Confused Lady.* He was particularly proud of the last comedy, considering it the equal of any of the "cloak and sword plays" that had been composed in Spain.

As royal librarian, Nasarre had an opportunity to examine rare books; and as early as 1732, under the pseudonym of Isidro Perales y Torres, he had reprinted Avellaneda's *Don Quijote,* which both he and his friend Montiano considered superior to the genuine second part. Spurred by Du Perron's criticism of the Spanish theater, Nasarre began to examine the contents of the National Library in an endeavor to find plays and critical works with which to refute the charge that Spanish plays had always been irregular. He was, of course, familiar with the forty-eighth chapter of the *Quijote* and probably also with Cervantes' statement in the "Addition" to the *Trip to Parnassus.* The clear expression of his opposition to current abuses in the theater, found in the *Quijote,* combined with his later remarks in the "Addition," quite naturally led Nasarre to believe that Cervantes must have attempted to observe the classic precepts in his early theater.* Unable to find any of the early plays of Cervantes to support his assumption that the author of the *Quijote* had set himself resolutely against the perversion of taste which at that time was threatening the theater, Nasarre examined with minute care the eight comedies that were extant, in an attempt to find some evidence that Cervantes had not belied completely the principles he had stated so vigorously in the *Quijote.* At this point he made a

---

*Martínez de la Rosa comments upon the detriment to Cervantes' glory which resulted from the discovery of these two early plays and the publication of the eight comedies. "None of these twenty or thirty compositions have come down to us, except the *Numancia* and the *Life in Algiers,* published in Madrid in 1784; and if to the good fortune of their author's glory, they had been lost as was commonly believed, and if the poverty of Cervantes had not forced him to sell the year before his death the plays which he had tossed into the corner of a trunk and condemned to perpetual silence and which came out in print because the actors were unwilling to buy them for performance on the stage, would posterity not have been deceived into believing that this famous writer was also an excellent comic poet?" (Francisco Martínez de la Rosa, "Apéndice sobre la Comedia Española," *Obras Completas de D. Francisco Martínez de la Rosa* [Paris, 1845], I, 171.)

startling discovery: Cervantes never intended that these plays should
be considered as serious examples of dramatic art. He had written
them as ingenious satires upon the new type of drama that was coming into vogue, and to make his purpose more obvious he had wilfully
violated all the dramatic precepts and had created monstrosities in
order to drive monstrosities from the theater. Nasarre's contention
was that Cervantes, seeing with grief and indignation that the
theater was in imminent danger of being corrupted,

> ... wished with these eight comedies, and eight *entremeses,* as with so
> many Don Quixotes and Sanchos, who exiled the portentous and ridicu-
> lous romances of chivalry which had turned the heads of so many men;
> he wished, I say, with comedies to mend the errors of comedy and to
> purge the theater of bad taste and bad morals, returning it to reason
> and to authority, from which it had strayed in order to please the rabble,
> with complete disregard for the sane and sensible portion of the
> population.[2]

Nasarre is forced to admit that the purpose is not so obvious as in
the *Quijote,* but he explains this by saying that Cervantes could not
express himself with his usual clarity because of the tyranny which
had taken possession of the theater. His new attempt to use satire to
correct a misguided public taste was thwarted, Nasarre says, by a
conspiracy on the part of authors and actors who were satisfied with
their profits and opposed any change in dramatic trends. He accuses these same interests of having practically withdrawn the edition of Cervantes' comedies and *entremeses* from circulation because
of their fear of its effect upon the public. This book, Nasarre says,
has become so rare that one can almost say the present edition is
new. He confesses that these comedies appear on the surface to be
just so many examples of the irregular theater and that without careful reading even those who pride themselves upon their powers of
discrimination may be deceived,

> ... so similar are these comedies to those which are considered to be good
> and pleasing; and the blunders are so well placed, the extravagancies so
> perfectly imitated, that they pass for excellencies and the reader will
> likely take for a seriously written comedy a work the purpose of which is
> to ridicule bad comedies by imitating them.[3]

The only plays in which Nasarre finds anything which approaches
an outspoken opposition to the new comedy are *The Fortunate
Ruffian* and *Pedro of Urdemalas.* His contention, however, is that in

all these comedies Cervantes sought to turn public taste by a ridiculous exaggeration of the irregularities of contemporary plays. *The Fortunate Ruffian* is, to be sure, the most irregular of the eight comedies. The first act takes place in Spain, and, with no preparation whatsoever, the second opens in Mexico. To explain the transition Cervantes uses a kind of prologue to the second act; and it is in this prologue that he appears to ridicule the irregularity of the new comedy. Nasarre is forced to base his entire case almost entirely upon a strained interpretation of this section, which he reproduces in its entirety.

In an attempt to explain Cervantes' failure to use more aggressive weapons against the irregularities of the new comedy, Nasarre paints the author of the *Quijote* as a defeated old man when, after years of separation from the theater, he again attempted to win acclaim in that field. Cervantes was not only old, he says, but poor; his enemies had succeeded in turning his patrons against him and in discrediting him with the public. The new writers of comedies, on the other hand, were applauded and well paid by the rabble and the middle class. These considerations made Cervantes cautious and hesitant, and prevented him from expressing himself with his usual vehemence and clarity. He chose, therefore, "to employ the Socratic method, with a fine irony, which reveals his opinions and sentiments and at the same time avoids a direct conflict with the masses, leaving to posterity, however, a testimony of his just desire to oppose irregularity in the theater." Nasarre suggests that Cervantes expressed somewhat similar ideas in his "Prologue." A reading of this prologue will suffice, however, to explain why Nasarre did not quote from it or press the matter further.

When he reached this point in his discussion, Nasarre must have realized that his arguments were not entirely convincing, for he admits that "a superficial reading of Cervantes' 'Prologue'" might give rise to doubts as to the validity of his contention. He therefore falls back upon the *Quijote*, where, he says, Cervantes was able to express his sentiments openly, and reprints the entire section which deals with comedy. He fails to note, however, that nowhere in this work does Cervantes mention Aristotle or any of his commentators, and that he confines his criticism almost entirely to glaring violations of the unities of time and place and to ridiculous distortions of historical facts.

All of Cervantes' efforts to oppose the irregularity and bad taste which had taken possession of the theater, Nasarre says, were in vain:

The number of comedies grew; and the fury of writing them was the only Apollo of their authors. Neither the hisses of the groundlings, nor the laughter of the serious minded, nor the example of famous poets, who wrote with art and good taste, were able to stem the tide of plays which were the unfortunate product of ignorance, vain presumption, and corrupted or prejudiced hearts; and, what is worse, which contained a seductive and perverse moral.[4]

The immorality which characterized the majority of the plays produced in Cervantes' time gave rise to a concerted attempt to ban all theatrical production, no distinction being made between the bad and the good. Spaniards, following the example of Cervantes, protested vehemently against the authors of foolish and irregular plays and wrote comedies of their own which were perfect and directly opposed to the type generally applauded. Some of these plays, Nasarre says, are still performed and are approved by all classes of society. Unfortunately Nasarre does not give the names of any of these perfect plays, and we are left in the dark as to his criterion of perfection. Certainly none of the Golden Age plays that were still in the repertoires in his day met the rigid standards set by neo-classicists. It is possible, however, that some of these plays were relatively free from the irregularities which Nasarre attacks throughout his prologue. One becomes convinced as he reads this work that the author is more concerned with morals than with rules, and that only glaring irregularities meet his complete disapproval.

Nasarre shows his sensitiveness to attacks that were being made upon the Spanish theater by foreigners and strikes back by accusing them of limiting their discussion to the bad plays in the Spanish theater and of appropriating the good ones for their own theater, either with obvious plagiarism or, as in the case of Thomas Corneille, with a frank admission of their indebtedness. Nasarre says that these foreigners either speak of Spanish plays without real knowledge of them or base their judgment upon the works of some authors, who, although admittedly famous, have no power of attorney to represent the nation as a whole. Before launching their criticism, they should have acquainted themselves with the history of the Spanish stage. They would have found that the very same plays which were censured in the *Spanish Theater*, published in Paris in 1738, had been consistently reproved by good writers in Spain. Nasarre uses

Du Perron's work as a steppingstone to his real purpose in writing the "Prologue." He now attempts to prove that not only Cervantes but numerous other critics had championed the classic precepts even at the time when the Spanish theater was giving most evidence of irregularity. It is a source of satisfaction to him that "the scholarly Juan Paez de Castro, chronicler of Carlos V, . . . saw, and communicated many manuscripts of Aristotle and collated his *Poetics,* which he translated and made well known to his countrymen before Castelvetro performed a like service for the Italians."[5]

Nasarre proposes to show that the early Spanish theater had been characterized by regularity, but that Lope, whom he calls "the first corrupter of the theater," arrested its development and started it upon the road to ruin. When Lope appeared the comedies were already "adult," but he put them back in "swaddling clothes." Nasarre resents keenly the stigma that Lope has put upon Spain:

> Spain would lose nothing in having Italy and France call the corrupter of our theater ignorant, or in having them place in the same category those who imitated him, especially the one who is called without any reason whatsoever the Prince of Comic Poets (Calderón). This censure holds true in some particulars, although the nation as a whole is innocent. Italy and France, however, have inferred that all Spaniards deserve the same scorn and so do us an evident wrong.[6]

It is unnecessary to speak of Lope, for his own words convict him. His *New Art of Writing Comedies* is "the most obvious proof of his irregularity," even though he tried to defend his comedies by laying the blame on the "bad taste" of his audiences.

Nasarre's principal attack is directed against Calderón, whom he calls the "second corrupter":

> It is true that they erected altars to Calderón as to a God of the theater, and that his superior genius at times stumbled upon some things which were inimitable, but which were accompanied by others so ignoble that one may doubt whether their baseness gives relief to the sublime, or whether the sublime makes that baseness less tolerable. . . . He drew everything from his own imagination; he abandoned his works to the care of fortune. . . . He scorned the study of the ancient comedies; his characters wander from the east to the west. . . . Haughtiness, the concept of honor, affrays, bravado, ceremony, armies, besieged fortresses, challenges . . . and all that which is improbable and foreign to comedy, he places on the stage. . . . It is true that to excuse him it is customary to say that he portrays the nation, as though it were entirely a nation of knight

errants and of imaginary men. And what shall I say of the women in his plays? All of them are noble; all have a fierceness at first, which inspires fear rather than love; but they soon, through jealousy, pass to the other extreme, representing before the public violent and shameful passions, and showing to chaste and unwary maidens the roads to perdition and the ways to incite and to maintain impure love, and to confuse and deceive their parents ... leading them on with the hope of unequal and secret marriages in scorn of parental authority and excused only by an extreme passion of love, which is painted as honest and decent; ... he gives vice a happy and laudable end; he sweetens the poison; he teaches the audience to drink it boldly, and takes away the fear of its havoc.

He makes his characters speak a seductive language with metaphors strung one after the other, so daring and unusual that the dreams of the feverish characters in Horace would be less wild. All sane people look with aversion upon the excessive sharpness of wit, and still more upon the false and untimely erudition dragged in by the hair, with which Calderón dresses and adorns his comedies. His lovers, his rejected suitors, resemble no one; and so he does not portray, but rather disfigures, and in so doing he sins against reason and against the art of comedy ... because all poetry should be like painting, which consists in the imitation of nature.[7]

None of Calderón's recognized faults are omitted by his relentless critic. His plots, Nasarre says, although ingenious, are almost always improbable; and the elegant and flowing diction is entirely out of place in comedy and would even be open to criticism in lyrical and tragic compositions. Anachronisms and errors in geography, mythology, and history appear at every step. Particularly does he censure the unnecessary scenes, and the handling of the exposition:

Many scenes and episodes are entirely impertinent, have nothing to do with the action, and fail to interest the spectators. The long narrations which have been substituted for the prologues, and which are sometimes necessary in order that the listeners may understand the comedy and look forward eagerly to the development of the plot, are almost always unskilfully handled by this poet and expressed in language that is too bombastic, lofty, and metaphorical.[8]

When he speaks of Lope and Calderón, Nasarre confesses that he allows himself to be carried away by his indignation and by zeal for his country. If all Spanish comedies had been in their beginning and throughout their development like those of Lope and Calderón, he admits that they would deserve all the censure that is being heaped upon them, but this is not and has never been true. He affirms with conviction that his nation has comedies which are rigorously adjusted to the rules of art and which "are in no way inferior to those of the famous Molière; to those of his imitator Wycherley, who is the English Molière; nor to those of Maffei and Ricchoboni in Italy."[9] It is not to be supposed from this statement that Nasarre had even a passing acquaintance with the English theater. It is evident that he was merely relaying to his countrymen the opinions of Voltaire, for he speaks in another part of his prologue of Wycherley, Vanbrugh, and Congreve, "who are the imitators of Molière in England and whose copies show even greater irregularities than the originals, if we are to believe Mr. Voltaire."[10]

Nasarre considers the frank admission on the part of Thomas Corneille of his indebtedness to the Spanish theater worthy of praise, and suggests that his brother, Pierre Corneille, with an equally frank admission, might have avoided a part of the censure directed against his *Cid*. All that Pierre Corneille wrote in defense of this tragedy, Nasarre says, could with equal right be applied to the defense of the Spanish theater, if his countrymen were disposed to claim that all the products of their theater were good and that an occasional departure from the rules of art is not only permissible, but laudable. But the Spaniards do not need to apologize for or to defend any irregularities, for "without incurring the risk of being accused of that vanity for which our nation is famous, we can affirm that we have a greater number of comedies which are perfect and written according to the rules of art than the French, Italians, and English combined."[11] He offers to prove his claim by printing comedies selected from those of Rojas, de la Hoz, Moreto, Solís, and other comic poets who "when they wished, observed the precepts of art religiously." The merit of these authors should not be questioned merely because they were sometimes careless, "because not even in Molière's comedies is his touch always recognizable." The Spanish theater is rich in plays

. . . written in accordance with all the rules of art: with natural and appropriate characters; with a good moral; with a probable plot and intrigue; with the much vaunted unities; with beautiful and fitting diction; and which please, amuse, and instruct the rabble and the courtiers, taking away the frown of the severe censors and purging with wit and laughter the vices of all.[12]

But it is useless to seek regular comedies among those of Lope and Calderón or among those of any of their imitators. Nasarre con-

veniently forgets that the above-mentioned authors were the principal imitators of Lope and Calderón.

In discussing Nasarre's proposal to publish in a collection a number of regular Spanish comedies, Menéndez y Pelayo makes the
following statement: "We do not know with much certainty to what
comedies Nasarre was referring; but from certain passages in his prologue it may be inferred that he had in mind some of the plays before
Lope, especially the *Celestinas*, the *Propaladia*, and the comedies of
Lope de Rueda."[13] Nasarre's statement, however, leaves no doubt
on this point; for, after his boast that Spain has more regular
comedies than France, Italy, and England combined, he adds that
the plays he proposes to print are "those which are selected from
Roxas, de la Hoz, Moreto, Solís, and other comic poets," and does
not even mention the dramatists prior to Lope. When Nasarre states
so positively that, although none of the plays of Lope or of Calderón
approach regularity, a great number of regular comedies by the
above authors can be found, he is, of course, guilty of a gross
exaggeration. Some of the plays of these writers are free from glaring violations of classical precepts, but none conform to all of the
requirements. It must be emphasized, however, that Nasarre is
inclined to overlook minor infractions, provided the moral purpose
of comedy is kept in mind, and provided the language is suitable
for comedy. He has apparently formulated no definite dramatic
creed of his own and has not thoroughly digested the treatises by
Luzán and earlier Spanish critics. He is guilty, therefore, of inconsistencies in the prologue. He practically ignores Luzán's *Poetics*,
in spite of their bond of interest and friendship and, in the expression of his dramatic precepts, contents himself with long quotations
from the Golden Age critics, Antonio López de Vega, and Cascales,
whose ideas he adopts without indicating exactly where their statements end and where the expression of his own opinions begins.
His failure to use quotation marks, as we shall see, confused his
opponents and made them ascribe to him statements which he had
taken without alteration from the above critics. The dramatic creed
of Golden Age neo-classicists was somewhat more liberal than that
of their eighteenth-century descendants. In turning away from
Italian and French preceptists as interpreted by Luzán and in relying
upon native exponents of the rules, men like Nasarre felt that they
were indeed vindicating their nation. They made no attempt, however, to ascertain the extent to which these Golden Age critics had

drawn their material from Italian commentators upon Aristotle and Horace. Nasarre was gratified to find that Antonio López de Vega set himself resolutely against the irregularity of the theater of his time and particularly against that of Lope, and he adopts as his own the following statement by that critic:

Let the propriety which is fitting to the characters be observed both in the invention of the subject and in the style. Let comedy be festive; tragedy, sad and always perturbed. Why should this be changed in any age? I do not say that the ancient rules should be observed with super-stition, for some concession must be made to changes of taste in different ages; nor that attention be paid to small matters, the violation of which, as modern usage has observed, mars neither the proper disposition nor the essential elements of the plot. It is, therefore, a matter of no conse-quence today that the number of acts be changed. I do not say that the action should be restricted to one or more days, or that the number of interlocutors be limited to four, in spite of the objection of Horace; nor, in short, do I object to the omission of other like nonessentials.[14]

In approving the above statement, Nasarre shows a more liberal attitude than Luzán and, but for his unreasonable animosity toward Lope and Calderón, and his extravagant claims in regard to Cervan-tes' reason for writing his last comedies, might have been a factor in modifying the narrowness of neo-classicism. Luzán almost com-pletely ignored the early Spanish preceptists and did not even men-tion López de Vega. Although no immediate results were notice-able in the quality of plays produced for the stage, Spanish scholars, following the publication of Luzán's *Poetics*, had become very active in historical research in the field of drama and literary criticism, spurred by their desire to vindicate the nation from the charge of barbarism. They became acquainted with the French theater and, probably to their surprise, discovered that a great part of that theater, which they had been prepared to hold up as a model for imitation by their countrymen, had been drawn from Spanish sources, and that many French plays were merely recasts of plays by the despised Spanish Golden Age authors. Nasarre had discovered some of these borrowings, and later neo-classicists were to complete the list. With obvious satisfaction he enumerates the plays which Molière, Scarron, and Thomas Corneille took from originals of Rojas, Moreto, and Solís, without the necessity of making any drastic changes. Even the many defects of Calderón's plays, he says, did not deter Thomas Corneille and Molière ("the great Molière," he adds, parenthetically) from adapting some of his works to the French theater, where they were received and continue to be received with enthusiasm. It is true, he admits, that considerable changes had to be made to make them conform to the rules. But

... this work was unnecessary in the comedies they copied from Guillén de Castro, Francisco de Roxas, Antonio de Solís, and others, who observed the moderation which the style of comedy requires. And, in passing, it is worthy of notice that the humor which is considered inimitable in Molière, and the buffoonery of Scarron, are found in their original form in the works of Rojas and Moreto.[15]

In the case of Rojas' *The Game Is Between Fools,* from which Thomas Corneille took his *D. Beltrán del Cigarral,* Nasarre makes an important concession with relation to the unity of place. In this comedy "all of the rules are observed except the unity of place, for the first act is in Madrid, and the second is in the Inn of Illescas; but this slip may be pardoned because of the ingeniousness of the plot and because it has a precedent in antiquity."[16]

All of the comedies upon which Nasarre puts his stamp of approval are *comedies of manners,* the same type which had found particular favor in the eyes of Luzán. Even at the height of the neoclassic movement critics were inclined to be lenient when they came to criticize a comedy of this type.

Nasarre's expression of what he conceives to be the moral mission of comedy is so thoroughly in accord with the ideas of later neoclassicists that Leandro Fernández de Moratín quotes it at length in his critical study, "Reseña histórica sobre el teatro español." According to Nasarre,

Calderón did not know that the authors of comedies, recognizing their usefulness, should clothe themselves with public authority for the purpose of instructing their fellow-citizens; being persuaded that the nation tacitly confers upon them the position of philosophers, and of censors of the ignorant, corrupt, or ridiculous multitude. It happens that the precepts of philosophy when they are put into books are dry and almost lifeless, and exercise little influence upon the spirit; but when they are presented in animated spectacles, they influence it profoundly. The austere philosopher disdains to appeal to the heart. The dominant tone of his maxims either offends or tires. The writer of comedies, on the other hand, drives a thousand passions from the soul; he uses them to introduce his philosophy; his lessons contain nothing that is not agreeable, and they are far removed from the magisterial severity which makes teaching detestable, and which increases the natural indocility of man. ...

The writer of comedies gives no lessons at all; we as listeners give them to ourselves, and we accept his ideas with no thought that he is trying to teach us.[17]

The writer of comedies, therefore, should not allow his didactic purpose to become too apparent. A closer adherence to this principle as expressed by Nasarre would have obviated much of the adverse criticism which was directed against the comedies of such writers as Tomás de Iriarte, and even to a certain extent against those of Leandro Fernández de Moratín himself. It may be significant that Moratín quotes the above passage *in toto* with the exception of the last sentence, where the indirect nature of the teaching is emphasized. It is an adequate testimonial to the influence of Nasarre's "Prologue" on subsequent neo-classic doctrine that Moratín, by his own admission, uses this passage as the basis for his well-known definition of comedy.

Nasarre does not claim that adherence to rules will in itself produce masterpieces. He recognizes the value of imagination and realizes that genius becomes restive under restraint, but he is quite convinced that unbridled imagination can only produce monstrosities.

I know well that the fire of the imagination does not always respect the rules which judgment prescribes, for the mind is as much the enemy of slavery as the heart. Correctness and regularity are qualities which make works of genius estimable. One should appreciate in a correct author not only the fire that appears in his productions, but also the fire which he holds back and which, had he permitted it to shine uncontrolled and at the wrong time, would have overswayed reason.[18]

He is not speaking of certain arbitrary rules based upon the authority of the ancients; he has in mind those fundamental rules by means of which enlightened minds subject the impetuosity of poetic genius to the exactness of reason. These rules, he says, even today in spite of the difference and the distance of times, of places, and of customs, make the comedies of Aristophanes, Plautus, and Terence pleasing on the stage, and cause those modern plays which most resemble them to be the best in all languages. He warns, however, of the danger of a too scrupulous observance of the rules:

Poetry is a proper, natural, and convenient imitation, or rather, it is a step well taken from truth to fiction. This idea is destroyed not only when writers scorn, but also when they observe with excessive scrupu-

lousness the rules of the ancients, which being based upon their customs
and manners, must yield to other rules based upon present conditions.[19]

Nasarre is as insistent as Luzán upon the *illusion of reality* which
comedy should produce:

> Poetry besieges our imagination on all sides with a vividly represented
> verisimilitude, and withdraws the image of contradictory things that
> might reveal the fiction of what the poet is presenting. In this manner it
> mixes fiction with truth; because the movements of our heart do not
> correspond to the true essence of external objects, but to the impres-
> sion they make upon the imagination. This impression does not always
> come from the real objects themselves, as is proven by the effect of
> dreams. And in order to produce in us the same emotions which are
> excited by the reality of objects, it suffices that the poet move our imagi-
> nation vividly with a well-sustained verisimilitude. With this verisimili-
> tude, and with a natural and minute expression, the poet achieves his
> purpose. Consequently, badly sustained characters and impossible actions
> ... are the greatest defects of poetry and the reefs of comedy.[20]

The author of the "Prologue" wishes to make it clear that the rule
of the three unities is not an invention of Italian and French critics,
nor even of the Greeks and Romans, but emanates from the principle of verisimilitude, or the imitation of nature, and is dictated by
good taste and reason:

> If among the Greeks and Romans we find the Aristophaneses, the
> Plautuses, and the Terences, and wish to draw from them models and
> rules with which to measure and construct comedies, it is not because
> they invented these plays, or because they set themselves up as law-
> makers; but because, having written at an age and in countries that were
> cultured and philosophical, they applied themselves carefully to the
> imitation of nature and manners, without withdrawing from the probable
> and rational.[21]

This insistence upon the rules as emanating from natural laws and
not as the invention of theorists forms a basic part of neo-classic doctrine in Spain and finds no clearer expression than in this "Prologue"
by Nasarre. Throughout his discussion, Nasarre carefully abstains
from giving any credit to Italy and France, in accordance with his
basic assumption that Spain has produced as capable commentators
on the classic precepts as any other nation. The condition of the
Spanish theater was not due to lack of scholars to direct it in the
channels of good taste; indeed, "our nation has less excuse than

other nations; because it preceded them in having masters to teach it, rules to direct it, and models to imitate."[22]

Nasarre, accordingly, quotes not only from Cervantes but from Manuel de Villegas, Christóbal de Mesa, Rey de Artieda, Cascales, and other Spanish writers to prove that cultured Spaniards were well acquainted during the seventeenth century with dramatic precepts and loud in their protests against the corruption of the theater. When he comes to a definition of comedy, he considers it unnecessary to formulate one of his own, or even to indicate his approval of the definition recently formulated by Luzán. He chooses rather to repeat the definitions of Cascales and of the Jesuit P. Rapin, the only foreign commentator whom he mentions in his entire "Prologue":

It is very easy to copy here from the Pinciano, from Cascales, or from Salas, what they wrote upon this subject, which surpasses all that has been said since by foreigners or by natives, who have spoken upon it with little knowledge of our theater. Nevertheless, I shall say with the Murcian historian [Cascales] that comedy is the dramatic imitation of a complete and properly proportioned action, humble and agreeable, which by means of diversion and laughter cleanses the soul of vices; or with the scholarly Jesuit, P. Rapin, that comedy is an image of ordinary life and that its purpose is to show on the stage private defects in order to cure public defects and to correct the masses with the fear of ridicule; the element of ridicule, therefore, being the very essence of comedy.[23]

After giving the above definition by Cascales, Nasarre para-phrases Cascales' analysis of its elements. In this interpretation, or elaboration, the following points are brought out: Comedy is imi-tation, because it would be neither poetry nor drama if the poet should speak directly. Although there must be only one action, this does not mean that there may not be other accessory actions or epi-sodes, provided they are so connected with the main action that all are directed to the same goal and all are solved by its solution. Comedy is "humble and agreeable" because its language is that of ordinary speech and because its characters are drawn from the humbler classes. The reason for this restriction is that the acts and conflicts of this class induce laughter, but

if a prince is ridiculed, he is aggrieved and offended; the offense demands vengeance; vengeance causes disturbances and unfortunate endings; all of which is purely tragic, because comedy, for the most part, is lascivious, and has as its characters procurers, prostitutes, knaves, and people of similar immoral nature. If some unmarried girl is introduced she is represented as a slave or a foundling.[24]

All violent emotions should be excluded from comedy. In order to accomplish this, "comedy observes a certain strict closure, which does not permit the entrance upon the stage of maidens, married women, or old men who set bad examples."[25]

The reason for this restriction is essentially the same as that given for the exclusion of persons of high rank: "Married women inspired by the passion of love should be excluded from comedy, not only because of the bad example, but also because their love intrigues give rise to jealousy, scandals, and deaths; which results are tragic, and contrary to the purpose of comedy."[26] Nasarre recommends as suitable for the drama of his own day rules which were formulated by Cascales at a time when the only criterion for judgment in treatises on poetics was the comedy of Aristophanes, Plautus, and Terence, in whose plays the stock characters were indeed officials, knaves, servants, slaves, prostitutes, procurers, citizens, and soldiers. He merely repeats what Cascales has said, without a thought of the consequences to public morals in Spain if these characters should be revived in comedy. It seems improbable that Nasarre had any real knowledge of the essential immorality of Roman comedy, especially that of Plautus.

Nasarre refrains from a more detailed discussion of the rules for comedy because he hopes "that the Royal Academy, when it enlightens the literary world with its promised *Poetics*, will relegate to oblivion all that has been written by the best authors and will give an eminent place to Cascales."[27] Menéndez y Pelayo does not believe that the Academy ever actually had it in mind to compose a *Poetics*:

> The Academy never thought seriously of composing a *Poetics*, although some writers jokingly affirm that it did. Too prudent to rush impetuously into the composition of a work upon such a debatable subject, which should always be left to individual initiative, it had no other relations with literature ... than that of having reprinted, as language texts, some of the works of classic authors and of having announced from time to time, since 1777, prizes for oratory and poetry.[28]

The above statement by Nasarre, however, was not made jokingly and it seems that he, as a member of the Academy, should have been well informed of its proposed plans. We have already noticed

that the composition of a *Poetics* was one of the three projects provided for in the constitution of the Academy.[29]

Nasarre's prologue, with its bitter and unreasonable denuncia-
tions of Lope and Calderón, probably contributed as much as the
satires of the *Diario de los literatos* to widen the breach between the
neo-classicists and the champions of the national drama. In regard
to the reaction of the public, Menéndez y Pelayo asks: "If the opinions of Luzán, so temperate in substance and form, had aroused such
resistance from wounded national pride, what violent opposition
might not be expected from this new and impertinent allegation, so
filled with self-satisfaction and pedantry?"[30] He adds that no fewer
than four refutations of Nasarre's work appeared in the short space
of two years. In one of these the author, Zavaleta, who signs himself
"a wit of this court," writes a scathing satire on the prologue and
testifies to the indignation which it aroused in Madrid:

> The criticism made against Don Pedro Calderón de la Barca is one
> of the most severe, violent, and unmerited that could be written by one
> whose custom was not to sully his reputation or his pen with the defama-
> tion of others. Many who have read the "Prologue" and those cruel accu-
> sations have been so aroused that they have almost been inclined to take
> a noisy and disproportionate vengeance. I have heard individuals of out-
> standing ability and scholarship say that one who writes such things must
> be possessed by a blind passion, capable of overthrowing reason itself,
> and must be devoid of patriotism.[31]

In spite of the fact that Zavaleta was clearly incensed at Nasarre's
condemnation of Calderón and Lope, he does not descend to personal invective, but confines his *Discourse* to a serious and, on
the whole, well-reasoned answer to the "Prologue." According to
Menéndez y Pelayo, Zavaleta's work, although written in a careless and confused style, "is filled with appropriate and elevated
thoughts which almost leave behind those we have read in the
works of Luzán and Don Juan Iriarte."[32] This critic adds that a part
of his arguments and the general spirit of his criticism are drawn apparently from the seventeenth-century apologists of Lope: Tirso de
Molina, Alonso Sánchez, Ricardo del Turia, Barreda, and Caramuel.
Like these critics, he says, Zavaleta

> pulverizes the system of the unities, and defends the imitation of nature
> as the only law of drama, not, however, in the exclusive and narrow sense
> of material imitation as understood by Nasarre and other pedagogues of
> his caliber, but with a broader and more fruitful interpretation of the
> words *verisimilar* and *nature*.[33]

Zavaleta finds true and regular imitations of life and passions in Spanish comedy.[34] Nature, he says, produces a countless number of emotions, and its greatness consists in its variety. Inasmuch as it subjects itself to no limits, why should we assume that the ancient writers of comedies exhausted its possibilities or even succeeded in making true portraits in their reduced and limited works? If the greatness of nature consists in its variety, how can its imitation be tied to invariable precepts? The ancient Plautuses and Terences, he says, remained at the doors and on the thresholds of nature without penetrating into its center and true essence.[35] The precept of the unities is embarrassing and useless, because it makes impossible the perfect representation of a great number of events, which neither in truth nor in fiction are subject to the unities.[36] Art, he believes, should open to men ways and means for the composition of their works and not present insurmountable obstacles. He has no objection to the establishment of rules of art, provided the benefit to be derived from their observance is manifest and proportionate to the difficulty involved.[37] But if comedies are imitations of nature, it is necessary that all rules be directed to this end. With a series of questions, Zavaleta attempts to show the inconsistency of Nasarre's interpretation of verisimilitude:

How then can this be effected when the unities oppress the mind, narrow the faculties, and limit the incidents? Can a precept be just, and accommodated to imitation, if it forces the events of three years to be represented in three hours? If an action began in Madrid, continued in Ireland, and finished in Morocco, how can it be truly imitated on a stage which represents a single place? If the poem imitates the life of a person, why should the series of events which compose it be truncated by making it imperfect with the representation of only one? If nature placed no measure, limit, or invariable end to actions, time, or place, what rule can justify the imposition of such burdensome rules upon its imitations?[38]

Nasarre had said that comedy is, or should be, "the mirror of life, the image of truth, and the imitation of nature and manners." Zavaleta calls attention to the fact that a mirror "copies faithfully all that is placed before it without excluding the high, the low, the good, the bad, the green or the blue."[39] Therefore, the entire truth should be represented in the theater, and, inasmuch as the pope, the king, the grandee, the common man, the proud, the humble, the gentleman, the private ciitzen, the plebeian, the thief, the slave, the ruffian, and the prostitute are all found in nature,

Nasarre, by his own definition, has proven that comedy has the right to represent these and many other characters.

Zavaleta accuses Nasarre of inconsistency in maintaining that the characters in comedy should be limited to humble folk, and that the higher the rank of the characters the less fitted they are to this genre. It is obvious that Zavaleta was misled by Nasarre's failure to use quotation marks, and, without comparing the "Prologue" with Cascales' Poetical Tables, assumed that the following remarks, which were taken literally from that work, were original with Nasarre:

The purpose of comedy being, then, to undeceive the world by means of ridiculous actions, it follows that comedy must deal with humble folk; and the higher the rank of the characters, the worse the comedy will be, for it will not achieve its purpose of inducing good customs and purging vices through the medium of laughter.[40]

Zavaleta denies that the representation of vices is capable of encouraging virtue; he believes rather that it propagates and spreads those vices.[41] Only the representation of noble actions, he says, can induce good manners. He objects also to Nasarre's statement, which again represents a direct quotation from Cascales, that the actions of the upper class cannot induce laughter. The natural consequence to be drawn from such a statement, he says, is that this class "does not live subject to error, vice, ridicule, or blame and enjoys the high privilege of being impeccable; and that nature reserved for the lower class the harsh burden of imperfection, weakness, ugliness, stupidity, absurdity, and sin."[42]

Zavaleta defends the mixture of the tragic and the comic in Spanish comedies. How can one imitate nature, he asks, by disfiguring its appearance and making pieces of its incidents? Did one ever see a sad incident unmixed with laughter? Did one ever see pleasure unmixed with suffering or happiness free from bitterness?

The insistence of neo-classicists that stage productions should create an illusion of reality strikes Zavaleta as particularly ridiculous. "Even the most stupid and ignorant spectators are able to distinguish and recognize quite well that everything they see on the stage is pretense and not reality, that it is painted and not alive, and that it is artificially imitated and not actual."[43]

He maintains that the very faults which Nasarre attributes to Calderón constitute that author's principal merit:

To blame Calderón because he wrote freely without imitating anyone
... and because all of his comedies deal with punctilious and valiant
gentlemen and noble ladies, haughty, serious, and reserved at first, and
later, amorous, jealous, and gentle ... is truly to convert light into darkness and virtue into vice. If Calderón preferred to follow a new course
in the broad field of nature and to choose for his imitations lofty objects,
noble passions, illustrious deeds, and elegant language, he deserves not
blame, but applause.[44]

While it must be admitted that Zavaleta very shrewdly pointed
out the inconsistencies in Nasarre's prologue, Menéndez y Pelayo
is guilty of exaggeration when he says that "the famous prologue was
literally torn to shreds," and that the chagrin occasioned by reading
Zavaleta's discourse was to a large degree responsible for Nasarre's
death. It is not surprising that Menéndez y Pelayo, in whom the
desire to find evidence of romanticism in almost all of Spanish literature assumes the proportions of an obsession, should enthusiastically praise the basic ideas in Zavaleta's discourse at the same
time that he condemns its defective style:

I am not surprised that D. Blas Nasarre died less from gout than
from the concern caused by reading this discourse, where his famous
prologue was literally torn to shreds.* Böhl de Faber took from Zavaleta's
book a good part of the arguments which he used in his romantic polemic,
where he mentions him several times with singular admiration, vindicating
him from the affected disdain of our *gallo-classic* critics of the past
century, who knew no other way to answer this beautiful outburst of patriotism and aesthetic freedom than to ridicule the book and its author,
a ridicule to which the work unfortunately lends itself because of its literary form, which, with the exception of those passages animated by
warmth of feeling and elevation of ideas, continually degenerates into
the macaronic. ... But those students who are not dismayed by the
thorns found in the taste of every age, when it is a matter of catching
the vicissitudes of the thoughts of our ancestors, must pass over this
Discourse with respect and observe in it the vein of native romanticism
which, through the whole of the eighteenth century, glides silently across
the field of our letters until it finds its great and majestic outlet in the
sea of modern criticism, of which all of these forgotten and slandered
authors are the more or less conscious heralds and precursors. Who can
hesitate today between Nasarre and Zavaleta, or fail to recognize in the
latter a true Spaniard and in the former a barbarous pedant of past ages?[45]

---

*The attribution of Nasarre's death to Zavaleta's discourse is found for the first time
in a note to García de la Huerta's *Defense of the Spanish Theater* (1786). Inasmuch
as the author was engaged at the time in a defense of Calderón, he would naturally
be inclined to exaggerate the effectiveness of Zavaleta's discourse.

The principal accusations which Nasarre makes against the plays of Calderón and Lope have stood the test of time. It must be remembered that nowhere does Nasarre insist upon a rigid adherence to the unities, and that he recognizes the difficulty of subjecting genius to the restraint of rules. Menéndez y Pelayo, in his discussion of Calderón, recognizes the same faults to which Nasarre calls attention, although he almost always dilutes any censure immediately with fulsome praise of other qualities. Indeed, what Menéndez y Pelayo says about Luzán's *Poetics* can be applied almost equally well to Nasarre's "Prologue." In negative criticism of Golden Age drama Nasarre is hardly more severe than Luzán. The difference between the two lies in their attitude toward the positive merits of Lope and Calderón. Luzán judiciously mixes praise with censure; Nasarre writes in the heat of anger and grants the enemy no quarter. He is obsessed with the desire to prove that his nation is not inherently barbaric and allows himself to be placed too much on the defensive by recent French criticism. He seems to believe that, by unloading upon Lope and Calderón the entire burden of responsibility for the transgressions of Spanish drama against the sacrosanct rules, he can exonerate the nation as a whole.

It is interesting to see how he covers these authors with a blanket condemnation, not even deigning to single out any particular work for censure, and attempts to hold up as patterns of regularity the works of the very men who imitated them, and who tended to follow them in their faults rather than in their virtues. He shows no evidence of having examined critically any substantial number of Golden Age plays. The faults to which he calls attention stand out with a superficial reading; the merits of the plays become apparent upon careful and unprejudiced examination. But it does not enter into Nasarre's plan to seek extenuating circumstances in the irregularity and frequent bad taste of the Golden Age theater or to find anything praiseworthy in Lope and Calderón. He is attempting to reform the theater of his time by purging it of all immoral or unmoral elements, by freeing it from the affectation of *Gongorism,* and by subjecting it to those dramatic rules which seem to him to be the outgrowth of the basic principle of verisimilitude. Certainly the theater was crying out for reform, and those forces which were opposing the innovations of neo-classicism had neither the ability nor the inclination to lift the drama from its low state.

All attempts to place upon neo-classicism the blame for lack of

positive accomplishment in the field of drama during the eighteenth
century fail to take into consideration the fact that for one hundred
years the Spanish theater had been steadily deteriorating. None of
the plays to which the nationalists could point with pride as equal
or superior to the plays of other nations were written after 1650.
Only a handful of Lope's plays had survived; the comedies of Tirso
de Molina had long since been forgotten; and even the name of
Alarcón was known only because Corneille had adapted one play
by this author to the French stage, and through another play,
The Weaver of Segovia, which is hardly characteristic of the
author's style. The Spanish theater during the first half of the
eighteenth century was almost completely dominated by the plays
of Calderón and his imitators and of that group commonly called
the "Calderonian decadents." In order to carry out any effective
program of reform it was essential, therefore, that these plays and
the form of dramatic art which they represented be completely
discredited. Neither the nationalists nor the neo-classicists were in
any mood for compromise. The latter soon realized that halfway
measures were futile and that as long as Calderón remained the
idol of the public and the model of dramatists, they could acomplish
nothing. Accordingly, the neo-classicists altered their strategy and
centered their attack upon Calderón and Lope. In this manner they
could point out the faults of Golden Age drama without seeming
to cast a stigma upon the entire dramatic production of that period.
Their attacks upon Lope were definitely secondary and were not calculated to arouse as much resentment as those directed against
Calderón. It is evident that the nationalists defended Lope more as
a matter of principle than of conviction, for the Calderonian decadents themselves were of a disposition to look with scorn upon his
theater.

Since the publication of Luzán's *Poetics* there had been ample
time for the neo-classicists and the nationalists to draw up their
battle lines. The same forces which had opposed so tenaciously Feijóo's attempt to modernize Spain's ideas in science and education,
and which had been responsible for the discontinuance of the *Diario
de los literatos,* now aligned themselves solidly against any innovations in the theater. To them the Spanish *comedia* represented the
pinnacle of perfection and any attempt to change it could only be
construed as evidence of lack of patriotism. Just as the tone of the
Diario de los literatos had grown progressively more bitter in the face

of blind and violent opposition to reform, so now the more rational
and equitable attitude of Luzán toward Lope and Calderón gives
way in Nasarre's "Prologue" to an equally blind and violent denunciation of the total dramatic production of these authors. An atmosphere has been created in which a calm consideration of the
merits and defects of Golden Age drama is impossible. Later, as we
shall see, the neo-classicists, feeling more secure, return to Luzán's
saner evaluation of that theater—without yielding an inch, however,
in their insistence upon its defects and the necessity for radical
reforms.

Montiano

Nasarre's defense of the Spanish theater was limited to comedy.
But Du Perron's censure had been directed at the whole Spanish
theater, and Spanish intellectuals did not feel that the honor of
their country had been sufficiently vindicated by Nasarre's "Prologue." The following year, therefore, Montiano sought to do for
tragedy what Nasarre had done for comedy. To this end he published
his first *Discourse Upon Spanish Tragedies*,[46] accompanied by an
original tragedy, *Virginia*, which he had composed with strict adherence to the rules, and which he hoped might serve as a model for
future Spanish tragedies. In the "Censure" by Juan de Aravaca,
which preceded the discourse, we see that criticism of the Spanish
theater by foreigners was primarily responsible for the work. Aravaca
says that Montiano's discourse

... not only restores to Spain the glory which foreigners have tried to
take away from her when they accuse her of being barren in erudite men,
perhaps in order to avail themselves of their works to build for themselves
the trophies of which they are so proud; but also demonstrates in a practical manner that even in this unenlightened century there is someone
who, with the greatest skill, can carry out all the rules prescribed for
tragedy by the best writers.[47]

Nasarre, whose "Censure" also accompanies the work, calls *Virginia*
"a tragedy written in conformity with the rules which the writers of
poetics have derived from reason and the practice of the Greeks,
Latins, and all the cultured nations." He adds that Montiano's work
is useful and necessary and should be read by those who, under the
illusion that they know the rules, constantly violate them.

Montiano confesses at the outset of his discourse that only his
love for Spain gives him courage to take up his pen. He recognizes

that the task he has undertaken is somewhat out of keeping with his age, his occupation, and even his previous training. Something must be ventured, however, for such a noble cause. Foreigners infer from the indolent silence of the Spaniards either that they have no defense against the charge which has been made against them, or that through cowardice they submit to the dishonor in order not to make it greater by the weakness of their arguments. Montiano is satisfied with the manner in which Nasarre has defended Spanish comedy and is certain that the latter, by the publication of his promised collection, will back up his assertion "that we have a greater number of comedies which are perfect and written in conformity with the rules than the French, Italians, and English."[48] He only wishes that someone equally competent would undertake the defense of Spanish tragedy. Since no one has shown any inclination to do so, he himself will assume the task with a clear consciousness of his limitations.

Montiano immediately takes Du Perron, whom he does not call by name but to whom he refers as the author of the work on the Spanish theater which appeared in 1738, to task for asserting that Spaniards have given the title of tragedy to *Celestina* and to *Ingenious Helen*.[49] If the French critic had taken the trouble to examine the *Bibliotheca Hispana,* published in 1581, by Nicolás Antonio, a work known throughout Europe, he would have seen that the *Celestina* had never been called anything but a *tragi-comedy* and that the *Ingenious Helen* was designated as a novel.[50] He would also have found in this work the names of many writers of tragedies. Indeed, tragedies are so old in Spain that before the year 1533 Fernán Pérez de Oliva had published prose versions of *The Vengeance of Agamemnon* and *Sad Hecuba,* taken from Sophocles and Euripides, changing and arranging them in such a manner that they have all the stamp of originality. These two tragedies are so correct that, in Montiano's opinion, they may be considered perfect. The three unities of time, place, and action, "which are not, as some believe, established arbitrarily or capriciously, but are the products of nature and reason,"[51] are rigorously observed.

Montiano is willing to concede that an anonymous play, *Policiana,* which was published as a tragedy, merits the censure of the French critic, for it has twenty-nine acts and deserves to be called a *tragic novel.* Two tragedies, published in 1577 with the title *First Spanish Tragedies: Pitiful Nise* and *Nise Crowned* under the name of Antonio de Silva, elicit Montiano's praise for their style and adherence to the rules.[52]

Montiano makes no attempt to defend the so-called tragedies of Juan de la Cueva. *The Seven Princes of Lara* would have been more properly called *The Punishment of Rui Velázquez*, since the play works up to its climax in the vengeance which Mudarra González takes upon his uncle and upon Doña Lambra. But even with a change of title the play would remain defective in its violation of the three unities.[53] Although Cueva wrote his *The Death of Ajax Telamon* in imitation of Sophocles, it bears little similarity to the original and violates the unities and verisimilitude.[54] *The Death of Virginia* has two actions. This defect, in Montiano's opinion, outweighs some marvelous passages in the work. *The Tyrant Prince* observes the unity of action but is completely implausible in its plot and incidents. Particularly does Montiano object to the use of allegorical figures, or rather ghosts, which, although accepted by the ancients, have been rejected by the moderns as contrary to the Catholic dogma and as injurious to the credulous public.[55]

Montiano has not seen *The Lovers* by Andrés Rey de Artieda, but he is willing to accept Cervantes' appraisal of the play in the *Galatea*, and to classify it as a regular tragedy.[56] He quotes with satisfaction Cervantes' praise of three other tragedies, *Isabela*, *Filis*, and *Alexandra*, in Part I of the *Quijote:*

"Do you not remember that a few years ago there were performed in Spain three tragedies composed by a famous poet of this country, which were of such a quality that they astonished, delighted, and held in suspense all who heard them, both the simple and the prudent, the common people and the nobility; and that these three plays produced more money for the actors than any thirty of the best that have been performed since?" "Doubtless," answered the actor, "you must be referring to the *Isabela*, the *Filis*, and the *Alexandra*." "I am," I answered: "and consider whether they observed the precepts of art well, and whether, because of observing them, they failed to appear what they were and to please everyone."[57]

Although he has been unable to find out any more about these tragedies, he is willing to take Cervantes' word for their merit. But Montiano's confidence in Cervantes' judgment was quite unwarranted. It has since been proven that the three plays were by Lupercio Leonardo de Argensola. Leandro Fernández de Moratín gives an analysis of *Isabela* in his *Origins of the Spanish Theater* and concludes that, although some scenes are well written and although the style is elegant and the verse excellent, the play lacks unity, simplicity, distribution, and verisimilitude, and, consequently, interest.[58] *Alexandra*, according to Moratín, is worse than *Isabela*, because "to the irregularity of the plan and to the implausibility of its atrocious characters and situations is added carelessness in style and versification." *Filis*, Moratín says, has remained unedited.[59]

Montiano is convinced that Cervantes' statement carries with it definite proof that the performance of tragedies was common in his time and that they appealed not only to the learned but also to the masses. He proposes to show that there was at that time in Spain a group capable of appreciating the delicacies of art, excellence of language, and rigorous observance of dramatic laws. He proposes also to show that tragedies began at that time to become perverted. After such a confident assertion one is surprised at Montiano's lack of success in unearthing regular tragedies.

He seems to be making a start when he cites five tragedies by Christóval de Virués, published in 1609: *The Great Semiramis, Cruel Cassandra, Furious Attila, Unfortunate Marcela,* and *Elisa Dido*.[60] But he has said at the beginning of his *Discourse* that he does not propose to treat his subject with partiality or to conceal what is worthy of censure. Accordingly, after quoting Virués' statement in the prologue that in the first four tragedies he has attempted to combine "the best of ancient art with modern practice," and that in the last he has completely conformed "to the style of the Greeks and Latins," Montiano does not hesitate to say that in *The Great Semiramis* Virués has not only fallen short of imitating the ancients but has also been unsuccessful in adjusting his technique to the best modern practice. The three acts of the play occur at different times; one act is at the Siege of Batra, the second is in Ninevah, and the third is in Babylon. By the author's own admission in the prologue the play might be considered as three tragedies instead of one. After an analysis of *The Great Semiramis* in which he points out the faults in plot structure, in characterization, and in verisimilitude, Montiano concludes that Virués, "intending to compose three tragedies, did not succeed in perfecting even one."[61]

Cruel Cassandra has one element which is lacking in *The Great Semiramis:* a plot and linking of the action; but in his attempt to conform to modern practice Virués has complicated the plot too much.[62] Montiano objects to the wholesale slaughter in the tragedy, where eight of the nine principal characters die, "because in addition to the excessive horror caused by so much bloodshed," such slaughter "makes the acting harsh, violent, and less credible."[63] He recognizes that examples of this practice are not wanting among the Greeks and more recently among the English, but he believes the sight of such terrible catastrophes has now become repugnant.

Montiano classifies Virués' third tragedy, *Furious Attila*, as regular, but the preponderance of the love element which is the sole motivating force of the action meets with his disapproval.[64] An over-emphasis upon love, in his opinion, is inconsistent with the majestic seriousness that should characterize tragedy. With obvious satisfaction Montiano backs his position with quotations from Voltaire, who in his *Dissertation upon Ancient and Modern Tragedy*, published in 1749, confessed, after emphasizing the superiority of the French theater over the Greek, "that gallantry has almost completely weakened the advantages we have in other respects," and added that "of almost four hundred tragedies which have been performed in the theater since it has achieved a measure of glory in France, there are not more than ten or twelve that are not based upon an intrigue of love, a thing more suitable to the comic than to the tragic genre."[65] If it is true, by Voltaire's own admission, that 388 out of 400 French tragedies are imperfect, should this fact not incline the French to look with more indulgence upon defects in Spanish plays?

Unfortunate Marcela, the fourth of Virués' tragedies, observes the unities, but fails to meet with Montiano's approval because it is "more a sentimental novel in verse than a true tragedy."[66]

Although Montiano has found fault on one score or another with the first four of Virués' tragedies, he has nothing but praise for *Elisa Dido*, and finds it unpardonable that a man like Virués with real poetic gifts and a knowledge of dramatic principles should "for the caprice of opening a new way, abandon the sure and well-worn road."[67] The unities, Montiano says, are observed so religiously in *Elisa Dido* that even the most scrupulous can find nothing to criticize. The time is limited to three or four hours; the scene to the Temple of Jupiter; and "the action to Dido's determination to be constant in her faith, in her love for the dead Sichaeus and in her endeavor to save her new city." The style, emotions, and manners are entirely in keeping with the tragic genre.

After this tragedy by Virués, Montiano finds none upon which he is willing to place his stamp of approval. In Christóbal de Mesa's

Pompeyo, published in 1618, the action moves from the island of Lesbos to the fields of Parsalia, to the sea, back to Lesbos, and finally to Egypt. In many of the scenes the stage is left deserted. There is also great inequality in the characters and in their language. As an evidence that Christóbal de Mesa wilfully violated rules well known to him, Montiano cites the "Dedication" which precedes the play:

> Tragedy is a poem which requires a Euripides or a Seneca; because, being limited to such a short period of time that Aristotle in his *Poetics* gives it only a day or a little more, the less time it consumes, the more unity it has; the more unity, the more perfection; and the more perfection, the more difficulty.[68]

Montiano's discussion has now led him to the so-called tragedies of Lope de Vega. An examination of the twenty-five books of Lope's comedies which the Royal Academy has been able to collect in its library reveals six plays that bear the title of tragedies: *The Duke of Viseo, The Burning of Rome, Beautiful Aurora, Innocent Blood,* and *The Most Constant Husband.* In discussing the works of Lope, Montiano realizes that he is on dangerous ground and begins his remarks with the following statement:

> And although I know that I am dealing with the darling of those who canonize works by the name of their author and not by their real merit, I intend to express my opinions freely; because without going into the right of such a prolific author to fame, or seeking to detract from the credit which he enjoyed during his lifetime and the praise which was showered upon him after his death, I consider it proper (inasmuch as it is necessary to speak of these poems) not to omit through fear of the insubstantial babbling of fashion, or for other equally unauthorized considerations, that judgment which sober reason and study dictate.[69]

Lope could not have chosen a better subject for a tragedy than *The Duke of Viseo* if he had limited the action to one subject; but with the introduction of the death of the Duke of Guimarans and the events which led to this death, the author has violated the first precept of tragedy. The violation of the unity of place is apparent since the scene shifts from the palace of the King to the house of the Duke of Guimarans, to the village of Viseo, to the seashore, and then to a street upon which the windows of the palace open. The transgression of the unity of time is evidenced by Evira's statement to the Queen in the third act that the Duke of Viseo has been absent for three days. Montiano objects also to the introduction into the action of peasants with their disputes and jokes which, he says, are only suitable to comedy. Nor are the student astrologer and the ghost characters that befit tragedy. He will not presume to criticize the language or the thought of the play "because Lope's verses usually carry the pedigree of good language and of the best concepts."

The Burning of Rome is a "small history of Nero starting during the lifetime of Claudius and ending with the death of Nero himself."[70] In order to conform to the account which Seneca gives of the reign of this emperor in his book, Clemencia, Lope found it necessary to place one scene in Armenia and another in Spain. Montiano refrains from saying more about the play because what he has pointed out is sufficient "to give an idea of what Lope calls a tragedy."

About Beautiful Aurora Montiano says: "The entire subject is comic in the manner of his art; there is nothing tragic except the death of Floris,"[71] which has no connection with the title of the play.

The Most Constant Husband, which is the story of Orpheus, "is not the most suitable for a tragedy." Plots taken from antiquity are implausible "and consequently the most foreign and repugnant to tragic precepts." When Lope has Fabio accompany his master on his journey into Hell with saddlebags and witticisms, he has "exceeded the limits of the most absurd imagination."[72]

Punishment Without Vengeance does not observe the unities of place and time, but is reasonably regular in its action. Lope introduces certain episodes, however, which are inopportune and improbable. Innocent Blood is equally irregular. Tragic situations are interrupted by comedy in the worst taste. The gloss which the lackey Morata reads to Doña Juana de Guzmán in her grave affliction and sadness "is a despicable folly at such a critical moment."[73]

Lope's tragi-comedies are in no respect different from his so-called tragedies; "but since he gave them another name (perhaps because he thought that, in this manner, he could excuse their breach of the ancient laws of tragedy),"[74] Montiano omits them from his discussion, merely giving the titles of the twelve plays of this type that he has been able to find.

Mexía de la Cerda belongs to Lope's school and commits the same errors of construction without approaching his master in language or thought. *The Seven Princes of Lara*, by Hurtado Velarde, does not observe the unities because the plot extends through twenty years; the scene shifts from Burgos to Córdova, then to the fields of Araviana, and to other places, and there are many actions instead of one.[75] *Angry Hercules* (1641) by López de Zárate, although the author asserts that it conforms to all the rules of dramatic art, is judged defective in its compression of events, places, and time. The "lofty, noble, and ingenious style" of the play is proof of the fact that "it is easier to write good verses than to form a good plot."[76]

From 1641 Montiano jumps to 1740, the year in which Tomás de Añorbe y Corregel published his *Paulino*. He does not feel disposed to waste his time discussing this play, which reveals the ignorance and ineptitude of its author. He only mentions it in order that the ignorant, reading this author's prologue and the title-page, may not be deceived into believing "that French tragedies, which he says he is imitating, are of such a nature."[77] He will refrain also from discussing a considerable number of tragedies of which he has knowledge, because they have remained unpublished. He will, however, make the blanket statement that most of them deserve a high rank. It is evident that Montiano is referring to plays written by some of his associates of the Academy of Good Taste. His statement indicates that, following the publication of Luzán's *Poetics*, the newly formed sect of neo-classicists had been quite busy testing the new formula. In spite of Montiano's praise, these tragedies must have been so disappointing to the authors themselves that they never circulated outside of the Academy.

The inclination of Spaniards for tragedy, Montiano declares, is so old that, not content with the translation of Aristotle's *Poetics* into Spanish, his countrymen wrote during the sixteenth century a number of commentaries upon Aristotle and Horace. Among such classical works he mentions the treatise on *Poetic Art* by Francisco Sánchez Brocense, written in Latin and printed in Amberes in 1582; a commentary upon Horace's *Poetics* by Thomás Correa, printed in Venice in 1587; the *Philosophia Antigua Poética* (1569) by Alonso López Pinciano; the *Tablas Poéticas* (1617) by Francisco Cascales and the *New Idea of Tragedy, or Commentary on the Poetics of Aristotle*, by González de Salas (1633), and finally Luzán's *Poetics* (1737).[78]

The same scholarly spirit and the same admiration for regular

tragedies impelled Pedro Simón Abril to translate *Medea* by Euripides, and González de Salas to translate *The Trojan Women* by
Seneca. The latter play, Montiano says, was so faithfully and ably
rendered in Castilian verse that it compares favorably with the
original in beauty and elegance of diction. A translation of Pedro
Corneille's *El Cinna* by the Marqués de San Juan in 1731 elicited
the statement by Don Juan de Ferreras in his "Aprobación" that

> ... it has been translated into our language with such success and such
> faithfulness to the spirit of the original that, if there were such a thing
> as the transmigration of souls of which the ancient misguided philosophers
> speak, one might believe that the author and the translator were the
> same.[79]

Montiano's desire to determine the time at which Spanish tragedies began to be corrupted was satisfied when he found the statement by Lope de Vega in *Apollo's Laurel* that Virués had written
"celebrated tragedies" and that, in addition, he was the author
"to whom the Comic Muse owed its best principles." Inasmuch as
Virués boasted that he had endeavored in his tragedies to combine
the ancient rules and modern practice, Montiano concludes that
the corruption of comedy and tragedy occurred at the same time, and
that Lope de Vega believed the combination advocated by Virués
had been responsible for the success of the Spanish *comedia*.
Had those who followed the example of Virués been content with
his moderation, Montiano says, "the change of method would not
have been so noticeable nor the errors of fantasy so serious."[80]

> But they forgot, almost at the same time, the ancient rules; and giving
> themselves over without reserve to the false rules which fashion and the
> fame of Lope had made authoritative, brought forth the new composi-
> tions, which are not in reality comedies, because of the affliction, offenses,
> vengeances, lie-calling, challenges, sword wounds, and deaths in which
> they abound; nor tragedies, because of the facetiousness and low rank
> of the personages, the languor of the sentences, the vulgar choice of
> expressions, and the happy endings which characterize them.[81]

Following Luzán, Montiano approves Cascales' statement that these
plays are "hermaphrodites, or monsters of poetry." He recognizes at
the same time that many Spanish plays have not committed such
grievous sins against dramatic precepts; that some imitate and show
respect for the ancients even to the point of giving a tragic ending
to the plot. At this point Montiano suggests the possibility of re-

working the least defective plays to make them acceptable, or at least less irregular. Plays so treated, he says, "would be more useful than the innumerable works we see on the stage at the present time, in which we do not find the slightest beneficial influence of those who have sought to imitate and to maintain the high level of Greek and Latin tragedy and comedy."[82] He does not wish his statement to be interpreted as a recommendation that imperfect works be imitated or approved; he wishes merely to divide plays into the good, the mediocre, and the bad. Montiano takes a step beyond Luzán in saying that many Spanish plays which imitate and show a certain respect for the ancients "with a little retouching could be made passable, or rather, less defective."[83] Luzán, in speaking of Moreto's ability to draw material from the "old farces," had been content to recommend that contemporary dramatists follow Moreto's example by availing themselves of ideas and scenes from old plays. It is doubtful whether Montiano was sufficiently familiar with French drama to realize that what he was recommending was precisely what the French dramatists of the preceding century had done in adapting Spanish originals to French standards of regularity and, in other cases, in drawing scenes and ideas from Spanish plays for the composition of original works. He could hardly have known the vogue of these translation-adaptations with which Pierre Corneille, Thomas Corneille, Rotrou, Scarron, and others had flooded the repertoires of the French theater. Certainly, however, he was familiar with Corneille's *Cid*, and would hardly fail to recognize that what could be done in a translation could with considerably greater ease be accomplished in the language of the original.

Montiano is convinced, or is trying very hard to convince himself, that the Spanish people like tragedies, and believes that this is proven by the popularity of such plays as Rojas' *The Asps of Cleopatra*, Calderón's *The Tetrarch of Jerusalem*, Vélez de Guevara's *A Queen After Her Death*, and Coello's *The Count of Essex*.[84] Everyone runs to see these works, Montiano says, without being deterred by the pity and terror produced by their tragic happenings. Even the crowd, which by nature is addicted to indecent lovemaking, low humor, showy staging, and manipulation of theatrical machinery, does not show itself entirely adverse to comedies adjusted to the rules of art or to tragedies, although the latter genre is contrary to their prevailing taste. If Spanish audiences receive defective tragedies with such favor, Montiano exclaims, "What would happen if they were written with the rigor of the law!"

As Montiano writes he seems to convince himself, if not the reader, that Spaniards have a definite propensity for tragic, serious, and magnificent themes. He has read some learned works that strengthen him in this conviction:

I inferred from this fact that since our nation is, according to the politician, Diego de Saavedra, in his work *Quid valeant vires*, of all nations the most amenable to reason and the most inclined to subject its emotions and passions to reason and, according to the Royal Academy of History in the dissertation which it published in the first volume of its *Fastos*, is a nation distinguished by its seriousness and proven clemency, fondness for truth and for the actual rather than the accidental; it is most natural that it should prefer tragic circumspection, with its pity, verisimilitude, profit, and rationality, rather than inopportune frivolities, insensibility of spirit, impossible happenings, sterile occupation, and absolute overthrow of reason.[85]

To the anticipated objection of those who claim that Spaniards are without experience or love for tragedy and that the masses with their fondness for irregular compositions have determined the type of plays performed on the Spanish stage, Montiano points out that by Voltaire's own confession about the theater of Paris, "if Cinna is played once or twice, the Venetian *fêtes* are played for three months." It is obvious, therefore, that the common people of France as well as of Spain prefer works that appeal to the senses rather than to the mind. Montiano concludes: "So if there the coarse extravagance of the people does not degrade the nation from the glory acquired by its good taste, the corruption of the masses will not be able to depose ours from the place it merits."[86]

A prodigious number of Spanish plays, Montiano confesses, belong to "this condemnable type of plebeian poems," but he calls attention to the fact that in Spain *comedies, tragedies,* and *tragicomedies* are all included under the heading of *comedias*. The index printed in 1735 by the heirs of Francisco Medel contained 4,409 *comedias* and reflected the custom of listing all plays in this way. Since many of the tragedies he mentions in his *Discourse* are included in this index, Montiano concludes that not all Spanish plays deal with "insubstantial love-making and ridiculous witticisms."[87]

He is aware that many will say that, although Spain may have devoted herself very early to writing tragedies according to the rules, the period of regularity was short and was succeeded by an era of corruption which has lasted up until the present time. He willingly concedes that this has been the history of Spanish tragedy; in fact, that is exactly what he has been trying to prove. But, he adds: "It is one thing to have withdrawn from the sure road of antiquity and to have put foot on unsteady and dangerous ground; and it is another thing never to have walked at all upon solid and safe ground."[88]

Montiano believes that he has adequately answered Du Perron and that from now on neither he nor anyone else will question the antiquity of tragedies or the inclination toward this genre in Spain. It only remains now to produce an example "which will, in part, re-establish the reputation of Spain in tragedy and which will recall achievements of some two hundred years before." He recognizes his limitations; he has done the best he can; let others better qualified then he carry on the work.

For my part I offer *Virginia* to the public, a tragedy which I have composed with considerable study and upon which I have worked until late in the night; if I have succeeded in writing a work that will not be scorned, that is all the reward I can expect for my labor. The incentive for my countrymen to imitate this pattern and to improve upon it (as it will be easier for any ordinary wit to do than it has been for me) depends entirely upon Providence in view of the obduracy of the many who remain enlisted in the ranks of the ignorant masses.[89]

Montiano analyzes his tragedy step by step to show how he has applied the dramatic precepts and, obviously, to forestall criticism of his methods. He insists that he will be as impartial in evaluating his tragedy as he has been in criticizing the works of others.

To this end I shall make a minute examination of the entire tragedy, touching where it is fitting upon the rules I have followed and the reasons which have induced me to observe them, in order that the analysis I make may serve as a defense, but without attempting to persuade anyone that my work contains no faults or departures from those principles.[90]

In order that we may follow Montiano in his analysis let us examine the plot of *Virginia*.

In the opening scene of the first act we are informed through a conversation between Virginia and her maid Publicia of the events which have preceded the opening of the play. We learn that Virginia is betrothed to Icilius and that she is the object of the lustful passion of Claudius the decemvir, who as yet has made no open declaration. She lives in constant dread of him and is reluctant to take part in a religious festival in the Forum because of her fear of meeting him there. When her betrothed, Icilius, notices that she seems disturbed and sad, he insists she tell him the cause. Misinterpreting her silence, he accuses her of inconstancy and thereby forces a confession from her. His first impulse is to take vengeance upon the decemvir; but at this moment Virginia's uncle, Numitor, enters and, having been apprised of the situation, counsels Icilius to attempt to enlist the aid of two senators, Valerian and Horace. Inasmuch as they have great influence over the common people, Numitor believes their support will be useful in the event Claudius tries to force his attentions upon Virginia. Icilius departs to look for the senators, and Numitor considers that the danger warrants dispatching a messenger to summon Lucius, Virginia's father, who is with his troops a short distance from the city.

At the beginning of the second act, Claudius, by means of a monologue, acquaints the audience with his side of the story. Because he controls the Roman empire he feels that his power should be supreme in all things, and he cannot understand why Virginia should resist him. His client, Marcus, advises him to impose his will upon her, saying that, as the ruler, he is not subject to ordinary moral laws. At this point, Valerian and Horace appear to question Claudius about the assassination of the Roman general Siccius. When they let it be known that Claudius himself is suspected of having ordered the assassination, the decemvir hotly denies the charge and flies into such a rage against his accusers that Valerian and Horace, convinced of his guilt, decide to take part in the movement to overthrow him.

In the third act, Claudius meets Virginia in the Forum and declares his love. When she rejects him, he resorts to threats. She hurriedly leaves the Forum, calling down the vengeance of the Gods upon his head. After her departure Claudius turns to Marcus for advice, and is assured that through a plan which he has conceived the girl can be forced to yield. Marcus is prevented from revealing his plan to Claudius by the arrival of Icilius, and the audience is kept in suspense. Icilius has come to offer his services to the decemvir but is rebuffed by the latter, whereupon the youth flies into another rage. The decemvir leaves the stage to be replaced by Virginia, who informs her lover of the declaration and the threats of Claudius. Icilius swears that he will take vengeance before sunset.

At the opening of the fourth act, we are informed of the client's plan. He proposes to accuse Virginia of being not the daughter of Lucius, but the offspring of one of his slaves; he will claim that Lucius adopted her, thereby depriving him of his property. When Marcus attempts to seize Virginia he is thwarted by the timely appearance of Icilius and Numitor, with an undetermined number of followers. Uncertain of the size of the force which accompanies Icilius and fearing a popular uprising, Claudius decides to throw a cloak of legality over his highhanded proceedings. He pretends to grant Virginia a fair trial at which he himself, of course, will act as judge.

In the fifth act, Virginia's father finally appears. At the trial he becomes convinced that there is no way to save his daughter from the clutches of Claudius. Accordingly, he pretends to acquiesce in the conduct of the trial upon the condition that he be allowed to speak privately with his daughter for a moment. Permission is granted and he retires, accompanied by Marcus, who is to stand near by to guard during the interview. In a few moments, during which Horace and Valerian have been keeping the audience entertained with threats against the decemvir, the father reappears with the announcement that he has killed both his daughter and Marcus. At this tragic news Icilius rushes at Claudius, who, realizing that he is in danger not only from Icilius but also from the mob, whose sympathies have been aroused by the tragedy, rushes off the stage closely pursued by Icilius. The latter returns shortly with a vivid description of how Claudius, seeing himself surrounded by enemies, has plunged his own dagger in his heart a bare second before Icilius' dagger descended. The mob departs to punish Claudius' accomplices, but Icilius refrains from accompanying them in order to officiate at the funeral pyre of his beloved. Overcome by grief, he announces his intention to give her a magnificent funeral and to erect a monument to her that will endure for many centuries. The curtain is held only long enough for Publicia to make certain that the audience does not miss the moral lesson of the tragedy:

> Let us go, Icilius, let us go; but may we
> be ever reminded by the examples
> of the two unburied delinquents
> and the funeral pomp you plan
> that never did virtue go unrewarded
> nor guilt fail to meet its punishment.

To forestall any possible accusation of plagiarism, Montiano states before he begins his analysis of *Virginia* that he drew his material from Livy and Dionysius of Halicarnassus, and that after he had finished his play he discovered two tragedies which dealt with the same subject; one by Juan de la Cueva and the other by the French dramatist, Campistron, printed in 1694.[91] He proceeds to show the dissimilarity between his plays and the two earlier works.

Montiano's first step in the composition of his tragedy was to draw up in prose the plan which he intended to follow, keeping always clearly in mind that a tragedy "is the imitation of a complete heroic action in which many persons take part in one place and in the space of one day; and that its principal purpose is to form or to correct manners by exciting terror and pity."[92] He believes the subject of his tragedy adequately meets the requirement that it be heroic and calls attention to Lucius' declaration that his daughter joyfully offered her breast to his knife in order to defend her chastity. To the anticipated objection that Virginia and her father are plebeians and, for that reason, not fit subjects for tragedy, Montiano answers that there is nothing little in Rome and that a Roman plebeian easily ranks with the most distinguished of other lands. Besides, he says, the beauty of Virginia easily makes up for any lack of noble blood.[93]

Montiano does not believe that there is more than one action in his tragedy, inasmuch as the activities of Valerian and Horace are directly connected with the main action. The exposition has been handled artistically, for the conversation between Virginia and Publicia acquaints the audience with the indispensible antecedents without making this purpose too obvious.[94] The action of the play starts when Icilius appears in the third scene of the first act. The revelation which Virginia has made in the first scene naturally leads the audience to expect that she will confess her fears to her betrothed. Montiano considers it more artistic to delay this confession until Icilius has wrung it from her by his unjustified suspicions. The meeting of Virginia and Claudius in the second scene of the third act has been adequately prepared and is expected by the spectators. Virginia's apparent inclination at first to leave her defense to Publicia, however, causes restlessness in the audience which is quieted when Virginia begins to speak, disillusioning the decemvir, reproaching him, and finally turning her back with an angry threat which leaves him speechless and incapable of action.

From the first scene of the fourth act the audience is anxiously waiting to learn the plan which Marcus has suggested to Claudius.[95] The tension increases with each scene until the audience fears that there is no way to prevent Virginia's falling into the clutches of the decemvir. The proposed trial offers temporary relief for the anxiety of the spectators. Montiano cannot conceal his enthusiasm for the effectiveness of the denouement. He is certain that the catastrophe or solution has been anticipated by no one, that the death of Virginia at the hands of her own father and her willingness to meet death to save her honor are sufficient to excite supreme pity. In the final scene everything is accounted for; Claudius and Marcus receive their just punishment and the audience is left with the consolation that the bright memory of Virginia's heroism will not be allowed to perish.

Montiano's detailed analysis of his tragedy leaves no doubt that he constructed it with great care. He must have kept Luzán's *Poetics* open before him as he wrote, using it constantly as a yardstick. To meet the strictest requirements of the unity of place, he limited the scene to the Forum of Rome. He hesitated for a considerable time as to whether to confine the action to twenty-four or thirty hours, to one period of the sun as recommended by Aristotle, or to three or four hours, which would make it conform exactly to the time of performance. Wishing to avoid both extremes, he chose a middle ground and reduced his tragedy to the hours of morning and afternoon.[96]

Not content to observe the three unities prescribed by previous critics, Montiano declares that he has endeavored to observe a fourth unity, that of character, and hopes that someone more competent than he will establish it as a convenient and useful precept.[97] As one reads the *Virginia* he is inclined to believe that Montiano's desire to make his characters conform always to recognized patterns of conduct explains in part, at least, their lifelessness and lack of interest. His characters become mere abstractions instead of human beings. To carry out his purpose Montiano has done everything he can to make Virginia speak and act at all times in a manner which will be in keeping with her modesty, her nobility of heart, and her characteristically Roman heroism. He has been equally careful with the other characters: Claudius is consistently cruel, insolent, domineering, and lustful; Marcus is base from the beginning to the end. Valerian and Horace attempt at all times to cover their ambitions with the cloak of patriotism; Lucius Virginius is always "suspicious, distrustful, cautious, and prepared"; Icilius is "intrepid, arrogant, confident, filled with a love for Virginia which detracts nothing from his patriotism"; Numitor shows at all times "prudence without timidity, good judgment without irresolution, and a restrained and proper conduct."[98] Montiano is mistaken in assuming that he has invented a fourth unity. He has merely carried to an extreme the four qualities which Aristotle prescribed for character: goodness, propriety, resemblance, and consistency.

Montiano defends at length his choice of blank verse. He recognizes that public taste favors pure rhyme, but he considers that true harmony consists principally "in the spirit and measure of the verse itself rather than in the uniformity and selection of the final syllables."[99] He has chosen, therefore, a verse form without pure rhyme because such a form "is more like prose, the common language of men in their daily lives." He finds ample precedent for his choice in the works of Garcilaso de la Vega, Gonzalo Pérez, Antonio de Silva, Christóval de Virués, Juan de Jáuregui, Francisco de Quevedo, and other writers of the sixteenth and seventeenth centuries. He also calls attention to the fact that Pinciano, Cascales, and Luzán all agreed "that meter is not necessary for epic and dramatic poems."[100]

The example set by "the great Corneille" is sufficient to induce Montiano to omit the tragic choruses. He has no confidence in the ability of contemporary Spanish musicians to achieve the effectiveness of classical music, and believes that "melody of the voices and the accompaniment will distract attention."[101]

Montiano is careful to keep the stage always occupied, "because although failure to link the scenes is not a capital sin, and may sometimes be violated, it is nevertheless a defect," and should be avoided as much as possible.[102]

In the formation of his plot, Montiano has chosen not only the possible, but the probable. To achieve verisimilitude he has consciously taken certain liberties with historical accuracy — not in fundamental facts, however, but in those which are accessory. He has exercised his discretion also in departing from Horace's precept that not more than three persons may speak in one scene. He has been moved to do so not only by the example of some of the best dramatic writers, but also because he has found in practice that the rule is unnecessarily strict.[103]

Finally, he has not completely ignored the *mise en scène*, because, although he considers it one of the least substantial adornments of tragedy, he recognizes that it may contribute to the success of the performance. In view of our limited information about the staging of plays in the first half of the eighteenth century, Montiano's ideas on effective staging have a definite historical value. He has not yet brought himself to accept and to recommend the French type of a fixed stage with no variation and admits some elaborateness of decoration. He realizes, however, the inadvisability of attempting to compete with the magnificence of the Italian opera, the influence of which was beginning to make itself felt in Spain, and which in the next century was to threaten the very existence of tragedies and comedies. Although he has not attempted to compete with the Italian opera, he has given some attention to the dignity of the spectacle.

... I realized that it was necessary not to compete (or even to attempt to do so) with the varied and magnificent decoration of the Italian operas because such decoration is impossible in tragedies, if the unity of place is to be observed; but I arranged for some attention to be given to the dignity of the spectacle by providing an opportunity for changing the stage setting and making the scenes ostentatious. So in the first act the view of some portion of the Forum and that of some distant perspective of the façade of the Temple of Palas may afford no mean mutation. In the second, third, and fourth acts, the successive alteration of the appearance of the Forum with no change in the scene of action, produces an effect that is natural, easily accomplished, and of no slight usefulness. And in the last act, the addition of the tribunal for the decemvir varies the setting and attracts attention with its novelty. The attendance of Romans of both sexes, ministers of justice, and soldiers not only fills and adds beauty to the stage, but also exalts the action... [104]

Montiano may have been influenced in his willingness to provide an elaborate setting for his tragedy by recent innovations in France. His friend Luzán, during his residence in Paris, had witnessed the first performance of Voltaire's *Semiramis* in 1748 and surely had conveyed to Montiano his impressions of the effectiveness of the staging of that tragedy. In Montiano's *Second Discourse* quotations taken from Voltaire's *Dissertation upon Ancient and Modern Tragedy*, which was published with *Semiramis*, show that Montiano was familiar not only with Voltaire's ideas on the proper staging of tragedies but also with the stage directions for *Semiramis* itself. As early as 1730 Voltaire had attempted to introduce scenery and spectacle in his tragedy *Brutus*. His criticism of French tragedy was that it had become mere conversation and that, inasmuch as the action was reduced to the barest minimum and no attention was given to the adornment of the stage, it had lost its popular appeal. The setting for *Semiramis* had shown a definite influence of the Italian opera, and the effect was intended to be spectacular. There was a large square with adjacent buildings which represented a palace and the entrance of a temple. Although the scene changed four times, some parts of the original setting remained in view to emphasize the observance of the unity of place. The setting proposed by Montiano does not differ in any essential respect from that used in Voltaire's *Semiramis*.

Montiano's Second Discourse

Although Montiano declares that the reception given to his first discourse exceeded his expectations, he believed that he could further strengthen the position of Spain in the field of tragedy against foreign attacks by the publication in 1733 of a second discourse, accompanied by a second model tragedy, *Athaulpho*.[105] He hoped by this work to prove conclusively the high position which tragedy held in Spain "during the happy times of Good Taste," and to excite in the present generation not only "a keen desire to restore that position by imitation," but also a determination to surpass anything which had previously been done. New research has revealed to him additional evidence of the antiquity of tragedy in Spain. Indeed he has found that it was older than he himself had thought. This new discovery is that Vasco Díaz Tanco de Frejenal composed three tragedies, Absalom, Amon, and Saul, published in 1552, but written some thirty years earlier. To establish the date of composition of these tragedies, Montiano starts with the *Triumpho Natalicio Hispano* which Frejenal wrote in middle life in honor of the birth of Felipe II. If the author had reached middle age at the same time he composed this work—in 1527—Montiano reasons that his tragedies, since they were the work of his youth, must have been composed about the year 1502 or before. Spanish tragedy, therefore, is even older than the Italian, inasmuch as Trissino's *Sophinisba*, which is considered to be the first Italian tragedy, was not performed until 1520 and not published until 1524.

Montiano notices that he failed to mention Cervantes in his first discourse as an author of tragedies, in spite of the fact that Gregorio Mayans y Siscar, in his edition of *Don Quixote* published in London, called attention to the fact that Cervantes had composed some trage-

dies "which were well received." Montiano is also pleased to note
two tragedies written by Guillén de Castro, *Dido* and *Eneas*, and two
others written by Salas Barbadillo. In the *Romancero* of Gabriel
Lasso he has found two tragedies, *The Honor of Dido Restored* and
The Destruction of Constantinople. Juan de Malara affirmed that
he had written a tragedy, *Absalom:* and Alonso López Pinciano, in
his *Philosophía Antigua Poética*, stated, as though the performance
of tragedies were a common occurrence, that he saw *Iphigenia* at
the theater of the Cruz. With the statement that Juan Boscán translated a tragedy of Euripides, Montiano brings to a close his evidence of the antiquity of Spanish tragedies. He insists even more
strongly than he had done in his first discourse, however, that
most of the so-called tragi-comedies which have been composed
in Spain, "with slight corrections, could be made into regular
tragedies."[106]

Montiano's investigation of early evidences in Spanish drama of
a familiarity with, and an adherence to, the principles of Aristotle
and Horace has suggested to him that in the period of good taste
the actors and the stage managers must have observed also the
principles of the ancient Greeks and Romans in stage *apparatus*,
"a part of the art of tragedy which contributes so much to perfecting the performance ... " Further investigation, he says, has convinced him that "the rules, which are perhaps unknown today, were
known even in the sixteenth century."[107] He has discovered in
Pinciano's *Philosophia Antigua Poética* a brief but able treatment of
the art of acting and staging as practiced by the ancient Greeks and
Latins. The remainder of Montiano's second discourse is a treatise
on the art of declamation and stage *apparatus*. He takes as his guide
the rules of Pinciano, and to these he adds what he has been able
to draw from the *New Idea of Tragedy* by González de Salas,
Julius Caesar Scaliger's *Poetics*, *The Art of the Theater in Paris*
by Riccoboni, and the *Literary Memoirs of Paris* by Luzán. The bulk
of his material is drawn from Pinciano, Riccoboni, and Luzán.
He is especially interested in encouraging the artistic performance
of tragedies, "a thing so completely forgotten today that I almost
dare to say it must be studied from the ground up." Montiano proceeds to give careful directions in regard to the actors' dress, declamation, bearing, and gesticulation, relying here principally upon
Pinciano and Riccoboni. He argues earnestly for historical accuracy
in dress and for naturalness in declamation and gesticulation. He has

noticed serious defects on the Spanish stage, particularly in the dress and arms of the supernumeraries, "due to a failure to study in histories or other documents the characteristics of each nation and of each profession."[108]

That the French theater at the close of the seventeenth and the beginning of the eighteenth century committed as glaring anachronisms as the Spanish is evidenced by the fact that in Racine's *Iphigenia* the scene is in the tent of Agamemnon, although at the time of Homer tents were unknown and it was to his hut, not to his tent, that the angry Achilles retired. A similar anachronism occurs when Agamemnon is represented as writing letters although the art of writing had not yet been introduced. As late as 1811 this tragedy was being performed in France with the same historical inaccuracies; at that time someone even conceived the idea of placing upon Agamemnon's table an inkwell with a goose quill, in order to add a touch of realism.[109] Examples of anachronisms in dress and manners abound in both the French and Spanish theaters of the seventeenth century and the early part of the eighteenth. Practically no attention was given to the *mise en scène*, and certainly no serious attempt was made to create an illusion of reality by stage decoration. Voltaire complains somewhat bitterly of the inadequacy and bad taste of the decoration used in his day:

I cannot sufficiently express my astonishment and displeasure at the lack of care which has been taken in France to make the theaters worthy of the excellent works that are performed. . . . *Cinna* and *Athalie* deserve to be performed in some other place than a tennis court, at the back of which a stage setting in the very worst taste has been set up, and in which the spectators were placed contrary to all order and reason, some standing on the stage itself and others in what is called the *parterre*, where they were cramped and pressed together outrageously, and where at times they rushed upon each other as in a popular riot.[110]

Although Montiano's goal is that speech, gesticulation, facial expression, and everything included under the term *acting* shall have the appearance of complete naturalness, he warns against the idea that imitation of nature suffices to make a good actor. "Many, although they know what they should do, cannot take a step until Art shows them the way and cannot succeed until repeated practice makes them adept."[111] Important as the movements of the body are, "let it not be thought that the fingers are to control the voice, and that the joints must be loquacious . . . because to represent materially with the hands and the body everything that the tongue articulates, would be to perform the ridiculous role of a mimic." Montiano has been speaking in generalities so far, but now he makes a direct reference to the Spanish stage, and to abuses he has noticed:

Our performances suffer at the present time from the defects which I am attacking. If there is narration with description (which usually is unnecessary and only serves to emphasize what is being represented) and a horse is being described, as in *The Scarf and the Flower*, the horse does not raise a foot or make a movement that the actor does not try to imitate with excessive zeal; he must even, by moving his hand backward, show where the tail falls; and if the firing of a gun is being described, he must act as though he had it against his shoulder, his right hand held forward, the left hand on the stock, and the index finger on the trigger, his head bent over and even one eye closed and the other looking down the barrel, just exactly as a hunter or a soldier does when he aims and fires. All the violent attitudes which could be assumed in the strangest situations (for example, in *The Most Prodigious Negro*, the struggle with the serpent; and in *The Genízaro of Spain and Scourge of Andalucía*, the fright of Mudarra when he saw the feet of Santiago's horse on his chest) are copied by contorting the body without respect for the nature, decorum, and seriousness of the character being represented . . .[112]

Montiano's rules for acting may seem to us today ridiculously detailed and mechanical, but they probably filled a definite need in a day when exaggeration of gesticulation and affectation in speech were in complete possession of the stage, when acting had kept pace with the decline in the quality of the plays themselves.

In regard to stage setting, Montiano believes that Pinciano gave the essential requirements when he said: "The adornment of the stage is necessary . . . and should vary according to the nature of the play; if it is a pastoral, there should be forests; if it is a city play, there should be houses."[113] Montiano expresses satisfaction and a certain pride in the new theaters which have recently been constructed in Madrid to replace the old *corrales*. With these theaters it is now possible to observe the proper rules of staging:

. . . Our theaters have the material proportions which any play may require; because within an oval form or shape, with reasonably good architecture, there is a vestuary, or scene of fair dimensions, which leaves free an adequate forum when such is necessary; a good-sized proscenium or *tablado;* a space for the wings or lateral machinery; a place above and below for the *appearances;* and in short, all the conveniences needed by the actors and the audience, although, of course, not on the scale which distinguished the Greek and Roman theaters, because the taste and wealth are lacking for such expenditures.[114]

He strongly recommends a careful examination of the nature of the plays to be performed and their supposed setting as well as the time of the action, in order that the temples, porticos, fortresses, palaces, and other buildings used in the performance may be historically accurate.

Since the composition of his first discourse Montiano has apparently given considerable thought to the proper staging of tragedies, and now he finds it hard to reconcile any change of setting whatsoever with that rigid application of the unity of place which he has come to accept as requisite for perfection in tragedy. His whole discussion of this unity shows a certain disturbance of mind. In the face of the practical difficulties that lie in the way of a fixed stage and of the unwillingness of dramatists to limit the action of their plays to one place, he is willing, however, to make certain concessions.

Although I am convinced (contrary to what I suggested in my first discourse) that the slightest change of scenery breaks the strict unity of place, which is such an aid to theatrical illusion . . . nevertheless, inasmuch as defects committed against this rule are not the work of the actors but of the authors, who sometimes conform in part and sometimes break the rule completely, I shall broaden the latitude I have given; or rather I shall suggest a way to facilitate the performance of such tragedies with less irregularity, and without altering the impressions made by the first view of the stage. The idea to which I adhered in my first discourse was that, if the scene permits, the stage should be set so that it has a different appearance in each act, always leaving some part which will call to mind the initial scene, in order to make it clear that the place is the same and that it is only being considered or seen from a different point of view, this change being made during the intermissions, when the audience is in suspense, the curtain which hides the stage is down, and the movement of the wings and drops cannot be noticed. Reflecting, then, that lowering and raising the front curtain will cause a notable interruption, it has seemed to me that this inconvenience could be avoided by arranging it so that the two or three wings next to the front of the stage would not move and by having them represent something suggestive of the changes that are to take place later, such as columns, arches, a hall, cliffs, trees, tents, or other like things. In this manner, with the main part of the stage reduced to these unalterable limits and with a curtain lowered behind the last of the immovable wings at the conclusion of each act, the forum may be made to appear in the following act with the desired changes, but with some part of the original scene still in view.[115]

Luzán's proposal that horizontal or perpendicular divisions be made on the stage does not completely satisfy Montiano; although, of all the modifications of a fixed stage which have been suggested by different writers, he confesses that he considers Luzán's plan the most practicable. Nevertheless, "it has the objection that the spectators will have continually before them three or four different places, which, recalling what has happened, or exciting curiosity about what is to take place, will cause their attention, which should be fixed on one spot, to stray from one to another."[116] Montiano realizes that serious objections could be raised to his own suggested modifications and returns to his advocacy of an absolutely fixed stage: "Therefore I advise that no change whatsoever be made in the stage setting; but that every effort be made to keep it the same from the beginning to the end, in order that the unity of place may be strictly observed."[117] The adoption of his plan would, of course, banish the *sainetes, entremeses,* and *bayles* from the theater. He agrees with Luzán that these interludes have no place in serious performances, inasmuch as their boisterous humor diverts the attention of the audience from that terror and pity "which are the two purposes of tragedy."

His desire that stage performances create an illusion of reality leads Montiano to a consideration of an abuse on the Spanish stage which is crying out for correction: the obvious and exasperating presence of the prompter. "The prompter, as he is commonly used to aid the actors, not only jars and distracts the audience, making it necessary for them to hear the play recited *in duet;* but also makes it apparent that everything which is heard is only pretended."[118] He is pleased to note that some improvement has recently taken place in the *comedias de teatro,* "that is, in those which have mutations and appearances executed with artificial light." Upon citing Luzán's *Memorias de París* he credits his friend with the innovation:

. . . The practice has been introduced in those plays commonly called *comedias de teatro* of having the prompter turn his back to the audience and face the actors, taking his position in an opening in the middle of the stage, disguised with a back-rest, or *niche,* which, although not very conspicuous, is sufficient to hide his presence. In this position he is heard less because he does not have to raise his voice so much.[119]

Nothing would please Montiano more than that his countrymen

should completely imitate the French practice of using the prompter only to remedy an occasional lapse of memory. If the actors had to rely less upon the aid of the prompter, they would study their roles more and would become ashamed of having to appeal to him. Montiano is unwilling to concede that the French have better memories than the Spanish and considers that the difficulty of learning the great number of plays in the repertoire constitutes no legitimate excuse. The only solution would be for actors to work more or for the number of plays to be reduced.

In his second discourse Montiano does not analyze his tragedy, *Athaulpho*. He refers to it a few times, however, to illustrate some of his remarks on staging and rules for acting. The scene is a palace hall upon which the rooms of the Prince and of Placidia, his wife, and other antechambers open. It is needless to say that the tragedy is rigorously neo-classic. Critics generally concede that it is superior to *Virginia*, in that the moral purpose is not so evident and the dialogue is somewhat more natural, but they are unanimous in terming it cold. Indeed, Cueto's statement that *Virginia* cannot be read in its entirety "without a powerful exercise of will power" is equally applicable to *Athaulpho*.

Neither *Virginia* nor *Athaulpho* ever reached the stage in Spain; but, curiously enough, they were given favorable reviews in France and in Germany. In April, 1751, the *Journal des Sçavans* welcomed the first discourse and the accompanying tragedy as evidence that the Spanish theater was beginning to see the evil of its ways, and in 1754 D'Hermilly published in Paris a translation of Montiano's discourses and tragedies. In Germany, Lessing, who for some years had been studying the Spanish language, and whose attention was called to Montiano's work by the review in the *Journal des Sçavans*, devoted a section of his *Theatrical Library* to a résumé of *Virginia*. His introductory statements show some enthusiasm but little real knowledge of the Spanish theater. In the preface to the *Beyträge zur Historie und Aufnahme des Theatres* (1749), Lessing had already evinced his interest in the Spanish theater:

> We shall direct our attention especially to the English and the Spanish theaters. . . . So it is with Lope de Vega, Agustín Moreto, Antonio de Mendoza, Francisco de Rojas, Fernando de Zárate, Juan Pérez de Montalván, Antonio de Azevedo, Francisco González de Bustos, and others. These are all men who have, it is true, as great defects as they have beauties, but from whom, nevertheless, a clever imitator can take much that is useful.[120]

It seems evident that Lessing was acquainted with Du Perron's
Extraits de plusieurs pièces du Théâtre espagnol and that the idea
had occurred to him, as it had to Du Perron, that the Spanish theater
might prove a rich source of exploitation for dramatists of his own
country. Lessing, even at that time, was interested in leading his
countrymen away from the monotonous imitation of the French
theater, but he had shown no disposition to depart from any of
the tenets of neo-classicism. His ideas on dramatic principles had
been derived principally from French translators of and commentators upon Aristotle, such as Dacier, D'Aubignac, Corneille, Boileau,
and Voltaire. Lessing's idol in 1749 was Voltaire, and indeed his ambition at that time was to become a German Voltaire. Those slight
heresies into which he was to fall after he shifted his allegiance to
Diderot had not made their appearance at this early date. He, therefore, welcomed, as had the French, an evidence that the Spanish
theater was on the up-grade, and saw in Montiano the initiator of a
type of drama which would elevate his country to a high rank among
European nations.

The works of the Spaniards are those which among all foreign
writings are the least known among us. In Germany we scarcely know
their contemporary scholars by name, although a closer acquaintance
with them would give us a quite different conception of Spanish literature
from that which is generally held. I flatter myself that the present account
will raise it to a higher level, and that my readers will be glad to learn
to know the greatest tragic poet that Spain can exhibit at present, a poet
worthy to compete with those of her neighbor. This man is Don Agustín de Montiano y Luyando, about whose life I shall give a report before I
present a detailed synopsis of the most excellent of his works.[121]

Lessing's knowledge of Montiano's discourses and of *Virginia* was
derived from D'Hermilly's translation, and his remarks were made
without a careful study of the play and with too much reliance
upon the French author's evaluation. Both Menéndez y Pelayo and
Pellissier exaggerate Lessing's praise. According to the former, Lessing said that "the tragic genius of D. Agustín Montiano could compete with the outstanding French writers of tragedy."[122] Pellissier
says: "... it gives him pleasure to make known to his countrymen the
life and works of the greatest tragic poet yet produced on the
Spanish peninsula, a writer whom his countrymen need not fear to
compare with those of their supposedly superior neighbors."[123]
As can be seen by the above translation, Lessing made no compari-

son between Montiano and earlier writers of tragedy either in Spain or in France. His statement concerns only Montiano's pre-eminence among contemporary Spaniards and his right to compete with the best French tragic poets of the day. Although Lessing was soon to repent his favorable estimate of *Virginia,* this later judgment must be considered against the background of his change of attitude toward the merit of Corneille and Racine which had been effected by association with the works of Diderot. In 1767 Lessing wrote in his *Hamburgische Dramaturgie:*

We know so little about Spanish works; I hardly know a single one which anyone has translated for us or of which abstracts have been made. *Virginia* by Agustín de Montiano y Luyando was written by a Spaniard, it is true; but it is no Spanish play; it is nothing but an experiment in the French manner, regular but frigid. I confess quite readily that I think by no means as favorably of it as I must have thought formerly.

If the second play of this author is not better; if the new poets of that nation who wish to tread that road do not succeed better; then they should not blame me if I prefer their old writers, Lope and Calderón, to them. [No. 68, December 25, 1767, p. 100.][124]

Pitollet suggests that Lessing's change of attitude toward the *Virginia* may have been influenced by J. A. Dieze's statement in a note to his translation of *Origins of Castilian Poetry* by Luis José Velázquez (1754), which was not published until 1769, but with the contents of which Lessing was probably familiar inasmuch as he and Dieze were friends. At all events, Lessing must have heard him express ideas similar to the following:

As far as his two tragedies are concerned, they unquestionably have the honor of being the most regular that the Spaniards have produced. But neither the careful observance of the rules prescribed by Aristotle and his followers, nor the very beautiful versification, has been able to make this play as interesting as many in which the rules are not so rigidly followed. They are entirely in the French pattern and lack even the characteristically national Spanish style.[125]

Neither Lessing's original estimate nor his later retraction can be considered the result of a sober and careful evaluation of Montiano's position in Spanish literature. In both cases, Lessing was merely following a leader.

A by-product of the desire of the Germans to acquaint themselves with the progress of dramatic art in Spain was an awakened interest in the contribution of Spanish dramatists to world drama during the Golden Age. This interest was stimulated through the reading of such works as Du Perron's *Extraits*, Lesage's *Spanish Theater*, and the French translation of *Origins of Castilian Poetry* by Luis José Velázquez.

German acquaintance with Spanish drama was obviously derived from French works, since few of the German writers at that time were familiar with the Spanish language. It is likely that Lessing was also acquainted with a little essay on the Spanish stage, by Johann Friedrich von Cronegk, published in Leipzig in 1765, which suggested that the world was more indebted to the Spanish drama than was commonly believed:

> It is to be regretted that we in Germany have so little opportunity to become acquainted with the new plays that come out of Spain. *Virginia* and *Athaulpho* are almost the last of which we know anything; and how far must the Spaniards have carried the development of drama, if they have followed these masterpieces? Although I cannot tell my readers anything else about the new Spanish stage, I believe they will not take it amiss if I undertake to give them some conception of the old Spanish theater: for even this information, which can be taken from the oldest writers in that language, is almost unknown in Germany; and I do not know why the admirers of French and Italian poets do not seek to investigate the sources from which the latter have taken so much, and quite forget those very writers who, next to the ancients, were the teachers of Corneille, Molière, and so many other great geniuses.[126]

Cronegk's confidence in the progress being made in writing regular plays in the pattern of Montiano's tragedies would have been shattered if he had known the true situation: that between 1751 and 1765 not a single tragedy or comedy written in the new manner had reached the stage in Spain and that only three original plays— *Jahel* (1763) by Sedano, and *The Fashionable Lady* (1763) and *Lucrecia* (1763) by Nicolás Fernández de Moratín—had been printed.

Montiano's discourses and tragedies probably received more favorable comment in France and Germany than in Spain itself. Praise for these works in the latter country was more or less limited to the circle of Montiano's friends in the Academy of Good Taste, who could hardly be expected to pass an adverse judgment. Even Porcel, who was, as we have seen, somewhat of a recalcitrant in the group, praised Montiano for his defense of Spanish honor and for the stim-

ulus he had given to the cultivation of regular tragedies. In his
Juicio lunático, Porcel says:

Lycurgus placed the statue of Euripides among those of the other
famous Greeks. Among them we should exalt that of our *Humble One*
[the academic name of Montiano] to a place beside that of Sophocles.
... Meanwhile, let us congratulate the nation that this, her generous
defender, should undertake, with such zeal and with such success, to defend her from the insults of foreigners and, with his example, to incite the
lazy writers of Spain to restore the theater.[127]

It is true that Porcel puts the above words in the mouth of the Golden
Age dramatist Francisco López de Zárate, "an uninspired writer like
Montiano, and one who a century before, in *The Mad Hercules,*
had insisted upon the rigid observance of classic precepts."[128]
Although there is reason to suspect that Porcel's praise might have
been given with tongue in cheek, the critical study of *Virginia*
read by Velázquez in the same academy was unquestionably
sincere.[129] In this study Velázquez calls *Virginia* "a model of all perfection," and in his *Origins of Castilian Poetry* he quotes the enthusiastic review of Montiano's tragedies by the editors of the *Memoirs
de Trevoux,* with whom, as Menéndez y Pelayo says, "the Spanish
reformers seem to have made a contract for mutual praise."[130]
Velázquez closes his discussion with this intemperate eulogy:
"In a word, no one until the present time has given rules more
precise, more minute, more comprehensive, more discreet, or
more judicious for the perfection and for the utility of tragedy
than Montiano, and no one has practiced them better."[131] Montiano
was able, of course, to count upon the support of the members of the
Academy of Good Taste, before whom he had read his first discourse
and the *Virginia* before offering them to the press. These works,
according to Cueto, "were received, if not with applause, at least with
a reverential appreciation, by that group of estimable humanists
who considered themselves restorers of Spanish poetry."[132]

Although the opposition aroused by Montiano's discourses could
not be compared to the storm of protest which greeted Nasarre's
"Prologue," the partisans of Lope and Calderón could not be
expected to remain entirely silent. Under the pseudonym of Jaime
Doms appeared a lengthy pamphlet which started with the pretense
of praising Montiano for his defense of Spanish honor, and soon
developed into a despicable attack upon his personal character
and the quality of his scholarship. The author, in a letter which

he represents himself as writing to Montiano, describes the enthusiastic reception of the first discourse by the erudites of France and
tells how he was engaged in writing a letter of appreciation to
Montiano for his able defense of Spanish drama when two friends
entered and began to attack not only the accuracy of the work
but also the author's motives in composing it. Doms makes a half-
hearted defense which only serves to make matters worse. His
friends accuse Montiano of ignorance of history and paleography
and even question his knowledge of the Spanish language. Nowhere
do they enter into a serious discussion of fundamentals. Their resentment has been aroused by what they consider Montiano's real motive
in the composition of his first discourse: the discrediting of Lope
de Vega.

> The purpose of Don Agustín is not, and has not been, to vindicate
> his nation, but to take two bites at Lope de Vega — as is evident by the
> manner in which he insults everyone who speaks well of him. [*Carta
> escrita por Don Jayme Doms Contra el Discurso sobre las Tragedias Es-
> pañolas y la Virginia de el Señor Don Agustino de Montiano y
> Luyando.*][133]

Not content to attack Montiano's work itself and his personal character, Doms taunts the author with having, so late in life, undertaken
a useless task.

An anonymous answer to Dom's work, probably written by Montiano himself, and a rejoinder by Doms, under the pseudonym of
Faustino de Quevedo, contributed nothing of real value to the
discussion.

At the close of his second discourse, Montiano adds the last word
to his controversy with Doms. After agreeing with the English critic,
Addison, that "since a perfect tragedy is one of the most noble productions of human nature, it is the most suitable for giving to the
soul the most delightful and the most instructive pleasure," he
declares that it was this consideration which prompted him to write
both of his discourses and that he expects the same type of criticism
that had greeted his first work.

> ... There was not lacking at that time someone who thought I should
> occupy myself with more serious work; and there will not be lacking
> someone now who will add to that censure, considering the subject
> still less decorous and useful; I pity his ignorance, and if that is not the
> source, I pardon his malice. I shall point out, nevertheless, that both in
> ancient and in modern times this matter has claimed the attention of the

greatest men, and that the most religious have not disdained to discuss it; taking into consideration always what I indicated at the beginning of my discourse: that the fault is not in the theater, but in those who misuse it.[134]

Montiano's earnest desire that his countrymen abandon Golden Age comedy and trage-comedy and fall in line with the exponents of regular drama went unheeded for several years. No dramatists of real ability existed in Spain at the time, and public taste certainly had not been trained to an appreciation of a type of drama that appealed to the intellect rather than to the emotions. The few works written according to the rules never reached the stage. One of Montiano's few followers declared in 1763,

In Spain such works are not written to be performed; nor are they compatible with the monstrosities which have taken possession of the theater, where art, regularity, and good taste are abominated or completely unknown; and where confusion, indecency, pedantry, and extreme barbarism reign, supported by ancient, shameful, and intolerable custom.[135]

It is interesting to note, however, that García de la Huerta, author of the one tragedy written and staged in the eighteenth century which has been most praised by the extreme partisans of the national school, gives Montiano credit for the restoration of tragedy in Spain: "To this worthy Spaniard is due the restoration of this type of poetry. His tragedies were criticized at the time with more wit than solidity; but these criticisms will not deprive him of the glory of having, by his example, promoted and almost revived these compositions."[136]

Velázquez

In 1754, Velázquez, the third preceptist of the Academy of Good Taste, published a treatise entitled *Origins of Castilian Poetry*, one chapter of which is devoted to comedy and another to tragedy. It is useless to seek originality in his treatment of either genre. In his discussion of comedy he follows Nasarre closely, going to the extreme of quoting at length this critic's denunciation of Calderón and concluding with the statement: "I give the words of this author because I am in complete agreement with him in this particular; although I do not approve the vehemence which he employs throughout his discourse in discrediting what has always been discredited by learned men and which will never be discredited among the masses."[137]

His chapter on comedy is made up principally of quotations from Nasarre, from Luzán, and from the *New Art* of Lope; and the section that deals with the history of the early Spanish theater is little more than a condensation of material taken from Nasarre's "Prologue." In his censure of Golden Age dramatists, Velázquez is no less severe with Lope than with Calderón, following Nasarre in calling the former "the first corruptor" and the latter "the second corruptor" of the Spanish theater. He goes more into detail in his denunciation of Lope than does the author of the "Prologue," although he is willing to concede to him "a prodigious facility of expression" and "the smooth and pleasing river of his eloquence." But Lope

... scorned the rules of the theater left to us by the ancients, banishing from his comedies verisimilitude, regularity, propriety, decency, decorum, and, in short, all that aids in maintaining the illusion of the plot and in fulfilling the principal purpose of dramatic poetry. It is useless to seek in his comedies the unities of action, time, and place: in his plays his heroes are born, crawl in their swaddling clothes, reach manhood, grow old, and die. They wander as though they were lost from the east to the west and from the north to the south. He carries them as though through the air; makes them fight a battle here, court a lady there, become friars in another place, die in still another, and even perform miracles after their death. He places one scene in Flanders, and the others in Italy, in Mexico, in Spain, and in Africa. The lackeys speak like courtiers, the princes like ruffians, and noble ladies like women without breeding or decorum. His actors come out on the stage as though they were driven in a throng and in armed squadrons. In his comedies there are frequently as many as twenty-four, thirty, and even seventy characters; and in *The Baptism of the Prince of Fez*, considering even this number inadequate, he adds a procession.[138]

Velázquez agrees with Nasarre that many Spanish comedies can be found without glaring irregularities, and to the list mentioned by Nasarre he wishes to add *D. Domingo de D. Blas, A Stranger Will Come to Throw Us Out of Our House, Open Your Eyes,* and other comedies by Francisco de Rojas, who, he says, was without doubt the Golden Age dramatist who most carefully observed the precepts of dramatic poetry. Velázquez expresses his sincere regret that Nasarre was unable to fulfil his promise to publish a collection of regular Spanish comedies, and is certain that

... if the author of the dissertation on Spanish comedy could have fulfilled the promise made in that work to publish in a collection the comedies selected from this and other Spanish authors with an appropriate analysis and criticism of each play, we would now have nothing left to desire on this point.[139]

Three comedies which have recently appeared in Spain as a result of the neo-classic controversy come in for brief mention. *Reason Against Fashion,* which Luzán has translated from the French of Nivelle de la Chaussée, although it belongs to the questionable type of *tearful comedy,* meets with Velázquez' complete approval. Even though it is a translation, "it has such an original air that one can scarcely discern its foreign origin."[140] This quality, however, is not found in two other works, *The Miser* and *The Sick Man,* translated from the French of Molière by Manuel de Yparraguirre and published on February 19 of that same year (1754). That Velázquez' judgment of their lack of merit is correct is attested by the facts that they never reached the theater and that those critics who deign to mention them speak of them in disparaging terms. The mention of these plays of Molière leads Velázquez to the statement that "when our nation possesses a genius comparable in merit to this great writer of comedies, it may expect the restoration of Spanish comedy."[141] This remark reveals a difference between his attitude toward the French theater and that of Nasarre, who, smarting under the insult which the Spanish theater had received from the pen of a Frenchman, carefully avoided giving credit to French writers.

Montiano's two discourses have, in Velázquez' opinion, anticipated all he can say about the origin and development of Spanish tragedy. He, therefore, contents himself with giving extracts from these works and concludes with the statement that Montiano's *Virginia* and *Athaulpho* are the most regular tragedies written in Spain up until that time. Those who speak with authority on these matters, he says, believe that their author "observes scrupulously and wisely all the rules of the theater," and that "it is difficult to find another play better conceived, and executed with more ability." A note to the 1797 edition of Velázquez' work reveals these experts on tragedy to be none other than the Fathers of Trevoux; the eulogy of Montiano's tragedies was taken from *Memoirs de Trevoux,* December, 1750.

Velázquez considers worth repeating the judgment which a "very ingenious writer of the day has just made of both tragedies":

The two exceedingly discreet and judicious discourses upon Spanish tragedies, together with the two tragedies, *Virginia* and *Athaulpho,* which, in the year 1750 and in the present year, 1753, have been published by D. Agustín de Montiano y Luyando ... will make apparent to other nations that we have in this century a Spanish Sophocles who can compete with the Greek. Far from imitating the two famous writers of tragedies, Corneille and Racine, he reveals and mends their defects. He does not weaken the action, or make it double with the inopportune episode of the cold love of Theseus for Dirsea, as Corneille does in his *Oedipus*. He does not distract attention with two spectacles as contradictory as the enamored Hippolytus and the furious Phèdre as Racine does in his *Phèdre*. He does not speak as majestically and as pompously as Corneille does in his *Cinna;* nor does he describe the death of Virginia at the hands of the punctilious Lucius Virginius, her father, to save the chaste Roman maiden from the brutal passion of the Decemvir Appius Claudius, with the untimely and flowery language with which Racine makes Theramenes announce to Theseus the death of his son Hippolytus, who has been torn to pieces by the claws of a dragon. In Montiano's tragedies the Romans speak with nobility but without pomp; the Goths with ferocity, but without ornament; passions are expressed with vigor, but without affectation; and although both tragedies are based principally upon the passion of love, it is not that type of love which is so justly condemned by the most severe critics. Mr. Salignac de Fenelon himself, who with equal reason and vehemence declaims against the pernicious abuse of tarnishing the severe purity of tragedy with scenes of profane love, and who calls attention to this intolerable impropriety in the works of the most famous dramatists of his nation, would admit without scruple the decent, pure, and most chaste love of Virginia for her betrothed Lucius Icilius, and that of Placidia for her husband Athaulpho. In a word, no one up until now has given rules more precise, more minute, more comprehensive, more judicious, more consummate for the perfection and for the utility of tragedy than Montiano; and no one has practiced them better.[142]

In a note to the 1797 edition we are told that the above extract was taken from Father Isla's prologue to his translation of Volume II of the *Christian Year* by the French Jesuit, Father Croisset. Pellissier attributes this praise to Father Croisset himself without noticing that the latter died in 1738, fifteen years before the above prologue was written:

> The articles of *L'Année Chrétienne* written by Father Croisset which Valázquez quotes as fairly indicative of the attitude of foreigners toward Montiano's plays may possibly have been a much-needed comfort to that author issuing wearily from the struggle with Jaime Doms. In it Montiano is called a Spanish Sophocles who, far from imitating Corneille or Racine, avoided the errors of those two authors and proved himself greater than either in his own dramatic productions ...[143]

Having failed to note that the praise given to Montiano was taken from Father Isla's own prologue to the translation of a work which gives the lives of the saints, distributed for each day of the year, and which is not even remotely concerned with drama, Pellissier feels it his duty to call attention to the possibility that "that notorious practical joker, Father Isla," may have been hiding "one more *gaminerie* under the fulsome praise of an author."

Just one detail casts a shadow over all this and makes one suspect that, after all, it might have been unsafe for Montiano to bask in the sunshine of so much praise. Velázquez tells us that the article was translated into Spanish by that notorious practical joker, Father Isla! The record for literary mischief-making established later by that talented writer through his *Diaz Grandes* [*sic*] *de Navarra* and through his *Gil Blas*, fills our minds with suspicion, and as we have not been able to compare the article in question with its supposed original, we feel it our duty to at least point to the possibility of one more *gaminerie* hidden by the witty Spaniard under the fulsome praise of an author, whose performance was palpably as modest as his own character.[144]

Father Isla was, however, wholeheartedly in sympathy with the neoclassic movement and was a personal friend both of Montiano and of Leopoldo Jerónimo de Puig, one of the editors of the *Diario de los Literatos*, exchanging friendly letters with the former and carrying on a regular correspondence with the latter.[145]

To establish conclusively Father Isla's sympathy with the reform movement and his familiarity with Luzán's *Poetics* one needs only read the "Prologue" to his *Fray Gerundio de Campazas* (1758), where he facetiously attempts to forestall objections that his story is improbable by taunting his anticipated critics for accepting in drama the most preposterous incidents:

But after all, will you not please allow my story to contain some slight improbability? Is it possible that you will be so inexorable with me, at the same time that you ignore and show yourself so acquiescent with others? Does it seem to you more probable that Sigismundo in the comedy, *The Castle with the Secret*, by the great Antonio de Solís, should throw himself into the sea on the coast of Epirus and should reach the shores of Cyprus supported only by his shield, even though the latter may be of cork and Sigismundo may be made of paper? Do the oracles who at each step interrupt our actors, anticipating what they are going to say, in order to make the event seem mysterious, appear to you more probable? Do those words, which come so opportunely from the music that they anticipate in song the very words which the actor is on the point of uttering, seem more true to life? Do those verses, thoughts, and concepts, spoken by two actors who come on the stage through different doors without seeing or hearing each other and who say exactly the same things . . . seem to you more natural? In short, if you wish to get a load of these improprieties, you have only to read the celebrated *Poetics* by Ignacio de Luzán and there you will find so many you will not be able to handle them.[146]

These words, written twenty years after the publication of Luzán's work, help to refute the claim that it was "little read and its influence negligible."

In the minutes of the Academy of Good Taste are found two discourses by Velázquez, one containing lavish praise of tragedy in general with particular emphasis upon Montiano's *Virginia* and the other dealing with the essential constituents of poetry. As might be expected, Velázquez prescribes for tragedy the rigid and conventional rules which the French and Italian preceptists had read into Aristotle's *Poetics*. He calls *Virginia* "the pattern of all perfection," and considers classical tragedy the height of sublimity in art. "The most excellent," he observes, "as well as the most arduous type of poetry is tragedy. For this reason Aristotle, when he came to write his *Poetics,* confined his work almost entirely to the rules for the composition of tragic poetry."[147] Spain, he says, had known and cultivated tragedy with marvelous art since the beginning of the sixteenth century but "suddenly lost her taste for it with the introduction of tragi-comedies."

Velázquez' *Origins of Castilian Poetry,* although it adds little or nothing in the field of drama to what had already been said by Luzán, Montiano, and Nasarre, contains some information of historical value, particularly in its brief summary of the activities of the neo-classicists in the translation of foreign works:

We have very few translations from French poets. The translation of *Cinna,* a tragedy by Corneille, published without the name of its author in 1713 and 1731, is by the Marqués de San Juan. Much superior to this work, although translated in prose, is Racine's *Britannicus,* published under the pseudonym of Don Saturio Iguren in Madrid in 1752, the real author of which is Don Juan Trigueros. This translation is well done and gives evidence of the good judgment and taste of its author, who through modesty concealed his name. In the translation of Racine's *Athalie,* done in good verse by Don Eugenio de Llaguno, one finds the same majesty and delicacy which everyone admires in the French original. Don Josef Antonio Porcel has translated in verse the French prose comedy, *The Scholarly Lady,* written against the Jansenists by an anonymous author. He is also translating in blank verse *Facistol,* a poem by Boileau. . . . Don Alfonso Dalda, a native of Granada, is at present engaged in the translation in blank verse of *Paradise Lost,* the only translation we have from the English.[148]

Spanish literature owes one debt to Velázquez that has seldom been recognized. His little book, more than the works of any of his contemporaries, served to acquaint the rest of Europe with the accomplishments of Spain in poetry and drama. No one prior to Velázquez had attempted to write a history of Spanish poetry. He was, therefore, cultivating new ground, and it was only natural that some of his evaluations and criticisms should be inaccurate. Menéndez y Pelayo is ruthless in his condemnation of Velázquez' work and does not hesitate to attribute its reputation in Europe to the additions made by Dieze in his German translation of *Origins of Castilian Poetry.* He says that the little book,

. . . in spite of the reputation it enjoyed for some time outside of Spain, not because of its own merit, but because of the copious additions with which Dieze, a professor of Göttingen adorned it, doubling its size, is (considered in its Spanish original) a memorandum of common information, much of which is erroneous and badly connected. As a book of erudition it is so out of date that it is of no use whatever to the student of bibliography. As a book of criticism it is still more unfortunate.[149]

So completely lacking in poetic feeling was Velázquez, according to Menéndez y Pelayo, that "when he reprinted the delicate and melancholy verses of Francisco de la Torre, he insisted upon attributing them to their first editor, Quevedo, without noticing the abyss which separates the poetic genius of the two authors."[150] This evidence of Velázquez' lack of poetic acumen is not so palpable, however, as Menéndez y Pelayo would have us believe. The fact that Luzán and Montiano were convinced by Velázquez' reasoning is to that critic but another proof of their complete aberration of taste. But by Menéndez y Pelayo's time the question of the authorship of *The Poems by Francisco de la Torre* had been debated by almost every historian of Spanish poetry and he, therefore, had the benefit of all of this discussion. Quintana, in the preface to his *Castilian Poetry* (1807); Estala, in his *Collection of Castilian Poetry* (1808); the German critic Wolf, in his *Jährbücher der Literatur* (1835), and Gil de Zárate, in his *Manual of Literature* (1844), had denied that it was the work of Quevedo. On the other hand, Alvarez y Baena, in

his *Life of Quevedo;* Sedano, in his *Spanish Parnassus;* and Bouter-
wek, in his *History of Spanish Literature,* had agreed with Velázquez. And as late as 1863, no less a critic than Tichnor, after a careful
consideration of the evidence, was strongly inclined to believe that
Quevedo was the author.[151] It appears then a bit unfair for Menéndez
y Pelayo to seize upon Velázquez' attribution of the poems of Francisco de la Torre to Quevedo and to hold it up to scorn as
supreme evidence of the worthlessness of *Origins of Castilian
Poetry.* He might, in all fairness, have called to the attention of the
world the fact that Velázquez discovered *The Book of Good Love,*
by the Archpriest of Hita, one of the masterpieces of Spanish literature which had lain unnoticed for some four centuries, and that he
gave a description and résumé of the poem in this same *Origins of
Castilian Poetry.* Velázquez announced this discovery in matter-
of-fact language without having had an opportunity to examine the
work carefully and evidently without a complete comprehension of
its significance:

> Around the year 1330, there flourished another Castilian poet of whom
> there is no notice, either in the *Biblioteca* by Don Nicasio Antonio, nor in
> the work of any other author, so far as I know. His name was Juan Ruiz,
> and he was Archpriest of Hita. His poetry is conserved today in a manu-
> script in the library of Toledo. Because the idea of the poem is unusual
> and ingenious, I shall give here a compendium which was made by a
> very learned individual, who, at my request, examined the complete
> manuscript.[152]

Much fairer than Menéndez y Pelayo's evaluation of Velázquez is
this statement by Cueto:

> One of the writers who must especially be taken into consideration in
> order to understand the epoch of transition which corresponds to the
> reign of Fernando VI and to evaluate properly the character which doc-
> trinal criticism took in the time of Carlos III is Don José Luis Velázquez,
> marqués de Valdeflores. His poetic genius, it is true, was not great; but
> his critical capacity was extensive; his good taste, as good taste was
> understood at that time, was sure; and his constancy in the difficult task
> of scholarship and investigation of ancient historical monuments was
> exemplary. Without doubt his *Origins of Castilian Poetry,* published for
> the first time in 1754, is all too brief and incomplete; but in it there are
> indications of a sound and elevated criticism, which was quite uncom-
> mon at that time; and, such as this historical sketch is, it does high honor
> to the discernment of its author and shows how much ground had been
> covered and how much strength had been acquired by the exotic doc-

trines which seventeen years before Don Ignacio de Luzán had sustained in dogmatic form.[153]

In spite of its lack of originality and its inadequate treatment of Spanish poetry, Velázquez' treatise was considered to have sufficient merit to justify a second edition in 1797, when the first edition had become exceedingly rare. The printer believes that the praise which was given to the work by Montiano in his "Censura" to the first edition is sufficient to silence all detractors, "who, exceeding the limits of fair criticism, reprove everything they read unless it suits their own palate and black bile."[154] This reprinting of Velázquez' work is of particular interest in the history of the neo-classic movement since it shows that the ideas expressed by Luzán, Montiano, and Nasarre, and which Velázquez so heartily approves, were still held even at that late date in spite of the concessions which the neo-classicists for tactical reasons had made to Calderón and Lope.

1. Blas Antonio Nasarre, *Comedias y entremeses de Miguel de Cervantes Saavedra, el autor del Don Quixote, divididas en dos tomos, con una Dissertación, o Prólogo sobre las Comedias de España,* Año 1749, con licencia, en Madrid, en la Imprenta de Antonio Marín.
2. *Ibid.,* pp. 1-2.
3. *Ibid.,* p. 2.
4. *Ibid.,* p. 13.
5. *Ibid.,* p. 22.
6. *Ibid.,* p. 24.
7. *Ibid.,* pp. 38-40.
8. *Ibid.,* p. 25.
9. *Ibid.,* p. 38.
10. *Ibid.,* p. 28.
11. *Ibid.,* p. 27.
12. *Ibid.,* p. 28.
13. Menéndez y Pelayo, *op. cit,* III, 245-46.
14. Nasarre, *op. cit.,* p. 34.
15. *Ibid.,* p. 26.
16. *Ibid.*
17. *Ibid.,* p. 41.
18. *Ibid.,* pp. 43-44.
19. *Ibid.,* p. 43.
20. *Ibid.,* p. 44.
21. *Ibid.,* p. 15.
22. *Ibid.,* p. 47.
23. *Ibid.*
24. *Ibid.,* p. 48.
25. *Ibid.,* p. 49.
26. *Ibid.*
27. *Ibid.,* p. 51.
28. Menéndez y Pelayo, *op. cit.,* III, 198
29. See p. 7.
30. Menéndez y Pelayo, *op. cit.,* p. 247.
31. Tomás de Erauso y Zavaleta, *Discurso crítico sobre el origen de las comedias de España, contra el dictamen que las supone corrompidas, y en favor de sus más famosos escritores, el Doctor Frey Lope de Vega Carpio y Don Pedro Calderón de la Barca,* escrito por un ingenio de esta corte, quien le dedica a M. I. S. la Señora Marquesa de la Torrecilla, etc., en Madrid, en la Imprenta de Juan de Zúñiga. Año MDCCL.
32. Menéndez y Pelayo, *op. cit.,* p. 250.
33. *Ibid.*
34. *Zavaleta,* op. cit., p. 115.
35. *Ibid.,* p. 130.
36. *Ibid.,* p. 212.
37. *Ibid.,* p. 223.
38. *Ibid.,* p. 224.
39. *Ibid.,* p. 247.
40. *Ibid.,* p. 248.
41. *Ibid.,* p. 249.
42. *Ibid.*
43. *Ibid.,* p. 235.
44. *Ibid.,* p. 236.
45. Menéndez y Pelayo, *op. cit.,* p. 254.

46. Agustín de Montiano y Luyando, *Discurso sobre las tragedias españolas*, Segunda impresión, en Madrid. En la imprenta del Mercurio. Año de 1750.
47. *Ibid.*, "Censura."
48. *Ibid.*, p. 4.
49. *Ibid.*, p. 6.
50. *Ibid.*, p. 7.
51. *Ibid.*, p. 8.
52. *Ibid.*, p. 10.
53. *Ibid.*, p. 17.
54. *Ibid.*, p. 19.
55. *Ibid.*, p. 23.
56. *Ibid.*, p. 24.
57. Cervantes, *Don Quijote*, Part I, Ch. 48.
58. Leandro Fernández de Moratín, *Orígenes del teatro español (Obras de Moratín, B.A.E.*, II, 210).
59. *Ibid.*, p. 224.
60. Montiano, *op. cit.*, p. 27.
61. *Ibid.*, pp. 28-35.
62. *Ibid.*, p. 35.
63. *Ibid.*, p. 38.
64. *Ibid.*, p. 39.
65. *Ibid.*, p. 40.
66. *Ibid.*, p. 42.
67. *Ibid.*, p. 43.
68. *Ibid.*, p. 47.
69. *Ibid.*, p. 48.
70. *Ibid.*, p. 50.
71. *Ibid.*, p. 51.
72. *Ibid.*, p. 54.
73. *Ibid.*, p. 53.
74. *Ibid.*, p. 56.
75. *Ibid.*, p. 58.
76. *Ibid.*, p. 59.
77. *Ibid.*, p. 63.
78. *Ibid.*, p. 65.
79. *Ibid.*, p. 66.
80. *Ibid.*, p. 69.
81. *Ibid.*
82. *Ibid.*, p. 70.
83. *Ibid.*
84. *Ibid.*, p. 71.
85. *Ibid.*, p. 73.
86. *Ibid.*, p. 75.
87. *Ibid.*, p. 76.
88. *Ibid.*, p. 77.
89. *Ibid.*, pp. 78-80.
90. *Ibid.*, p. 81.
91. *Ibid.*, pp. 83-84.
92. *Ibid.*, p. 85.
93. *Ibid.*, p. 87.
94. *Ibid.*, p. 89.
95. *Ibid.*, p. 94.
96. *Ibid.*, p. 101.
97. *Ibid.*, p. 105.
98. *Ibid.*, p. 106.
99. *Ibid.*, p. 111.
100. *Ibid.*, p. 113.
101. *Ibid.*, p. 115.
102. *Ibid.*, p. 116.
103. *Ibid.*, p. 119.
104. *Ibid.*, pp. 119-20.
105. Montiano, *Discurso II, Sobre las tragedias españolas*, Madrid, en la imprenta del Mercurio, Año de 1753.
106. *Ibid.*, p. 14.
107. *Ibid.*, p. 16.
108. *Ibid.*, p. 29.
109. Eugene Despois, *Le Théâtre Francais sous Louis XIV* (Paris, 1874), pp. 132-33.
110. Voltaire, *Oeuvres Complètes*, IV, 499.
111. Montiano, *op. cit.*, p. 82.
112. *Ibid.*, p. 85.
113. *Ibid.*, p. 30.
114. *Ibid.*, p. 31.
115. *Ibid.*, pp. 35-36.
116. *Ibid.*, p. 39.
117. *Ibid.*, p. 40.
118. *Ibid.*, p. 47.
119. *Ibid.*, p. 48.
120. G. E. Lessing, *Sämtliche Schriften*, ed. K. Lachman, 3rd ed. revised by F. Muncher, Stuttgart, 1886-1924. IV, 52. See J. G. Robertson, *Lessing's Dramatic Theory* (Cambridge, 1939), p. 293.
121. Lessing, *Theatralische Bibliothek*, i, p. 117; *Schriften*, vi, p. 70. See Robertson, *op. cit.*, pp. 293-94.
122. Menéndez y Pelayo, *op. cit.*, III, 257.
123. Pellissier, *op. cit.*, p. 81.
124. Robertson, *op. cit.*, p. 294.
125. *Ibid.*, p. 295.
126. Johann Friedrick von Cronegk, *Schriften* (Leipsig, 1765-66), pp. 389 ff. See Robertson, *op. cit.*, p. 294.
127. Cueto, *op. cit.*, p. lxxxiii.
128. *Ibid.*
129. Luis Josef Velázquez, *Orígenes de la poesía castellana*, segunda edición (Málaga, 1797).
130. Menéndez y Pelayo, *op cit.*, III, 260.
131. Velázquez, *op. cit.*, p. 125.
132. Cueto, *op. cit.*, p. lxxxii.
133. Pellissier, *op. cit.*, p. 83.
134. Montiano, *Discurso II*, p. 118.
135. Juan Joseph López de Sedano, *Jahel, tragedia sacada de la Sagrada Escritura* (Madrid, 1763), p. xliv.
136. Vicente García de la Huerta, *La Es-*

cena Hespañola Defendida en el Prólogo del Theatro Hespañol, segunda impresión, Madrid, MDCCLXXXVI.
137. Velázquez, *op. cit.*
138. *Ibid.,* p. 91.
139. *Ibid.,* p. 99.
140. *Ibid.*
141. *Ibid.*
142. *Ibid.,* pp. 103-4.
143. Pellissier, *op. cit.,* p. 83.
144. *Ibid.,* p. 84.
145. See the "Letters of Father José Francisco de Isla" in *B.A.E.,* XV, pp. 24, 36.

146. José Francisco de Isla, "Prólogo," *Fray Gerundio (B.A.E.,* XV, 59).
147. Cueto, *op. cit.,* p. cxx, "Nota."
148. Velázquez, *op. cit.,* p. 127.
149. Menéndez y Pelayo, *op. cit.,* III, 260.
150. *Ibid.,* p. 261.
151. George Ticknor, *History of Spanish Literature* (4th ed.; Boston, n.d.), II, 332-35.
152. Velázquez, *op. cit.,* p. 35.
153. Cueto, *op. cit.,* p. ccx.
154. Velázquez, *op. cit.,* "Advertencia del Impresor."

IV

Early Attempts to Improve the Theater

The Theater During the Reigns of Felipe V and Fernando VI

In spite of the efforts of the neo-classicists, the Spanish theater remained until after the middle of the eighteenth century in the same state of decadence which had characterized it for nearly a century. It is true that the old *Corral de la Cruz* and the *Corral del Príncipe*, which had not been materially changed since their construction in 1579 and 1582, were replaced with modern structures, the former in 1743 and the latter in 1745; but, although Montiano spoke with some pride of the new theaters and of the facilities they offered for more realistic staging of plays, Leandro Fernández de Moratín, in his "Historical Sketch of the Spanish Theater," assures us that the stage, the manner of performance, and the costumes remained very much as they were in the old courtyards.

The curtains continued, as did the cap and the candle of the prompter, who moved from one place to another behind the curtain. The Alcalde de Corte, or Judge of the Municipality, still continued to preside over the performances, seated in the proscenium with a clerk and two constables behind him. The wretched orchestra, made up of five violins and a bass viol, furnished the music as before.... The propriety of the costumes was in keeping with the rest. Let it suffice to say that Semiramis appeared before the audience with her hair done up in curls, with earrings, coat of changeable silk, hooped skirt... and high-heeled shoes. Julius Caesar appeared with a crown of laurel, curled periwig, plumed hat under his left arm, tissue jacket, velvet coat... short sword, and a lace neckpiece. Aristotle (as an ecclesiastic) wore a cleric's garb, a round wig with a calotte, a closely buttoned coat, a black collar bound with linen, mulberry-colored hose, and gold buckles, and carried a crutchlike cane.[1]

Ridiculous as the above costumes may appear to a modern reader, it should be borne in mind that equally glaring anachronisms characterized the French stage until after the middle of the eighteenth century. The editors of the *Library of Spanish Authors,* when they reprinted Moratín's work in 1846, could not refrain from inserting a note to this effect in defense of the Spanish theater:

Here it is necessary to point out that such improprieties were not limited to the Spanish stage. The same thing occurred in foreign theaters; and to be convinced of this, one needs only to examine the evidence of many French and English laminas of this time. This condition lasted until the latter part of the century. In the middle of the century the hoop skirts, the high-heeled slippers, and the powdered headdress formed in France also a part of the costumes of the Greek and Roman matrons as well as of the nymphs, until Mlle. Clairon was heroic enough to appear before the audience without the rigid costume prescribed by custom, at the same time that Lekain was suppressing the plumed hats which up until that time always covered the heads of Oedipus, Herod, and Julius Caesar. But in spite of these reforms, other anachronisms continued, which did not disappear entirely until in 1791 Talma introduced upon the stage the studies of costumes which David was making on canvas.[2]

During the reigns of Felipe V and Fernando VI the government adopted a hands-off policy with reference to the popular theater. Even those plays which were performed at the Spanish court for the entertainment of Marie Louise of Savoy, the first wife of Felipe V, were not restricted to neo-classical plays, but included many of the old Spanish comedies. The Princess des Ursins, who was responsible for this attempt to lessen the gloom that pervaded the court, wrote in 1713:

Every evening we have Spanish and French plays; the latter are beautifully performed by the servants of the King. The others have neither rules nor decorum for the most part. In them women are made to speak to men with a freedom which is entirely improper, and Monsieur le Marquis de Villena, who is a cultured man, agrees with us that there is no rhyme or reason in these plays and that Calderón and Solís cannot be compared with Corneille and Racine.[3]

Any chance that the court might have had to be a factor in popularizing neo-classic plays was cut off by the death of Felipe's French wife in 1714 and his subsequent marriage to an Italian princess, Isabel Farnese. During the remainder of Felipe's reign he was completely under her influence; the aged Princess des Ursins was sent back to France, and Italian influence replaced the French at court. Isabel Farnese, who had been accustomed to the elaborate performances of the Italian opera in her homeland, had no interest either in Spanish comedies or in neo-classic plays. Finding the theater of the *Caños del Peral,* which had been constructed at the beginning of the century for the performance of Italian comedies, entirely inadequate for her purpose, she caused it to be rebuilt and elaborately equipped for the performance of Italian operas. Farinello, the foremost singer of Italy, was brought to the Spanish court, either to soothe the melancholy of Felipe V or to satisfy Isabel Farnese's love for the opera, and remained there during the reign of Fernando VI. Bárbara de Braganza, the wife of the latter, was as fond of the Italian opera as was Isabel Farnese, and the court theater, the *Buen Retiro,* was given over to the direction of Farinello, who immediately ordered it redecorated on the most magnificent scale. Moratín gives us an account of the elaborateness of the spectacles which were offered for the entertainment of the court:

He brought to Madrid the best professors of vocal and instrumental music, mechanics, and painters of stage scenery, and adorned the performances with sumptuous magnificence. When performances were given in the hall called *de los Reinos,* the floor was covered with exquisite carpet, and the walls were hung with drapes of gold tissue, mirrors, carved work, and paintings, between which statues were placed. The illumination was in keeping with all the rest. The musicians in the orchestra wore scarlet uniforms with gold lace. For one opera, the stage was decorated entirely with crystal; on another occasion the hall was illuminated with two hundred chandeliers; in the opera *Armida placata* the stage represented a delightful place with eight fountains of natural water, one of which sent a jet seventy feet into the air. Among the trees could be heard the song of a multitude of birds, most skilfully imitated. The richness of the costumes, furniture, and stage equipment, the retinues (which at times were made up of fifty women and two hundred men), the sight of armies with numerous horses, elephants, chariots, war machines, arms, insignias, military music, fireworks which could be seen beyond the stage at the close of the spectacle . . . , all of this was worthy of a great monarch who squandered the wealth of his treasury on this diversion.[4]

Such brilliant spectacles, which were directed by an Italian and acted by Italians, could have no influence upon the popular theaters. The operas were sung in Italian; the actors with only one exception were Italian; and all of the workmen employed in stage decoration and machinery came from Italy. Only the spectators were Spanish, and in order to enable them to follow the performance with some comprehension, it was found necessary to translate the plays and to distribute these translations at the first performance. The theater of the *Buen Retiro* opened in 1747 with Metastasio's *Clemency of Titus,* the translation of which was made by Luzán in the space of a few hours. Subsequent translations were made by an Italian physician who had no real knowledge of the Spanish language.

According to Moratín, popular performances presented a wretched contrast to these magnificent spectacles. Abandoned by the court, "the Spanish stage in the hands of ignorant actors and inept poets was sustained by the enthusiasm of the masses."[5] Only a few new plays were being presented at that time, however, and it may be assumed that the repertoires were made up almost exclusively of the plays of Calderón, Moreto, Solís, and other Golden Age dramatists, who certainly did not deserve to be called "inept." One thing is certain, however, and that is that neo-classicism had in no way altered popular performances. Cañizares was still writing plays in the old manner and even held the position of censor of comedies from 1702 until 1747. So little effect did the neo-classical rules have upon his plays that even his *Sacrifices of Iphigenia,* which he wrote before 1716 in imitation of the *Iphigénie* of Racine, in order to show, as he himself says, "how plays are written in the French style," bears so little resemblance to the original that it might easily be taken for a Golden Age play. After Italian influence had become prevalent at the Spanish court, Cañizares attempted to turn Metastasio's *Temistocles* into a comedy with music; but again he adapted his play so completely to Spanish taste and manners that only the subject matter distinguishes it from his other works. He increased the number of characters, made them act and talk like Spaniards, added to the complication of the plot, and even introduced a *gracioso* to increase the popular appeal.

It was certainly too much to expect neo-classicism to have any real effect upon those inferior dramatists of the time who had been content, and even proud, to follow in the footsteps of Calderón, and who had been responsible for a continuance of the very condition which the neo-classicists were determined to eradicate. Even if such writers had been converted to the new ideas, their native ability would have been entirely inadequate to enable them to succeed in regular comedy and tragedy, just as it had proven inadequate for the production of passable works in imitation of Golden Age drama. One dramatist, it is true, made a feeble attempt to show that he could conform to the new rules if he chose. It will be recalled that one of the two plays reviewed by the *Diario de los Literatos* was Añorbe y Corregel's *The Tutoress of the Church.* Añorbe's first reaction to the unfavorable criticism by the *Diario* was to publish the next year an indignant answer in the prologue to a musical drama, *Jupiter and Danae,* in which he maintained that Spanish dramatists had no obligation whatsoever to follow rules of art formulated by Plautus and Terence and accused the editors of the *Diario* of having wilfully misled at least a portion of their readers: "... and what is most irritating is that they maliciously conceal the fact from their less informed readers that the art of which they speak is that which was followed by Plautus and Terence, and not by Lope, Calderón, or any other Spanish writer."[6]

It appears that Añorbe either was not entirely satisfied with his defense or wished to silence his detractors with a demonstration of his versatility. Accordingly, he published in 1740 *El Paulino,* a tragedy based, as he himself says in a "Note to the Reader," on Corneille's *Cinna.*

> The motive which has induced me to leave the Castilian road is an assertion made in my presence that Spanish writers are incapable of composing a tragedy in conformity with the laws of Horace and the practice of Corneille in his *Cinna.* This statement rankled with me, although I said nothing at the time. I secured a copy of Corneille's *Cinna,* read it carefully, and, following his steps as well as I could, composed my *Paulino.*[7]

In this same "Note" he leaves the impression that the style and content of his previous plays had been a concession to popular taste: "I well know, Reader, that this work will not be to your liking, but, having written so many times to please you, this time I write to please myself, at the risk of your unburdening your anger with a couple of coarse expressions that will leave me unaffected."[8]

As we have seen, Añorbe's new play was received with scorn by the principal exponent of neo-classic tragedy, Montiano, who disposed of it with a single unflattering remark.[9] The fact that Añorbe wrote no more plays of any kind for the theater may or may not have been due to neo-classic criticism; but, in any event, the Spanish theater was not the loser.

Comedies of Saints and Sacramental Plays

Although the popular theater successfully withstood all attempts at reform on the part of the neo-classicists during the reigns of Felipe V and Fernando VI, it was not so successful against attacks by the church. Certain ecclesiastics had waged a relentless warfare against all theatrical performances during the entire seventeenth century, condemning the immoral lives of the actors and insisting that the theater was a school of lasciviousness. Friars and clerics even attributed disasters of war and pestilence to this institution, claiming that they were a divine punishment sent upon the nation for permitting its continuance. As a result of this type of propaganda by the church, every death of a member of the royal family and every outbreak of pestilence was a signal for a royal decree forbidding theatrical performances. In the first half of the eighteenth century the clergy increased its efforts and succeeded in closing many of the theaters in the provinces. In the diocese of Calahorra performances were prohibited in 1700. The theaters of Andalucía were closed in 1734, those of Pamplona and Valencia in 1721 and 1748. In Andalucía many theaters remained closed until 1789.

Neo-classicists took their cue from the church in their condemnation of the immorality of the Golden Age theater as a whole but insisted that a thorough housecleaning was all that was necessary. It is quite likely that their emphasis upon the moral function of tragedy and comedy was largely an outgrowth of a desire to counteract church opposition. The ban upon Comedies of Saints during the reign of Fernando VI was the result of combined efforts of the church and the neo-classicists. Church opposition to these comedies had been gathering force during the seventeenth century, and by the latter part of the century it manifested itself in such unqualified condemnations as that issued by Father Camargo in 1689:

The truth is that the Comedies of Saints are much worse and less tolerable than those on profane themes, called Cloak and Sword plays. And the reason is very clear. Because in addition to the fact that they contain the principal incentives to lasciviousness, which are courtships, impure love, immoral actresses, music, disguises, dances, and obscene interludes, these comedies which are called *Divine* have the horrible monstrosity of mixing the sacred with the profane, of confusing light with darkness, and of joining earth with heaven, which is a monstrous indecency that holds within itself a great number of indecencies. What greater indecency can there be than to see the virtues and purest actions of the saints alternating with lewdness and lascivious love; acts of penitence with comic interludes; and tears with the dissolute dances of the actors and actresses? What is more discordant than to see the *gracioso*, or fool of the comedy, dressed in the sacred garb of a cleric and to hear him utter buffoonery and see him play the role of a rascally and worldly man, who is often a drunkard and of dissolute character?[10]

In 1751, shortly before the Comedies of Saints were banned by royal decree, the Jesuit Father Moya y Correa wrote a belated answer[11] to the "Aprobación" which had accompanied the *Genuine Fifth Part of the Comedies of the Celebrated D. Pedro Calderón de la Barca,* published in 1682 by Vera Tassis y Villaroel. This "Aprobación" by the Trinitarian Father Manuel de Guerra y Ribera had aroused a storm of protest among the Jesuits immediately upon the publication of the work. In this controversy, as indeed throughout the campaign against the immorality of Golden Age comedy, the church by no means presented a solid front. Many of the clergy were enthusiastic in their praise of the plays of Lope and particularly of those of Calderón, in whom they could see only perfection. Father Guerra had said in his "Aprobación":

With no intention of wronging the great number of poets who have ennobled and continue to ennoble the theater of the world and of this court, I take the liberty to say that our D. Pedro Calderón alone was sufficient to make comedy illustrious and to free the theater from all scruples. This man of great judgment, scholarship, and wit climbed with such courage and majesty to the pinnacle of achievement in comedy, that the envious can only aspire to imitate him. It is not necessary that my love and respect pay this tribute; his comedies speak for themselves. . . .

The Comedies of Saints are exemplary, those based upon history serve to correct error, and the comedies which have love as their theme produce only innocent diversion.[12]

Father Moya, on the contrary, saw in the comedy of his day only an incitement to sin. Although he divided comedies into the good and the bad, as Luzán had done, his every effort was directed at proving that the plays which were being performed on the stage at that time and which, with few exceptions, were products of the Golden Age, belonged to the latter class. He was particularly horrified at the lack of modesty of the actresses. They were adept, he said, in adding to their natural beauty false charms to attract the eye. In the dances which were given in the interludes and at the close of the comedy, all their movements were calculated to arouse sinful passions:

. . . to fill the spaces or intervals between the acts and *interludes,* or at the end of the comedy, one of those women comes out to dance. But, what dances! What motions! Tossing their heads, casting their eyes here and there, looking now at one, now at another, with such gestures, with such movements, and such leaps that they endanger their own and the audience's modesty.[13]

Father Moya was much concerned over the effect which attendance at the theater produced upon the youth of the land, particularly the students:

In addition to the above, comedies give rise to many serious sins of omission. The diversion of comedies distracts students from their studies; they waste the money their parents have taken from other brothers in the hope that the student will become the support of the entire family. . . . The father believes that his son is making progress with his studies when he is only becoming schooled in perversity. The students come out idlers; they marry to the displeasure of their parents in order to imitate one of the adventures which they have witnessed in comedies, and they kill with grief the very ones who gave them being. Others, from the instruction which they have received from comedies, prepare themselves for the high calling of the priesthood with such saintly habits that they are better equipped as priests of Venus or of Mars than as ministers of Christ.[14]

Among the bad comedies Father Moya cited many by Calderón, Lope de Vega, Vélez de Guevara, and other Golden Age dramatists. He was especially bitter in his condemnation of the so-called *devout comedies:*

However saintly a comedy may be, there is introduced in it for no reason whatsoever a marriage, a wooing, or an immodest solicitation. No sooner has the saint finished an ejaculatory prayer to God or the Virgin when, in order to alleviate the seriousness (which has been maintained for some time), the *gracioso* blurts out some shameless remark as big as one's fist. The saint invokes the love of God, and immediately a devilish lay-friar appears, and affronting religion and ecclesiastical dress, breaks out with a half-dozen endearing expressions directed at the *graciosa*, and, turned into a veritable bobbin, overcome with love, he approaches her, showering upon her a thousand caresses, and with this salad of good and bad things the audience weeps and laughs in turn, one thing undoing what the other seems to be building up. The saint sighs out his love for God, and the *graciosa* sobs because her gallant scorns her.

The saint retires from the world and turns his back upon the one who has been the cause of his perdition, and she, in order not to lose her illicit commerce, carried away by love, pulls at his cloak like another wife of Potiphar, with amorous reproofs, caresses, expressions of tenderness and flattery. What a fine battery directed at the audience!

If the comedy deals with some repentant sinner, in the performance his falls are painted with more vivid colors than his virtues. *Interludes* are thrown in, which abound in indecencies; afterward comes the music and then the dances.[15]

Although the *Autos Sacramentales* were designed more than any other theatrical performances to increase religious devotion, they sinned almost as much as the Comedies of Saints in their introduction of profane elements, which served to negative any salutary effects. These *Autos,* which were subsidized by the municipalities as an important part of the festival of Corpus Christi, originated during the last quarter of the sixteenth century and continued with little change and without interruption until 1765, when they were finally suppressed by royal decree. The nature of the *Autos Sacramentales* and the extravagant ceremonies which accompanied them may be judged from the account of a Dutchman, Francis van Aerssen, who visited Spain in 1654-55:

On the 27th of May we saw all of the ceremonies of the festival of Corpus Christi, which is celebrated more and lasts longer in Spain than any other. They begin with a procession, in the first ranks of which march a great number of musicians and Biscayans with their tambourines and castanets. With these there are a number of people dressed in various colors, who dance, leap, and pirouette with as much abandon as they might at Shrovetide. The King goes to the Church of Santa María, which is not far from the Palace, and after Mass, comes out with a taper in his hand. In front goes the Tabernacle with the Host, attended by the Grandes of Spain and the members of the Council. On this day, to avoid dispute, no order of rank is observed; so that the members of the Council *de Hacienda* are mixed with those of the Council of the Indies. Also at the front move some gigantic machines, that is, statues made of cardboard, and controlled by men who are hidden inside. They are of different shapes, some quite hideous; all of them represent women, except the first, which is only a monstrous painted head worn by a man of small stature, so that it seems to be the head of a giant on the body of a pygmy. (This is called *la Gigantilla.*) Among these fanciful monsters there are two who represent Moorish or Ethiopian giantesses. The rabble call these figures *Neighbor's Children,* and also *Mamelinas.* I have heard also of another frightful machine which rolls along through the streets on that day, called the Tarasca, from the name of a forest, which is supposed to have been at one time in Provence, at the site of the present town of Tarascon on the banks of the Rhone, in front of Beaucaire. They say that a serpent lived there, who was as much an enemy to the human race as the one who deceived our ancestors in Paradise. The story goes that Santa María subjected it and killed it with her girdle and with her prayers. Whether this be history or fable, the *Tarasca* is a Serpent of enormous size, with its whole body covered with scales, a broad belly, a long tail, short feet, twisted talons, frightful eyes, and a large gaping mouth. This bugaboo moves through the streets, and those who are concealed inside the cardboard and paper of which it is made, control and handle it with such skill that they can make it remove the hats of those who are not on their guard. The simple villagers are very much afraid of it and when it lays hold of them the people laugh heartily. The most pleasing and striking act which I saw these giants do, was to bow before the Queen when they came in front of the Palace balcony. ...In the afternoon at five o'clock *Autos* are represented. These are spiritual comedies, interspersed with several comic *Interludes,* which are quite extravagant and are designed to season and enliven the seriousness of the drama. The two companies of players that are in Madrid close their theaters at this time and for a month perform only these devout plays before the public on a stage erected in the street for this purpose. They are obliged every day to give their performance in front of the house of the President of one of the Councils. They begin at the Palace square where a stage is built with a canopy under which their Majesties sit. The theater or forum is at the foot of these catafalques or stages, and since the actors perform with their backs to the public, they place around the theater some little painted houses on wheels, where the actors dress, make their entrances, or retire at the end of each scene. Before the *Autos* begin the dancers who have taken part in the procession dance and leap, and the giants amuse the people.[16]

As early as 1598 the incongruity of immoral actors and actresses playing the roles of the Virgin and Joseph in an *Auto Sacramental* had shocked the dramatist Lupercio Leonardo de Argensola, who felt impelled to write a protest to Felipe II. After condemning the actresses for their use of dress and suggestive dances to effect the downfall of men, he covers both actors and actresses with a blanket accusation of immorality in their private lives.

And what can scarcely be said or written is that the dress and representation of the holy Queen of the Angels has been profaned by these wretched instruments of sin. And so true is this, that in a comedy performed at this court, which dealt with the life of Our Lady, the actor who played the role of Saint Joseph was living in concubinage with the woman who represented the person of Our Lady; and this fact was so notorious that the audience was scandalized and laughed boisterously when they heard from her mouth the answer of the Holy Virgin to the angel: *Quo modo fiet istud, etc.* And in this same comedy when they reached that part which dealt with the mystery of the birth of our Redeemer, this same actor who was playing the role of Joseph reproved the woman in a low voice because he thought she was looking at a man of whom he was jealous, calling her by the most shameful name that can be given to a bad woman. These things are unworthy of your Majesty's ears, but they are more unworthy of performance in the theater.

With this kind of people and in this manner they celebrate the festival of the day of the Sacrament.[17]

The theaters had been closed the year before because of the death of the Princess Catalina, and Argensola was adding his voice to those who opposed their reopening. He urged the king that, in the event he lifted his prohibition, he at least forbid the representation of sacred subjects.

The immoral lives of certain actors who represented Mary Magdalene and Christ were condemned by Father Juan de Mariana in his *Treatise Against Public Diversions*, published for the first time in Latin in 1609:

In the last few years, in a certain theatrical company, as we heard it told by the very judge who investigated the incident, a certain woman of that flock, who played the role of the Magdalene, was convicted in Alcalá de Henares of living in concubinage with the actor who with pomp and majesty, voice and actions represented Christ, the Son of God himself.[18]

The incidents cited by Argensola and Mariana were used over and over again as ammunition against the *Autos Sacramentales* during the seventeenth century and reappear with little change in 1751 in the work by Moya y Correa, already cited.

When the neo-classicists added their voices to that of the church in protest against the *Autos Sacramentales,* the complete suppression of this peculiarly Spanish type of drama was soon effected. The church had shown no interest whatsoever in dramatic rules, being concerned only with the moral issues involved. Luzán, as we have seen, did not choose to include the *Autos* among the types of Golden Age drama which he attacked in his *Poetics,* although he did express his strong disapproval of the Comedies of Saints. But when the neo-classicists entered resolutely upon their campaign to regularize the theater and to purge it of those elements which had elicited the scorn of foreigners, they concentrated their attack first upon the Comedies of Saints and, when these were prohibited during the reign of Fernando VI, turned their attention to the *Autos.* In both of these cases they could, of course, count upon the support of the church.

Clavijo y Fajardo

The leader of the neo-classicists at this stage in the fight against the *Autos* was Clavijo y Fajardo, who, having been educated in France, returned to Spain imbued with the ideas of Voltaire and Buffon and convinced of the cultural inferiority of his native land. As a result of his firsthand acquaintance with the French theater he became the leader and, to a certain extent, the spokesman of the neo-classic party. As the most effective means of disseminating his ideas, Clavijo y Fajardo began in 1762 the publication of *El Pensador*,[19] a series of essays in newspaper form in imitation of the *Spectator Papers* of Addison. Among these *Thoughts*, as the essays were called, which deal with a variety of subjects, there are a number that constitute an aggressive campaign against the irregularities of the Spanish stage. He initiates his attack in his third *Pensamiento* with a burlesque defense of Spanish comedies:

Is there no way to restrain the boldness with which foreigners make fun of us to our faces? Gentlemen, where are we? What untimely forbearance is ours? And then afterward comes a lot of noise, much boasting, a great deal of

> A fierce people are the Spaniards,
> for when they take a thing to heart,
> the sea trembles before them,

with other boastful speeches of the same caliber. I say that it is all noise, that the soil of Spain has changed, and the sulphur and pitch of the Spaniards has been converted into sugar-paste and caramel....

Only yesterday I found myself in a conversation, where, among many Spaniards, there were two foreigners. At first we talked of matters of no consequence; but these two gentlemen who, according to the praiseworthy custom of their nation, seem not to be able to live without trying to satirize us, were getting their ammunition ready, and began to make war with flags flying, and on what? ... On the darling of our eyes, on the precious jewel of Spain; in a word, on our beloved comedies.

What abominations! What iniquities! What lies these two critics told about our comedies! I do not know how I had the patience to listen to them, and much less to witness the senseless tolerance of our beloved compatriots, who, without parting their lips, without saying even "this comedy is mine," endured the whole volley.

The two gentlemen opened with the three unities, which they say should be observed in comedy: *unity of place, unity of time, and unity of action,* with the explanation of each, as if we knew nothing whatever of the unity, denary, or centenary. They dwelt a long time on this nonsense, displaying their erudition, and trying to prove that the three exalted unities are not observed in Spanish comedies. "All right, Gentlemen," I asked them, "Why, and to what end should they be observed? I know that you will tell me it should be done because the masters of art established it so. And who are these masters, and these doctors, whose documents and lessons we must follow blindly? Aristophanes, Menander, Plautus, Terence, and others of the condemned? Fine models they are, on my word! Is it your wish that some men who are burning in hell give us lessons and that we take them as oracles?" ... "Let us consider now the purpose which the unities serve. You gentlemen say that the rule of the unities has been prescribed by good taste and reason, and that it serves to maintain the illusion. ... And who has told you that we wish to deceive people? No, gentlemen, quite the contrary: we are men of good faith, and in truth, we do not sell a cat for a hare, and we call bread, bread. ... And if you don't believe me, look at our theaters and our actors. They seem hired hands; and with the exception of raising or lowering their voices wherever the whim strikes them with no method or discernment whatsoever, and without knowing what they are doing, they play the role of parrots, repeating what the prompter tells them; but this they do well and faithfully because in the most distant part of our *Corrales* (and make fun of the name, if you wish) the prompter's voice is heard before theirs. And in the comedy, *Esopo el Fabulador,* I have seen a lady defend herself singlehanded against four or five grown men all armed with swords, that did not even touch her clothing, because the points were looking at the stars. Now this could not have happened if any attempt had been made to maintain an illusion of reality, for they would have turned her into a sieve; and it is better beyond question to give up deception than to be sanguinary and cruel to a poor girl who has done no wrong and is not to blame because the simpleminded poet placed her in that predicament. Our theaters themselves could not deceive even the most uneducated. The lights which are supposed to illuminate the stage appear before they should, go up and down, and weave behind the curtains so that they seem to be penitents carrying torches; and when an attempt is made to represent lightning flashes, the boy who burns the pitch, and the hemp itself, are usually in the view and knowledge of everyone, as if they wished to say: "Don't be afraid; all this is in fun." In short, neither in ourselves nor in what we do is there any illusion, or anything that resembles it; and we are very proud of the fact in spite of all that two million foreigners may say, for, after all, the world and men of judgment will support us.[20]

Under the guise of defending the Spanish theater Clavijo y Fajardo continues to ridicule the self-satisfaction of the nationalists who persist in clinging to the Golden Age tradition. From the beginning of the controversy, one of the principal arguments of these partisans of the Spanish *comedia* against the neo-classical rules had been that they cut off the flight of genius and were an evidence of poverty of imagination. Keeping up his pretense, the *Thinker* says that he could easily confound his opponents with the authority of Lope, Calderón, Solís, Cervantes, and a great number of others; but, inasmuch as their testimony might be considered prejudiced, he prefers to avail himself of the weapons of the foreigners themselves, since the insult has come from that source. He takes Boileau's famous statement that a single action performed in one place and limited to one day should keep the theater filled and the audience in suspense. He agrees thoroughly with the words of Boileau, but maintains that these rules, which have been adopted by all civilized nations, are observed absolutely in the Spanish theater. The only trouble, he says, is that the foreigners in their poverty of invention, and because of their compliant nature, have given a distorted interpretation to this rule. He continues:

You gentlemen understand by this expression that if the action of a play starts in Vienna, it should not have its middle in Babylon, nor its end in Mongolia. If this interpretation of yours is not violent, I do not know anything that could be so in the world. It is all right for me in my room, by means of an optical camera, to see in a few minutes the Square of Saint Peter in Rome, the Gardens of Hamptoncourt and of Versailles, the Square of Saint Mark in Venice . . . and a thousand other things, which present themselves before my eyes as if they were actually present in body and soul; and yet, in the two or three hours that the performance of a comedy lasts, I am not to be allowed to see the Palace of Schombrun, the Seraglio of Constantinople, and the Court of Agra, with its bands of Germans, Turks, Eunuchs, and Mongolians, although this is the prettiest and the most entertaining thing in the world.[21]

Spaniards, he says, observe the rule incomparably better, and in its literal sense, which means that the play should end in the place where it begins, for it would be very inconvenient to witness the first act in Rambla in the province of Córdoba, and to have to go to the Encante to see the second, and to Barceloneta for the third.

In regard to the unity of time, he says, any schoolchild knows that this means a comedy should not last two or three days, for the performances would have to be continued through the night. Foreigners misinterpret this unity and take it to mean that the action represented in the play should be such that it could reasonably take place in one day. This again, the *Thinker* claims, is a ridiculous interpretation. If he can read the life of Methusaleh in an hour's time and can find out what happened to him over a space of nine hundred years, why should he not be allowed to see in a comedy, which lasts at least two hours and a half, what happens during two thousand two hundred and fifty years? This, he says, can be proved by simple arithmetic.

The poverty of genius among the French, English, and other Europeans is evidenced, he says, by the fact that on the flyleaf of none of their plays will one see the term *famous* accompanying the title, while six or seven thousand Spanish comedies are so styled. In the verse form of their plays the French also reveal the poverty of their genius, for from the beginning to the end of their plays they use only eleven-syllable couplets. "On the contrary, in our comedies beauty and pleasing variety hold complete sway. Ballad meter, *décimas, redondillas, quintillas, endechas,* sonnets, and octaves, all are brought into play making a most beautiful and delicious salad."[22]

He denies that the invention of the telescope, pneumatic and electrical machines, printing, and other things show any superiority on the part of foreigners, for, in their comedies, do not the Spaniards make monkeys talk, and do they not represent supernatural voices? Both of these miraculous things are found in the "famous" comedy, *The Modern Pythagoras,* by Lope de Vega: and in *King Bamba* by the same author, a newborn babe plays his role like a grown-up man. Nor have foreigners invented the method of bringing four infernal spirits on the stage and making them dance and figure in the intrigue of a comedy as Lope has done in *Poverty of Reynaldo.* Foreigners have also shown their lack of genius by limiting the number of characters in a play to six or seven. Spaniards are much more liberal, for in the comedy *The Modern Pythagoras,* in addition to the guards of the King of Morocco, a troup of Moorish sailors, a talking monkey, a statue, two pairs of great angels, and a supernatural voice, there are at least twenty-five other characters. The *Thinker* is confident that foreign detractors of Spanish comedy will say no more about the three unities when they see a recent comedy by Melchor Fernández de Leon, one of the new comedies performed on the Spanish stage, the title of which is *Civil Wars from the Creation of the World, Taken Directly from the Annals of Cardenal Baronio,* and that they will be ready to confess their own inferiority in inventive genius.[23]

This clever and scathing satire of the *Thinker* could but add fuel to the flame in a controversy that had already become bitter. Clavijo y Fajardo's adversaries called him an enemy of his country, and even those who were disposed to recognize the extravagance of the Golden Age comedy were offended by the virulence of his attack. We shall see in the next chapter how an anonymous author came to the defense of Lope and Calderón in a lengthy reply, entitled *The Spanish Nation Defended from the Insults of the Thinker and His Followers* (1764).

In *Thought IX*, Clavijo y Fajardo makes the accusation that Lope, Calderón, and Solís had corrupted the Spanish theater, but finds that contemporary dramatists like Antonio Bazo have written plays that are equally monstrous. Particularly is he annoyed that this author, whom he avoids calling by name, should have turned Metastasio's opera, *Artaxerxes*, into a Spanish comedy with the title, *The Piety of the Son Overcomes the Cruelty of the Father, or the Royal Oath of Artaxerxes*. The *Thinker* uses the reactions of a South American gentleman, who has recently come to Spain for the first time, as a basis for a bitter condemnation of the contemporary theater in Spain. In order to acquaint his new friend with the life and manners of Madrid, he takes him to the theater of the Cruz, where the above play is being performed. The South American expresses surprise to a gentleman sitting beside him that the title of *comedy* should be given to a play, the theme of which could serve only for a tragedy. He says that although there is no theater in his own land, he has familiarized himself with the theatrical art of the ancients and with the best practice of the moderns, and can find no authority in either for giving the title of *comedy* to a play whose characters are kings and illustrious persons. The gentleman replies with an air of condescension:

... Your studies may have been very good; but they have availed you little, when they allow you to be surprised that princes and kings play roles in comedy. For that reason it is profitable to travel, and you have done well in coming to Madrid, where in six months you will have seen many comedies in which not only kings and princes, but also bishops, cardinals, popes, and friars with their lay-brothers, speak. And you will also see how one of these lay-brothers rolls up his sleeve, as if he is drunk; you will hear his witticisms, and see him take out his dagger and struggle with temptation. You will see how he resists this temptation to the edification and good example of the people. ... But you will have seen nothing yet. You will then hear Death, Envy, and the Devil speak, and at the same time you will hear Saint John the Baptist, the Holy Virgin, the Eternal Father, and all the Celestial Court; although, if I must tell the truth, it is somewhat repugnant to me to see the rascal, who two hours before was amusing himself in the tavern, come to play the role of

Christ; and to see the indecent woman, who has just left her gallant, come to play the role of the Holy Virgin.[24]

Talking through his South American friend, Clavijo y Fajardo voices his opposition to the opera as a genre and particularly his irritation at the contemporary vogue of adapting the works of Metastasio to the Spanish stage in the form of comedies.

As the result of the popularity of the Italian opera at the Spanish court during the reign of Felipe V and Fernando VI, those Spaniards who prided themselves upon their culture had become acquainted with the principal works of Metastasio. Probably those operas which Bazo and Nipho adapted to the Spanish stage either as comedies or as tragedies were the very ones that were most popular at the theater of the Buen Retiro. The vogue of the Italian opera had ended, but its influence persisted. Inasmuch as the opera had made little attempt to conform to the neo-classical rules which were applied to tragedy and comedy, Spanish dramatists found that they could be adapted better than the regular genres to the taste of the public, particularly with the addition of the *graciosos,* whose antics and witticisms never failed to gain applause.

Clavijo y Fajardo pays his respect to the genius of Metastasio but regrets the misuse of his talents:

... To make a comedy out of an opera! It seems a dream. The opera, Sir, is not a regular play. The Italians in their fondness for music have invented this spectacle for the delight of the senses to the sacrifice of reason. Wishing to represent an action entirely in song, they have had to tolerate many improbabilities and extravagancies which reason condemns and good taste rejects. I shall say nothing now of the lack of verisimilitude of a man who is about to die beginning to sing an aria; of his beloved stopping to sing another when she goes to free her lover, whose death is imminent. I shall say nothing about the same words repeated a hundred times, and a thousand other improprieties, which only bad taste can endure with patience; I shall only say that since this spectacle has for its end the pleasure of the senses and not of the intellect, all the emphasis is placed upon the music and decorations; and almost no attention is given to drama.[25]

The celebrated Metastasio, he says, unfortunately dedicated his great talents to a work for which any ordinary poet would have sufficed. Either because the opera was at the time the vogue in his country, or because he was incapable of writing regular plays, he used the best materials to build very defective structures. No one can deny the sublimity of his thoughts or the superior quality of his poetry. Few mortals have had such great gifts, but "in spite of this, all of his plays sin against judgment and against art."[26]

Clavijo y Fajardo is disposed to overlook the errors of Metastasio as inherent in the genre which he is cultivating, but he cannot pardon the wretched translator who chooses to translate and to put on the stage, with the name of *comedy*, "an opera, a spectacle which is monstrous and recognized as such by the very nations that adopt it."[27] If the translator had freed the work from its irregularities, he might have made of it a fair tragedy; and if he had been a man of genius, he might even have composed a good tragedy since all of the elements are tragic; but no amount of genius would have sufficed to convert it into a comedy, which, by its very nature, must be merry and festive and must ridicule vices and defects. Perhaps, the *Thinker* says, the purpose of the translator was to produce a work that was less irregular than those customarily seen on the Spanish stage. If so, he praises his intention; but he pities his choice. To avoid one error, the translator did not need to fall into another. If he felt a burning desire to compose a play, why did he not compose a comedy according to the rules of art? Or if he did not care to go to that trouble, why did he not translate one of the many excellent foreign comedies? (As we shall see, this was precisely what Clavijo y Fajardo himself was doing at the time, and it constituted an important part of the program of the neo-classicists in their attempt to replace Golden Age comedies and contemporary monstrosities with regular plays.) The *Thinker* recommends even more strongly than Luzán and Montiano the reworking of Golden Age comedies:

... Why has he not taken one of our many comedies which, in order to compete with the best that have been written in other lands, are only awaiting the hand of a master capable of polishing them? I know that this is not as easy as it appears, and that this task requires a mastery of art, a refined taste, a delicacy, a fine touch, an exact discernment, and a special study of the human heart and of manners; and unfortunately the translator possesses none of these qualities.[28]

When the so-called comedy begins, the South American notices that the translator has done nothing but substitute for the beautiful versification of Metastasio a vulgar poetry, or rather a humble, trivial, and wretched prose. He remarks:

... There is no way to get our poets to take a middle ground in their style; either they must mount to the clouds, in order to lose sight of judgment and reason, and to say in affected language terrible nonsense which they themselves could not explain, giving all of their attention to piling up high-sounding and sonorous words; or they must drag themselves shamefully along the ground.[29]

The appearance of the *graciosos* so exasperates the South American that he breaks out into an angry tirade against the introduction of coarse humor in a work that should be a serious tragedy:

... I thought he would arouse the *Patio*, the *Gradas*, the *Cazuela*, and the *Aposentos* when he saw the *graciosos* come out. The South American bit his lips, stamped his feet, and gave an extreme show of his emotions. "Where are we?" he said. "What barbarism is this? Can people be so ignorant? Can they applaud this? Would this plaster be tolerated among savage Negroes, even without having the *graciosos* come out on the stage in a troupe?[30]

The gentleman at his side expresses surprise that he should find distasteful what amuses others so much and assures him that if there were no *graciosos* the audience would do nothing but yawn, because all of the spice and humor of the plays depends upon these characters. By their use, he says, the Spaniards have no difficulty in making any tragedy, no matter how sad and melancholy, pass for a comedy. The South American says that he is beginning to understand, and asks:

So then, to turn any tragic play into a comedy here, one needs to do no more than to stick on, even though it may be with chewed bread, a couple of *graciosos* wherever it suits the whim of the poet, without their fitting the situation or serving for anything except to interrupt with silly observations the most critical incidents, and especially those that move or should move to compassion?[31]

The gentleman answers that it is true and that all of the plays commonly called *tragi-comedies* in Spain are constructed in that manner.

The following day the South American goes to the Cruz alone to see a comedy entitled *Risk, Slavery, Disguise, Fortune, Chance, Deity;* and that night he informs the *Thinker* of his reactions to the comedy:

... Just imagine! The King of Egypt (any king will do, for we do not know his name), and the Princess Clotolisa, an Egyptian name of unusual meaning, and the Prince Aristeo (prince of any country you wish, and the betrothed of my lady Doña Clotolisa) come out on the stage on a hunting party. All of this family then separate, each going his or her own way; and then the good Princess, who has remained all by herself in the woods, reappears at the right of the stage. Now what could happen to a pretty girl alone in the woods except for her to meet bold people who do not show her respect? And so it does happen. Walking around those rocky places where he has been reared, without knowing any other world except their ruggedness, or any human being except a good old man with whom he lives, appears the rustic *Persino* (it develops later that he had been born in Persia, and for this reason the name suits him marvelously well), a smart and arrogant lad, who has played truant from his cave and is running around those mountains in search of adventure. And what does the Devil, who mixes everything up, do? He tempts Clotolisa to sing, and she immediately yields. (How could a Princess who has gone out on a hunting party keep from singing in the wood, especially when there is an orchestra so conveniently at hand?) Persino, who doubtless has never in all his life heard even a Gayta Zamorana, is dumfounded and stands with his mouth open. He also takes a notion to sing, and he does it as if he had spent six years in a College of Music. The Princess comes out from ambush; the two see each other and get along admirably. The Princess declares glibly and simply to the rustic that he does not look like any tiger or wildcat to her. The artful Persino is encouraged by this statement and rushes to kiss her hand. ... The Princess defends herself, although half-heartedly; she cries out, and behold, here come the King, Prince Aristeo, and the whole gang. They ask her why she has shouted. Clotolisa finds a good answer. She says that her fear was greater than the provocation warranted; and the King takes the rustic to the palace and offers him his protection. Artemisa, the Queen of Persia, comes in dressed as a man and accompanied by a giant Negro, called Ascombroto, with whom it seems she has been traveling. She declares that in her kingdom she had become involved in a love affair with a foreigner, whose name and rank she did not know at the time of the incident; that a child had been born to her, whom she abandoned in the woods, doubtless because she had no way to rear it, or because she had no scruples against infanticide.[32]

The *Thinker* interrupts him at this point and begs him to tell him no more lest he burst with rage. He cannot understand how actors can perform or an audience approve such monstrosities. Is it possible, he asks, that the Spanish theater is so backward? Is it possible that his countrymen are ignorant of the most elementary rules of drama, and that a man who sets himself to write comedies should forget, not only the dignity and decorum which befit persons of high rank, but also the decency which humanity and reason demand even among those of the lower class? He wishes to know whether the audience applauded this play as wildly as they had applauded the

comedy the day before at the Príncipe. The South American
answers that there had been some applause, but that it had not been
strong or sustained; that only in the *sainete,* which was the only
good thing in the whole performance, did the audience clap their
hands and applaud with spirit. This statement is seized upon by the
Thinker, who enters upon a defense of the masses against the accusation so often brought against them, that they are responsible for the
bad taste and irregularity of the Spanish theater:

> Look what happened in this case, and yet those poets who have taken
> it upon themselves to furnish the public with foolish and barbaric plays
> come to us and say that they compose bad comedies because the taste of
> the masses is depraved. Barbarians! It is not the public that is to blame;
> it is your ignorance, your laziness, your lack of taste and of instruction.
> In the comedy at the Cruz, as you have told me, one sees nothing but a
> fabric of foolishness, of delirium, of improprieties, and of indecent
> coarseness. In the comedy at the Príncipe, even though the play is so
> defective, there is interest, a continuous action, decency, and characters
> that are well or poorly sustained. So the people appreciate it more than
> the other, because, at least, they understand it and do not find anything
> immoral in it . . .[33]

The public goes to witness these comedies, the *Thinker* says, because
it has no choice. The same thing happened in Greece and Rome,
and more recently in France, for their plays were even more irregular
than Spanish comedies until Menander, Plautus, and Terence appeared in the former countries, and Molière in the latter. The
Thinker is confident that when a genius of the first order appears in
Spain and writes comedies as they should be written, the public will
give a demonstration of what it really thinks of the contemporary
monstrosities.

The neo-classicists realized very early that their only chance of
success was to win the general public to their cause. To adopt the
attitude that public taste was inherently depraved would be to admit
defeat before a shot had been fired. The blame must be put upon
the writers of comedies during the Golden Age, and now upon those
who followed in their footsteps. Occasionally, a neo-classic critic
would lose his temper and berate the public, but in the main the
leaders of neo-classicism were consistent in exonerating the public.

In his definitions of tragedy and comedy, Clavijo y Fajardo adds
no element not already found in Luzán's *Poetics,* which he cites with
profound respect on more than one occasion. He seems to be con-

cerned in all his remarks upon the theater with what he considers to be the moral function of that institution. In *Thought IX* he says:

The object of tragedy is to inspire horror for great sins and love for sublime virtues. To achieve this end the poet seeks an action which is, in itself, great and heroic; and limits his characters to personages of the highest rank.... He contrasts virtue with vice, and causes innocence to be persecuted by tyranny. He places virtue in the most terrible straits, in the most violent conflicts, and makes it suffer with constancy.[34]

His definition of tragedy is only another restatement of Aristotle's definition: "Tragedy is a serious action, performed by illustrious persons, with a majestic tone, and a sublime style.... Its purpose is to purge the passions by means of terror and pity."[35]

Clavijo y Fajardo is convinced that the theater is one of the most effective means of correcting the evils of society. About tragedy he says:

...A heart accustomed to these impulses which are produced by the magic of the theater becomes gentle, more beneficent, more merciful. All the moral virtues, the seeds of which are already in the heart, and which are cultivated by the good examples seen in the theater, are made to germinate. There the horror of sin and the beauty of virtue are painted with all the power that poetry and eloquence combined can give them. There the spectator learns to detest the one and to love the other; and the impressions left by the good examples presented to him are so vivid that there is no man, no matter how bad he may be, who if he were free to choose the lot of any one of the characters, would not prefer that of the innocent who is oppressed to that of the delinquent who prospers. So all the great masters call tragedy the school of virtue and the art of making men humane and good.[36]

Although in *Thought XXVII* Clavijo y Fajardo says that "there is no drama, and probably no writing of any kind that can compete in seriousness with tragedy," this does not mean that he considers it a more important genre than comedy. Indeed, in *Thought XXIII* he praises comedy first and then adds: "Tragedy is no less useful, nor is its object less clearly defined."[37] His definition of comedy emphasizes its didactic function: "Comedy is an imitation in action, designed to cleanse the spirit of its defects and folly by means of delight and laughter."[38] In *Thought IX*, he goes into detail in his discussion of the object of comedy and its effectiveness in the correction of vice:

Comedy is simple and jocose. Its object is to correct the folly of men, who, by nature, are perverse and filled with self-love. We see the defects of our fellow-beings with complacency; but we are so sensitive to ridicule that our self-esteem suffers, and anyone who has any knowledge of the human heart knows that it is controlled and corrected more by the fear of scorn and mockery than by the horror of sin or the fear of punishment.[39]

The moral purpose of comedy must always be kept in mind, because it is destined for a public that reads no other books and receives no other instruction:

... Its influence is powerful over men; and so a good comedy is as capable of reforming a people and of keeping it reformed as a comedy that presents bad examples is capable of perverting it and of keeping it perverted. For this reason great men have always said that this should be one of the principal objects of the government, since it provides public education and it alone can shape the manners of the people. Therefore all enlightened nations have given great attention to their theaters, and it has been observed that this institution has thrived at the very time when letters and arms were at their highest point.[40]

Throughout his articles on the theater in the *Pensador,* Clavijo y Fajardo makes a bid for government intervention to the end of purifying and regularizing the theater. Luzán and others had suggested the advisability of imposing a censorship upon all plays offered to the theater. The *Thinker,* however, is more outspoken in his insistence not only that it is to the interest of the government that a regular and moral theater be established and that bad plays be banned, but also that it is the duty of government to promote the theater as an important part of public education. He, more than any of his contemporaries, prepared the way for the subsidization of the theater undertaken by the prime minister, Aranda, in the reign of Carlos III.

Constantly in Clavijo y Fajardo's mind, as in the minds of all the leaders of neo-classicism, was the fear of what the numerous Frenchmen in Madrid would say about the backwardness of Spain as evidenced by the bad taste, immorality, and irregularity of its theater. In *Thought XX* he quotes at length from a review of a Spanish comedy, *The Valiant Aeneas, or Dido Abandoned,* by Joseph de Ybañez y Gassia, that had appeared in a French periodical, the *Encyclopedic Daily:*

Although the King of Spain is encouraging the sciences and the arts ... and although the Spaniards are a very intelligent nation, nevertheless we do not see letters making the progress that should be expected. Perhaps it will be believed that, if Spain is not distinguishing herself in philosophy, she is at least successful in cultivating the fine arts; but such is not the case. All of the dramas that are presented to the public now are modeled upon those of Lope de Vega, Calderón, and Moreto. Although one must recognize the talent of these poets, the barbarism of their age is so evident among the traces of genius that at times shine in their works, that they should not serve as models for the moderns who write for the theater. And so it is that, in spite of great genius, this nation has produced up until now nothing but shapeless and monstrous plays, where all that is base and comical is mixed with the sublime and the pathetic.[41]

After admitting that the French periodical was more than justified in its condemnation of *The Valiant Aeneas,* Clavijo y Fajardo exclaims: "What Spaniard, who has any blood in his veins, does not become kindled with just indignation against the bad taste of his country, when he sees how much reason foreigners have to treat us as they do, and to call us barbarians?"[42] He knows quite well, he says, that sensible and cultured Spaniards regret and cry out against this abuse, urging the reform of the theater; but when, he asks, will the entire nation recognize the need for such reform? In *The Valiant Aeneas* the transgressions committed are against the rules of art, but in most of the plays presented on the stage the sins are of an even more serious nature. In them lawlessness is approved and crime is exalted; corruption is preached, and vice is praised. At this point Clavijo y Fajardo abandons his role as an exponent of theatrical regularity to don the robe of a cleric, and to preach a veritable sermon against the evil consequence of attendance at the theater in its present condition:

Fathers, Mothers do not send your sons and daughters to the theater. There they will see what education tries to hide; there your daughter will learn to marry against your wishes, following a blind caprice. There she will see the leading lady go veiled to the house of the gallant; and she will see that the father is jeered and the lady is applauded. Your son will learn the laws of punctilious honor, contrary to the laws of the gospel and of the King; and he will come to believe that he is dishonored unless he resists what the King and Jesus Christ command him. In short, there they will see purity and innocence made ridiculous and brazen boldness and lawlessness held up to esteem. No, do not send them to the theater; wait until that fair day dawns in Spain when the theaters are reformed. Then you may indeed send them safely. Fortunate will be the Spaniard be who witnesses such a happy day![43]

In *Thought XXIII* Clavijo y Fajardo makes it clear that he is by no means in agreement with those moralists who would ban the theater entirely:

I know very well that much has been said and is being said by some men, who look with horror upon any kind of worldly diversion and would like to see even the most innocent pleasures destroyed. I know equally well that many others, insensible by nature to all that which does not conform to their ideas, censure in good faith anything that seems to distract them from the narrow road which they, leaning upon the principles of a rigid doctrine, propose to follow.[44]

Neither of these two types of moralist, he says, is a competent judge in the matter. Before pronouncing their sentences, they should bear in mind that large cities are not, and should not be, monastic cloisters. It is necessary, therefore, that there should be forms of public entertainment to keep the idle from harmful pursuits and to provide innocent recreation for those who need rest after they have fulfilled the duties of their professions. He is certain that, if due consideration is given to these reasons, it will be conceded that theatrical performances are not only useful, but necessary; and that, far from being banned, they should receive every encouragement from the government. When they are convinced of the salutary effect of tragedy and comedy upon manners, the opponents of the theater will diminish in number, and those who feel inclined to cultivate these genres will be encouraged to study their respective rules.

Can there be, in fact, any lesson more profitable than a comedy, where one sees painted with that vividness which is inseparable from theatrical action, and with the jocularity inherent in this form of drama, the anxiety and suffering of a miser; the false generosity of a rich man; the misdirected magnificence of a grandee; the infamous remarks of a slanderer; the disorders which occur in a family as the result of the bad conduct of a husband; or the series of griefs and sorrows of a girl who marries against the decorum of her blood and against the sacred laws of parental authority?[45]

Clavijo y Fajardo is not writing a work on poetics in the manner of Luzán, nor endeavoring, like Montiano and Nasarre, to prove that Spanish drama in its origin had been regular and had been corrupted by Lope de Vega and Calderón. He makes no attempt to salve the pride of his countrymen, but confines himself to a relentless campaign against the continuance of the Golden Age tradition. He maintains that, in doing so, he is showing more genuine patriotism and concern over the well-being of his nation than those who are content to allow the theater to wallow in the mire of indecency and bad taste that has made it the object of scorn of all civilized nations.

Who is the enemy of this nation? The one who, without wishing to deprive it of this diversion, which can be very useful if it is well directed, cries out and proves that our theater is not as it should be; that it is a school of corruption; that our youth learn in it to lose their innocence with the licentious expressions and images that it presents; . . . or the one who places the honor of the nation on a false foundation, and having no other reason to justify the theater in its present state than the fact that it has been so in the past, and that the plays performed are genuinely Spanish, overlook the obscenity and bad examples that are found at every step?[46]

In *Thought LXII* he takes Moreto's *A Woman Cannot Be Guarded* as a typical Golden Age comedy, and, after making an analysis of the play, concludes: "This is what is performed in theaters that were destined to correct the vices of society, and in this manner men without intelligence or will have converted into poison the very thing that should be its antidote."[47] If this evil were without remedy, he says, it would indeed be better to close the theaters.

Over and over again, Clavijo y Fajardo gives evidence that his primary concern is to vindicate Spain in the eyes of cultured nations; and in using the term *cultured* he obviously has in mind France, where he received his early training.

And what judgment will be formed of us in view of such customs by those who, not knowing us, measure and evaluate us by our plays? Without doubt they will believe us a barbarous and bloodthirsty people; and it is not surprising that many believed and still believe that our nation is incorrigible and that no degree of caution is excessive in our towns where on every corner they expect to meet assassins armed with daggers.[48]

Menéndez y Pelayo and Cotarelo y Mori limit their discussion of the role that Clavijo y Fajardo played in the neo-classic movement almost entirely to his attacks upon the *Autos Sacramentales*. His campaign against the *Autos*, however, was only a part of his program, and was not instituted until he felt he had adequately expounded his views on Spanish comedy. It is true that he had touched lightly in *Thought III* upon these religious plays, but not until *Thought XLII* did he make them the real target for his attack. He begins his remarks by expressing surprise that the royal ban against the Comedies of Saints has not been extended to include the *Autos Sacramentales:*

> In truth it seems incredible that such a Christian nation could see without horror the profanation of the mysteries of its religion and the signs, representations, or images of the most sacred things. Not many years ago performances of comedies that have for their theme the lives of the saints were banned, doubtless because in them was seen a pro-fanation of virtue. . . . And who would have believed that, in a prohibi-tion so well considered and so useful, first place would not have been given to the *Autos Sacramentales* that represent the life of Jesus Christ and are filled with material from the Scriptures?[49]

With little of the violence and open indignation that had charac-terized his attack upon Golden Age comedy, Clavijo y Fajardo gives systematic and well-reasoned arguments against the *Autos*, basing his contention that the king should issue a ban against them upon four points: the purpose of the *Autos*, the place where they are per-formed, the actors who play the different roles, and the manner of their performance.

No person of average education, he says, should be ignorant of the fact that the purpose of the theater is to correct manners by ridicule. How then can anyone consider it fitting to carry the high-est objects of religious veneration to such a place? And if it is an act of irreverence to represent evangelical truths in the theater, it is even more irreverent to have them come from profane mouths:

> The persons who represent the *Autos*, apart from their personal virtues or vices, contribute to make the performance indecent and odious. People who are accustomed to see an actress play the role of a woman of the lower class, a laundress, or a shop-woman, which, for all its serious-ness, is no less indecent, and in which modesty and purity are often tarnished, cannot be deceived when they see her play the role of the Holy Virgin.[50]

Clavijo y Fajardo admits that there are passages in the *Autos* that incite tenderness and devotion, but, he says, any benefit that might be derived from them is negatived by discordant elements:

> To see a man, who, in a comic interlude, was dressed as a rascal, covered with rags and smoking a cigar, come to play in an *Auto* the role

of a Person of the Holy Trinity (as I have seen), produces the same discord as to see the one who represents the Eternal Father in the *Auto, The Food of Mankind,* transformed in the *sainete* into a doorkeeper and making some indecent remarks about the register to a girl who has previously played the part of an angel.[51]

The costumes of the actresses, he says, are calculated to cause gossip and scandal rather than inspire devotion. Equally to be censured are the glaring anachronisms committed in the costumes of the actors. Who, he asks, could refrain from laughing boisterously when he sees a Levite come out on the stage dressed as a priest and wearing a miter?

The criticism that Clavijo y Fajardo makes of the *Autos* is directed primarily at their profanation of sacred material and at their injurious effect upon public morals. He does not attempt to evaluate them in the light of neo-classic rules, considering, as Luzán had done, that they constitute a separate genre.

The *Autos* may be considered in two respects: in relation to the belles-lettres and to religion, whose mysteries they represent. . . . If they are considered from the aesthetic point of view, it will be very difficult to determine to which class of poetry they belong, since in subject and workmanship they fit into none. By their subject matter they are excluded from profane poetry. The sacred mysteries of our religion and the respectable truths of the Gospel are infinitely distant and diametrically opposed to everything that is profane. . . . This is not to condemn all religious poetry . . . Moses, Job, and David left us the best models of religious poetry, destined to sing the marvels of the Most High, and his mercies.[52]

The *Autos,* he says, cannot be called epic or lyric poetry, and certainly do not deserve to be classed as dramatic poetry, since they lack completely the requisites dictated by reason and good taste, and taught by the masters of art. The *Autos,* he concludes, are nothing but allegorical dialogues in metrical form; they try to bring within the grasp of our comprehension that which would cease to be supremely great if our humble reason were capable of conceiving it. What Catholic who makes even an average use of his reason, he asks, can fail to be shocked when he sees a Host painted on a theater curtain?

Romea y Tapia

Menéndez y Pelayo tells us that popular indignation was aroused "against the insults that the Frenchified and Voltairian publisher, under the cloak of piety, directed at the *Autos*,"[53] and that a number of articles appeared in their defense, although he confesses that he is familiar with only one. The author of this energetic defense of the national theater, he says, was Juan Christóbal Romea y Tapia, who published in opposition to the *Pensador* a periodical entitled *El Escritor sin Título*. Romea y Tapia attributes the supposed defects of Calderón, and the ardor with which he painted ideal and improbable things, to the taste of a nation more inclined to subtlety than to pathos, and asserts that the failure of writers to equal the nonsense of Calderón can be explained only by the fact that the defects that are attributed to him contain something of the sublime. He also declares that if Calderón's critics would undertake to write one comedy "as bad" as those by Calderón, he would compose ten better than those of Molière. Following Zavaleta he exclaims:

Who is ignorant of the fact that each nation has its genius, its propensities, dress, language, vices, virtues, and character, and that, consequently, the diversions are and should be different in different nations? If we differ in human actions, why should we not differ in the manner of applauding or condemning them, which should be the object of comedy?[54]

He distinguishes between the works of Nasarre, Luzán, and Montiano, whom he mentions with respect, and other works that have been written without real knowledge of Spanish drama or of the rules of art. He then adds:

It is not my intention to go into the reasons that either party has for its position, nor to make a catalogue of many of our plays, that have no other defect than their failure to conform to the much vaunted unities and to a badly understood and poorly explained principle of verisimilitude; for, inasmuch as these rules are not the decisions of any general council, that which is called an abuse, when sanctioned by the whole nation, becomes a custom and even a law.[55]

He hastens to say, however, that he does not approve all Spanish comedies, for "it is unquestionable that there are some so monstrous that not even the lash of satire can punish them as they deserve."[56] Romea y Tapia defends the *Autos* as legitimate sacred poetry and insists that Calderón's *Autos* have every right to be considered as drama. He finds ample justification in the Bible for the use of allegory and considers that the fact that God assumed human form justifies man in portraying the Divine Being. But Romeo y Tapia limits himself to defending the *Autos* on aesthetic grounds as legitimate works of art; he is far from defending their manner of performance.

... One must confess that D. Joseph Clavijo was reasonable in his criticism on this point, since it is beyond dispute that the changing of costumes and other plagues for which he condemns the actors have no other justification than a stupid abuse, detested by some of them, but stubbornly followed because they do not dare to oppose a custom established through the years.[57]

There are other defects in the Spanish theater, he declares, that deserve serious and vigorous reproof. The elimination of these defects would necessarily result in the reform of the theater, the reform of the manner of performance, and even the reform of the plays themselves. After this broad assertion the reader is disappointed to learn that Romea y Tapia's panacea for the evils of the theater actually amounts to the suggestion that this institution should be converted into an aristocratic diversion by excluding the turbulent masses from the performances:

... the source of all the evils that beset our performances is the wretched quality of the audience, due to the low price of admission. There is no diversion of this kind in any of the famous cities of Europe that is not far more costly and for that very reason less harmful. This, which seems a paradox, can be proven positively by a visit to our *corrales* that are commonly filled with poor people and wretched artisans who, enrolled under the banners of the *Chorizos* and the *Polacos,* leave their houses in abandon and in their obstinate blindness disregard their duties as heads of their households. Covered with rags from head to foot, they shout and clap their hands as if their entire happiness depended upon Anfriso's reciting a ballad well, Lisi's singing gracefully a *tonadilla,* or Bato's making the crowd in the pit roar with laughter. Is it not a deplorable shame that, spending the greater part of the day in idleness, they neglect their work and lose their customers?[58]

Like other moralists of the theater Romea y Tapia is much concerned about the effect of attendance at theatrical performances upon the youth of the land, but he differs from them in that he attributes the demoralization of the youth to the act of attendance itself and not to the bad example found in the plays or to the detrimental influence of immoral actors. He is not concerned over the quality of the plays themselves and believes that the evils he deplores would persist even though the neo-classicists succeeded completely in regularizing the theater:

Let us consider now whether these vices and others equally bad would be remedied by the performance of comedies written in strict conformity with the rules of art, in the manner of the ancients, and according to the desires of modern critics. It is evident that they would not be, because these defects have no connection whatsoever with the performances, and for the consummation of all their evil effects it is of no consequence that the plays have one form or another. Therefore, if the Spanish theater is to be reformed, it is necessary to have recourse to another method and to apply a better corrosive than that offered by a play carefully and skilfully written, because the theater has cancerous fistulas that cannot be reached by physical perfections . . .[59]

It matters little to the actors whether they perform well or badly, whether the plays themselves are good or bad, provided the theater is filled and their efforts are applauded. Romea y Tapia is convinced that, even though a new crop of Plautuses should appear, their plays would neither attract larger audiences nor produce more money than existing plays, even including those that are most defective and fantastic. The harm being in the ear, it matters little whether the instruments be tuned or untuned. The only solution for the evils of the theater, therefore, lies in the improvement of the audience: "Let the audience be improved, exclude the uncultured, the wretched artisans, the uneducated youth, those who go to the theater from malignant and inveterate habit, the large number of women who, unfortunately, attend, and we shall see many wounds healed with this single caustic."[60] All these effects can be achieved, Romea y Tapia says, by the simple expedient of raising the price of admission to two pesetas. He forgets that the national theater of Spain owed its peculiar form to the fact that from its origin it had been designed to appeal to all the people, and particularly to the very rabble he would now exclude from the performances. He forgets also that the *Autos Sacramentales* were designed to appeal to the masses, not to the aristocracy or the erudites. While his wounded patriotism impels him to defend the Golden Age theater against the neo-classicists, his recommendation, if it had been carried out, would have dealt a death blow to that very theater. Menéndez y Pelayo praises the "solid erudition with which Romea y Tapia proves that the *Autos* are legitimate sacred poetry" and his "brilliant defense of allegorical art," but says nothing whatsoever about his ridiculous solution for the evils that beset the theater. Romea y Tapia's defense of national drama and of the *Autos* deserves little more consideration than his recommendation that the theaters be converted into an aristocratic diversion. He confines himself to generalities and presents no effective argument against the attack by Clavijo y Fajardo, Nicolás Fernández de Moratín, and Mariano Nipho upon the irregularity and bad taste that characterized so much of Golden Age comedy.

1. Leandro Fernández de Moratín, *op. cit.*, p. 447.
2. Moratín, "Discurso preliminar," *Obras (B.A.E.,* I, 311).
3. *Collection of Letters of the Princess des Ursins,* by Louis de la Trémoille, Vol. V. See Pellissier, *op. cit.,* p. 15.
4. Moratín, *op. cit.,* p. 314.
5. *Ibid.*
6. Thomás de Añorbe y Corregel, *Jupiter y Danae* (Madrid, 1738). See I. L. McClelland, *Origins of the Romantic Movement in Spain* (Liverpool, 1937), p. 14.
7. Añorbe y Corregel, "Note" to *El Paulino.* See McClelland, *op. cit.,* p. 15.
8. *Ibid.*
9. See p. 114.
10. Cotarelo y Mori, *Biblioteca de las controversias sobre la licitud del teatro en España* (Madrid, 1904), p. 127.
11. *Ibid.,* pp. 473-80.
12. *Ibid.,* p. 336.
13. *Ibid.,* p. 476.
14. *Ibid.,* p. 477.
15. *Ibid.,* pp. 478-79.
16. Casiano Pellicer, *Tratado histórico sobre el origen y progresos de la comedia y del histrionismo en España* (Madrid, 1804), pp. 259-63.
17. Cotarelo y Mori, *op. cit.,* p. 67.
18. *Ibid.,* p. 432.
19. *El Pensador Matritense.* Discursos críticos sobre todos los asumptos que comprehende de la sociedad civil. Con Real Privilegio que tiene Don Pedro Angel de Taragona, Barcelona. Por Francisco Generas, Impresor. This is a reprint of *El Pensador* (published in Madrid, 1762).
20. *Ibid.,* Tomo primero, pp. 51-57.
21. *Ibid.,* pp. 59-60.
22. *Ibid.,* p. 66.

23. *Ibid.,* pp. 71-72.
24. *Ibid.,* p. 194.
25. *Ibid.,* pp. 204-5.
26. *Ibid.,* p. 207.
27. *Ibid.*
28. *Ibid.,* p. 209.
29. *Ibid.,* p. 211.
30. *Ibid.,* p. 212.
31. *Ibid.,* p. 213.
32. *Ibid.,* pp. 216-18.
33. *Ibid.,* p. 220.
34. *Ibid.,* p. 197.
35. *Ibid.,* Tomo segundo, Pensamiento XXVII, p. 308.
36. *Ibid.,* Tomo primero, Pensamiento IX, p. 198.
37. *Ibid.,* Tomo segundo, p. 219.
38. *Ibid.,* p. 314.
39. *Ibid.,* Tomo primero, pp. 199-200.
40. *Ibid.,* pp. 201-2.
41. *Ibid.,* Tomo segundo, pp. 147-48.
42. *Ibid.,* p. 149.
43. *Ibid.,* p. 156.
44. *Ibid.,* p. 216.
45. *Ibid.,* pp. 219-20.
46. *Ibid.,* Tomo cuarto, Pensamiento LXV.
47. *Ibid.,* Pensamiento LXII.
48. *Ibid.,* Pensamiento LXV.
49. *Ibid.,* Pensamiento XLII.
50. *Ibid.*
51. *Ibid.*
52. Menéndez y Pelayo, *op. cit.,* III, 278.
53. *Ibid.,* p. 279.
54. *Ibid.,* p. 280.
55. Cotarelo y Mori, *Biblioteca de las controversias,* etc., p. 529.
56. *Ibid.*
57. *Ibid.,* p. 530.
58. *Ibid.*
59. *Ibid.,* p. 531.
60. *Ibid.*

V

Mariano Nipho and The Spanish Nation Defended

THROUGHOUT the conflict between the neo-classicists and the nationalists there were certain individuals who were in sympathy with the former in their insistence upon the necessity for reform in the theater and in their condemnation of certain extravagances and bad taste in Golden Age comedy, but who found a cool welcome in the ranks of the neo-classicists because they at times flared up at the unqualified indictment of the Golden Age theater by foreigners and by the most rigid exponents of regularity among their own countrymen. We have noticed that at the beginning of the controversy Porcel found it impossible to renounce entirely his allegiance to the traditional theater. Luzán, following a conciliatory policy, had recognized good and bad qualities in Golden Age comedies, but his successors, Nasarre and Velázquez, did not see fit to mix praise with censure; and Clavijo y Fajardo allowed no word of commendation for the national theater to come from his pen. As Spaniards became more familiar with contemporary dramatic criticism in France they could not fail to notice that there was a swing in that country away from blind adherence to neo-classical precepts as they had been evolved by such rigid theorists as Boileau and D'Aubignac. They became aware that the rules which extreme neo-classicists regarded as essential for dramatic excellence had been unwillingly followed by Corneille and had been regarded with some degree of scorn by Molière in his *Critique de l'Ecole des femmes*. They noticed also that among contemporary French critics there was a growing tendency to overlook violations of the unities of time and place when they believed better results could be achieved by their breach than by their rigid observance. Conspicuous among those Spaniards who had come to question the infallibility of the rules was Mariano Nipho.

The inconsistency, either apparent or real, of Nipho's position on the national theater made him the object of attack by both nationalists and neo-classicists. As the author and editor of *El Diario extranjero*, the first Spanish periodical to attempt a regular criticism of plays performed on the Spanish stage, he incurred the ill will of Romea y Tapia by his failure to see only perfection in the works of Calderón and his followers. Although, as he says, "he professes an almost idolatrous respect for the talents of Calderón," he admits that he is filled with confusion when he sees the extravagances committed by this genius in plays like *To Conquer Love One Must Wish to Conquer It*. He admires Calderón's *Life Is a Dream* but condemns the impossible plot and the absurdities found in *The Emotions of Hatred and Love*, and when Romea y Tapia in *El Escritor sin Título* accuses him of being a traitor to his country and of seeking to lower Spanish drama in the estimation of foreigners, he replies with some heat:

> The new critic, or "The Writer Without a Title," deserves no other answer for the time being than to request that, since he finds Calderón so good and Rojas so exact in everything, he show us a single comedy by either writer that is good and that observes the proper regularity and correctness of manners.[1]

In the same periodical he admits the sins of Spanish comedies, not confining his remarks to inferior eighteenth-century plays, but obviously having in mind also the dramatic production of the Golden Age. He differs noticeably, however, from Nasarre, Montiano, and Velázquez in that he attributes the defects of the Spanish theater, not to the bad example set by Lope and Calderón, but primarily to the ineptitude of the actors and to the depraved taste of the public:

> What is to blame for all the sins of our comedies? The ignorance and at times the excessive boldness of the actors; the heedlessness and the depraved taste of the spectators; and the lack of exactitude and the vaporous ardor of the writers. . . . The poet would willingly follow verisimilitude, propriety, and decency; but he is forced to write dreams and delirium, because the frenzy and the fever of the people wish it so.[2]

His condemnation of the excessive use of the love motif in Spanish comedy is as severe as any to be found in the works of Luzán, Nasarre, Montiano, or Clavijo y Fajardo:

> In fact, is it not a very ridiculous thing that in the theater one is always forced to hear lovers open up their hearts to each other and give vent to their amorous passions with expressions full of tenderness, or lament the cruelty of their ladies or their mistresses, or abandon themselves

to the indiscreet mental disorder of jealousy, or sigh and become desperate because they are unable to overcome the obstacles that prevent the licentious satisfaction of their desires? Can there be anything more vexatious than forever to see rivals and competitors in affairs of love, and men and maidservants who are ready to aid them in their folly and extravagances? Always the same thing![3]

Nipho is taking his cue here directly from Voltaire and Fontenelle rather than from previous Spanish neo-classic critics. Both of these writers had taken a definite stand against the prevalence of the love element in French drama, particularly in tragedy. Nipho extends this criticism to comedy and appeals for a type that will concern itself more with the correction of manners through ridicule than with love intrigues. His position on this point was sufficiently orthodox to suit even the most rigid neo-classicists. His praise of Calderón in other places, however, is distinctly inconsistent, inasmuch as that author invariably built his comedies and tragedies around a complicated love intrigue and, especially in his cloak and sword plays, used with monotonous frequency the very devices Nipho is holding up to ridicule. It should be noted, however, that in the articles which appeared in the *Diario extranjero*, Nipho never gives unqualified praise to Calderón. Under the heading "Noticias de moda" of April 12 appears a tribute, not so much to the superior quality of Calderón's comedies as to the sustained popularity of his theater in the face of the most vigorous opposition on the part of the exponents of the rules. He admits Calderón's defects but asserts that his popularity will endure until the neo-classicists produce examples with which to back up their theories. This is the passage from which Menéndez y Pelayo quotes as indicative of Nipho's admiration for Calderón:

> In the *Diario extranjero* . . . he had already inserted encomiastic judgments of several of the comedies of Calderón, whom he calls "an admirable poet, never more glorious than when most impugned, but not conquered. . . . There is no doubt that Calderón as a man had his defects, but until now I have seen no one who has corrected them."[4]

For a correct evaluation of Nipho's position, it is necessary to place the words cited by Menéndez y Pelayo in their proper setting, for Nipho is laying the foundation for recommending the reworking of Calderón's comedies, not only to improve their style by modifying the imaginative flights, but also to make them less detrimental to public morals:

The theaters of Madrid, always appreciative, have paid their characteristic reverent homage to the memory of Don Pedro Calderón de la Barca
by opening the theatrical year with a comedy by this author, never more
glorious than when most impugned, but not conquered; since, although
the invasions have come very close the conquest is still beyond the realm
of the imagination because of lack of models. There is no doubt that
Calderón ... had his defects; but until now I have seen no hand that has
corrected them.[5]

Nipho is doing little more than Luzán, Montiano, and others had
done in paying tribute to the genius of Calderón in the same breath
that they decried the misuse of that genius. He also aligns himself
with the neo-classicists in his recommendation that recasts of Calderón's plays be made:

It is well to point out a harm; but then it becomes inevitable to offer a
remedy. It would be advisable, extremely advisable, to curtail in Calderón
some flights of poetic ardor, and other efforts of the imagination that are
badly sustained and injurious in their effect; in this no less honor would
be done to the reputation of this admirable poet than benefit to our peninsula; since, by taking away from him that which is superfluous and perhaps detrimental, we would make his works cease to be an object of
criticism and become pleasing and effective instruments for public instruction. There are prudent hands that can perform this service for the
fatherland; and in so doing they will pay the best and highest tribute
to Calderón. It would not be bad, since people are *thinking*, for the day
to come when they will act.[6]

In the first number of the *Diario extranjero* (April 5, 1763),
Nipho had inserted in his review of the French comedy *Dupuis et
des Ronais* both praise and censure of Calderón, while setting up the
French drama as a model of the type of play he would like to see
imitated in the Spanish theater, and at the same time showing his
impatience at the failure of the neo-classicists to back up their
theories with action:

The purpose of the above has been not only to give an idea of what a
good French comedy is, but to show how fitting it would be if Spanish
comedies were of such a nature. Our old poets, if they were living today
and the taste of the nation were favorable to this type, would write plays
not only as good but much more sublime. Calderón was a genius, and a
great genius; he did what fitted his times; and although he is called bad,
it will be necessary for those who say this to write better plays in order
to support their opinion. In the present condition of the nation, it is not a
time to say that if Peter was bad, Anthony was worse, but to leave the

dead in peace, and for the living to exercise themselves in virtue and uprightness.... Let us see a good comedy, and let bad criticism cease. Such a comedy will be the most effective criticism, ... Spain does not need arid reflections, but concrete examples. The theater is crying for a good comedy, and the public will appreciate it. We have critics by the handful. Let us leave off sterile rules and bring our work to light....[7]

Even in his discussion of the *Autos* Nipho refrains from giving Calderón unqualified praise. He defends the fundamental purpose of these plays but recognizes that their manner of performance justifies the attacks to which they have been subjected. Again he praises the "prodigious genius" of Calderón and his "ingenious fancy," qualities which even the most rigid neo-classicists were willing to concede. In his remarks on two *autos* by Calderón, *The Food of Man* and *Love Thy Neighbor as Thyself*, played at the Príncipe and the Cruz, June 10 to July 5, 1763, he says:

Criticism, whether just or given in the heat of passion, exaggerates the defects of these allegorical dramas; but it cannot deny that, if their performances were carried out with the candor and purity required by sacred subjects, they would serve not only as entertainment but also as very sound documents for the instruction of the public.... I have heard many speak of these ingenious and fanciful works of Calderón with a mistaken criterion, whether they recognize in him inimitable excellencies or reprehensible extravagance; but with a careful examination of either judgment, Calderón emerges victor because of his prodigious genius. This alone makes him worthy of all applause; and it is quite certain that if the setting were in keeping with the spirit of the *autos*, which is moral teaching, these diversions would be of a different nature; but, however criticism may consider them, they will always be plausible because of their exquisite fancy; although the vice that the theater communicates to them causes no little concern in pious minds.[8]

The comments upon the theater in the *Diario extranjero* certainly did not place Nipho among the ardent partisans of the national drama, nor did his occasional recognition of Calderón's genius and his impatience at the lack of action on the part of neo-classicists suffice in themselves to make him *persona non grata* in the ranks of the latter. As the prolific editor of some ten periodicals, three of which were devoted primarily to foreign affairs he, as much as any man of his time, was instrumental in drawing the attention of his countrymen to what was going on beyond their frontiers. The full titles of these three periodicals will perhaps be sufficient to indicate how well posted Nipho presumed to be on foreign affairs: *The Lon-*

*don Courier: A Periodical Made Up of Various Letters That Manifest
the Procedure of England with Reference to Her Customs, Industry,
Arts, Literature, Commerce, and Marine Affairs* (1762); *General
Messenger of Historical, Literary, and Economic Matters of Europe
(in Continuation of the London Courier), in Which Will Be Found
Useful Notes on Sciences, Agriculture, Arts, and Commerce of
France, Holland, Germany, Italy, and Other Countries and Provinces
in Europe That Owe Their Prosperity to a Prudent and Well Directed Public Economy, etc.* (1763); *The Foreign Daily: Important
and Curious Notes on the Best Works on Arts and Sciences That
Appear in the Most Civilized Nations of Europe, Together with
Many Important Secrets for Effective Conduct of the Arts, of Agriculture, and of Mechanics, etc.* (1763).[9]

It was only natural that a man who prided himself so greatly
upon his knowledge of world affairs should take an active part in the
neo-classic controversy. Probably as much as any critic of his time
Nipho tried to strike a happy medium between the blind allegiance
to the national theater that characterized such men as Zavaleta and
Romea y Tapia and the narrow-minded scorn for that theater so
volubly expressed by uncompromising neo-classicists like Nasarre
and Clavijo y Fajardo. He could see qualities in the French theater
worthy of imitation on the Spanish stage, without closing his eyes
completely to the merit of Spanish Golden Age comedy. His attitude,
however, toward some of the contemporary monstrosities that surpassed in extravagance and bad taste anything produced during the
Golden Age was no less severe than that of Clavijo y Fajardo. In his
account of the opening performance on April 8, 1763, of Antonio
Bazo's *To Sacrifice Love on the Altar of Honor: Cleonice and De-
metrius*, he exclaims:

> Already the pompous titles are beginning: may God grant that we
> not vomit again. . . . I do not believe the theatrical rejoicing is very
> healthy, because it appears that the disease of the spleen is being felt.
> [A play on the word *bazo*, which is both the name of the author and a
> term meaning spleen.][10]

He characterizes this play as a monstrosity taken from the opera
of Metastasio and is no less severe in his criticism of another comedy
by Bazo, *The Peace of Artaxerxes with Greece*. It seems that Romea
y Tapia, Clavijo y Fajardo, and Nipho could agree upon one thing
at least: the complete lack of merit of Bazo's plays, for Romea y

Tapia wrote in *El Escritor sin Título:* "To judge the merit of this work, I beg my readers to read it, for they will find there all the art of combining improprieties, stringing fiction together without discernment, long and short verses, and low and almost meaningless expressions."[11] As we have seen, Clavijo y Fajardo had nothing but contempt for another comedy on the same theme by Bazo, which had been performed in 1762 and which was also an adaptation of an opera by Metastasio.

Miss McCelland, in her work, *The Origins of the Romantic Movement in Spain,*[12] has adequately vindicated Nipho's name from the scorn expressed by Leandro Fernández de Moratín, who branded him as the *pestilent Nipho,* and from lack of appreciation on the part of Menéndez y Pelayo for his merit as a theatrical critic. Miss McClelland does not believe there is any actual inconsistency in Nipho's position with reference to the national theater and the neoclassic movement. Those passages in his writings that may seem to be contradictory can be understood, she says, when they are considered in the light of his insistence on national independence. In support of her contention, Miss McClelland cites in *The Origins of the Romantic Movement in Spain* the following extract from Nipho's *General Messenger:*

> This is the reason why . . . one of the best critics said about the present war waged against the theater that it is a waste of time to point out and to argue about faults; each nation has its particular taste; the French like illusion, the Spaniards like variety, etc. . . . *Taste* is an elf that everyone says exists, but no one has determined where. Each nation has its character; the test of excellence is in knowing how to direct it. For one nation to make rules for another is to try to make the whole world one nation.[13]

It is not, however, in the *General Messenger* or in the *Diario extranjero* but in *The Spanish Nation Defended Against the Insults of the Thinker and His Followers* (1764)[14] that Miss McClelland finds abundant evidence of Nipho's admiration for Golden Age drama and of his insistence upon literary freedom. The abrupt change from a rather general censure of the national theater, mixed with an occasional recognition of the genius of Lope and Calderón, found in the *Diario extranjero,* to the unqualified endorsement of that theater in *The Spanish Nation Defended* seems to justify the charge of inconsistency that has been directed at him by subsequent critics and even by his own contemporaries, if indeed he was the author of the latter work. It would be difficult to explain this about-face on the part of

Nipho except as the result of personal animosity toward Clavijo y Fajardo, or unless he felt that his denial of authorship contained in the "Foreword" to *The Spanish Nation Defended* left the road open to him to express ideas which would guarantee a favorable reception for the work among the large section of the public that had never faltered in its allegiance to the traditional theater. It should be borne in mind that Nipho depended for his livelihood upon his publications.

The title, *The Spanish Nation Defended from the Insults of the Thinker and His Followers*, and the explanation of the purpose and scope of the two *Discourses* into which the work is divided constitute a definite appeal to prospective buyers. Following the title of the first part appears this somewhat extravagant claim, which, as we shall see, the author fails to support in the body of the text: "In this work it will be shown with French testimony that Spanish comedies, in addition to being original, are the best in Europe and that the famous Spanish poets should be celebrated and not reproved." Nipho assures the reader in the "Foreword" that he is not the author of the work; that, indeed, his role has been limited to arranging for its publication:

This work, the merit of which is so great, is obviously not from my pen; but in case it may be believed necessary that I make a declaration to this effect, I protest with the greatest candor that my part in it has been limited to copying it from the original. A gentleman who loves Spain, and who is very much disturbed that Spaniards should be termed barbarians because they are fond of their theater, has wished to show in this paper, and in another that will follow, the injustice of the insult. His studies have been constant and well directed in almost all branches of knowledge; he is well instructed in several languages and has a mastery not only of the dead languages, but also of almost all the living languages of Europe. His inclination to acquire the highest form of knowledge has led him to journey through the principle provinces and states of Europe, in which school he has acquired valuable knowledge that is not conceded to those who limit themselves to the prejudices of their native land. He arrived last year at Madrid, and having seen the conflict that was being waged in the periodicals, he regretted very much that some of these, in discussing comedies, should treat the subject with such ignorance and that others should show so little courtesy. Irritated but not infuriated, he composed the present discourse; and because of the sincere affection that he has always professed for me, he sent me his work. I told him without flattery what I thought about it; and availing himself of our genuine friendship, he urged me to secure its publication. . . . This is the truth. I present this work to the public only because of the pleasure that it will afford to many; the merit belongs entirely to someone else, and only the arrangement for its publication is due to my efforts.[15]

This "Foreword" by Nipho has been consistently ignored by the few critics who have deigned to discuss *The Spanish Nation Defended*. Indeed, it is not even mentioned by Menéndez y Pelayo, Cotarelo y Mori, or Miss McClelland, all of whom evidently dismissed it as a literary fiction. Sempere y Guarinos, some twenty-three years after the composition of the work, attributed it to Nipho without comment. It appears that at the time of its publication and for some time thereafter it was accepted as the work of an anonymous author, for Sebastián y Latre in his *Experiment on the Spanish Theatre* (1772), after complaining that certain "defenders of bad taste" take up arms against any drama whose craftsmanship is beyond the reach of their meager understanding, adds the following comment on other writers whose education should be sufficient to enable them to distinguish the good from the bad, and refers repeatedly to the *anonymous* author of *The Spanish Nation Defended*:

I would be contented if this obstinacy were confined to such people, but the pity is that there are others who, having all the instruction necessary to decide the question, perhaps in order to make a show of the magnanimity of their spirit, or because they know that applause is certain, follow the popular party, which gathers courage from seeing on its side someone who defends its opinions with arguments even though they be false. It seems that the *anonymous* author of the paper entitled *The Spanish Nation Defended from the Insults of the Thinker and His Followers* belongs to this group. He was probably confident that the work would have an immediate and wide acceptance; and, in order to expedite this acceptance, he began and continued his work by scorning and attacking the well-founded criticism of *The Thinker* and by applying to the latter and to those who shared his opinions indecorous expressions rarely used among enlightened people. The truth is that anyone who has clear vision and studies *The Thinker* and the *anonymous* author with impartiality will recognize without difficulty in which direction the weight of reason inclines.[16]

In view of the prevailing practice in literary polemics of the day for writers to use pseudonyms in their critical articles and to disclaim authorship when these articles were attributed to them, it is perhaps presumptuous to suggest that Nipho may have been telling the truth when he claimed to have had no part in the composition of *The Spanish Nation Defended*. Miss McClelland suggests that he probably wrote these discourses in order "to convince such persons as Romea y Tapia of his regard for Spanish genius." It is curious that he should disclaim authorship in the "Foreword," if this indeed was his purpose.

It is known that Nipho at times acted as an intermediary in the publication of works of other authors. In 1765, or shortly after, Ramón de la Cruz refers directly to such activity on the part of Nipho:

> I am not surprised at what Nipho says about me or his manner of saying it, because he speaks ill of everyone and later contradicts himself. He is an unfortunate wit, and, although he makes free use of tricks, we know that the few pesetas he has earned from his works were stolen from foreigners and poets. I do not regret that he shows his violent anger at me so unjustly, but I do regret that he should lie at the expense of my reputation. He is a man without religion, *because if a critical work of mine could be interpreted as malignant censure of someone, when I consulted him about it and entrusted its publication to him, why did he applaud it?*[17]

There is no record of any work of criticism published by Ramón de la Cruz prior to that time, except the prologue to his comic opera *Sacrifices Are Pleasing to the Deity*, published in 1757. Could Ramón de la Cruz have been referring in 1765 to *The Spanish Nation Defended*, which came out the year before? Cotarelo y Mori says that Ramón and Nipho had been friends, and that the latter had given Ramón advice about some of his writings, but that for some unknown reason their friendship terminated. It is possible that the rupture developed from the publication of the above-mentioned work. It may be significant that Ramon's brother Juan returned to Spain in 1764 from a long residence in Paris, where he had gone at the expense of Fernando VI to develop and perfect his natural artistic faculties. We are told that after his return he communicated to Ramón ideas and translations of short plays from the French, and that he had a deep interest in the theater.[18] This work could have been written by Ramón de la Cruz in collaboration with his brother, or this brother could have been the repatriated Spaniard to whom Nipho refers in his introduction as the real author of *The Spanish Nation Defended*. In view of the animosity that existed between Ramón de la Cruz and Clavijo, the bitter tone of the work would be quite understandable. On the other hand, there is no evidence that any such animosity ever existed between Nipho and Clavijo.

Ramón de la Cruz composed and staged in 1765 a one-act farce, *Complaining People*, directed at the *Pensador* and his followers, in which he expresses ideas similar to those found in *The Spanish Nation Defended*. Referring obviously to Clavijo y Fajardo, one of the characters exclaims in mock condemnation of the irregularity of the Spanish theater:

> Oh, sectarians of bad taste! Oh, deluded people! What good does it do to preach a sermon to you once a week? Do you think that in these sermons they say hastily whatever strikes their fancy through self-interest or caprice, and that it is some fantasy they have invented. . . . By no means, friends. Do not think that they claim originality, for they say that before them the rules had already been championed by Salas, Cascales, Cervantes, Luzán, and other competent writers. . . . They cite the authority of great critics and say it is necessary that the theater be corrected. Madam Director, if we must stage dramas to suit the taste of these gentlemen, put on your coat and go forth to seek poets who, mindful of the fact that we suffer the blame for their shortcomings, will improve our performance by mending their faults.[19]

When the Director answers that she has been told the public wishes only nonsense and turmoil, a shout comes from the pit, from the stands, and from the boxes, that this is not true. Speaking for the section occupied by the nobility, one of the characters, García, defends Spanish comedies, saying that their sustained popularity is due to their gaiety, lively fancy, intricate plots, clever conceits, wit, and language. Where so many have been written, it is sufficient that some be good and not all bad. He then exclaims: "Oh, Spaniards! Who would say that foreign nations have translated more of our comedies than we have of theirs? This is the strongest evidence that they find merit in them."[20] And still, he says, there are people so narrow-minded and prejudiced that they think the worst plays are to be found in Spain. These critics presume that they can achieve more fame by the criticism they conceive or transfer against Spanish comedies than they could by putting their theories into practice. If they would reduce their lofty doctrines to practical and original works for the stage, they would render their nation a double service. Speaking then directly to Clavijo and Moratín, he says: "Let it surprise no one that *those who speak to the public* be told by the public to go forward on the road that leads from saying to doing, since they have already prepared the ground so thoroughly."[21]

Later four actors come out, representing the audience seated in the stands and boxes. As the spokesman for the stands, Martínez asks what regular tragedies or comedies have been witnessed and rejected by them that they should be branded as "barbarous," that is, as "people without faith, religion, politics, art, letters, and without respect for the memory of their heroes." He answers his own questions by saying that Spaniards have been too busy enriching their nation with conquests and spreading the clear light of religion to give their attention to observing in the theater "three or four kickshaws that are good if they have already been established; but if not, are unnecessary and are missed only by idlers."[22]

In the second discourse of The Spanish Nation Defended, in the form of a note by the editor, there is a vicious, irrelevant, and gratuitous attack upon Sedano's tragedy, La Jahel, which had recently been published. The author of this note says that "one scene of Calderón or of Lope is worth more than all that has been written in Spain for the past twenty years, not excluding the new tragedy, La Jahel, composed by Don Juan López Sedano," the theme of which "is not suitable for tragedy or for any other dramatic composition."[23] This attack elicited an immediate response from Sedano himself in El Belianís Literario. Nowhere in this article does Sedano accuse Nipho of being the author of The Spanish Nation Defended. Indeed, he repeatedly speaks of the author and the editor as two different persons. He holds Nipho responsible, however, for approving and publishing the work and taunts him for inconsistency in view of his previous attacks upon Golden Age drama:

It is quite true that our critics hold primarily responsible the one who lent his name and his efforts to the publication of this work and are filled with surprise at his inimitable candor and docility. In view of the fact that he has been the most tenacious and irreconcilable partisan of the Reformation and has said more bad things about our comedies and their authors than all other critics combined, calling them "ridiculous, indecent, inhuman, lascivious, false in their ideas, affected and inflated in their language, filled with impure thoughts, and animated only by the fire of lust," . . . and has called those who applaud them "barbarous, prejudiced, and uncivilized," . . . they marvel that he should dare to affix his name to, and be responsible for, the publication of a writing that is diametrically opposed to his vaunted system of "Civilization and Reform," and in which it is claimed that the comedies of Spain, in addition to being original, are the best in Europe and that the famous Spanish poets should be praised and not reproved.[24]

People are asking themselves, Sedano says, whether it is believable that a man who allows his name to accompany such a writing should be the same one who, in the Diario extranjero of July 9, 1763, made the statement: "The theater is in need of reform and correction everywhere; but nowhere in the world more than in Spain. . . . As it exists today the Spanish theater should be not merely reformed, but completely abolished."[25] Like Ramón de la Cruz, Sedano comments upon Nipho's practice of arranging for the publication of the works of others and accuses him of altering some of them until they bear little resemblance to the originals. In view of Nipho's frank confession made in an earlier work that he only wrote to make money, Sedano believes that, recognizing the profit that could be made from the publication of *The Spanish Nation Defended,* he "willingly took upon himself the task of polishing it, commenting upon it, adding to it, and finally publishing it."[26]

The author of *The Spanish Nation Defended* represents himself as a Spaniard who has recently returned to Spain after having spent more than eleven years in Paris, two in London, three in Italy, and more than a year and a half in Germany. His long residence in foreign lands has enabled him to form an accurate estimate of European drama and to appreciate the superiority of the Spanish theater. During his absence from Spain he has read carefully everything that has been written about dramatic art and has been constant in his attendance at the theater wherever he has been. These statements are made with the express purpose of proving that he is eminently better qualified than the *Pensador* to pass upon the relative merit of Spanish and foreign plays, inasmuch as the latter can claim familiarity only with the French theater. There is no evidence that Nipho himself had ever been outside of Spain, and certainly since 1742, when he published *The Deceptions of Madrid and Snares of Its Inhabitants,* his numerous publications were evidence of a constant residence in the capital. Writing under his own name he could claim no firsthand acquaintance with any theater except that of his native land, and any judgment he might make of the relative merit of that theater would be discredited. It is, therefore, possible that in order to give weight to a defense of the Spanish theater he chose to represent it as coming from one whose direct acquaintance with the European theater far exceeded that of Clavijo y Fajardo or any of his followers.

The author says he would never have determined to take up his pen against the *Pensador* if he had not heard repeatedly that the latter was treating the Spanish theater scornfully, and that, not content with violent condemnation of Spanish comedies, he was branding as barbarous all those who went to see them. Even then he would have overlooked his arrogance had he not feared that his ridiculous criticism of contemporary plays might lead the youth of the land to regard all Spanish drama with contempt, without making the proper distinction between the good and the bad. The *Pensador*, he says, leaves the impression that no good play has ever been written in Spain and compares the bad plays he censures to *The Annals of Baronio*. The author of *The Spanish Nation Defended* apparently started his work shortly after the publication of *Thought III* and gives no evidence of having read the remaining thoughts, since no reference is made to any of the others, even though several of them contained dramatic criticism.

Early in the first *Discourse* we find what Miss McClelland calls Nipho's clear and complete "declaration of faith":

> I did not fail, nor do I fail today, to find pleasure in reading the plays of the French, Italian, English, and German theaters; but although they have marvelous beauties, truths, and other prerogatives which are attributed to them by the *críticos de moda* who, passing over many imperfections which they are incapable of recognizing or of which they affect ignorance, busy themselves solely with finding defects in the Spanish theater, I say, and I shall prove my assertion, that I find Spanish comedies much more perfect, original, and worthy of esteem than those of foreign nations. Notwithstanding the idea that was impressed upon my mind by the beauties I have seen in such fine countries of Europe, I confess that when I returned to Spain I felt a secret joy in my heart, believing myself fortunate to live among my beloved fellow-countrymen and to see our comedies again; but as there is no pleasure in this life that is not mixed with sorrow, all my contentment was soured when I heard that Spaniards were being called barbarous because they like the inimitable comedies of Lope de Vega, Calderón, Rojas, Moreto, Molina, Diamante, Candamo, and many others. Moved by a certain impulse of patriotism and by a spirit of pure grief, I exclaimed: "If they call barbarous the natives of this country, who have not seen the theaters of France, Italy, Germany, and England, because they are fond of their exquisite theater, what will the new critics say of me if they find out that, after having seen so many beauties, I still maintain my affection for Spanish comedies? . . . I say in the first place that the three unities so extolled but misunderstood are not included among the essential rules of the theater, and that it is permissible to violate them and even to sacrifice them to pleasure when they prevent the realization of the beauties and graces that a subject may contain in itself.[27]

Here the author deals directly with the thorny question of the unities. If Nipho had expressed in the *Diario extranjero* or in works subsequent to the publication of *The Spanish Nation Defended* a similar attitude toward the unities, this statement could with more reason be considered his "declaration of faith"; but in none of these works do we find anything that approximates a definite stand on this subject; nor do we find in his other works the term "inimitable" applied to the plays of Golden Age dramatists. As we have seen, he was far from giving unqualified praise in the *Diario extranjero* even to Lope de Vega and Calderón. In his review of the latter's *Emotions of Hatred and Love,* which he considered typical of this dramatist's plays in its mixture of wisdom and absurdity, in its excellent diction and its impossible plot, there is no suggestion of the unrestrained admiration that characterizes every reference to him in *The Spanish Nation Defended.*

The author of this work proposes to prove not only that the unities are not necessary for dramatic excellence, but also that the beautiful comedies of the Spanish theater have never been equaled either in ancient or in modern times, and that France and other nations have freely admitted their indebtedness to the Spanish theater. He will prove his assertions, not by recourse to native writers, but by the authority of those very foreigners whom the deserters of the Spanish theater hold in such high esteem. Indeed, throughout the two discourses he makes such extensive use of French sources that it is difficult to determine where he is expressing his own ideas and where he is merely paraphrasing the ideas of French critics. In France, as we have seen, the neo-classic rules were being subjected to careful scrutiny, and many writers were expressing their disapproval of a rigid interpretation of these rules. The author, it must be admitted, has done a rather thorough job of examining the critical works of Corneille, Voltaire, Fontenelle, Saint-Evremond, and particularly of Houdard de La Motte, in all of which he finds varying degrees of dissatisfaction with the hampering restrictions of the rules. He takes particular satisfaction in citing the words of "the great Corneille, the father of the French theater" in the preface to his *Clitandre:*

> ... If I have held this play within the rule of the unity of one day, it is not because I repent not having done so in the *Mélite,* or because I have resolved henceforth to conform to this exact limitation. Today some worship this rule; many make light of it. For my part I say that I have only wished to demonstrate that if I depart from it, it is not because I am unfamiliar with it, but because it does not suit me.[28]

M. Duval, another great French dramatic poet and a contempo

rary of Corneille, he says, ridiculed the unities of time and place in the preface to his *Agarita;* and more recently M. de Fontenelle had admitted in his *Reflections on Poetics* that these unities should be observed when the subject permitted it, but that when the matter treated could not be brought within such narrow limits, it was necessary to deviate from the rules to some extent and to endure their breach patiently, since in themselves they were not very important or necessary.

The author notes that even Voltaire, who was the most outspoken exponent of regularity, confessed that at times greater beauty could be attained by the breach of the rules than by their observance. Most of the ideas the author of *The Spanish Nation Defended* expresses relative to the unities are direct translations taken from Houdard de La Motte's *The Three Unities and the Unity of Interest,* of which he gives a rather complete digest. Even though, he says, there are a number of copies of this work in Madrid, he does not have it before him as he writes and depends entirely upon his memory. La Motte wrote, the author says, to free the French theater from "the yoke, or superstitious servitude to the unities,"[29] maintaining that a strict adherence to the unity of place was inconsistent with the principle of verisimilitude because all the parts of an action could not occur in one place. The scene changes frequently in operas, and such changes serve to strengthen rather than destroy the illusion. The unity of time, the French critic asserts, is no more rational than the unity of place, particularly if it is applied rigidly. Recognizing the difficulty of limiting the action to one or two hours, critics have been willing to stretch the time to twenty-four. La Motte objects that there are many subjects which cannot be restricted even to this period, but says nothing to indicate that he would favor any extended lapse of time between acts. The author of *The Spanish Nation Defended* does not attempt to prove that La Motte or any other French critic favors the complete disregard for the unities of time and place which characterized so much of Golden Age drama. He realizes that even such latitude as La Motte advocates is inconsistent with his own practice, for in all his plays he observes the rules scrupulously. The author explains this inconsistency by saying that "in France, everyone, even the sovereign himself, is subjected to the rule of fashion."[30]

In many cases it is difficult to determine whether the author is quoting, paraphrasing, or expressing his own ideas. For instance, he begins his discussion of the unities with the following declaration, which is only a restatement of the ideas of La Motte:

... The three unities not only are not essential but are not even necessary. It is the office of the poet's genius to know when it is fitting to observe them in the interest of verisimilitude. The man of taste never allows himself to be chained; he listens to the voice of the rules, but follows his imagination.... I am not endeavoring to destroy the rules that have been established for the composition of works of genius; from such an idea I am far removed. Although I know quite well that they do not give genius to those who lack it, I recognize no less the importance and necessity of establishing rules to prevent the confusion of things in imitation of those irregularities so censured by Horace; because when one lacks principles, he is capable of all manner of extravagance.[31]

It is necessary, he says, to compare the rules with each other, and to determine which should be preferred in the event it is necessary to make a choice.

As was the practice among neo-classic critics, the author of *The Spanish Nation Defended* takes Aristotle and Horace as his points of departure. About the former's *Poetics* he says:

Aristotle formed his plan of the rules of dramatic poetry from long and serious reflection on the works of contemporary poets. Considering these rules with prudence, one notices that they were made only for the purpose of reducing nature to a method, in order that poets might be able to follow it step by step and not lose sight of its tracks. By observing the rules one is able to give things harmony, proportion, and naturalness.[32]

His position on the rules formulated by Aristotle is essentially the same as that of Luzán, Nasarre, Montiano, and, for that matter, of all the neo-classicists. These rules, he says, "are based on judgment and reason, rather than on authority and example." Although Aristotle wrote in a very solid manner in his *Poetics*, his order is inexact and inconsistent. The author has the same criticism of the "beautiful precepts" of Horace. Both of these poetics, in his opinion, "are not so much a method for composing good works as instruction on how to avoid writing bad ones."[33]

The author agrees with Horace that the action should be unified and simple. There may be subordinate actions, he continues, but these must be so linked with the main action that they will not destroy the unity of the whole or detract from the continuity of interest. The action should be simple in order that it may be easily followed; but in spite of its simplicity, it should be sufficiently diver-sified to hold the interest of the spectators. At this point he pauses to pay tribute to the great Spanish poets for their skilful handling of plot.

He bases his arguments against a rigid interpretation of the uni-ties of time and place upon that same principle of verisimilitude which the neo-classicists were so fond of invoking. It is clear, how-ever, that he opposes any flagrant violation of these unities, and favors only a reasonable modification in the interest of verisimilitude.

The unities of *time* and *place* are neither essential nor important to the extent that some claim: this depends upon the genius of the poet, who may sacrifice them at his discretion, provided he conforms to the most exact verisimilitude; because no one can ever approve that some persons who are supposed to be in Germany and others who are supposed to be in Italy should appear on the same stage; not only making the theater as large as the whole earth, but endeavoring to make a fixed place repre-sent in the same hour things so distant with no cause whatsoever for such a prodigious variation.[34]

As further evidence that the author is recommending only a moder-ate relaxation of the unity of place, we may consider the one example he cites from the English theater. After saying that English poets sacrifice this unity whenever they consider such a sacrifice conven-ient, he backs up his assertion only with Murphy's comedy *The Apprentice,* which he says was performed a short time before with astonishing success at Drury-Lane Theater in London. As an evi-dence of the complete violation of the unity of place in this comedy, he says that a part of the action takes place in Wingate Castle, the scene then changes to another street where the apothecary lives, and the rest of the action occurs in the jail.[35] Such a moderate infrac-tion of the unity of place would have met with no marked dis-approval, however, on the part of Luzán, Nasarre, or Velázquez, and probably would have been tolerated even by the *Pensador.*

After his assertion that so long as verisimilitude is observed the unity of time is purely arbitrary and without authority, it is some-what surprising to find that he does not attempt to justify the free-dom of Golden Age dramatists, but confines his discussion to the various interpretations that have been given to Aristotle's "period of the sun," and concludes by saying that the Greek philosopher cer-tainly never meant to limit the action of a play to the time of performance.[36]

In his criticism of *Russian Resemblance* Nipho had condemned the play partly on the basis of its transgression of the unities of time and place, although his objections are directed only at excessive changes. He speaks of "the improprieties of too little and too much action, and of making time run and halt" in violation of the unity of time. Particularly does he object to the fact that the action moves "through palaces and gardens, forests and graveyards with almost no distinction of scenes," which, he says, alters ridiculously the unity of place. While it is not difficult to reconcile these statements with the position taken on the unities by the author of *The Spanish Nation Defended,* Nipho's declaration in the *Diario extranjero* that "since all of our comedies are defective in this respect," the infractions of the unities of time and place in *Russian Resemblance,* "if not tolerable, at least (since those who are able do not remedy them) deserve some kind of passport,"[37] is hardly consistent with the unqualified praise lavished upon Golden Age drama in *The Spanish Nation Defended,* and with the complete absence of any criticism in that work of the glaring infractions that characterize the plays of that period.

Although the author boasts in his foreword to the first discourse that he will prove with French testimony that Spanish comedies are not only original, but the best in Europe, he comes to the end of this part without having given sufficient evidence to support his assertion. He now proposes in the second discourse to trace "with propriety and exactitude the development of the theaters of Greece, Rome, Italy, England, and France,"[38] in order to show by comparison the superiority of the Spanish theater. The great Spanish poets, he says, preferred not to imitate the Greeks, but to compete with them, and, for this reason, have a beauty of their own. On the contrary, Roman taste was a more or less perfect copy of the Greek; Italian taste in the time of Leo X was only a copy of the Greek and Roman; and the most favorable thing that can be said of French taste is that it is a happy combination of the Greek, Roman, and Italian, altered only by the influence of climate, government, and manners. The author devotes five pages to the theater of the Greeks; less than two to the theater of the Romans; four pages to the Italian theater; and six pages to the English. All of this discussion is accurate in the main, but superficial. The author seems content to show his erudition and makes no attempt to compare these theaters with the Spanish in support of his thesis. He devotes twenty-six pages to the theater of France, which is, after all, a natural allotment of space, since his discourses were intended as an answer to those Spaniards who had shown themselves so keenly sensitive to French criticism.

Although the *Pensador* has chosen as representative of the Spanish theater one of its worst contemporary comedies, the duration of which he compares to the *Annals of Baronio*, the author of *The Spanish Nation Defended* says he will not stoop to such tactics, but will pass over in silence the entire production of the French theater of the fifteenth and sixteenth centuries when France had as yet produced nothing worth while. He will completely ignore Jodelle, Rotrou, Garnier, Hardy, and Mairet, who were the immediate predecessors of Corneille. This great poet and sublime talent, he says, "was the first who gave a rational form to the French theater, carrying it on the wings of his prodigious genius to the highest pinnacle of perfection."[39] His praise of Corneille paves the way for the assertion that this author achieved his greatest success with a tragedy borrowed from one of the inferior plays of the Spanish theater. What must be the nature of our good plays, he asks, if a reworking of Guillén de Castro's play, *The Youth of the Cid*, which was below the Golden Age average, could win such acclaim in France?[40]

He concedes more originality to Corneille than to Racine and suggests that Racine "probably would not have been what he was, if Corneille had not preceded him."[41] Although he does not deny "the seductive graces, and the sweet eloquence" of Racine, he criticizes his tragedies for their sameness. "Almost all his plays," he says, "are directed toward the same goal: a declaration of love, a rupture of relations, a reconciliation, and a show of jealousy."[42] Inasmuch as the author immediately cites Saint-Evremond as the first who called attention to this defect in Racine's plays, it may be assumed that his remarks are largely an echo of this critic's ideas, rather than the result of independent study. Saint-Evremond, he says, claimed that Corneille "was the only one who possessed the good taste of antiquity,"[43] and later Voltaire confirmed this opinion in his *Essay on Poetics*, acknowledging that in France tragedies "are conversations, rather than the representation of an action." According to Voltaire the excessive delicacy of the French forced them to give in narration what should have been presented to the eye. Saint-Evremond accused the French theater of failing to produce any strong impression, and added that what should arouse pity only causes a feeling of tenderness. The author of *The Spanish Nation Defended* agrees with Voltaire that French dramatists are afraid to present new types of plays to a nation "accustomed to consider ridiculous anything that departs from accepted usage."[44]

The author doubts that tragedy will ever be successfully introduced upon the Spanish stage. This he infers from the example of Rome, whose two million inhabitants, because of their grave, circumspect, and retired life, never favored this genre. How could Spaniards, who are so similar to the Romans in their way of life, care for tragedy? In the situation in which Spain finds herself, people go to the theater to laugh, not to cry. Even if tragedy could be acclimated in Spain, he is convinced that plays written in the manner of Racine would be detrimental, although he pays tribute to his beautiful versification and noble thoughts. Tragedy, he says, should incite love for virtue and accustom men to take up arms in its defense. It should offer great examples of patience, constancy, and zeal, in the manner of Greek tragedy. In Racine's plays, on the contrary, the characters, although virtuous, are too commonplace. They have a softening effect upon the spirit, and produce in the spectators a feeling of weakness and discouragement. Although the author is in general agreement with Aristotle that tragedy makes men modest and compassionate by showing them the unforeseen misfortunes that befall even those of the highest rank, he warns of the danger that, through tragedy, men may be led to the other extreme and become too timid or too compassionate.[45] Aristotle, he says, recognized two defects in man that need correction: pride and hardness of heart. In view of the fact that Spaniards are by nature compassionate, the author believes tragedy could be used effectively in Spain to cure the above weaknesses. At this point he pauses to pay a tribute to Montiano for having opened the way for the cultivation of this genre in Spain:

... If we consider this matter as philosophers and as politicians, and are mindful of the use that our people make of their pity and compassion, it will be easy to show that a remedy such as tragedy would serve to cure them of the defects we have mentioned. The philosophy of the theater is to correct man with great examples. For this reason we should give grateful homage and applause to the studious application and noble labor of one of our academicians who gave us two tragedies, with which he opened the road for the composition of such works by showing with all clarity in the discourse which precedes one of them the glory that genius acquires by dedicating itself to the tragic poem; but we should not become prejudiced in favor of the new system upon which a great number of French tragedies base their narrowness and their excellence. The dawn of tragedy introduced into Spain by our academician would have satisfied completely the desires of the erudite if he had observed the taste of antiquity somewhat more closely.[46]

The ancients, he says, recognized that tragedy should be restricted to the representation of great objects of terror and pity. The use of any other emotion serves only to degrade it and deprive it of its majesty. Particularly will this be so if tragedy turns from fear and pity to avail itself of love, which, because of its burlesque character, is ill suited to the seriousness that befits this genre. As though oblivious to the fact that Golden Age drama in Spain almost invariably represented a mixture of genres and made use of love as the dominant motif even in those plays which were essentially tragic in nature, the author continues:

... In fact, tragedies mixed with gallantry never produce the admirable effect of Greek tragedies. The ancients recognized the exclusive nature of this genre and never mixed gallantry and love except in comedy, because love is of such a character that it always detracts from that air and heroic circumspection which are essential to tragedy.[47]

The author apparently chooses to consider all Golden Age plays as comedies, for he adds that "love has sufficiently established its jurisdiction in our comedies, and therefore nothing should induce those authors who wish to cultivate the taste for the heroic to mix love in their tragedies."[48] Having condemned Racine as too effeminate, he finds that Crebillon approaches more nearly the taste of the ancients. The tragedies of the latter, he says, "are clothed with a lofty grandeur; but without falling short of the heroic, they inspire terror and pity, which are the two principal functions of tragedy."[49] The tragedies of many authors, however, are so filled with gallantry that they produce no effect whatsoever.

Like most Spaniards of his day, the author of *The Spanish Nation Defended* found himself in an embarrassing position in evaluating the works of Voltaire. He recognizes the relative merit of Voltaire's tragedies, but at the same time that he praises his genius, he feels impelled to condemn his religious views:

It is necessary to make an exception among the moderns of M. Voltaire, who, in addition to his accomplishments in tragedy and the magic power of his style, has embraced many branches of the sciences with great success; but it is a matter of pity and grief that he should have caused the Christian religion so much concern, and that he should have placed upon it the sad necessity of reproving him and of condemning some of his errors, the stains of which it is almost impossible for him to wash away.[50]

In his opinion comedy is more popular than tragedy in all countries because it deals with things known to everyone, while tragedy concerns itself with subjects removed from common knowledge. Inasmuch as comedy takes as its model public manners, it must vary as these manners vary. If critics will study Spanish life of the past century, they will find that Lope, Calderón, and their followers gave an accurate picture of their time.

In addition to cultivating the three basic types of comedy— comedy of character, comedy of situation, and comedy of emotion— Spaniards have invented another type, a comedy of intrigue, "the ingenious comedy of Spain." The revolutions which comedy experienced in its origin and the changes it has undergone have arisen from the nature of the peoples and their forms of government. This explains, he says, the peculiar characteristics of Spanish comedy.

For this reason (besides the many comedies of character, situation, and emotion, that we have) we, who affect in our manners a haughty gravity and in our sentiments a romanesque or novelesque grandeur and among whom women live in a certain retirement, have developed another kind of comedy filled with intrigue and incidents, mistaken identities, disguises, intercepted letters, nocturnal adventures, and disguised princes, in the treatment of which subjects our poets have excelled all those of Europe.[51]

Foreigners, particularly the French, are fond of comedies of this type, but they lack the imagination to invent them, and for that reason must content themselves with copying the works of others. After citing a number of French comedies based upon Spanish plays of the preceding century, he says:

Many other plays, up to the number of two hundred, could be mentioned, which were translated into French by the best writers of the past century, the period in which France produced such prodigious talents in dramatic poetry; but those that have been mentioned will suffice to show how esteemed our comedies were and still are in France. What does not admit of doubt is that while Corneille, Racine, and Molière were still alive (the three columns of the French theater) all of these plays were translated, and at that time, probably because of their help, the French became so ingenious. This being so, why do their critics today insult Spain by calling her barbarous?[52]

The author of *The Spanish Nation Defended* is doing here exactly what Nasarre had done fifteen years earlier. Spaniards, both nationalists and neo-classicists, continued to find new evidence of French borrowing from the Spanish theater during the seventeenth century. The author probably was not aware of the extent to which Thomas Corneille, Scarron, Lesage, and others had freely admitted this indebtedness in the prefaces of their works. He has promised to prove with French testimony that "Spanish comedies are not only original, but the best in Europe and for that reason the famous Spanish poets should be praised rather than censured." To accomplish this purpose he has recourse first to various statements by Voltaire, whom he calls "the right eye of the critics of the Spanish theater." These statements are taken principally from the *Essay on Epic Poetry*, and are not directly in point. The frank recognition on the part of Voltaire of the indebtedness of the French to the Spanish theater is to be found in his prefaces to the works of Corneille, which had not appeared in 1763. What satisfaction the author would have derived from the following statement by Voltaire in his preface to the *Cid!*

When Corneille wrote the *Cid*, the Spaniards exercised the same influence upon all the theaters of Europe that they did in their politics; their taste, as well as their political power, was dominant; and even in Italy their comedies, or tragi-comedies, were given preference by the nation that had produced the *Aminte* and the *Pastor fido,* and which, inasmuch as it had been the first to cultivate the arts, seemed fitted to give laws to literature rather than to receive them.

However it may be, people prided themselves then upon knowing Spanish as they pride themselves today upon speaking French. It was the language of the court of Vienna, of Bavaria, of Brussels, of Naples, and of Milan. The marriage of Louis XIII to the daughter of Felipe III had made the Spanish language so fashionable that is was almost a disgrace at that time for men of letters not to know it. The greater part of our comedies were imitated from the theater of Madrid.[53]

He bases his claim of the superiority of Spanish comedies principally, however, upon the statement that Corneille, "the great Corneille, that illustrious genius, restorer and father of the French theater," makes in the dedication and the prologue to his comedy, *The Liar,* and takes pleasure in quoting the former in its entirety:

Considering that I owed my first reputation to the comic genre, I could not abandon it without a kind of ingratitude. It is true that when I took the risk of leaving it, I did not dare to rely upon my own strength; and in order to elevate myself to tragic dignity, I sought the aid of the great Seneca, from whom I borrowed all that which is rare and unusual in his *Medea;* for this reason, when I determined to return from the heroic to the natural and simple, I did not dare to descend from such a height without relying upon a good guide, and, for that reason, I allowed myself to be led by the ever famous Lope de Vega, fearing to lose my way in the web of intrigue spun by my *Liar.* This play, in short, is nothing but a simple copy of an excellent original, which Lope de Vega published with the title of *Truth Suspect;** and relying upon Horace's statement that poets, like painters, may take any liberties they wish, I thought that, although our two nations were at war, it was permissible for me to have business dealings with Spain. If this kind of commerce is a crime, I have been guilty of such for a long time. I am not saying this because of the *Cid* alone, which I composed with the aid of D. Guillén de Castro, but also because of the *Medea,* which I have just cited, and because of *Pompey* itself, since, thinking to avail myself of the aid of two Latins, I found myself being helped by two Spaniards, Séneca and Lucanus, for both were natives of Córdoba. Those who were unwilling to approve my dealings or understanding with our enemies at that time, will approve, at least, that I make raids upon their Parnassus, and whether this is considered as a pillage or as a loan, I am satisfied with this kind of plundering. At any rate, my intention is that this shall not be the last robbery that I shall commit upon the Spaniards.[54]

The author of *The Spanish Nation Defended* cites also with great satisfaction the following tribute Corneille pays to the genius of the Spanish author:

... If I may be allowed to say frankly what I feel about a thing in which I have so little part, I shall confess that the invention of this comedy by Lope has won my heart to such an extent that I find nothing that so suits my taste or is comparable in this genre either among the ancients or the moderns. This comedy by Lope de Vega is completely ingenious from beginning to end, and the incidents are as proper as they are amusing. This is so true that one would need to have a very ill-humored temperament to disapprove of the economy and conduct of this play and not enjoy its performance.[55]

Feeling that he has adequately proven his point, the author passes to a brief discussion of the merits of Spanish actors. At this time an effort was being made in Spain to introduce French technique in what was called "declamation," which embraced every

*Corneille was unaware at this time that Ruiz de Alarcón was the real author of *Truth Suspect.*

phase of acting. He concludes that even if French declamation were superior, which he does not admit, it would never be acceptable to Spanish ears. He supports his contention that Spanish recitation is more natural than French by citing an incident that has just occurred in Madrid:

A Frenchman, who recently came to Madrid, . . . saw himself obliged to witness the performance of our comedies; and the recitation of almost all our actors and actresses pleased him very much. Some days later, by chance, or through curiosity, he went to the rehearsal of a much heralded tragedy, where some fellow was making formidable efforts, and terrible mechanical gestures, in order to teach our actors the supposed new French method of declamation. Our good French officer was very much displeased to see that, although the Spanish manner of acting was the best and most natural in Europe, they were trying to replace it with another that was not only inferior, but violent, impertinent, and completely unnatural.[56]

The author defends the *Autos Sacramentales* by claiming that all the nations of Europe have been fond of allegory, but he does not try to establish any definite connection or show any similarity between the allegorical plays of the rest of Europe and the peculiar type represented by the Spanish *Autos*. To meet the objection that the most sacred roles are often played by the most immoral actors and actresses, he suggests somewhat facetiously, it seems, that even this objection could be overcome by requiring the actors and actresses, "who are to represent saints or biblical characters in the *Autos*, to perform Christian acts for a period of a week prior to the performances, confessing and taking communion, in order to be able to play their roles decently and with respect."[57]

The principal value of *The Spanish Nation Defended* lies, not in its defense of Golden Age comedy, but in the fact that it served to acquaint the reading public with the changes that had taken place in dramatic criticism in France. Just as Luzán's *Poetics* had informed Spaniards of all the critical works that had appeared in Italy and in France from the beginning of the Renaissance to the opening of the eighteenth century, so this work made available the ideas of Fontenelle, Saint-Evremond, Houdard de La Motte, and Voltaire. It may be said that it "brought Spanish criticism up to date."

Probably no one in Madrid was more familiar with the theater in all of its aspects than Nipho. In the *Diario extranjero* he had initiated theatrical reviews in Spain, and many of his articles had dealt with actors and with their problems. As a rigid moralist he had added his voice to those who cried out against the prevailing immorality in the theater; but he differed from them in that he believed the evils could to a large extent be eradicated by increasing the remuneration of the actors. He admitted that the theater in Spain "as it is found today should be not only reformed, but entirely abolished." His solution was for the government to assume complete control of the theaters and to pay the actors a salary that would enable them to live decently and comfortably. In this way they would not be dependent upon the attendance at the plays and the result would be

... a double benefit for the theater in the fact that the actors themselves would be more attentive to their obligation and more subject to law; they would provoke fewer scandals, because one who has what he needs ... will not likely abandon himself to obstreperous vices. Today an actor or actress who has only the income derived from performances scarcely has enough to buy a coarse cloth coat, because what he spends on wigs and other incidentals consumes not only what he earns but somewhat more.[58]

Nipho had commented frequently in the *Diario extranjero* upon the quality of acting on the Spanish stage and had particularly praised José Espejo and Nicolás de La Calle for their performance in Calderón's *Ladies Also Have a Code of Honor*, with which the theater of the Cruz opened the season of 1763-64. To Nipho the earnestness and vigor with which these two actors struggled on the stage represented the height of dramatic art. "This is the way for actors to play their roles, truly imbued with the spirit of the characters that are being represented, and to fulfil the rigorous laws of their profession that require that an actor make a lie pass for truth and fiction for reality."[59] The author's most flattering remarks were reserved, however, for the young actress, María Ladvenant, whose scandalous life did not prevent her from winning recognition as one of the outstanding actresses of the eighteenth century.

Nipho's interest in the theater at this time was not confined to dramatic criticism, but was also evidenced by the composition of an allegorical and satirical *sainete*, entitled *The Tribunal of Dramatic Poetry*, to accompany the comedy *A House with Two Doors Is Difficult to Guard*, by Calderón, with which the winter season of 1763 opened, and by a translation and adaptation of an opera by Metastasio with the title *Hipsípile, Princess of Memnos*. This opera, which was turned into a comedy, was by far the most successful play of the season, having a run of twenty-one consecutive days, while the plays of Calderón, Moreto, Montalban, Rojas Zorilla, and other Golden Age dramatists were enjoying runs of from two to five days. In view of Nipho's activity and his firsthand knowledge of the theater and its problems, it is not surprising that when the government decided to take an active part in the control of the theater it should choose him to draw up a plan for reform. This plan, which was never put into effect, concerned itself primarily with the improvement of acting and theatrical management, and gave little attention to dramatic precepts. Nipho's suggestions for the selection and training of actors, the supervision of rehearsals, the formation of two groups of actors in each theater that could alternate in the performance of plays (thereby enabling each group to have sufficient time to learn and practice new roles), careful research on the part of the producers to avoid inaccuracies and anachronisms in dress and scenery, and the establishment of a fund to provide for actors during periods of sickness or enforced idleness, were far in advance of his time. It seems that Spanish actors were never allowed enough time to learn their roles, for we are told that the prompter was often the most active member of the company. Frequent references to this deficiency on the part of the actors are found in the *Diario de Madrid*, the *Correo de Madrid*, and other periodicals in the latter half of the century.

1. *Diario extranjero*, June 7, 1763.
2. *Ibid.*, p. 40.
3. *Ibid.*, p. 170.
4. Marcelino Menéndez y Pelayo, *op. cit.*, III, 283.
5. *Diario extranjero*, "Noticias de Moda," April 12, 1763.
6. *Ibid.*
7. *Diario extranjero*, p. 27.
8. *Ibid.*, p. 172.
9. Eugenio Hartzenbusch, *Apuntes para un catálogo de periódicos madrileños desde el año 1661 al 1870 (Madrid, 1894)*, pp. 8-9.
10. *Diario extranjero*, April 8, 1763.
11. *El Escritor sin título*, 1763, p. 57. See Ada M. Coe, *Catálogo bibliográfico y crítico de las comedias anunciadas en los periódicos de Madrid desde 1661 hasta 1819*

(Baltimore: Johns Hopkins Press, 1933), p. 177.
12. I. L. McClelland, *The Origins of the Romantic Movement in Spain* (Liverpool, 1937).
13. *Ibid.*, p. 74.
14. *La nación española defendida de los insultos del Pensador y sus secuaces.* Dalo al público D. Francisco Mariano Nipho (Madrid, 1764).
15. *Ibid.*, pp. 3-5.
16. Sebastián y Latre, "Prólogo del autor," *Ensayo sobre el teatro español* (Saragoza, 1772).
17. Cueto, *Poetas líricos del siglo XVIII* (*B.A.E.*, III, 512). The italics are mine.
18. Cotarelo y Mori, *Don Ramón de la Cruz y sus obras* (Madrid, 1899), p. 17, "Note."

19. *Ibid.*, p. 89.
20. *Ibid.*, p. 90.
21. *Ibid.*
22. *Ibid.*, p. 92.
23. *La nación española defendida*, Discurso segundo, p. 196.
24. *El Belianís Literario*, 1765, Número VI, p. 149.
25. *Ibid.*, p. 150.
26. *Ibid.*, p. 151.
27. *La nación española defendida*, Discurso primero, pp. 13-15.
28. *Ibid.*, p. 84.
29. *Ibid.*, p. 87.
30. *Ibid.*, p. 100.
31. *Ibid.*, pp. 70-71.
32. *Ibid.*, p. 72.
33. *Ibid.*
34. *Ibid.*, p. 80.
35. *Ibid.*, p. 83.
36. *Ibid.*, p. 81.
37. McClelland, *op. cit.*, p. 77, footnote.
38. *La nación española defendida*, p. 109.

39. *Ibid.*, p. 130.
40. *Ibid.*, p. 131.
41. *Ibid.*, p. 138.
42. *Ibid.*
43. *Ibid.*, p. 140.
44. *Ibid.*, p. 141.
45. *Ibid.*, p. 144.
46. *Ibid.*, p. 146.
47. *Ibid.*, pp. 148-49.
48. *Ibid.*, p. 149.
49. *Ibid.*
50. *Ibid.*, p. 150.
51. *Ibid.*, p. 171.
52. *Ibid.*, p. 180.
53. Pierre Corneille, "Le Cid, Préface de Voltaire," *Oeuvres* (Paris, 1849).
54. *La nación española defendida*, pp. 179-80.
55. *Ibid.*, p. 184.
56. *Ibid.*, p. 206.
57. *Ibid.*, p. 212.
58. *Diario extranjero*, pp. 251-52.
59. *Ibid.*, p. 27.

VI

Nicolás Fernández de Moratín

THE YEARS 1762 and 1763 were particularly significant for neo-classicism in Spain, for in those years Clavijo y Fajardo published the first numbers of the *Pensador;* Sedano published *Jahel* (1763), an original Spanish tragedy in the manner of Montiano; and Nicolás Fernández de Moratín published three works that may be considered landmarks in the history of the movement: a comedy, *The Fashionable Lady* (1762); three pamphlets entitled *Censure of the Spanish Theater* (1762-63); and a tragedy, *Lucrecia* (1763).

Jahel, which Qualia calls a "frigid imitation of the Racinian sacred tragedy,"[1] is accompanied by a long preface in which the author prescribes rules for sacred drama and indulges in a typical neo-classic condemnation of the *comedia*. Sacred subjects, as they have been treated by Spanish dramatists, he says, have "violated truth, chronology, verisimilitude, and decency," and have been characterized by "violent interpretations, false information, insipid allegories, and extravagant metaphors." He has no hope that his tragedy will be accepted by the theater because "in Spain such works are not written to be performed, nor are they compatible with the monstrosities which have taken possession of the theaters, where art, regularity, and good taste are abominated or completely unknown and where confusion, indecency, pedantry, and barbarism hold full sway, sustained by an ancient, shameful, and intolerable tradition."[2]

Tomás de Iriarte, who, it must be admitted, was not an impartial judge, submerged the play with ridicule in his satire, "Give and Take" (1778):

Intelligent people, who saw that composition when it appeared in print, did it full justice. There is scarcely a person who remembers that such a tragedy was ever written or who has any desire to read it;

and only by tradition is it known that the play has only one defect, which is apparent from the first to the last scene, namely, complete frigidity.[3]

This tragedy, Iriarte says, is full of languid and interminable speeches. There is almost no character from the principal to the least important who does not have at least one of considerable length. "Jahel begins with a speech of ninety-one verses; her husband answers with another of one hundred and thirty-three, ninety of which are given consecutively with no pause whatsoever."[4]

Moratín's comedy, *The Fashionable Lady*,[5] represents the first attempt on the part of the neo-classicists to write a comedy in accordance with the rules. As we have seen, Montiano had written two tragedies, *Virginia* (1750) and *Ataulfo* (1753), accompanied by discourses in which he gave a history and a defense of tragedy in Spain and a careful analysis of *Virginia*. Nicolás Fernández de Moratín, according to his son, undertook the composition of his comedy "at the instigation of his friend, Montiano."[6] As in the case of the latter's works, the "Dissertation" that accompanied *The Fashionable Lady* is more important than the play itself, for, while the comedy was never performed, the "Dissertation" apparently was widely circulated. This work, more than any other exposition of neo-classic principles since Luzán, approaches the general tone and policy of that critic. The author abstains from the bitter and all-inclusive denunciation of Calderón de la Barca and of Lope de la Vega that had characterized the works of Nasarre and Velázquez, although he does not yield an inch in his disapproval of the irregularities of the Spanish theater. This represents a change of policy, if not of heart, from the denunciation of the *comedia* and of Calderón found in two satires composed in his youth, which he published in 1764 in *The Poet*, after his disapproval of the irregular theater had been given fresh impetus by the unfavorable reception accorded his attempt to set a standard for future comedies with *The Fashionable Lady*.

In his first satire he condemns the fundamental immorality of Calderón's theater: "Do you not notice how audaciously the youth of Spain, corrupted by the fertile inspiration of Calderón, throws off the bridle? Do you not see virtue always oppressed by his muse in the comic theater, and evil rewarded and applauded?"[7] In the second he gives a summary of all the censure the neo-classicists had hurled against the *comedia:*

You will see no semblance of truth represented, nor a single action finished in one place and at one time.

If it starts in Madrid, it ends in Flanders; years pass by the hundreds and the thousands, and one action stumbles upon another.

Old popular manners are mixed with the most modern, and the coarser they are the more they are esteemed.

Those who at the beginning are of tender years, at the middle are grown up, and at the end their legs tremble with age. . . .

Do not mention Terence and Plautus, for there are ignorant people here who scorn them because their style is simple.[8]

It is not surprising that when the author of these *Satires* gave warm praise in the "Dissertation" to some elements in the Spanish *comedia* and paid tribute to the native ability of Calderón, he succeeded in fooling no one. His real views at that time were too well known, and his injured attitude at the reception of *The Fashionable Lady* was somewhat incongruous.

However, when he wrote his comedy and the accompanying "Dissertation" he was inclined to be magnanimous, evidently realizing that the neo-classicists had been pursuing the wrong course. The attempts of such critics as Nasarre to whip the recalcitrants into line had failed. Not only the critics but the lowly public must be induced to support the new ideas if they were ever to become anything more than theory.

Like his predecessors, Nicolás Fernández de Moratín admits that he is impelled to action by a desire to vindicate his country from the attacks of foreign critics. In his initial paragraph he gives clear expression to his motives:

Although for one to throw himself into impossible tasks is rightly censured by the wise, there are passions so vehement that they confuse the mind and prevent it from recognizing the rashness of an undertaking. I recognize that mine are of such nature; but my love for my country is so great that in order to vindicate it in so far as I am able from the insults of foreigners, I expose myself openly to the insults of local critics and slanderers.[9]

He is well aware that it seems blasphemous to speak of perfecting a genre that has been cultivated by such men as Lope, Calderón, Moreto, Solís, and Candamo. Yet it is a fact that foreigners and even some natives ridicule the Spanish *comedia* and even affirm that the Spanish theater has not produced a single perfect comedy. Although Lope claimed to have composed six regular comedies, they are not

extant, and, by his own admission, all of his other plays are irregular
and therefore imperfect. Moratín does not consider the excuse given
by Lope to justify the irregularity of his theater worthy of the great
intellect of that genius, for he believes that, although the crowd may
applaud an irregular play, it would be no less willing to applaud one
written "according to art." In support of this conviction he recalls
instances that have come under his own observation where even
the crowd marveled that small children should become men in
the short space of three hours and that the garments worn by the
actors should last thirty or forty years. At this point, he voices
the criticism so frequently heard throughout the neo-classic controversy that the *comedia* invades the field of the epic in depicting
the past, present, and future.

Not only is it improper that a whole chronicle should be represented in the short space of three hours, but it is equally unfitting
that in such a short time the scene should shift twenty, thirty, or
more leagues from the place where it started: "This does not need
to be proved by authorities or subtleties; for it will seem impossible
to any man of judgment that, without moving from his seat, he can
see the façade of the New Palace, the Capitolio of Rome, and the
bay of Algiers."[10]

It will be observed that at no time do neo-classic critics condemn
a play for minor infractions of the unities; rather, they confine their
censure to flagrant violations. Had they been equally liberal in their
own application of these principles, they would surely have obviated
much of the adverse criticism that has been directed against their
plays and against the movement as a whole.

Moratín considers that the violation of the unity of action has
been responsible for the violation of the other unities: "for since they
have piled up in their comedies such a multitude of incidents, it has
been necessary to lengthen the duration and to travel many leagues
in order to unravel them all."[11] According to Menéndez y Pelayo,
this is the only statement in the "Dissertation" which reveals any
critical perspicacity, for it is "the only serious argument that has been
brought forth in support of the doctrine of the unities."[12]

The author of this preface anticipates the objection of the ignorant, who will call him "bold, rash, sacrilegious, blasphemous, and
unpatriotic," because he dares to censure authors who have won
world recognition.

In support of his contention that the crowd does not applaud comedies merely because they are irregular, he cites the example of Molière, whose comedies in the not distant past have been the admiration not only of the cultured class but even of the common people in France. The plays of Metastasio are applauded by the masses throughout Europe, and the common people flock to the theater in Italy to see the comedies of Goldoni. To please the public it is not necessary to abandon art, "and if some comedies or tragedies written without art have been well received, it is not necessarily because they are irregular; for if they had been written according to the rules of art, they would have been doubly applauded."[13]

Moratín frankly confesses that his ideas are not new, having already found expression in the works of Cascales, Cervantes, Luzán, Mayans y Siscar, and more recently in Montiano's discourse on tragedy in Spain. But since there has been no improvement in the Spanish theater and since "the few comedies that are produced today have the same defects, and even greater defects than the old," it seems that the efforts of these illustrious men have been in vain. A reiteration of the classic principles is, therefore, not out of place.

So numerous are the errors of the Spanish *comedia* that the scorn of foreigners is not without justification. The author enumerates some of the most frequent of these errors, frankly following the procedure of Luzán. After dealing with the various infractions of the principle of verisimilitude, he finds particularly culpable the failure of the *comedia* to fulfil its basic mission: the correction of vice.

After enumerating the irregularities of the *comedia*, by way of palliation the author pays a high tribute to the native ability of such men as Calderón, Lope, Solís, Rojas, Moreto, Candamo, and Montalbán:

... Who would not be pleased and extremely fascinated by the prodigious and natural fluency of the profound Calderón, through whose mouth the muses spoke so sweetly? Who does not admire the discretion of Solís, of Don Francisco de Rojas, of Don Agustín Moreto, of Candamo, of Montalbán, and many others? And what man can be so dull witted that he is not amazed by the natural facility and the sonorous elegance of the prolific Lope, who was so excellent in lyric poetry that he is not even excelled by Petrarch?[14]

The recognition of the merits of these men is made to prove that he has "no hatred, or envy for such eminent men, who did not abandon art through ignorance, but only through caprice and for the sake of novelty." Not all of their plays are completely defective, since there are many which, if not good, could with slight alteration be made so. Among the comedies the author of the "Dissertation" lists as relatively free from defects are *My Lady Comes First, The Pawns of Chance,* and *The Worst Is Not Always True* by Calderón. That Moratín's judgment in regard to these comedies was shared by later neo-classicists is indicated by various statements to be found in reviews of these plays which appeared in *El Memorial Literario* over twenty years later. In the November, 1785, number of that periodical there is a criticism of *My Lady Comes First,* in which the reviewer says: "The genius of Calderón is revealed in the intricate plot and clever solution, and it is fairly regular in time and place." About *The Pawns of Chance* the reviewer says in March, 1786: "The good plot and solution, and the comic situations that result from various mistaken identities, which are sustained until the end, place this in the number of regular and ingenious plays of Calderón that are always agreeable to the Spanish spectator." And in regard to *The Worst Is Not Always True,* we are told in the April, 1785, number of the *Memorial:* "This is one of the ingenious comedies of Calderón that are sufficiently regular in place, time, plot, solution, and action." All this is in marked contrast to the attitude of Nasarre, who would not admit that Calderón had ever produced anything worthy of commendation.

Having concluded the theoretical and critical part of this "Dissertation," the author says: "It only remains to give an example, and to see if these theoretical rules can be put into practice."[15] He therefore presents *The Fashionable Lady,* with no claim to setting himself up as a master, but with the sole desire of inciting others more capable than he to compose original comedies. He proceeds to make what he calls a disinterested criticism of his own comedy. He has chosen the subject, he says, because it seemed a proper and natural theme for comedy. He has intentionally left the beaten path where all the characters are "lovers, duelists, and bullies," although he has not entirely disregarded such characters "because they are characteristic and pleasing to the Spanish people." The moral is evident without the necessity of a multitude of axioms. Although such well-known authorities as Pierre Corneille and Luzán allow as the scene of the action an entire city and its outskirts, he has not wished to avail himself of such license, but has without violence restricted the action to a single room. The unity of time is so carefully observed "that the action lasts no longer than the performance," for, although he is aware that the action may extend through twenty-four hours, he has limited it to what seems to him more natural. He has avoided introducing a complicated plot, since the time and the fixed stage would not allow it. Nor will there be found in his comedy that "sublime and elegant style" so characteristic of the *comedia*, since, even if he were capable of rising to such heights, he would not deem such a style in keeping with the simplicity of comedy. He does not deny that there are faults in his work; but without boasting, he feels justified in saying that "few comedies will observe the precepts so religiously." He closes his "Dissertation" with the following plea, by means of which he evidently seeks to forestall in his case the adverse criticism that had greeted the attempt eleven years earlier by Montiano to produce a model tragedy:

> To correct my defects I do not need satires or nicknames. I shall be very grateful to anyone who, better informed than I, will point out my mistakes, and I shall publicly confess him to be my master, for I am not ashamed to learn. I hope my country will appreciate my intention, for I am exposing myself in order to defend it. If I have not succeeded, at least my intention was noble, and I shall be happy if some learned compatriot, stimulated by my example, will carry to perfection what I have so roughly started.[16]

This comedy is only of historical interest as representing the first attempt to carry out in an original comedy the theories which had been so often expressed since the time of Luzán. Even the most ardent neo-classic critics have not been willing to go beyond conceding to the author that his intention was, in his own words, "at least noble." In the execution, they have been unanimous in condemning the work as cold, devoid of technical merit, and completely lacking in comic force. This lack of merit is adequately attested by the evaluation given to the comedy by the author's son:

> This work . . . lacks comic force, propriety, and correctness in style; the defects of our old comedies combined with the violent regularity to which its author tried to subject it produced an imitation of uncertain character that could hardly have sustained itself on the stage if an attempt had ever been made to perform it.[17]

All the efforts of the author and his friends to present *The Fashionable Lady* in Madrid met with complete failure. Moratín, who attributed this failure to the opposition of the partisans of the national theater and particularly to that of Ramón de la Cruz, who was in virtual control of the theaters of Madrid, launched a vicious attack against the Spanish theater and its adherents in three articles, entitled *Desengaños al teatro español (Censure of the Spanish Theater).*[18] Whether rightly or wrongly, the neo-classicists blamed Ramón de la Cruz for preventing the performance of their plays and declared war upon him. In the first *Desengaño* Moratín is clearly referring to Don Ramón when he says:

> ...And bear in mind that it is not the members of the Royal Academy of Spain, nor those of the Academies of London or Paris, nor of the Arcadians of Rome, but the actors themselves and particularly the poetasters or composers of *sainetes* and *entremeses* who pass upon the merit of plays in Spain.[19]

Cotarelo y Mori attributes the conflict between Ramón de la Cruz and the neo-classicists, not to any fundamental difference in literary creed, but to the fact that the public received the *sainetes* of the former with enthusiasm and the regular plays of the latter with complete aversion. In his longer plays, he says, "Cruz was of their school; he also translated and imitated the French and made an effort to adjust himself to those highly vaunted *rules of art;* some of his *sainetes* themselves give clear indication of that moralizing tendency which the neo-classicists believed to be indispensable."[20]

In the first *Desengaño* Moratín also gives violent expression to that disapproval of the *comedia* which, in the "Dissertation," he had seen fit to temper with words of praise. Angered by the reception given his model comedy and no more able to stand criticism than the champions of the national school, he now loses his head completely and calls the Spanish theater "the school of evil, the mirror of lasciviousness, the picture of effrontery, the academy of impudence, insults, mischief, and rascality."[21] Following Nasarre, he calls Lope and Calderón the first and second corruptors of the Spanish theater, knowing full well that this accusation never failed to arouse the admirers of these authors to a feverish heat of indignation. As a striking example of the lack of verisimilitude and absurd style of Calderón's plays, he cites the opening lines of *Life Is a Dream,* and adds sarcastically:

> I should like to know whether a woman who falls headlong down a mountainside with her horse, instead of complaining about the places where she hurts, will say to him all those inappropriate pedantries, which

the audience does not understand any more than the horse. If some passionate lover of Calderón falls from his horse and lands on his ears, let him call him a "violent hippogriff" and he will see how it relieves him.[22]

In the second and third *Desengaños* the author goes to the aid of Clavijo y Fajardo, who in the *Pensador* had opened an attack upon the *Autos Sacramentales*. We see that Moratín has returned to the uncompromising attitude which characterized his earlier *Satires,* and which prompted Menéndez y Pelayo to call him "in theory the most violent, and the most furious of all those who at that time swore by the authority of Boileau."[23] In the second *Desengaño* he also defends himself against the persecution to which he expects to be subjected because of his remarks in the first:

I have committed no crime except to point out some defects in deference to truth for the honor of my country and to prove to foreigners that intelligent Spaniards do not approve such performances and that Don Pedro Calderón has no power of attorney to speak for Spanish literature. There are others alive and dead who surpass him; but, in payment for my efforts, you will see my ungrateful nation rise up angrily against me. The writers are already trimming their pens to overwhelm me with their satires and insults.[24]

The contents of the second and third *Desengaños* are adequately summarized in this statement by Moratín's son:

In the following discourses he proved that Calderón's *Autos,* so admired by the masses, should not be tolerated in a nation that prides itself upon being enlightened and catholic, both because of their abandonment of all the rules of drama, and because of their falsification of the dogmas of religion, the violence with which the text of the Holy Scripture is interpreted and adapted, and the very serious inconvenience of presenting to the view of the people, with all the illusion that the theater offers, actions, the dramatic interpretation of which degrades the majesty of the law and its high mysteries, worthy only to exist for our edification in sacred books or to be heard in the temple as a peculiar theme of its most eloquent ministers.[25]

Moratín especially ridicules the use of allegory, which is such an essential element in the *Autos:*

Is it possible for Spring to speak? Have you ever heard Appetite say a word? Do you know the timbre of the voice of the Rose? Can anyone ever think it possible for divine and human characters of remote centuries and from different nations to assemble and speak, as for example, the Supreme Trinity, the Devil, Saint Paul, Adam, Saint Augustine, Jeremiah, and others, committing in this manner horrible and insufferable anachronisms?[26]

As Menéndez y Pelayo points out, Moratín exaggerates the immediate effect of the *Desengaños* when he says that "the third *Desengaño* had hardly been published when the government banned the performance of *Autos*." The fact that they were not prohibited until some two years later, however, does not bely the importance of these discourses in the controversy.

After the failure of *The Fashionable Lady,* Moratín turned to tragedy and in 1763 published *Lucrecia,* with a short preliminary discourse on neo-classic tragedy. In this discourse he insists upon the complete conformity of his play to the unities and the difficulty of adjusting it to the rules. It is much easier, he says, to write a nonsensical and irregular play. He declares, as he did in the preface to *The Fashionable Lady,* that he is motivated by a desire to incite others more able than he to write regular plays. In the periodical *Aduana crítica* (1763) appeared an unfavorable review of the tragedy:

> According to the laws of drama this is not one of the best plots, since it is double in that the passions are confused and weakened, and excite neither terror nor pity, for the punishment of a perfidious person produces satisfaction and joy in view of an outraged innocence. The unities are not observed with the completeness the author claims, since the violence and the death of Lucrecia constitute a complete action, and, although it was the origin of the vengeance against the aggressor, his death and its manner make up a separate action. The unity of time also is not perfectly observed. . . . The language lacks the sublimity required in tragedy.[27]

The author of this review was Miguel de la Barrera, who remonstrated with the *Pensador* for its attacks on Lope and Calderón and rather halfheartedly defended the *Autos Sacramentales.* He takes no determined stand in the controversy between the neo-classicists and the champions of the national drama, for after affirming that "the unities of action, place, time, and character arise from the observation of nature and are necessary to achieve the illusion of reality," and that sins committed against these precepts deserve severe correction, he adds that "the other precepts, which were derived from the whims of the ancients, do not require a perpetual and universal obedience."[28]

Moratín was not to be deterred by the rejection of *The Fashion-*

able Lady and *Lucrecia*, and in 1770 offered another tragedy, *Hormesinda*, to the theater. According to his son Leandro Fernández de Moratín, this play was performed only through the influence of Aranda, the prime minister, "such was the opposition on the part of the actors to what they called the French style."[29] To prove the mistaken judgment of both actors and public the following incident is cited. When the play was read to the actors, those who were to play the leads questioned their ability to perform such roles, and Espejo, a good friend of Moratín, who was to play the part of Trasamundo, waited until he could speak to the author alone and said:

The tragedy is excellent, Señor Moratín, and worthy of your genius. For my part, I shall do all I can. But, tell me the truth. Why do you insist upon writing in the French manner? I don't say for you to take a single line away from the play; but it wouldn't be any trouble for you to add a couple of *graciosos*, would it?[30]

Moratín is reported to have grasped his hand, crying with laughter, and to have answered: "You are a good man, Uncle Espejo; study your role very, very carefully, and I will take the rest upon my conscience."[31]

In the opening scene of the tragedy we learn through a conversation between Hormesinda and her servant Elvira that Munuza, the Moorish governor of Jijon, has taken advantage of the absence of her brother, Pelayo, to force her to marry him. It appears that the Christians are living under the rule of the Moors but that the peace between them is unsteady. Through trickery Pelayo has been sent by Munuza to Córdoba where the Moors have been given orders to kill him. Munuza's plan fails and Pelayo returns. Hormesinda has resisted every amorous advance of the Moor and is his wife in name only. She anxiously awaits the return of her brother, confident that he will avenge her.

When Pelayo arrives he talks first to his betrothed, Gaudiosa, and to her father, Trasamundo. Before he sees his sister and, of course, before anyone has told him of her forced marriage, Gaudiosa requests that he give all the details of the defeat of the Spaniards by the Moors. This Pelayo does at great length, giving an account of the invasion, the final battle at Guadalete, and the last words of Roderick, the king of the Goths, in which he confessed that his lust had caused the downfall of Spain and commended his kingdom and its defense to Pelayo, as the son of Fávila. After Pelayo has finished his account, Trasamundo hints that a far more terrible thing has befallen him than his defeat by the Moors, but says that it would be better for him to find it out through Munuza.

Angry at his failure to win Hormesinda's love, the Moorish governor has planned a diabolical revenge, aided by the suggestions of his servant, Tulga. By means of a forged letter he convinces Pelayo, for whom he professes friendship, that his sister has yielded to an impure love and has dishonored his name during his absence. Tulga informs Munuza that the Spaniards are planning an uprising and are basing their hopes for success on the leadership of Pelayo. He suggests that Pelayo be induced to drink a toast to a peace treaty proposed by Munuza. The wine will, of course, be poisoned, and the Moorish governor will be free from a threat of rebellion and, by arranging that Pelayo himself order the execution of his sister, will discredit him in the eyes of his followers.

Pelayo proves to be incredibly stupid and refuses to listen to Hormesinda when she tries to tell him what Munuza has done. Seeing his sister in tears, he assumes that this is conclusive proof of her guilt. When his future father-in-law urges him to take vengeance, he thinks the old man is referring to the stain Hormesinda has cast upon his honor, although he is, of course, speaking of her forced marriage to Munuza and hopes in this way to incite Pelayo to lead an immediate rebellion against Moorish tyranny. Pelayo never seems to question for a moment the good faith of the Moor and prefers to believe him rather than to listen to his sister. Everything could have been cleared up immediately upon Pelayo's arrival if any one of Pelayo's friends, or Hormesinda herself, had ignored his remonstrances and blurted out the truth.

Munuza is finally unmasked in the fifth act, after Hormesinda has already been led away to be executed. Fortunately at this very moment a band of Cantabrian horsemen arrive, Hormesinda is saved, and Pelayo joins in the battle in time to prove his bravery and to kill Munuza with his own hands. Tulga is forced to drink the poison intended for Pelayo, and all the culprits receive their just reward. The plot ends happily with the promise that Pelayo will be successful in freeing Spain from the Moors.

The plot of this tragedy is so improbable and unnecessarily involved that neo-classic critics themselves were almost unanimous in their censure. The following statement by Tomás de Iriarte is by no means exaggerated:

In the plot of *Hormesinda*, in its thoughts, and in its style, the public has noted almost the same defects as the learned, and seldom has there been such unanimity among the intelligent and the unintelligent. . . . The principal part of a drama being the intrigue, the defects that stand out in *Hormesinda* can hardly be excused. One notices the lack of clarity and of explanation in the first scenes: Hormesinda's forced marriage to Munuza, with no information as to how it was effected; and Pelayo's trip to Córdoba, with no indication of the urgent motive that prompted it, or why he should play the role of ambassador. Another serious error is the unexpected credulity on the part of Pelayo, who with no other information than an account (and a very slight one) by a Moor whom he should not have trusted so much, and a few words Trasamundo has told him, does not hesitate to believe his sister guilty.[32]

It is inconceivable, Iriarte says, that Pelayo should have remained so long in ignorance of the facts:

In short, neither Fernández, nor Gaudiosa, nor Elvira, nor Trasamundo, nor Hormesinda herself . . . has the courage to manifest to him immediately the treachery of Munuza; so that from the beginning of the drama the audience forsees that the instant the hero takes the trouble to listen to any one of them he will be disillusioned, and that the plot is not solved as early as the fourth scene of the second act because the poet does not want it to be solved.[33]

Hormesinda was performed at the Príncipe by the company of Juan Ponce and lasted from the 12th to the 17th of February, 1770, with satisfactory receipts, but was never revived. Leandro Fernández de Moratín says that the play was a success in spite of the organized resistance of the partisans of the national school:

In fact, neither the corrupted taste of the public, nor the deadly announcements circulated by cheap poets who composed *tonadillas*, nor the words of sedition with which one of the most audacious pedants of the day stirred up the fearful mob of the *chorizos*, could prevent the play from being received with applause on its opening day and on the successive days of its performance.[34]

He attributes to this effort on the part of his father the original tragedies that began to be composed from that time on and affirms that "he disproved the absurd idea that Spaniards had no liking for tragedy, and, at the same time, confused the ignorant who considered it impossible for a play written with regularity and good taste to meet with the approval of the public in Madrid."[35]

For the theme of his third tragedy, *Guzmán the Good*, published in 1777, Moratín chose a subject that had already been treated in the Golden Age by Vélez de Guevara, with the title *The King Outweighs Blood*. In the earlier play the action does not start until the end of the second act, all of the first part being taken up with a confused medley of political intrigue. Moratín narrows the action to the struggle in the heart of Guzmán between his love for his son and his duty to his king. He follows the account found in the *Chronicles of the Kings of Castile*, which tells of the collaboration of the Moorish king, Aben Yacob, and Prince John in the siege of the frontier fortress of Tarifa and the defense of that city by Alfonso Pérez de Guzmán:

... And the prince captured the young son of Alfonso Pérez and sent a message to this Don Alfonso Pérez saying that, if he did not surrender the city to him, he would kill his son, and Don Alfonso answered that he would not surrender the city to him; that, as for his threat to kill his son, he himself would give him a sword with which to kill him, and, throwing his own sword over the wall, he said that he would rather have his son killed and five other sons, if he had them, than to surrender one city that he held in the name of the king, his lord; and Prince John, in his rage, ordered the son killed before his father's eyes; and with all this he was unable to take the city; and when the Moors, who were with Prince John, saw that he went to such extremes to take the city and could not do so, they lifted the siege and went back across the sea.[36]

Moratín removes Prince John entirely from the plot and gives his role to the Moor, Jacob Aben Juseph. He also adds a number of episodes to the bare account given in the chronicle, in an attempt to afford dramatic interest and to provide enough intrigue to hold the attention of a Spanish audience. The capture of the son, Don Pedro, is made to take place on the day of his wedding to Doña Blanca. Fatima, the daughter of Aben-Jacob, is represented as hopelessly in love with Don Pedro, and aids him to leave the Moorish encampment upon his promise to return to prison after he has seen his parents. Doña Blanca goes in disguise to the Moorish camp to offer herself as a prisoner in exchange of her husband's freedom. As a last and rather hasty attempt to complicate the plot Fatima is captured and Guzmán threatens to kill her if his son is executed, but finding himself unable to match the brutality of the Moor, allows her to go free. In Moratín's play Guzmán is not only torn between his love for his son and his duty to his king, but forced to resist the frenzied and tearful entreaties of his wife. Don Pedro also finds himself compelled to choose between his honor and his love for Doña Blanca.

The neo-classic critic Sempere y Guarinos, who wrote a review of this tragedy ten years after its publication, could find nothing to praise in it except the fact that it did not follow the prevailing practice of making tragedies end happily by punishing vice and rewarding virtue. This tragedy, he says, is not the best tragedy in the Spanish theater, and perhaps not even the best of those written by Moratín, for, in his opinion, *Hormesinda* is superior,

... because in *Guzmán* the constant pleas of the tearful Doña María, who seems an unworthy wife of such a great hero as Don Alfonso, far from causing any emotion, produce such boredom that the reader has difficulty in finishing the play. Moreover, the few episodes that are introduced, like Don Pedro's release from imprisonment, arranged by Fatima under his word of honor to return to her; the capture of Fatima herself; and the visit of Doña Blanca to the tent of Aben-Jacob might have been treated with more delicacy.

But this tragedy has one thing worthy of note in the solution of the plot; and that consists in the fact that it does not end like almost all modern tragedies by punishing vice and rewarding virtue; but, on the contrary, leaves the innocent Don Pedro to be persecuted and killed, his wife filled with bitterness, and his mother disconsolate; so that, in spite of the surprise caused by Don Alfonso Guzmán's action in throwing his sword over the wall to the Moor so that it may be used to kill his son, rather than surrender the fortress of Tarifa to secure his freedom, and in spite of the fact that this decision should suspend all other emotions, nevertheless, to see innocence and valor punished, even though the latter is rash, leaves in the spectators a certain feeling of terror and compassion that is appropriate to tragedy.[37]

Although this play was never performed and has hardly been considered by critics worthy of mention, it nevertheless gave the legend its definitive dramatic form. Those critics who condemn Moratín's tragedy have only words of praise for Gil y Zarate's *Guzmán the Good* (1847), which does not differ essentially from the earlier work in plot.

1. Charles Blaise Qualia, "French Neo-classical Tragedy and the Comedia," *Publications of the Modern Language Association* (March, 1939), p. 191.
2. Juan López Sedano, *Jahel*, tragedia sacada de la Sagrada Escritura (Madrid, 1763), "Preface," p. xii.
3. Tomás de Iriarte, *Colección de obras en verso y prosa* (Madrid, 1805), VI, 129.
4. *Ibid.*, p. 130.

5. Nicolás Fernández de Moratín, *La Petimetra*, comedia escrita con todo el rigor del arte por Don Nicolás de Moratín, criado de la Reyna Madre, nuestra señora. Con licencia. En Madrid, en la oficina de la viuda de Juan Muñoz, calle de la estrella, año de 1762. When this comedy was reprinted in the second volume of the *Biblioteca de Autores Españoles*, the dissertation was unfortunately omitted.

6. Leandro Fernández de Moratín, "Discurso Preliminar," *Obras (B.A.E.*, II, 316).

7. Quoted from Menéndez y Pelayo, *op. cit.*, III, 286-87.

8. *Ibid.*

9. "Dissertación" to *La Petimetra*.

10. *Ibid.*

11. *Ibid.*

12. Menéndez y Pelayo, *op. cit.*, III, 288.

13. "Dissertación."

14. *Ibid.*

15. *Ibid.*

16. *Ibid.*

17. Leandro Fernández de Moratín, *op. cit.*, p. 458.

18. Nicolás Fernández de Moratín, *Desengaño al Theatro español. Respuesta al romance liso y llano y Defensa del Pensador. Desengaño II al Theatro español, sobre los autos sacramentales de Don Pedro Calderón de la Barca. Desengaño III, al Theatro español sobre los autos sacramentales de D. Pedro Calderón de la Barca*. The first of these articles was published in November, 1762, and the other two in September and October, 1763.

19. *Desengaño I*, p. 8.

20. Cotarelo y Mori, *Iriarte y su época*, p. 83.

21. *Desengaño I*, p. 12.

22. *Ibid.*

23. Quoted from Menéndez y Pelayo, *op. cit.*, III, 286.

24. *Desengaño II*, p. 37.

25. Leandro Fernández de Moratín, "Vida de Don Nicolás Fernández de Moratín," *B.A.E.*, II. p. ix.

26. *Desengaño II*, p. 50.

27. Ada M. Coe, *Catálogo bibliográfico y crítico de las comedias anunciadas en los periódicos de Madrid desde 1661 hasta 1819* (The Johns Hopkins Press, 1935), pp. 134-35.

28. *Aduana crítica, o hebdomadario de los sabios de España*, 1763-4, Núm. II, pp. 77-80. (See McClelland, *op. cit.*, pp. 63-64).

29. Leandro Fernández de Moratín, *op. cit.*, p. xi.

30. *Ibid.*

31. *Ibid.*

32. Cotarelo y Mori, *op. cit.*, p. 435.

33. *Ibid.*, p. 437.

34. Leandro Fernández de Moratín, *op. cit.*, p. xi.

35. *Ibid.*

36. *Crónicas de los reyes de Castilla, desde Don Alfonso el Sabio hasta los Católicos Don Fernando y Doña Isabel*, colección ordenada por Don Rossell (*B.A.E.*, Vol. 66).

37. Sempere y Guarinos, *Ensayo de una Biblioteca Española de los mejores escritores del reinado de Carlos III* (Madrid, 1787), IV, 125-26.

VII

Concerted Efforts to Reform the Theater

NEO-CLASSICISTS from the time of Luzán had favored some form of government control of the theater and censorship of plays, but until the accession of Carlos III to the throne, no attempt on the part of the government was made to coerce or even to influence Spaniards to accept neo-classic doctrines. Under this monarch, however, this passive attitude was abandoned and a policy of sweeping reforms was instituted to the end of regularizing the theater.

The leader of this campaign was the prime minister, Aranda, who seems to have been actuated by a sincere desire to improve the theater of his native land. The first step was taken in 1763 when Nipho was directed to draw up a plan of reform. As we have seen, Nipho was so convinced of the need of reform that he believed it would be better to abolish the theater entirely rather than allow it to continue in its corrupted state. Yet, as Cotarelo y Mori points out, Nipho's constructive ideas were not very far-reaching and, indeed, were limited to converting the theater into a school of morals. Because of political disturbances, the reforms proposed by Nipho were never put into effect, and "governmental power did not become also a literary legislator."[1]

When political conditions became more settled Aranda continued his efforts, directing his attention first to improvements in the stage itself and to promoting harmony between the partisans of the two rival theaters, the Cruz and the Príncipe. To accomplish the first purpose he suppressed the cloths or curtains which had been the only adornments of the stage from the time of the old *corrales*, except in the case of occasional productions called *de teatro*, for which more elegant settings were provided. Aranda spent more than twenty thousand duros on painted sets and, by increasing the price of box seats two reals per person, established a decoration fund for continued improvement of stage properties. Prior to that time functions had been given during the summer season only on Sundays and on festival days. Beginning in 1768, Aranda arranged for daily performances at night during this season, thereby putting the theater upon a much sounder financial basis.

In order to curtail the disturbances provoked by the *chorizos* and the *polacos*, Aranda mixed the personnel of the theatrical troups and forced them to change theaters with the change of seasons.[2]

These modifications and innovations were, however, only external and did not affect the repertoire of the theater. The neo-classicists were clamoring for the suppression of those plays which were considered injurious to public morals and which, because of their irregularity, had provoked the scorn of foreigners. It was, of course, out of the question to take these plays from the stage without an adequate substitute. Two courses were open to the reformers: translating foreign plays and reworking the old Spanish comedies. The latter course had already been suggested indirectly by Luzán and openly by nearly all subsequent neo-classic critics, inasmuch as, by their own admission, not all of the old comedies were objectionable and many, they said, could be made regular with slight changes. In the meantime, in order to meet present needs of the theater, Don Bernardo Iriarte was commissioned to choose the most regular plays from the old theater. As a result of his search some seventy plays were selected to form a provisional repertoire. Among these plays were included twenty-one by Calderón, eleven by Moreto, seven by Rojas, five by Solís, three by Lope de Vega, one by Alarcón, and none by Tirso de Molina. Cotarelo y Mori says that Don Bernardo made certain changes in these comedies, making them conform more nearly to the unities and suppressing inopportune passages. In an "Informe," or report, by Don Bernardo to Aranda, the former approved also the idea of replacing native plays with French comedies, provided they could be made to conform to Spanish customs.[3]

In regard to the changes he thinks should be made in plays retained from the old theater, he says in a letter to his friend, Don José Manuel de Ayala, who had been appointed *corrector of dramas:*

It is important to correct so far as possible the plays of Calderón, because of their general acceptance and because their plots are ingenious even though they are characterized by sameness; but in correcting his plays as well as those of other authors like Rojas, Moreto, Solís, etc., an attempt should be exerted to make them conform as far as possible to the unities; to suppress asides, poetic comparisons, and everything that smacks of flowers, rivers, cliffs, mountains, meadows, stars, etc., etc.; to curtail the untimely witticisms of the *graciosos,* especially in serious and essential scenes; and to remove completely everything that destroys the illusion.[4]

These recommendations by Don Bernardo are significant in that they point the way to the method employed in later recasts of old comedies, where at times so many changes were made that the resultant work might almost be called original. It was recognized that in many cases Golden Age comedies could not be forced within the limits of the unities without violence and without sacrificing verisimilitude and that a compromise had to be made. The recommendation that asides be suppressed was very sensible, since the frequent use of this device in Spanish comedies constituted one of their principal offenses against verisimilitude.

Don Bernardo is very insistent that all personal allusions and all indecency and obscenity be removed from *sainetes.* He is referring to the works of Ramón de la Cruz and does not hesitate to call him by name. He is violently opposed to glosses in comedies and insists that they be suppressed along with "descriptions of horses, birds, ships, tempests, battles, lions, and all kinds of wild animals, monsters, and vermin."[5] In this way, he says, "ignorant actors will have no occasion to attempt to represent the mane of a horse, the wings of an eagle, the horns of a bull, the roar of a lion, the motions of a swimmer, a rower, or a fighter, etc."[6]

He would banish from the stage all comedies of magic, of friars, and of devils, as well as those that have a second, third, fourth, and fifth part, even though he recognizes that this would meet with howls of indignation on the part of idiots and of the actors. The fact that the latter make money with them is no reason for the government or for rational people to permit their continued performance. The comedies of magic and those that dealt with friars and devils were, indeed, the principal source of income of the theaters. It is doubtful whether they could have made enough money to remain open without these plays. In 1795-96 five comedies of magic— *Venus' Ring, Pedro Vallalarde, Don Juan de Espina, Marta la Romarantina,* and *Fineo the Magician*—produced 405,714 reals in 65 performances for an average of 6,241 reals, while 32 Golden Age plays were producing 402,146 reals in 127 performances for an average of 3,266 reals. That is, five comedies of magic produced more than all the comedies of the Golden Age. In 1800 the picture had not changed, for three comedies of magic and three religious plays, which held the same appeal for the public—*The Trials of Job, The*

Prince of Mogul, The Trials of Tobías, The Two Friends of God, The Magicians of Astracán, and *The African Magician*—in 76 performances, produced 489,318 reals for an average of 6,438, while 33 Golden Age plays in 137 performances were producing 393,194 reals for an average of 2,862. It is readily understandable that the actors should oppose the removal of these comedies from the repertoire, for their livelihood depended upon them. The appeal of these plays was as much to the eye as to the ear. After *Sacramental Plays* and *Comedies of Saints* were banned comedies of magic stepped in to satisfy the appetite of the public for spectacle. Spaniards as a whole were obviously tired of Golden Age comedies that made use of word pictures in lieu of stage decoration. It did not matter that the tricks of the magician or of the devil were clumsily done. The public was easily satisfied and received the transformations and the appearances with enthusiasm. Samaniego, in the *Diario de Madrid* (May 4, 1788), makes some amusing comments upon the staging of comedies of magic:

> The changes of scene, the flights, the dives, and the transformations are the best that can be performed. It is true that stage art only concerns itself with the success of the operation, without bothering about promptness, propriety, and other things, which, although they contribute to the illusion, might also cause the stage machinist to be regarded as a sorcerer. So, if a donkey is supposed to fly, you will see a quarter of an hour in advance the enormous cable to which he is to be harnessed, and for an equal length of time you will see the wide opening which is to vomit forth some enchanter or some devil. The creaking of the ropes, the knocking of the counterweights, the noise of the wheels and pulleys, and all the operations of the skilful machinists can be heard at least from Cuatro Calles. So even the most stupid person knows how these tricks are performed, and with stage art reduced to such easy and simple principles, we can be sure that we will never lack stage operators, and, what is more important, the Inquisition will never bother them.[7]

As a practical method of spreading neo-classic precepts Aranda conceived the idea of establishing theaters in the Royal Residences, or *Sitios Reales,* of Aranjuez, San Lorenzo, and La Granja, where plays translated from the French might be performed under the most favorable conditions and before audiences that would be predisposed in their favor. Clavijo y Fajardo was named director of this theater and, in addition to this duty, took upon himself the task of translating various French plays. To him are credited translations of *Andromaque* by Racine; *The Universal Heir,* by Regnard; and

Vanity Humbled, from *Le Glorieux,* by Destouches. In addition to
these translations by Clavijo, Pablo de Olavide translated for the
theater of the Sitios Regnard's *The Gambler,* Voltaire's *Casandro y
Olimpia,* Racine's *Phèdre,* Le Mierre's *Lina* and *Hypermenestra,*
Maffei's *Mérope,* Du Belloy's *Celmira,* and Mercier's *The French
Deserter.* His daughter, Engracia Olavide, translated Mme de Graf-
figny's *Paulina,* and Gaspar de Jovellanos translated Racine's *Iphigenia.* Many of these plays were also performed in the theaters of
the Príncipe and the Cruz.

Among those who contributed in this manner to the spread of
neo-classicism was the young Tomás de Iriarte. In the collection of
his works made by the author himself, we are given an account of
his connection with the theater of the Sitios. In the preface to Volume V, Iriarte says:

> During the years 1769, '70, '71, and '72, immediately following the es-
> tablishment of a new Spanish theater in the Royal Residences, the author
> was charged with translating several dramatic compositions from the
> French. Among these plays were *The Spendthrift, The Scotchwoman, The
> Bad Man, The Man Who Imagined He Was Sick, The Sensible Ward,
> The Merchant of Esmirna,* and others. And since in that theater prose was
> preferred to verse because it was a more natural imitation of a conversa-
> tion, had been adopted by cultured nations, and had been equally well
> received in our own, the above mentioned plays were translated into
> that medium.[8]

The preference of the audiences at the Sitios for comedies in prose
was in keeping with the general trend throughout Europe, a trend
already noticeable in the time of Luzán, who gave them at least a
qualified approval. Iriarte thought, however, that prose translations,
although they might be well received on the stage, would lose their
effect when read; and therefore he admitted to his published collection only two translations which he had made in verse: the comedy,
The Married Philosopher, and the tragedy, *The Chinese Orphan,*
the former from Destouches and the latter from Voltaire. In this same
preface he gives the method he uses in his translations: "He [the
author] translated them without following the original very closely
and added or omitted what he considered advisable in order to make
them conform to our manners and language, and in order to prevent the inclusion of any maxim, or expression, that might offend our
delicacy."[9]

Cotarelo y Mori says that *The Married Philosopher* lacks interest and comic force and that Iriarte's translation, though well done, could not give the work qualities it did not originally possess. In reviewing this play in 1811, the *Gaceta de Madrid* says: "Destouches is the first comic author of the eighteenth century both in chronology and in literary merit. . . . The most complete eulogy that can be made of Iriarte's translation is to say that the comedy seems to be original."[10] An examination of the list of performances in the theaters of Madrid reveals that *The Married Philosopher* was performed fourteen times in 1782 and that it was given sixty-two performances between 1786 and 1831. We know also from the incomplete records available that it was performed frequently on the stage in Barcelona at least from 1779 to 1792. This play must, therefore, be counted as one of the most popular neo-classic comedies translated from the French, and, indeed, one of the most popular plays performed on the Spanish stage during this entire time. It should be borne in mind that throughout the period from 1786 to 1831 the bulk of the plays borrowed from the French theater are properly classed as dramas or as sentimental comedies. These plays, in which considerable attention was given to the *mise en scène*, were much more favorably received than true comedy or true tragedy, especially in the closing years of the eighteenth century and in that part of the nineteenth which preceded the romantic period.

Those critics who consistently minimize the success of the neo-classic movement have had much to say about the aversion on the part of both actors and public for tragedies and comedies translated from the French. Cotarelo y Morí, speaking of performances in 1788, says:

> The aversion of actors at that time for classic tragedy in the French manner, because of the hatred it inspired in the general public is well known. But as a part of the public and certain important personages requested it, they had brought from Cádiz an actress, famous for her ability in tragic roles, whose name was María Bermejo. Not without great opposition on the part of the actors was she able to perform on the 23rd of April, 1788, Le Mierre's tragedy, *Hypermenestra*, which had been translated by Olavide.[11]

In November, 1796, *Hypermenestra* had a run of five consecutive days with average receipts of 6,453 reals, producing 7,335 reals on the fifth day. During this same year 32 Golden Age comedies averaged 3,266 reals in 127 performances, while four neo-classic plays translated from the French were given 15 times with an average of 5,893 reals. We have already noted the proceeds realized from comedies of magic during 1795-96.

Golden Age comedies are represented by these same critics as consistently holding their popularity with the public, although they were so vigorously condemned by the "furious neo-classicists" that Calderón himself began to lose his pre-eminence on the stage and to be replaced by "extravagant dramas" and "detestable" translations. Speaking of the performances of María del Rosario Fernández ("The Tyrant") in 1787, Cotarelo y Mori says that during the month of April she performed only well-known Golden Age plays. "But not even for a moment did she fail to win the applause of the public."[12] During this month the Golden Age comedies performed at the Príncipe included *I Love All I See, Pleasures and Displeasures of This Life, The Pretended Arcadia,* and *The Spirit Lady.* These plays were given twelve performances and averaged 2,961 reals, which is a very meager amount considering the fact that the season opened with the first of these comedies and the attendance might be expected to be larger at the beginning. In fact, this play ran for five days with average receipts of 4,054 reals. Excluding this play, the others averaged only 2,180 reals. If all the plays during the year had won equal "applause" from the public, the theaters would have had to close their doors. In evaluating the popularity of Golden Age plays during the neo-classic period it is customary to cite the number performed or their percentage of the total. The only accurate estimate than can be made, however, is on the basis of average receipts. The lack of popularity of Golden Age comedies with the general public, in spite of all that has been said to the contrary, accounts for the popularity of translations from the French theater and of the extravagant plays of Comella and his school during the closing years of the eighteenth century and the first decade of the nineteenth. Golden Age comedies had not been driven from the stage by neo-classic propaganda; they were dying a slow death because they no longer reflected Spanish customs, and therefore had lost their appeal to the public.

A considerable number of second- or third-rate plays that were popular on the French stage at the time found their way almost immediately into Spain and, in spite of the opposition of the nationalists, came to dominate the Spanish theater to such an extent that they discouraged original productions. It seemed to make no difference whether the plays were neo-classic or whether they fell under the classification of the *drame,* a genre that was replacing regular comedy and tragedy in popular esteem in France and which was the immediate forerunner of such extravagant and irregular plays as Ducange's *Thirty Years, or the Life of a Gambler,* which produced a sensation when it was performed in Spain in 1828, filling the theater and rivaling the success of the Italian opera. The principal purveyor of French plays at this time was Enciso Castrillón, followed closely by Rodríquez Arellano and from a distance by Teodoro de La Calle. Encisco's translations—*We All Build Castles in the Air,* from Collin d'Harleville; *Vanity Humbled,* from Destouche's *Le Glorieux; The Absent Minded Man,* from *Le Distrait* by Regnard; *The Reconciler,* from *Le Conciliateur* by Demoustier; *The Aragonese Muse,* from *Le Metromanie* by Piron; and *The Oppressor of His Family,* from *Le Tyran Domestique* by Alejandre Duval—were well received on the Spanish stage, *The Absent-minded Man* and *Vanity Humbled* having 32 and 34 performances respectively from 1802 to 1818.

Two of the outstanding triumphs of the career of the famous actor Isidoro Máiquez were achieved in translations by Teodoro de La Calle. The first of these was a translation of a neo-classic arrangement, or recast, of Shakespeare's *Othello,* composed in French by Ducis. It is somewhat ironical that the most famous of English dramatists should have owed his popularity on the Spanish stage to works that bore so little resemblance to the originals. *Macbeth,* also translated by La Calle, and *Romeo and Juliet,* translated by Dionisio Solís, were both taken from recasts by Ducís. Cotarelo y Mori considers Máiquez' success in *Othello* convincing evidence of his remarkable histrionic ability.

Although La Calle's work is not entirely bad, since it has passages that are well and boldly versified, the strongest argument that can be advanced in proof of the merit of Isidoro Máiquez is the fact that with such a weak version of a renowned original, twice mutilated and degenerated, he was capable of producing an unforgettable effect upon the public. This tragedy lasted for ten days on its initial run in 1802 and was played six more times the same year. From 1802 to 1818 it had a total of fifty-four performances. The only play in which Máiquez approached this success was another translation by Teodoro de La Calle. This was Arnaud's tragedy, *Blanca and Moncasín or the Venetians,* or, as it was called in French, *Les Vénetiens,*

which had been enthusiastically received when it was performed in
Paris in 1799. La Calle's translation, which was neither good nor
bad, was made in the same verse form as *Othello*, that is, in hendecasyllabic *romance*, which had come to be used exclusively for
tragedy in Spain both in original works and in translations. *The Venetians* was given eight performances on its initial run with receipts
of 11,309 reals on the first night and 11,988 on the last when the
average for all plays that year was considerably less than half that
sum. Again Cotarelo y Mori attributes the success of the tragedy
almost entirely to the acting of Máiquez. *The Venetians* was viciously
attacked by critics in *El Memorial Literario* and in *El Diario de
Madrid*. The former published a detailed synopsis and analysis of the
tragedy which concluded with this statement: "This work lacks a
quality that is essential in tragedy because it inspires neither terror
nor compassion.... The style is ordinary, obscure, and redundant;
there are errors in grammar and language, padding in the verses and
inconstancy in the assonance."[13] The *Memorial* also published in the
same year a long satire in hendecasyllabic couplets that had been
written and widely circulated in manuscript form by Juan Bautista
Arriaza, a well-known poet of the day who prided himself upon his
critical ability and knowledge of neo-classic precepts. This satire,
which bore the title *Reflections Between Acts*, made obvious and
unflattering references to Máiquez and to the style of declamation
he had recently brought from France, where he had studied under
the well-known French actor, Talma. If any of the readers missed the
point in the *Satire*, they could not fail to understand a note by the
editor of the *Memorial:*

> The author of the satire appreciates, as is proper, the effort, the appli-
> cation, and the success with which the roles in *Othello*, *Vanity Humbled*
> ... and in many others have been performed ... but reputation should not
> be leased to anyone for periods of time nor should applause be given
> through partiality or as a routine matter. It should be observed that
> when characters are weakly drawn by the poet, it is useless for the actor
> to try to give them energy; the forcefulness of the expression forms a
> marked contrast with the weakness of the words. French acting as it is
> found today is defective, exaggerated, and unnatural even in the eyes
> of Frenchmen themselves, whose clamor against Talma and his followers
> resounds continuously in the periodicals.[14]

The *Memorial* at this time was highly critical of the French plays
chosen for translation and even more critical of the translations

themselves. If these had been as bad as the *Memorial* claims, they certainly would have been rejected by the public. The following statement seems to have been the product of wishful thinking:

[This satire] destroys a foreign production, and perhaps this will be its greatest fault to many of our countrymen who are accustomed to look with stupid admiration upon everything that is foreign while they smother in infancy the laudable efforts of every national writer.... Certainly those who secretly lament the blind choice by which the degenerate fruits of the French theater ... are transferred to our stage will not deny the usefulness of the publication of this satire.[15]

From the remarks made by the *Memorial* it is evident that nationalistic critics, or neo-classicists themselves under the impulse of an aroused patriotism, were opposing the introduction of French plays.

Such barbarous things should be banished from any civilized theater. If the public applauds them, what does the public not applaud? ... Even if this satire had no other recommendation than that of having been the first to interrupt with ironical laughter the general cry of applause in favor of such an atrocious spectacle, it would be acceptable to those intelligent people who do not want to see the pleasure derived from sympathy degenerate into a desire to witness suffering.[16]

Articles in the *Diario de Madrid* for and against foreign plays became more and more frequent during the rest of the year 1803, the most violent of the attacks coming from the pen of one who signed himself *El Muñidor de los de aquende*, which, freely translated, means a "partisan of the national theater." At this time Máiquez had been placed in charge of the theater of the Caños del Peral, and in choosing plays had shown a marked preference for translations. The attacks against his management and manner of acting seem to have come in many cases from neo-classicists themselves. Angered by what he considered unfair treatment and feeling that he was being betrayed by the party with which he had affiliated himself, Máiquez struck back at the "Partisan of the National Theater" and at the *Diario de Madrid:*

It is bad to satirize actors even though it be in general terms, because, as they are made up of a small number of individuals, general satire runs a great danger of becoming personal. Moreover, actors are not slaves but honorable citizens who have their place in society and who are more useful than many of those who satirize them. The management of the theater, Mr. Partisan, is not a jewel that is thrown into the street to be picked up by the first one who sees it; it is a commission given by the government and, therefore, to satirize the director of the theater is to insult the government itself. . . .

The intention of the government when it recently authorized the opening of the theater of the Caños del Peral was doubtless to make available to the public the amusement and the instruction which the theater is capable of affording; and it is certainly extremely odd that, when its director has tried to put this intention into effect and to offer the public plays by the best modern writers he has only succeeded in making himself a target of satire and mockery in the *Diario*. . . .

All the writers, all the papers, and especially the *Diario de Madrid* itself cried out against the absurdities, the improbabilities, and the defects of the old comedies; they demanded the observance of the rules and the unities; they called in loud voices for a reform of the theater and sighed for true comedies that would teach the harmful effects of vice and the reward of virtue and which, at the same time, would keep the rules of the theater, those rules that are not derived from the authority of the Greeks and Romans but from nature itself, of which the theater should be an imitation. All of this promised a good reception for French plays, especially since they were cited as models by all those who declaimed against our old comedies. These plays were presented and immediately those same critics, those same periodicals that desired them declared their opposition to them, detested them, ridiculed the director of the theater in which they were performed and, becoming enthusiastic with a kind of literary patriotism for the concepts and puns of the gallants of Calderón and Moreto, treated the director of the theater as an enemy to the literary glory of his nation and a stalwart partisan of the French theater. Despicable and malicious critics! How is the director of the theater to blame for your not knowing yourselves what you want? If foreign writers were wrong in criticizing the defects of the old Spanish comedies, why did you join them by asking for a reform of the theater? . . .

Perhaps you will say that some of the plays were good and some bad and that all of them were badly translated; but how, I ask, is it possible for all of the works to have equal merit? Should I set myself up as a censor of translations and discharge the functions of a literary censor as well as those of a stage director? The government charged me with the latter task, and it alone has the right to examine my conduct; especially when it has designated an ecclesiastical judge to examine their moral content and a scholar to see that they conform to the rules of art.[17]

In taunting his critics for their inconsistency, Máiquez shows familiarity with the arguments advanced by neo-classic critics in favor of a regular theater. Many of this school seemed to swing like pendulums from a condemnation of Golden Age comedy and an advocacy of regularity to an extreme nationalism. This constant conflict between mind and heart accounts to a considerable extent for the violent antagonisms that developed within the ranks of the neo-classicists.

The *Memorial Literario* in the last third of its life, according to Menéndez y Pelayo, reflected the ideas of Capmany, who had changed from an earlier worshiper at the altar of French culture to a relentless antagonist who broke "into invectives against the French language and against the taste and style of her writers" in a work entitled "Critical Observations Upon the Excellence of the Castilian Language," which preceded his *Historical-Critical Theater of Eloquence*.[18] The vehemence that characterizes the attitude of the *Memorial* in its reviews of translations of French plays certainly corroborates Menéndez y Pelayo's statement. This periodical professes to be in sympathy with the precepts of neo-classicism and with the purpose of that school to regularize the theater. It recognizes the role that translations could play in such a program, but decries the almost complete lack of ability on the part of those who have exercised themselves in this field. In reviewing *The Beautiful Peasant Girl*, a comedy translated by María Rosa de Gálves, the *Memorial* says: "This drama is translated from French but not into Castilian, for it has remained in the hybrid language so much in vogue among the crowd of bad translators, who have taken possession of the theater in order to destroy our language more quickly and surely."[19] And in discussing the translation of *The Manners of the Day*, from Collin d'Harleville, it makes this comment:

And since these common translators have determined to continue in their noble and apparently easy task of destroying the Castilian language, we also shall continue with equal constancy to point out their defects; and if we do not succeed with our admonitions in getting them to mend their ways, we shall at least be able to laugh and to make the public laugh by calling attention to their inanity and stupidity.[20]

The *Memorial* admits that the French theater is very rich in excellent works but says that the translations of these plays have failed to bring out their merit. Repeated proof of this fact is to be found in the works of Molière, Regnard, Destouches, Fabre d'Eglantine, and Collin d'Harleville, which are filled with wit in the French originals and with nonsense in the translations. The *Memorial* laments that, in the attempt to replace Golden Age comedies, the gain has been more than offset by a loss:

In everything true reform consists not in destroying but in rebuilding; not merely in uprooting an abuse but in preventing another from occurring; in producing new beauties and in retaining the old. Because, after all, we usually had in our comedies good language, good and even excellent versification, at times lofty thoughts, ingenious ideas, interest, action, characters, and all the wealth of drama, even though these qualities were submerged by defects that are so well known. Everything was overthrown and, by observing the three unities that are so easy to keep when nothing else is desired, we thought we had brought about a great reform; but it was necessary that Lope, Calderón, and Moreto should be followed, if not by a Molière and a Racine, at least by a Regnard, a Destouches, or a Rotrou. Lope and Calderón were the idols of a barbarous age, but they will also be read and esteemed in an enlightened one; but who will read our bright, new comedies?[21]

Unfortunately, the *Memorial* says, in the translation of French plays more attention has been given to quantity than to quality:

If translations are one of the best means to enrich the literature of a nation, there is no doubt that ours must be very wealthy, since for a century we have been busy in transferring to our language the literary compositions of the rest of Europe, particularly of France. It is true that most of the best works remain there; but, on the other hand, most of the insignificant and bad ones attain the honor of being naturalized in Spain. In that way we become rich, if abundance constitutes wealth.[22]

Inasmuch as these translations were generally well received by the public in spite of all the defects to which the *Memorial* calls attention, it seems evident that good translations and original neoclassic comedies would have met not with opposition but with enthusiastic approval from that group. It is not surprising, therefore, that a comedy like Moratín's *The Consent of Young Maidens*, which combined genius and regularity, should have produced such a sensation with twenty-six consecutive performances in 1805.

1. Cotarelo y Mori, *Iriarte y su época*, p. 49.
2. *Ibid.*, p. 65.
3. *Ibid.*, p. 66.
4. *Ibid.*, p. 421.
5. *Ibid.*
6. *Ibid.*
7. Cotarelo y Mori, *La Tirana* (Madrid, 1897), pp. 186-87.
8. Tomás de Iriarte, *Colección de obras en verso y prosa* (Madrid, 1782). The edition of 1805 is used in this study.
9. *Ibid.*, "Prefacio," Vol. V.
10. *Gaceta de Madrid*, May 9, 1811.
11. Cotarelo y Mori, *Isidoro Máiquez y*

el teatro de su tiempo (Madrid, 1902), p. 26.
12. Cotarelo y Mori, *La Tirana*, p. 165.
13. *El Memorial Literario*, Tomo IV, Año tercero, 1803, pp. 177-78.
14. *Ibid.*, p. 214.
15. *Ibid.*, p. 208.
16. *Ibid.*, pp. 209-10.
17. *El Diario de Madrid*, Jan. 11, 1804.
18. Menéndez y Pelayo, *op. cit.*, III, 375.
19. *El Memorial Literario*, Tomo II, 1802, p. 97.
20. *Ibid.*, p. 247.
21. *Ibid.*, p. 56.
22. *Ibid.*, p. 243.

VIII

Iriarte and His Times

Tomás de Iriarte

WHILE Iriarte was busily engaged in translating French plays for the theater of the *Sitios*, he found time for one original composition, *The Busybody*, a comedy in three acts and in verse, which he published in 1770 under the anagram of D. Tirso Imareta.[1] Cotarelo y Mori comments upon the rarity of this play, which, he says,

... was not included in the edition of his works made by the author, or in the one made by his family after his death, nor has it ever been reprinted, so far as I know. Forner, who even makes a mistake in giving its title, says in a satire in prose against Iriarte ... that *El finge negocios*, "a comedy written to dwarf those of Terence and Molière, was printed without the name of the author, and after being printed has disappeared" ... which indicates that he was not able to examine it ...[2]

Iriarte tells us in the "Prologue" to the comedy that his purpose is to ridicule a type which "is one of the most common in Madrid, and one that is calculated to be less tiresome to the audience than those ordinarily found in comedy because of the variety of scenes produced by the disposition of a busybody ..." Iriarte so exaggerates the character, however, that the result is a caricature. Cotarelo y Mori says that he is not a busybody but rather "a fool who could never exist as a type, not being, therefore, a character or a social defect, but a case of a particular mania."[3]

Plot interest is almost entirely lacking in *The Busybody*, for it is evident from the beginning that Don Gil will never win the hand of Doña Elvira. He rushes around through the entire play, complaining about the infinite number of things that occupy his time. All of his supposed business is of no importance whatsoever, consisting of the most trivial tasks. He does not even allow himself time to talk to Doña Elvira, or to her father when the latter seeks to discuss the projected marriage with him. In the end he loses Doña

Elvira to Don Pablo because of his eccentric character. Although Don Gil is most ridiculous, he is never brought to realize that fact and therefore there is no question of repentance. Nor is he sufficiently in love with Doña Elvira to feel his loss. There is a minor action in the love affair of Don Miguel and Doña Vicenta, the sister of Don Gil, the solution of which does not necessarily depend upon the solution of the main plot, although there is an attempt to tie them together in the third act. The principal merit of the play lies in its natural dialogue and smooth versification. The introduction of the two notaries is entirely without justification. They enter, hide, and leave without affecting the development of the plot to the slightest degree.

In this comedy, of course, the unities are religiously observed. Contrary to the general custom of the neo-classicists, Iriarte varies the verse form to include both octosyllabic *romance* and *redondillas.* As has been noted, however, the preceptists never expressly barred *redondillas,* only specifying that the verse form in comedies should be natural and should approximate prose as nearly as possible. Next to assonance the *redondilla* most nearly filled this requirement.

The author boasts in the prologue that he has avoided "the sub-lime style of versification, which is suitable for lyric poetry but out of place in comedy." It will be remembered that this same claim was made by Nicolás Fernández de Moratín in the preface to *The Fashionable Lady.* Iriarte also avoids "the witty remarks of a *gracioso,*" who, he says, is usually the only pronounced character in the Spanish *comedia.* Here Iriarte evidently has in mind the criticism made by Luzán and repeated by other critics that writers of comedy in Spain were accustomed to make "serious and even at times tragic all the principal subject matter of their comedies and to entrust the humor to servants, to whom they gave the name of *graciosos.*"[4]

Although he condemns the theme and development of this com-edy and its lack of comic force, Cotarelo y Mori praises the versifica-tion and language, which he says reveal the future master. The por-trait which the servant, Mateo, draws of the protagonist, according to this critic, seems the work of a poet of the seventeenth century. It might well have been suggested, however, by the numerous ex-amples of this device that had filled French literature since the middle of the seventeenth century. More than any other neo-classic writer, Iriarte uses this method of characterization. The same tech-nique is especially apparent in *Winning Ways,* where Doña Elena gives a portrait of all the characters except Rosalía.

Iriarte has enough confidence in the merit of his comedy to say in the prologue that if the public does not approve his play,

...we shall reach the conclusion that, in order to please it, modern writers should not take as the subjects of their comedies fixed characters, copied from originals that are seen in life, nor should they represent the manners of society with the propriety which the theater requires; but rather they should transform the theater into an academy of poetry which will be attended only to hear odes recited by heroes, madrigals by lovers, and epigrams by servants.[5]

If the comedy meets with approval, one can no longer doubt that a comedy written without affected language, with a clear, consistent plot, in which "a single character is made to stand out and which contains only those incidents necessary to the development of the plot, and which in the end rewards or punishes the principal personage," is capable of instructing and amusing an audience perhaps more than those in which the crowd applauds "the confused and at times improbable series of purely amorous incidents, the sublime style that is suitable in lyrical poetry but out of place in comedy, and the witticisms of a *gracioso.*"[6]

Iriarte believes his comedy will lose in being read, since its effectiveness depends upon careful staging and natural acting. He has little confidence, however, in the ability of the actors to interpret the characters properly, and fears also the organized resistance of certain persons who, as is well known, "have done everything possible to prevent its performance."[7]

The public, indeed, had no opportunity to pass judgment on the play, for it never reached the stage. Iriarte attributed this failure to the opposition of Ramón de la Cruz, that "tyrant and monopolizer" of the theater, who, because of the popularity of his *sainetes,* had gained such ascendancy over the actors and over the public that his approval was necessary for the production of any new comedy. He was even accused of having retained this comedy, which was sent to him for approval, and of having turned it into a *sainete* with the title *The Conceited Man.*[8] Ramón de la Cruz was probably the greatest obstacle to the reforms advocated by the neo-classicists, since his *sainetes* seemed to satisfy the need the public felt for comedy.

As has been pointed out, Ramón de la Cruz embarked upon his dramatic career with translations from the French and at that time aligned himself with the neo-classicists, clamoring as loudly as any for theatrical reform. In the preface to his operetta, *Sacrifices Are*

Pleasing to the Deity (Madrid, 1757), he goes to the extreme of advocating a censorship of drama in order that the Spanish theater may
not remain the laughingstock of foreigners, and strongly condemns
"the pitiful spectacle of the *sainetes,* which are characterized by
ridicule alone." He promises to continue his study of dramatic precepts in order that he may better equip himself to translate from the
French, but sees little chance for the acclimatization of neo-classic
tragedy or comedy in Spain, because before this could be accomplished the old plays would have to be withdrawn entirely from the
stage. It would then be necessary to maintain neo-classic drama
artificially until the taste of the people should change.[9]

It may well be that this last statement accounts for the change
of heart experienced by Ramón de la Cruz. Unquestionably, he was
an opportunist, who chose to follow rather than oppose popular
taste. It is true that in so doing he succeeded in dominating the
stage, but one cannot help wondering whether, with his unquestionable gifts as a comic poet, he might not have been the answer to the
prayer of the neo-classicists for a leader with qualities similar to those
of the great Molière. Once embarked on his course as a writer of
sainetes, he soon became a victim of the attacks of the neo-classicists
and was goaded to reprisals. With an assumed air of innocence, he
taunts the neo-classicists with their continuing failure to produce
original works:

I want to correct myself, I want to imitate you, and I ask you not for
precepts, for I know where they are written, but for examples; I am waiting for models of those perfect works produced by your invention and
composed by your pens in order that they may serve as a foundation for
that correctness you rant about.[10]

These taunts by Ramón de la Cruz may have been instrumental in
provoking the neo-classicists to action.

Three years after the publication of *The Busybody* Iriarte composed, under the pseudonym of Don Amador de Vera y Santa Clara,
an ingenious satire on the prevalent bad taste among authors and
public, probably inspired by Cadalso's *Superficial Erudites,* which
had appeared the year before. In this work, *Writers in Lent,* the
author expresses his shame that his fellow-countrymen are still dis-
puting about the unities while other nations are bending their efforts
toward the improvement of theatrical art, and that Spaniards have
not yet admitted that the rules are based on natural reasons and have
been sanctioned by long practice. Years will pass before the public

can be made to understand that these laws were discovered, not invented. Dramas in Spain are still not to be distinguished from novels and chronicles.

To emphasize the lack of verisimilitude occasioned by non-observance of the unity of time, he takes the extreme case of the famous Christian Jacobsen Drakenberg, who had died the year before at the age of 146, and proposes that a drama be composed, the first act of which will represent the birth of the protagonist and the last act his death and funeral. He concludes: "The avoidance of this is what is called 'observance of the unity of time' . . . and when this unity is not observed no man of intelligence will say 'I am going to a comedy, or I am going to a tragedy'; but, 'I am going to see a chronicle, or a novel.' "[11]

To illustrate what is meant by the unity of place, he takes the hypothetical case of a comedy based on the conquest of Mexico by Cortés, in which the scene will shift from Santiago de Cuba to Vera Cruz, then to Mexico City, then back to Vera Cruz, with the final scene taking place in Toledo, and concludes that this "is what we call not observing the unity of place; for whenever this unity is broken, no one should say 'I am going to a comedy, or I am going to a tragedy' but 'I am going to roam, or to see the world.' "[12]

The unity of action means simply that only one action should be presented, although it may be adorned with different incidents, and that there should not be two equal heroes to divide the interest. Otherwise a drama might embrace all the wars of Alexander or all the adventures of Don Quixote.

Iriarte warns against the idea that the mere observance of the unities suffices to make a drama perfect. Among the other requirements he lists cleverness in plot, verisimilitude in episodes, variety in dialogue, purity of style, suitability of theme, and finally that elusive quality so necessary to move and to hold the listener in suspense—interest.

After a play has been composed which combines all these qualities, the audience remains to be reckoned with. The success of a play frequently depends upon "the quality and the education of the people who make up the audience."[13] Iriarte probably has in mind here the failure of his own play The Busybody even to reach the theater. At this point he describes various types of listeners who are so addicted to the abuses of irregular comedy that they cannot appreciate one which follows the rules. Iriarte gives a picture of the

theater as seen through the eyes of an ardent neo-classicist, but contributes nothing new to the theory of comedy.

Iriarte recognizes the debt of gratitude the neo-classicists owe the
government "for having given its attention to correcting the theater
by beautifying its physical plant; by taking steps to make the audience observe the proper silence, attention, and decorum; and by
trying to introduce the performance of regular plays."[14] He expresses
confidence that the Spanish theater will be improved by adopting
whatever is good in the theater of other nations without excluding
the commendable qualities of its own and that authors will be
induced to compose original tragedies and comedies "when they
see that those which are performed according to the rules of art and
decency gain applause, and when the actors improve in their profession, because upon the latter depends the success of any theatrical
performance."[15] But the best elements of native and foreign works
were not combined in Iriarte's own plays, and not until Bretón de
los Herreros were they successfully fused.

Iriarte might be expected to defend the art of translation, since
he had been one of the most active in that field; and indeed, in this
article he does so with considerable warmth, carefully distinguishing
between those careless and incompetent writers who translate by
contract and those who possess "a smooth, clear, correct, and persuasive style." Probably feeling keenly his own failure to produce a
successful original comedy, but still confident of his ability, he
exclaims: "A fine task it would be to try to prove that learned men
who have devoted their energies to translations do not have sufficient genius to write original works!"[16]

Translations, Iriarte says, are applauded only by critics who appreciate the difficulties involved, the utility of such translations, and
the fact that great men of all nations have exercised their talents in
this field. Many people believe a translation even in verse to be a
simple task, undertaken only by those incapable of writing original
works. These critics would change their minds

...if they themselves were forced to look for proper equivalents, to
correct, or at times to conceal errors in the original, to polish the translation so that it will not appear to be such, and to naturalize oneself (so to
speak) with the author whose work is being translated, absorbing his
ideas, emotions, and opinions, and expressing all of this in another language with equal conciseness, energy, and fluency.[17]

Iriarte advises Spanish authors that, without conceding to foreign nations, especially France, absolute superiority in all matters, they lay aside their vanity and translate French works,

... in the first place because it is difficult for others to write works that are as good and to write without repeating or copying a great part of what the French have already said; and in the second place because in translating their writings we would in many cases only be recovering what is ours, for it is well known that foreigners have been making use of works that we have quite forgotten.[18]

These statements reveal one of the principal weaknesses of the neo-classic program. To start with the assumption that the French had already exhausted the possibilities of classic comedy was to admit the impossibility of original creation in that genre. This attitude was not limited to Spain. In France, Voltaire expressed the opinion that comic types did not exist in sufficient number to keep neo-classic comedy alive. Everything has its limits, and

... high comedy has its limits. There are in human nature not more than a dozen characters, at the most, that are truly comic and sharply defined. L'Abbé Dubos ... believes that men of genius can still find a great number of new characters; but it would be necessary for nature to create them. He imagines that the slight differences that exist in men's characters can be handled as successfully as great subjects. The shades, it is true, are innumerable, but the striking colors are few; and it is these primary colors that a great artist uses.[19]

Molière himself had expressed confidence in the almost limitless possibilities of the comic genre, saying in L'Impromptu de Versailles:

... Do you think that he has exhausted in his comedies all of the ridiculous types of men? Without leaving the court are there not twenty that he has not touched? Why, why, Marquis, Molière will always have more subjects than he needs; and all he has treated so far are only a trifle compared to what remains![20]

Many Spanish writers of no mean ability were content to fritter away their genius with translations under the illusion that their adaptations of French plays were almost, if not quite, as meritorious as original works. Of course there were extenuating circumstances. It must be confessed that there was little incentive to originality when audiences seemed to make no distinction between French translations and Spanish originals, and even seemed at times to prefer the former to the latter.

Following Iriarte's lead, nearly all later translators, including Moratín, sought to justify their work by pointing out the difficulties involved in a well-made translation. Although a Corneille might adapt a Spanish original like *The Youth of the Cid* by Guillén de Castro to the French stage and still have his work considered original, times had changed and an adaptation remained the property of the original author, at least in the opinion of Spanish critics, no matter how much ingenuity the adapter revealed in making the work conform to the manners of his native land and even though he might enlarge a comedy of one act into a full-length work.

The statement so frequently made by neo-classicists that in translating from the French they were in many cases simply returning to Spain what had been taken from her, is rather naïve and was only a method of salving their pride. Even after his recommendation that the Spaniards borrow from the French stage, Iriarte feels impelled to insist that the French themselves were not inventors:

> We are doing little favor to the ancients and to ourselves, in supposing that the French are authors of what they only imitate or improve. Good oratory and dramatic poetry adjusted to art flourished in Athens and in Rome before they did in Paris; and I do not know why a comedy that observes the precepts dictated by natural reason should be called a comedy in the French manner and not in the Athenian or Roman.[21]

Iriarte is particularly vexed at the Gallicisms which have come into the Spanish language. It is interesting to note, however, that most of the expressions he censures so strongly have made a place for themselves in Spanish and are used today with no thought of their origin.

The bitter polemics which resulted from the intense antagonism between the neo-classicists and the champions of the national school form an unpleasant but interesting chapter in Spanish literary history. These literary quarrels were constantly augmented by jealousy and dissension within the neo-classic group itself. Following the publication of *Writers in Lent,* Iriarte was moved by his enthusiasm for Horace to translate in 1777 the *Poetic Art or Epistle to the Pisones* by that author. Having incurred the enmity of Sedano because of his criticism of the latter's *Spanish Parnassus,* he soon saw himself the victim of a vicious attack. This came from one who had revealed a sympathy for the regular theater by translating such comedies as Molière's *Misanthrope,* Goldoni's *The Fortunate Landlady,* and a tragedy by Metastasio, *To Be Conquered and Conqueror,*

Julius Caesar and Cato. In imitation of the tragedies of Montiano, as we have noted, he had even published a tragedy, *Jahel,* preceded by a preface in which he claimed to be actuated solely by a desire to contribute to the restoration of good taste in Spanish literature. His attack on Iriarte was motivated, therefore, not by differences in literary creed but by personal animosity. Iriarte came to the defense of his own work in a clever satire in dialogue form, entitled "Give and Take," which was published in the *Gaceta* on October 16, 1788.

Throughout the remainder of his life Iriarte was almost constantly engaged in polemics. The most relentless of his assailants was Juan Pablo Forner, whose position in the neo-classic controversy is somewhat difficult to define. Like Sedano he expressed his dissatisfaction with the low condition to which the literature of his native land had fallen and composed an original work, the comedy *The Philosopher in Love,* as a practical demonstration of the precepts. But Forner's malignant nature allowed him to spare no party or author. For Iriarte he seemed to cherish a particular dislike, and every new work of this author was the object of an unreasonable and relentless attack. Although Iriarte's defenders were numerous, these polemics embittered his life and unquestionably impeded his creative work.

Hardly less disturbing to his equanimity was the attitude displayed by Ramón de la Cruz toward the principles advocated by neo-classicists. The *sainetero* did not engage in polemics with his adversaries but instead availed himself of a much more dreaded weapon. In his *sainetes* he not only constantly held up to ridicule the supposed pedantry and coldness of the neo-classicists, but indulged in personalities. Iriarte was enraged at the methods of attack used by Ramón de la Cruz, and in a letter to a friend in mild defense of Nicolás de Moratín's tragedy *Hormesinda* he expressed fear that he would see himself made the butt of ridicule in a *sainete.*

I have the consolation that during Lent he does not compose *sainetes,* and, therefore, until Easter I am free of being satirized on the stage, unless in the meantime he makes use of the Harlequin of the *volatines* to ridicule me in some farce or in the puppet shows of the Máquina Real, managing in that way not to have his tireless muse idle during these forty days. All of this may take place; but I swear to you that if in this or any other way I should see my person serve as a diversion for the public on the stage as other honorable citizens of this city have seen themselves, I would be forced to take satisfaction with some other instrument than the pen. I do not understand why the *abbés* have not thought about using

their swords already, after all the insults they have received from Don
Ramón, and why they have not given him a ... Pardon me, Sir, for I
am furious![22]

Although Iriarte was perfectly aware of the defects of Moratín's
work, he resented keenly the implication that since *Hormesinda*
was a failure no regular tragedy could find acceptance, and that
the products of bad taste must continue to dominate the stage.

In truth, not only that poet [Ramón de la Cruz], but also his followers
and many who were not of this opinion before the publication of the
Hormesinda, have believed that the bad reception of this tragedy proves
the merit of those works that have been propagating bad taste in our
theater; and others who are more ignorant and with whom the arguments
of reason are of no avail have even inferred that tragedies cannot meet
with favor in Spain in view of the rejection of *Hormesinda.*[23]

Iriarte attributes Nicolás Fernández de Moratín's failure to lack of
experience. The inferior quality of Ramón de la Cruz's *sainetes* he
ascribes to "lack of principles":

Don Ramón has been writing for the stage for many years and has no
excuse for not having made progress in this career except a lack of principles. Moratín perhaps would compose a reasonably good tragedy if he
were given a well-organized plan and if he allowed it to sleep for a
couple of years and smoothed it with a dull and slow file. Don Ramón
would spoil this same plan with low thoughts and forced expressions ...[24]

So morally pernicious are Ramon's *sainetes* that "they deserve to be
censured, not in a letter, but in a very serious criticism, or perhaps
in a denunciation to the government."[25]

There seems to be little doubt that Iriarte's well-known fable,
"The Donkey and His Master," was directed at Ramón de la Cruz
and his literary principles:

"The foolish crowd is accustomed to place
an equal value on the good and the bad:
I give it the worst, for that is what it praises."
In this manner a writer of indecent farces
was wont to excuse his errors;
and a sly poet who heard him
answered in the following way:
A master gave straw to his
humble ass and said to him:
Take this, since with this you are content.

He said this so many times that one day
the ass became angry, and answered, "I take
what you are willing to give me; but, unjust man,
do you think that I like nothing but straw?
Give me grain and you will see whether I eat it."
   Let those who work for the public know
that perhaps they blame the public in vain;
for if it eats straw when they give it straw,
when they give it grain, it eats grain.[26]

The neo-classicists found in this fable a constant source of comfort and were fond of quoting it in support of their contention that failure of dramatists in the past to discipline their comedies had been responsible for the bad taste of the public. The audience must be educated to appreciate regular comedy.

   Since the failure of Nicolás Fernández de Moratín's *The Fashionable Lady* and Iriarte's first play, *The Busybody*, to find a producer, no further attempt had been made to stage a regular comedy. The theaters of the *Sitios* had been suppressed by Floridablanca when he succeeded Aranda as prime minister, and the French director of theaters, appointed by Aranda in 1770, had made himself so unpopular with the actors by his attempts to induce them to adopt a more natural style of declamation, that he was forced to resign in 1776. Cotarelo y Mori resents the statement made by Leandro Fernández de Moratín that the Spanish stage was abandoned to "inept writers of farces." Having examined the record of performances in the two theaters of Madrid for a period of forty years preceding Leandro Fernández de Moratín, he declares that almost half the plays performed were by Calderón; a fourth by Moreto, Solís, Hoz, Córdoba, and other Golden Age dramatists; and that a large portion of the remainder were *sainetes, zarzuelas,* and *heroic comedies* by Ramón de la Cruz.[27] Among the works of these authors, he says, preference was given to

dramas as absurd, in the opinion of the neo-classicists, as *Disdain Conquered by Disdain, The Alcalde of Zalamea, García of Castañar, The King the Best Alcalde, The Grandee of Alcalá, The Gypsy Girl of Madrid, The Misfortune of the Voice, Juan Labrador, The Liar at Court, The Worst Is Not Always True, One Will Come from Outside, Jealousy the Greatest Monster, Which is the Greater Perfection?,* and so many other supremely beautiful productions of our renowned theater of the seventeenth century.

It is true, he goes on, that alternating with them were found *The*

Magician of Salerno, The Magician of Astracán, The Magician of Mogul, Marta la Romarantina, etc., which drew the largest audiences because they were produced on festival days and because the public has always seemed to favor this type of play. But the works of Bazo, Solo de Saldívar, and Laviano, he continues, "in addition to being few in number, lasted only one or two days." The theater of the seventeenth century was dominant, and "the Spanish people continued to be faithful to their great poets, and, if not in real life, at least on the stage, they wanted to see that national romanticism which reminded them of their days of glory."[28] The statement by Moratín with which Cotarelo y Mori is taking issue is as follows:

The presidency of the count of Aranda and the ministry of the marquis of Grimaldi terminated; and the theaters of the *Sitios* were closed. The theaters of Madrid continued to mix the translations they had acquired with their old repertoire; and as they enriched themselves every day with new absurdities, the result was that when at the Cruz they were performing the *Misanthrope* or *Athalie*, at the Príncipe the crowd was applauding Ildefonso Coque in the role of the *Most Prodigious Negro* or *The African Magician*. Never has there been seen a more monstrous confusion of old and new plays, of "hits" and "misses." The muses of Lope, Montalbán, Calderón, Moreto, Rojas, Solís, Zamora, and Cañizares; those of Bazo, Regnard, Laviano, Corneille, Moncin, Metastasio, Cuadrado, Molière, Valladares, Racine, Concha, Goldoni, Nipho, and Voltaire, all alternated in discordant union; and from these contradictory elements the repertoires of both theaters were formed.[29]

In evaluating the popularity of plays the number of performances of a given play and the amount of money it produced are much more important than the number of plays or their percentage of the total repertoire. For instance, in 1781-82 the *Magician of Astracán* had a run of twenty-four days; Golden Age plays almost never lasted for more than two performances. The works of Bazo, Solo de Zaldívar, Laviano, and Moncín, which according to Cotarelo y Mori lasted only one or two days, were, on the contrary, quite popular during that year. *The Beautiful Shepherdess,* by Solo de Zaldívar, was given thirteen performances; *The Sun of Spain,* by Laviano, seven; and *The Royal Oath of Artaxerxes,* by Bazo, five. The outstanding success of the year 1782 was achieved, with nineteen performances, by *The Conquest of Saint Philip,* by Danieli y Armendáris, a play of such little merit that we do not find it mentioned afterward. An examination of the *Diario de Madrid* for the year 1787 will give us an idea of the relative popularity of Golden Age comedies and those of such an inferior dramatist, for instance, as Laviano. In that year Laviano's *The Dark People of Aragón* ran for ten days with average receipts of 5,064 reals; his comedy, *The Sun of Spain,* was given seven times with an average of 3,670 reals, and in 1795 it was repeated for five performances with an average of 5,307. In the year 1787 Calderón's *The Constant Prince* and Lope de Vega's *The King the Best Alcalde* lasted only two days each and produced 2,170 and 2,330 reals respectively. In 1788 Moreto's *The Aunt and the Niece* averaged 1,838 reals in two days; *The Grandee of Alcalá,* by the same author, produced 1,397 in one performance; and his *A Woman Cannot Be Guarded* averaged 1,576 reals in two performances. Calderón's *To Conquer Love One Must Wish to Conquer It* lasted two days with average receipts of 2,170 reals; his *Apeles and Campaspe* two days for an average of 1,277; his *It Is Better Than It Was* two days for an average of 1,387; and his *Life Is a Dream* three days for 2,168 reals; and Lope de Vega's *The King the Best Alcalde* produced an average of 1,044 reals in two performances. It is interesting to note that in this same year the neo-classic tragedy *Hypermenestra* was revived for five performances for an average of 5,146 reals. It is true that Golden Age plays account for about 40 per cent of the total in 1781 and 1782; but an equal number of plays were written by thoroughly incompetent dramatists during these years and for at least the next decade. It appears, therefore, that Moratín's statement was fully justified. The public showed a marked preference for new plays of any type over the products of the Golden Age.

In spite of the seeming failure of their plan to replace irregular comedy, neo-classic partisans had definitely increased in number and the novelty of their ideas seems to have worn off somewhat. The public was decidedly better prepared and more willing to accept a comedy of the new school than it would have been at the time of the composition of *The Busybody.*

Iriarte was the first to test his maxim on the stage;

> Let those who work of the public know
> that perhaps they blame the public in vain;
> for if it eats straw when they give it straw,
> when they give it grain, it eats grain.

And the reception accorded his *The Pampered Youth,* a three-act comedy in verse (1788), seemed to prove its truth.

For his second attempt in the comic genre, Iriarte chose a theme with a wider application than that of *The Busybody*. Spanish society at the time probably offered many examples of irresponsible and dissipated youth, which conflicted sharply with Iriarte's ideas of the value of a severe mental and moral discipline.

There is evidence that Iriarte sought to make his play a kind of laboratory experiment in the rules of neo-classicism. The original plan and sketch of the comedy shows that the author gave particular attention to the unities:

> Unity of place: the scene is a room in the house of Doña Dominga ...; unity of time: the action begins at eight o'clock in the morning, and ends when the uncle says that as soon as they eat dinner Don Mariano will leave for his exile; unity of action: the punishment of the excesses of a badly reared son, all of the horror being concentrated in him...; unity of interest: all of the characters influence the action, which is single.[30]

The theme of the comedy is reduced to the misdeeds of a headstrong and dissipated youth, condoned and even abetted by his mother, which find their just punishment as prescribed by the moral code of the neo-classicists.

Don Christóval returns to Madrid after an absence of fifteen years to find that his nephew, Don Mariano, has been ruined by the excessive indulgence of his mother. Having yielded to her entreaties and relinquished the youth to her guardianship during his absence, he now reassumes his duty and seeks to correct his misguided nephew. He finds that through dissipation Don Mariano has incurred numerous debts and that the estate is in a deplorable condition. When Doña Dominga seeks to defend her son. Don Alfonso turns upon her, blaming her for everything. The mother has deceived him consistently in regard to the development of his ward, always writing that he was studious, obedient, and courteous. Don Christóval finds instead that he is "stubborn, effeminate, superficial, insolent, lazy, and incapable of following a decent career of any kind." From the confidential servant Pantoja the uncle learns the extent of the dissipation of Don Mariano: that he spends much of his time in the company of a certain widow, Doña Mónica de Castro, and that the house in which she lives belongs to the estate. Don Mariano is engaged to marry Flora, the daughter of Don Alfonso, an old friend of Don Christóval. Don Alfonso, who has been in Madrid only a short time, wishes to break the engagement when he learns the true character of his prospective son-in-law. Doña Dominga insists that the marriage contract be fulfilled, and all agree to give Don Mariano a chance to reform.

The situation is complicated by the attentions of another suitor for Flora's hand, Don Fausto, who discovers that a portrait given by the young lady to Don Mariano is in possession of Doña Mónica. He succeeds in purchasing the portrait from the widow and returns it to Flora, who begins to realize the mistake she has made. Don Christóval visits the widow's house and finds that it is a gambling den and a meeting place for vicious characters. He orders her to vacate the house. Angered by what she calls an insult to her character, she confronts Doña Dominga with a promise of marriage signed by Don Mariano and demands that the son fulfil his promise. Aided by an accomplice who poses as her brother-in-law, the widow has completely duped the youth and, during a wild evening spent in her house, has induced him to sign the paper. Don Alfonso recognizes her as a notorious character from Granada, the daughter of a landlady. This recognition comes at the close of the second act.

The action of the third act is complicated by a final attempt on the part of Doña Mónica to induce Don Mariano to marry her. Pretending to be reconciled to giving him up, she returns a paper which she says is the marriage contract, but which proves to be a forged love letter from Don Fausto to Flora. Don Mariano demands satisfaction; and, although he denies authorship of the letter, Don Fausto accepts the challenge for the following morning.

Don Christóval has informed the Alcalde of the disorderly house run by Doña Mónica, and a raid is planned for that afternoon. In order to prevent his nephew from being caught with the other offenders, he orders him to remain at home. As soon as his uncle leaves, however, Don Mariano goes to the widow's house to recover Flora's portrait, which he supposes to be still in her possession. When the Alcalde arrives he finds Don Mariano playing the role of banker. Through the influence of Don Christóval the youth is not sent to prison but exiled from Madrid. The uncle proposes to take him to Valencia, where he may start life anew under his guidance and removed from his mother's influence. The play ends with a typical neo-classic injunction:

> What? You are confused?
> That is not a bad sign. And
> if some day you have children,

you can cite this example to them;
but if you do not give them
better instruction than you have received,
what is happening to you today
will happen also to them.

From the initial scene we are never allowed to forget the didactic purpose of the author. The play itself has sufficient intrigue to hold the interest of the spectators, although some violence is done in the final act in order to observe the unity of time, insufficient time being allowed for Don Mariano to leave his house, arrive at that of Doña Mónica, and assume his role of banker. All of this, with the arrest of the offenders and the arrangement between the Alcalde and Don Christóval, would necessarily consume more time than that allowed.

Iriarte is much more concerned than Leandro Fernández de Moratín with public morals. Gambling seems to be his particular aversion, for we find this vice playing a prominent part in both *The Pampered Youth* and *The Ill-bred Miss.* His description of the scene the uncle witnesses in the house of Doña Mónica is detailed and realistic.

The language of the play is completely free from affectation; in fact, at times it descends almost to the level of a *sainete,* especially in the speeches of Don Mariano. The characters of Don Mariano and his mother are admirably done and thoroughly consistent throughout. The author is not so successful with the minor characters, Flora and Don Fausto; but since his primary purpose is to paint the character of an overindulgent mother and a profligate son, this is not a serious defect. The play is not entirely devoid of comic force, although the humor is frequently furnished by the side remarks of the servant, Pantoja.

Spanish dramatists had not yet learned the art of giving comic force to the principal characters in their comedies. The long practice of relegating this element to the *graciosos* could not be dropped suddenly. Comedy of character and situation is rare even in the best neo-classic plays.

The play is written in octosyllabic *romance,* which remains constant throughout an act, but which changes with the act.

After some difficulty occasioned by the unwillingness of one actress, La Paca, to play the role of the mother, Iriarte succeeded in persuading María Bermejo to accept it; and on September 9, 1788, the play was presented at the Príncipe by the company of Manuel Martínez. The author had directed the rehearsals of the play himself and apparently was successful in aiding the actors to interpret their roles without exaggeration.

The success of this comedy was complete. The initial run was eight days, with an attendance more than double that of the plays that preceded and followed it. The "Censure" by Don Santos Díez González, who had succeeded Don Ignacio de Ayala as Corrector of Comedies, could not have been more flattering. This comedy, he says, is clear proof of the excellency of the dramatic precepts; and the adversaries of regularity "who have tyrannically taken possession of our theater" can no longer taunt the exponents of these precepts by saying that writing good works is quite different from talking about them. "Don Tomás de Iriarte . . . has answered such an objection by publishing this original comedy, in which I not only can find no defect, but, if necessary, I would challenge any critic and even the most envious man to point out a single defect."[31] Such is the merit of the play, in Díez González' opinion, that not only does it deserve to be performed, but its author should receive public thanks "in order that, in view of this example of honor and distinction, other writers may be encouraged to imitate him by presenting original plays, which is the best way to improve and correct our theaters."[32]

The review of the comedy which appeared in the *Memorial Literario* was highly flattering:

The theme is not as lofty as in many of our comedies, nor as low as in others that might pass for *entremeses;* it is in between, being taken from civil life, which is appropriate for comedy. Its language is pure and correct; its style is uniform and stable, there being no necessity for changes. The action is single and the interest is lively and well sustained. It observes the proper decorum of the characters. . . . Virtue is everywhere placed in contrast with vice, the latter being punished and the former always emerging triumphant. The plot is well handled and the solution is prepared without leaving any loose ends, the whole forming a thing of beauty, made up of well-proportioned parts and combined with the proper magnitude and grandeur . . .[33]

In the *Diario de Madrid* for October 3, 1788, however, an anonymous writer published an *octave* in which the success of the play was attributed not to its merit, but to the skill of the actors. This was answered in the *Diario* on October 6, by a friend of the author, with another *octave*. On the 11th of the same month, the first critic accused Iriarte of having taken the plan of his comedy from Goldoni and the plot from a *sainete* by Ramón de la Cruz. This accusation was answered by the author himself so effectively in the same periodical on October 18 that the unknown critic ceased his attack.

Leandro Fernández de Moratín, while abstaining from giving the comedy his unqualified endorsement, does give Iriarte credit for having composed the first original neo-classic comedy to be produced in the theaters of Spain.

... *The Pampered Youth* ... very well performed by the company of Martínez, received the applause of the public because of its moral object, its versification, and its style. Perhaps it deserved the censure of those who noted in it a lack of dramatic movement, of lightness, and of mirth; but these defects are easily tolerated in view of the many qualities that made it estimable both in the performance and in the reading. This was the first original comedy performed in the theaters of Spain to be written in accordance with the essential rules dictated by philosophy and good criticism.[34]

The Pampered Youth was played occasionally until 1811 and was revived for four performances in 1822.

In the same year (1788), Iriarte published another comedy, *The Ill-bred Miss*, which is a variant of the theme of *The Pampered Youth*. In this case an indulgent father spoils his daughter. His indulgence is caused by an epicurean philosophy which forbids him to worry over anything. He welcomes the opportunity to entrust the care of his daughter to a young widow, Antonia, who cherishes the hope of ensnaring him. She flatters and humors the girl, giving her the worst possible advice. There is in this comedy as in *The Pampered Youth* a careful use of balance. Against the Marqués, who is an affected fop, superficial but calculating, we find the thoroughly moral and sensible Eugenio, and against the irresponsible father we have his sensible sister and her husband, who try to show Pepita the error of her ways. The girl hesitates for a time between her two suitors, but, not being able to tolerate the preaching of Eugenio, she decides definitely on the false Marqués. In the end the latter is exposed as an imposter, with a wife whom he has abandoned in want. He is also identified as the swindler who was responsible for the loss of the fortune of Antonia's dead husband. As the Marqués is carried away to prison, Pepita turns to Eugenio and signifies her willingness to marry him. The young man, however, replies that the bad habits produced by her education are obviously more deeply rooted than he thought, and that he gladly yields her to some man less particular than he. The comedy closes in true neo-classic fashion with Don Gonzalo's repentance and a warning to other fathers:

> My dear sister, from today on
> I shall learn to be more prudent;
> And may other negligent fathers
> profit by my example.

In many respects this comedy is superior to *The Pampered Youth*. The character of Pepita is entirely convincing and consistent. Iriarte uses the Marqués to give vent to his dislike for those Spaniards who affect foreign manners and speech, a dislike which he had already expressed in *Writers in Lent*. Some of the same Gallicisms censured in that work are now put into the mouth of the Marqués. The scene where the Marqués asks Eugenio for his opinion about some verses that he has written, but which he pretends are anonymous, suggests a scene in Molière's *The Misanthrope* (Act I, Scene 2), although there is certainly no direct plagiarism.

There is much more humor in this comedy than in the earlier play, and the humor derives more from the nature of the characters themselves.

Cotarelo y Mori points out the change in Iriarte's method:

And as the principal defect noted in *The Pampered Youth* was the lack of comic force, Iriarte did not wish to incur the same criticism again; so from the beginning this work has more movement, the first scene opening with several couples singing and dancing *seguidillas*. And during the course of the action there is also a profusion of humorous incidents.[35]

The *Diario de Madrid* published a lengthy criticism of the comedy giving first the plot and then a "Scenic Analysis of the Comedy" by acts with another section entitled "Merit of This Act." At the end of the article appears a paragraph with the heading: "Merit of the Drama in General:"

The three unities are rigorously observed, since the principal action concerns the bad training of a girl; the time is limited to four or five hours of one morning, and the place to a country house. The character of the personages is well sustained in a negligent father, a badly reared daughter, a haughty and foolish neighbor lady, a commercial traveler who is a liar and a swindler, a faithful and wise friend, a prudent and decorous sister, a sincere brother-in-law, and a gossiping servant. The style is simple and familiar in the main characters and humble and low in the servants. The verse is unadorned, being octosyllabic assonance throughout.[36]

La Espigadera was loud in its praise of the play and of its author, quoting the judgment of the Italian critic, Signorelli, which had appeared in his *Critical History:*

The plot deserves much praise for its regularity, for its excellent moral aspect, and for its natural portrayal of the characters of Pepita, Doña Ambrosia, Don Gonzalo, and of the Marqués particularly, in whom the pedantry of those who confuse the Castilian language with French words and phrases is ridiculed with much wit, after the manner of the famous author of the *Gerundio . . .*

and continuing with its own evaluation of the comedy:

. . . Would that many plays as regular and worthy of praise as this one were being performed in our theater and that those who furnish the stage with farces might devote themselves to studying nature more and to following the straight path of regularity and good taste along which this author has traveled.[37]

The "Censure" which Don Santos Díez González, as corrector of comedies, made of the play was most flattering and ended with the same recommendation he made in the case of *The Pampered Youth* —that is, that Iriarte be given thanks for his contribution to the culture of the theater, which, we are told, the mayor of Madrid, Don José Antonio de Armona, did with great pleasure.[38]

For some unexplained reason the performance of this comedy was not entrusted to the company of Martínez, which had been so successful with *The Pampered Youth,* but to the company of Eusebio Ribera, which at that time was distinctly inferior in personnel. This company, Cotarelo y Mori says, had as its leading ladies two "beautiful statues," Juana García Hugalde and Andrea Luna, and for male leads Vicente Merino, "who was always sick," and Manuel García, "who was only notable for his love for the profession, because his declamation was extremely affected, and he was considered by intelligent people a very mediocre actor."[39] In spite of the poor performance of the actors, the comedy lasted on its initial run from the 3rd to the 9th of January, 1791, with receipts that ranged from 7,336 reals on the first day to 3,876 on the seventh, which far surpassed the average for the plays performed that year. It appears that the partisans of the national school had organized their forces and that they did their best with noisy demonstrations to prevent the success of the comedy, for *La Espigadera* comments bitterly on the conduct of this element of the audience:

... in spite of the efforts of educated people, we have seen to our sorrow the comedies, *The Trickster Nobleman* and *The Ill-bred Miss*, cried out against, while applause has been given to *The Good Son, Aragon Restored, The Conquest of Milán,* and other monsters produced by barbarism, in which there is no connection, coherence, plot solution, *agnicion, peripecie,* unities, or any of the intrinsic and essential qualities of comedy.[40]

While the comedy was still on the stage the following comments appeared anonymously in the form of an *octave* in the *Diario de Madrid:*

> No matter how the actors ruin it,
> no matter how ruffians detest it,
> and foolish critics regard it with disdain,
> while they applaud the plays of silly authors;
> to the impartial public
> and to truly intelligent people
> the *Ill-bred Miss* is a very moral
> and a most exquisite comedy.[41]

Iriarte's last play, *Winning Ways,* in three acts and in verse, was composed during his residence in Sanlúcar in 1790. The comedy was performed in the palace of the Duchess of Osuna but never reached the theaters of Madrid. Not until after the author's death was the play published. There is in the National Library of Madrid a rough draft of this comedy in which the author reveals how carefully he sought to follow the classic precepts, even going so far as to count the number of verses for each scene. In one of its articles on dramatic precepts the *Diario de Madrid* had said that "each scene should consist of sixty hendecasyllabic verses at the most in a tragedy or of seventy octosyllabic verses in a comedy."[42]

In *Winning Ways* Iriarte abandoned to a considerable extent the moralizing tone that had characterized his previous comedies. There is no attempt to correct through ridicule.

A young lady, Rosalía, of noble parentage, is shipwrecked en route from Havana. Her uncle is drowned and she is rescued. She makes her way to Madrid, where, because of lack of funds, she is forced to enter the house of Don Alberto as a servant. Without revealing her identity she soon succeeds in winning the admiration and affection of all except Elena, a young widow, who, having been disillusioned by her former husband, has developed misanthropic tendencies and sees only faults in her associates. Don Alberto and his son, Leandro, both aspire to win the hand of the charming servant. Don Alberto learns her identity and, since there is no difference in their social positions, is eager to lead her to the altar. Don Leandro, believing her to be a servant, is still willing to marry her. However, since she is really from the upper class, Iriarte cannot be accused of advocating the abandonment of class distinctions. This play hardly goes beyond the position taken by Lope de Vega in *The Water Maid,* where the heroine is a noble lady in disguise. Although Leandro does signify his complete willingness to marry out of his class, it is unnecessary, as it turns out, for him to oppose tradition, and the solution is conventional. At the close of the comedy, Leandro, of course, wins Rosalía's hand. No one is punished and no one is ridiculed. The play is rather an exaltation of feminine virtue in the person of the heroine.

The element of intrigue is furnished in this comedy by the machinations of Elena, who seeks to prevent the marriage of Leandro to the charming servant because he has previously paid court to her. Her jealousy is, however, only superficial, being rather piqued pride than a consuming passion. If the author's intention was to contrast Rosalía, who possesses that rare quality *don de gentes,* or winning personality, with Elena, he only partially succeeds, since Elena never becomes a disagreeable character. She has many qualities found in Molière's *Misanthrope.* It is possible that Iriarte received some suggestions from this play and made Elena a combination of Célimène and Alceste. The portrait scene in *Winning Ways* may have been suggested by the well-known scene (Act II, Sc. 4) in *Le Misantrope,* where Célimène gives a word painting of each of her suitors. Cotarelo y Mori would trace this technique back to the Spanish dramatists of the Golden Age. It seems much more likely, however, that the immediate source was French.

In *Winning Ways* Iriarte comes dangerously close to violating the unity of action. The love affair between Doña Teodora and Don Melchor is really solved before the solution of the main plot, although its solution does depend in a measure on the latter's solution. Iriarte may have derived the idea of this minor action from the numerous examples of the *bachillera* in Golden Age comedy, who in the end allows herself to be ruled by her heart rather than by her head. The character of Teodora, who is "inclined to platonic love," is, however, only sketched.

The construction of *Winning Ways* is rather loose for a neo-classic comedy. There is a profusion of minor interests. Don Alberto is described in the "List of Characters" as an "old man prejudiced in favor of everything that is old. An eccentric character." We are led to expect from the initial scene that there will be a definite conflict between his ideas and those of Elena, and that this conflict will play a prominent part in the solution of the play. This contrast is dropped, however, almost immediately. Don Alberto's rivalry with his son becomes the main issue, but never seriously threatens the happy solution of the comedy as it does in Molière's *L'Avare*. The character of the Marqués is well drawn. He was doubtless a rather common type in Spanish society at that time. The comedy is indeed more a gallery of prevailing types than a well-constructed play. The interest drags at the close, since the audience is already informed of the solution. The revelation of Rosalía's identity comes too early in the play to furnish any element of suspense. The appearance, in the final scene, of the sailor who rescued Rosalía is entirely extraneous, for he contributes nothing to the interest or to the solution of the plot.

Recasts of Golden Age Comedies

While Iriarte was achieving a measure of success with original comedies in winning the public to an acceptance or tolerance of the neo-classic theater, another author was carrying the fight to the stronghold of the national school. In 1772 Sebastián y Latre published his much censured *Experiment on the Spanish Theater*.[43] Following the plan already suggested by Luzán in his *Poetics* and recommended directly by Don Bernardo Iriarte, the author of the *Experiment* sought by model recasts to incite his countrymen to rework the mass of irregular Golden Age comedy which held the boards so tenaciously, thanks to the predilection of the actors for this type of play and to the untiring efforts of partisans of the national school, more than to the popularity of such plays with the general public.

In the "Prologue" to the *Experiment*, the author recognizes the natural ability of the Golden Age writers Lope de Vega, Calderón, Moreto, Solís, Salazar, and Rojas, but laments that they should have misused their talents:

If our poets had controlled their imagination as they should, what perfect models we would have today to imitate! The plays would be fewer in number, but much more useful and more in keeping with the moderation of a Christian theater and with the seriousness of the Spanish nation. These great men, being too sensitive to the applause of the blind crowd, allowed themselves to be carried away by its flattery; and even after they came to recognize that the road they had been following was not the right one, they did not dare to oppose the bad taste of their age, fearful perhaps of jeopardizing the reputation acquired from their first productions.[44]

After serious reflection the author has determined to risk the disapproval of the crowd in order to aid in bringing order out of chaos. Although the ignorant masses insist obstinately "that our comedies are in keeping with the character of the nation, and that, therefore, their duels, quarrels, incidents, and adventures are characteristic of us,"[45] the author maintains that this defense is motivated by a ridiculous caprice and a despicable pride which brands as unpatriotic any censure of Golden Age dramatists. More difficult, however, to combat than the prejudices of the crowd is the opposition to reform on the part of those whom he calls "protectors of bad taste," whose education should make them allies rather than adversaries of the proponents of a regular theater.

The author traces his own classical education from the time he wrote the prologue to his tragedy British, when he was not entirely convinced of the defects of the Spanish dramatists. After diligent study of Aristotle, Horace, Cervantes, Cascales, Luzán, Nasarre, Velázquez, and other critics he has determined "to follow their thought in regard to taking the plots of our poets" and adapting them to the rules.[46]

To carry out his purpose he has chosen two plays: Progne and Filomena by Rojas and The Resemblance by Moreto. He has not been moved to choose these two works by admiration for them or because they are in any sense regular. On the contrary, he says, his motive was that "it seemed to him that he was doing a great service to the public in trying to remove them from the theater" in their original form.[47]

In commenting on The Resemblance in 1785, the Memorial Literario misinterprets the motives that impelled Sebastián y Latre to make his recast:

The beautiful arrangement of the plot and the amusing situations that result from the incidents place this comedy among the most regular and delightful in our theater. Nevertheless, Don Sebastián y Latre, in the reform of the Spanish theater which he started, tried to correct some slight defects in the comedy, choosing it at the same time as one of the best.[48]

The author of the recast says that his principal objection to these plays is not their numerous irregularities but their detrimental moral influence. A "pernicious example for wild youths and a scandalous spectacle for uncautious maidens,"[49] they are especially harmful since they are in everyone's hands and frequently performed.

Like all the neo-classicists, Sebastián y Latre believes firmly in dramatic illusion. In order that this may not be destroyed at the end of each act, he recommends that the *sainetes, entremeses,* and *tonadillas* be omitted between acts because they "destroy the illusion and the poet loses all the effort he has expended to kindle interest in the spectators during the act..."[50]

This same idea is later voiced by Leandro Fernández de Moratín in a note to his *New Comedy* (Act II, Sc. 4). The distribution of the performance was as follows: "The comedy started, and after the first act an *entremés* was given; after the second there was a *tonadilla,* a *sainete,* then another *tonadilla,* and finally the third act."[51] All of this, Moratín says, destroyed the illusion and unity of the comedy, for "there is no way to describe the distraction, the discordance, and the lack of unity and interest, that resulted from this strange mixture."[52]

Sebastián y Latre closes his prologue by expressing his purpose: "The sample I present can only serve to indicate the course that should be taken in order to remove from our theater so many comedies like those of Rojas and Moreto."[53] His efforts, however, met with a cold reception not only from the public but even from extreme neo-classicists, who considered it absurd to attempt to rework the old comedies. Menéndez y Pelayo summarizes the result of these recasts: "Sebastián y Latre's attempt satisfied no one. The public still understood Moreto and Rojas and wanted the old comedies and not the recasts, which they considered sacrilegious; and the fanatics who favored French taste cried out that it was absurd to attempt to correct *our terrible comedies.*"[54]

From the number of performances and the average receipts of Golden Age plays at this time it appears, as we have seen, that it must have been the nationalist critics much more than the masses who objected so strenuously to any tampering with their beloved *comedia.*

In his recast of *The Resemblance* Sebastián y Latre seeks in every way possible to make the play regular. Only assonance is used and the unities are carefully observed. To make this observance possible, it is necessary to reduce much of the action of the original to a narrative. The only thing he could not do was to make the comedy an active exponent of morals. He seeks to remedy this defect, however, by dragging in a moral in the last speech:

> ... Nevertheless
> in these and other matters,
> my children, proceed with caution.
> Don't trust in appearances
> and form your opinions as I have done.
> Let what you have observed
> serve as a lesson to you.

Sebastián y Latre certainly did not succeed in driving Moreto's play from the theater, for it continued to be played until 1813 and enjoyed a renewed popularity from 1820 to 1831, being played eighteen times during the latter period.

The time was not yet ripe for recasts. Not until 1800 did a reworking meet with public approval. In that year Cándido María de Trigueros converted Lope de Vega's *The Star of Seville* into a regular tragedy with the title *Sancho Ortiz de las Roelas,* which Menéndez y Pelayo hails as "one of the greatest theatrical events of that epoch."[55]

The reviews of this work, however, were not all favorable; for, while the *Diario de Madrid* praised the play, calling it one of the best tragedies ever presented on the Spanish stage, the *Gaceta de Madrid* and the *Regañon General* found nothing to commend in the recast. The review that appeared in the *Diario de Madrid* on February 15, 1800, was written apparently by an ardent admirer of Lope, who, at the same time, professed to be eager for reform in the Spanish theater. This reform, he says, will depend to a large extent upon improvement in the talent and training of actors. His comments on *Sancho Ortiz* begin with a eulogy of Lope and a denunciation of contemporary dramatists:

A few days ago I saw the tragedy *Sancho Ortiz de las Roelas,* taken from an original comedy by the incomparably fertile Lope de Vega, who gave it, if I am not mistaken, the title *The Star of Seville.* When I call Lope de Vega incomparably fertile, it is because many are not able to appreciate the fecundity of this writer in view of the irregularity of his comedies, and

do not realize that in all or in most of them he knew how to introduce
interesting incidents, sometimes comic and sometimes tragic, and that
his language is always pure and his style natural and fluent, although the
versification is too artificial at times. A man, in short, who hardly knew
how to write a bad verse, should not be confused because of the great
flaws in his comedies with the present purveyors of our theaters, who have
never been able to write a good line in their lives, much less to express
an emotion capable of touching the heart.[56]

In spite of his admiration for Lope, it is evident that this critic has
not read the original work, for he continues:

... I think that the recaster of this tragedy has not touched the verses, a
matter which we could determine by a comparison of the recast with the
original. What he has probably done has been to cut out some episodes
in order that the scene may not change except between the acts; a fine
idea, since the unity of place, which is not so rigorous as that of action
or even that of time, is kept to a certain extent, if in the same act we are
not made to pass from one place to another...[57]

The reviewer would prefer, however, that the recaster had not
caused the corpse of Bustos Talavera to be taken to the room of his
sister Estrella, and that the killer had not been brought to the same
room and into the presence of the sister of the dead man. These
defects, of course, are due to the attempt to observe closely the unity
of place within the act. This review was answered on the 22nd of
the same month in the Diario de Madrid by another critic, who
defended Sancho Ortiz against the objections that had been raised
and ended with strong praise of the recast:

... The tragedy Sancho Ortiz de las Roelas, if not the best, is at least one
of the best that have been presented in our theater, and is superior in
merit to most of those that have appeared in foreign countries. We cherish
the hope, therefore, that in a short time we shall see many other arrangements of our old plays performed.[58]

The recast was published in 1800 and was preceded by a lengthy
"Foreword," in which Trigueros gives due credit to Lope de Vega as
the original author.[59] In his Life of Lope de Vega, Rennert gives free
rein to his contempt for neo-classic precepts and does Trigueros
an injustice by accusing him of altering the original completely. He
even goes to the extreme of insinuating that Trigueros appropriated
Lope's play without giving him credit:

In England the degenerate taste of the period of the Restoration altered the plays of Shakespeare. Here the Shadwells and the Tates thrust them into the strait jacket of the unities. About a century later we find Trigueros, in Spain, accommodating some of the comedies of Lope de Vega to the same system. Of *The Star of Seville* not a line of Lope's is left. It is divided into five acts and, in the copy I have, the poet's name is not mentioned. The title is *Sancho Ortiz de Roelas, Tragedy, arranged by D. Cándido María Trigueros.*[60]

Rennert obviously did not have access to the first edition of the recast and was not aware of the "Foreword," in which Trigueros dwells at such length on the merits of Lope as a dramatist and of *The Star of Seville* in particular. It is obvious also that he did not compare the recast with the original; for, if he had, he could not have made the statement that "not a line of Lope's is left." As a matter of fact, Trigueros preserves a great many of Lope's lines intact and makes very slight alterations in many others.

Inasmuch as the first edition of this comedy is rare and the "Foreword" did not accompany the reprints in 1804, 1813, 1815, and 1818, it may be well to examine Trigueros' statement in detail:

When Lope composed the present drama, calling it a comedy and giving it the title *The Star of Seville,* he knew very well that he was composing a true tragedy and said so himself through the mouth of Clarindo. . . . It is true that the author overloaded it somewhat, beginning the action before it was necessary and directing it with the same disorder that has been so common since those times; but we should not attribute these defects either to ignorance on his part or to lack of aptitude and talent for tragedy. . . . If we analyze this tragedy intelligently and without prejudice, we shall find in it the greatest proof of the true dramatist and tragic poet. A well-chosen and well-handled action, sublime and well-sustained characters, excellent and magnificently pathetic situations, either expressed or suggested; appropriate expression, and a versification that is characteristically Lope's, are qualities rarely found to such a degree in writers of any nation. . . . The action of this drama is unified and simple, but full of that marvelous and indescribable something that entertains and charms at the same time that it moves and instructs.[61]

After paying this warm tribute to Lope, Trigueros explains the method he has followed in making his arrangement:

Since I have not had to make any change at all in the action or in its conduct, it is obvious that the same unities of time, place, and interest which are in the present work were also in the original. . . . The only difference consists in the fact that I have made these unities more apparent and have not permitted changes except between the acts. This difference, however, has forced me to make various changes in the disposition and order of the scenes; but the most notable alterations have been due to other reasons. It seemed to me I should omit everything that precedes the real action of the drama; and, although in the old comedy this was put into action, it was really more suitable for narration and for a "hidden prologue." With this single change an entire act and the greater part of another were omitted, which could perhaps furnish material for another drama. Although Lope's comedy was very long, reducing it to a little more than half of its length would make it too short, and the acts, which, because of place requirements, should be five, would be left very brief and very unequal. To avoid these objections it has been necessary not only to interpolate a great number of new verses, but also to add scenes and to develop, so to speak, some excellent situations which in the original were only suggested. In spite of these changes, since all the substance of the invention and the greater part of the arrangement is Lope's, as well as the greater number of verses, some of which have been slightly retouched, it must be confessed that the principal merit of this tragedy is his, and any lack of merit it may have . . . should be attributed to the corrector alone. . . .[62]

Sancho Ortiz de las Roelas was presented for the first time on January 22, 1800, and ran for eight days. It was repeated for seven days in December of the same year. The total production for the year was 87,293 reals, an average of 5,819. This one recast, in 15 performances, produced almost one-fourth as much that year as 33 original Golden Age plays in 137 performances. It was played 49 times from 1800 to 1814. In view of the outstanding success of this recast, Trigueros was not long in reworking three other plays by Lope: *The Water Maid, The Prudish Lady,* and *The Female Sharper.* Of these recasts *The Water Maid* proved to be one of the most popular plays on the Madrid stage for the next thirty years, having 65 performances from 1803 to 1818 and 20 performances from 1820 to 1833. It was performed for the first time on April 18, 1803, and lasted for fifteen days. The next year it was repeated for nine consecutive performances.

A review of *The Water Maid* in the *Memorial Literario* praised the plan of the recaster and expressed the hope that others would follow his example:

Without renewing here the much debated question of the merit of our Spanish theater, it will suffice to observe that it would be a very good idea for some of our writers to reform many old comedies as Don Cándido María Trigueros has done with this one that we are going to discuss, and with his well-known recast of *The Star of Seville,* both the product of the fertile wit of our Lope.[63]

In this recast, Trigueros followed the same procedure as in *Sancho Ortiz.* The *Memorial Literario* says that

... the modern reformer has done no more, as he himself confesses, than to omit all of the first act and a few lines in the others, interpolating only some verses in order to prolong the duration of the drama. In so doing he has not made the comedy regular, since its defects are inherent, but he has corrected the most glaring errors, and this seems to have been his plan.[64]

While the reviews in the *Memorial Literario* and the *Diario de Madrid* were favorable, the *Regañón General* found the recasts of *The Star of Seville* and *The Water Maid* "wretched and ridiculous." After censuring the overwhelming preference shown in the theater of the Caños del Peral for translations of foreign plays, and the indecent jokes, guffaws, and jests which marred the performances in that theater, the *Regañón* says:

In the theater of the Cruz we notice more moderation and respect in the performances. Here, it seems, they have proposed to follow a different system from that followed in the Caños del Peral. Almost all the comedies are from the old poets of the seventeenth and sixteenth centuries. Since all extremes are vicious, a middle course should be followed. Some of the old comedies are so well known that they are boring; others deal with such antiquated subject matter that they do not interest us; and others are so nonsensical that we cannot endure them. It is true that in almost all there is excellent language; but skill is necessary in order to choose those which lack the above defects and which will be pleasing on the stage, a thing we do not find in the plays that are being performed at present. One of the means by which we might have an excellent national theater would no doubt be to correct and arrange the multitude of theatrical works of our poets, but who dares to undertake such a task? After the attempts that have been made by so many wise and able men, who have failed so badly, will anyone have the audacity to correct a nonsensical verse written by Calderón, Lope, and the others? It may well be that someone with extraordinary talent will succeed in doing so, but up until now we have seen nothing but the wretched and ridiculous recasts of *The Star of Seville* and *The Water Maid.*[65]

Eleven years later the *Gaceta de Madrid* objected strenuously to Trigueros' attempt to transform *The Star of Seville* into a regular tragedy:

To try to make a tragedy that will conform to the rules of art from a comedy, in which the plan, workmanship, incidents, style, and everything else is defective, is a task not only bold but impossible. So it happened that when Don Cándido María Trigueros transformed *The Star of Seville,* a comedy by Lope de Vegas, into the tragedy, *Sancho Ortiz de las Roelas,* he succeeded in tearing down the former and making from its pieces a monster that is neither Lope's work nor a drama with any sense in it. . . . So it remains only as an evident proof of the bad taste of the recaster and of the ridiculousness, harmfulness, and uselessness of recasts, a new branch of literature invented in Spain in the last century.[66]

In his recasts Trigueros had pointed the way, however, and had proven that the public would welcome arrangements of Golden Age plays, if they were made with a genuine appreciation and affection for their good qualities and a desire to accommodate them to a modern theater. Although Trigueros did not live to see his last three recasts performed, his work was taken up almost immediately by Vicente Rodríguez de Arellano, who reworked Lope's *To Leave the Certain for the Doubtful* in 1803, and by Enciso Castrillón, who presented his arrangement of Lope's *Dorotea* in 1804. Arellano's recast proved to be very popular, having an initial run of eight days and being performed thirty-seven times from 1803 to 1818.

A note in the periodical *Efemérides* calls attention to Castrillón's attitude toward the original of the play he was reworking: "The author of this comedy is one of the greatest admirers of the grace, the style, and the versification of the old Spanish poets, and particularly of the phoenix of them all, Lope de Vega."[67]

Sebastían y Latre's attempt to rework Golden Age plays failed because he had no sympathy or appreciation for the *comedia* and was actuated solely by a desire either to alter them until they conformed completely to neo-classic precepts or to drive them from the stage. The new generation of recasters, however, approached their task with an entirely different attitude. They chose a play because they considered that it had genuine merit and could, without too great violence, be made to conform to the rules.

It may be said that through the efforts of Trigueros a number of Lope de Vega's plays were restored to the Spanish stage, for, prior to that time, *The King the Best Alcalde* was the only one of his comedies that had remained in the repertoire of the theater, and even this play was unenthusiastically received when it was returned to the stage for an occasional performance. Following the procedure used by Trigueros, and motivated by an equal love and admiration for Golden Age plays, Dionisio Solís, the prompter at the theater of the Principe, turned his talents to arranging such well-known comedies as Lope's *The King the Best Alcalde* and *The Simple-minded Lady;* Calderón's *The Alcalde of Zalamea, The Pretended Astrologer, Emotions of Hatred and Love, I Love All I See, The Hidden Man and the Veiled Woman,* and *The Spirit Lady;* Moreto's *The Grandee of Alcalá;* Tirso de Molina's *Pious Martha* and *The Peasant Girl of Vallecas;* Rojas' *García del Castañar;* and Cuellar's *The Pastry Cook of Madrigal,* nearly all of these recasts being made between 1810 and 1819 at the request of Máiquez, who played the leading roles. Hartzenbusch, his biographer, says that no one surpassed Solís in his ability to remodel old comedies, "a difficult but ill-appreciated task," and gives the titles of sixteen recasts of Golden Age plays made by him. These and many other comedies of the old theater, Hartzenbusch says, "owed to him their revival on the stage from which they had long been exiled." "The skill with which Solís imitated the style of the author whose work he was remodeling was such," he continues, "that a famous humanist and poet of the time, having attended the performance of one of these comedies, and having written later a review of the play, praised, as the best part, a passage that was entirely the work of Solís..."[68] In the period immediately preceding the advent of romanticism, Hartzenbusch, Carnerero, Bretón de los Herreros, and many others reworked a very considerable number of Golden Age comedies, subjecting them to the precepts in so far as it was practicable to do so but respecting the general plan and versification of the original works.

In addition to these recasts, it appears to have been a recognized practice to "correct" Golden Age plays. In the "General Regulation for the Direction and Reform of the Theaters," adopted in 1807, provision was made for the renumeration of those who made such corrections:

> Art. 6   The translations in prose, the old plays which are only corrected, the *tonadillas, sainetes,* and all kinds of interludes will be paid for in a lump sum.

There is no way to determine the number or the titles of the comedies that were subjected to this "correction," but it is likely that few of the old comedies were presented in their original form. We have in this same "Regulation" a definition of the term *refundición,* or recast, as it was interpreted at that time:

> Art 4.   The same price will be given for every old play that is *refundida* [recast], this term being applied to all those in which

the *refundidor* [recaster], using the argument and many scenes and verses of the original, varies the plan of the plot and inserts new incidents and scenes of his own invention.[69]

At no time were the recasts given the wholehearted support of neo-classic critics, who tolerated them as more regular than the originals, but considered the task impossible. There was a strong tendency, even among those neo-classicists who were unwilling to concede that the *comedia* was entirely bad, to consider that it had outlived its day and had no meaning for a new age.

Only two original comedies remain to be treated in the period which preceded Leandro Fernández de Moratín and his school. These are the ill-fated *The Tradesmen*, by Cándido María de Trigueros, and the equally unsuccessful *The Trickster Nobleman*, by Alvaro María Guerrero, the prolific poetaster of the *Diario de Madrid*.

The Tradesmen

Trigueros' comedy, *The Tradesmen*, was awarded one of the two prizes given by the municipal government of Madrid on the occasion of the public festivals in 1784 in honor of the birth of the princes, Carlos and Felipe, and the signing of the treaty of peace in Paris, which terminated an ill-advised war in which Spain had been a pawn in the hands of France in her rivalry with England. Two prizes of fifty doubloons each were offered for dramas "which, because of their novelty, merit, and subject matter, are considered worthy of such a signal honor." The conditions were that the plays be original and "if a tragedy, it must be taken from our history; if a comedy, it must ridicule national manners or vices. These plays must be written in verse, not being operas or *zarzuelas*, and must be performed within two months."[70]

A preference was expressed by the municipal government for plays adjusted to "the rules of art." Fifty-seven dramas were presented in competition for the prizes, and the committee of judges headed by Gaspar de Jovellanos, after due deliberation, announced as the winners Trigueros' comedy and *The Wedding of Camacho*, a pastoral comedy by Juan Meléndez Valdés. The only other play that seemed to have received consideration was a tragedy *Atahualpa*, by Cristóbal María Cortés y Vita, which was recommended as worthy of publication, but was never performed, so far as the records show, in any of the theaters of Madrid. Jovellanos says that an extraordinary clamor was raised against the plays selected, because those who had failed in the competition took advantage of the opportunity to question the decision of the judges.[71] It is quite likely that this attitude on the part of the disgruntled competitors found noisy expression during the performances. It certainly accounts for the mass of satires that circulated almost immediately against *The Tradesmen* and *The Wedding of Camacho* in the form of sonnets, ballads, and *décimas*.

In the preface to *The Tradesmen* Trigueros explains his choice of subject and makes it quite clear that his primary concern is the correction of vice. To be worthy of respect, he says, the theater must conform to the intention of the "August Sovereigns."

In order to achieve this purpose it is indispensable that the dramas that are performed in it be agreeable and capable of entertaining the spectators without containing anything detrimental to morals or harmful in any way.

But the glory of being agreeable is a foolish glory if public benefit is not attained at the same time. To be agreeable and useful is the end to which every poet and philosopher should aspire.

This object can be attained if a vivid portrait of harmful manners is drawn, and these manners are presented in such a way that they will excite laughter by taking advantage of those situations that are calculated to produce such a result.

The abundance of such manners is very noticeable in any nation; and in this great and universal bazaar of ridiculousness our Spain is in no way inferior to the others.

Feudalism, Gothic nobility, and Arabic-Scholastic pride have left a considerable number of prejudices that offer a stubborn resistance to the wise efforts of the government and to the enlightenment of a philosophic century which, in spite of its present state of ignorance, will some day be the epoch of greatest honor to humanity.

One of the prejudices that are the products of vanity and ignorance is the low esteem in which the trades and tradesmen are held, as an immediate effect of a false idea of nobility.

From this unjust scorn has come a mania on the part of most of the tradesmen to rise above their social class, with the result that they neglect or forsake their trades in the belief that they will be more highly regarded in other positions. Everyone recognizes how detrimental this foolish notion is to the public good.

Among the many methods that might be found to combat this evil by ridiculing it, the author of this comedy has chosen the one which seemed to him most effective: that is, not only attacking it directly but also opposing indirectly and in the same manner other vices that arise from the same cause.[72]

The vice he intends to attack, then, is the prejudice on the part of the upper class, which has its origin in the feudal age, against the artesans or *menestrales*. As a result of the low esteem in which they are held, many of the latter class are dissatisfied and wish to abandon their trades. By ridicule the author seeks to correct this evil.

The Tradesmen, contrary to the prevalent practice in comedy, is written in hendecasyllabic *romance* meter, a meter that had been reserved exclusively for tragedy. The author yields to popular taste, at least in the inclusion of a comic character, Pitanzos, who has all the qualities of the *gracioso,* and whose role was played by Mariano Querol, the outstanding comic actor of the day. He also takes into consideration the fondness on the part of the public for singing and dancing and not only has the servants sing in the second act as they are adorning the garden, but introduces one scene where Rufina, Clara, and Rafa, three of the principal characters, sing and dance.

This comedy was played from July 16 to July 26, 1784, at the Príncipe by the company of Eusebio Ribera. No attention or expense was spared in its staging. A new front curtain, painted by Zacarías González y Velázquez, represented in the foreground an old man, naked and holding a kind of scoop in his left hand, leaning over a large jar and pouring water into it in representation of the timid river Manzanares. To the left and in the middle of the curtain there was the figure of a woman sitting on some clouds and representing comedy, with a mask in one hand and a trumpet in the other. In the upper part Apollo, seated on a throne of clouds, was crowning three handsome matrons, who represented the three noble arts, Painting, Music, and Poetry; and in the background appeared the temple of Fame.[73]

The decoration of the prologue, or "Loa," which was written by Ramón de la Cruz, was a garden with flowers, statues, and a horizon. Dawn appeared in the figure of a matron, crowned with seven stars, seated in a chariot drawn by four bears, with a madrona tree in full fruit at the back. Shepherds and shepherdesses could be seen dancing in the garden.

The stage for the comedy itself represented a magnificently adorned garden in Chamaartin, with a summerhouse, or bower, in the foreground. During the second act the servants, who are engaged in decorating the garden for a festival, sing in a low voice from time to time, while an orchestra is playing behind the scene.

The effect of the comedy is marred not so much by its regularity and strict adherence to the unities as by its constant moralizing. The spectator is not allowed to forget that the purpose of the play is to ridicule the evil effects of excessive ambition and vanity on the part of the artisans. In the closing scene, Don Juan, the *barba*, who, as the old man, represents the voice of wisdom, pronounces a typical neo-classic sermon:

Stop all that nonsense; nobility is based on virtue and work. Everyone is born to sweat; he who earns his living with his labor is fulfilling his duty and is a good man, worthy to be esteemed as such. The fact that others, through either fortune or misfortune, may have been condemned to idleness, and may have other caprices, is of little importance. One who opposes reason is rash, for we are all branches from the same trunk. No one is more noble than a good citizen, and he who is most useful to society is most noble, whether he be of high or low degree. . . . Let us live where Heaven has placed us, for only in that way will we be happy; and let us realize that what is good can never be bad.[74]

In spite of the efforts of the author and the elaborateness of the stage setting, *The Tradesmen* was a failure, as was also its companion, *The Wedding of Camacho*, which was played simultaneously at the Cruz. Jovellanos confesses that "the fortune of these two plays in the theater could not have been worse," but attributes their failure primarily to the bad performance of the actors. They have been, he says, "diabolically ruined." Although this critic, who, as one of the judges, might be expected to defend *The Tradesmen*, calls it "one of the best plays that have been produced for our theater and one of those most in keeping with our nature and manners," other critics have dealt harshly with the comedy. The *Memorial Literario* published a review of *The Tradesmen* in July and August, 1784. Though the critic points out merits in the play and is obviously trying to be fair, the article's general tone is unfavorable:

. . . The comic character Pitanzos pleased with his witty remarks directed at the tradesmen, his exaggerations of mountain nobility, and the story of the donkey loaded with straw. . . . The spectators also found agreeable the benign character of Cortines' wife, who regretted the disorders of her husband. They were also pleased with the goodness of the daughter Rufina and the chaste and simple love of Justo. The complaints that Cortines makes about the bad opinion the rich and noble class have of the tradesmen seemed well founded to many people. The audience also enjoyed the sweet and delicate tunes sung by Rufina, Clara, and Rafa. . . . Notwithstanding these appreciable qualities in a comedy that should have as its object the reproof of vice and the triumph of virtue, the most scrupulous did not find all the qualities prescribed by the rules of art, and noticed an inconsistency in the purposes of the various personages. . . .[75]

The criticism directed against *The Tradesmen* aroused in Trigueros a spirit of defiance. He refused to admit that his comedy was not excellent, and from that time until his death, which occurred around 1803, the numerous critical articles on the theater written by him for the *Diario de Madrid* were signed with the initials E.A.D.L.M. (El Autor de *Los Menestrales*).

The Trickster Nobleman

The Trickster Nobleman,[76] in three acts and in verse, was performed a few months after Moratín's comedy *The Old Man and the Young Girl*, and provoked almost as much adverse criticism as *The Tradesmen*. Its author, Alvaro María Guerrero, was an ardent partisan of the neo-classic precepts and had come to the defense of Iriarte's *The Pampered Youth* with a sonnet published in the *Correo de Madrid* on November 12, 1788. A *letrilla* published in the *Diario de Madrid* on January 16, 1791, in defense of the same author's *The Ill-bred Miss*, has also been attributed to him. Guerrero's enthusiasm for regular comedy led him to compose *The Trickster Nobleman* and to make it conform as nearly as possible to the precepts and moral purpose of neo-classicism. Cotarelo y Mori says that this comedy was performed at the Príncipe a few months after the performance of Moratín's *The Old Man and the Young Girl* but that it met a less favorable reception. Indeed, to judge by the comments made in the *Memorial Literario* and *La Espigadera*, it must have been a complete failure. The play is not without merit, however, and, as the first dramatic attempt of the author, gave definite promise. The unfavorable tone of contemporary reviews seems to have discouraged the author from further efforts. Cotarelo y Mori says that a friend of the author, Don Lucas Alemán y Aguado, directed at the play this friendly gibe:

> As the afternoon was cold
> and the thought thin
> Guerrero's comedy
> died of apoplexy.*

*Guerrero and Alemán had engaged in tilts in the *Diario de Madrid* and in the *Correo de Madrid* over literary questions. The latter was very definitely aligned with the opponents of neo-classicism, although his attacks were humorously satirical and never bitter or caustic. The impression left by Cotarelo y Mori is a trifle misleading, since the above gibe came from a literary opponent rather than from a friend.

The Trickster Nobleman was not without its defenders. The editor of *La Espigadera* replied angrily to Alemán's joke. In his review, the editor, while admitting the defects of the comedy, carefully calls attention to its regularity and purity of language, and praises the willingness of its author to oppose the popular taste. The reviewer recognizes the scarcity of real comic talent and the difficulty of composing a regular comedy which combines comic force with moral teaching:

The subject is suitable for comedy, the purpose of which is to correct vices by means of amusement and laughter. Since there are few people who are capable of recognizing the ridiculous and painting it with wit and sprightliness, it is not strange that the author of this comedy (even though he has shown imagination and ability in other forms of poetry) has not been able in this one to please the public, whose displeasure at seeing its performance was not entirely unfounded. . . . But it is not fair to confuse the author with the mob of versifiers who, without having made the acquaintance of the elementary principles of art, flood our theater with monstrous and nonsensical dramas, since, at least, his language is pure and suited to the genre; the verse is free and without euphuism, metaphors, puns, or Gallicisms; the plot is comic without a mixture of the heroic and the ridiculous; the unities of place and of time are very well observed; and, in a word, it is evident that the author, if he has not had the ability and dexterity that genius gives to paint the ridiculous with wit and delicacy, at least knows the rules of art and has preferred to avoid the usual extravagance that leads writers to temporize with the perverted taste of the crowd. . . .[77]

The Trickster Nobleman indeed has all the negative qualities prescribed by the neo-classic code. But the positive qualities, which genius alone can give, are lacking. There is no reason to suppose that the author would have been more successful even if he had allowed his imagination more sway. Frequently plays written under the neo-classic rules are harshly censured and the impression is left that the failure of the work was due to suppressed imagination when, as a matter of fact, the author would probably have done no better under any other system. Not only were there no outstanding plays produced by the neo-classicists before Moratín, but none were produced by the nationals, who were certainly not hampered by oppressive rules.

1. Tomás de Iriarte, *Hacer que hacemos,* comedia por D. Tirso Ymareta, con licencia en la Imprenta Real de la Gazeta, año de 1770.
2. Cotarelo y Mori, *Iriarte y su época* (Madrid, 1897), p. 77.
3. *Ibid.,* p. 78.
4. "Prólogo" to *Hacer que hacemos.*
5. *Ibid.*
6. *Ibid.*
7. *Ibid.*
8. Cotarelo y Mori, *Don Ramón de la Cruz y sus obras* (Madrid, 1889), pp. 140-41.
9. See Charles Blaise Qualia, *op. cit.,* pp. 189-90.
10. Quoted from the fly-leaf of *Don Matalote,* an anonymous *sainete,* published in 1833. The above lines are ascribed to Ramón de la Cruz.
11. Tomás de Iriarte, *Los literatos en Cuaresma,* por Don Amador de Vera y Santa Clara (Madrid, 1773), republished in *Obras de Iriarte,* VII, 39.
12. *Ibid.,* p. 39.
13. *Ibid.,* p. 40.
14. *Ibid.* p. 46.
15. *Ibid.*
16. *Ibid.,* p. 48.
17. *Ibid.,* p. 33.
18. *Ibid.*
19. Voltaire, *Oeuvres Complètes* (Paris, Garnier Frères, 1878), XIV, 553.
20. Molière, *L'Impromptu de Versailles,* Scene IV.
21. Iriarte, *op. cit.,* p. 35.
22. Cotarelo y Mori, *Iriarte y su época,* "Apendice," IV, 442.
23. *Ibid.,* p. 434.
24. *Ibid.,* p. 444.
25. *Ibid.,* p. 445.
26. Iriarte, *Obras,* I, 41-42.
27. Cotarelo y Mori, *Iriarte y su época,* p. 333.
28. *Ibid.*
29. Leandro Fernández de Moratín, "Reseña histórica sobre el teatro español," in *Orígenes del Teatro español* (Paris, 1883), pp. 460-61.
30. Cotarelo y Mori, *op. cit.,* p. 345.
31. *Ibid.,* p. 348.
32. *Ibid.,* p. 348-49.
33. *El Memorial Literario,* Oct., 1788.
34. Moratín, *op. cit.,* p. 462.
35. Cotarelo y Mori, *op. cit.,* p. 359.
36. *El Diario de Madrid,* April 29, 1789.
37. *La Espigadera,* Num. 14, II, 1790, pp. 49 ff.

38. Cotarelo y Mori, *op. cit.,* p. 363.
39. *Ibid.*
40. *La Espigadera,* Num. 15, 1791.
41. *El Diario de Madrid,* January 7, 1791.
42. *Ibid.,* August 7, 1789.
43. Thomás Sebastián y Latre, *Ensayo sobre el teatro español,* Zaragoza, En la Imprenta del Rey nuestro Señor, Año de 1772.
44. *Ibid.,* "Prólogo."
45. *Ibid.*
46. *Ibid.*
47. *Ibid.*
48. *El Memorial Literario,* February, 1785.
49. Sebastián y Latre, *op. cit.,* "Prólogo."
50. *Ibid.*
51. Leandro Fernández de Moratín, *Obras Póstumas* (Madrid, 1867), I, 137.
52. *Ibid.*
53. Sebastian y Latre, *op. cit.*
54. Menéndez y Pelayo, *op. cit.,* p. 314. Menéndez y Pelayo says in a note that the words underscored are quoted from Sempere y Guarinos, *Ensayo de una biblioteca de los mejores escritores,* V, 126.
55. *Ibid.*
56. *El Diario de Madrid,* February 15, 1800.
57. *Ibid.*
58. *Ibid.,* February 22, 1800.
59. Cándido María Trigueros, *Sancho Ortiz de las Roelas,* tragedia arreglada por D. Cándido María Trigueros. En Madrid, en la imprenta de Sancha, 1800.
60. Hugo Albert Rennert, *The Life of Lope de Vega* (Philadelphia, 1904), "Note," p. 186.
61. Trigueros, *op. cit.,* "Advertencia,"
62. *Ibid.*
63. *El Memorial Literario,* Tomo V, January, 1804, p. 29.
64. *Ibid.*
65. *El Regañón General,* June 22, 1803.
66. *Gaceta de Madrid,* June 16, 1811.
67. *Efemérides de la ilustración de España,* 1804. See Coe, *op. cit.,* p. 76.
68. Juan Eugenio Hartzenbusch, "Noticias sobre la vida y escritos de D. Dionisio Solís," published first in *La Revista* de Madrid, 1839, pp. 488-507; and republished in *Ensayos poéticos y artículos en prosa, literarios y de costumbres* (Madrid, 1843), pp. 173-214.
69. Cotarelo y Mori, *Bibliografía,* p. 701.
70. Cotarelo y Mori, *Iriarte y su época,* pp. 284-85.

71. "Carta de Jovellanos," Archivo municipal. Sección de Espectáculos. See Cotarelo y Mori, *op. cit.*, p. 293.

72. Cándido María de Trigueros, *Los menestrales*, comedia premiada por la Villa de Madrid para representarse en el Teatro del Príncipe con motivo de los festejos públicos que executa por el feliz nacimiento de los Serenísimos Infantes Carlos y Felipe y ajuste definitivo de la paz (Madrid, 1784).

73. Cotarelo y Mori, *op. cit.*, p. 289.

74. *Los menestrales*.

75. *El Memorial Literario*, July, 1784, and August, 1784. See Coe, *op. cit.*, pp. 151-52.

76. Alvaro María Guerrero, *El hidalgo tramposo*, comedia de figurón, en tres actos, en verso. Representada por la compañía de Ribera en este presente año de 1790. (This comedy is included in *Comedias de varios autores*, Tomo VI, Yale University Library.)

77. *La Espigadera*, 1791, No. 15, p. 171.

IX

Neo-classic Tragedy

Cadalso

THE YEAR following the performance of *Hormesinda*, Moratín's friend José Cadalso, who is known principally for his *Gloomy Nights, Superficial Erudites,* and *Moroccan Letters,* presented a tragedy, *Sancho García* (1771), in which María Ignacia Ibañez, who had played the part of the sister of Pelayo in the earlier play, appeared as the Countess of Castile. Leandro Fernández de Moratín tells us that Cadalso, who was very much in love with this actress, was unwilling to have her appear in his play until she had won the approval of the public by her performance in *Hormesinda.*[1]

The subject of this tragedy by Cadalso, which is very inferior to his other works, presented insurmountable difficulties. A Moorish king, Almanzor, in order to gain control of Castile, pretends to be in love with the widowed countess of that region. She, in spite of her rather mature age, falls blindly in love with him and is willing to sacrifice her honor, her kingdom, and even the life of her son to hold his affection. There is no suspense or interest in the play, for early in the first act the Countess listens without horror or indignation to Almanzor's proposal that she kill García and, after wavering a while between giving up her lover and shedding the blood of her son, she makes the decision in the second act and pronounces his death sentence. At the end, through an error of a servant, the mother drinks the poisoned wine intended for García and dies unrepentant. Realizing what she has done, she urges her son to drink, and when he refuses she angrily and spitefully confesses her guilt and her love for Almanzor. García pardons his mother as she is dying, and Almanzor stabs himself.

If an unhappy ending can be considered essential to a well-constructed tragedy, this play, at least, meets this requirement. The defects in plot are not even compensated for by beauty of style. The fact that the poet chose to write his tragedy in hendecasyllabic couplets further detracted from its effectiveness, for this closely repeated rhyme with its heavy beat has always been unpleasant to Spanish ears.

In spite of the efforts of the heroine and the other actors, the play was a complete failure, lasting only five days at the Cruz and being performed in an almost empty theater. On the first day it produced only 1,184 reals and on the fourth and fifth 320 and 155 respectively.[2]

Even though these first attempts by the neo-classicists to write regular tragedies either never reached the stage or else met with a cool reception from the audience, it cannot be said that their lack of success was due to their observance of classic precepts. At the same time that the public was rejecting these original plays it was accepting with considerable enthusiasm works translated from the French and the Italian in which the same precepts were followed. One is forced to the conclusion that the neo-classicists were not entirely wrong in accusing Ramón de la Cruz of responsibility for the unfavorable reception of their plays, when he considers that Ramón de la Cruz's tragedy, *Sesostris,* an imitation of an Italian work by Zeno and Pariati, was performed for fourteen days in 1767; that another tragedy, *Triumphant Aecius,* a translation of *Ezio* by Metastasio, ran for twelve days in the same year; that *The Shepherd King,* another imitation of a play by the same name by Metastasio, had a run of fourteen days in December of that year; that *Man Can Conquer Love,* still another translation from Metastasio, was performed for twelve days in 1768; that *The Proud Bayaceto,* a translation of Racine's *Bayaceto,* ran for twelve days in 1769; that *The Scotchwoman,* translated from Voltaire, was favorably received; that comedy *The Gleaner,* based on *Les Moissonneurs* by Favart, lasted some fourteen days and was frequently repeated; and that *Eugenia,* translated from Beaumarchais, ran for eight days at its first performance in 1772 and was revived twice in the same year. All of these translations and adaptations were made by Ramón de la Cruz himself and were as neo-classic in form as the original tragedies that were being rejected.

Inasmuch as Golden Age plays during this same time were running from one to five days at the most, the success of the above plays is evidence either of their merit or of the influence of Ramón de la Cruz. If the first is true, then the failure of such tragedies as *Hormesinda* and *Sancho García* must be attributed more to their

inherent weakness in plot and style than to the insistence of their
authors upon following neo-classic rules. That there may be some
truth in the second supposition is not impossible inasmuch as, by
Cotarelo y Mori's own admission, Ramón de la Cruz had by the
year 1765 become the master of the theaters of Madrid. Cotarelo
insists, however, that the rejection and unfavorable reception of neo-
classic plays was in no way due to Cruz's intervention. "The translations or imitations of foreign plays," he says, "were performed with
difficulty or were ill received not because he abused the authority he
had over the theater, but because of the unfailing aversion the public
felt for the *gallo-classic* innovations."[3] The tragedies and comedies
we have just cited were all well received, however, and they certainly
fall within the category of "translations or imitations" of foreign
plays. When we consider also that *Andromaque,* an adaptation from
Racine by Pedro de Silva, ran for fourteen days in May of 1764, and
for ten days in November of that year, and was frequently performed
for over half a century, and that *Hypermenestra,* a tragedy by Le
Mierre, translated by Olavide, lasted for nine days in the same year
and proved to be one of the most popular plays on the Spanish stage
for the next fifty years, we become convinced that lack of original
talent, far more than the rigidity of neo-classic precepts, was responsible for the poor quality of Spanish drama during the eighteenth
century, and that the public did, in fact, welcome a change from a
steady diet of Golden Age comedies.

López de Ayala

The composition of regular tragedies presented a particular challenge to neo-classic intellectuals, and the few that appeared were
written by men who were primarily scholars or critics and only sec-
ondarily dramatists. Armed with the rules, they invaded a field in
which they had little practical experience and frequently little
genuine aptitude. It is highly improbable that their plays would
have been any better even if they had given free rein to their imagination and had violated the unities at will.

The above statements are applicable in part at least to Ignacio
López de Ayala, professor of Poetics in the Royal College of San
Isidro and member of the Royal Academy of History. Among numer-
ous scholarly works, he published nuptial songs in Castilian, Latin,
Greek, Hebrew, and Arabic to celebrate the marriage of the Prince
of Asturias (later Carlos IV) to María Luisa de Parma, and an epi-

taph in Latin, Greek, and Hebrew upon the occasion of the death of the Queen Mother, Isabel Farnese. As a historian, he published the first volume of a *History of Frederick the Great* (1767), and a *History of Gibraltar* (1782). As a scientist and philosopher, he published a dissertation on the *Aurora Borealis,* observed in Madrid on the night of October 24, 1768, and another dissertation on the nature of comets. In 1772 he published the *Moral Philosophy of Aristotle,* with an original prologue.[4] With this background, he offered to the theater a neo-classic tragedy, which was printed in 1775 but not performed until February, 1778, when it had an initial run of seven days. This tragedy, *The Destruction of Numancia,* has little in common with Cervantes' *Numancia.*

Publio Cipión Emiliano has been besieging Numancia for a long time, preferring to make its inhabitants yield to hunger rather than to risk the lives of his men in an attack. The priest, Dulcidio, has consulted the oracle of Hercules, which has answered:

> Dulcidio, the Duero is blood, the Tiber tears;
> Rome is mourning and fears. The name
> of your country will be immortal, if in its pain
> it chooses the sword and rejects the chain.

Megara, the general in command of the city, is basing his hopes of resisting the siege upon the words of the oracle, which he misinterprets, and upon expected aid from the forces of Lucian and an African ally, Yugurta. The latter has offered to come to the aid of the city provided Olvia consents to marry him, and she, although in love with Aluro, in order to save her country has agreed to his proposal. She finds, however, that Yugurta was the slayer of her brother, Olón, whose death both she and Aluro have sworn to avenge. Her love for her country and the entreaties of the priest, Dulcidio, finally overcome her aversion for Yugurta and she arranges a meeting with him that night. Aluro, informed of the meeting, comes to the trysting place and in the darkness mortally wounds Olvia, thinking she is Yugurta. The Numantians learn that the forces of Lucian, while coming to their aid, have been surprised and defeated by the enemy. A sword and a chain sent to them by the consul reveal to them the true meaning of the oracle upon which they have relied. Realizing that they must choose between slavery and death, they set fire to the city and throw themselves into the flames.

The diction and versification of this tragedy, which is written in

hendecasyllabic *romance* meter, elicited the warmest praise from
Martínez de la Rosa:

> The diction of *Numancia* is pure and in general appropriate and facile;
> and as for the versification, it is so replete and sonorous that it has con-
> tributed powerfully to the favorable reception of the play. It may well be
> affirmed that as long as the hearts of Spaniards beat as they remember the
> past glories of their country, and as long as their ears are charmed by
> beautiful versification, *Numancia* will endure on the stage.[5]

Lista, writing in the *Censor* in 1882, forty-seven years after the publication of *Numancia*, comments upon a recent recast of the tragedy
made by Antonio Sabiñón. In this recast, he says, the lack of dramatic interest, which is the principal defect of the play, has been
carried to the extreme. If in a tragedy the situation of the hero
never changed, if he were always threatened by a great and inevitable calamity, the result would be monotonous; the play would lack
interest, and every scene would seem a catastrophe. This is exactly
the case with *Numancia*, where the spectator sees no possible way
for that heroic city to avoid its doom. Ayala recognized this defect,
Lista says, and attempted to remedy it with the love episode of
Yugurta and Olvia, which, if it had produced its effect, would have
given the Numantians some hope of salvation. In Sabiñón's recast,
however, this episode, which in Ayala's play relieves the sad monotony of the plot, has been suppressed, leaving the play completely
devoid of dramatic interest. Lista says that Ayala, a pupil of Luzán
and a friend of Moratín, the father, was one of the first in the
eighteenth century to have the glory of contributing to the restoration of Spanish poetry and to the re-establishment of good taste.
His versification "is rhythmical and vigorous like that of his master,
Luzán, although it also resembles Luzán's in being somewhat un-
graceful and inflexible. At a time when such bad poetry was written,
Numancia must have seemed to the lovers of true poetry an extraordinary phenomenon." Lista finds in the tragedy frequent imitations of Virgil, the final scenes being particularly filled with movement and vigor. The last curses of Megara merit, in his opinion, an
honorable place in Spanish classic poetry:

> The blood of destroyed Numancia,
> an innocent and just blood, calls to heaven
> against you, ambitious Rome. These ruins,
> the skeleton of a sad and bloody city,

the witnesses of my glory and your injustice,
will exist as eternal monuments
against your perfidy. A just heaven
will choose my soul as the instrument
with which to avenge my country and to humble
the proud arrogance of your empire.
Yes, Megara's soul, a wandering spirit,
will be a fury that walks through the
towns of Spain and drives them to vengeance.

Although Lista says that Sabiñón's recast was unfavorably received, its initial run of eight days in September, 1814, twice as long as that of any other play that year, its revival for two days in November of the same year, and its repetition for several performances in each of the years 1815, 1816, 1818, and 1819 bely this statement. During the season 1814-15 at the Príncipe not even Comella's play, *María Teresa of Austria,* had as long a run. Indeed, from the first performance of *Numancia* in 1775 through more than half a century, this tragedy was one of the most popular plays on the Spanish stage, having consecutive runs or from three to six performances every time it was returned to the theater.

García de la Huerta

In the year 1778 another original tragedy, written in complete conformity with the rules, was favorably received by the Madrid public. This play, *Raquel,* by Vicente García de la Huerta,[6] has received more flattering reviews, from nationalist as well as neo-classic critics, than any other tragedy composed during the eighteenth century. According to a note by its editor, shortly after its initial performance and before its publication more than two thousand copies were made and circulated in Spain, France, Italy, Portugal, and America. Although *Raquel* was not performed in Madrid until 1778, it was played in Barcelona as early as 1775 and was almost as popular there for the next twenty years as an adaptation of Racine's *Andromaque,* by Pedro de Silva, which had appeared some five years earlier. In the "Foreword" which precedes the editions of 1778 and 1786, the author declares he composed the play to prove to foreigners that Spaniards had an aptitude and a liking for tragedy. Although the division into five acts, as allowed by the classic precepts, facilitates the development of the action, he has voluntarily "reduced his tragedy to a single act, since the two inter-

missions are not necessary in reading and only because of the exi-
gencies of the stage does it appear divided into three acts."[7]

Cotarelo y Mori, as an uncompromising nationalist, who concedes no merit to any neo-classic play as such, says: "And this is the
only thing classic about this composition: the framework, the skeleton. In everything else, plot, ideas, sentiments, characters, and versification, it is indigenous. It is a drama of the seventeenth century."[8]
He admits that modern critics in foreign countries have not favored
the work, and "in fact, one must agree that it suffers from lack of
verisimilitude and poverty of characters." But on the other hand,

it is distinguished by other positive merits, such as its excellent language,
its vigorous and harmonious versification, the strange and appealing
chivalry of some of its characters, and its wealth of monarchical spirit
and ardent Spanish nationalism. . . . For these reasons, *Raquel* has been
and will be fervently applauded whenever it is performed in our
theaters.[9]

Menéndez y Pelayo calls *Raquel* "the great theatrical event of the
reign of Carlos III." For the first time, he says, there appeared a
tragedy written in accordance with classical precepts, which not
only pleased, but aroused the delirious enthusiasm of the public.
Raquel became popular in the noblest sense of the word because
"only in appearance was it a classical tragedy, in that its author submitted to the dogma of the unities, to a majestic uniformity of style,
and to the use of a single kind of verse." In everything else it was a
heroic comedy, like those of Calderón, Diamante, or Candamo, "with
the same spirit of honor and gallantry, with the same love and
bravery expressed in pompous, florid, and fine-sounding verse. . . .
Raquel could not fail to triumph because it was genuinely poetic and
genuinely Spanish. It is the only tragedy of the past century that
has life, energy, and noble inspiration."[10]

A comparison of the stage success of *Raquel* with that of a number of the much maligned imitations and translations of French neo-
classic tragedies reveals some rather startling facts. From 1791 to
1819 *Raquel* had only thirteen performances, against forty-six for
López de Ayala's *Numancia*. Racine's *Athalie*, translated by Eugenio
Llaguno y Amarola (1754), had twenty-four performances from 1804
to 1815; Le Mierre's *Hypermenestra*, translated by Pablo de Olavide,
was played forty-four times from 1788 to 1810; Arnaud's *Blanca y
Moncasín*, translated by Teodoro de la Calle, had thirty performances from 1802 to 1816; Du Belloy's *Celmira*, translated by Olavide,

was played fifty-one times from 1785 to 1810; Racine's *Andromaque*,* adapted by Pedro de Silva, was performed thirty-eight times from 1786 to 1816.

A Golden Age play on the same theme by Juan Diamante, *The Jewess of Toledo*, had long been popular on the Spanish stage. Signorelli tells us that "all the leading ladies of the Spanish theater learn the role of the Jewess of Toledo in the comedy of that title by Diamante in order to demonstrate their talent."[11] Diamante apparently derived his theme from a poem composed in the reign of Felipe IV by Luis Ulloa. The subject had also been treated by Lope de Vega in *The Peace of the Kings and Jewess of Toledo* and by Mirá de Amescua in *The Unfortunate Raquel*. Although there is no indication that Huerta consulted either of these plays, he unquestionably borrowed freely from Diamante and particularly from Ulloa, but in doing so he altered his material sufficiently to be credited with an original work rather than a recast. Huerta had easy access to Ulloa's epic poem, inasmuch as it had recently been republished in Sedano's *Spanish Parnassus*. Diamante's play is a tragi-comedy covering at least seven years, with the usual Golden Age intrigue and with a *gracioso* who interrupts the action at the most serious moments with his buffoonery.

The Jewess of Toledo continued to be popular even after the appearance of *Raquel*, having had twelve performances from 1786 to 1791, during which time there is no record of any performance of Huerta's tragedy on the Madrid stage, although it was played ten times in Barcelona from 1775 to 1793 against five for *The Jewess of Toledo*. The fact that *Raquel* was being played in Barcelona proves that Signorelli was mistaken in affirming that it was banned by the government shortly after its second performance in Madrid. Cotarelo y Mori says that it was taken off the stage after a week's run in order to substitute another play in honor of the return of the Court to

---

*Cotarelo y Mori calls this work a translation and attributes it to Clavijo y Fajardo (*María Ladvenant* [Madrid, 1896], p. 111), but Qualia has conclusively proven that the tragedy with this title, that had an initial run of fourteen days in June, 1764, and was repeated for ten performances in December of the same year, was Pedro de Silva's extremely free adaptation, *Andrómaca, o al amor de madre no hay afecto que la iquale*, by D. Joseph Cumplido (pseudonym of Pedro de Silva). (Charles Blaise Qualia, "Racine's Tragic Art in Spain in the Eighteenth Century," *PMLA*, December, 1939, pp. 1065-68.) It seems evident also that this is the version that was so popular from 1786 to 1816, inasmuch as an edition, entitled *Andromaca, o al amor de madre no hay afecto que le iquale*, was published in the same year by the Librería Quiroga and another edition, entitled *Andromaca y Astianacte, o al amor de madre no hay afecto que le iquale*, was published in the same year by the Librería Escribano. The author in each case is given as Joseph Cumplido.

Madrid, and that it was not prohibited by the government until 1802. This prohibition evidently did not remain in force, for the play had a seven-day run in 1809 and another run of five days in 1813. There is no record of any other performances on the Madrid stage, at least from 1793 to 1819.

The tragedy is written in hendecasyllabic *romance* meter with the usual shifts of assonance to avoid monotony. All three acts take place in the reception hall of the old castle of Toledo. At the opening of the play, the city is celebrating the seventh anniversary of the victory of Alfonso VIII over the Moors at the battle of Las Navas de Tolosa. The manifestations of joy are clouded, however, by the realization that the monarch has become a slave to the charms of Raquel, a beautiful Jewess, who has taken advantage of her influence to become the virtual ruler of the kingdom. Hernán García de Castro, the nobleman who gives expression throughout the play to those lofty and noble sentiments of patriotism and unswerving loyalty to the king which were so dear to Spanish hearts and which account to a considerable extent for the success of the tragedy on the Spanish stage, gives in a short speech in the first scene all the exposition necessary for the comprehension of the action:

> Yes, Garcerán, I gratefully admit your courteous expression; but do not recall to me memories that are either completely erased, or have been so notably obscured. Let us wait, yes, to see with indolence how the disorder and abandonment of the kingdom continues amid such an enormous subversion. Let us see the tyranny of an intruder, the overthrow of public government, dishonor, luxury, avarice, and, in short, all manner of vice, for everything evil is condensed in Raquel, in that basilisk, who has so benumbed the senses of Alfonso with her sight that only the blunders he commits give indications that he is still alive. Seven years ago Alfonso VIII returned in triumph and joy to Toledo, and seven years ago he turned into base chains the green laurel that crowned his brow. Then why, when you speak of his deeds, Garcerán, do you not dwell upon the ignominy with which a Jewess has held him so long entangled in her bonds? Why, when you relate to us his triumphs, do you forget the shameful servitude of an unfortunate people, sacrificed to the cupidity of that despicable courtesan? Who do you omit the outrage and the stain cast upon the nobility and upon their rights?[12]

The people rise up and demand the death of Raquel. When the king angrily prepares to punish the rebels, the noble Hernán García, as their spokesman, gives him a forceful account of the grievances of his subjects and finally convinces him that his duty is to exile the Jews and with them Raquel, who has been responsible for all the harm that has befallen the kingdom. Torn between his love for Raquel and his duty to Spain, Alfonso at the close of the first act communicates his decision to the Jewess.

In the second act the Jews appeal to Raquel through her evil counselor, Ruben, to make an attempt with her charms to regain the king's affection and to induce him to revoke the order of banishment. When Alfonso finds himself alone with her he is powerless to resist her beauty and seeks only to find a way to retain his mistress and to force his subjects to accept her. Relying upon the traditional loyalty of Spaniards to their monarch, he seats Raquel on the throne and announces that all must pay her homage as queen. The Jewess immediately takes advantage of her new position to say to Alvar Fañez and to García, who, coming to seek an audience with the king, find her on the throne:

> I am Raquel, Raquel, whom you insulted a short time ago so proudly and boldly. I am Raquel, whom Alfonso has chosen to rule in his stead; whom he himself has placed upon his royal throne and with whom he has divided all his power; to whom already his loyal vassals render the most submissive allegiance. I am one who intends to punish traitors; one who will cause the sword to fall on treacherous necks; one who will make proud spirits a carpet for her feet.[13]

The king decides to go on a hunting expedition, and when Raquel expresses fear for her safety during his absence, he reassures her:

> What do you fear, my Raquel? What do you suspect? Are you not in command now in Castile? Are my kingdoms not subject to your will? Does not your hand move everything? In my dominions do not all respect and obey you? Do you not have the power now to avenge yourself, if anyone is so foolish as to offend you?[14]

As soon as the king leaves, the people, led by Alvar Fañez, clamor for the death of the Jewess; and in spite of the efforts of García, who maintains a steadfast loyalty to Alfonso, they enter the castle with drawn swords. They find Raquel with her counselor, Ruben, and, in order to achieve their purpose without staining their own hands with the blood of their queen, they make him the instrument of their vengeance, forcing him to choose between losing his own life and stabbing Raquel with the dagger he has drawn to defend himself. The king returns in time to hear from the dying lips of his mistress that her crime has been her love for him and that Ruben has been her assassin. Alfonso immediately stabs Ruben and, after an all-too-brief show of emotion over the fate of the one whom he has adored so much, admits his own responsibility for the tragic outcome of their love and pardons his vassals. García closes the play with a moral in typically neo-classic fashion:

> Let excessive pride take warning, for when heaven wishes to punish arrogance, no privilege or power can defend it.

As Sempere y Guarinos points out, the tragedy is neo-classic not only in its observance of the unities, but in the consistency of its characters. Throughout the play Raquel is haughty and presumptuous; Alfonso a good king, but in love; García a patriotic nobleman unswerving in loyalty to his monarch; Manrique a fawning minister; Ruben an astute and treacherous Jew; Alvar Fañez an intrepid Castilian.[15]

In its lofty sentiments *Raquel* may have much in common with the Golden Age *comedia,* but the fact remains that in form it is ultra-classic and its versification shows none of the variety so characteristic of the drama of the seventeenth century. Moreover, if the tragedy indeed enthralled the public, it did so without the aid of a *gracioso.*

Huerta's contribution to the theater is limited to *Raquel,* to an adaptation of Fernán Pérez de Oliva's tragedy, *The Vengeance of Agamemnon* (1530), which he published in 1778 in his *Poetical Works* with the title *Agamemnon Avenged,* and to a reworking of a translation of Voltaire's *Zaïre,* the title of which he chose to transform into *Faith Triumphant Over Love and Scepter, or Xayra* (1784).[16] *Agamemnon Avenged,* according to Quintana, is nothing more than Oliva's prose translation of Sophocles' *Electra* turned into hendecasyllabic *romance* meter. Quintana proves his assertion conclusively by placing the opening lines of Oliva's and Huerta's works side by side.[17] No effort was ever made, apparently, to stage this tragedy.

Just as Huerta in *Agamemnon Avenged* did not translate Sophocles' work, but availed himself of Oliva's arrangement of the Greek tragedy, so when he offered his version of Voltaire's *Zaïre* to the theater he did not consult the original play, but rephrased an existing translation. In his "Advertencia," Huerta says that many translations of this tragedy have been made in Spain, but that only two have been printed, one by Juan Francisco del Postigo in Cádiz in the year 1765, and another a few years before in Barcelona. The latter, which was reprinted in 1782, is, he says, the one upon which he is basing his work. Curiously, the greater part of this "Advertencia" is devoted to a denunciation of bad translators and an explanation of the proper technique for translations. A translator, he says, "should treat the original of the work he is translating with all the courtesy a host is supposed to observe with a guest whom he voluntarily takes into his home." This observation serves Huerta as a starting point for a condemnation of Linguet's *Spanish Theater*, printed in Paris in 1770, in which the French author translated fifteen Golden Age comedies and five *entremeses*. Although Huerta concedes that Linguet's intentions may have been honorable, as evidenced by the fact that the collection was dedicated to the Spanish Academy, he says that unfortunately his choice of plays and his skill in translation did not match these intentions.

The Barcelona version of Voltaire's work was very popular on the stage of that city from 1775 to 1789, being performed almost every year. It was also performed frequently in the theaters of Madrid from 1790 to 1794. No record of the performance of Huerta's *Xayra* appears before 1804, during which year it was given seven times. It was repeated four times in 1806. It does not seem, therefore, that Huerta improved upon his model in the estimation of the theatergoing public.

While Huerta posed as a defender of the Golden Age theater, nowhere does he show a well-developed and consistent dramatic creed. In the prologue to his *Spanish Theater* (1785-86),[18] he declares that his intention is to vindicate the Spanish theater by presenting to the public a select collection of its best plays. Nasarre, he says, promised to publish such a collection, but was prevented by his early death from fulfilling his promise; and more recently, Ignacio López de Ayala undertook to form a collection of Spanish plays, "choosing the best and correcting them in the places where they might be considered defective." Huerta is certain that under Ayala's able hand an excellent collection will be made. His own work, he says, will not be so ambitious, and the public must not expect the comedies he includes in his collection to be free from defects. He has been unable to find any regular plays among the works of the dramatists cited by Nasarre.

My investigations and my diligence have not enabled me to find a single one of the many comedies completely free from defects that Nasarre affirmed could be found in the Spanish theater; for, although I have searched the authors he cites, neither in Rojas, nor in Hoz, nor in Moreto, nor in Solís have I been able to find anything except a certain

number of comedies that, without including substantial offenses against a
reasonable verisimilitude, nevertheless sin against some of those rigid
rules, the product of pure convention, that are observed ... by those who
hide their lack of fire and invention with the specious pretext of being
exact and scrupulous.[19]

Nasarre, he says, must have understood regularity in this sense, or
else he promised more than he could fulfil. His proposition would not
be so open to criticism if he had limited himself to affirming "that an
extraordinary number of Spanish plays could be presented to
foreigners, which, in spite of occasional irregularities, contain more
genius, more invention, more grace, and generally better poetry
than all their correct and regular productions."[20] One seeks in
vain in Huerta's prologues to *Xayra* and to the *Spanish Theater* for
any clear-cut expression of dramatic creed. He seems to be chiefly
concerned with venting his spleen upon French dramatists and upon
all foreign critics who have at any time said anything unflattering
about the Spanish theater. He is particularly incensed against Signorelli, Voltaire, and Beaumarchais, and expresses his contempt for
Racine by saying that his *Athalie* clearly reveals that it was written
for a girl's school.

Huerta's choice of plays in his *Spanish Theater* has been assailed
by almost every critic who has deigned to mention it. Menéndez y
Pelayo says its quality can be judged by the fact that "it does not
contain a single comedy by Lope de Vega, Tirso de Molina, Alarcón,
Guillén de Castro, Montalbán, or any other poet of the richest, most
original, and most brilliant epoch of our theater."[21]

A comparison of the plays included in Huerta's collection with
the list of performances in the theater at the time reveals that
Huerta did little more than choose the most popular plays of the day
for inclusion in his collection. Of the authors cited by Menéndez y
Pelayo, only Montalbán's *The Lovers of Teruel* was being played at
the time Huerta published his work, whereas twenty-nine of the
thirty-six comedies he includes were in the repertoire of the theaters,
twenty-four of them actually being played from 1784 to 1786, during
which period his *Spanish Theater* was being published. It is understandable that Huerta should not have chosen to include in the
limited scope of his collection plays that were completely unknown
at the time. As for Lope de Vega, it is evident that Huerta did not
place him in the same category with Calderón. In commenting upon
Linguet's translations, he says:

The first comedy of this collection is *The Slave of Her Gallant*, one of the many incorrect and defective plays with which the extremely fertile genius of Lope de Vega flooded the theaters. For these reasons it is also one of those that are seldom performed even by the companies that tour the provinces.[22]

As a matter of fact, it was the Spanish actors and public rather than Huerta who had placed their seal of disapproval upon the authors he omits from his collection.

The publication of the *Spanish Theater* immediately involved its author in a heated polemic with Felix María Samaniego, Juan Pablo Forner, and Tomás de Iriarte. The first of these, whose culture was primarily French and who was a profound admirer of Voltaire, answered Huerta in a paper entitled *Continuation of the Critical Memoirs of Cosme Damián*. He criticizes Huerta for inconsistency in his defense of the Golden Age *comedia*, maintaining that he might have made a better case for his opinions by coming out openly and saying that

genius is superior to rules; that the latter are the work of men; that the pretended legislators of the theater had no authority whatsoever to impose upon the rest of the human race a yoke that was contrary to natural liberty; and that, in short, poets are not wretched vassals of a sad and severe reason, but the most brilliant courtiers of a noble and generous imagination, their queen and natural mistress.[23]

Samaniego leaves no doubt as to his own dramatic creed and cites Lope de Vega, Calderón, Moreto, and their followers "before the tribunal of reason to answer the charge of having adopted, promoted, accredited, and made almost invincible, the defective form of our theater."[24] In Samaniego's opinion, "order is the first law and first principle of all things; without it there can be no beauty or perfection." The laws that have been set up for each class of dramatic composition "are based upon the continuous and profound observation of nature" and are therefore "eternal, universal, and appropriate to all ages and all countries."[25] Menéndez y Pelayo points out that if Huerta had accepted the challenge of Samaniego and had followed the course laid down by Golden Age apologists of the *comedia*, he would have brought "face to face two aesthetic systems, each a worthy adversary of the other, because each of them contains an equally true principle, an element equally necessary, the principle of liberty and the principle of order."[26] Huerta, incapable of such rational thinking, launched a veritable tirade of invective against his opponents. They, in turn, matched his insults, laughed at his vanity, pointed out his lack of erudition, and qualified him as ignorant and insane. The result was one of those long-drawn-out polemics so common in Spanish literary life during the seventeenth and eighteenth centuries. Even Huerta's onetime friend, Tomás Iriarte, added his voice to the dispute in a mock epitaph: "Lacking in reason, although not in genius, here rests the audacious Huerta, leaving a vacant place on Parnassus and an empty cage in Zaragoza."[27]

Probably the most reasonable criticism contained in Huerta's works is to be found in the prologue to the second part of *Spanish Theater*. Of all Calderón's plays, his *cloak and sword* comedies, he says, are most applauded by intelligent men. In them one ordinarily finds "better observed that Hellenistic regularity so esteemed beyond the Pyrenees, although, to tell the truth, the rules are not observed as religiously by their authors as these classicists recommend, because it is certainly easier to learn the precepts of an art than to put them into practice." The following statement, although not at all original with Huerta, is a reasonable evaluation of the rules and an effective argument against a narrow interpretation of dramatic illusion:

> I am firmly convinced that, although dramatic faults relative to the three unities are real faults, that is always the least substantial thing about a theatrical work. No one doubts that the ancient and modern preceptists who favor such a close adherence to these unities base their opinion and argument upon illusion, a phantom that can only exist in idle brains, supposing that it is easy to transport spectators in such a manner to the time and place of the action that they will forget themselves. I challenge all those who have heard the most pathetic and regular tragedies to say honestly whether they have ever for a single moment imagined themselves outside of the theater where the performance was taking place.[28]

Cienfuegos

Over twenty years elapsed between the first performance of *Raquel* and the next original neo-classic tragedy worthy of mention. On June 29, 1798, Alvarez de Cienfuegos' *Zoraida*[29] was performed at the theater of the Caños, where it was favorably received. This work, which is generally conceded to be his masterpiece and which was chosen by Ochoa for inclusion in his *Treasury of the Spanish Theater*, deals with the love of the tyrant, Boabdil, for a beautiful Moorish maiden, who is already betrothed to Abenamet, a leader of the Abencerrajes. While pretending to favor the lovers, Boabdil treacherously causes Abenamet to lose the sacred standard in the defeat of his men at the battle of Jaen, a loss which, according to Moorish law, is punishable by death. When Zoraida seeks to persuade the king to intercede in behalf of Abenamet, Boabdil tells her that he will do so only on the condition that she become his wife. To save her lover, Zoraida consents and Abenamet is sentenced to banishment. When he comes to take leave of his beloved, his friend, Almanzor, in order to dissuade him from his purpose, is forced to tell him that Zoraida is already the bride of Boabdil. Abenamet insists upon seeing her, and in a rapidly moving scene the lovers are surprised by the king and his guards. Realizing the hopelessness of the situation, Abenamet stabs himself and removing the dagger from his breast extends it to Zoraida with the words: "If you love, this steel is beautiful; take it and test it." Zoraida obeys, plunging the dagger into her heart.

Cienfuegos should have terminated his tragedy with this dramatic catastrophe, but instead he weakens its effect with two more scenes in which the people of Granada rebel against Boabdil and restore his father, the noble Hacen, to the throne, which he had renounced for some unexplained reason before the opening of the play. Hacen closes the tragedy in a declamatory fashion by sentencing his son to life imprisonment in the same tower that had held the unfortunate Abenamet, and by admonishing the Zegríes and the Abencerrajes to forget their differences and unite for the defense of the kingdom.

The play observes the unities with some difficulty. It is true that a single action takes place in one day and within a palace garden; but, to satisfy the unity of place, it is supposed that Zoraida, an orphan of noble blood and a ward of the king, lives in the palace itself and that the tower where Abenamet is imprisoned is adjacent to the garden. To observe the unity of time it is necessary to crowd the action in the third act and to have Abenamet's departure on his exile and his return occur almost simultaneously.

Zoraida was returned to the stage from April 30 to May 2, 1803, with Máiquez playing the role of Almanzor. The receipts on these days were satisfactory, but for some reason the tragedy was never performed again. Menéndez y Pelayo, speaking of Cienfuegos' poetry, says that he was born to be a romantic and regrets that he did not live at a time when he could have given free rein to his temperament. Although the basis of his ideology was the humanitarian philosophy of the time, "a vague and melancholy coloring reveals the influence of the false Ossian and of Young."[30]

Nowhere does Cienfuegos reveal his sentimentalized melancholy more strikingly than in the dedication of *Zoraida* to Celima:

> When I recall my loves in order to give to each its place in my affections, could I forget Celima, the lovable Celima, that Celima who made my heart the nest of her love? Time passed and our love took wings; but the nest remains and will only perish with my dying breath. Meanwhile, I find pleasure in her memory. I visit those places that were the solitary witnesses of our tender love; I recall those serene days in which a look from her eyes, a smile from her lips gave pleasure to my soul. In the midst of such fantasies, I cannot help exclaiming a thousand times: Where are you, Celima? And Celima does not answer. Why was our love not eternal? Alas! It only seems to have died, for it lives and will live forever in the tenderest part of our hearts. Yes, my adored Celima, I know that you cannot forget Cienfuegos, nor can Cienfugos be ungrateful to the one who loved him so much. Ask my verses and they will tell you whether it is possible for me to cease to love one who has inspired entire poems, one from whose mouth I heard for the first time many of the passionate expressions which Zoraida made her own. Zoraida is yours; it wishes to be; it cannot help being yours, and it will consider itself well repaid if sometime you lay it aside and stop your reading to shed a tear, a single tear to the memory of Nicasio Alvarez de Cienfuegos.[31]

The Countess of Castile,[32] another tragedy by Cienfuegos, was performed for the first time on April 23-25, 1803. It was repeated twice in May and twice in September of the same year with average receipts but was never revived. The subject, which is the same as that of Cadalso's *Sancho García,* was foredoomed to failure. The denouement is improbable and overly sentimental. The Countess, after handing her son the poisoned cup, repents, snatches it from him, and drinks its contents herself. The final scene finds her son and her Moorish lover kneeling beside her dead body, each clasping one of her hands and swearing a mutual friendship.

Two other tragedies by Cienfuegos, *Idomeneo* and *Pítaco,* were never performed, but were printed in the second edition of his works, published in 1816 by the order and at the expense of Fernando VII. The first of these plays has a plot very similar to that used by Euripides and by Racine in *Iphigenia in Aulide.* To save his country, Idomenio has promised to offer his son, Polimenes, as a sacrifice to the gods. The priest, in whom he has confidence, is urging that the sacrifice be made in order that he may place his own son on the throne. When Polimene is led to the sacrificial altar, the people rise up in indignation, free him, and threaten the lives of Idomeneo and the priest. The latter's son dies defending his father; Polimenes is fatally wounded; his mother, Brisea, kills herself because of her grief; the priest meets a tragic end, confessing his guilt before he dies; and Idomeneo resolves to give up his throne and, like Oedipus the King in Sophocles' work, seek asylum in distant lands.

The tragedy follows the unities without effort and, unlike Cienfuegos' other tragedies, contains no love episode. The principal defect of the play consists "in the abuse of a certain novelty which Cienfuegos introduces in imitation of the Greeks, in whose tragedies effective use was frequently made of silence and music." Cienfuegos abused this device, "allowing entire scenes to pass, and even two in succession, without a word being uttered, having actors appear and disappear gesticulating."[33] In addition to this defect, the tragedy is characterized by a euphuistic style, exaggerated emotion, an artificial and violent use of bold metaphors, and a certain tendency to philosophize and to preach directly to the audience, which is so noticeable in Voltaire's Oedipus.

The plot of Pítaco[34] is quite similar to that of Sophocles' Electra. Faon, accompanied by an intimate friend, Alceo, returns to Mitelene to find that the king, his father, has been assassinated and that, by vote of the people, Pítaco, one of the wise men of Greece, is now on the throne. Pítaco, who, unlike Egistus in Sophocles' play, is noble, magnanimous, and generous, immediately offers his friendship to Faon and Alceo and restores their property that has been confiscated. The two conspire, however, to assassinate him; their attempt fails; Alceo is taken prisoner; and Faon escapes in a boat. Pítaco, tired of the dangers and uneasiness that beset a ruler, announces his intention to abdicate. Martínez de la Rosa objects particularly to Cienfuegos' use of the love episode between Faon and Safo. The prince pretends to love her only to make her an accomplice and, as he himself explains later, in order that Pítaco may see before he dies that everyone, even Safo, whom he loves as a daughter, has forsaken him. This design also fails, for the girl rejects with horror her lover's proposal, and Pítaco, after a brief period of anger at her supposed ingratitude, learns that she is innocent and has, indeed, tried to thwart the plan of the conspirators.

Pítaco is written in complete conformity with the rules. The unities are rigidly observed, even though the conspirators must discuss their plan in the palace itself, the scene of the entire action.

Although this tragedy, which was presented at one of the poetic contests suggested by Jovellanos and sponsored by the Royal Academy, did not receive the prize, it did open the doors of that society to its author in 1799.

Alcalá Galiano says that Cienfuegos' tragedies were praised only by a few of his friends, in the additions made by Quintana and others to Muñarriz' translation of Hugo Blair's *Lessons Upon Rhetoric and Belles-Lettres* (1798).

Posterity (the additions to Blair's *Lessons* say) will give their place to the tragedies of D. Nicasio Alvarez de Cienfuegos, the first among us who has given to this genre its proper style, coloring, and tone.

Posterity has come and has pronounced a verdict diametrically opposed to what Cienfuegos' ardent admirer predicted. It seems impossible that anyone today would dare to put such works on the stage. They lie completely forgotten and it is well that they should. This is said with grief by one who respects the memory of Cienfuegos as a most worthy man; although as a poet, he was generally only mediocre, sometimes good, but usually bad, especially in his tragedies.[35]

Quintana

At the same time that Cienfuegos was achieving a small measure of success with his *Zoraida* and *The Countess of Castile,* his good friend, Manuel José Quintana, presented two tragedies that remained in the repertoires of the theaters for a number of years and, from the standpoint of attendance, must be reckoned among the most successful attempts of the neo-classicists to introduce regular tragedy in Spain. The first of these plays, *The Duke of Viseo,* is little more than a recast of an English musical drama, *The Castle Specter* (1796), by Matthew (Monk) Lewis, a work which, although of no great literary merit, was very popular on the English stage. Quintana's tragedy bears no resemblance to a comedy of the same title by Lope de Vega.

The tragedy is written in hendecasyllabic *romance* meter and is divided into three acts. The entire action takes place in the Duke's fortress in Portugal. The unities of action and place are observed without difficulty, but the usual lack of verisimilitude is encountered when so much action is crowded into one day. There are no stage directions for the first act, but we are told that the second act takes place at night and that the scene will be illuminated by a single taper at the side of the stage. The directions for the third act are more elaborate. "The scene represents a dark subterranean chamber with several arched galleries. A stone bench covered with straw serves as a bed for Eduardo. Near the bench there will be a post from which hang the chains which have held him prisoner. It is supposed that he has just awakened."

The Duke of Viseo[36] was performed for the first time on May 19, 1801, and lasted eleven days. This initial run with average receipts of 5,010 reales places it among the most successful plays of the year. It was repeated in 1803 for seven days and for two days in 1804, but was not played again until 1811. It was performed twice in 1812, four times in 1815, and five times in 1818, presumably after it had been corrected and reworked to some extent by its author.

Enrique, the present duke of Viseo, sees Matilde, the beautiful daughter of one of his vassals and, against her will, brings her to his castle, where he dresses her in fine clothes and loads her with jewels. The exposition of the tragedy is furnished by a conversation between Enrique and Ataide, the jailer of the castle and Enrique's trusted adviser. Enrique and his older brother, Eduardo, had both loved Teodora. After she had rejected him and married Eduardo, in an insane fit of jealousy he had killed her and stabbed his brother, leaving him for dead. He had ordered his henchmen to kill all of Eduardo's followers, as well as his infant daughter, Violante. He confesses to Ataide that he has never been able to forget his love for Teodora and that he has transferred all his passion for her to Matilde, who resembles her so much. Ataide, who was implicated in these evil acts against his will, confesses to Matilde that she is Violante, the daughter of Eduardo and Teodora, and tells her how he saved her from death and arranged that she be reared by one of Eduardo's trusted vassals. He also tells her that, having discovered that Eduardo had been severely wounded, but not killed, he has kept him in confinement all these years without informing Enrique of the fact.

The duke tells Matilde of his love, and when she rejects him and informs him that she is betrothed to Leonardo, a vassal of the Count of Oren, he becomes angry and allows her only one day to make her decision, threatening to use violence if she refuses him. Leonardo, who is actually the Count of Oren, has discovered Matilde's abduction and comes to free her. Enrique surprises the lovers and orders the Count to be imprisoned, even though the latter reveals his identity and reminds Enrique that he is also a powerful nobleman.

In his dreams the apparition of Teodora comes to Enrique and holds out her arms to him. As he goes to embrace her, blood begins to flow from her breast. She suddenly turns into a skeleton and encircles him in her arms. Terrified, he tells his experience to Ataide, who says it was a warning from heaven. When Enrique indicates that he repents of his evil deeds, Ataide informs him that his brother is still alive and that he may find peace for his troubled spirit by freeing him and imploring his forgiveness. Enrique seems to welcome the suggestion for a while, but is soon informed that Ataide has released the Count of Oren, who is now advancing to attack the castle. He then regrets his momentary softness of heart, and having forced Ataide through torture to reveal the place where Eduardo is imprisoned, goes with his guards and two Negro slaves to the dungeon to kill him.

In the meantime, Violante has been carried away by Ali, one of the slaves, to the very dungeon where her father has been imprisoned so many years. The two meet and shortly reveal their respective identities. A touching reunion takes place, which is interrupted by the entrance of Enrique and his guards. The two brothers meet again face to face. When Enrique learns that Matilde is really his brother's daughter, he shows no horror at the idea of incest, and offers to spare Eduardo's life if Violante will consent to marry him. At this moment the Count of Oren and his soldiers force their way into the castle and free Eduardo and Violante. Eduardo shows the magnanimity of his heart by offering to pardon his brother, but the latter, consistently evil to the end, chooses to die by his own hand rather than owe his life to one whom he has wronged so much and stabs himself, falling into the arms of Ali. With his last breath he requests his slave to carry him to die where he will not have to look upon the face of his hated brother.

After the first performance of this tragedy in 1801, a long review appeared in the *Memorial Literario,* in which the anonymous critic prefaces his remarks with the statement: "True criticism is a friend of the arts which it directs and supports, not an envious enemy that persecutes and harasses them.... Let us try, then, to apply impartially the invariable laws of tragedy to *The Duke of Viseo,* without losing sight of the motives that should incline us to indulgence."[37]

From the detailed summary and analysis of the tragedy given in the *Memorial Literario,* it is evident that Quintana made many alterations in his work before it was republished in his *Obras Completas* in 1821. Some of the suppressions he made were ill advised, since they

destroy the connection. We wonder, for example, in the later edition
how and why Violante came to the dungeon where her father was
imprisoned. In the original this is made clear, for the second act ends
with these words by Enrique: "Take her away; put her under the
towers of the castle; let her die there." This speech was omitted in the
1821 edition.

The critic in the *Memorial* regrets that the author, who shows
such familiarity with the rules of art, did not choose an original subject and one that was appropriate for tragedy:

> *The Duke of Viseo,* or rather, *The Castle Specter,* since it is all the
> same, is nothing but a web of atrocities, an improbable story, loaded with
> unconnected incidents and forced situations. In short, it is one of those
> monstrous dramas composed only to horrify the spectator which, unfor-
> tunately, are too much in vogue in certain foreign theaters. It is all right
> for people in London and elsewhere to entertain themselves with such
> specters, but let them leave us with the amusing extravagancies of
> Calderón and Moreto until they can give us tragedies that will make us
> shed sweet tears, born of compassion and terror; or comedies which, with
> a well-executed painting of our vices, will excite us to an agreeable
> smile.[38]

In pointing out inconsistencies in the plot, he asks how it is possible
for Enrique, who is represented as cowardly, barbarous, and atrocious, to manage with the assistance of only three men to kill the
duke, his wife, and his family, and to take possession of all his titles
and property and to maintain himself in peaceful possession of them.
This play, he says, is a tragedy only in name, because the principal
personages do not have the character, the manners, or even the
noble language which befits them. Even more notable is the defect
of mixing in the tragedy people of high and low rank—that is, two
black slaves with dukes—not giving them silent roles, but making
them take an active and important part in the play.

This review is mild compared to a long letter signed D. P. L.
that appeared a short time later in the same periodical. In this letter
the author gives a long list of repetitions of words: *barbarous, horror,
fury, destiny, fatal, agitation, frantic, snatch, agitation, breast, drag,
echo, eagerness,* etc. He takes delight in calling attention also to
Quintana's abuse of figures of speech, inverted word order, and caco-
phonous verses. All of these things, he says, form

the heroic tone of the gloomy tragedy of the barbarous, frantic, and
furious Duke of Viseo, who has more of the traits of a Moor than of a

Christian; a play which, instead of drawing tears, has injured the ears of the spectators, crushing them in every verse with horrible sounding words that inspire horror rather than terror.[39]

Quintana himself, when he published this tragedy in 1821, freely admitted its faults and his own lack of experience at the time of its composition:

It was not possible to give to *The Duke of Viseo* the verisimilitude, the historical interest, and the dignity its subject matter lacks. The author was led astray by a few novel and energetic passages in the English drama from which he took the theme of his play; and he thought that, if he adjusted them to a picture less removed from our scene, they might produce an effect upon a Spanish audience. But he did not see then, as he sees now, that to take these beauties from their environment was to deprive them of a great part of their native value. The license of drama, the prestige of music, and the more open system under which the English and German writers work, authorize freedom, cover up lack of verisimilitude, and enlarge the proportions; so that exaggeration and violence are less noticed and the beauties the subject affords are developed with greater vigor. To reduce these compositions to the severity of the rules established by the poetic legislators of the South is to mutilate them, to do violence to their character, and to render them ineffective.[40]

Quintana's second tragedy, *Pelayo*,[41] is divided into five acts and is written in hendecasyllabic *romance* meter. The first act takes place in the house of Veremundo, the second, third and fourth in a large hall in Munuza's castle, and the fifth in an underground dungeon. There are no stage directions. The unities are observed but not enough time is allowed for the logical development of the action. The play was performed for the first time on January 19, 1805, with Máiquez playing the title role, and lasted seven days. The following year it was given six consecutive performances. It was not returned to the stage during the French domination of the peninsula—that is, from 1807 to 1813. Within a month after the final withdrawal of French troops from Spanish soil in 1813, *Pelayo* was performed again for a run of four days. It was performed seven times in 1814, four times in 1815, five in 1816, and three in 1818. As an original Spanish tragedy it was second in popularity only to López de Ayala's *Numancia*. Both plays, of course, owed their enthusiastic reception on the Spanish stage to their noble expressions of patriotism.

Quintana's tragedy differs from Moratín's *Hormesinda* and Jovellanos' *Munuza* primarily in its treatment of Pelayo's sister. The earlier works follow closely the legendary account in which Hormesinda is forced against her will to marry Munuza and in which she is unjustly accused by her brother and finally vindicated. The ending is happy in the legend and in the earlier tragedies. Quintana departs entirely from the established story and represents Hormesinda as being in love with the Moorish leader. To save her city from destruction at the hands of the invaders, she has thrown herself at Munuza's feet. He, in turn, has been moved by her beauty and soon by his love for her to treat the city and its inhabitants with the utmost leniency. Believing her brother to be dead, Hormesinda has yielded to Munuza's suit and on the very day Pelayo returns has agreed to be his wife. When he learns that his sister is going to marry the Moor, Pelayo enters the castle in disguise and berates her for the dishonor she has brought upon him and upon her country.

After he has been acclaimed king by voice of the people, Pelayo organizes a rebellion. His identity is discovered by Munuza. The Christians attack without their leader and the Moor goes out to lead his men in battle. Believing that the Spaniards have no chance of success, Hormesinda, to save her brother's life, opens the door of his prison and urges him to flee. Pelayo, of course, chooses to fight with his men and his presence turns the tide. After the battle the defeated Munuza returns to the castle to kill Pelayo. When Hormesinda tells him that she has freed her brother, he realizes that his love for her, which has prompted his clemency toward the city, has caused his downfall. Although she vows her love, he stabs her at the very moment Pelayo enters to save his sister and to slay Munuza. To avoid death at the hands of the Christians, the Moor kills himself. As he dies he points to Hormesinda, declaring that he has avenged himself. With her last words Hormesinda reminds her brother that she is dying for him. Pelayo's final speech must have been particularly popular with Spaniards, whose patriotism was at fever heat at the time the tragedy was performed:

Spaniards, Pelayo's blood is bathing the cradle that holds your new-born empire. . . . You see the tyrant dead before you. There is no rest now; let the struggle last for centuries and centuries; and if an insolent people at some future time should try to tie to the chariot of its triumph the nation we are freeing today, may our grandsons defend their independence with equal force and may the glory and liberty of Spain be made eternal by your heroic example.[42]

When *Pelayo* was performed in 1805 and 1806 it was almost a prophecy of the French invasion, and when it was returned to the stage in 1813 it was like the triumphant cry of a victorious people. After its initial performance in 1805, it was both praised and censured in the periodicals. José María de Carnerero wrote a review in the *Memorial Literario* that was on the whole commendatory: "The action could not be better prepared. ... How well the protagonist sustains his character from the beginning to the end of the drama! The verses of this tragedy are generally fluent, rhythmical, and poetic; but the style is not appropriate at times, and the metaphors are usually too lofty."[43] But in the *Diario de Madrid* a critic who signed himself E. A. de S. J. wrote a scathing denunciation of Quintana's work:

I read the aforesaid tragedy a few days ago and on each page I found expressions so inhuman, exotic, and violent, with such incoherent metaphors, with verses so euphuistic and weak, so confused, harsh, and silly, and with such unevenness of language and style throughout the work that if I should tell the public what I think of it, the public and I would be sickened and satiated for many days.[44]

When Quintana reprinted his tragedies in 1821, he chose, he says, not to recall the debates they aroused at the time of their performance; how the author was censured, satirized, and slandered; and how he met slander with scorn, satires with silence, and honest criticism with docility. Profiting by the latter, he continues, he revised the plays, and in their new form they were received favorably whenever the actors gave proper attention to their performance. The success of *Pelayo*, he admits, was due to its timeliness, its many defects being covered up by the patriotic interest of the theme.

The free and independent sentiments that animate the play from beginning to end, and its direct application to the oppression and degradation that were humiliating our country at the time won the approval of the spectators, who saw reflected there the indignation pent up in their own hearts, and they gave evidence by their applause of their sympathy with the political purpose of the author.[45]

To understand the acrimoniousness of the attacks upon Quintana's tragedies we must take into consideration the fact that as early as 1801 the neo-classicists were divided into two groups, one of which was headed by Moratín and his friends and the other by Quintana and Cienfuegos. Each group took pleasure in weighing the plays of the other in the balance of the classic precepts and in finding them wanting. A witness to the turbulent political and literary life of the first years of the nineteenth century, Antonio Alcalá Galiano, gives a detailed account of the formation, composition, and literary creeds of these two factions. Literary activity in Madrid in 1806, he says, was divided between two bands, although some individuals preferred to take no part in the disputes, either because of friendship or of enmity toward members of both groups, and at times there were desertions from one group to the other. Differences or antagonisms existing between members of the two parties were not confined to literary doctrines, but could be traced, in many cases, to clashes of personalities or to ambition and jealousy. One group was sponsored by the government—that is by Godoy, the Prince of Peace—and was led by Leandro Fernández de Moratín. This group included such men as the Jesuit priest Pedro Estala, who contributed frequent articles to periodicals and whose authority as a literary critic was highly respected, and the Abbé Melón, who held at that time the important position of censor of printing. The other party, led by Quintana and Cienfuegos, numbered among its members Juan Nicasio Gallego, Blanco White, Manuel María de Arjona, and Eugenio de Tapia, all of whom were well known for their lyric poetry and for their espousal of the precepts of neo-classicism.

According to Alcalá Galiano, the ideas of Quintana's party were those of the French philosophers of the eighteenth century and of the French revolution. Its classicism was less pure than that of its adversaries, being based on the writings of Voltaire and his group, while the followers of Moratín continued to be orthodox in their adherence to the tenets of Boileau and Racine. Each band had a kind of catechism of its faith, or rather a book in which it proclaimed its doctrines. The *Philosophical Principles of Literature* (1797), by the French writer Batteux, translated into Spanish by Agustín García de Arrieta, served the party of Moratín, while Quintana's group swore by the *Lessons Upon Rhetoric and Belles-Lettres* (1798), by the English author Hugo Blair, translated by Joseph Luis Muñarriz.

There was no fundamental difference in the literary creed expressed in the two works in so far as neo-classic precepts were concerned. The battlefield of the opposing factions was rather the appendices written by the translators or by their friends. This section was devoted to an evaluation of Spanish literature of the Golden Age and of the contemporary period. Moratín's party gave preference to the former and the followers of Quintana to the latter. Golden Age literature was to the first group an object of

admiration, although they confessed that it had sinned in not conforming to the precepts of Aristotle. The second group held that if
there was anything good in Golden Age literature, the bad prepon-
derated and contaminated the whole.

Moratín's contempt for Muñarriz' translation of Blair and the literary production of his collaborators was still very much alive in
1824 when he gave vent to his condemnation in a letter to Mariano
and Pedro Nougués:

In general I shall say to you that the style and poetic language of
these pieces belong to the school, if it could be called a school, of Cienfuegos, Quintana, and Mor de Fuentes, and, in truth, I should like for
you to form your taste and style upon what is good in our own poets.
To write verse I would study Garcilaso, Herrera, the Argensolas, Luis
de León, Francisco de la Torre, Arguijo, Rioja, Lope (the extravagant
Lope), Valbuena, and others of the sixteenth and seventeenth centuries.
... The leaders of modern *culteranismo* have done none of this ... they
have devoted themselves exclusively to French literature, without bother-
ing to cultivate the language they learned at the cradle. They have heard
that considerable defects of judgment and taste were to be found in our
poets and have chosen not to read them and to scorn them, as if a Spaniard
could find the language of the Muses anywhere else.[46]

In order to indoctrinate the present and future generations, Moratín says, this school prepared a manual of instruction; and in order to
do so

...they found a poor man, who, without any literary qualities except
the ability to read and write, translated from the French in barbarous
jargon what Blair had composed in English for Englishmen, and who had
recourse to his friends to supply the great void in that work relative to our
literature. This afforded his collaborators an opportunity to show off their
critical ability and their exquisite taste. ... It is needless to call attention
to the mass of nonsense in these wretched additions; suffice it to say
that with the support of his helpers, he saw his work transformed into
an elementary textbook by order of the Council, which decreed that the
good taste of Muñarriz should be studied in the schools.[47]

The *Memorial Literario* published from 1802 to 1804 a very complete digest and criticism of Arrieta's translation of Batteux's work.
The reviewer is warm in his praise of the French original but finds
the translation incorrect and inadequate. The translation, he says,
departs so much from the original that he cannot use it to give a
true analysis of Batteux's *Principles of Literature*. He must, therefore,

make his compendium by using both the original and the translation. When he reaches the section devoted to Spanish drama, he says that "the translator, following his custom, alters and adds to the original, and interpolates bits taken from here and there, forming long appendices upon Spanish tragedy and comedy."[48] All that is good in this medley, he says, is taken bodily from Luzán, whom the translator despoils without even mentioning his name. Arrieta has followed the established practice of defending the Spanish theater by calling attention to more than fifty comedies that were appropriated by Pierre Corneille, Thomas Corneille, Molière, Rotrou, Regnard, and other French dramatists. The reviewer answers, quite reasonably, that "true literary glory does not consist in starting first but in going farther."[49]

The translator has said that to Spain belongs the credit of being the inventor of a new theater which was imitated by the other cultured nations of Europe, and that no other nation can show an equal number of comedies characterized by original invention, variety of incidents, and elegance of style. The reviewer answers that he does not understand what the translator means by a new theater because the only new theater worthy of consideration has been that of Corneille, Racine, and their imitators, and even this is nothing but the theater of the Greeks, modified to meet modern conditions. It is true, he says, that Spaniards formed a new kind of theater, but it was monstrous and irregular and, strictly speaking, belonged neither to comedy nor to tragedy. The mere fact that the early French dramatists translated and imitated Spanish comedies, just as Spaniards are now translating and imitating the French, is really without significance unless it can be proved that those plays upon which the reputation of the French theater rests can be traced to Spanish sources. Only in the case of the *Cid*, the reviewer says, can this be claimed. The tragedies upon which Corneille's fame really rests, that is, *Horace, Cinna, Polyeucte*, and *Rodogune*, derive their beauty from the study of the Greek and Latin theaters. Molière, at the beginning of his career, may have derived inspiration and ideas from Spanish plays, but the three comedies that have raised him to the front rank of comic poets—*Tartuffe, The Misanthrope*, and *The Miser*—are completely original. The reviewer concludes:

The momentary influence that Spanish literature had upon French occurred at the time of our decadence. Their bad writers, or at least those that were still bad, took from us something that was good and much that was bad; they imitated us for the most part in our affected and overnice style, in our false and euphuistic thoughts, in our confused and improbable plots, and in all the jargon of our novels and comedies.[50]

It is evident that in giving so much space to a digest of Arrieta's translation the *Memorial Literario* was motivated primarily by a desire to condemn and ridicule the nationalistic ideas contained in the additions. In its pro-French and antinational criterion it surpassed Luzán, Montiano, Nasarre, Nicolás Fernandez de Moratín, or even Clavijo y Fajardo.

The second edition of Muñarriz' translation of Blair's *Lessons* elicited a review, signed by Quintana, in the *Variedades de Ciencias, Literatura y Artes* (1805). In this review Quintana praises the clearness of the ideas and the simplicity of style in Blair's treatise:

... Such is Blair's work: without system, without pedantry, without affectation, he was able to explain the best doctrines of the earlier preceptists and to treat the most difficult questions of the theory of the art of writing, reducing them to the clarity and simplicity that the spirit and the mind require for their comprehension and approval.[51]

He has only praise for the additions, in which an extensive application of Blair's principles is made to Spanish language and literature. He attributes these additions entirely to the translator and says nothing of his own work as a collaborator. This is the section, dealing with the Spanish Golden Age, which was particularly condemned by Moratín. Quintana says:

The principal Spanish poets and prose writers are judged by him [Muñarriz] with exactitude and with a severity that may seem excessive. But perhaps the translator wished to put an end to the immoderate and unreasonable praise which others up to that time had showered upon them. It was said openly that Garcilaso, Herrera, the Argensolas, Mendoza, Mariana, and other authors of the so-called Golden Age were models, each one in his class; they were compared to the authors of antiquity; one was called Horace, another Sallust; and as a result the youth of Spain conceived a blind and pernicious admiration for these authors: their taste was perverted and they turned away from the road that led to perfection. In view of this condition the translator of Blair has done a service to our letters, manifesting with complete frankness that in these mines there is a great deal of slag mixed with the gold.[52]

Muñarriz himself answers, in the same periodical, an attack launched by Arrieta against his translation and makes it clear that the principal "bone of contention" has been his criticism of the poetry and prose of Bartolomé Leonardo de Argensola, Fray Luis de León, Fray Luis de Granada, and Father Mariana. In the same answer Muñarriz disavows complete responsibility for the additions: "Let it be understood as a general point that Blair spoke of our literature only twice. All that is found in the translation relative to our authors is my own work or the work of my friends."[53]

Shortly after the first performance of Moratín's *The Female Hypocrite*, on May 19, 1804, a long review and criticism of the comedy appeared in the *Variedades*. This article was signed by Quintana and is written with the same attention to detail and in the same style as the reviews of two of Moratín's earlier comedies, *The Old Man and the Young Girl* and *The New Comedy*, that had been included in Muñarriz' additions. Quintana begins his remarks with a statement of the difficulties that confront a critic who publishes his evaluation of a work of literature. If he praises the work, people say that he is a wretched flatterer; if he censures it, he is a detractor who aspires to gain a name for himself by attacking those who have already won renown.[54]

In this review Quintana carefully mixes praise with censure. In fact, he says so many good things about the author and his work that it is difficult to understand how the review could have stirred up a controversy. Nevertheless, a writer who represented himself as a friend of Moratín wrote an equally long answer to Quintana's review, saying that he agreed with him in his praise of *The Female Hypocrite*, but disagreed with him in every case where he had seen fit to censure the play. Quintana published this answer in the *Variedades*, accompanied by his own remarks upon each of the points under discussion.[55] It is possible that this controversy might have degenerated into another bitter polemic if Moratín had not put an end to it in a letter to the editor asking that *The Female Hypocrite* not be made the object of further discussion and expressing the fear that some might think he himself had written the recent defense of the play:

. . . Appreciating, as is just, the good intentions of the one who has spent his time in answering you and in vindicating my cause, I am of the opinion that he made a mistake in not signing his name. This neglect might cause people to believe (and there will be many who will want to believe it) that I avail myself of the well-known and unfortunate device of answering my critics by supposing the existence of a charitable person who favors and defends me.[56]

In language very similar to that used later by Quintana in speaking of his critics, Moratín says:

I never answer the censures that are made of my works. I always appreciate them, because, if they are well written, they instruct me; they aid me with their observations and I remain silent. If they are absurd, they contribute indirectly to my fame; I laugh at them, at their authors, and at the spirit that moved them, and I also remain silent.[57]

From its inception the neo-classic movement was characterized by dissension within its ranks almost as much as by its opposition to literary irregularity. The classic precepts, as elaborated by a long succession of commentators, constituted an invitation to a display of pedantry. Every new play that appeared was immediately measured, weighed, and dissected with the new instruments of dramatic criticism. In the additions to Blair, Moratín's comedies, *The Old Man and the Young Girl* and *The New Comedy*, were subjected to a thorough analysis. The result was about nine parts of censure to one part of praise. This verdict certainly must have influenced Moratín's attitude toward Quintana and his followers and may account, in part at least, for the adverse criticism that greeted the latter's tragedies when they first made their appearance.

When the administration of the theaters was returned to the municipal government of Madrid on November 3, 1806, a committee was appointed to draw up a new set of regulations, and it was specified that these regulations should be subject to the approval of Quintana and of the two well-known actors Isidoro Máiquez and Antonio Pinto. The position of civil censor of the theaters, which had been held by Santos Díez González from 1789 until his death in 1804, had passed to Casiano Pellicer, and upon the death of the latter in February, 1806, had been entrusted to Quintana. Inasmuch as Quintana was the only literary man on the committee, it may be assumed that he was largely responsible for the provisions and the wording of the document. Although these regulations remained in force only a little more than a year, they contained many sound innovations and formed the basis for subsequent reforms. It is significant that Quintana should have had an important part in drawing up regulations that replaced a previous plan sponsored by Moratín. In spite of their difference of opinion with regard to the merits of Golden Age poets, Quintana and Moratín were equally convinced of the necessity for reform in all phases of Spanish literature. Moratín would certainly have subscribed to Quintana's evaluation of Luzán's *Poetics:* that it

...has the merit of being a well-written book, the best of those published at the time. Sound and true in its principles, opportune and moderate in erudition and doctrine, judicious in plan, and clear in style, it presented qualities of intellect, art, and good taste which were not to be found among the writers of that period, some of whom were depraved by the prevalent bad taste while others were addicted to an undigested medley of knowledge that was childish, inopportune, and always tedious.[58]

Quintana resented the accusation, so frequently heard in his day, that the imitation of French literature and the tenets of neo-classicism had been responsible for the corruption of Spanish literature:

It is a common and frequent thing among those critics who pride themselves upon being purists, to accuse French letters of having corrupted and destroyed the proper and native character of Castilian poetry. But in reality this is not true; because long before French writers began to be taken as models, Spaniards had already abandoned all good principles in the imitative arts and had allowed the torch of genius to be extinguished in their hands. Painting had died with Murillo, eloquence with Solís, poetry with Calderón; and in the half-century that intervened between them and Luzán, no book, no writing, with the exception of an occasional comedy by Cañizares, sufficed by its literary merit to attract the attention and the interest even of the most indulgent. What is nonexistent cannot be degraded or corrupted. Imitation of French writers may well have given a different character to our taste and to our literature, but it could not disfigure something that no longer existed or kill something that was no longer alive.[59]

Quintana's interest in the theater was evidenced at an early age by his composition of a short *Poetics,* or, as he called it, *Rules for Drama,* which he entered in 1791 in a contest sponsored by the Spanish Academy. This work was published for the first time in 1821 with corrections and notes. The most significant thing critics have observed in the notes is a change in the author's attitude toward the unities. In his *Rules* he had said: "Let a single action be presented in a fixed and designated place and in a single revolution of the sun." He now adds this comment:

Such is the precept of the unities in all the rigor of the school. The author, who wrote this work upon leaving school and with the milk of rhetoric still on his lips, could not help advocating their strict observance. Now he does not think so rigidly about the unities of time and place; and he notices that, if there are strong reasons in their favor, there are also striking examples against them.[60]

Quintana is still very cautious, however, about advocating any marked relaxation of the rules; and he adds that he is not attempting to resolve "a question which the present disputes over the relative merits of the two genres, classic and romantic, or romanesque, have made more and more complicated."[61] He still insists upon the necessity of achieving verisimilitude, and would permit relaxation of the precepts only to the extent that such relaxation contributes to greater beauty in a composition.

Quintana declares that the indulgent reception accorded his *Pelayo* motivated him to undertake the composition of other tragedies and that he had already made considerable progress upon three, *Roger de Flor, The Prince of Viana,* and *Blanca de Borbón,* when his work was interrupted by the French invasion and the revolution. From that time, he says, "the obligation of attending to work of a quite different nature, the necessity of moving from one place to another, and the well-known avalanche of persecutions and imprisonments the author has suffered, destroyed his papers, together with the best years of his life and all his literary projects."* He hopes that other writers will enjoy quieter times and will be more fortunate. Indeed, political and economic conditions throughout the eighteenth century and well into the nineteenth were unfavorable to literary production. Critics who condemn the lack of original works during the so-called neo-classic period, and who express contempt for the accomplishments of this school, fail to take sufficiently into consideration the difficulties under which its writers labored.

*Upon the return of Fernando VII Quintana was imprisoned in the fortress of Pamplona, where he remained six years (1814-20), without being permitted during this time to have visitors or to write even to pass away the time.

1. Leandro Fernández de Moratín, *op. cit. (B.A.E.,* II, ix).
2. Cotarelo y Mori, *Iriarte,* p. 97, note.
3. Cotarelo y Mori, *Don Ramón de la Cruz,* p. 206.
4. Sempere y Guarinos, *op. cit.,* I, 154.
5. Francisco Martínez de la Rosa, "Apéndice sobre la tragedia española," *Obras Completas* (Paris, 1845), p. 111.
6. Vicente García de la Huerta, *Raquel.* (Reprinted in *Tesoro del Teatro Español* [Paris, 1899], Vol. V.)
7. Cotarelo y Mori, *op. cit.,* p. 191.
8. *Ibid.*
9. *Ibid.,* p. 192.

10. Menéndez y Pelayo, *op. cit.,* III, 318.
11. Pietro Napoli Signorelli, *Storia critica de'i teatri antichi e moderni,* quoted from Schack, *Historia de la literatura y del arte dramático en España* (Madrid, 1887), V, 165.
12. *Raquel,* Act I, Sc. I.
13. *Ibid.,* Act II, Sc. 9.
14. *Ibid.,* Act III, Sc. 4.
15. Sempere y Guarinos, *op. cit.,* III, 104.
16. Vicente García de la Huerta, *La fe triumfante del Amor y Cetro,* tragedia francesa, traducida al español por Don Vicente García de la Huerta de la Acad-

emia Española. Quarta Edición, con licencia, en Segovia. En la imprenta de Don Antonio Espinosa, n.d.

17. Manuel José Quintana, *Obras Completas (B.A.E., XIX, 149)*.

18. García de la Huerta, *La Escena Hespañola defendida en el Prólogo del Theatro Hespañol* (Madrid, 1786).

19. *Ibid.*, p. 148.

20. *Ibid.*

21. Menéndez y Pelayo, *op. cit.*, III, 320.

22. "Advertencia" to *Xayra*.

23. Menéndez y Pelayo, *op. cit.*, III, 323.

24. *Ibid.*

25. *Ibid.*

26. *Ibid.*, p. 324.

27. Quintana, *op. cit.*, p. 150.

28. García de la Huerta, *op. cit.*

29. Nicasio Alvarez de Cienfuegos, *La Zoraida*, tragedia en tres actos (Valencia, 1815).

30. Menéndez y Pelayo, *op. cit.*, III, 408.

31. Cienfuegos, *op. cit.*

32. Cienfuegos, *Obras Poéticas* (En la Imprenta Real, Año de 1816), 2nd ed.; Vol. II.

33. Alvarez Espino, *Ensayo Historico Crítico del Teatro Español* (Madrid, 1876), p. 271.

34. Cienfuegos, *Obras Poéticos*, Vol. I.

35. Antonio Alcalá Galiano, *Recuerdos de un anciano* (Madrid, 1878).

36. Manuel José Quintana, *Obras Completas (B.A.E., XIX, 41-59)*.

37. *El Memorial Literario*, 1801, I, 161.

38. *Ibid.*, p. 166.

39. *Ibid.*, p. 279.

40. Quintana, *Obras Completas*, p. 41.

41. *Ibid.*, pp. 58-73.

42. Manuel José Quintana, *Pelayo*, Act V, Sc. 5.

43. *El Memorial Literario*, 1805, II, 201.

44. *El Diario de Madrid*, March 19, 1805.

45. Quintana, *op. cit.*, p. 42.

46. Leandro Fernández de Moratín, *Obras Póstumas*, III, 12.

47. *Ibid.*, p. 13.

48. *El Memorial Literario*, 1803, IV, 77.

49. *Ibid.*, p. 86.

50. *Ibid.*, p. 87.

51. *Variedades de Ciencias, Literatura y Artes*, Año segundo, Tomo Primero (Madrid, 1805), p. 346.

52. *Ibid.*, pp. 355-56.

53. *Ibid.*, p. 102.

54. *Variedades*, Tomo Segundo (Madrid, 1804), p. 356.

55. *Ibid.*, III, 295-305.

56. *Ibid.*, p. 306.

57. *Ibid.*

58. Quintana, *Obras Completas*, p. 116.

59. *Ibid.*, p. 146.

60. *Ibid.*, p. 81.

61. *Ibid.*

Theory and Dramatic Criticism

WHILE Iriarte, Trigueros, María Guerrero, and Sebastián y Latre were attempting to present regular comedies on the stage, the fight against the irregular theater was carried on vigorously in the periodicals, including *El Correo de Madrid, El Diario de Madrid,* and *El Memorial Literario.* Nor were the neo-classicists less active in discourses and other formal expositions of their theories. Indeed, the period from 1780 to 1792, immediately preceding Moratín's *The New Comedy,* may be considered as the peak of the campaign against the irregular theater.

Sempere y Guarinos

In 1782 Sempere y Guarinos published a free translation of Muratori's *Reflections upon Good Taste in the Sciences and in the Arts,* accompanied by a discourse on the contemporary taste of Spaniards in literature.[1]

The author calls attention to the fact that the French have freely admitted the debt owed by their theater to early Spanish dramatists. With considerable relish he quotes a statement by Saint-Evremond: "Let us confess frankly, says M. de Saint-Evremond, that the writers of Madrid are more fertile in invention than ours; and that is the reason for our taking from them the greater part of our subjects."[2] He also quotes a statement by the author of the *Library of a Man of Taste:* "Spain has been especially fertile in dramatic poets. There are more Spanish comedies than Italian and French comedies and tragedies combined from their origin to the present time. Therefore the Spanish theater is the source from which many of our writers of tragedies and comedies have drawn their material."[3] Sempere y Guarinos reasons that since the French are so ready to acknowledge their indebtedness to the Spanish theater, there is no reason for Spaniards to consider unpatriotic a recognition of the merits of French neo-classic plays. "Our countrymen should match the sincerity with which the scholars of that enlightened nation confess their debt to us by recognizing with good will how much she surpasses us at the present time in art and in style."[4]

But the Spanish *vulgo* is not willing to concede any defects in its idols and considers any criticism an insult to the Spanish nation, believing that no geniuses can ever equal Lope de Vega, Calderón, and Góngora. The author traces briefly the history of neo-classic criticism in Spain from the time of Luzán and concludes that as a result of the efforts of these critics the Spanish theater has come to find itself "on a very nice footing." No longer do men of good taste appreciate "comedies filled with flying, enchantments, and apparitions." He does not claim, however, that these have lost their appeal for the crowd. Among the regular plays which have been performed "with great acclamation" on the stage he lists the following translations: *Pamela, The Scotchwoman, The Gleaner, Albert I, The Good Wife,* and *The Beautiful Shepherdess;* and among the original plays he names *Raquel,* by García de la Huerta; *The Destruction of Numancia,* by López de Ayala; *Hormesinda,* by Nicolás Fernández de Moratín; *Jahel,* by Sedano; *Ana Bolena,* by Villarroel; and *Sancho García,* by Cadalso.

Although Sempere y Guarinos says that all the above plays, both translations and original works, "have produced much money," his statement is evidently based on wishful thinking rather than upon fact. There is no record of any performance of Villarroel's *Ana Bolena* in the theaters of Madrid, and Cadalso's *Sancho García* when it was performed produced 1,184 reals the first day and on the fourth and fifth days produced only 320 and 155 reals respectively. On the other hand the people flocked to the Príncipe at the same time to see *The Reapers of Vallecas,* by Ramon de la Cruz.[5]

Sempere y Guarinos finds comfort also in the progress made by the actors in their declamation, which he attributes to the influence of the French and Italian school of opera. These, he says, "have reformed the violent manner of acting, and have introduced another that is more natural and more in keeping with the nature of the subject matter and the dramatic characters."[6]

The dearth of original plays does not prove that genius is dead in Spain. He believes the reason is to be found in the fact that it is harder to win fame since the introduction of the rules: ". . . good taste that has been generally introduced does not allow praise to be given so easily to dramatic and lyrical works, and this fact should discourage those who have not added to their native talent a great deal of application and study of the rules."[7]

Dramatic Criticism in Periodicals

In 1773 Iriarte had expressed regret that, while in France and Italy newspapers were published to criticize contemporary literature, Spain had had no such papers, after envy forced the abandonment of the *Diario de los Literatos* in 1742.

Years ago there was published in this city a very useful work of that nature with the title *Diario de los Literatos*, which was the product of persons of solid erudition and refined taste. That same envy, the ugliness of which I have painted for you, and the satirical attacks to which these authors saw themselves subjected gave them sufficient reason to desist from their laudable undertaking. Would that it might be revived in our time to the glory of science and of the fatherland![8]

The *Pensador* by Clavijo, which had appeared in 1762, and the *Censor*, which ran from 1781 to 1786, could hardly be called periodicals in the sense Iriarte had in mind, because all the articles of the former were written by one man and the latter was published in the form of discourses. The discourses devoted to drama were rather a general attack upon the *comedia* than reviews of contemporary plays.

In 1784 appeared the first number of the *Memorial Literario,* which came nearer than any other periodical of the time to the dignified and reasonable tone that had characterized the first numbers of the *Diario de los Literatos*. In the initial number of January, 1784, the *Memorial* indicates the policy it expects to follow in its articles on the theater:

In these articles we propose to give the argument or constitution of the comedies that are being performed on the stage and to collect the opinions of men of good judgment with reference to their good qualities or their defects.[9]

To serve as a basis for subsequent criticism of comedies the following definition is given:

Comedy is a representation (by means of interlocutors) of an action that is not great, illustrious, and severe like tragedy, but moderate, low, or commonplace, and agreeable, directed to the correction of manners by portraying them skilfully and reproving with wit those that are vicious.[10]

If comedies written in Spain conformed to this rule, the theaters would be "moral, political and economic schools"; but the ignorance of many poets, the desire on the part of others to please the *vulgo*, or the condition of the taste of the nation has kept the theaters from fulfilling this mission and has given free rein to the belief that comedies can be novels on the stage, with heroic adventures and battles which take place in a moment; and that the coarse buffoonery of the *graciosos* is suited to the theater.

In justification of its intention to pass judgment on the comedies performed in the theaters of Madrid, the *Memorial* quotes from Luzán:

> Granting then the singular merit of these and other poets and in view of the esteem and appreciation I have shown for their successes, their partisans will have no reason to be offended if I pause to call attention here to some of their defects and negligence for the instruction of those who write in the future; just as it is the custom to mark and to give warning on maritime maps and navigator's charts of the reefs and shoals found by other pilots . . .[11]

Following this statement there is an analysis and criticism of the plays which had appeared recently at two theaters, the Príncipe and the Cruz.

In February, 1784, under the heading "Theaters" the *Memorial* quotes a passage from the *Notes to the Poetics of Aristotle*, by Batteux, in which the vices considered as fit subjects for ridicule in comedy are limited to those that are ridiculous or odious by their very nature, "like love in an old man, vanity among noblemen when it is exaggerated or when it is ill fitting; avarice, or all those caprices or passions that are believed to be good or unimportant rather than bad by those who have them."[12] At the side of vice, virtue must always stand in pronounced relief.

In 1784 and 1785 the *Memorial* continued to comment on the rules that should govern comedy. The following extracts will serve to show how closely these comments followed the established neoclassic code:

> Since comedy must give definite manners to its principal personages, or traits that will indicate the nature of each, . . . a comedy that does not bring out these qualities, or in which they are vague and undetermined, or in which they change without reason or sufficient necessity, will neither imitate nature nor conform to the rules based upon it.[13]

> . . . As comedy imitates civil life it follows as a natural consequence that

its speech should imitate familiar language. Knowledge of this principle is all that is necessary for us to see at once how careless most of our writers of comedy have been in imitating nature on this point.[14]

... Clearness of expression is one of the principal requirements of good language and good poetic idiom and since comedy imitates humble style, it seems that it should endeavor to avoid obscurity and to use clear language. The basis of clearness is purity and propriety.[15]

At this point the *Memorial* censures the use of Gallicisms like *destroza mi corazón* and *batirse en duelo*, expressions which had met the disapproval of Iriarte in *Writers in Lent*. Propriety not only pertains to "expressions that are appropriate and pure," but also to the character of the personages, since it is not fitting for a servant to speak like a gentleman or for a gentleman or lady to speak "in the style used in the Lavapies district."

Some comic poets, either following the custom of introducing *graciosos* in comedies, or being directed by the maxim that comedy should excite laughter, consider that all the wit consists in puns, or plays upon words. It is true that comedy should excite laughter, but it must be the kind of laughter that results from ridiculing vice to make it odious or despicable.[16]

In the light of the ideas expressed above, it is not surprising to find much of Golden Age comedy considered objectionable. The *Memorial* follows closely the judgments expressed by Luzán in his *Poetics* with reference to individual plays. For instance, after pointing out some defects in Moreto's *Disdain Conquered by Disdain*, the reviewer concludes, "But Don Ignacio Luzán in his work excuses these and other defects." *Pretty Don Diego*, also by Moreto, is praised more highly than any other Golden Age comedy. These plays would naturally meet more nearly the approval of the neo-classicists, since, as Luzán had said, they were "those that could properly be called comedies." Even in *Memorial* reviews of plays by Calderón, however, there is an obvious attempt to be fair. The reviewer at times finds them "fairly regular" and usually concedes that they have the quality of interesting the spectators. It is apparent that Luzán's *Poetics* is the norm in all the reviews. For example, in the review of *Gratitude, but Not Love*, by Calderón, this statement is made: "It has amusing episodes and a regular plot but improbability in the valor of the women. It does not seem to me, says Don Ignacio de Luzán, ... that the language Laurencio uses in *Gratitude, but Not Love* can ever be considered good and appropriate in comedy."[17] The reviews of *Emotions of Hatred and Love* (1784), *His Own Jailor* (1787), *My Lady Comes First* (1784), *Welcome but Unwelcome if You Come Alone* (1784), *To Give Time to Time* (1784), *Eco and Narciso* (1786), *Pawns of Chance* (1785), and *The Hidden Man and the Veiled Woman* (1784), all by Calderón, contain more praise than censure. *The Misfortune of the Voice* even arouses enthusiasm:

... If it did not violate the unities of place and time so much, ... it would be one of the best comedies in our theater; and even with all that, its good qualities are not obscured; for it has much interest in the intrigue, a great contrast of emotions, incidents that are well arranged and entangled, a natural and facile solution, and an agreeable invention ...[18]

The plays of Calderón which meet with complete disapproval are those considered detrimental to morals, notably his tragedies built around the so-called *pundonor* theme: *Jealousy the Greatest Monster and Tetrarch of Jerusalem; The Physician of His Honor;* and *The Painter of His Dishonor.* In regard to the latter play, for example, the critic sums up his review with this statement: "It is an action that is not only rash and unjust but perverse in its example."[19]

Comedies which vie with a novel in their multiplicity of episodes are certain to draw the fire of the *Memorial.* Thus it finds *Count Lucanor,* by Calderón, filled with improbabilities: "To put within the confines of a comedy a romance of chivalry filled with nonsense is to multiply absurdities, by violating verisimilitude in time and place, and by piling up incidents and episodes that are unconnected and very much apart from the main action."[20]

In its criticism of Lope, Tirso, Alarcón, Moreto, and other Golden Age dramatists, the *Memorial* shows no noticeable animosity, its scorn being reserved primarily for plays of the Calderonian decadents. In regard to Cañizares' *To Intercede for His Offender and Baron of Pinel,* the *Memorial* says: "If there are such things as extravagant comedies, this unquestionably is one of them. It is useless to look for the unities of time, place, and action. And what shall we say about its lack of care and moderation in handling decency and decorum of manners?"[21] This is typical of the reviews of Cañizares' plays with the exception of *Dómine Lucas* and *The Little Rogue in Spain,* which, since they are comedies *de figurón,* are not found particularly objectionable. The *Dómine Lucas* review again quotes Luzán.

In regard to contemporary authors, the *Memorial* is inclined to be eminently fair and at times overly indulgent. Both merits and defects are always noted. But in the "Introduction to the Theatrical Year" that appeared in the issue of April, 1786, the *Memorial* announces a change of policy. Irritated at the prevalence of "pernicious comedies, of evil manners and bad example," this periodical says it will emphasize the necessity of a serious, quick, and effective reform of the theater. Since the actors have it in their power to choose the plays to be presented, an effort must be made to convince them that the primary purpose of the theater is not to amuse but "to portray manners, reproving the bad and proposing the good." The theater must be made "a school of good manners," which will ridicule vice and exalt virtue. There is, however, no violent attack upon the old theater and the *Memorial* still mixes praise with censure.

This moderate attitude on the part of the *Memorial Literario* is in marked contrast to that of the *Diario de Madrid.* The tone of the critical articles on the theater and of the few reviews of individual plays which appear in the latter periodical is as extreme as any found in *El Pensador* by Clavijo y Fajardo. To be sure, the *Diario de Madrid* prints articles for and against neo-classicism as they are submitted, but the editorial policy of the periodical is never left in doubt. The difference between the attitude of the *Diario* and that of the *Memorial* may be seen by a comparison of the receptions accorded Calderón's *Life Is a Dream.* The *Memorial* concludes that "its wealth of opportune reflections and serious moral maxims . . . make it worthy of public esteem".[22] In the *Diario de Madrid* appeared the following denunciation written by Cándido María de Trigueros, and signed with the initials E. A. D. L. M. (*El Autor de los Menestrales*):

Gentlemen: I have just witnessed the performance of *Life Is a Dream* and my anger has been aroused to such an extent that I cannot remain silent, but I do not know where to begin. . . . I shall say very little about its execution in order to be able to devote more space to the play itself. The costumes of the actors could not be more inappropriate. Poles and Russians of ancient times are dressed in modern French fashion . . . and the execution is in keeping with the costumes. One hears almost nothing but a hail of verses; I mean, a continuous discharge of . . . verses following each other in rapid succession like stones thrown down upon a patio. . . .
"But what is this?" those who do not stop to examine things will say. "Who is this new slanderer? Who is this insignificant author of articles signed with five letters, who so shamelessly speaks of the comedy *Life Is a Dream,* the admiration and delight of our elders? Who is this insipid

detractor of the most famous composition of the famous Don Pedro Calderón de la Barca?" Those who believe me to be such do not know me well. I esteem the talent of Calderón much more than these vain admirers who only appreciate him through prejudice or habit; and because I esteem him I wish this comedy were not his . . . a good language and a facile and sonorous versification are its only good qualities. The absurdities of this comedy cannot be enumerated in a few lines. Neither art, nor verisimilitude, nor manners, nor history, nor natural law, nor religion; nothing is respected in it. It is readily believable that all the copies that can be found of it are not burned only through respect for the great talent of its author. . . .[23]

In the same year that saw the publication of the second edition of Luzán's *Poetics* the *Diario* began a series of articles under the titles "Scenic Poetry" and "Poetics of the Theater." These articles, of course, reached a much larger group of readers than did Luzán's work. On December 31, 1788, the *Diario* promised to discuss dramatic principles. This promise was not carried out until May 20 of the following year, when an "Introduction to Dramatic Poetry or Poetics of the Theater" was published. In the preface we are told:

The "Poetics" we are going to publish is vast and will exceed one hundred articles in as many days. . . . We shall talk . . . about all aspects of the theater and about drama in general. We shall explain the rules and laws that are applicable to all forms of drama and shall point out particularly those that apply to comedy, tragedy, and opera.[24]

The articles themselves, which begin on the following day, represent an attempt to explain in simple language the neo-classic precepts. The theater is considered "a school of manners." The utility of this institution can be defended only by assuming that its purpose is to reprove vice and exalt virtue. Since man is by nature more inclined to the former, the theater performs a definite service to the government by keeping a goodly number of the population occupied for three or four hours, thereby preventing them from indulging in their favorite diversions: gambling and drinking. This is but a repetition of Luzán's statement.

Although there are some who would like to abolish the theater entirely as vicious and immoral, many plays like *The Punishment of Avarice, Bewitched by Force, Domine Lucas, One Will Come from Outside, Beware of Still Water, A House with Two Doors, The Gambler, The Deserter, The Father of the Family, The Pampered Youth, The Ill-bred Young Lady, The Foreigner, Eugenia, The Gleaner, Clementine, The Good Friend,* and some *sainetes* by Ramón de la Cruz are "very decorous, instructive, and moral plays from which much profit and edification can be derived."[25] It will be noted from the above list that the approbation of the *Diario* is not limited to neo-classic comedy, but includes plays by Juan de Hoz, Calderón de la Barca, Moreto, Zamora, and Cañizares, in addition to translations from the French theater.

To be condemned are plays of vicious and corrupt morals like *A Woman Cannot Be Guarded, The Avenger of His Affront,* and *Jealousy the Greatest Monster.* Particularly objectionable are the comedies of magic: *Pedro Bayalarde, Marta la Romarantina, The Contest the Devil Had,* and *The Magician Brancanelo,* which can only interest children and ignorant people.

To the plays which meet the disapproval of the *Diario* are added all those "which sin noticeably against dramatic rules and laws, destroying verisimilitude, history, geography, etc., and trampling upon unities and precepts."[26]

It would be unprofitable to attempt any extensive analysis of these critical articles in the *Diario,* since they are clearly based on Luzán. There is no vicious attack on the *comedia,* and only extremes are condemned in contemporary plays. The only types which should be excluded from the stage completely are tragi-comedy ("because it is not natural to combine grief and pleasure, laughter and tears, heroism and baseness, or the serious and the ridiculous"); Comedies of Saints; comedies of magic; and Sacramental Plays.[27] The *Diario* shows a much more moderate attitude toward the *sainete* than that held by Iriarte and restricts its discussion of this genre to the statement: "It is unnecessary to make any observations about *entremeses* and *sainetes* because, since they paint the ridiculous, they always have the nature of comedies."[28]

The *Diario's* discussion of the unities follows closely that of Luzán. This periodical is very explicit, however, about certain technical requirements, and lists seven which pertain to the scenes: (1) Each act should have "at least six, ordinarily eight, and ten at the most." (2) Each scene should consist "at the most of sixty hendecasyllabic verses, if it is in a tragedy; or of seventy octosyllabic verses, if it is in a comedy; regularly forty, and not less than twenty to thirty." (3) Every scene should affect the principal action and include some "incident, episode, or intrigue that pertains to it." (4) In every scene not more than three nor less than two characters should speak. (This recommendation is taken directly from Luzán.)

(5) There should be no monologue scenes "because it is ridiculous and unusual for people to talk to themselves." (6) The first time an actor appears on the stage he should "bow to the audience." (7) The stage must never be empty. In addition to these requirements, it is essential that every entry or exit be sufficiently motivated.[29]

In regard to the verse form to be used in drama, the *Diario* only stipulates that, since comedy is a "humble poem, civil, domestic, and commonplace, the only object of which is to excite laughter and portray the ridiculous," verses should be of seven or eight syllables. Therefore the most appropriate forms for comedy are the "octosyllabic *romance*, the *redondilla*, the *quintilla*, the *décima*, and the *endecha*." Each *jornada*, or act, may begin with *décimas* or *redondillas* for two or three scenes and continue with *romances*, the assonance of which should vary with each act.[30] The *Diario*, therefore, even though ardently neo-classic, would admit all the verse forms which were later "reintroduced" by Bretón de los Herreros and which were considered such a radical departure from the neo-classic precepts.

The *Diario* is also more specific than other commentators about the length of a tragedy or comedy.

... Spanish comedies and pastorals may be lengthened to 3,000 octosyllabic verses (whether they are *romances, redondillas, quintillas,* or *décimas,* or any combination thereof); and tragedies to 2,000, or at the most 2,500 hendecasyllabic verses (whether they are heroic *romances* or blank verse).[31]

The discussion of the unities varies only slightly from Luzán's *Poetics.* In order that the unity of place may be observed, the author should choose for a comedy "a reception room, a hall, an antechamber, a kitchen, etc.," and for a tragedy "some stately hall, temple, or amphitheater." For comedy, however, all the rooms of a private house may be used and for tragedy all the rooms of a palace. An entire city may not serve as the scene of the action. Going back to Roman comedy, the *Diario* adds:

... Many think, and with much reason, that it is most fitting for the stage to represent some street, plaza, portico, shop, garden, field, promenade, fair, market, or other public place within the view of everybody, in which it may be pretended and supposed with verisimilitude that various people go and come, enter and leave while attending to their affairs.[32]

The unity of time is interpreted to mean "one morning, one afternoon, one night, or perhaps eight, twelve, or fourteen hours, and to avoid doubts, it is better to pretend that the action lasts from sunrise to sunset or the equivalent."[33] The statement of the unity of action is entirely conventional.

The *Diario* was publishing its articles on the rules when Iriarte's *The Pampered Youth* was first presented and, in view of its warm defense of this comedy and the similarity of its ideas to those of that author, may well have been influenced by him. The only important divergence in ideas is found in the brief comments in the *Diario* on the *sainete*, which show none of Iriarte's bitterness toward that type of play.

El Correo de Madrid, which ran from 1786 to 1790, was a kind of open forum of public opinion, although, as in the case of *El Diario de Madrid*, its editorial policy is never left in doubt. Some of the strongest condemnations of irregular comedy are found in its columns. Many of these criticisms are in the form of anonymous letters to the editor.

In the *Correo* the actors and the staging of the plays particularly come in for censure. An article by the editor himself on October 10, 1786, gives an interesting account of a dispute between the *Polacas* and the *Chorizos* in regard to the defects of the actors:

... It is amusing at times to hear the disputes that arise between those who attend the theaters. The *Polacos* and the *Chorizos* form opposing factions who attack each other and defend themselves alternately with heat or phlegm according to their temperaments. But the oddest thing is that the target usually comes to be the actors in the two theaters. A few days ago we witnessed one of these affairs at a certain party. The battle began with remarks about the thrusts that had been made in the papers against the *Polacos*. The *Chorizos* who were at the gathering deduced from this an unanswerable argument in favor of the superiority of their band. Their opponents said that, since the crowd likes what is worse, it prefers to attend the theater of the *Chorizos*. They came to blows then; that is, they brought into the discussion the principal actors of the theaters and compared their persons and their merit. There were no long, tall, or broad bodily characteristics of the ladies that were omitted from the discussion. About one actress they said that her corpulence alone and her labored speech were sufficient to justify her removal; another was too affected and shouted too much; one was cold; another had a disagreeable voice; some cut off the verses badly; others always talked in the same tone. After discussing the ladies they passed to the men. One leading man was compared to a mechanical doll that walked up and down on the stage without bending its knees and swaying the upper part of its body. His gesticulation, they said, was stiff, consisting of horizontal motions that started from his breast and went as far as he could reach with his hand, which he closed suddenly at the end of the movement as though he were catching a fly in the air. One actor was described as perpetual motion, and another as a buffoon who interrupted the most serious passages with inopportune grimaces.[34]

That this description was reasonably accurate is indicated by an anonymous response to the article published a week later. The writer agrees with the editor but thinks that any censure of the actors and of irregular comedy "is preaching in the wilderness." He cites the unfavorable reception given to the *Memorial Literario's* condemnation of Alarcon's *The Weaver of Segovia* and other "monstrous comedies." The *Memorial*, he says, has also objected to the fact that the actors show themselves behind the scenes. This criticism, however, has produced no results, for "they show constantly the full length of their bodies and bow to the orchestra and to the boxes."[35] The writer believes it is useless to oppose the predilection of a certain type of spectator for the *comedia*.

... Don't waste your time. Those who like only Calderón, Moreto, etc., and the manner in which their plays are performed, are innumerable. There are people who can hardly keep from neighing when they see a gallant, who, in order to describe a beautiful mare, puts himself on all fours, rears up, cavorts around, and snorts. The women ordinarily like nothing but amorous figures of speech and endearing expressions. When the gallants and the ladies melt with sentiment in their conversations, everything is fine.[36]

Since neo-classic comedy required the most complete naturalness on the part of the actors, it suffered much more from bad performance than the *comedia*, which relied more upon intrigue and action than upon characterization. We have observed that the first neo-classic comedy to achieve success on the stage, Iriarte's *The Pampered Youth*, was directed by the author himself, and no small part of the effectiveness of the play was attributed to the natural manner in which it was performed. Certainly the style of acting which had developed in Spain as a natural consequence of the exaggerated and metaphorical language of Calderón and his followers must have been a serious obstacle to the development of neo-classic comedy. It is doubtful whether even Molière could have succeeded in France if he had had to entrust his plays to such actors.

Even the most ardent neo-classicists were perfectly aware that little progress had been made in educating the *vulgo* to an appreciation of regular comedy. Governmental censorship is frequently urged in the periodicals of the day. At least one commentator of 1789 has not given up hope of reforming public taste by persuasive methods. In the *Correo de Madrid* of November 3 of that year we find the advisability of a strict governmental censorship questioned. The writer says:

> ... it is necessary to temporize with the *vulgo* and even with the actors themselves, who for the most part are even more deluded than the former, and to accept and follow their taste until they are freed from prejudice. The best thing to do, as soon as a drama is announced, would in my opinion be for some able person to advise the public whether the aforesaid drama is regular or not, both in general terms and with reference to some of its particular beauties or defects. ... In this way the public would come to notice the good and bad points in plays, would acquire proper ideas, and would learn what a true comedy or tragedy is.[37]

In the following year, after recognizing the "complete lack of success of those who, longing for the reform of the Spanish theater, declaim against its defects," an anonymous writer announces a remedy he believes will be effective. He suggests that, since there are many talented amateurs in Madrid who appreciate regular comedy, the Board of Hospitals should choose those who are outstanding, make available the theater of the Caños del Peral, defray all expenses for costumes, music, lighting, etc., and form a company which would be capable of performing regular plays. He realizes that the number of good plays is very limited but believes that if the Board would offer annual prizes to stimulate the production of regular comedies and if competent critics were selected to examine and to correct the least defective of the old plays, this situation could soon be remedied. He suggests finally that nothing would be more fitting than that the Board should inaugurate the performances of the new company with *The Pampered Youth* by Iriarte.[38]

In April of the same year the following recommendation was made in the *Correo:*

> ... In order to separate good comedies and tragedies from the bad and to reform and correct those that are susceptible of reform, and in order to throw away completely those that are useless, extravagant, and harmful, it would be very fitting for a board of censors to be set up, composed of six persons, two of them to be theologians to look after morals and dogma, and the four remaining to be men of good taste and competent literary

judgment, whose duty it would be to examine all plays presented to the theater for performance.[39]

Eleven years later, a similar plan was put into operation with the formation by royal decree of a Board of Censors.

In 1790 appeared the first number of *La Espigadera,* which more than any other periodical may be considered the mouthpiece of the neo-classic movement at that time. Among the subscribers are found the names of most of the ardent champions of the school. The initial number carried these verses from Horace's *Ars Poetica:*

> Omne tulit punctum qui miscuit utile dulci
> Lectorem delectando, pariterque monendo,

together with Iriarte's translation:

> Y todos con su voto contribuyen
> Al que enseñar y deleytar procura,
> Y une la utilidad con la dulzura.*

The first article of this number was entitled "Impartial and True Discourse upon the Present Condition of the Spanish Theater." Nowhere do we find a more severe indictment of the defects neo-classicists considered inherent in the *comedia,* or a more scathing denunciation of the contemporary monstrosities, which appealed to the depraved taste of the *vulgo.* According to the anonymous critic the theater in Spain lies "in such an indecorous and debased condition that if it is not completely barbarous, it is at least not very far from coarseness, indecency, and the greatest disorder which this kind of an institution can reach."[40] Not only are the "stage sets and decorations niggardly, absurd, and indecent" and the "stage direction confused, vague, and calculated to maintain and to perpetuate bad taste," but the actors whose obligation it is to express with truth and naturalness the roles assigned to them are so incompetent that "theatrical performances... in Madrid have reached such an extreme of irregularity and ridiculousness that if the culture of a capital were to be judged by that of its theater (as many foreigners wish) ours could not fail to pass for the most uncultured and uncivilized in Europe."[41] The author attributes the condition of histrionics in Spain to the type of drama the actors have had to interpret.

*And everyone approves with his vote the one who seeks to instruct and to entertain, thus combining utility with pleasure.

... It is easy to conjecture that absurd comedies must produce actors of the same type. Pompous and high-sounding speeches, metaphorical verses, extraordinary imagery, subtle concepts, sophistry, rhymed argumentations, epic and lyric features ... in short, all that mass of poetic ornamentation in all kinds of meters, styles, and species in which most of our comedies are written inevitably produces actors who resemble inspired priests of Cybele or witches of Pythia. In order to be able to recite all that poetic enthusiasm and fury, the actors must become equally enraptured and exalted.[42]

In proof of his contention the author cites *The Old Man and the Young Girl* and *The Pampered Youth*, which were directed by their respective authors and whose success was due, in part, to the natural manner in which they were performed. In order that the art of acting may reach a state of perfection it is necessary not only that the actors receive proper instruction but also that the plays performed "be written rationally and be adjusted to the precepts of art and good taste."

The plays which were written in Spain during the Golden Age are so irregular and so immoral that they have provoked heated discussion of the advisability of discontinuing the theater. The author declares that "if they are to perform, and offer to the public monstrosities, vice, and corruption, it would certainly be better for the theaters not to exist."[43] The purpose of the theater is "to teach and correct while entertaining," but in Spain it may well be said that until the present the purpose has been "to corrupt while entertaining."

The indictment the author of this article makes of the *comedia* is of the same nature as that made by Nasarre, Velázquez, and Iriarte. Following the plan of these critics, he enumerates the many faults which have characterized the *comedia*. It should be borne in mind always that the program of the neo-classicists was not confined to advocacy of the unities but included a systematic and continued attack against the extravagances and immorality of the old theater. The statement of the *Espigadera* in 1790 is very similar to that made by Moratín three years later in a letter to Godoy, suggesting the creation of the position of Director of Theaters.*

La Espigadera does not believe that the extravagances of the *comedia* should be tolerated merely because of the fact that

*This entire article in the *Espigadera* was apparently written by Juan Pablo Forner, since the section directed against the *comedia* is included almost without change in his *Exequias de la lengua castellana*.

Lope and Calderón were men of "fertile and marvelous imagination":

...What does it matter that our dramatists have been eminent poets, men of fertile and marvelous imagination, if they have for the most part offered us nothing but great extravagances, sustained with all the pomp of poetry, or indecorous actions and intrigues animated with the lively fancy of the incidents and with the elegant and rapid gaiety of the dialogue, which makes agreeable what would be horrible if it were presented in its nudity? In our dramas one sees painted in the most delightful colors the most indecent solicitations, elopements of maidens, scaling the walls of noble houses, resistance to law, duels and challenges that are rash and based upon a false concept of honor, approved abductions, attempted and executed acts of violence, insolent buffoons, man and maidservants who glory in and profit by their infamous mediations; and all of this is presented not to make it odious by making it laughable (as should be done) but to fascinate the spectators by keeping them hanging upon the suspense of the incidents until finally two or three marriages bring to an honest end the boldness of the gallants and the wantonness of the ladies, vicious actions remaining in this way unpunished and the audience schooled in the art of love-making without consideration for honor and justice or respect for public morals.[44]

According to the *Espigadera* all drama should be "parables in action, natural examples taken from life, vivid reproofs which improve society by painting with verisimilitude what really happens."[45]

Realism should replace the extravagances of the *comedia*. The only legitimate drama is that which copies "the temperament, the designs, the manners, the characters, the thoughts, and the effects that are experienced in association, in rank, and in the occupations of men."[46] If the theater does not do this it will never be more than it is at present in Spain, that is, "an imaginary region where, without any other purpose than to enthral or produce laughter by any means, people of all kinds appear to recite long passages of high-sounding verse, to rant, and jest, and to perform acts that would not even pass for dreams if they were told by a rational man."[47]

The position of the neo-classicists in 1790 does not differ materially from that held by Luzán, who, while conceding to the Golden Age dramatists remarkable capacity for interesting the spectators and unusual natural talent, regretted the misuse of these gifts. After such a detailed enumeration of the defects of the *comedia* as that contained in the article in *La Espigadera*, one is inclined to regard the brief tribute paid to Golden Age writers as a reflection of national pride or as a concession to popular taste made for tactical reasons. It must be remembered, also, that the *comedia* is being compared with the contemporary monstrosities of the Calderonian decadents and of Comella and his school and not with works of art:

... Men with great talent withdrew from the task of writing good works in order not to have to face the competition of those who furnish the theaters with farces. The latter, attributing their delirium to the depravity of popular taste and being incapable of imitating the excellencies of our old dramatists, do nothing but emphasize their defects. The result has been such disorder that in the comedies written for the theaters in the last fifty years one sees nothing but absurdities, delirium, enormous and intolerable nonsense in which there is not even a shadow of the beauties of Calderón and Lope, and one sees accumulated all the improbable, violent, prodigious, and foolish incidents found in the multitude of those comedies of ours that are considered most laden with absurdities. In short, in our theaters ... very great writers, as were almost all the dramatists of the past two centuries, shirking the rigidity of the rules of art and wandering from the straight road of imitation (the soul of poetry), wrote dramas which with all their irregularity contained admirable scenes, interesting situations, and excellent incidents. When they did not try to soar, their style was elegant, pure, attractive, smooth, fluent, and harmonious; they often painted characters admirably and manners very vividly and appropriately. Some of their comedies are equal to the most celebrated of those composed in foreign lands. The epoch of these great men passed ... and after them came wretched poetasters who not only continued to maintain their defects but added to them constantly in order to fascinate the *vulgo*.[48]

It is evident that the *Espigadera* is referring here particularly to such contemporary works as Comella's drama *The Good Son, or María Teresa de Austria*. In Number 10 of this periodical there is an extended article in which the reviewer seeks to prove by numerous examples the extent to which this work violates all the rules dictated by reason and good taste.

The School of Comella and Zavala y Zamora

It would be a mistake to assume that the new school of writers which had sprung up in Spain in the last quarter of the eighteenth century, and which was headed by Comella and Zavala y Zamora, had been unconditionally condemned from the beginning by all neoclassicists. The *Memorial Literario*, whose indulgence has already been noted, found in their plays much that it considered worthy of commendation. In 1784 the *Memorial* praised *The Good Wife* by Fermín de Laviano, saying: "This comedy is sufficiently regular and the characters are well expressed. The expressions and maxims and the reflections on decorum were rather pleasing, and the reform of the dissolute young man brought out doctrine and manners by contrasting virtue with vice."[49] And the review published in 1789 of Comella's *Louis XIV the Great* is on the whole favorable:

> ... One notices in this play a good arrangement of the plan, episodes that are appropriate and subordinated to the main action, a facile solution, suspense, well-sustained characters, appropriate maxims and expressions ... and a language that is rather clear, animated and natural. All of this can excuse some objections that may be raised against some incidents.... But this, as we have said, is obscured by the beauty that results from other incidents, from the well-prepared and motivated emotions and from the skilful arrangement of the entire action, as well as from the decorum of the characters and the subject.[50]

It is difficult to believe that such praise could be given by a neo-classic periodical to any work of that writer whom we find so ridiculed by Moratín in *The New Comedy*. The attitude of the *Memorial* is indeed puzzling. One is inclined to think that the reviewer found himself admiring some of these works in spite of himself, but, realizing that such admiration was not in keeping with his allegiance to the rules and might brand him as devoid of that essential quality, *good taste,* hastened in his next article to condemn the irregularity and extravagance of the new comedy. One feels, upon examining the reviews of this period, that the reviewers frequently found their taste in conflict with the rules which their intellect impelled them to accept. The praise which *El Memorial* accords the works of Comella and his school at times gives evidence, at least, of its determination to examine impartially all new plays and, whenever possible, to combine praise with censure.

In the same year (1790) the *Memorial* finds that in Zavala y Zamora's *The Coppersmith of San Germán or Mutual Gratitude,* "with the exception of the unity of time, which is notably violated, everything else follows the regular order; the characters are well sustained, the action is very appropriate, the episodes are well handled, and the intrigue and solution are natural. There are very tender and interesting passages."[51]

The attitude of the *Espigadera* contrasts sharply with the indulgence of the *Memorial.* In 1790 the former says of Zavala y Zamora's *Aragon Restored by the Valor of Her Sons:*

> ... This subject is absolutely alien not only to comedy but also to tragedy.

... It is one of the most nonsensical that the human mind can conceive. Now the sins of our old dramatists are imitated but there is not a shadow of their beauties. The play observes neither unity of action, place, nor time and cannot fail to be branded as one of the most stupid imaginable, because it has neither interest, illusion, important situations, characters, manners, nor morals. . . . We are astonished that anyone should think that our theater is reformed.[52]

The plays of the school of Comella and Zavala y Zamora which received the greatest acclaim from the public at this time were the *heroic comedies*. The *Memorial* is almost as severe as the *Espigadera* or the *Correo de Madrid* in its condemnation of these monstrosities. Zavala y Zamora's *Charles XII* is called "an aggregate of incidents and battles... reduced to one place and to one time, although they happened in different places and through a period of eight or nine years."[53] When the third part of this drama was played in June of the next year, the *Memorial* was sarcastic in its condemnation:

... But let our apprentice dramatists bear in mind that if occasionally the review of troops by the king himself has been received in our theaters (as being very appropriate to a comedy), how much more pleasing it must be to see the King direct the drill of his troops in preparation against an attack, as happens in this play ... in which one hears him shout: Attention! Load! Aim! Fire! and one sees all this done with exquisite realism, and then he sees the king rush with naked sword at his soldiers and they at him, as at the end of an *entremés*.[54]

This is the type of play which is justly ridiculed by Moratín in *The New Comedy* and which has been so consistently condemned by subsequent critics. Since the popularity of such plays constituted a much greater menace to regular comedy than did the *comedia*, Moratín naturally directed at them the shafts of his satire. The *comedia* received a respite while the neo-classicists turned to face this new enemy.

It seems that the public at this time had developed an inordinate taste for plays with spectacular stage settings. The opening of the Italian opera on January 20, 1787, had introduced to Madrid audiences a type of performance which not only offered an attraction to lovers of music, but also, in the splendor of its settings, stood out in marked contrast to Golden Age comedies and to neo-classic translations of tragedies and comedies from the French and Italian theaters. Only comedies of magic and the new sentimental and heroic dramas of Comella and Zavala y Zamora could stand this

competition, and the former could appeal only to uncritical spectators, to judge from a contemporary account of the performance and
staging of *The Magician of Salerno:*

I have seen just recently the old and noisy comedy of magic, *The Magician of Salerno,* at the theater of the Príncipe, and the displeasure I have
experienced there impels me to write you in order to give vent to my
annoyance. My first disagreeable experience was to enter through a narrow lane or funnel, which, although it is probably only three yards long,
has nevertheless two stations at which I, together with a string of men
who were in front of me and behind me, paid successively the customary
admission fees. As soon as I had come out into the open court, I began to
look around for a seat, but I looked in vain, for all were taken. I determined not to remain standing because I did so once and it cost me dearly.
The great surging of the crowd, the extreme heat, the obnoxious odors
that came from some near-by places, and at times from the bystanders
themselves, and finally a water vendor who appeared frequently with his
large decanter, crowding between the great number of people, disturbing a thousand in order that two or three might wet their lips; all this
annoyed me so much that my head reeled and my stomach was upset for
several days. . . . I left this part of the theater and I was fortunate enough
to meet some friends, who took me to their box. The performance started
soon with one of the four or five overtures which they play alternately
during the entire year and which have our ears completely worn out. An
old curtain was raised and the first thing that presented itself to the view
of the audience was the devil. . . . It is useless to say that in none of the
plays of this type should one expect a grain of substance. The only profit
that can be derived from them is reduced to visual delight or to the suspense of the imagination when the decorations are pleasing and when the
stage machinery is operated with delicate and hidden art. There was
none of this in that blessed *Magician of Salerno.* The stage sets that represent gardens, halls, etc., have been so frequently used that we are tired
of seeing them. The same thing can be said about the cave-ins, and besides
it is perfectly obvious how they are effected. The figure of the walking
bass viol is so bulky that it immediately announces the presence inside of
a boy (and it could easily be a mule), who makes it move forward.
The flying of the two male and female characters is not executed with any
artfulness, but by main strength; and one needs only to turn his eyes
toward the second row of balconies to see the stage machinists swinging
their arms.[55]

A month later the same critic gives a similar account of the performance of *The Magician Brancanelo:*

. . . The first scene represented a blacksmith's shop, but there was so much
hardware hanging on the walls that it looked like a royal armory and gave

every indication of being the house of a blacksmith who was rich and
not poor as he was supposed to be. In a short time a devil by the name of
Caupolicán came out. This devil must have been very peaceful, for he
did not dare to tempt the blacksmith (Brancanelo, if you please) and
remained quiet until he was called. Now the festival is all set up. The
wonders and the amazing things commence: flights, transformations, cave-
ins, and all manner of nonsense. But after all, as there are a few reasonably good stage tricks and some showy decorations, the performance is
not so intolerable as that of the *Magician of Salerno*.[56]

To understand the great popularity of the Italian operas at this
time one need only notice the complete contrast between the physical plant of the theater of the Caños del Peral, where they were
presented, and that of the Príncipe and the Cruz. Of course, the
quality of the acting and the general dignity of the performances
were no small factor in the preference of the cultured class for the
opera. A detailed description of the theater of the Caños appeared
in the *Correo de Madrid* some three months after the account of the
performance of *The Magician Brancanelo:*

... The entire theater of the Caños del Peral, which has recently been
remodeled and equipped for the performance of operas, besides filling a
void that was noticed by foreigners as soon as they became acquainted
with Madrid, is majestic and worthy of the capital of Spain. It has four
levels and on each level there are sixteen boxes, divided in this manner:
Levels 1, 2, and 3 are for general admission; and the fourth (which is the
most elevated) serves for what is called the "stew pan" for the women
and the "corridor" for the men. ... There is, in addition, a gallery entirely
around the boxes on the first level, but a little below them so as not to
obstruct the view of those in the boxes; they have comfortable seats and
sufficient room. ... The ceiling is flat, and from it hang three crystal chandeliers, two on each side and another, larger and more beautiful, forming a triangle with them. The larger chandelier has twenty-four holders
with lighted candles. The proscenium arch of the theater has four doric
columns. The forum appears rather large. The decorations present a beautiful sight and their taste is such that it suggests the perfection of the three
noble arts. The music consists of eighteen violins, four violas, one bassoon,
one clavichord, three contrabass viols, two bass viols, two clarinets, two
oboes, two flutes, and two bugles. It is needless to say that the effect of
all these instruments is distinctive and harmonious. *The Medonte*, which
is the opera that is being performed at this time, and which I have seen,
is probably excellent; but as I do not understand Italian and have only
been able to catch an occasional word ... I cannot pass upon its merit. ...
The costumes are in excellent taste, very fine and quite costly. The actors
in the opera and the dancers are very good looking; the prima donna has a
very pretty face and the principal ballerina is just as pretty. ... All of them

sustain, and obviously lose themselves in, the characters they represent. There is no whispering between them, no signals, or hand salutes to the spectators, nor are gazers seen between the wings; they perform with dignity and are masters of the stage. In short, in many particulars our best actors could take lessons from them . . .[57]

The new comedies of Comella and Zavala y Zamora, both the sentimental and the heroic, made full use of scenery, stage devices, and mass effects to enthral the spectators. Although in *Cecilia as a Widow* Comella makes an obvious attempt to conform to the unities and other neo-classic precepts, he gives careful attention to the *mis en scène:*

The scene is supposed to be a village of the Marqués, situated four leagues from Portugal in Old Castile.

Act I

The theater represents a part of the village. On the left there are buildings and on the right a forest. The background will be a hill. It is night, and in the west the moon is beginning to go down below the horizon. The theater will grow light by degrees; a gentle symphony will imitate night, then dawn, and sunrise. It will end when the cries of the countrymen going to Castañar are heard. Don Fernando comes out, looks at the sky and then says: . . .

This play is lacking in humor and overflowing with sentimentality. The moral lesson is emphasized in the final speech by the Marqués:

> And since we have seen
> the effects of vice
> and how virtue is protected
> by God in the greatest danger,
> let everyone love virtue;
> let everyone detest vice.

All the actors chime in on the last two lines.

In Zavala y Zamora's *Triumphs of Valor and Cunning*,[58] the first of his *Charles XII* trilogy, we have this picturesque scene in the first act:

Act I

A high mountain and a ravine at the back of the stage with a dense wood on one side of the mountain slope; along the back of the mountain in the distance can be seen merlons and fortified towers, which indicate the proximity of Moscow. To the tune of a military march soldiers and the Muscovite officers, Menciof, Augusto, Pedro, and the Czarina come on the stage in battle order.

In the "Prologue to the Reader," which accompanies the 1787 edition of this work, Zavala y Zamora expresses his appreciation for the reception accorded the first, second, and third parts of his *Charles XII* series. He defends himself against his critics, using some of the same arguments Lope de Vega had used more than a century and a half earlier, but insisting more upon the poet's right to exercise his imagination:

... don't stop (as so many ridiculous critics in the republic of letters have done) to criticize a few passages which may violate historical truth with episodes that can add brillance to the scene and force to the characters. Moreover, even though the rigid and ridiculous laws of our dramatic preceptist may not allow a writer this freedom, the condition of our theaters would force him to take it.

His next statement is entirely in Lope's vein, and like the latter's *New Art of Writing Comedies,* is a plea of confession and avoidance:

... So it is that the author sees himself forced to repudiate a fine and regular drama that he has conceived, because he knows how little such plays are adapted to public taste, upon which he must depend. Hence the poet who writes more to conform to the general idea than to a particular historical background, more to enrich himself and the actors than to win praise from intelligent people, is forced to commit these errors with complete knowledge of what he is doing. The spectator who stops to consider these points is willing to excuse the monstrosities of all kinds which he observes in many compositions; but one who is deprived of this ability slashes and cleaves to his heart's content, making the wretched author the target for his criticism; but if he wishes to see a dramatist, who has been writing in accordance with the taste of the people, adjust himself more easily to the observance of art, let him correct first the evil habits of the public, and let him then offer a proper reward for a correct drama, for I know that authors will not be lacking to fill the void. I do not say that those errors which some writers commit because of lack of knowledge of geography and chronology deserve indulgence, but I do say that critics should look with less impatience upon the sacrifice of perfection to custom. If my critics should do this, they would save their breath; they would be my friends; but if not, I declare war upon their bad comedies and worse *sainetes*...[59]

Zavala y Zamora ends his foreword with this defiant note. Moratín was not long in picking up the gauntlet, and his clever satire in *The New Comedy* delighted the partisans of neo-classicism but, as we shall see, had little effect upon public taste and did not drive his adversaries from the field.

1. Sempere y Guarinos, *Reflexiones sobre el buen gusto en las ciencias y en las artes,* traducción libre de las que escribió en italiano Luis Antonio Muratori, con un discurso sobre el gusto actual de los españoles en la literatura (Madrid, 1782).
2. Sempere y Guarinos, *op cit.,* p. 230.
3. *Ibid.*
4. *Ibid.,* p. 231.
5. Cotarelo y Mori, *Iriarte,* p. 97, Note.
6. Sempere y Guarinos, *op. cit.,* p. 235.
7. *Ibid.,* p. 237
8. Iriarte, "Los literatos en Cuaresma," *Obras de Iriarte,* VII, 28.
9. *El Memorial Literario,* January, 1784.
10. *Ibid.*
11. *Ibid.*
12. *Ibid.,* February, 1784.
13. *Ibid.,* April, 1784.
14. *Ibid.,* November, 1784.
15. *Ibid.,* December, 1784.
16. *Ibid.,* April, 1785.
17. *Ibid.,* November, 1784.
18. *Ibid.,* May, 1786.
19. *Ibid.,* May, 1785.
20. *Ibid.,* February, 1786.
21. *Ibid.*
22. *Ibid.,* September, 1785.
23. *Ibid.,* May, 1788.
24. *El Diario de Madrid,* December 31, 1788.
25. *Ibid.,* May 30, 1789.
26. *Ibid.*
27. *Ibid.,* June 9, 1789.
28. *Ibid.*
29. *Ibid.,* August 7, 1789.
30. *Ibid.,* August 24, 1789.
31. *Ibid.,* June 27, 1789.
32. *Ibid.,* July 7, 1789.
33. *Ibid.*
34. *El Correo de Madrid,* October 10, 1786.
35. *Ibid.,* October 17, 1786.
36. *Ibid.*
37. *Ibid.,* November 3, 1787.
38. *Ibid.,* January 9, 1788.
39. *Ibid.,* April 23, 1788.
40. *La Espigadera,* No. 1, 1790.
41. *Ibid.*
42. *Ibid.*
43. *Ibid.*
44. *Ibid.*
45. *Ibid.*
46. *Ibid.*
47. *Ibid.*
48. *Ibid.*
49. *El Memorial Literario,* August, 1784.
50. *Ibid.,* November, 1789.
51. *Ibid.,* October, 1790.
52. *La Espigadera,* No. 12, II, 1790.
53. *El Memorial Literario,* July, 1786.
54. *Ibid.,* June, 1787.
55. *El Correo de Madrid,* December, 1786, p. 96.
56. *Ibid.,* January 20, 1787.
57. *Ibid.,* April 18, 1787.
58. Gaspar Zavala y Zamora, *Triunfos de Valor y Ardid, Carlos Doce, Rey de Suecia* (Madrid, 1787).
59. *Ibid.*

XI

Moratín

FIFTY YEARS of constant effort on the part of the neo-classicists to reform the theater in Spain had been so unproductive of positive results that the movement seemed destined to remain almost entirely in the realm of polemical discussion. No leader had appeared with sufficient ability to put the precepts into practice in a manner that would be acceptable on the stage. With *The Pampered Youth* Iriarte had produced the first neo-classic comedy which lasted beyond its initial performance. His second play, *The Ill-bred Miss*, met with less favor, and his last comedy, *Winning Ways*, never reached the public stage. Javier de Burgos sums up the accomplishments of the neo-classic movement both in tragedy and in comedy during the reign of Carlos III, which lasted from 1759 to 1788:

... The men who worked to replace our theatrical practices with the doctrines proclaimed in Greece in ancient times and adopted in France in modern times recognized that, in order to spread these doctrines and make them take root in our soil, they had to support precept with example; and after Montiano's original tragedies, *Virginia* and *Athaulpo*, Moratín the father published a tragedy entitled *Hormesinda*, which seemed more tolerable than the former works only because its subject was national. *The Fashionable Lady*, a comedy by the same author, was coldly received on the stage; and almost the same fate befell *The Pampered Youth* and *The Ill-bred Miss* by Don Tomás de Iriarte a short time later. Don Vicente García de la Huerta produced *Raquel*, an adaptation of a theme already treated in the old theater with the title *The Jewess of Toledo*. Don Ignacio López de Ayala in *Numancia* brought out again a subject treated in a play of the same name by Cervantes; and Don Gaspar Melchor de Jovellanos based his *Munuza* on the same theme as Moratín's *Hormesinda*. All the efforts of the champions of the new theater were limited during the reign of the third son of the founder of the new dynasty to the above plays; to *The Honorable Culprit* by Jovellanos; to the translations, *The Married Philosopher*, *The Chinese Orphan*, *Agamemnon*, *Zaïre*, *Hypermenestra*, and *Athalie*, made by Iriarte, Huerta, Don Pablo Olavide, and

Don Eugenio Llaguno; to two or three anonymous productions by obscure authors; and to the recasts of *Progne and Filomena* by Rojas and *The Resemblance* by Moreto, which Don Thomás de Sebastian y Latre tried to accommodate to the new theater...[1]

Javier de Burgos concludes that with sixteen to twenty plays "produced with great effort in twice as many years" it was obviously impossible to establish a theater. Although this statement was made after criticism of the author's own plays had made him an opponent of neo-classicism, it is substantially correct.

Leandro Fernández de Moratín saved the neo-classic movement from an inglorious death. Although today critics are disposed to deny him creative genius or comic force, for more than fifty years he was a dominating figure in the Spanish theater. Before the performance of Iriarte's *The Pampered Youth*, he had already composed his first comedy, *The Old Man and the Young Girl*, a three-act play in verse. In 1786 he read this play to the company of Manuel Martínez, whose members doubted that it would be successful on the stage because of its simple plot, but agreed to accept it. In the "Foreword" to the 1825 edition of this comedy, Moratín gives an account of the obstacles he encountered before the play was finally performed. He experienced no little difficulty, he says, in obtaining a license for its performance, and was able to do so only by making so many suppressions that the scenes were left truncated, the dialogue was made inconsistent, and the entire work was almost ruined. An insurmountable obstacle to the performance of the play then presented itself, for "the second lady of the company (who was bordering on forty years of age) refused to play the role of Doña Beatriz, in order to preserve, at least in the theater, her unalterable youth." The play was returned to its author, who abandoned for the time being his attempts to have it presented. Two years later, believing that conditions were more favorable, Moratín offered his play to the company of Eusebio Ribera, but here he encountered another unforeseen obstacle:

...An actress, who for a period of thirty years had performed with applause in various cities of Andalucía and in the Royal Residences, a woman of great talent, sensibility, and understanding of the delicacies of art, and who was at that time employed as an understudy in the company, read the comedy, applauded it, and determined to play the role of Doña Isabel. That estimable actress was still able to play the roles of Semiramis, Athalia, Clitemnestra, and Hecuba; but it was impossible for her to play that of a nineteen-year-old girl without subjecting herself to the derision of the audience. The conflict in which the author saw himself was very great, for it was obvious that he would either have to sacrifice his work through timidity or take upon himself the unpleasant task of disillusioning a lady, whom neither her birth certificate nor her mirror had been able to convince that she was no longer young.[2]

It was necessary to resubmit the comedy to the censors for approval, and Moratín was very much pleased when the ecclesiastical judge refused to give his permission for its performance. Two years later, in 1790, through the influence of the prime minister, Godoy, the comedy was finally presented at the Príncipe by the company of Ribera. Moratín was allowed to direct the rehearsals himself and the success of the play was due in large measure to the natural manner in which the actors performed their roles.

In *The Old Man and the Young Girl* Moratín attacks the custom of arranging marriages without consideration for the desires of the contracting parties, a theme which is to recur in *The Baron* and is to find its most successful treatment in *The Consent of Young Maidens*. In *The Old Man and the Young Girl* Don Juan and Doña Isabel have been in love since childhood. The guardian of the girl, however, is a heartless miser, who prefers that she marry Don Roque de Urrutia, a ridiculous old man, since the latter has agreed not to demand an account of his administration of her affairs. Not being able to overcome Isabel's resistance with entreaties or threats, the guardian, by false testimony, convinces her that Don Juan has already married in Madrid, where he is living with his uncle. Overcome with jealousy and motivated by spite, Isabel marries Don Roque. Upon the death of his uncle, the youth returns to Cádiz to arrange certain details pertaining to the estate. Ignorant of the relations which have existed between his wife and Don Juan, the old man offers him his hospitality. The youth, who has received no notice of Isabel's marriage, gladly accepts the offer. When the lovers meet there are mutual recriminations until each is convinced of the constancy of the other. Don Roque discovers the situation and by threats forces his wife to receive her lover and to dismiss him with the declaration that she no longer loves him. During this scene the old man is hidden in an adjoining room. No happy solution is possible with such a plot. Don Juan leaves for the Indies convinced of Isabel's unfaithfulness, and the girl announces her determination to leave her husband and enter a convent. This comedy marks a radical departure from the love theme which had been prevalent in the *comedia* in that it starts rather than ends with a marriage.

The Old Man and the Young Girl was received enthusiastically by the neo-classicists. The *Memorial Literario*, while recognizing certain defects in the work, saw in its author a fit disciple of the school of Terence and Molière.

... This comedy is rightly considered to be well written and well executed. The author, by making some characters sentimental and others ridiculous, has been able to mix pathetic and comic scenes in such a manner as to keep the spectators interested and amused from the beginning to the end. He shows that he has caught the spirit of Terence and Molière and has been able to imitate them successfully.[3]

... Nevertheless, some have noticed that there are occasional repetitions and that Muñoz is at times more intelligent than he should be; that there are scenes too pathetic for a comedy; and that Isabel could not leave her husband to enter a convent against his will without the permission of the civil or ecclesiastical court, etc....[4]

In the *Diario de Madrid* for June 28, 1790, María Guerrero published a *letrilla* in defense of Moratín's play. Since this poem gives a rather complete summary of the faults neo-classicists found in the *comedia* and in the contemporary theater, as well as the qualities considered essential in a regular comedy, it will be given in full:

> Because it is a play,
> perfect and finished in form,
> a thousand things are said
> about *The Old Man and the Girl*.

> As this comedy
> has no appearances
> of proud Kings
> or lascivious Queens,
> on familiar terms
> with their lackeys,
> a thousand things, etc.

> As the reader finds
> the three unities
> prescribed by art
> carefully observed
> and does not see Spain
> dance with the Indies,
> a thousand things, etc.

As it has no
Moors with buckles,
Persians with dress-coats,
Greeks with ruffled collars,
Ambassadors and other
things of like manner,
a thousand things, etc.

As there are no assaults
and no artillery,
councils of war,
horses on friezes,
music and cymbals,
or Swiss trumpets,
a thousand things, etc.

As there are no women
with swords at their side
who defend forts
better than Ruy Díaz,
and spend their lives
without sleep
and without food,
a thousand things, etc.

As there are no Leopolds,
crowns, or miters,
or men who die
of pure nobility
when the notion strikes
or the author wills,
a thousand things, etc.

As the machinists
are so idle and
do not conjure up
seas, caves, grottos, mountains,
lightning flashes, thunder,
rain, snow, and wind,
a thousand things, etc.

As Don Juan remains
quietly in Cádiz half a day
when he could easily
go to Lombardy
to eat and then
sup in Manila,
a thousand things, etc.

These and other things
are much in vogue
in all the dramas
played these days;
and as it lacks
all these jewels,
a thousand things are said
about *The Old Man and the Girl.*
— Guerrero[5]

Moratín takes pride in inserting in his "Notes" to *The Old Man and the Young Girl* this tribute to the play by his friend, the Italian critic Napoli-Signorelli, who was later to translate *The New Comedy* into Italian:

I have read the manuscript of *The Old Man and the Young Girl.* It seems to me an estimable work by a writer who is following the path of true taste. The moral lesson derived from a vivid representation of the unhappiness caused by the marriage of an old man with a young girl is worthy of the comic genre.[6]

Signorelli praises the simplicity of the plot, the skilful characterization, and the regularity of the entire play. He is particularly pleased with the manner in which Moratín has combined the best elements of the language and versification of Calderón and Lope without yielding to any of their extravagance; and he believes that "this comedy can form a glorious epoch in the Spanish theater, if it has imitators as it deserves to have."[7]

In the *Lessons on Rhetoric and Belles Lettres*, the translator Muñarriz (or his collaborators) analyzes this comedy in detail and dwells at length upon its defects, but concludes that "all the faults of *The Old Man and the Young Girl* are covered in part by the good versification, the rapidity of the dialogue, the truth and the freshness of the coloring, and the happy portrayal of the characters of Muñoz and Don Roque, who are always amusing, always comic."[8] Most of the defects which are noted in Muñarriz' criticism are fairly obvious. One is inclined to agree that the comedy is faulty in its plan because there is no particular problem to solve. From the moment Don Roque learns of the former love affair between his wife and Don Juan he is obliged to insist that his guest leave, and from the moment Isabel learns that she has been tricked into marriage with Don Roque, she is forced to regard him as an enemy. The element of ridicule in the comedy yields almost completely to sentiment. The end is melancholy, for all the suffering is borne by the young lovers. The final statement of Don Roque to the servant, Muñoz, carries no conviction:

> Be silent, for in all you tell me
> You are probably right;
> But allow me to curse myself;
> For I, through my folly,
> Have been to blame for everything.
> I am paying for it now, and though
> It be late, I realize now
> That at my age one should
> Not think of marriage.[9]

In 1822 Lista in *El Censor* is warm in his praise of the comedy. He considers it absurd to attempt to analyze a play that should be known by heart by all people of "taste and culture." He declares that the appearance of this play in the midst of the frightful corruption of the theater at the time "formed a new era in the annals of the Spanish theater and let Spain know that she had a Terence and gave her the hope of having a classic theater."[10] Lista also believes that this play contains more sentiment than Moratín's other comedies, since the spectator forgets the punishment of Don Roque and is left profoundly moved by the unhappy fate of Isabel. In the later plays of Moratín this critic notes more humor and less sentiment.[11]

The initial performance of *The Old Man and the Young Girl* ran from the 22nd to the 31st of May, 1790, at the Príncipe, with average receipts of 4,629 reals, which marked it as one of the most successful plays of the season. During the same year it was performed five more times at the Príncipe and seven times at the Cruz. The play remained in the repertoire of the theaters until 1814 and was performed frequently. From 1821 to 1832 it enjoyed a renewed popularity, being presented fifteen times at the Cruz, nine at the Príncipe.

Two years later Moratín produced his famous three-act prose play, *The New Comedy*, which elevated its author into the first rank of the advocates of regular comedy. The reviews of this play were most enthusiastic. The *Diario de Madrid* says of it:

... Everything in this comedy is estimable. The artifice is as true to life as the events are practical in substance; the moral purpose is excellent since it encourages the theater to be what it should be, that is, a school of good manners and the temple of good taste; the situations are most natural; the episodes are as opportune as they are joined to the principal action; and the style is natural, familiar, and suited to the characters of each personage; in short, the three unities and the other precepts are observed without, for that reason, detracting from the cleverness and other delicate beauties that are found scattered throughout the play . . .[12]

The problem to be solved in *The New Comedy* is very simple. Everything depends upon the success of the play Don Eleuterio has composed, which is to be performed that day for the first time: the marriage of his daughter to the pedant Don Hermógenes and the remedy for the financial distress of the family. This, however, is simply a framework for a scathing attack upon the monstrosities which have taken possession of the Spanish stage.

In a letter to Juan Pablo Forner, later published in the *Semanario Pintoresco Español*, 1844, the author gives an account of the cabal formed against the comedy by Comella, Zavala y Zamora, and others who believed themselves attacked. In fact, the play was subjected to five *censuras* before it was finally admitted to the stage on February 7, 1792. In the "Foreword" which precedes the edition of Parma (1796), the author says that the actors studied their roles "with particular care." When the day of the performance arrived, "those who had said before that it was an insipid dialogue, fearing that it might not seem so bad to the public as it did to them, tried to band together in great number and put an end to it at its first performance."[13] In his letter to Forner, Moratín describes this first performance:

. . . The crowd of *chorizos*, pedants, street-corner critics, worthless authors and their partisans occupied a great part of the court and the ends of the galleries. Everything went well; the public lost none of the remarks and applauded at the proper places; but, when in the second act Don Serapio speaks of the peppers dipped in vinegar, such was the commotion on the part of the *chorizos* and the clamor they raised that I thought they would commit the comedy and its author to the infernal regions; but those who do not eat peppers made them hush, and so the performances came to an end with general applause, which sufficed to avenge me for the trials I had endured.[14]

So heated was the discussion the following day on all the street corners of Madrid and so violent were the epithets hurled at the play that its success remained in doubt until the second performance when, as Moratín writes: "The success on this day as well as on the seven that the play lasted was so complete that it exceeded all our expectations and surpassed that of Don Roque *(The Old Man and the Young Girl)*."[15] The acting, Moratín says, was very good, and

even Juana, "the frigid and stiff Juana, performed miracles, astonishing all who heard her." In spite of the public's favorable reception of
The New Comedy, Moratín questioned the ultimate success of its
attack upon the irregular comedy of Comella and his school: "Well-
meaning people think that a work like this should bring about the
reform of the theater; but I believe that it will continue in the same
state it has been in; and that Comella will enjoy his dramatic crown
in peace."[16]

That this misgiving was not unfounded is proved by the fact
that a large part of Zavala y Zamora's production and most of
Comella's is subsequent to 1792 and the very works which are so
strongly satirized in *The New Comedy* continued to hold the boards.
Although the critics, who had been excessively indulgent in the past
with these authors, became much more severe in their judgments
and rarely found anything to praise in their works, they did not
lose their popularity with the public. From January 1, 1795, to
July 13, 1796, fifteen plays by Comella and Zavala y Zamora produced 337,026 reals, which was more than four-fifths as much as all
the Golden Age comedies produced during that period and more
than three-fourths as much as all the comedies of magic; and as late
as 1800 we find six plays by these two authors earning a total of
236,656 reals in forty-nine performances, for an average of 4,830
reals, while Golden Age plays were averaging 2,862 reals. And it is
evident that as late as 1803 the exponents of the regular theater
did not consider that *The New Comedy* had had much effect on the
popularity of the monstrosities of Comella and his school. *El Regañón General* in that year testifies that

> ... the old delirium and extravagances are nothing compared to what
> we see in modern works that are applauded by the *vulgo.* We have a good
> example of this in the interminable caravan of long, tedious comedies of
> the eighteenth century like those in several parts that deal with Charles
> XII, Catharine, Frederick, and an infinite number of others that are
> entirely devoid of plan, intrigue, common sense, and even the Castilian
> language ... [17]

The *Regañón,* however, has nothing but praise for the attempt made
by Moratín: "Oh, admirable author of *The New Comedy!* Your pen
alone has been capable of painting the conduct and absurdities of
these wretched authors, and anyone who dares to write on this subject from now on will do no more than copy your expressions."[18]

Although Moratín insists in the "Foreword" to the edition of

Parma that "Don Eleuterio is, in fact, the compendium of all the bad dramatists who wrote in that epoch and the comedy he is supposed to have written is an imaginary monster, composed of all the extravagances that were being performed at the time in the theaters of Madrid,"[19] it is obvious that his attack is directed against Zavala y Zamora and Comella because of the popularity of these two writers. The drama, *Carlos XII*, in four parts, by the former had drawn the fire of the neo-classicists during the years 1786 and 1787. This play was a heroic comedy of the type ridiculed in *The New Comedy*. The *Correo de Madrid* was violent in its condemnation of the play:

... Have original comedies been performed? Yes, out of deference for the truth we must confess that there have been; but what original plays they are! ... These comedies have carried the new art to its perfection; from them our Spanish theater will form a new epoch—by making clowns out of kings; by putting a battle in each act, with all the stage effects of trenches and stockades, and with cannons and mortars that shatter the ear drums and delight the eyes with their fireworks . . .[20]

It would seem, however, from certain references within Moratín's play that he had in mind particularly Comella's *Frederick II*, the first part of which had a run of seventeen days in 1789. In 1790 Comella brought out a second part with the title, *Frederick II in the Field of Torgau*. This play was only slightly less successful than the first part, running for fourteen days and producing 86,147 reals. Up until this time only comedies of magic had produced as much on consecutive runs as these plays by Comella. In the same year Moratín's own comedy, *The Old Man and the Young Girl*, had produced only 46,560 reals in a run of ten days. *Frederick II* would certainly have a reason to occupy a prominent place among the new plays that were so unpopular with Moratín.

On July 31, 1789, the *Diario de Madrid* commented upon the popularity of Comella's play but maintained that this was no evidence of its merit. The critic says that the author has not succeeded in portraying the true greatness of Frederick and that the play as a whole lacks dignity and nobility because every character speaks as if he belonged to the lowest class. He objects strongly to the picture the author paints of the wretched condition of a poor family. "The horror of destitution," he says, "is not a thing that should be represented in the theater to such an extreme." Another scene he finds particularly objectionable is "that of the dagger." This suggests to us immediately statements made in *The New Comedy*, where a scene of "a dagger" is twice mentioned and where a pathetic scene of a hungry mother and child is made to figure prominently in *The Great Siege of Vienna*, the drama that Don Eleuterio has written.

Moratín does not mention *Frederick II* in the following list of plays which he gives in his "Notes" to *The New Comedy* as models for *The Great Siege of Vienna*. The omission may have been intentional.

... The conquest of a kingdom, a battle, the siege of a city, are not fit subjects for comedy.... Those dramas Don Eleuterio took as models for his comedy belong neither to the comic, the tragic, nor the epic genres. These were, for example: *The Conquest of Madrid; The Capture of Oczakow; The Defense of Barcelona by the Strongest Amazon; The Siege of Calahorra; Asturias and Leon and the Victories of Pelayo Gave Glory to Spain; To Use His Dagger Against His Own Blood Because of His Loyalty and Nobility and the Capture of Milán; The Restoration of Astorga; A Lone Woman Overcomes the Greatest Danger; The Castilian Champion and the Capture of Sepúlveda; Hernán Cortés in Tabasco; The Hero's Wife Exceeds Him in Heroism; Charles V Before Dura; The Restoration of Madrid; The Valor of the Murcians Against the African Crescent; The Siege and Capture of Breslau; The Most Heroic Spartan Lady; The Siege of Calés; Jerusalem Conquered; Triumphs of Valor and Cunning; The Destruction of Sagunto; The Capture of Stralsundo; The Siege of Toro; Aragon Restored by the Valor of Her Sons; The Conquest of San Félipe by Spanish Arms; The Siege of Pultova; The Burning of Troy.*

From this list, which represented actual plays and not products of Moratín's imagination, it may be readily seen that the type of drama written by Don Eleuterio was the rule rather than the exception on the Spanish stage at the time of the composition of *The New Comedy*. Zavala y Zamora enjoyed the questionable distinction of having eight of his plays in this list; Valladares had two, and Comella only one: *The Siege of Calés*.

Not only are the titles of the works of Comella, Zavala y Zamora, and their school extravagant, but the names of the characters are unpronounceable. Moratín says:

... They make the characters in their dramas Irishmen, Russians, Scandinavians, or Wallachians, and suppose the scene to be Schaffhausen, Hangeorgenstadt, Sichartskirchen, Plaffenhofen, or Schabenmunchen. Who can keep from laughing at these plays, that bristle with names so exotic and harsh that our language cannot admit them without violence; our tongue cannot pronounce them, nor our ears endure them ...[21]

Among the exotic names found in these plays by Moratín are:

... Drunch, Apragin, Grothau, Patcul, Morosow, Mencicoff, Mollen-
dorff, Meknoff, Ramanuff, Mirowitz, Kultenoff, Fiedfel, Dieforf, Eschel-
emburg, Kruger, Kulmen, Kenverhuller, Dening, Dumang, Neuperg, Ros-
ling, Reychel, Renchild, Stoffel, Torfen, Strambol, Strugaw, Stronow,
Vakerbat, Harcolth, Newmark, Zastrow, Brank, Goerts, Keit, Roht, Zrin.[22]

Moratín adds: "These were the interlocutors of the comedies Don
Eleuterio was imitating. Who will deny that Doña Mariquita was
more than justified in ridiculing the barbarous jargon that resulted
from such names?"[23] It is not surprising that Moratín should consider
the *comedia* preferable to such contemporary extravagances. He
adequately explains his reason for directing his attack against living writers rather than pointing out defects in the works of the
Calderonian decadents by saying that "if the errors of Cañizares,
Añorbe, or Zamora had been ridiculed it would have been a useless
task to censure those who could no longer reform or defend
themselves."[24] Quite naturally Moratín makes no attack in *The New
Comedy* against the *comedia*. Indeed, he says through his mouthpiece, Don Pedro:

... No Sir, any of our old comedies vex me less, no matter how bad they
may be. They are irregular; they contain nonsense; but that nonsense
and that irregularity are the products of genius and not of stupidity. They
have enormous defects, it is true; but among these defects there are
things that, upon my life, hold in suspense and move the spectator so
much that they make him forget or excuse all the mistakes that have
gone before. Now compare our sorry authors today with the old ones;
and tell me whether Calderón, Solís, Rojas, and Moreto are not worth
more when they rave than the others when they try to speak sensibly.[25]

It should be noted that whenever Moratín praises the *comedia*, it is
against the background of the pernicious and extravagant contemporary theater. When he wrote *The New Comedy* an attack against
the writers of the Golden Age did not enter into his purpose. It was
even to his interest to propitiate the *vulgo* by admitting that their
"irregularity" was the product "of genius, and not of stupidity."
  The New Comedy contains, in addition to its satire against
Comella and his school, a condemnation of the pedantry that made
a fetish of the dramatic terms borrowed from Aristotle. In this section Moratín was only following Molière's lead in his *Critique de
l'Ecole des femmes.*[26] The stock language of dramatic criticism had

found its way into Luzán's *Poetics* and had been repeated by subsequent critics. Instead of speaking of tragedy and comedy, it was much more fashionable to speak of Melpómene and Thalia and of the buskin and the sabot. Moratín has the pedant Don Hermógenes give the rule in regard to the two kinds of plots, the *simple* and the *implexa*, first in Latin and then in Greek, "for greater clearness." The following statement by Don Hermógenes recalls the passage already cited from the *Critique de l'Ecole des femmes:*

> ...I understand now. Although, to make it clearer, it would be well to explain what the critics understand by *protasis, epítasis, catástasis, catástrofe, peripecia, agnición,* or *anagnorisis,* elements that are essential in every good comedy, and which, according to Scaliger, Vossio, Dacier, Marmontel, Castelvetro, and Daniel Heinsio... (Act I, Sc. IV)

Moratín's satire against this pedantry was a master stroke. In order to overcome the prejudice of the *vulgo* against regular comedy, it was necessary to strip it of its foreign clothing. The critical terms cited above had become symbols of the antinational drama. Moratín himself generally shunned the use of these terms in his own discussion of the classic precepts.

Moratín's next comedy, *The Baron,* which was originally composed as a *zarzuela* in 1787, was intended only for private performance. For some reason, however, this did not take place, and the work circulated for some time in manuscript form.[27] During the absence of its author it was altered and performed without music several times in private homes, and in this form it reached the public stage in Cádiz. Upon his return, Moratín recognized the necessity of correcting the play.

> The genial indolence of the author could not stand this, nor could his self-love allow a composition everyone attributed to him to acquire every day new defects and to be publicized in like proportion. He examined it with particular care; ... he tried to improve it; he suppressed the music; he varied the intrigue to a considerable extent, giving it more movement and interest; he added force and expression to the characters; and stripping it of many faults of his own and of others, if he has not formed an excellent work, ... he thinks that, at least in the form in which it is published today, it will not displease those who know how difficult it is in such matters to approach that perfection so desired but never attained.[28]

Moratín delivered the corrected comedy to the actors at the Cruz. Resentful at the preference shown, the company of the Caños del

Peral took vengeance by having a recast in three acts made of the original *zarzuela*. This recast, which was given the title *The Proud Village Girl*,[29] was the work of a certain cavalry officer, Don Andrés de Mendoza, whose only claim to literary distinction seems to be this pirated play. Mendoza was not content with pilfering Moratín's play but followed the example set by Avellaneda in his continuation of Cervantes' *Don Quijote* and insulted the author of *The Baron* in the prologue to his comedy. Moratín says:

... Without ever having suspected it, he suddenly found himself a poet; he gave to his badly joined pieces the title *The Proud Village Girl;* he called it an original comedy; he insulted the author of *The Baron* in the introduction; and the counterfeit play was studied, printed, and performed at the theater of Los Caños before Moratín's play could be presented at the Cruz.[30]

When Moratín's comedy was performed on January 28, 1803, it was known beforehand that it would be hissed. At this initial performance the conspirators were unsuccessful until the final scene, when "voices, shouts, knocks, whistles, frightful uproar, everything was used, and those in the audience who had liked the comedy contributed with their applause to increase the din and confusion."[31] The following day, however, there was no noise except that of applause. The public avenged the former insults with its manifest approval and retained many passages in its memory as proverbial expressions, "and since then the spectators always listen with attention to this story, which is simple, true to life, comic, instructive, and in which the precepts of art and good taste are observed as they are in all the works of this author."[32]

Cotarelo y Mori declares that *The Proud Village Girl* is no worse than *The Baron* and believes that Moratín probably weakened his own work in order to make it as different as possible from that of Mendoza. The role of the *galán* has, according to this critic, more character in *The Proud Village Girl* than it seems to possess in *The Baron.*

The plagiarized version was played so often at the Caños, according to the *Regañón General*, that the public almost knew it by heart. This repetition, however,

... was caused not by any extraordinary applause the work received (although it is true that it did not displease), but by the fact that in this theater they continued the practice of the Italian opera companies of filling in an entire theatrical year with a couple of dozen productions by repeating them continually.[33]

Cotarelo y Mori concludes from his reading of the article in the *Regañón General* that this periodical recognizes "that the comedy of Mendoza is not bad."[34] This statement is misleading, however, since it does not accurately interpret the tone of the article, which is wholly condemnatory. The *Regañón* calls attention first to Mendoza's statement in the prologue to *The Proud Village Girl:*

... my first intention ... was to purge that despicable embryo of its many errors, in order to read it to a group of friends; but when I set to work, I realized that it was a very arduous task, and that it would be easier for me to write a play on the same subject, the object of which would be to satirize the actions of many parents who, because of a ridiculous vanity, sacrifice their children without consulting their wishes or their real interests.[35]

The *Regañón* objects strongly to the term *original,* which has been applied to Mendoza's work, and maintains that not only is the play admitted by the author himself to be plagiarized but also an examination of the two plays shows that "it is neither a translation nor an imitation, but a wretched and servile copy of the *zarzuela* which Mendoza criticized with such urbanity."[36] In proof of this assertion the *Regañón* cites the following facts:

... The characters of the principal personages have been taken entirely from it, although the names of some have been changed; more than three hundred verses are found in *The Proud Village Girl* that do not differ from those in *The Baron* even by so much as an accent mark; the plot is almost the same, the only difference being that some new characters have been introduced into the drama to aid in its solution.[37]

Whatever merit *The Proud Village Girl* has belongs, in the opinion of the *Regañón*, entirely to the *zarzuela*, because "all that the recaster has added and changed is untrue to life and not very well digested."[38]

As has been indicated, the theme in the two plays is the same. A mother, through vain ambition, seeks to marry her daughter to a supposed baron. At the close the baron is unmasked and forced to flee, leaving the girl free to marry the youth with whom she is in love. The mother, properly repentant, asks forgiveness.

The *Memorial Literario* praises Moratín's comedy and holds it up as a model for future dramatists:

... Combining true talent with a profound knowledge of art, he makes

Thalia speak in our language in an appropriate manner and presents true Spanish comedy to us for the first time. . . . He proved to the intelligent that if nature had endowed him with a talent for comedy, he had also known how to find the road followed by Terence and Molière.[39]

In 1822, after *The Baron* had been reintroduced into the repertoire of the theater, Lista published in *El Censor* a review in which he ranks this comedy below Moratín's other plays "in its plot and in its moral" but insists that it is not inferior in language and versification.[40] This judgment is sound, although the inferiority is not surprising when we take into consideration the history of the composition of the comedy.

The public, however, seemed unaware of this inferiority. Both *The Baron* and *The Proud Village Girl* held the boards almost without interruption until 1833. From 1820 to 1832 the advantage was with *The Baron*, which was performed twenty-one times against nine for *The Proud Village Girl*. The history of these two plays is unique in that a plagiarized play and its model remained in competition for thirty years.

In Moratín's play, as Lista points out, Leonardo resembles a *galán* of Calderón in his passionate love for Isabel. For this reason the versification in his speeches "is more animated and artful, and approaches more the manner of our old writers of comedies."[41]

The early history of Moratín's next comedy, *The Female Hypocrite*, is to a certain extent similar to that of *The Baron*. The comedy was composed by Moratín prior to 1791, and before it had been corrected to the satisfaction of the author, it was circulated in manuscript form. During Moratín's absence from Spain, it was produced several times in private performances in Madrid and was played frequently in the provinces. Upon his return, he corrected the play and presented it to actors at the Cruz, where it was performed on May 19, 1804, without opposition.

There were no factions, or vengeances, or conspiracy, or uproar, experience having shown the uselessness of these methods, and the name of the author now assured applause. The public received it with particular appreciation; but falsely devout people and the critics did not. The former abominated it with reason; the latter published delicate observations in which they manifested on one hand their laudable desire to see art attain perfection and on the other their own lack of ability to indicate the means of achieving this result.[42]

The length of its initial run testifies to the reception given the comedy. It lasted from the 19th to the 29th of May, 1804, and was repeated in August of the same year. In 1807 the comedy was brought out again and was performed frequently until 1815. From 1820 to 1823 it enjoyed another period of popularity. The success of the initial performance was due in no small measure to the quality of the acting. Cotarelo y Mori tells us that "it was very well performed because Don Leandro was tireless in training the actors, going to the house of Virg and Pinto, and to the theater, in order to get them to rehearse all the incidents of the play with minute exactitude."[43] Moratín himself says:

> Ponce performed to perfection the role of Don Claudio. Pinto showed his well-recognized ability in that of Don Luis, as did Francisco Vaca in that of Don Martín. Josefa Virg, an estimable actress, whose versatility has enabled her to represent the most difficult and varied characters, brought out skilfully the effrontery, the impatient desire for freedom, the astuteness, and the false devotion of Doña Clara. María García stood out in the character of Doña Inés. To indicate that the role of Perico deserved the approbation of the spectators it is sufficient to say that it was played by Querol. Francisco López caused the audience to regret that the role of messenger was not longer, because he represented excellently a little old man as pusillanimous, inept, timid, cold, silly, and feeble-minded as the author had conceived him.[44]

The Female Hypocrite aroused a storm of protest from those who believed they saw in it an attack against true piety. This reaction calls to mind the controversies which resulted in France from the composition of Molière's *Tartuffe,* from which the Spanish author drew his principal idea. Although we are told in the "Foreword" to *The Female Hypocrite* that both the attacks on this play and the eulogies of it were written "with urbanity and moderation,"[45] this does not seem to have been the case. José Yxart, in his edition of the *Selected Works* of Moratín, says: "The most violent polemics and incredible intrigues followed the performance of *The Female Hypocrite,* as always happens when hypocrisy, the most fragile and shy of all vices, is attacked."[46]

We have seen that a long review of the comedy by Quintana in the *Variedades de Ciencias y Artes* provoked an answer by an admirer of Moratín, which was believed by some to have been written by the author himself, and in which *The Female Hypocrite* was represented as a perfect comedy. A letter from Moratín to Quintana, which was also published in the *Variedades,* nipped this potential polemic in the bud.[47]

The general debt of Moratín's comedies to Molière and the particular debt of *The Female Hypocrite* to *Tartuffe* and *The School for Husbands* have been treated in detail by Vezinet.[48] This debt was never denied by Moratín and has been repeatedly emphasized by critics.

The comedy is directed against the hypocrisy of a young girl, who uses a pretended piety to cover her escapades. The characters of Don Luis and Don Martín are well drawn and are obviously based upon the brothers in Molière's *The School for Husbands,* which, in turn, derives from Terence's *Adelphi.* Against the character of the hypocrite, Doña Clara, we find the lovable and sincere Doña Inés. Unlike the hypocrisy of Tartuffe, which proceeds entirely from the malice of his character, the false piety of Doña Clara finds a measure of justification in the fact that her father wishes her to take the veil in order that he may profit from the inheritance he supposes will come to her from a relative. She pretends to have no interest in worldly things only in order, by deceiving him, to accomplish her ends. Don Luis accuses his brother of being responsible for the perversity of Doña Clara, a perversity which he blindly and stubbornly refuses to see.

> Pretended,
> And the cause is manifest.
> When she was a girl she showed
> Candor, and excellent qualities;
> But you, wishing to see
> Greater perfection in her,
> Harshly and inflexibly set out
> To correct her slightest faults;
> You shouted at her; she did
> Nothing that suited you.
> Your severity produced in her
> Only dissimulation, and cunning;
> Your oppression, a greater desire
> For freedom. The frequency
> Of punishment produced fear,
> And lacking true virtues,
> Virtues that you were unable
> To inspire in her, she
> Pretended to possess them.
> You made her hypocritical and false;
> And as soon as she acquired skill
> In deceiving her father,
> She deceived him so completely

That only when she had the most vices
Did he believe she was perfect.[49]

The methods Doña Clara uses are to be condemned, for she attempts to throw the blame for her misdeeds upon the innocent Inés. The character of the protagonist has been criticized for not always being "as astute and farsighted as a hypocrite should be."[50] It is true that at times she seems somewhat stupid. Although the plot of *The Female Hypocrite* is more involved than Moratín's earlier plays, it still suffers from excessive simplicity, and from lack of suspense and interest. The action is closely knit, however, and the treatment of the characters is, on the whole, admirable. The language is simple and appropriate and the facility of the verse contributes to the naturalness of the dialogue.

In 1810 the *Gaceta de Madrid*, in discussing *The Female Hypocrite*, laments that Moratín's plays are not seen more often on the stage, since they would prove profitable not only to the actors but also to the public:

... to the former because they would have a good attendance, and to the spectators because they would see original plays that can compete with the best of the theaters of our neighbors, the only ones among modern nations who with the most truth and justice can boast of having a theater that is complete, pure, and regular.[51]

The *Gaceta* praises the "sound and exquisite moral," which in this comedy is within the understanding of all classes, the vividness and naturalness with which manners are depicted, and the dialogue, which is consistently "natural, amusing, and pleasing."[52]

The *Censor* did not devote an article to *The Female Hypocrite*, but in its discussion of *The Consent of Young Maidens* pays its tribute to the earlier play. This article contains a good statement of Moratín's purpose:

In *The Female Hypocrite* he proposed to banish from society the language taught by hypocrisy and preserved by habit and stupidity. He proposed to make it clear that morality and especially Christian morality does not consist in vicious practices or in sterile phrases, but in the fulfilment of duties and the exercise of virtues. As a moralist he attacked a vice that, more than any other, was corrupting the Spanish people who, from the cradle, had been lulled by prudery.[53]

In 1834, after the censorship which had been imposed upon this comedy had been lifted, Larra says:

Upon seeing it performed again today, we do not know whether to praise the enlightened action of a government of restoration or to marvel at the gross ignorance which enveloped it for so many years in the ruin of a cause momentarily lost. So hypocritical is the party that has fanaticism as its emblem that it believed itself attacked in *The Female Hypocrite!*[54]

Larra thinks that since *The Female Hypocrite* was already known by heart by everyone, the importance attached at that time to the revival of the play was due to its long prohibition, especially since others of Moratín's comedies, which had escaped the ban of the censor, were poorly attended. The public, he says, applauded the play and in addition paid a very hearty tribute to "the memory of Moratín."[55]

In this comedy, as in *The Old Man and the Young Girl*, Moratín rejects the typical Golden Age solution. In 1821 the *Censor* published an article entitled "Reflections Upon Spanish Drama in the Sixteenth and Seventeenth Centuries," in which it called attention to the fact that the *comedia* never fails to end with the marriage of the ladies and the gallants, and added: "This nuptial fury has ceased now, and we have even seen in *The Female Hypocrite* that the hand of the prude is granted to Don Claudio for their mutual punishment, and that the virtuous Inés in reward for her virtues remains unmarried."[56]

Moratín's last original comedy, *The Consent of Young Maidens*, in three acts and in prose, marks the peak of his dramatic achievement. The initial performance of this play was one of the outstanding successes of the Spanish theater. Moratín gives this account of its reception:

The Consent of Young Maidens was performed at the theater of the Cruz on the twenty-fourth of January, 1806, and if there is any doubt as to which of the author's comedies is the best, there is certainly no doubt that this is the one that was received by the public with the greatest applause. The first performance lasted for twenty-five consecutive days until, with the arrival of Lent, the theaters were closed according to custom.[57]

The comedy was taken to the theaters of the provinces at the same time it was enjoying such acclaim in Madrid. Four editions of the play were made in that same year, "and all were necessary to satisfy the desire of the public to read it after they had seen the performances in the theater."[58]

According to Moratín, public approval restrained his opponents from publishing the multitude of articles which had been composed against the play. But this did not entirely deter these adversaries, for "many were the accusations made against the comedy before the tribunal of the Inquisition."[59] Don Christóbal Cladera (El Abate) was the most violent in his protest against the comedy. The author himself tells us that "a minister, whose principal obligation it was to favor good studies, spoke the language of the most ferocious fanatics and announced the ruin of the author of *The Consent of Young Maidens* as that of an offender who deserved a serious punishment."[60] But the tempest which threatened the comedy was dispelled by the presence of Godoy, the Prince of Peace, and Moratín's enemies were forced to defer their vengeance. The *Minerva o el Revisor General* reports that the comedy lasted twenty-five days and produced 194,672 reals.[61] In the *Memorial Literario* there appeared an extended review of the play signed J. M. de V., in which the attacks against the comedy are answered:

The slander of those who are envious of the exquisite merit of Inarco Celenio, or, in order that all may understand, of Don Leandro Fernández de Moratín, has reached such a point that they accuse him of plagiarism in his unusual comedy *The Consent of Young Maidens*. Some say that it is the work of his father; others that it is taken from a French play, *L'Oui des Couvents (The Consent of the Convents)*; others say that there are in it scenes copied almost literally from a comedy in one act, the *Contract Annulled*, by Marsollier.[62]

The reviewer asks the calumniators whether they have ever found in any ancient or modern comedy the peculiar style which characterizes all the dramatic works of the author of *The Consent of Young Maidens*, and the "delightful wit" which abounds in all of them. He contrasts the comedy of Moratín with the type of play so popular in Spain at the time: "*The Deaf Man at the Inn, The Bachelor and His Servant, Armida and Reynaldo,...The Wife with Two Husbands*, etc., and other farces of the type called "tearful" and ... the gallicized translations with which we have seen the Spanish theater inundated."[63] The reviewer is most enthusiastic in his enumeration of the excellencies of this comedy, which, he says, meets all the requirements of the neo-classic rules:

A plan well conceived and happily executed; the action prepared, conducted, and unraveled with complete naturalness and verisimilitude;

the propriety of characters well sustained through the entire drama; the interesting contrast between the emotions of Don Diego and Doña Francisca, which hold the attention of the spectators to the end of the play; the incomparably amusing and animated dialogue; the purity and beauty of the language; ... in short, the infinite beauties and wit that make up the *vis comica* of the ancients, scattered through the whole comedy and its excellent moral could not fail to please all those who retain the sensibility, wisdom, and the ready exercise of their faculties. ... The moral, yes, the moral, when has it been expressed with better chosen and more important maxims than in *The Consent of Young Maidens?*[64]

In 1820, following a performance of this comedy, the *Censor* gave a short review in which it says that *The Consent of Young Maidens,* without yielding to the author's other plays in language and characterization, exceeds all of them in the intrigue and interest of the plot. The reviewer, Lista, calls attention also to the catastrophe in Moratín's plays, which always presents "a picture of virtue and compassion" except in the case of *The Old Man and the Young Girl.* This similarity with the author of *Andriana,* together with the perfection and urbanity of language and the sententious gravity in which he rivals him, will make future generations honor Moratín with the title of "Spanish Terence." The Spanish author is superior, however, to Terence in *vis comica* and is a worthy rival of Molière and Moreto.[65]

Larra insists upon the sentimental element in *The Consent of Young Maidens* as well as in all of Moratín's comedies:

This is the time to make an essential observation. Moratín has been the first comic poet to give a lachrimose and sentimental character to a genre in which his predecessors had wished to present only the ridiculous. We do not know whether it was the effect of the epoch in which Moratín lived, in which sentiment was beginning to take possession of the theater, or whether it was the result of profound and wise meditations. This is the essential difference between him and Molière, who speaks always to the mind and convinces it by presenting the laughable side of things. Moratín introduces certain personages in order to feed the desire of the crowd for mirth, but he seems to be trying to appeal to more delicate spectators by the predicaments in which he places his heroes.[66]

It seems, indeed, that Moratín delights in placing his protagonists "on the brink of a precipice" as in *The Consent of Young Maidens* and *The Baron;* or in plunging them cruelly into an abyss as he does in *The Old Man and the Young Girl* and *The Café (The New Comedy).*[67] Larra considers this to be the peak of dramatic art, since

in actual life tears always accompany laughter. Larra's own sentimental nature made him appreciate particularly this element in
Moratín's plays. *"The Consent of Young Maidens,"* he says,

has been heard with applause, with indescribable applause, and not
only has the beautiful sex wept, as one periodical, which is ashamed to
show emotion, says; but we men have also wept and with our tears
have revived Moratín's laurels which ignorance and oppression had
tried to dry and wither.[68]

This critic also points out that, while the problem attacked in
the comedy has practically disappeared in his day, it was of major
importance at the time of the composition of Moratín's play.

Our grandparents, accustomed not to reason or feel for themselves,
did not allow their children to reason or feel. A scholastic education in
the universities was the only one that men received; and if a girl came
out of the convent at the age of twenty to give her hand to the one designated by parental interest, it was said that she was well reared . . .[69]

Moratín censures this custom and defends the right of young people
to choose their own mates. Although such a worthy theme was sufficient to inspire the author to write a great comedy, Larra does not
believe it will enjoy a lasting popularity like Molière's *The Miser*
and *The Hypocrite,* but that it is rather "a true comedy of the epoch;
in a word, a comedy of entirely local circumstances, destined to
serve as a historical document or as a literary model."[70] In spite of
this, however, it is, in his opinion, Moratín's masterpiece and his
greatest claim to immortality.

Larra's judgment has been borne out only in part by the subsequent history of this comedy. Through the remainder of the neo-
classic period it was the model of writers of comedies, who sought
to imitate its excellencies but despaired of surpassing or even of
equaling the master. Larra was mistaken, however, in assuming that
the comedy would not enjoy a lasting popularity. Parental control of
marriages was not to be so easily terminated in a country so deeply
rooted in its traditions, and *The Consent of Young Maidens* continued to have meaning for the spectators. This theme, as we shall
see, was used frequently by the imitators of Moratín.

Moratín's dramatic muse was almost sterile compared even with
that of his contemporaries. Five original comedies form an inadequate foundation upon which to build a theater. Moratín's biogra-

pher, Silvela, relates that on one occasion he jokingly called him lazy, comparing his meager production with that of Comella, Zavala, Moncín, and Valladares. Moratín answered: "The Spanish theater would have at least five or six more comedies of mine, if I had not been harassed so much."[71]

Even if Moratín had been entirely free to write, it is doubtful whether his production would have been much larger. In the "Notes" to *The New Comedy,* he condemns the fertility of Lope and Calderón and even finds that Goldoni has prostituted his talent in order to maintain his position as a purveyor of comedies. To Moratín, "to write much means to write badly."[72] He believes that a writer should write only under the urge of his muse and should turn a deaf ear to the demands of the public.

> Let an author never assume the task of supplying the theater with compositions. . . . Let him concern himself only with the study of nature and the precepts dictated by sane reason; let him write only during those few brief and happy moments when he is inspired; let him be the severest judge of his own works.[73]

Moratín's remaining neo-classic comedies are limited to two free translations from Molière. The first of these, *The School for Husbands,* was performed at the Príncipe on March 17, 1812, and met with applause. In the prologue to the first edition of this comedy, Moratín seeks to justify the liberties which he has taken with the original:

> He has translated Molière . . . with the liberty he considered proper in order to translate him accurately and not to spoil his true meaning; and he takes pleasure in advance in considering the surprise of the critics when they notice his lack of exactness in putting the original expressions into Spanish and when they find entire pages in which scarcely a word can be said to have been scrupulously translated.[74]

This same procedure is followed in his translation of Molière's *A Physician in Spite of Himself,* which met with an equally favorable reception. In this play, as in *The School for Husbands,* Moratín endeavors to make the action and manners conform to Spanish taste by suppressing, adding, and changing whenever he considers such alteration advisable. He proceeds with the complete confidence that "if Molière were living, he would make in this and other works of his the same corrections with more severity and greater skill."[75] So well did Moratín succeed in adapting these plays to Spanish man-

ners that hardly a trace of their origin is apparent. He was fond of
saying that comedy in Spain should wear a Spanish "skirt and man-
tilla" and he follows this precept closely in all his original comedies
and in his translations from the French, making Spanish everything
he draws from Molière.

Moratín's attitude toward the English theater forms a marked
contrast with his admiration for the French. During his residence
in England from September, 1792, to August, 1793, he had an opportunity to familiarize himself with the theater of that country, and
before his return to Spain in 1796 he had composed a translation of
Shakespeare's *Hamlet*. His introduction and notes to this translation,
published in 1798, indicate clearly that his primary motivation was
not admiration for the English work. His purpose, he declares, is "to
present to the Spanish people one of the best plays of the most
famous English writer of tragedies," inasmuch as they "do not have
the slightest idea of the dramatic performances of that nation or of
the merit of their authors."[76] The acquaintance of the Spanish public
with the tragedies of Shakespeare had been derived, as we have
seen, from translations of French neo-classic arrangements of these
plays. In his "Notes" Moratín methodically and thoroughly picks
Shakespeare's tragedy to pieces, calling attention to its anachronisms,
inconsistencies, bad taste, and numerous violations of classic precepts, pausing occasionally to pay a mild tribute to the genius of its
author, which he finds revealed in some particular scene. A passage
of evaluation taken from the "Foreword" will suffice to show how
barbarous and cruel the theater of Shakespeare appeared to the
leader of Spanish neo-classicism:

In this work there will be seen a great, interesting, and tragic action,
which, from the initial scenes, is announced and prepared by marvelous
means that are capable of firing the imagination and filling the heart
with excitement and terror. At times the plot moves at an animated and
rapid pace; at others it drags because of the inclusion of inopportune
events and poorly prepared and useless episodes unworthy to be mixed
with the great interests and emotions that are being presented. It rises
again and acquires all the agitation and tragic movement that befit it in
order to fall and change its character suddenly, causing those terrible
passions, worthy of the buskin of Sophocles, to cease and give place to
the coarsest dialogues, capable only of exciting the laughter of the *vulgo*.
The denouement comes and the author breaks rather than unties the
knots that have been unnecessarily formed by piling up improbable circumstances which destroy all of the illusion; the dagger of Melpomene
having been drawn, he bathes it in innocent as well as guilty blood; he

divides the interest and brings into question the existence of a just providence...[77]

Moratín insists that he has carefully refrained from following any existing translations and has endeavored to make his own as accurate as possible, "neither adding defects, nor trying to cover up those he found in the original." In order to facilitate comparison of his translation with the original, he publishes the two side by side. This play, of course, was never intended for performance on the Spanish stage.

Moratín's Dramatic Theory

Probably few authors have left behind them a more complete account of their literary activities and ideas than Moratín. His *Posthumous Works* in three large volumes, his *Origins of the Spanish Theater* with its "Historical Sketch of the Spanish Theater," *The New Comedy,* and the prefaces to his comedies afford ample material upon which to base a study of this phase of his work. In the *Posthumous Works* are included prologues to his comedies and extensive notes on *The Old Man and the Young Girl* and *The New Comedy.*

The formal expression of Moratín's dramatic creed is found in the "general prologue" to his comedies, which Menéndez y Pelayo calls "his literary testament."[78] According to this critic, the concept of comedy which Moratín held in 1825, even after Lessing and Schlegel, and when the romantic school was triumphing everywhere, "was the narrowest that can be imagined, much narrower than the formula Moratín himself had practiced."[79] Moratín's definition of comedy, in fact, does not differ materially from that of Luzán and is as rigid as that of any of the neo-classicists:

Imitation in dialogue (written in prose or verse) of an action that happens in one place and in a few hours between private individuals, by means of which and through the opportune expression of which emotions and characters, vices and errors that are common in society are ridiculed and truth and virtue are, as a natural consequence, recommended.[80]

Although Menéndez y Pelayo says that this concept is much narrower than the formula Moratín followed in his own works, there is no evidence to support such a claim. In all of his original comedies he followed the rules scrupulously. Ruiz Morcuende concludes that Moratín "was a dramatic genius, *in spite of the three unities.*"[81]

After giving his definition of comedy, Moratín discusses each element. Since comedy portrays men as they are, it imitates national and contemporary manners, common errors and vices, and incidents of domestic life. This conception of the approximation of comedy to everyday life had been held from the beginning by Spanish neo-classicists. In this respect neo-classic comedy may be considered as a forerunner and a preparation for the numerous essays on manners that found their most finished form in the articles of Mesonero Romanos and Larra which coincided with the brief vogue of romanticism in Spain. It is also likely that the impulse to compose realistic satires on contemporary faults and foibles found its outlet principally in this objective type of writing because the opposition on the part of the *vulgo* and nationalistic critics was still too strong to permit its full realization on the stage. Instead, then, of one character so charged with some ridiculous defect that he could carry the weight of a comedy, we find a multitude of minor defects realistically portrayed in these essays on manners. The school of Moratín, if it accomplished nothing else, prepared the way in Spain for a literature of the middle class.

Moratín reasons from the realistic nature of true comedy that the proper vehicle of expression is either prose or verse. In verse,

Neither *quintillas, décimas,* lyrical stanzas, sonnets, nor hendecasyllabic verses are admissible in comedy; only octosyllabic *romance* and *redondillas* approach the simplicity which should characterize it, the first doing so much better than the second.[82]

In discussing the unities of place and time, Moratín quotes Boileau: "Let a single action, in one place and one day, keep the theater full to the end."[83] He then summarizes his own conception of the unities: "If a theatrical composition is to be good it must have a single interest, a single action, a single plot, and a single solution. The unities of time and place should accompany the unity of action, which is indispensable.[84] It is useless, according to Moratín, to cite the example of great poets who did not observe the unities, since, if they had followed them, their success would have been greater.

The expression in his definition, "between private individuals," Moratín amplifies as follows: "A writer of comedies must avoid all the extremes of sublimity, of horror, of amazement, and of lowliness. Let him seek his arguments, personages, characters, passions, and the style in which they are to be expressed in the middle class of society.[85]

The defects which serve as a target in comedy should not be

physical, involuntary, and incapable of remedy. No physical defect
should be portrayed in the theater unless it is accompanied by some
moral defect. Comedy should limit itself to the presentation of those
frequent excesses

... which arise from the nature and particular inclination of men, from
absolute ignorance, from errors acquired through education or through
association; from a multitude of contradictory, ferocious, useless, or
absurd laws; from the abuse of domestic authority and the false rules
that direct it; from civil, religious, or political biases; from community,
class, or national spirit; from custom; from laziness; from example; from
personal interest; from a combination of circumstances; from emotions
and ideas that produce effectively vices and disorders capable of disturbing harmony, decency, and social pleasure and of affecting private and
public interests.[86]

It cannot be denied that Moratín's formula is exceedingly narrow
and would bar from the theater a great number of plots that have
met with notable success on the modern stage. It should be emphasized, however, that neo-classicism in Spain can be understood only
as a reaction against the lack of restraint which produced in the
Spanish Golden Age a mass of absurdities along with strokes of
genius. It should also be remembered that Moratín and his school
were not composing scholarly, historical criticisms of a dead
theater, but were attacking a living force. In spite of the fact that
the *comedia* no longer reflected Spanish customs, it tenaciously held
the boards and discouraged the composition of original plays. Most
of the dramas composed in Moratín's day were still patterned after
those of the Golden Age, unfortunately choosing to perpetuate this
theater in its worst aspects. Before any constructive work could be
done, it was necessary to dispel many false notions inherited from
the past. If one examines the criticisms of the *comedia* in almost
any contemporary history of Spanish literature, he will find an admission of the very faults the neo-classicists saw in it. Mérimée compares it with the Italian *commedia dell'arte* in its improvisation and
in the fixity of its characters:

These are the elements which the public never wearied of and never
ceased to demand: motion, quick succession of romantic events, surprises,
abrupt turns brought about by chance or caprice, not logic; repetition of
the same intrigues and the same characters, or better, of the same types
reproduced over and over. Psychology, truth, style, artistic composition,
deep emotion, delicate sentiments ... for these the public cared not a

whit. . . . That job required no genius, or even talent; a certain sleight
of hand answered the same purpose and produced the same results.
A hundred and fifty years later the public still applauded with equal
enthusiasm and *for the same reasons,* the plays of Comella.[87]

It is a mistake to think that romanticism revived the *comedia*
in Spain. It had never died and was, in fact, more active in the period
which immediately preceded romanticism than in that period itself.
As late as 1841 Javier de Burgos expresses his keen regret that, while
the plays of Shakespeare are still being presented in England and
those of Corneille, Racine, and Molière are frequently performed
in France, "only an occasional play by our most celebrated dramatists is seen in our theaters and hardly a single one by Calderón."[88]
Even those Golden Age plays which were performed in the romantic
period were for the greater part recasts, many of which were composed by such neo-classicists as Bretón de los Herreros, Gorostiza,
and Mesonero Romanos, who attempted at least to minimize their
irregularities.

Moratín was relentless in his attacks on the *comedia* because it
represented the antithesis of those principles which he considered
so essential to the establishment of regular comedy. Although his
work was destructive in part, he, more than any other dramatist of
his time, pointed the way to *high comedy,* and approached the modern comedy of manners with its middle-class background. Probably
no Spanish writer of modern times has been more enthusiastically
praised and more violently attacked than Moratín. To many of
his contemporaries he was a literary idol, and even today most critics
praise his comedies in the same breath with which they condemn
the narrowness of his literary creed. In 1821 his works were highly
commended by Lista in the *Censor.* In an article entitled "Announcements upon Theaters," the author declares that an impartial policy
will be followed in that periodical in its reviews of plays. He insists,
however, upon the moral purpose of drama and condemns the irregular theater. His summary of the condition of the Spanish stage in
1821 shows that little progress had been made in regularizing the
theater since Moratín's *New Comedy.* He considers, however, that
Moratín has definitely fixed the pattern for this genre.

The immortal author of *The Old Man and the Young Girl* and *The
Female Hypocrite* has fixed forever the character of true Spanish comedy,
combining Calderón's versification with Moreto's wit and Molière's profound morality. In him we possess the precious model for comedy; and

for that reason corruption of public taste in this genre at least is unpardonable, although in tragedy we still cannot compete with our neighbors of the French theater. Our theater will weep for a long time over the civil discord and the six years of despotism that deprived it of new compositions by the Spanish Terence.[89]

Although by no means so enthusiastic as Lista, Menéndez y Pelayo pays Moratín as high a tribute as his own intensely nationalistic nature will permit. He calls him "the most eminent of our comic poets in the classic style, and one of the most correct and most nearly perfect writers in our language or in any other."[90] He considers that Moratín was to a certain extent a martyr to the literary doctrine the chains of which he seemed to bear so easily. The first error of Moratín, in his opinion, was his obstinate imitation of Molière, with whose talent he had nothing in common. When Moratín is himself, he reveals unusual poetic gifts and is outstanding in two different genres: "literary criticism carried to the theater ... and a certain kind of urbane, sentimental, and serious comedy where comic elements are given secondary consideration."[91] Menéndez y Pelayo is unwilling to admit that this comedy bears any resemblance to the type which Diderot wished to implant in France. On the contrary, Moratín's muse avoids any strong expression of sentiment. He is rather of the school of Terence. "Both," Menéndez y Pelayo says, "lack comic force and originality, and both have as their characteristic note a gentle and benevolent sadness."[92]

1. Francisco Javier de Burgos, "Discurso sobre el teatro español," pronunciado en el Liceo de Granada, in El Panorama, Tercera Epoca, Vol. V, Núm. 121, pp. 170-71.

2. Moratín, Obras Póstumas, I, 60. The actress to whom Moratín is referring is obviously María Bermejo, who played the role of the mother so successfully in Iriarte's El señorito mimado.

3. El Memorial Literario, 1790, Vol. XX, Num. 111.

4. Ibid.

5. El Diario de Madrid, June 28, 1790.

6. Moratín, Obras Póstumas, I, 84-85.

7. Ibid.

8. José Luis Muñarriz, Lecciones sobre la retórica y las bellas letras, por Hugo Blair, translated from the English by D.

José Luis Muñarriz. 3rd ed., IV, 321-24.

9. Moratín, El viejo y la niña, Act III, Sc. 14.

10. El Censor, May 25, 1822, pp. 342-44.

11. Ibid.

12. El Diario de Madrid, February 21, 1782.

13. Moratín, Obras Póstumas, I, 90.

14. Antonio Cánovas del Castillo, Arte y Letras (Madrid, 1887), p. 277.

15. Ibid.

16. Ibid., pp. 277-78.

17. El Regañón General, June 18, 1803.

18. Ibid., June 22, 1803.

19. Moratín, op. cit., I, 93.

20. El Correo de Madrid, September, 1787, p. 446.

21. Obras Póstumas, I, 131.

22. Ibid., p. 132.

23. *Ibid.*
24. *Ibid.*, p. 93.
25. Moratín, *La Comedia Nueva*, Act II, Sc. 5.
26. *Ibid.*, Act II, Sc. 6.
27. Moratín, *Obras Póstumas*, III, 197.
28. *Ibid.*, p. 198.
29. Andrés de Mendoza, *La lugareña orgullosa*, comedia original en tres actos representada por primera vez en el coliseo de los Caños del Peral el día 8 de enero de 1803, en Madrid, en la imp. de Sancha.
30. Moratín, *Obras (B.A.E.*, II, 373).
31. *Ibid.*
32. *Ibid.*, p. 374.
33. *El Regañón General*, June 25, 1803.
34. Cotarelo y Mori, *Máiquez y el teatro de su tiempo*, p. 157.
35. *El Regañón General*, June 25, 1803.
36. *Ibid.*
37. *Ibid.*
38. *Ibid.*
39. *El Memorial Literario*, 1804, V, 198.
40. *El Censor*, June 1, 1822.
41. *Ibid.*
42. Moratín, "Advertencia," *La Mojigata* (*Obras de Moratín*, p. 392).
43. Cotarelo y Mori, *Máiquez*, p. 212.
44. Moratín, *Obras*, p. 392.
45. *Ibid.*
46. José Yxart, *Comedias escogidas de Moratín* (Barcelona, 1884), "Prólogo," p. 11.
47. See p. 307 above.
48. Vezinet, *Molière, Florian et la littérature espagnole* (Paris, 1909), pp. 11-178.
49. Moratín, *La mojigata*, Act I, Sc. 1.
50. Muñarriz, *op. cit.*, p. 328.
51. *Gaceta de Madrid*, February 9, 1810.
52. *Ibid.*
53. *El Censor*, October 27, 1821.
54. Mariano José de Larra, "Representación de la Mojigata," in *Revista Española*, February 2, 1834.

55. *Ibid.*
56. *El Censor*, April 21, 1821.
57. Moratín, "Advertencia," *El Sí de las Niñas* (*Obras de Moratín*, p. 418).
58. *Ibid.*
59. *Ibid.*
60. *Ibid.*
61. *Minerva o el Revisor General*, March 18, 1806.
62. *El Memorial Literario*, May 16, 1806.
63. *Ibid.*
64. *Ibid.*
65. *El Censor*, October 27, 1821.
66. Larra, *op. cit.*
67. *Ibid.*
68. *Ibid.*
69. *Ibid.*
70. *Ibid.*
71. Manuel Silvela, "Vida de Moratín," in *Obras Póstumas*, I, 36-37.
72. *Ibid.*, I, 98.
73. *Ibid.*, pp. 98-99.
74. Moratín, *La escuela de los maridos* (*Obras de Moratín, B.A.E.*, p. 442).
75. *Ibid.*, p. 460.
76. *Ibid.*, p. 474.
77. *Ibid.*, p. 473.
78. Menéndez y Pelayo, *op. cit.*, III, 421.
79. *Ibid.*, p. 422.
80. Moratín, *Obras*, p. 320.
81. Federico Ruiz Morcuende, "Prólogo" to *Moratín, Teatro (Clásicos Castellanos*, p. 51).
82. Moratín, *Obras*, p. 321.
83. *Ibid.*
84. *Ibid.*
85. *Ibid.*
86. *Ibid.*, p. 322.
87. Ernest Mérimée, *A History of Spanish Literature*, translated by S. Griswold Morley (New York, 1930), p. 346.
88. Javier de Burgos, *op. cit.*, p. 161.
89. *El Censor*, January 13, 1821.
90. Menéndez y Pelayo, *op. cit.*, III, 419.
91. *Ibid.*, p. 420.
92. *Ibid.*

XII

The Plan of Reform of 1799

MORATÍN'S participation in the neo-classic controversy dates from his *Satire Against the Vices Introduced in Castilian Poetry,* published in 1782. In this work, which he composed at the age of twenty-two, Moratín has already formulated the dramatic theories that are to be his guide through the remainder of his life. There is the same antagonism to the *comedia* which is to be so often reiterated in his later writings. The author's own analysis of this satire gives an adequate idea of his attitude:

The author accuses our old poets of having confused in drama the tragic and comic genres; of failing to observe the unities; of ignorance of uses and manners; of having applied epic arguments to the theater; of not having given a moral or didactic object to their plots, but of flattering the gross vices of the crowd or recommending those of another more elevated class as positively laudable actions. He does not overlook the impertinent buffoonery of those who are called *graciosos;* the affected language of the ladies and the gallants; the fatidical daggers; apparitions of specters; disorderly princesses; patrols; hiding places; swordplay; false concepts of honor; incidents (thousands of times repeated) of the ribbon, flower, and portrait that give rise to such euphuistic concepts; and the voluntary and trivial solution of those involved plots. The comedies of magic, of saints and devils, and those of mythological subjects (the ultimate extreme of error) are also disapproved by this writer.[1]

Yet Menéndez y Pelayo says that nothing is more false than to consider Moratín "an enemy of the old Spanish theater." He says that in the prologue to his comedies, written in Paris in 1825, and in all of his works Moratín "shows clearly that he felt for the colossi of our theater all the esteem compatible with his narrow theories and his own nature which was not at all inclined to admiration or to enthusiasm."[2] Those who would, through national pride, seek to make Moratín an admirer of the *comedia* are easily comforted when they balance the meager praise he occasionally accords Golden Age dramatists against the violent condemnation cited above and against this indictment of the pernicious moral content and the extravagance of their productions:

In the old comedies that are being performed it seems that our authors taxed their ingenuity in painting in the most flattering manner all the crimes imaginable, not only embellishing their deformity, but presenting them to the eyes of the public with the name and appearance of virtue.

Maidens admit their lovers to their houses, while their father, the brother, or cousins are asleep; they hide them in their own rooms; they leave their houses and go to look for them in order to accuse them of infidelity or to account for their own actions; they flee with them and abandon themselves to the most reprehensible aberrations of love as if they were the most profligate and dissolute women. Paternal authority is insulted, mocked, and ridiculed. Honor is based upon chivalrous and absurd notions which laws cannot suppress and extinguish as long as the theater gives them its sanction. One is not a gentleman who does not occupy himself in indecent love affairs, breaking down doors, climbing in windows, hiding in corners, bribing servants, profaning, in short, the most sacred honor and trampling upon those considerations which should restrain the most violent passions of every good man . . . in a word, all that which can inspire a relaxation of morals, false ideas of honor, quixotism, boldness, effrontery, disobedience to magistrates, scorn for law and supreme authority, is combined in such works. These plays are performed in the theaters of Madrid and the government tolerates them with indifference.[3]

Occasionally, it is true, when it serves his ends, Moratín praises such writers as Lope and Calderón for "their exquisite sensibility, their ardent imagination, their natural fluency," etc., but he never fails to condemn the products of these qualities. In 1827 he writes to Augusto Bobée:

I shall tell you also that in the number of comedies by Lope, Calderón, and their imitators, it is useless to look for anything perfect; for all those that can be chosen will be defective and all will have estimable qualities that recommend them in the midst of the disorder and carelessness with which they are written; but if you demand that I point out a good comedy of that period, I shall not be able to do so, because I know none.[4]

So strongly did Moratín feel the disgrace the irregular theater had brought upon Spain that he was one of the most active in seeking reform through governmental intervention. The ideas of Moratín, Jovellanos, and Urquijo are so similar in this regard that it is difficult to determine which of the three was primarily responsible for the direction this reform was to take. In 1790 Jovellanos, at the request of the Academy of History, composed a long report on the most popular forms of public spectacles and diversions in Spain. Inasmuch as the primary purpose of this report was to inform the Council of Castile of the condition of these matters throughout the kingdom, this report had a semiofficial character. Jovellanos is concerned almost entirely with the moral aspects of the problem and says very little about precepts. After condemning vigorously the immorality of the *comedia* and after paying the usual neo-classic tribute to the genius of Golden Age dramatists, he gives his solution for overcoming the dearth in the theater of plays that contain the desired qualities of morality and regularity and which are capable at the same time of interesting the spectators. This solution is to arrange contests in which authors would be encouraged to compete by offering two prizes annually of a hundred doubloons and gold medals for the best dramas presented. Nobody, he says, would be more competent to arrange the contests, examine the dramas offered in competition, and serve as judges, than the Royal Academy of Language. These contests would insure in a short time, he believes, a supply of good dramas. At the beginning, of course, it would be necessary to exercise indulgence because "the human spirit is progressive and the goal of perfection is so distant that it would be impossible to reach it in one flight."[5]

Even though an adequate supply of good dramas was provided, no reform in the theater could be effected, he says, without a drastic change in the performances themselves. In view of the carelessness with which actors are selected it is remarkable that they have any good qualities at all. The few of outstanding ability who appear from time to time owe their success to native talent alone, for they have had no instruction in the art of acting. Even the best of these, however, are only capable of playing the roles of low characters on the level of their own social position and never rise above mediocrity in the representation of persons of higher rank. Declamation, Jovellanos declares, "is an art and, like all imitative arts, has principles and rules derived from nature."[6] It would not, in his opinion, be "a task unworthy of the zeal and foresight of the government to seek foreign teachers or to send young men to travel and study outside of Spain and to establish later a practical school for the education of our actors."[7]

Any reform in the theater must also include a complete over-
hauling of the physical plant of the theaters and a modernization of
stage decorations and properties. If the condition of the arts in Spain
were to be judged by her theaters, it could be said with justice that
they were still in their primitive state:

Such are the lowly, narrow, and inconvenient structures of the coliseums; the barbarous and ridiculously extravagant architecture and perspective represented in their curtains and wings; the lack of propriety
and the poverty and slovenliness of the costumes; the sorry material, the
bad and niggardly appearance of the furniture and sets, and, in a word,
the indecency and wretchedness of the entire stage apparatus.[8]

Jovellanos realizes that such a radical and complete reform would
require a considerable expenditure of money, but he believes that
with proper management the theaters are capable of producing the
necessary revenue. He dares to suggest that they be taken completely
out of the hands of the so-called hospitals, or charitable institutions,
which, from the time of the initial construction of the theaters of
the Príncipe and the Cruz, have owned and leased them to the
theatrical companies, receiving as rent a certain percentage, not of
the net profit, but of the gross revenue of both theaters. If all of
the income could be devoted to maintaining and improving the
physical properties and to increasing the remuneration of the actors,
the situation could soon be remedied. "What is the reason," he asks,
"for the poverty of our best theaters?" The answer, he says, is
obvious:

Who can fail to see it? The reason consists in the fact that they have
been a means of levying contributions. What relation is there between
the hospitals of Madrid, the friars of San Juan de Dios, foundling children,
the municipal government, and the three coliseums? Nevertheless, they
are participants in a goodly portion of the revenue of the theaters. . . .
The consequence is that the actors are badly paid, the stage decorations
ridiculous and badly maintained, the dressing rooms improper and indecent, the lighting inadequate, the music wretched, and the dancing
abominable.[9]

Another result of this situation is that the authors, the artists, and
the composers who work for the theaters are so poorly paid that
only the dregs of genius are attracted. "What could be done," Jovellanos exclaims, "with the abundant revenue of the theaters if all
this income were distributed with judgment and good taste!"[10]

In 1791 Mariano Luis Urquijo, who was soon to be raised to the position of minister of state, expressed in the preface to his translation of Voltaire's *The Death of Caesar*[11] ideas quite similar to those of Jovellanos and Moratín, although he exceeds both in his admiration for the French theater and in the violence of his attack upon the actors who control the performances in the theaters in Spain. He calls French authors "sublime geniuses, zealous lovers of the public good, who dedicated themselves to dissipating" the dark shadows that had obscured the French theater and by constant work, meditation, and study have brought to it "the beautiful light of reason and good taste." He brands Spanish actors as "people without training or talent to discern the good from the bad," stupid and uneducated people from the lower classes, and blames them for rejecting good works when they are presented or performing them so badly that their authors prefer to withhold them from the theater. He is particularly concerned over the backwardness of his nation in the production of tragedies and believes that public acceptance of the original tragedies *Hormesinda, Raquel, The Destruction of Numancia,* and *Guzmán,* and the enthusiastic reception of translations of *Zaïre, Phèdre, Iphigénie, Electra,* and other tragedies by Racine and Voltaire have proved beyond all question that the taste of the public in general is changing and that it is time to abandon the *comedia.*[12]

Urquijo is more specific than Jovellanos in his suggestions for reforms in the theater and anticipates those made by Moratín the following year. He recommends recasts of Golden Age comedies, the complete elimination of the *sainetes,* the foundation of a school of dramatic art, and the establishment of a board of control for the theaters, the duties of which would be "to examine for itself all the old and modern dramas; to order corrected those that are susceptible of emendation; to prohibit the performance of those that are bad; and, by bestowing laurels, prizes, and honors upon good poets who distinguish themselves, to encourage the youth of the nation to study such an important science."[13] Like Luzán he deplores the Golden Age dramatists' misuse of their talents. If Lope, Calderón, and their followers "had disciplined their imagination as they should have, what perfect models we would have today to imitate! Their dramas would be fewer, but much more useful and in keeping with the moderation of a theater which should be a public teacher of manners."[14] If the reforms he proposes are adopted, he is certain that

...the theaters of the capital, which are the principal theaters in the
nation, would not be as abandoned as they are now. The *Federicos* and
the *Carlos XII's* would not be staged, but in their place good dramas
would appear, performed well and with proper decorum by the actors.
The actresses would not be seen in the wings during the performances, as
they are today; and when the play is over they would not be seen in
between the curtains, giving a bad example to the spectators with their
lascivious and indecent gestures and depriving the play of all its illusion.
Voices and shouts would not be heard, which at the present time keep
the people from hearing and the actors from performing. There would
be another culture in the theaters, which would no longer be illuminated
with tallow candles, or be left in darkness, as frequently happens when
the drama is long because the candles are consumed and others are
not lighted.[15]

Two years after Jovellanos presented his report to the Academy of
History and through that body to the Council of Castile, and the
year following the publication of Urquijo's discourse, Moratín wrote
a letter from London to the king in which he proposed the creation
of the office of "Director of the Theaters of Madrid," and offered
his own services in that capacity. This letter, together with another
which contained a long article on the condition of the theaters in
Madrid and terminated with a plan for their reform, was sent by
Moratín to the minister Godoy. Moratín's article follows the general
pattern of Jovellanos' report in condemning the immorality and
irregularity of the *comedia,* insisting upon the advisability of establishing a school of declamation, and characterizing the costumes as
"improper, ridiculous, and indecent," the stage scenery as "unworthy," and the decorations as "grotesque." He speaks also of the
clumsiness and bad taste of the stage sets and machinery, the general lack of comfort in the theaters, the lack of order observed by
the spectators, and a great number of other defects. The music in
the theaters, he says, is as poor in quality as the plays and the
performance of the actors.

To his condemnation of the *comedia* Moratín adds a severe indictment of the *sainetes:*

Since the theater has fallen into such disrepute that the *vulgo* makes
up the larger portion of the audience, the authors of *sainetes,* who lack the
ability to compose works worthy of the esteem of a decent and enlightened
public, have preferred to please the vile rabble and have succeeded. They
represent in the theater with admirable fidelity the life and customs
of the lowest class of the populace: tavern keepers, fishmongers, rag-
pickers, rogues, pickpockets, jailbirds, and in short, the filthy dregs of

the slums of Madrid. These are the characters of such plays. Gambling dens, daggers, drunkenness, dissipation, abandonment, all the vices that are characteristic of such people, are painted with deceptive coloring in order to expose them to the view of the ignorant *vulgo,* which applauds them because it sees itself portrayed in them.[16]

He will not pause to consider the comedies of magic, "nonsensical compositions that perpetuate the stupid ignorance of the *vulgo,*" or fill their minds with errors that are "no less opposed to sane reason than to the august truths of our most holy religion"; nor will he speak of modern comedies, "which are so insufferable because of their lack of invention, art, and decorum that they give foreigners a bad impression of our culture."[17]

Like Jovellanos, Moratín attributes the economic plight of the theaters to the fact that such a large part of the revenue must be paid to the hospitals:

It is a well-known fact that well-managed theaters produce an income very much in excess of their expenses . . . but because of a bad arrangement and a combination of circumstances . . . the theaters in Madrid can scarcely support themselves in spite of the wretchedness and indecency of their performances, which are unworthy of a capital like ours and completely out of harmony with the condition of the arts, literature, enlightenment, and national opulence. As long as considerable sums are withdrawn from the receipts of the theaters for purposes that have no connection whatsoever with them and which should be taken care of by other means, we see to our shame and discredit that there is no financial inducement to stimulate the wealth of competent writers that are to be found in the nation to compose works of a quality sufficient to drive from the theater the nonsensical plays that are being performed.[18]

Moratín's solution for the ills that beset the theaters is the appointment of a director of the theaters of Madrid, who would have all the authority necessary to direct them, who would be responsible to the government for the political and moral content of the plays, and without whose approval no play, old or modern, could be performed. In the case of the old plays that were susceptible of correction, the director could alter or suppress passages as he might choose, and only with these reformations could they be performed. The director would have "absolute authority in all that pertains to the reforms and perfection of the theater."[19] Moratín's objection to the existing plan for the control of the theater is based upon the contention that, while the magistrate of Madrid holds the position of judge protector of the theaters, the actual control is so divided as to be ineffectual. The plays to be presented, he says, are subject to the examination and approval of the magistrate, the vicar, a censor appointed by the vicar, a censor appointed by the magistrate, and a religious censor. In addition to these, the director of the theatrical companies, the *galán*, the *dama*, the *gracioso*, or any member of the troupe has the right to pass upon a play and accept or reject it at his whim. As a result of this method of selection, there is no work of merit that is not scorned, censured, altered, or disfigured with abridgments and corrections by people who have no ability whatsoever. Almost insurmountable obstacles are placed in the path of regular plays while, on the other hand, "there is no nonsensical, indecent, or absurd play that is not immediately approved and performed."[20]

Moratín's proposal was forwarded by Godoy to Don Juan de Morales Guzmán y Tovar, the magistrate of Madrid, for his examination and consideration, inasmuch as the latter, in his capacity of judge protector of the theaters, was primarily responsible for their conduct and management. The magistrate, in a dignified and reasonable answer, expressed his admiration for Moratín but insisted that the picture he had drawn of the condition of the theaters of Madrid was "exaggerated and unjust." He does not deny that some of the old plays are highly defective and detrimental to morals, but to say that such defects are peculiar to the Spanish theater, in his opinion, "is to do little justice to national and too much to foreign authors."[21] He freely confesses that the theater is in need of reform and that most of the plays that are being written are bad. Obviously referring to Luis Moncín and Fermín del Rey,* he says that the actors who assume the task of writing plays for the theater are, for the most part, "mercenaries who write a comedy to earn sixty or seventy pesos." The magistrate explains that, since his duties are so heavy and since his ability in such matters might be open to question, he has named two censors, one ecclesiastical and one lay, to pass upon plays that are offered for performance. The lay censor, he says, is Don Santos Díez González, a professor of poetics in the College of San Isidro,

---

*Luis Moncín was a *galán* and Fermín del Rey the prompter in the company of Manuel Martínez at the Príncipe. The former composed more than twenty-five plays, and the latter some ten, for the theater. Among the most popular of these was *A Mountaineer Knows Best Where the Shoe Pinches* by Moncín, which had a run of eleven days in 1795 and produced 48,794 reals; and *Hernán Cortés in Tabasco* by Fermín del Rey, which ran for eleven days in 1790 and produced 54,111 reals. Their works, in spite of the fact that they were usually well received by the *vulgo*, were entirely devoid of literary merit and deserved all the ridicule to which they were subjected by neo-classic critics.

who is considered eminently qualified in this field. Plays, therefore, are actually subjected to only one censorship, that of Santos Díez. "But if the censor is well qualified and has the power to reject bad plays, why are they permitted?" people may ask. The magistrate says that the anwer to this question is easy: *"Because there are no others."*

...The people of Madrid must have some decent diversion so that they will not go astray into things that may have unfortunate consequences. *The old comedies do not attract, but drive people from the theater.* For this reason it is a custom of long standing to perform new plays at certain times, and the censor is aware that those that are presented to him are not regular. He must, however, be contented so long as they contain nothing contrary to religion or detrimental to morals.[22]

One of the most illuminating sections of this report relates to the remuneration of actors:

Actors could get along all right today if they earned enough to pay for their food; but Sir, they are perishing with hunger. For the information of Your Excellency, I have before me the statement of the theatrical accountant, which gives the total amount of money received by each of the individuals in the theatrical companies during the season 1791-92, and it appears that the maximum pay was 18,654 reals and the minimum 6,113.

Well, Sir, if the leading lady of the theater, after working hard and running the risk of being insulted in public by some ruffian, earns 18,000 reals, an amount scarcely sufficient to pay for her shoes and headgear, and as a result can neither dress herself nor pay for her food unless she increases her income by some questionable means, what inducement is there for any woman to become an actress?[23]

Although all this activity produced no immediate results, the matter was not allowed to rest. In 1796 Jovellanos' report was read with applause before the Supreme Council of Castile, and the following year the magistrate of Madrid forwarded to Godoy a plan, formulated by Don Santos Díez, which was sent to Moratín for his examination and comments. Inasmuch as this plan was in line with the recommendations he had made to the minister, differing only in the fact that it did not specify the duties of the director, Moratín did not hesitate to give it his approval. Santos Díez' plan provided that the actors should not be permitted to intervene in the selection of plays and should be assigned fixed salaries. Moratín believes that the plan obviates the only difficulty or objection that might arise:

> The actors are interested in attracting large crowds in order to earn more money; they are afraid if they do not stalk around on the stage and howl and do not perform nonsensical comedies in an unbecoming manner, the public will not attend; ... this interest and this fear gives them a certain right to select the plays and to choose the worst ones. Let a fixed salary be assigned to the actors in proportion to their class and ability and all objections will be met.[24]

According to this plan, a certain per cent of the revenue derived from the production of a play would be paid to the author. Inasmuch as his profit would depend directly upon the popularity of his work, he would have the strongest possible incentive to write good plays. The plan also provided for the distribution of three annual prizes in the form of gold medals for the best plays presented. Moratín believes that these prizes, "added to the percentage of the receipts and to the honor which would result to the winners from having their works chosen in a public contest, would be sufficient inducement to attract authors of genuine merit."[25] The management of the theaters would be in the hands of a board presided over by a judge, and composed of a director, a censor, and teachers of declamation and music. The absurd classifications of *gallant, lady, comedian, fool,* etc., which had resulted from the constitution of the plays of the old theater, would be abandoned, and the number of actors in each company would be reduced to nineteen, a number adequate, in Moratín's opinion, for the performance of any play. Moratín was thinking, of course, of plays that would conform to neo-classic precepts and not of the heroic comedies of Comella, Zavala y Zamora, and their school, or of the comedies of the Golden Age. This represents a rather drastic reduction in personnel, inasmuch as in 1797-98 the number of actors in the two companies was fifty and by the time the plan of reform actually went into effect in 1800-1801, the number had mounted to fifty-nine.

Urquijo became minister of state in 1799. Santos Díez' plan was approved by royal order on November 29 of that year, and a board of control was appointed to take over the management of the theaters the following April at the beginning of a new theatrical season. On this board General Gregorio de la Cuesta was to serve as president, Moratín as director, Santos Díez González as censor, and Francisco González Estéfani as secretary.

As it was finally approved, the plan provided for six first, second, and third prizes in the form of gold medals for the best original tragedies and comedies entered in public competition, and in addition gave to their authors the right to collect for a period of ten years 3 per cent of the receipts at the performances of these plays in all the theaters of the kingdom. From the plays that were awarded prizes, a collection would be formed and published with the title *New Spanish Theater of Prize-Winning Plays*. The same privilege without the medals would be given to all writers of original plays which were not entered in competition, or did not receive prizes, but which were accepted by the theaters of Madrid for performance. A separate collection of these plays would be made and published with the title *New Spanish Theater*. This collection would also include newly translated plays, and their authors would receive the same reward as the authors of original works until the number and merit of the latter should be sufficient to meet the needs of the theater.

When Moratín was informed that he had been appointed director, and before the formal approval of the plan, he wrote a letter to the minister, José Antonio Caballero, insisting upon his lack of qualifications for the position and requesting that he be allowed to decline the offer. Although Cánovas del Castillo doubts that Moratín gave in this letter his real reasons for renouncing a position which he had so eagerly solicited six years earlier,[26] these reasons seem entirely adequate in the light of the storm of opposition that had been aroused by his satire on the contemporary theater in *The New Comedy*. At the time he made his proposal, Moratín was in London, having left Madrid some three months after the performance of this play. When he returned to Spain the latter part of 1796 and to Madrid on February 5, 1797, he found that the theater had not changed during his absence, that the comedies of magic had lost none of their popularity, and that Comella was indeed still wearing "his dramatic crown." It would have taken a very brave and confident man to assume the virtual dictatorship of the theaters of Madrid under such circumstances. He insists in his letter that no one should accept such a position "who does not have the energy, fortitude, and constancy required to struggle with the passions of other men, to combat their cunning, and to correct deeply rooted abuses." He assures the minister that no one could be found less qualified than he in this regard. He continues:

My temperament, my inclinations, my health, which is beginning to fail, my love for study, and my complete lack of training in making myself respected and obeyed, are such powerful obstacles that I would be false to my conscience and to my honor if, in spite of them, I should accept an obligation I would certainly be unable to discharge.[27]

His reputation, he declares, such as it is, he owes to a few plays that have been received favorably by people of discernment; but there is no reason to infer from this that he would make a good director of the theaters. The scarcity of good plays alone has made his comedies stand out. If indeed they are the least defective that have been performed and he is the best qualified to write such works, it would be harmful to the theater for him to cease writing and to devote all his time to management. Nothing can be expected of him, he concludes, except that the few works he has contributed to the theater will be followed by others less imperfect; and "this can take place not amid the continuous anxiety of a direction so extensive and so difficult, which requires such vigilance and for which I recognize my lack of qualification, but in the tranquillity of a life entirely removed from cares and disturbances."[28] Moratín's renunciation was accepted on December 6, 1799, and Don Andrés Navarro, a professor of moral philosophy at the College of San Isidro, was appointed in his stead. Cotarelo y Mori says that the new director was "a man whose ignorance in theatrical matters was such that, according to a contemporary of his, he did not even know where the two theaters were located."[29] Moratín was induced to serve on the board in the capacity of "Corrector of Old Comedies," a position created expressly for him. His duties in this position were clearly defined:

The King has been pleased to appoint Don Leandro Fernández de Moratín to the position of Corrector of Old Plays in order that, after examining those that make up the present repertoire of both companies and others that belong to them, he may remove and send to the Royal Library those which, in his opinion, should be completely prohibited and select those suitable for performance. He shall correct the latter both with regard to rules of art and to moral, social, Christian, and political considerations.... He shall return the plays he has examined and corrected to the repertoire of the theatrical companies, and only in their corrected form shall they be performed in the capital or in any other part of the kingdom....

These will not be included in the collection of plays to be published every year, as provided by the plan of reform which will be in effect in the future, but will form a separate volume, entitled *Old Plays That Have Been Corrected*....

The task which His Majesty wishes Don Leandro Fernández de Moratín to assume is limited to that of correcting, arranging, and reducing to a better form the old compositions of the most famous Spanish dramatists, which, among a great number of beauties, contain defects of such a nature that they cannot be tolerated in a well-directed theater. In this way the theaters will have the abuandance of plays they require; the old plays will make up for the lack of new ones; and, stripped of the many defects that render them useless in their present form, they will retain most of their excellent qualities and will be worthy of performance until they are replaced by better plays.[30]

Although Moratín's duties included not only the selection of old plays that were to be prohibited, but also the correction of those that were judged to be worthy of preservation, Cotarelo y Mori assures us that he carefully abstained from committing such a profanation and gave his attention only to the first of these tasks.[31] This critic tells us that before his resignation from the Board on July 15, 1800, because of dissension between him and the president, General Cuesta, Moratín had formed a list of comedies that were to be banned, to the number of several hundred, and that 616 titles were included in the introductory pages of the six volumes of the *New Spanish Theater* before it ceased publication in 1801. He says that among the banned plays "were included *Life Is a Dream, A Woman's Prudence, The Jewess of Toledo, Loved and Hated, The Constant Prince, The Weaver of Segovia, The Marvelous Magician, The Catalan Cain*, and a hundred other excellent works." The impression is left that most of the plays banned belonged to the old theater.[32]

Cueto (the Marqués de Valmar) goes even farther in his condemnation of the prohibition of "hundreds of plays that were the recreation and delight of the public."[33] "It seems incredible," he says, "that among the works prohibited should be found many of the most precious and admirable jewels of our great dramatic literature."[34] He lists a total of forty-two Golden Age plays and adds:

This sample of the long catalogue of prohibited dramas more than suffices to show the insane spirit with which neo-classicism, which had won the support of the government, robbed the Spanish people of the legitimate pleasure of theatrical works that had sprung from their nature, from their hearts, and from their period of glory. The illustrious names of Calderón, Tirso, Moreto, Montalbán, Matos Fragoso, Vera Tassis, Alarcón, Lope, Diamante, Candamo, Cañizares, and other popular poets found no mercy before the tribunal of the preceptists. Calderón is treated, as can be inferred from the catalogue, with true anger, in spite of his being, among all the old poets, the greatest, the most Spanish, and the purest in sentiment and doctrine. To ban from the Spanish stage *Life Is a Dream* and *The Marvelous Magician* is to carry despotism to the point of insanity.[35]

Cueto clearly implies that the titles he lists were only a part of the Golden Age plays that were banned, when, as a matter of fact, he has omitted almost none of those that appeared in *The New Spanish Theater*. He says nothing of some six hundred others on the list, which any critic would be rash in defending, if for no other reason than that they are not available for examination, the majority of these plays never having been published. Only some fifteen of the Golden Age plays he mentions had been played during the preceding ten years, and these were among the least popular plays of the period. Not a single Golden Age comedy that could be called popular at the time was prohibited.

A vast majority of the plays that met with the disapproval of Moratín were works only the titles of which are known today. Included in his list, of course, were all the comedies of magic and a number of the works of Comella, Zavala y Zamora, Moncín, and Fermín del Rey. More than thirty Golden Age plays were actually performed during the year 1800-1801, when the theaters were under the complete control of the board.* To replace the Golden Age plays that were banned, Cotarelo y Mori declares, the two theaters began to perform "translations from the French like *Cecilia and Dorsán, The Abbé l'Epée, The Miser, Acelina,* and a few others, translations that needed translation themselves."[36] Two of these plays proved to be very popular on the Spanish stage for the next ten years. *The Abbé l'Epée* produced 84,503 reals in a run of sixteen days in 1800 and 61,074 reals in ten days in 1801. *Cecilia and Dorsán* produced 67,269 reals in fifteen days in 1800. If the board had been equally fortunate in selecting all of its plays that year, the theater would indeed have entered into a period of prosperity.

*Golden Age plays that were performed during this year included: *You Are Welcome but Unwelcome if You Come Alone, Ladies Also Have a Code of Honor, Enchantment Without Enchantment, Fortune and Misfortune of a Name, To Give Time to Time, Three Vengeances from One Punishment, The Hidden Man and the Veiled Lady,* all by Calderón; Moreto's *The Force of Nature, The Power of Apprehension, The Resemblance, Disdain Conquered by Disdain, A Woman Cannot Be Guarded, Pretty Don Diego, The Grandee of Alcalá,* and *The Aunt and the Niece;* Rojas' *Don Lucas del Cigarral* and *García del Castañar;* Lope's *The King the Best Alcalde;* Zamora's *Bewitched by Force;* Tirso's *To Love by Signs;* Montalbán's *The Persecuted Prince* and *The Most Constant Wife;* Matos Fragoso's *The Wise Man in His Retirement;* and Cañizares' *The Castilian Band, I Understand Myself and God Understands Me, King Henry the Infirm,* and *The Little Rogue in Spain.*
(Taken from the record of performances in the *Diario de Madrid* for this year.)

As soon as the municipal government was informed that it would no longer have control of the theaters, it presented a memorial to the king protesting the action, declaring that the theaters had been constructed by the city and therefore belonged to it, and predicting the failure of the new plan. The hospitals could, of course, foresee that in the not distant future their connection with the theaters would be terminated. With the reduction in the personnel of the companies, those actors who found themselves unemployed quite naturally added their voices and their influence with their former comrades to the mounting opposition to the plan. Those actors and actresses who were to remain in the two companies were encouraged by the municipal government to refuse to sign the new contracts presented to them by the board. According to the new plan, the actors would be required to perform roles as they were assigned to them without regard to the old classification of *gallant, lady, old man, fool,* etc., and, of course, would no longer be able to select the plays to be performed. It is quite understandable that they should have misgivings about the success of a new regime that would not permit the performance of comedies of magic, spectacular comedies based upon religious themes, or the heroic comedies of Comella, Zavala y Zamora, and their school.

Although the actors were forced to yield and finally signed their new contracts, there is no question but that they did everything in their power to hinder the success of the reform plan in order to bring about a speedy reinstatement of the old system. Cotarelo y Mori speaks of the many satirical articles that came out against the plan and of the sharp decline in attendance at the theaters. He asserts that at the end of the theatrical year of 1800-1801 the Board had incurred a debt of 234,959 reals and it was estimated that this debt would mount to 734,759 reals by October, 1801.[37] This critic is relentless in his criticism of the reform plan and notes with satisfaction that the receipts at the Príncipe on one day at the end of May, 1800, were 610 reals, that on June 9 they were 721 reals at the Príncipe and 848 reals at the Cruz, and that on June 19 the receipts at the Príncipe were only 410 reals. He exclaims: "The authors of the reform should have been satisfied!" What he does not tell us, however, is that the play that produced 610 reals was *To Love by Signs* by Tirso de Molina; that the play that produced 721 reals was *Don Lucas del Cigarral* by Rojas; and that the play that produced 848 reals was *Enchantment Without Enchantment*

by Calderón. Nor does he say that it was a translation by the
thoroughly incompetent actor-dramatist, Fermín del Rey, that produced 410 reals.* Almost without exception the plays that attracted
the fewest spectators during the year 1800-1801 were Golden Age
comedies. It is obvious, then, that the proposed curtailment of these
plays had nothing to do with the decline in attendance. The deficit
during the year in question was due to the determination of the
actors to sabotage the plan by the quality of their acting, and to the
elimination during this year of comedies of magic and heroic comedies. For a number of years the solvency or insolvency of the
theaters had depended to a large extent upon these two types. At all
events, a number of the plays which had been rejected by Moratín
and which were popular with the vulgo were returned to the theater
in August 1801 at the request of the censor, Don Santos Díez, who
affirmed that "although defective, they were innocent and popular."[38]

The organized resistance to the reforms instituted by the board
was so effective that the government was forced to return the
theaters to the control of the city of Madrid on January 24, 1802.
The efforts of the neo-classicists for the past fifty years had been
directed toward regularization of the theater through government
control. These efforts had culminated in the Plan of Reform, and its
failure left the neo-classicists so completely discouraged and disillusioned that advocacy of government intervention never again
formed a part of their platform.

*On May 20, 1800, Calderón's Ladies Also Have a Code of Honor produced 751 reals;
on June 30 Lope's The King the Best Alcalde produced 693 reals; and on July 12
Moreto's The Aunt and the Niece produced 763 reals.

1. Quoted from Hermosilla, Juicio crítico
de los principales poetas españoles de la
última era, obra póstuma (Paris, 1855),
p. 81.
2. Menéndez y Pelayo, op. cit., III, 424.
3. Moratín, "Carta al Excmo. Sr. Duque
de la Alcudia (Godoy)." See A. Cánovas
del Castillo, Arte y Letras (Madrid, 1887),
pp. 285-86.
4. Moratín, Obras Póstumas, III, 113.
5. Angel del Río, Jovellanos, Obras Escogidas (Clásicos Castellanos, II, 35).
6. Ibid., p. 36.
7. Ibid., p. 37.
8. Ibid., pp. 39-40.
9. Ibid., p. 46.

10. Ibid.
11. Mariano Luis de Urquijo, La muerte
de César: tragedia francesa de Mr. de
Voltaire, traducida en verso castellano, y
acompañada de un discurso del traductor,
sobre el estado actual de nuestros teatros,
y necesidad de su reforma (Madrid,
1791).
12. Ibid., "Discurso," pp. 55-57. See
Charles Blaise Qualia, "The Campaign
to Substitute French Neo-Classical Tragedy for the Comedia, 1737-1800," PMLA,
March, 1939, pp. 184-211.
13. Ibid., pp. 70-71.
14. Ibid., "Discurso," p. 18.
15. Ibid., p. 79.

16. Cánovas del Castillo, *Arte y Letras*, pp. 286-87.
17. *Ibid.*, p. 286.
18. *Ibid.*, p. 282.
19. *Ibid.*, p. 289.
20. *Ibid.*, p. 284.
21. *Ibid.*, p. 291.
22. *Ibid.*, p. 296. The italics are mine.
23. *Ibid.*, p. 298.
24. *Ibid.*, pp. 303-4.
25. *Ibid.*, p. 305.
26. *Ibid.*, pp. 316-20.
27. *Ibid.*, p. 318.
28. *Ibid.*, pp. 318-19.
29. Cotarelo y Mori, *Máiquez*, p. 78.

30. See C. E. Kany, "Plan de Reforma de los Teatros de Madrid aprobado en 1799," *Revista de la Biblioteca, Archivo y Museo*, Año VI, Julio 1929, Numero 23.
31. Cotarelo y Mori, *op. cit.*, p. 79.
32. *Ibid.*, p. 85.
33. Marqués de Valmar (Cueto), "Don Antonio Gil y Zárate," *Autores Dramáticos Contemporáneos* (Madrid, 1881), II, 229.
34. *Ibid.*
35. *Ibid.*
36. Cotarelo y Mori, *op. cit.*, p. 85.
37. *Ibid.*, p. 120.
38. *Ibid.*, pp. 88-89.

XIII

Moratín's Contemporaries

Juan Pablo Forner

ONE OF the most popular comedies written in conformity with the classic precepts was Forner's *The School of Friendship, or the Philosopher in Love* (1795),[1] in three acts and in verse. Menéndez y Pelayo calls this comedy cold, a judgment which has been followed by those critics who have deigned to mention the play. Cotarelo y Mori gives an account of the reception accorded the comedy upon its initial performance and attributes the poor quality of the acting in the principal roles to the aversion which Rita Luna and García Parra felt for the "gallo-classic theater." The success of the play, he tells us, was only moderate.[2] The basis of this assertion appears to be a statement made by Pedro Estala to Forner:

> The three or four who have followed my directions, that is, Querol, La Polonia (Rochel), La Porta (Gabriela), and Cubas (Felix de) have played their roles perfectly; but the main characters, García (Parra), and Rita, who would have nothing to do with the rehearsals, have performed very coldly. You should thank Querol because he has done his best.[3]

The play, however, ran for eleven days with average receipts of 4,806 reals, and was frequently performed from 1795 to 1830. The continued popularity of the work belies to a certain extent the judgment of the critics. The author was confident that he had produced an outstanding comedy, and with his characteristic lack of modesty wrote, in answer to an attack upon it in the *Diario de Madrid*, March 28, 1796: "With the exception of the comedies of Moratín the younger, *The Philosopher in Love*, alone and by itself, contains more beauties than all those the Spanish theater has engendered for the last hundred years."[4] In the same article he boasts that he had spent no more than two weeks in conceiving and writing it.

The comedy itself is not without merit, and possesses certain qualities which conformed rather well to Spanish taste, without being guilty of the irregularity so often found in the *comedia*. The unities are observed, although the scene shifts from the home of Don Silvestre to that of Don Felipe. The verse form is the octo-syllabic *romance*, with the assonance varying with each act. The language, however, is strongly reminiscent of the *comedia*. Speeches are frequently long and are packed with the type of gallant language and noble sentiments which were so dear to the Spanish public. The action is unified but sufficiently involved to keep the play from dragging.

Don Silvestre, who thinks only of money, wishes to marry his sister, Inés, to the Marqués de la Espina because the latter is rich and will not insist upon a large dowry. Inés is in love with Fernando and with the aid of the servant, Benita, and her cousin, Luisa, seeks to thwart her brother's plan. At the suggestion of Benita, Fernando persuades his friend, Felipe, to pretend affection for Inés and to ask Don Silvestre for her hand. Felipe is a rich philosopher and a misanthrope, past fifty years of age, who lives in retirement. The humor of the play lies in the change which takes place in his attitude toward women from his first meeting with Inés. What starts as pretense becomes truth, for he falls in love with her. There is then a conflict between his own love and the loyalty he owes to his friend. The plan agreed upon is that Felipe will remain Inés' suitor only long enough to cause Don Silvestre to send the Marqués away. The latter is a dissolute egoist who boasts constantly of his numerous conquests. There is never any chance that Inés will accept him, for she repeatedly affirms that she will take the veil first. Felipe meets with such favor in the eyes of the avaricious Don Silvestre that the Marqués has recourse to a despicable trick to rid himself of his rival. He accuses Felipe of having challenged him to a duel. The judge, however, is reluctant to believe that Felipe is guilty and sets a trap for the Marqués. In the end the philosopher is exonerated and the real guilt is shown to lie with the Marqués. With a magnanimous gesture, Fernando offers to yield Inés to Felipe. The girl herself, through gratitude for the kindness of the philosopher, is willing to marry him. Felipe, however, is equally generous and insists that Don Silvestre give his sister's hand to Fernando.

The moral lesson of the play is emphasized in the closing lines of Felipe:

Enjoy, enjoy the delights

of love in sweet calm
and in blessed innocence.
I am old now and
death will call me soon;
I shall, therefore, retire
into solitude and live
removed from the world
and detesting its ungrateful
tumult; my consolation
will be to know I have made
two hearts happy and that
they repay with their virtue
the wishes of a friend
who loves them; may
they always keep stamped
on their memory this lesson,
and may they come to be a glory
and an honor to their country.[5]

This play conforms to the idea of comedy which the author expresses in his *Exequies of the Castilian Language* and which had already been enunciated in *La Espigadera* in 1790.[6] Critics have all apparently overlooked this article in *La Espigadera* and have assumed that the mention made in the *Exequies* of a previous manuscript from which Cañizares is supposed to read is a literary fiction. The entire section in the *Exequies* relating to the drama is merely an extract from the long article that had appeared in *La Espigadera*. The ideas in this article conform so well to those expressed by Forner in works known to have been written by him that there appears to be no reason to question his authorship.

In his *Exequies* Forner repeats the statement made in *La Espigadera* in regard to the purpose of drama:

The purpose of theatrical representation has been, from its very origin, to correct and to teach. The vices of the people are corrected by making them appear ridiculous; those of persons in high positions by the atrocity of the punishments or by the important fatality of what is called fortune, the principal object of this art being to present examples that will make people flee from vice or place little confidence in grandeur. If these examples are not paintings or faithful portraits of life, they will be useless, vain, or vicious, because that which is either impossible or rare is not applicable to the possible and common. From this fundamental rule are derived naturally all the rules that make up the art of writing dramas. The latter are not, and should not, be anything but parables set to action, natural examples of human life, reproofs that improve society by painting with verisimilitude what actually happens in that society.[7]

In *The Philosopher in Love* we find a practical application of these principles. The viciousness of the Marqués is flagellated and the avarice of the brother is made the butt of ridicule. Virtue emerges triumphant. The struggle that takes place in Don Felipe between love and loyalty and the noble manner in which he solves this conflict afford enough sentiment to appeal to a public accustomed to the tearful comedy. The speeches on the whole are much too long and frequently serve only to enable the author to expound his ideas.

The principal theme of the comedy is expressed in this speech by Don Felipe:

> Philosophy! What a fatuous
> word for one who understands it well!
> Philosophy! ... A poor devil
> wears himself out filling
> his head (entirely bald
> from the effort of study)
> with exaggerated maxims
> that sound very solemn;
> somewhere in his mind he prints
> magnificent documents
> on virtue, decency, constancy,
> fidelity, heroism. And then
> what happens? Our wise man
> makes a visit and sees
> a girl, attractive, gay,
> alluring, with playful eyes,
> with light complexion
> and rosy cheeks, and then
> goodbye! all the poor scholar's
> wisdom disappears in the trap.[8]

The Madrid edition of this comedy is preceded by "A Defense of the Vulgo in Relation to Dramatic Poetry." Since critics have derived their conception of Forner's dramatic principles almost entirely from the *Exequies* and have contented themselves with a mere mention of this "Defense," it may be well to examine it in detail as the final expression of the author's creed.

In the opening paragraph Forner takes Lope de Vega to task for affirming in his *New Art of Writing Comedies* that in order to please the public it is necessary to strip comedy of all regularity and to entrust it entirely to caprice and unbridled imagination. It seems that Lope believed "that the *vulgo* has received rationality only in order to love absurdity and to admire extravagance."[9] Forner constitutes himself the defender of the *vulgo* and accuses would-be dramatic poets of seeking to cover up their own inability:

Poor *vulgo!* The mediocre writers of comedy load upon it the blame for their own lack of ability; and proud and triumphant with the happy outcome of their inanities and delirium, they become more secure in their unjust recrimination as they see that, in fact, the greatest absurdities are the most applauded.[10]

According to Forner, those erudites of the Golden Age who were capable of leading drama along the path of regularity disdained to cultivate the genre, and mercenary poets with no literary principles flooded the stage with plays entirely devoid of truth and decency. In this depravity of taste "the *vulgo* was never to blame for anything except for not having stoned the first writers who taught them to like nonsense."[11] Lope used the theater as a means of earning a living, and his earning capacity depended entirely upon the quantity of his production. "He also loved glory, and in order to retain his laurels he chose to attribute to the stupidity of the *vulgo* the delirious works which the needs of his stomach impelled him to write."[12]

Forner believes firmly that the purpose of the theater is "to instruct through entertainment by means of credible actions." The rules which govern artistic creation are "sure, certain, constant, and essential in order that the mind may discharge its functions in a manner that befits the purposes and goals of human rationality."[13] If human nature were not depraved and subject to error and extravagance, the rules would be unnecessary; but "the danger of depravity inspired the rules; and in them the intellect possesses a guide line that enables it to travel without becoming lost in the labyrinth of its own works."[14]

It is not enough that dramatic compositions be true to life; they must also be beautiful. Beauty derives in part from craftsmanship and in part from talent. Both verisimilitude and beauty should be adjusted to the purpose of each type of dramatic composition. In Forner's opinion, the end of tragedy "is to teach the powerful the inconstancy of human grandeur," and the purpose of comedy "is to correct the vices of the people by means of ridicule."[15] It is necessary, therefore, that in this last genre everything be popular, nothing lofty, nothing sublime, that nothing rise above the ordinary limits of civil life. Even the defects of the upper class, however, find their antidote in the picture or mirror of vicious manners. Forner hastens to add that he has no intention of reducing dramatic works to the two types of tragedy and derisive comedy:

I am very far from agreeing with the impertinent rigidity of certain crabbed scholars, who, tied to a mass of purely arbitrary little rules, have tried to clip the wings of human genius and narrow the limits of verisimilitude, as if it were only possible to teach in the theater by producing tears or laughter. There are a thousand delightful sentiments in man, independent of pity and laughter.[16]

He cites the example of Terence, who has been censured because his plays do not provoke mirth like those of Plautus or Aristophanes. Terence may not excite laughter, "but he charms, enraptures, and fascinates as he paints on the scene with a skilful brush not exaggerated pictures of men, but real men as we see them in life."[17]

Forner turns at this point to a discussion of *The Philosopher in Love.* The applause which has been accorded the play would be doubtful proof of its merit, he says, "if one saw in it the stage effects that are customarily used to draw the applause of the *vulgo.*"[18] But the situations of the comedy are not taken from the storehouse from which mediocre writers are wont to draw. In the main they are new and are the product of the genius of the author. Forner enumerates the merits of his play:

The principal characters are also entirely different from those ordinarily seen, being limited to a philosopher, a miser, a madcap marquis, and a lady who is gay, wise, and of very mature spirit. The plot is conducted with great simplicity and naturalness; there are no intricate incidents, carousals, turbulences, or confusions of persons because of darkness; there are no lost papers, discovered portraits, fear-inspiring swordsmen, servants who act as go-betweens, criminals who go to the gallows with pale and cadaverous faces, preaching kings, heroines from romances of chivalry, military trials, gloomy caverns, shipwrecks, battles, monstrous toads or serpents. There is a very simple action, developed in a few necessary situations, that terminates in a solution foreign to the action, but necessarily arising from it.[19]

Twelve years before, in 1784, Forner had composed a comedy entitled *The Captive Girl* which failed to pass the censor, Don Ignacio López de Ayala. Angered by the failure of his play to reach the theater, Forner gave vent to one of his characteristic personal attacks, in which he expressed ideas almost identical with those contained in his "Defense of the Vulgo" in regard to the irregularity of the *comedia* and the rules that should govern dramatic compositions:

Let the loathsome custom of repeating on the stage our old improprieties triumph, then. What are the fundamental rules? The unities, verisimilitude, decorum, characters, manners, diction. . . . I have no interest in seeing my play, *The Captive Girl,* performed. On the contrary, I would be ashamed to have it appear as a work of mine on a stage which has been given over to buffoon saints, lackeys, brutal kings, politicians, duelists, princesses in love with gardeners, and other inanities of equal caliber . . .[20]

After citing this statement, Menéndez y Pelayo makes the following comment:

These were the ideas that Forner held about the theater in 1784 and when he wrote his *Reflections of Tomé Cecial,* directed against Huerta, in 1786. He held more or less the same ideas in 1796 when he composed his cold comedy, *The School of Friendship or the Philosopher in Love,* preceded by a ludicrous "Defense of the Vulgo in Relation to Dramatic Poetry." But when he finished the most excellent and mature of his works, *The Exequies of the Castilian Language,* he had modified a great deal his critical rigidity and looked with undisguised sympathy upon the boldness and dash of the old poets.[21]

At this point he quotes from the *Exequies* in support of his theory of the supposed evolution in the attitude of Forner toward Lope and Calderón, and in a note cites a passage which he calls "another precious confession by Forner in favor of our theater." His enthusiasm impels him to declare that "these *Exequies* are by all odds Forner's masterpiece, and one of the most notable works of the eighteenth century," and to ask, "Why are they not printed in a separate volume?" This question by Menéndez y Pelayo was given as justification by Sainz y Rodriguez for his edition of the *Exequies,* which was published as one volume of the *Clásicos Castellanos.* The very passage cited forms a part of that section of the *Exequies* taken from *La Espigadera* and originally published in 1790, that is, six years before the composition of the "Defense of the Vulgo," which Menéndez y Pelayo characterizes as "ludicrous" and which he admits reveals a strong antagonism toward the *comedia.* This critic fails also to note that Forner's death in March, 1797, would hardly have allowed time for any pronounced modification in the antagonism toward the national theater which he expresses so forcefully in the

"Defense of the Vulgo" in 1796. Moreover, the *Exequies,* which were left unpublished at Forner's death, were almost certainly composed before 1796. No evolution is to be found either in Forner's dramatic creed or in his attitude toward the *comedia.* The leaders of the neo-classic movement from its beginning recognized the genius of Golden Age dramatists, but deplored the misuse of their talents. Forner pays tribute to the genius of Lope and Calderón not only in his *Exequies* but also in his "Satire Against the Abuses," in his "Letter on the Captive Girl," and in the "Defense of the Vulgo." A close examination of statements made in all these works will reveal that they do not vary in any essential respect.

The fate of his comedy *The Captive Girl* and the attacks which had been launched against *The Philosopher in Love* awakened all the ire of Forner, who, even without such an incentive, was capable of the most violent satire. He vents his spleen in the "Defense" upon those who have dared to call his latest comedy a "monster," against those "pedantic and stupid dictators who, because they have learned by heart four little rules of poetics, think they are qualified to per-ceive merit or lack of merit in works of literature."[22] He insists that his comedy is most regular in its action, manners, episodes, con-nection, and solution. No character is superfluous and none fails to observe the rule of constancy. He disclaims any intention of aspiring to the glory of a writer of comedies, and is content if he has enter-tained his fellow-citizens "decorously and rationally" in a time when the Spanish stage has reached such a low state "that even mediocrity must be considered excellence and the absence of raving as real merit."[23]

After his insistence that his own comedy observes the rules so faithfully, the following passage, in which he censures excessive scrupulousness in their observance, can only be attributed to his animosity toward those neo-classic critics who had dared to criticize *The Philosopher in Love* for not being entirely regular:

Since the beauty of works is entirely the product of genius, the peda-gogues cannot understand that at times it is necessary to ride rough-shod over some unimportant rule in order not to lose a very beautiful stroke, which would be very languid if it were adjusted exactly to this little rule. .. Excessive exactitude almost always degenerates into dryness, just as great license produces monstrosities. ... Old comedy was ignorant of the rules of art; new comedy tries to know them too well.... The rules will be of little use to spirits that are cold and frozen; and great and persuasive writers cannot subject themselves entirely to the servitude of a rigid regularity. Without this tolerance the restoration of the theater is impossible.[24]

If one confined his reading of Forner's "Defense" to its final statement, he might well believe the author to be a most reasonable and liberal critic. Indeed, there is ample evidence that Forner was not entirely satisfied with the results which the neo-classic movement was producing. In his *Exequies of the Castilian Language,* after lamenting the dearth of dramatic genius in Spain, he adds:

I tell you frankly that, while recognizing how much many of the poets of the reign of Felipe IV and Carlos III strayed from the path of good taste, I prefer their sophisms, insolent metaphors, and thoughtless flights of the imagination to the cold and semibarbarous dryness of most of those who write poetry today in Spain; because, after all, in the errors of the former, I see and admire the wealth and fecundity of a language that was able to serve as an instrument for such extraordinary phrases and images, but in the modern poets I see only indigence, poverty of genius, and a low and babbling language.[25]

Like Moratín, however, Forner never compromised in the essentials of his literary creed and continued to believe that the purpose of drama was to correct and teach. His limited praise of Calderón and Lope arose only from the profound contempt he felt for the contemporary theater and reminds one of Moratín's statement in *The New Comedy:* "Calderón, Solís, Rojas, and Moreto are worth more when they rave than these when they try to speak sensibly."[26]

María Rosa Gálvez de Cabrera

Among the immediate imitators of Moratín, Alonso Cortés would give first place to a woman, María Rosa Gálvez de Cabrera.[27] This judgment seems to be based almost entirely upon the similarity between Moratín's *The New Comedy* and *The Literary Nitwits* by this authoress. In a letter written in 1801 to the Board of Control of the Theaters, Rosa Gálvez refers to her tragedy, *Ali-bek,* which had been accepted for performance and publication, and for which she requests the payment of twenty-five doubloons in lieu of the percentage of receipts provided by the Plan of Reform, alleging an immediate need for money. She mentions in this same letter the fact that she is composing several other dramatic works which she hopes will be accepted by the board for performance. These are obviously the plays that were included in the three volumes of her *Poetical Works,* published in 1804.[28]

Inasmuch as five of the seven full-length plays in this collection are tragedies, it may be assumed that Rosa Gálvez gave her attention first to this genre and that only later did she become interested in writing comedies. Indeed, in a letter to the king, dated November 21, 1803, in which she requests that he authorize the publication of her works at the expense of the state, she emphasizes the fact that they will be made up principally of tragedies and says nothing about comedies. She is motivated primarily, she says, "by the desire to present to the public a work, the like of which has never been attempted by any woman in Spain or in any other nation, since the most celebrated French authoresses have limited themselves to translations, or, at the most, have published an occasional dramatic composition; but none of them has presented a collection of original tragedies like that of the petitioner."[29] Through her influence with Godoy, with whom she is said to have been on very intimate terms, her request was immediately granted, and her works were published at government expense. Although she had expressed the hope in her letter to the Board of Control that other dramatic works of hers would be approved for performance, it appears that the unfavorable reception accorded *Ali-bek* in 1801 forced her to abandon any plans she may have had for the performance of her other tragedies and to content herself with their publication.

Included in her *Poetical Works*, along with lyrical compositions, were the following plays: *Bion*, a lyrical opera in one act, translated from the French; *Saul*, a one-character dramatic scene; *Safo*, a one-act tragic drama; two original comedies in three acts and in verse, *The Egoist* and *The Literary Nitwits;* and five original tragedies in verse—*Florinda*, in three acts; *Blanca de Rossi*, in five acts; *Amon*, in five acts; *The Negress Zinda*, in three acts; and *The Delirious Woman*, in five acts. In addition to these plays she composed a one-act comedy, *One Fool Makes a Hundred*, which was judged worthy of publication in *The New Spanish Theater* in 1801; two original comedies in three acts, *The Modern Family* and *The Amazon Slave Girls*, which were left unpublished; a comedy in three acts, translated from the French with the title *Catherine or the Beautiful Peasant Girl*, which was published separately in 1801 and also included in *The New Spanish Theater;* and the ill-fated tragedy, *Ali-bek*, which, like her one-act comedy and the translation just mentioned, was published in the same collection.

When *Ali-bek* was performed at the Príncipe in August, 1801, it ran only eight days with receipts that were well below the average for the year, falling as low as 607 reals on the sixth day and ending with 997 reals. There is no record of subsequent performances. The only mention of the tragedy in any of the periodicals, it seems, was a review which appeared shortly after its publication in the *Memorial Literario* and which was caustic in the extreme. It is quite evident that the critic has a strong bias against the participation of women in the field of literature. Without going into the opinions that have been expressed for and against such participation, he will only say "that there are some men who believe that nature has destined women for occupations which, if not incompatible, at least are not favorable to the cultivation of letters; and so, although they have due respect for learned women, they esteem and prefer those who, being content to discharge their obligations, seek in study only that which will heighten their natural charms, without making of it their principal occupation."[30] A few women, he admits, particularly in France, have cultivated dramatic poetry, but their compositions have not even reached the level of mediocrity. They have limited themselves to composing simple dramas in prose and have never attempted to wear the tragic buskin, this honor being reserved, apparently, for the Spanish nation. "So then, we may praise the native talent, the enthusiasm, and above all the noble arrogance of the authoress of *Ali-bek,* since all of these qualities are necessary to compose an entirely original tragedy in five acts and in verse, in which the three unities are observed."[31]

The following summary in the *Memorial,* although clearly influenced by prejudice, gives a fairly accurate idea of the plot and the episodes of the tragedy, the principal defects of which are not so much the confusion and horror of the incidents as the inconsistency of the principal characters and the failure of the author to define their motives clearly:

Let us imagine a timid and innocent lamb, surrounded by ferocious tigers that roar, attack, wound, and tear each other to pieces, and we shall have an idea of Amalia, who is the heroine of the drama, and of Ali-bek, Hassam, Mahomad, and their crowd. Bloody and exterminating battles, daggers and poison at every step, treason and more treason, this is the action of the tragedy.

Ali-bek is a rebel, who for the good of Egypt bathes it in blood and covers it with horror; he spends all his time arguing with himself over whether he should take poison or not, and while he is making up his mind, he gives it to his doctor to drink. Morad is a good Musselman, a hero by profession, noble and valorous to the extreme, who for his part fights, kills, burns, and destroys, all with the good intention of meeting Ali-bek face to face, killing him, and taking his wife, with whom he has been madly in love since childhood. The other characters are so bad that these can pass as good in comparison. Hassam is the most horrible monster that has ever been seen; he has renounced the Christian faith, has sold his daughter to the honorable Ali-bek, and, having learned medicine, amuses himself by poisoning everybody around him. It is true that he does these things to avoid greater evils and that he experiences certain scruples in his heart, but this does not interrupt his evil deeds.

Mahomad is a Mameluke who is so bad and so infamous that everybody hates him and he hates everybody; some flatter him, others insult him, but all try to kill him and he tries to put an end to all of them. Finally Ismael, the last person in the tragedy, is a poor devil who does not bother anybody and who speaks as little as he can, always fearing, apparently, the results of such a violent tempest.

Some timid spirits, frightened at such bloody and atrocious carnage, will probably condemn the plan and conduct of the drama as horrible and improbable; but those who are well informed about the modern history of Egypt will find it very true to life and the customs of those people faithfully portrayed; for this the authoress doubtless should be praised.[32]

Ali-bek is, indeed, one of the weakest, least interesting, and most confused of all tragedies performed during the neo-classic period. It is hard to understand how it could have been chosen for inclusion in *The New Spanish Theater* or any other collection, unless it was through the intercession of Godoy.

In the "Foreword" to Volume II of her *Poetical Works* Rosa Gálvez gives a typical neo-classic explanation of her purpose in devoting herself to the composition of regular tragedies:

The tragedies I offer the public are the fruit of my fondness for this genre and of my desire to prove that the scarcity of these works in our literature is due more to the fact that our writers have not given their attention to them than to any ineptitude on their part. In fact, up until now it can almost be said that we do not have a perfect tragedy; but how can there be any in a nation that has such little liking for this type of play and whose actors, a short time ago, were so unwilling to perform any play that bore the name of tragedy, although this genre gives such pleasure in other cultured nations and makes up the greater part of their theatrical performances? In truth, it seemed that the fortune of tragedies in Spain was improving lately; some have been favorably received by the public, but unfortunately we cannot take much pride in this, because only foreign tragedies have been applauded.[33]

Quintana is more than kind in his evaluation of Rosa Gálvez' trage-

dies when, after giving rather mild praise to the talent of the authoress as it is revealed in her poetry, he makes these remarks in the
Variedades:

We shall limit ourselves to saying that the style of her tragedies is
rather colorless; that some of the subjects she has chosen are not very
interesting; and that her facility in composition has led her to produce so
many plays that she has not been able to polish any of them properly.
Several scenes in *Amon* and the second act of *The Delirious Lady*, which
show her genius and capacity, make one regret that she has not devoted
all the time and effort that she has expended on all of her plays to these
two alone.[34]

Although Rosa Gálvez' comedies are superior to her tragedies,
they do not rise above mediocrity. Her first attempt in the comic field
was made in 1801 with the one-act comedy in prose, *One Fool
Makes a Hundred*. She explains in the "Foreword" that this comedy
was written to serve as a *fin de fiesta* to her tragedy, *Ali-bek*. The
reasons for the choice of subject were:

The opinion of some people that dramatic compositions of this type
could not be written in Spain comparable in grace, invention, and animation of dialogue to those in this genre that have come from other
countries and that we have seen translated; and certain notions held by
many young pople, who almost without having breathed the air on the
other side of the Pyrenees, return home scorning everything in their
native land, and showing that all they have derived from their visit is a
ridiculous ability to dress, speak, and conduct themselves in an extraordinary manner.[35]

One Fool Makes a Hundred was presented at the Príncipe on
August 1, 1801, and was revived for five performances at the same
theater in 1821. In 1816 it was reworked as an opera.[36] In its review
of this comedy, the *Memorial Literario*, after giving the purpose of
the author, concedes that the idea is good but believes it could
have been better handled, "since, although there are occasional
witticisms that produce laughter, most of them are common jests
and buffoonery, the entire humor consisting in what the Italians
call "caricatures."[37] This comedy fell under the ban of the ecclesiastical censor in May, 1801, because it was feared that since the play
was a satire on those who affected French manners and speech, it
might offend many of the officials of France who were stationed at
the time in Madrid. Doña María Rosa protested this action to the

judge protector of the theaters and succeeded in inducing him to submit it to another censor, whereupon it was duly approved both for performance in the theater and for publication.

The Literary Nitwits, María Rosa Gálvez' first full-length comedy, is an imitation in verse of Moratín's The New Comedy, and like its model rigorously observes the neo-classic precepts. It is written entirely in octosyllabic romance; the scene in all three acts is the study of Don Panuncio; and the action lasts only a few hours. The principal role is that of Don Panuncio, who believes himself to be a prodigy of erudition. His house is a meeting place for eccentric characters: the inventor, Don Cilindro; the antiquarian, Don Epitafio; the poet, Don Esdrújulo; and the foppish Baron de la Ventolera. All of these flatter the vanity of Don Panuncio, although each is engrossed in his own mania. Don Panuncio wishes to marry his niece, Doña Isabel, to the antiquarian because the latter is rich and has promised to use his money and influence to insure the success of a comedy Don Panuncio has written. Fearing to jeopardize his own reputation, Don Panuncio has decided to have the play performed in the name of his son, Don Alberto, who has just returned from his studies in Salamanca. The young man is very much in love with Doña Isabel, who, although somewhat mischievous and plain-spoken, returns his affection. The only problem to be solved in the play is the prevention of the marriage of Isabel to Don Epitafio and the arrangement of her marriage to Don Alberto. Much against his will the young man is forced to allow the comedy, which bears the ridiculous title Contrast Contrasted, to be produced under his name. Of course, the play is a complete failure and its erstwhile supporters turn against its supposed author, each declaring that he had foreseen the result. Don Epitafio writes the following letter to Don Panuncio:

Since your son's comedy is detestable, it will not be performed again nor will it be printed; and therefore the rough draft will in time become a manuscript which will serve as a record of our bad taste. Send it to me so that I may place it among other papers of the same class which adorn my museum.[38]

Angered at Don Epitafio's attitude, Don Panuncio readily consents to the marriage of his son to his niece.

The satire of the author is directed not only at the would-be dramatic author, but also at the poet, Don Esdrújulo, and at the

affected Baron. Don Esdrújulo boasts of having been a writer
of *comedies of magic:*

> I have been a dramatic
> author, and I used to study
> the popular taste; then
> I wrote comedies of magic,
> and in all the solutions
> the devil came and carried
> off the actors; in others
> of better taste the heroes
> went to the gallows;
> and from there they escaped
> without anyone's knowing when or how.
> I kept them invisible
> on the stage, although they were
> surrounded by the other actors;
> and afterward I granted them
> pardon for no other reason
> than that the play might end
> and because I so willed it.[39]

The bad taste of the public, which reveals itself in a predilection
for miserable translations, is ridiculed through the speeches of the
Baron, who, upon hearing of the new play, says to Don Alberto:

> Your play must not be
> original, but a rare
> translation. Translations
> all please much, *beaucoup.*
> Although their originals may be
> detestable; although they may
> limp and be crippled in the hand;
> although they may be headless and
> although they may be bad in their
> influence and untrue to life;
> no matter. They are translations
> and that is enough. *Rien de plus.*[40]

The Baron has composed a comedy himself, and in the last act he
offers to read it to Don Alberto, who turns angrily upon him:

> Because of you and other ignorant
> people like you, our theater
> finds itself with an epidemic
> of modern translations,
> most of them very bad,
> since to our misfortune

> the jewels of the foreign theater
> are seldom chosen.[41]

The character of the Baron bears the brunt of the satire. His speech is an unintelligible mixture, at times, of French and Spanish. For the latter language he has a profound contempt. He is engaged in translating into French "the opaque verses of Góngora" and is uncertain of the meaning of the word *parler* in Spanish:

> The word
> *Parler* is in Spanish
> *to speak?* Oh! I have forgotten
> our wretched language.
> I will see whether I can
> find it in the dictionary.[42]

The comedy apparently never reached the stage, probably because of the popularity of the type of drama it so severely satirizes. The criticism the *Memorial* makes of *One Fool Makes a Hundred* may well be applied to *The Literary Nitwits,* since all the characters except Don Alberto, Doña Isabel, and the servant, Lucas, are so overdrawn that they become nothing more than caricatures.

The Egoist, which is termed an original comedy in three acts, belongs rather to the pathetic genre. The comic element is completely lacking, the protagonist Milord Sidney being a heartless villain who leads a wild life, shows no affection for his young son, Charles, and breaks the heart of his faithful and loving wife, Nancy. In the final act, in order that he may be free to devote his attentions to another woman whom he has seduced by false promises, he attempts to poison his wife. Because, according to his philosophy, "an egoist does not feel remorse," he has no compunction in carrying out his plan. After he has administered the first dose of poison his guilt is discovered. Nancy turns upon him:

> Wicked man,
> incapable of a sense of guilt
> or of love, man of stone,
> here is my decree of
> divorcement. Here is the record
> of your infamy and my death,
> my death, which you have tried
> to hasten, and since Heaven has
> saved me from your wickedness
> until now, in the future,

far from you, burying
my complaints and my misfortune,
I hope to live a safer life.[43]

In the final scene Sidney is carried away to prison and the play ends
with the type of tableau recommended so strongly by Diderot. The
stage direction is as follows:

The Governor and the guards carry Sidney away; Nancy and Charles
follow him to the middle of the stage and stand, as do the other actors,
in an attitude that reveals consternation and emotion. The curtain falls.[44]

This play reveals in a striking manner the influence of the pathetic
genre on one who is correctly regarded as a staunch supporter of the
classic precepts. The character of the egoist might easily have been
given comic treatment. The author, however, chooses to correct vice
not by ridicule, but by chastisement, and by making it odious. The
perversity of the villain causes two virtuous women the most intense
suffering and in the end must meet its just punishment. This is truly
a lachrymose comedy. There is no evidence that *The Egoist* was ever
produced, nor did it arouse sufficient interest upon its publication
in the *Poetical Works* of the author to be reviewed in any of the
periodicals.

Another comedy by Doña María Gálvez, *The Modern Family,* in
three acts and in verse, was first played April 14, 1805, at the theater
of the Caños, where it ran for four days. It was repeated on the 2nd
and 3rd of the following month and in October, 1807, was played
twice. In 1824 it was revived for two performances at the Príncipe.
According to Cotarelo y Mori, this play was chosen to inaugurate the
performances of the new company at the Caños after the revamping
of the theatrical companies by the Subdelegate of Theaters, the
Marqués de Fuerte-Hijar. At the last moment it appeared that the
performance could not be given because the vicar, an ecclesiastical
censor, decided to withdraw his permission, calling the play immoral
and a school of libertinism. The authoress appealed to the governor
of the council and finally succeeded in overriding the ecclesiastical
censorship. The play met with only moderate favor, although Máiquez himself played the role of the music teacher, a servile and
treacherous Italian. From the brief discussion of the play by Cotarelo y Mori, it seems to suffer from the same exaggeration we have
observed in *One Fool Makes a Hundred* and in *The Literary
Nitwits.*[45]

The only remaining original play by Rosa Gálvez to be performed on the Madrid stage was *The Amazon Slave Girls,* which ran for only two days in November, 1805, at the theater of the Caños del Peral. The only recognition it received was a short review in the *Memorial Literario,* which was almost as unfavorable as the review of *Ali-bek* in the same periodical four years earlier, although not so caustic:

It seemed to us that the subject is not very interesting and that it lacks novelty. Strange subjects can be found which in spite of their strangeness are uninteresting; but the subject of this drama is not only very commonplace, but awakens no curiosity whatsoever. In fact, we are weary of seeing on the stage meetings between brothers who have been separated for a long time, recognitions by husbands and wives, friends, etc.[46]

After reading Rosa Gálvez' satire on the detestable translations that had flooded the Spanish stage, it is somewhat surprising to find that a translation by her was made the object of pitiless censure in the *Memorial Literario* in 1802. Following the publication of *Catherine or the Beautiful Peasant Girl,* the *Memorial* commented:

This drama is translated from the French, but has not been transferred to Castilian, for it has remained in that half-breed jargon so much in vogue among the mob of bad translators, who, to destroy our language more quickly and surely, have taken possession of the theater. There is scarcely a Castilian phrase in the entire composition, or a sentence that does not violate grammatical rules. The play is also to be condemned for the inclusion of a great number of words recently introduced or entirely unknown in our language.[47]

During the entire neo-classic period there was an open season on translators. When the Plan of Reform in 1799 offered the same reward to them as to authors of original compositions, an almost incredible number of foreign plays soon made their appearance on the Madrid stage. The majority of the plays performed at the Caños del Peral from 1801 to 1808 were importations principally from the French theater, most of these being the work of incompetent writers. Neo-classic critics were particularly fond of directing the barbs of their satire at these translations, whether they were the work of nationalist writers or of members of their own school. It was rare, indeed, for a neo-classicist to please another neo-classicist with either an original play, a recast, or a translation from the French or the Italian theater.

The precedent had been set, however, and the tide of importations from these theaters was not to be stemmed. For the next fifty years the French repaid with compound interest what they had borrowed during the seventeenth century.

Meseguer

In the present state of decadence of Spanish literature we willingly praise productions if they are even mediocre.[48]

With this doubtful praise the *Memorial Literario* begins its review of Meseguer's *The Talebearer*, a three-act comedy in verse. This play is neo-classic in its observance of the unities, in its verse form which never departs from the octosyllabic *romance*, and in its purpose, which is to ridicule a talebearer. There is no scene division.

The plot, while unified, is complicated by the schemes of the talebearer. Don Luis de Osorio, a gentleman who is forced for political reasons to live under the assumed name of Diego, and his daughter, Inés, have entered the service of Don Pedro. The latter, who is most favorably impressed by the obvious nobility of his servant and by the beauty and modesty of Inés, treats them as equals in spite of the remonstrances of his wife, Doña Laura, and her sister, Doña Martina. Inés and Don Juan, the supposed son of Donavert, a German colonel, are secretly in love. Don Fermín, the talebearer, discovers their secret love affair and by a mass of intrigue seeks to prevent their marriage, first by slandering Don Juan to the girl's father and then by fostering the jealousy of Doña Martina, who aspires to catch the handsome youth. Doña Laura and her sister urge Don Pedro to dismiss Don Diego. When it seems that Fermín is on the point of succeeding in his scheme, there is a *recognition*. It develops that Don Juan is the son of Don Diego and that Inés is the daughter of the German colonel. Don Diego is informed by Donavert that he has been pardoned by the government and may now assume his rightful name. The circumstances which gave rise to the confusion of parentage are most improbable. The *recognition* removes all obstacles to the marriage of Don Juan and Inés, the tale-bearer is unmasked, and the comedy ends in Golden Age fashion: "And may this effort evoke, if not applause, at least no severe censure."

Almost from the beginning of the play the audience is informed that Don Fermín's malevolence is really inspired by his secret love for Inés, and that he hopes to reduce the girl and her father to such a state that they will be willing to accept him as a suitor. The *Memorial Literario* points out that the character of Fermín, while well done on the whole, does not represent a real talebearer:

The best part of the play is the character of the talebearer, which stands out above the others and stirs them to action. In the first verses he reveals his restless and malign nature. Nevertheless, it would have been more appropriate to have made his actions stem from his nature alone and not from his interest in Inés.[49]

The *Memorial* is more than fair in its evaluation of the comedy: "For this reason we say that the main characters are comical and are well sustained and contrasted, the scenes are varied, the language expressive and pure, and the versification regular."[50] The principal defects are a lack of verisimilitude and originality in the solution and "the very long speeches, which are exceedingly tiresome and interfere with the rapidity of the action."[51]

Notwithstanding the apparent fairness of this review, Meseguer believed he saw in the article evidences of malice. In 1803 he published a defense of his play in the *Regañón General*. After declaring himself satisfied with the reception given his comedy in Madrid and in "all the theaters of Spain," he directs his attention to the review in the *Memorial:*

... Number 6 of the *Memorial Literario* has just reached my hands with its censure of my comedy, and although I did not come out as badly as I had expected, because I had certain little suspicions that it would be severely criticized even though my dramatic talent might be praised ... I felt nevertheless a bit of annoyance since it seemed to me that partiality or lack of intelligence had been responsible for that censure; for, as I have said, I was not and am not on the best terms with one of the publishers, compilers, or, as they call themselves, editors of the *Memorial*. I suspected, therefore, that he would have a particular motive in greeting and upbraiding my poor *Talebearer*.[52]

In answer to the *Memorial*, he publishes a burlesque poem entitled "Pasagonzalo" ("A Light Stroke"), in which he takes up point by point the criticism of that periodical. A comparison that had been made between his play and those of Molière arouses his resentment: "Molière wrote many like this? Perhaps they think we have not read this Molière, or that we have grown up in some uncivilized region. Neither Molière, nor any of his many admirers, has written an original comedy that can be compared with *The Talebearer*."[53]

His play is so perfectly constructed, Meseguer declares, and so carefully observes the unities, that it could easily be staged as one act with no interruption whatsoever. This "Pasagonzalo," though clever in parts, was so long that it occupied half of Number 21 of the *Regañón* and all of the following three numbers. It was answered in the *Diario de Madrid* on September 21, 22, and 23, 1803. This polemic, which was characterized by personalities from the beginning, became more and more heated. On October 22 Meseguer replied to the article in the *Diario*, addressing his unknown opponent as Mr. Perhaps-Dirty.*

The patience of the readers of the *Regañón* became exhausted, and on November 5 a subscriber wrote a protest to the editor in which he threatened to discontinue his subscription "if you continue printing such articles." This was followed on November 16 by a letter from another subscriber which began as follows: "Mr. *Regañón General:* I wish you good day. For a long time your periodical has been arousing my ire because, instead of finding in you a serious and judicious censor, I find only an indulgent supporter of tedious bagatelles."[54] These remonstrances seem to have been effective, for we hear no more from Meseguer or from "Mr. Perhaps-Dirty."

When one recalls that the polemic between Miñano and the so-called Pedro Rico occasioned by the performance of *The Taste of the Day* was running concurrently with the above polemic, he must conclude that the patience of the readers was truly astounding. These polemics were not without their amusing side, however, and must have served as a basis for many a conversation in the cafés.

Meseguer shows considerable talent in *The Talebearer*, but he seems to have lacked the ability to stand criticism. No other play of his is mentioned by critics except a translation of Terence's *Andria*, which was probably never published, although the author declares in a note to his letter of October 22 that he has already completed this play together with two others, *The Treasure* and *The Fainting Fit*, and may publish them.

Mor de Fuentes

José Mor de Fuentes, who is called "extravagant" by Alonzo

---

*A critic published in the *Diario* on September 22, 1803, a severe indictment of an arrangement in Spanish of Corneille's *Cid*, and signed his article *Quizásusi*. Quite obviously this is the critic who was engaging in the polemic with Meseguer at the same time. The latter chooses to alter the pseudonym to *Quizá-sucio*, which means "perhaps dirty." The original pseudonym is untranslatable.

Cortés,[55] composed in 1800 two comedies, *The Rake* and *The Masculine Woman*. Another comedy, *The Egoist*, is listed by Cejador y Frauca, but without comment or date of composition.[56] Moratín does not mention the play in his "Catalogue of Dramatic Works." One is forced to agree with Alonso Cortés that *The Rake* is "bad in every respect, in spite of the moral lesson contained in the solution."[57] Azorín was certainly not referring to his comedies when he said that Mor de Fuentes "deserves more than four insipid lines in our compendiums of literary history."[58]

Judged by any standard, *The Rake*,[59] a comedy in three acts and in verse, has little to recommend it. It conforms easily to the unities because of the excessive simplicity of the plot. In the play, Rodrigo, a profligate with no sense of propriety or honor, abuses the kindness of his rich guardian and seeks to marry his daughter, Inés, for her money. The girl, who constantly expects a letter from an absent suitor, Don Gonzalo, rejects his advances. It develops that Rodrigo has been intercepting Don Gonzalo's letters. He is also involved with a woman of questionable character whom he tries to use as a decoy to further his plans with Inés. The absent lover turns up, the villain is exposed, and the comedy ends happily. The character of the profligate might have served for a true comedy or for a sentimental comedy, but Mor de Fuentes succeeds in making it neither, for the principal character is neither ridiculous nor odious.

In the violence of his judgments, Mor de Fuentes may be compared to Forner, although he lacks the latter's critical insight. Cueto gives this summary of Mor de Fuentes' opinion of his contemporaries:

To Mor de Fuentes the illustrious and discreet statesman, the Count of Floridablanca, was nothing but an extremely superficial and even ignorant man; in Cienfuegos, to whom he had entrusted the correction of his poetical compositions before offering them for publication, he sees only queer discords and heavy, harsh, and enigmatic language; Moratín's comedies are, in his opinion, long *sainetes,* sprinkled with more or less witty expressions which the author was accustomed to pick up from the market women; he calls Salvá inane and a criticaster, and his renowned grammar a medley of Valencianisms; he characterizes Juan Nicasio Gallego as too Gallician; he says that the admirable *Don Alvaro,* by the Duke of Rivas, is a tedious comedy in the manner of the comedy of magic, *Pedro Bayalarde.* The style of Martínez de la Rosa, in his eyes, is the stiff prosiness of the droll Martínez; the lofty poetry of Quintana is high-sounding jargon, alternating with lines that drag the ground; and, finally, the ideal inspiration of Lamartine is the stiff sobs of a whining poet.

Only Rosa Gálvez and Meléndez find favor before the dreadful tribunal of this inexorable and bilious critic.[60]

Mor de Fuentes' literary creed is given in the preface to his second comedy, *The Masculine Woman*.[61] In this preface the author condemns "tearful comedies or tragicomedies," following the French critic, La Harpe, whom he cites. His definition of comedy conforms to the neo-classic pattern:

> Comedy becomes an imitation of what happens in society. . . . Furthermore, in the midst of the most pleasant happenings, there are occasions that deeply affect the heart. In this regard, the greatest philosopher is Molière himself, who affords so much pleasure with his wit, since the essence of true comedy consists in alternating humorous and moral scenes, the tendency of this genre being to provoke in the audience a gentle smile, the inseparable companion of satisfaction, rather than to excite boisterous laughter.[62]

He declares that in *The Rake* as well as in *The Masculine Woman* he has tried to be original, following not the rules of Aristotle or any other preceptist, but the laws of nature. He has, therefore, suppressed all asides and soliloquies. He has excluded from the cast all servants, who, as far as he has been able to observe, "do not intervene, outside of the theater, in important and confidential family matters."[63] He recommends the octosyllabic *romance* as the only verse form for comedy. At this point he makes a statement which reveals his egotism and accounts for the "unpolished versification" which Alonso Cortés notes in *The Rake*:

> In this regard I can say that versification is easy for me, and, if anyone criticizes my spending an almost incredibly short time in composing a comedy, I shall answer him by saying that this profession does not offer sufficient recompense to justify forcing my impatient nature to concentrate upon an object for several days.[64]

The Masculine Woman is, like *The Rake*, a three-act comedy in verse, and it is even less interesting. The title and some of the lines in the first act promise a character modeled somewhat along the lines of Lope de Vega's *The Avenger of Women* or of Moreto's *Disdain Conquered by Disdain*, both of which plays Mor de Fuentes may well have had in mind; but the characters of Leonor, the masculine woman, and the Marqués, whose indifference is interpreted at first as a mere ruse to overcome Leonor's resistance, are not sustained.

The Marqués is not at all in love with Leonor and marries the sensible and very feminine Felisa; while the masculine woman, for no reason at all, gives her hand to Marcelo, a friend of the Marqués. No one is ridiculed in the play and no one is punished at the end. In this comedy, as in *The Rake*, Mor de Fuentes has completely misused the material at his disposal.

From 1800 to 1803 there appeared a number of neo-classic comedies in addition to those already mentioned. None of these, however, influenced the development of drama. But they have a certain historical interest, since they indicate that, following Moratín's initial successes, and with the encouragement offered by the Plan of Reform for the composition of original plays, there was a short period of relative activity in the production of neo-classic comedies. The writer of *sainetes*, González del Castillo, was moved to compose three comedies in 1800: *The Proud Girl in Love, An Imprudent Passion*, and *The Hypocritical Mother*.[65] Only the last of these seems to have attracted any attention, and that not until several years after its composition. In 1820 and 1821 *The Hypocritical Mother* was played at the Príncipe and failed to meet the approval of the critics, whose objections were based not upon the failure of the play to observe the rules, but upon the failure of the protagonist to measure up to the title of the play. In *El Censor* Lista emphasizes this point and denies that the character of the mother is made ridiculous:

The term "hypocrite" does not fit her. She is a weak mother, for whom it is not hard to sacrifice a daughter to the interest and pleasure of a son who is ill-bred and given over to evil practices; she is a prude who believes that virtue consists in phrases and superficiality; she is a stupid woman, who implores the favor of heaven to promote slander and deception, which are calculated to send the innocent Clara to a nunnery; but she is not a hypocrite. . . . Most of the characters of this comedy are odious without being ridiculous. How much more detestable Tartuffe is, and yet what a dose of ridiculousness his inimitable author gives him! The prudery of Doña Tecla, the only comic element in this play, is more burlesque than comical, because it is genuine and not pretended as in the case of Moratín's *The Female Hypocrite*.

Any man who has feeling and education will be furious and will not laugh at *The Hypocritical Mother*.[66]

Simón de Viegas

The Pettifogger,[67] a three-act comedy in verse by Don Simón de Viegas, takes its place in the graveyard of those neo-classic comedies which were the product of a misguided attempt on the part of writers with no dramatic talent to incite Spaniards to the composition of original works. In a note which precedes the play, the author explains his motive in writing the comedy: "The author did not send it to the theater through self-interest or vain presumption, but to stir other writers to compose original works instead of devoting their time to translations." A precedent for this type of explanation had been set at the beginning of the neo-classic movement by Montiano and by Nicolás Fernández de Moratín. A half-century later we find the same motives inspiring neo-classicists to what they liked to believe was unselfish self-sacrifice for a worthy cause.

The title of this comedy, *The Pettifogger*, or ignorant and vociferous lawyer, is not entirely accurate. The protagonist, Don Melitón de Brincoces, is a law student who is on the point of taking the bar examination. With a superficial display of erudition, he succeeds in dazzling Don Zenón, a rich merchant, who is eager to have such a promising young man for a son-in-law. Don Melitón is a pedant who is addicted to Latin quotations and who dominates every conversation with his loquacity. The author contrasts his shallowness with the common sense of the doctor, Don Luciano. Much of the comedy is taken up by the arguments of the would-be lawyer and the doctor, in which the former is always defeated. The comedy is intended as a satire on pedantry; but although there seems to be abundant material for comedy in such a theme, the author misses his goal completely. Brincoces is a conceited fool, but never provokes a smile. The intrigue is furnished by his attempt to win the hand of the daughter of a rich merchant. This marriage is made to hinge upon the outcome of the examination the young man is to take. Although the girl is in love with the sensible but extremely timid Don Jacinto, this love affair is entirely devoid of dramatic interest. The young man takes no active steps to prevent the marriage, nor do the doctor and the brother of Don Zenón, although they all see through the shallowness of Brincoces. At the close of the play, Brincoces is notified that he has failed the examination; Don Zenón realizes that the supposed prodigy is in reality an ignorant pedant; and Jacinto wins the girl. The only element of suspense lies in the uncertainty over the outcome of the examination.

The play was presented at the theater of the Caños del Peral on September 7, 1803, and was such a complete failure that it ran for only one night. The author seeks to explain this failure in the above-mentioned note. Having observed that in the performance at the Caños many of the speeches were omitted and that the play was merely recited, not acted according to the rules of declamation, he publishes the play in order that its merits may be impartially judged. He is particularly bitter in his condemnation of the acting of the grandmother and the servant, Paca. The actresses, he says, were "an old automaton whose face was a mask and showed no emotion whatsoever, and a young girl who, as a servant, acted and spoke as well as could be expected from her very limited experience."[68] Cotarelo y Mori insists, however, that the play was performed by the best actors in the company, with the exception of the role of Paca, which was given at the last moment to Francisca Camino. After reading the comedy one is inclined to agree with this critic that the actors could not express character which did not exist and that "the whole thing is completely bad, including the verses."[69] In the comedy the unities are carefully observed, the verse form is octosyllabic *romance* throughout, varying with each act, and there is an attempt to correct vice through ridicule. The play is, therefore, distinctly a neo-classic comedy, the product of rules but not of genius.

Dámaso de Isusquiza

In the same year, 1803, an attempt was made by Dámaso de Isusquiza to fuse elements of the neo-classic comedy and the *comedia*. *The Jealous Man and the Foolish Girl,* a three-act comedy in verse, was presented for the first time at the theater of the Caños from the 10th to the 13th of October, 1803, together with *The Translator,* an operetta. The play is obviously an imitation of two comedies by Molière: *The School for Wives* and *The School for Husbands.* Lista in *El Censor,* June 2, 1821, gives Hurtado de Mendoza's *The Husband Makes A Wife and Association Changes Manners* as the source. Isusquiza, however, was well acquainted with the works of the French dramatist, having translated his *L'Avare* in 1800. It hardly seems necessary to trace the source of Isusquiza's play to the earlier Spanish comedy, in spite of the obvious similarity of themes.

The Jealous Man and the Foolish Girl has more intrigue than most neo-classic comedies of the day. Don Nicasio is a modified Arnolphe who expects to marry his ward, Doña Isabel. In the Spanish play the exposition leaves much to be desired since we are only told that the father of the girl, upon his death, has entrusted her to the care of Don Nicasio.

In *The School for Wives* Arnolphe has had Agnes brought up in ignorance in order that she may be too stupid to deceive him. The supposed stupidity of Isabel, however, is not adequately explained. Nor do we know why the marriage between the guardian and the ward has been delayed. As in *The School for Wives*, the girl shows that she is by no means a fool, succeeding in outwitting her guardian at every point in order to attain her desire, which is to marry Don Jacinto, a handsome young man with whom she has fallen in love at first sight.

The secondary plot is taken from Molière's *The School for Husbands*. Don Pío is in love with Doña Margarita, the sister of Don Nicasio. His confidence in the faithfulness of his betrothed is in marked contrast with the jealousy of Don Nicasio. He even encourages his friend Enrique to observe the admirable qualities of Margarita and intentionally enables him to be alone with her. This complete confidence on his part is taken for indifference by Margarita, who would prefer that he show himself to be a more passionate suitor.

When Don Nicasio learns that Don Jacinto has become interested in Isabel upon seeing her once at the theater, he seeks by every possible means to prevent his friend from meeting her. Aided by Margarita, Isabel prevails upon her guardian to take her again to the theater. Don Nicasio, however, stipulates that she go disguised as a boy. This precaution is of no avail, since Jacinto accompanies them and, although he does not penetrate the disguise, is charmed with the supposed youth who bears such a strong resemblance to the girl he loves. The two succeed in evading the vigilance of the guardian and escape to a café where they have an extended conversation. When Don Nicasio finally discovers them, he takes Isabel home at once and forces her to write a letter to her suitor, forbidding him to continue his attentions. The girl, by a ruse, causes her guardian to leave the room for a moment, thus enabling her to add a postscript in which she explains the letter and affirms her love for Jacinto. Showing himself more stupid than his ward, Don Nicasio delivers the letter to Jacinto without examining it. Later, when he surprises her writing to the young man, she pretends that she is writing a letter for Margarita, who is in love with Jacinto rather than with Don Pío. Don Nicasio is more than pleased with this explanation. By marrying his sister to Jacinto he can accomplish two things: he can remove one whom he has considered a dangerous rival and triumph over Don Pío, who has maintained that women should not be guarded too jealously.

At the suggestion of the servant, Lucía, Doña Isabel persuades Don Nicasio to marry his sister to Jacinto immediately. She explains that Margarita is ashamed to face him after her secret love affair has been discovered and that she wishes to come veiled to the ceremony. Don Nicasio agrees, and, thinking to keep Isabel safely guarded in the meantime, tries to lock her up in her room. By a trick, however, it is the servant who is locked up and Isabel comes out dressed as Margarita and heavily veiled. The overjealous suitor with his own hand delivers his ward to her lover. Don Pío believes that Margarita has been unfaithful to him and shows sufficient concern to convince her of his impetuosity. He is not so generous as his prototype in *The School for Husbands*. A double wedding is arranged and Don Nicasio, taking a cue from *The Misanthrope*, leaves in anger, declaring that he is going away "to the most uninhabited wilderness where I can be free from faithless women and stupid men."

A very unfavorable review of this comedy was published in *El Regañón General* on November 2, 1803. Among many other comments, the writer, who signs himself *The Impartial Critic*, says:

In this play it is useless to look for verisimilitude or regularity, for it has no incident that is not absurd and unnatural; the characters are queer, since the jealous guardian, who is the protagonist, can rather be called a fool, who is wrapped up in himself, than a jealous man. This is shown from the beginning to the end of the comedy. What man, no matter how foolish he might be, would ever think of taking his wife to a café dressed as a man so that no one would make love to her?[70]

In 1807 the comedy was reviewed in *Minerva o el Revisor General*. This review is brief but hardly less unfavorable than the review in the *Regañón:*

Not just the girl, but all or almost all of the characters are stupid. The incidents, although fairly amusing and not displeasing on the stage, are poorly conceived and improbable. In contrast with the jealous guardian there is another character who is extremely gullible, but even though he is stupid, he is not so bad as the former.... The language and the versification could be worse.[71]

In 1821, after the comedy had been revived, Lista published in *El Censor* a review in which he admits the popularity of the play but objects to the treatment of the subject:

The characters of the jealous guardian and the foolish ward always produce a good effect on the stage and the scene in the café, and those of the letter and the delivery of Isabel to her lover, Don Jacinto, by the jealous guardian himself produce a great deal of laughter. But in every dramatic action it is necessary that the means used by the author be in proportion to the results; and this principle is openly violated in all the combinations of this comedy. . . .[72]

Although written as three acts, *The Jealous Man and the Foolish Girl* was divided into four acts on the stage, in order not to change the scene within the first act.

The fact that this comedy remained in the repertoire of the theater until 1830 is evidence that the public did not agree with the critics in regard to its merit. In 1816 it was reworked as a three-act comedy and played as *The Jealous Guardian* with Máiquez in the leading role. In 1821 the play reappeared at the Príncipe as *The Jealous Man and the Foolish Girl or the Astute Village Girl*, and in 1823 it was played in four acts at the same theater as *The Jealous Guardian and the Astute Village Girl*, and termed a recast of a play by Tirso. It seems evident, however, that these plays are the same. Under the title *The Jealous Guardian and the Astute Village Girl* the comedy was played ten times from 1825 to 1830.

Although this comedy did not meet with the approval of the critics, it was clearly written under the influence of the rules. The violation of the unity of place is slight, since the scene is shifted only once and then to a house in the same city. As has been observed, even Luzán did not prohibit such license. There is an obvious attempt to imitate the *comedia* in the versification by using different meters: *redondillas, quintillas, décimas, romances,* etc. Further concession is made in this play to popular taste in the parallel love affairs of Jacinto and Isabel and Don Pío and Margarita. In cloak and sword plays this dualism is rarely absent. It must be remembered, however, that the first preceptist of the neo-classic school had recommended what he called the *fábulas implexas* as more likely to maintain the interest of the spectators in a comedy, and the *Diario de Madrid* in its *Poetics* had reiterated this recommendation.

The continued popularity of this play in spite of its obvious defects may be due to its points of similarity with the *comedia*. It has many scenes with real comic force and sufficient intrigue to hold the interest of the spectators. After noting all its defects, we must admit that *The Jealous Man and the Foolish Girl* at least is not cold, as are so many neo-classic plays of the period.

1. Juan Pablo Forner, *La escuela de la amistad o el filósofo enamorado*, comedia, precede una apología del vulgo con relación a la poesía dramática, con licencia en Madrid, imp. de Fermín Villalpanco, 1796.
2. Cotarelo y Mori, *Máiquez*, pp. 63-64.
3. Marqués de Valmar (Cueto), *Bosquejo de la poesía castellana en el siglo XVIII (B.A.E.,* LVII, 143).
4. Cotarelo y Mori, *Iriarte y su época*, p. 398.
5. Act III, Sc. 3.
6. Juan Pablo Forner, *Exequias de la lengua castellana (Clásicos Castellanos,* [Madrid, 1925]), pp. 180-87.
7. *Ibid.*, pp. 184-85.
8. Act III, Sc. 1.
9. Forner, *op. cit.*, "Apología," p. iii.
10. *Ibid.*, p. iv.
11. *Ibid.*, p. vi.
12. *Ibid.*, p. xiii.
13. *Ibid.*, p. xv.
14. *Ibid.*, p. xvi.
15. *Ibid.*, pp. xxiii-xxv.
16. *Ibid.*, p. xxvi.
17. *Ibid.*, p. xxvii.
18. *Ibid.*, p. xxix.
19. *Ibid.*, p. xxx.
20. Menéndez y Pelayo, *op. cit.*, III, 327.
21. *Ibid.*
22. Forner, *op. cit.*, p. xxxi.
23. *Ibid.*, p. xxv.
24. *Ibid.*, pp. xxvi-xxvii.
25. Forner, *Exequias*, pp. 146-47.
26. Moratín, *La Comedia Nueva*, Act II, Sc. 5.
27. Narciso Alonso Cortés, "Prólogo" to *Bretón de los Herreros, Teatro (Clásicos Castellanos* [Madrid, 1929]), p. x.
28. María Rosa Gálvez de Cabrera, *Obras Poéticas* (Madrid, en la Imprenta Real, 1804), 3 Vols.
29. Manuel Serrano y Sanz, *Apuntes para una biblioteca de escritoras españolas desde el año 1401 al 1833* (Madrid, 1903), p. 449.
30. *El Memorial Literario*, May, 1802, II, 11.
31. *Ibid.*, p. 12.
32. *Ibid.*, pp. 12-13.
33. Rosa Gálvez, *op. cit.*, "Advertencia."
34. *Variedades de Ciencias, Literatura, y Artes*, 1805, I, 163-64.
35. Rosa Gálvez, *Un loco hace ciento*, "Advertencia" (Madrid, 1801).
36. *Un loco hace ciento*, drama original

en un acto, escrito por Doña M. R. G. y refundida para ópera por D. A. S. V. (Cádiz, 1816).
37. *El Memorial Literario*, 1801, II, 64.
38. Rosa Gálvez, *Los figurones literarios*, Act III, Sc. 12.
39. *Ibid.*, Act I, Sc. 9.
40. *Ibid.*
41. *Ibid.*
42. *Ibid.*, Act. I, Sc. 8.
43. Rosa Gálvez, *El Egoista (Obras Poéticas)*, Act III, Sc. 11.
44. *Ibid.*, Act III, Sc. 13.
45. Cotarelo y Mori, *Máiquez*, pp. 215-16).
46. Serrano y Sanz, *op. cit.*, p. 452.
47. *El Memorial Literario*, 1802, II, 97.
48. *Ibid.*, 1801, I, 213.
49. *Ibid.*
50. *Ibid.*
51. *Ibid.*
52. *El Regañón General*, August 10, 1803.
53. *Ibid.*
54. *Ibid.*, November 16, 1803.
55. Alonzo Cortés, *op. cit.*, p. viii.
56. Julio Cejador y Frauca, *Historia de la lengua y literatura castellana* (14 vols; Madrid, 1915-22), VI, 291.
57. Alonso Cortés, *op. cit.*, p. viii.
58. Azorín (Martínez Ruiz), *Lecturas españolas*, 1920, p. 130.
59. José Mor de Fuentes, *El calavera* (Madrid, en la imprenta de Cano, 1800).
60. Quoted from Cejador y Frauca, *op. cit.*, VI, 291.
61. Mor de Fuentes, *La mujer varonil* (Madrid, en la imprenta de Cano, 1800). This comedy is rare; Cejador y Frauca and other critics do not mention it.
62. *Ibid.*, "Prefacio" pp. 3-4.
63. *Ibid.*
64. *Ibid.*, p. 10.
65. Juan Ignacio González del Castillo, *Obras Completas* (3 Vols.; Madrid, 1914).
66. *El Censor*, October, 1821, II, 189-91.
67. Simón de Viegas, *El Rábula*, comedia en tres actos (Madrid, 1803).
68. *Ibid.*, "Nota."
69. Cotarelo y Mori, *Máiquez*, pp. 184-85.
70. *El Regañón General*, November 2, 1803.
71. *Minerva o el Revisor General*, 1807, V, 130-31.
72. *El Censor*, June 2, 1821.

XIV

Sentimental Comedy

THE LATTER PART of the eighteenth century saw the Spanish stage overrun by the type of sentimental comedy which, starting in France with Nivelle de la Chaussée's *Le Prejugé a la mode,* had dominated the French theater to the practical exclusion of true comedy. Luzán, in Spain, had yielded to the attraction of that play and had translated it into Spanish in 1751 with the title *Reason Against Fashion.* In 1791 Jovellanos achieved a marked success with *The Honorable Culprit,* which met with the almost complete approval of neo-classic critics. Comella, Zavala y Zamora, and others of their school filled their plays with sentiment mixed with melodrama. The type of sentimental comedy which was further developed in France by Diderot and his followers was supposed to bridge the gap between tragedy and comedy, and came to be known in that country as the *drame.*

In Spain sentimental comedy found many defenders even among the staunchest neo-classicists. Santos Díez in the preface to *The New Spanish Theater,* published in 1799, declares that

... those plays that the moderns call *serious* or *tearful* comedies, or *urbane* tragedies, will not be excluded, for, although this new dramatic genre was not well received at first by many men of authority in the field of dramatic poetry, it has, nevertheless, made for itself such a place in all the cultured theaters of Europe that it would be odd not to admit it into ours.[1]

The preface quotes at length from the *History of All Literature* (IV, 356), in which the author, Don Juan Andrés, defends the new genre:

I do not see why a theatrical composition should be scorned which, under any name that may be given to it, is able to touch the heart with the keenest emotions and inspire a useful morality, and which completely fulfils the purpose of the theater, which is to delight and to instruct . . .[2]

In 1800 the Spanish stage was taken by storm by the sentimental comedy, *Misanthropy and Repentance*, by the German dramatist Kotzebue. This play had been recast into French by a certain Madame Molé and had achieved an almost unprecedented triumph in Paris. Following the well-established precedent of not consulting original works but of translating French recasts, Dionisio Solís, the new prompter at the theater of the Príncipe, took Madame Molé's version and turned it into Castilian verse. On its initial run the play lasted from January 30 to February 16, 1800, and produced 128,404 reals. It was given its second run in January, 1801, and produced 69,386 reals in ten performances. No play on the Spanish stage, except comedies of magic, had ever attracted such crowds. In February, 1801, this play was warmly praised by the *Memorial Literario:*

We have seen the drama entitled *Misanthropy and Repentance* performed for the second time; and for the second time we have seen the public flock to see it with the same interest; which is an unmistakable proof that it is one of the most interesting plays in the modern theater and one of the most worthy of appreciation by sensitive hearts and by lovers of virtue and good taste. In fact, it would be hard to find among modern productions one that has made as deep, as general, and as lasting an impression on the spectators as this work by the famous Kotzebue in all the theaters of Europe . . .[3]

After the first wave of enthusiasm had died away many critics realized that their praise had perhaps been too lavish. The *Memorial Literario* modified its judgment in its issue of February 22 of the same year, although it later found itself again in the position of defending this work and sentimental comedy in general.

Shortly after the initial performance of *Misanthropy and Repentance* a writer who signed himself P. Z. saw in the popular acclaim that it received evidence that "good comedies do not need brilliant decorations, dances, or battles like those found in *The Masquerade of Amiens* and *Alexander in Soghiana* to attract a crowd." He also noted with satisfaction that for some time interest in the performances of plays had not been interrupted during the intermissions "by the mixture of *sainetes* and *tonadillas.*"[4] Later in the same month a writer who signed himself Z. praised the original work and the French recast, both of which were in prose and in five acts, but objected to the liberty Solís took in reducing the play to three acts and putting it into Spanish verse. As a result, he says, "at each instant one finds obscure and languid thoughts, and disarranged passages." In April of the same year another critic with the initials Y.B.M. recognized the immense popularity of the play, but dared to question its real merit, denying that it possessed the characteristics of a good comedy:

> *Misanthropy and Repentance,* the comedy that has been performed recently with so much applause and such attendance, and which has pleased and should please everyone with its theme, is a bad comedy, although it is a very good, very moral, and very tender story. Do not be displeased that I should criticize this comedy when the general acclaim with which it has been received, and the tears that it has made so many shed, including myself, give such evidence of its merit. I say that we must make an effort not to confuse a good comedy with a good story. One is quite different from the other. There is scarcely a writer of average ability who is not capable of forming a story that will hold the spectators in suspense and touch their hearts, but not all those who can do this are able to write a comedy. . . .[5]

From 1800 to 1803 the periodicals were filled with articles for and against Kotzebue's play and sentimental comedy in general. The popularity of these plays with the public increased so much that they threatened for a while to supplant all other types. In an attempt to meet this competition, heroic comedies were given a strong injection of sentiment, and even neo-classic comedies paid their tribute to sentimentality. In 1802 Andrés Miñano attacked the *tearful comedy* with the same weapon Moratín had used against the extravagant heroic comedies of Comella and Zavala y Zamora. Using *Misanthropy and Repentance* as a target, he sought by ridicule to drive such plays from the theater. In the "Preliminary Discourse" to his comedy *The Taste of the Day* (1802),[6] he traces briefly the history of the *pathetic genre.* He states that his object is to "arrest the progress of sad, doleful comedies." He admits that sentimental dramas have in themselves a great attraction since they share the interest which accompanies any novelistic action. The public is predisposed in their favor and does not readily forget the emotions they arouse. To this incentive to compose works of this type is added the difficulty of writing good comedies, since an author of true comedies must combine great talent and poetic genius with long study, close observation, and especially the gift of presenting in a humorous manner the extravagancies of his age. Miñano voices at this point the oft-repeated idea that the government should subsidize regular comedy, since through it many disorders are corrected which cannot be successfully attacked by law.

According to Miñano, the French, not finding a successor to the immortal Molière, opened their doors to the pathetic genre which offered more variety in scenic effects and made easier the road to fame. The works of this type that have appeared in France and in other nations are legion, but the most popular of all has been *Misanthropy and Repentance* by Kotzebue. Miñano admits:

It must be confessed in good faith that this drama is superior to all that have been written in its class, if we consider only the seductive delicacy, or rather that species of magic with which the author controls our most intimate emotions, moving, melting, and even breaking at will the hearts of the spectators.[7]

In *The Taste of the Day,* Miñano has the Marqués say:

Don't laugh, gentlemen, the drama, *Misanthropy and Repentance,* has caused in Paris two hundred epileptic fits, forty abortions, and seven sudden deaths. When, oh when will we achieve such glorious triumphs here in Madrid![8]

Don Alfonso answers ironically:

I am certainly filled with shame when I see the stupid people who have performed and who have attended *Misanthropy and Repentance* walking around the streets without at least having their mouths twisted and their eyes out of their sockets, and without crutches.[9]

After pointing out the improbable situations in the play, its faulty technique, and its atrocious moral, the author gives his attention to the defects of the pathetic genre in general. Basing his argument on Muñarriz' translation and additions to the work of Hugo Blair on *belles lettres*, he limits drama to tragedy and comedy, the tools of the former being terror and compassion and of the latter ridicule. He concludes that "this definition, which is as exact as it is adjusted to the precepts established by the masters of art, should close the door completely to any innovation."[10] Miñano believes that Spaniards have less reason to admit the pathetic genre than other nations because the Spanish theater abounds in "most pleasing comedies, which, in spite of the defects that were perhaps unavoidable at the time they were written and the disorder which is characteristic of an ardent and too poetic imagination, at least have the advantage of not provoking that ennui which we notice in foreign plays."[11] He also believes that the Spanish *comedia* is a faithful picture of the manners of its age and that it has always been characterized by "ridicule, wit, and comic force." The solution, according to Miñano, is for the government, in addition to encouraging original works, to put into execution the idea proposed in the creation of the Board of Control of the Theaters in regard to reworking *cloak and sword* plays and comedies that deal with ridiculous figures.

In order that the public may see that his criticism is based upon good authority, Miñano quotes at length from "one of the greatest French dramatists," without, however, giving his name. According to this French critic, no play which was even tolerable was produced in France from the death of Molière to the year 1697, in which Regnard wrote his *Le Joueur (The Gambler)*. Since nothing is so difficult as to make educated people laugh, the theater was reduced to presenting romantic comedies which were less faithful pictures of the ridiculous aspects of men's characters than "experiments in that urbane tragedy, or illegitimate poetic genre, which being neither tragic nor comic, manifests the inability of their authors to compose either tragedies or comedies."[12] From this time on, the French critic is represented as saying, the comic element was banished from comedy, and sentiment was substituted in its place. He does not deny that two or three pathetic scenes may be very effective in a comedy, since examples of such moderate use of sentiment are found in Terence and even in Molière; but he insists that it is necessary to return immediately to the simple and humorous depiction of manners. In short, declares the French critic, when French dramatists lost their ability to make audiences laugh, comedy became disfigured and tragedy soon met the same fate, with the result that now only monstrous plays are seen in each genre.

Although the principal object of his attack is *Misanthropy and Repentance,* Miñano states in the "Preliminary Discourse" that in the subordinate episodes he wishes "to oppose the frivolity and bad taste which the blind imitation of everything that is seen in or comes from foreign countries produces in our young people."[13] In this matter Miñano aligns himself with Iriarte, who, in his *Ill-bred Miss,* had introduced as a secondary character the exaggerated type of marquis who affected French culture and who looked with scorn upon everything Spanish. Like its model, *The New Comedy* by Moratín,

The Taste of the Day is written in prose and is divided into two acts. The plot is reduced to a minimum.

Don Ruperto Escamilla and his wife, Doña Eulalia, have arranged the marriage of their daughter, Doña Jacinta, to the Marqués of Bombonera. At the opening of the comedy they are awaiting his arrival. Doña Eulalia, who is an ardent supporter of tearful comedies, in order not to arrive late at the performance of *Misanthropy and Repentance,* which is scheduled for that evening, leaves for the theater, telling her husband to accompany the Marqués, when he arrives, to her box.

When the Marqués comes in, Don Ruperto receives him and delivers his wife's message. The Marqués is a most ridiculous character who speaks a jargon of French, Italian, and Spanish, and who has a profound scorn for everything Spanish. An argument follows between him and Don Alfonso, a friend of the family and a secret admirer of Doña Jacinta, over the merits of sentimental comedy, Don Alfonso ridiculing the genre and the Marqués warmly defending it and attacking the Spanish *comedia.*

Don Alfonso and the Marqués go to the theater to join Doña Eulalia, leaving Don Ruperto to make the necessary arrangements for supper. In a short time Don Alfonso and the Marqués return bringing with them Doña Eulalia, who has been overcome by emotion during the performance of the play. The lady begins to rave about her infidelity to her husband. She says she has been unfaithful to him and declares herself unworthy of his forgiveness. It soon becomes apparent to those who have witnessed the performance that in her delirium she is repeating lines from the play. Don Ruperto believes his wife is making a true confession and remembers a certain youth who has frequently been seen in her company. Don Alfonso finally convinces the husband of the true state of affairs. The Marqués reproves Don Ruperto for being so ready to condemn the supposed affair between his wife and the youth and insists that even if his wife had been guilty he should have emulated the husband in *Misanthropy and Repentance* and overlooked her unfaithfulness. Don Ruperto becomes angered upon hearing the extravagant ideas of the Marqués and realizes that his daughter has been right in not wishing to marry him. The Marqués becomes incensed in his turn when he sees that they do not appreciate the beauties of *Misanthropy and Repentance,* and he leaves. Don Alfonso asks for Jacinta's hand, which the father readily grants.

According to the *Memorial Literario,* the success of the play was due in no small measure to the imitation of the raving of Doña Eulalia and the affected mimicry of the role which the actress performed with such skill that she drew repeated and sustained applause from the audience. The *Memorial* adds: "The play ends then in a parody, making a serious role ridiculous. In the same manner all good plays can be ridiculed, as happens in the tragedy *Manolo,* which affects a tragic style although its subject matter is despicable."[14]

But just as Ramón de la Cruz's play was unsuccessful in its attack upon tragedies, good comedies will be unaffected by parody and mockery. The *Memorial* hastens to say that it is not attempting to pass upon the merits of *Misanthropy and Repentance,* since this is such a debatable subject. True, the play does not excite laughter, which seems to be the test the author of *The Taste of the Day* would apply to comedy; but it is well known that it would be difficult to find thirty amusing plays among the many thousands that have been performed in all the modern theaters of Europe. The *Memorial* cites, in support of its position, the French critic Marmontel, who divides comedy into *comedies of character, comedies of situation,* and *comedies of tenderness.* Although it has been frequently stated that the purpose of comedy is to ridicule the eccentricities and vices of men, the *Memorial* denies that this rule is observed in either ancient or modern comedy and maintains that "every action on the stage which can agreeably entertain people of intelligence and taste without arousing vehement passions or very strong feelings is a good comedy."[15]

If we compare this definition with that given by the *Memorial* in its first number of January, 1784,[16] we see clearly the change in the attitude of that periodical. The first definition is only a restatement of that of Luzán. Now the *Memorial* leaves out entirely any allusion to the didactic purpose of comedy or to its essentially comic nature. It says that Aristotle's idea of comedy as "a representation of that which is laughable, reprehensible, or extravagant in men's characters and actions" adequately described comedy as it was in his time, but that it believes modern comedy is rather "the representation of that which is agreeable and pleasurable in civil life, and in the characters, manners, and actions of men."[17] By experience everyone knows that reasonable and virtuous actions, manners that conform to nature, and characters free from eccentricities and extravagance

may and do please on the stage. This definition in no way excludes
sentimental comedy and is even broad enough to include much of
the romantic drama that came later.

The Taste of the Day soon involved its author in a polemic with
a translator who, signing himself Pedro Rico, launched an attack in
the Regañón General. The articles by this adversary and the answers
by Miñano run from July 2 to September 24, 1803. Pedro Rico
resents the criticism of contemporary translations contained in
The Taste of the Day and wishes to make it clear that he is not one
of those miserable translators who, without native ability or study,
translate everything that falls into their hands. On the contrary, he
says, he has worked hard—very hard—to learn the exact equivalent
of French words and expressions, both cultured and colloquial, in the
Castilian language.[18] In the following number he viciously assails
Miñano's comedy. It must be confessed that much of his criticism of
the technical defects of The Taste of the Day is just. He scoffs at
Miñano's statement that his purpose is "to arrest the progress of sad
and doleful comedies," for he considers that this is only one episode
of the comedy:

But this is only an episode of the action; an attempt is made to
achieve this object with the words of a fatuous person, a meddler, who
contributes nothing to the play, and with an improbable event; consequently, you do not achieve your purpose; nor, since this episode is
alien to the principal action, could it aid in the development of the plot.
If the cold lover, Don Alfonso, and the insipid sweetheart, Doña Jacinta,
had prepared this stratagem to get out of their difficulty, perhaps, perhaps
it might have been justified.[19]

Pedro Rico does not believe that The Taste of the Day will have any
effect whatever upon the general popularity of Misanthropy and
Repentance:

Who do you think will refrain from going to see Misanthropy, though
it be given a thousand times, if he likes it, just because of the fear of
being left maimed, crippled, epileptic, or dead with emotion? No, Mr.
Taste of the Day, this is not the way to correct men's manners. The sad
effects must be possible; and not only possible, but the necessary consequence of the vices that are being ridiculed; otherwise the ridicule is
useless, impertinent, and despicable like your composition.[20]

The success of The Taste of the Day on the stage was probably
due, to a considerable extent, to the performance of Máiquez in the

role of the Marqués. This actor had resented keenly a criticism of his performance in *Blanca and Moncasín, or the Venetians,* by Arnaud, and of the style of acting he had acquired in France. This criticism, which had been published earlier that year in the *Memorial,* was written by Juan Bautista Arriaza, who enjoyed considerable reputation as a poet and critic, but who apparently affected French mannerisms. In playing the role of the Marqués, we are told, Máiquez came out "imitating Arriaza so perfectly in dress and mannerisms that the likeness was immediately apparent to everyone."[21]

The Taste of the Day was performed eight times during December, 1802, but since it was composed to meet a particular situation, naturally did not enjoy a lasting popularity. Miñano expressed himself as entirely satisfied with the reception accorded the comedy and was unwilling to concede that the success was due entirely to the acting of Máiquez:

The truth is (no matter how much it may displease the *Regañador* and others who have been badly wounded) that the clever handling of ridicule was what caused *The Taste of the Day* to be applauded at all of its performances, in spite of the fact that it is entirely lacking in stage effects; and although I shall never deny that the one who played the role of the Marqués did so with great effectiveness, it is also necessary to call attention to the fact that no one has ever extracted juice from dry fruit.[22]

Miñano also believes that his comedy has adequately fulfilled the purpose for which it was written:

Translations have improved and doleful comedies have completely lost their popularity; the last time *Misanthropy and Repentance* was performed at the Cruz, the fact that it produced but a slight effect on the spectators was quite evident; these spectators even laughed at the very situations which formerly had made them weep.[23]

Although *The Taste of the Day* seems to have been effective in diminishing the popularity of *Misanthropy and Repentance,* it had no effect upon the pathetic genre in general, which gained rather than lost in popularity during the early part of the nineteenth century, and which was not without its influence upon those who are considered the chief exponents of neo-classic comedy—Moratín, Gorostiza, and Martínez de la Rosa. As will be noted, the sentimental element is especially apparent in the later works of Gil y Zárate.

In 1821 the thoroughly classic periodical *El Censor,* after recognizing that the defects which have been attributed to the Spanish *comedia,* to the English theater, and to the German innovations are real defects which must be avoided in any drama that aspires to perfection, adds:

Our severity will not be such that we will banish sentimental dramas or historical tragedies from the theater, although we shall always attend the *Miser* and *Zaïre* with greater pleasure; but we shall never approve the adoption on the stage of the monstrous romantic dramas that break all the rules of the theater.[24]

The attitude of Jovellanos toward the pathetic genre may be easily inferred from the fact that he chose to write his *The Honorable Culprit* in conformity with that type. In the introduction to his edition of the *Selected Works* of this author, Angel del Río insists upon the difference between the ideas expressed in his *Report on Public Spectacles* and those generally held by neo-classicists and suggests their closer affiliation with Rousseau's *Letter on Spectacles.* Jovellanos' position with regard to the Spanish *comedia,* to contemporary plays, and to the rules which should govern drama does not, however, differ in any essential respect from that of other neo-classicists. He evidently considered that *The Honorable Culprit* did not violate the precepts of the school. In the *Report on Public Spectacles* he says:

The reform of our theaters should begin with the banishment of almost all the dramas that are being performed at the present time. I am not speaking only of those for which the spectators today show a foolish and barbarous preference, those that are the abortions of a gang of hungry and ignorant poetasters, who have taken possession of the stage in order to drive from it all decorum, verisimilitude, interest, good language, civility, humor, and Castilian wit. Such monsters will disappear at the first glance cast upon the stage by reason and good sense. I am speaking also of those that are justly celebrated among us, which at one time served as a model for other nations, and which have been and are still regarded by the wisest and most enlightened portion of our nation with enthusiasm and delight. I shall always be the first to confess their inimitable beauty, the novelty of their invention, the beauty of their style, the fluency and naturalness of their dialogue, the marvelous craftsmanship in their plots, the facility of their solutions, the fire, the interest, the jokes, and the comic wit that shine so brilliantly in all of them.[25]

But all of these estimable qualities are unimportant, in his opinion, if, considered in the light of the precepts and of common sense, they are accompanied by vices that make them detrimental to public interest. At this point he quotes from the article by Forner that had appeared in the same year in *La Espigadera:*

Who can deny that in these comedies, *according to the vehement expression of a modern critic,* one sees painted in the most delightful colors the most indecent solicitations, elopements of maidens, scaling the walls of noble houses, resistance to law, duels, and challenges that are based upon a false concept of honor, approved abductions, attempted and executed acts of violence, insolent buffoons, man- and maidservants who glory in and profit by their infamous mediations?[26]

It is necessary, Jovellanos declares, to replace these comedies with others, "that will be capable of delighting and instructing by presenting documents which will perfect the spirit and the heart of the class of persons who attend the theaters most frequently."[27] He is very explicit in enumerating the qualities that dramas should have in order to justify their performance on the stage. The theater, in his opinion, should be an instrument for the propagation of the highest forms of religion, morality, and patriotism. In the theater one should see

. . . continuous and heroic examples of reverence for the Supreme Being and the religion of our fathers; of love for the fatherland, for the Sovereign and the Constitution; of respect for hierarchies, laws, and constituted authority; of conjugal fidelity; of paternal love; of tenderness and filial obedience; a theater which will present good and magnanimous principles, humane and incorruptible magistrates, citizens filled with virtue and patriotism, prudent and zealous heads of families, faithful and constant friends; in a word, heroic and strong men, lovers of public good, zealous of their liberty and their rights, protectors of innocence and stalwart foes of iniquity. . . .[28]

He is equally explicit in enumerating the vices which he considers fit subjects for ridicule in comedies:

. . . pride and baseness, prodigality and avarice, flattery and hypocrisy, supine religious indifference and superstitious credulity, loquacity and indiscretion, the ridiculous affectation of nobility, of power, of influence, of wisdom, of friendship; and, in short, all the manias, all the abuses, all the bad habits into which men fall when they leave the path of virtue, honor, and good breeding to abandon themselves to their passions and caprices.[29]

Although he would banish from the theater the tiresome emphasis upon effeminate love affairs such as were never found in the "beautiful and sublime tragedies of the ancients," he does not object to the use of love as a motivating force provided it is held in restraint "by the laws of honor and decency." Certainly, the severest neo-classicists could find nothing objectionable in any of the above statements. And yet Jovellanos composed a sentimental comedy in prose, his only incursion into the field of comedy. He probably felt that his work met the neo-classic requirements for this genre, since it conformed to the unities and was designed to correct human defects.

Menéndez y Pelayo calls *The Honorable Culprit* the "first Spanish work worth remembering in that type of urbane tragedy or lachrymose comedy that La Chaussée and Diderot popularized in France,"[30] and declares that lachrymose comedy is the germ of the modern drama of manners.

In his "Historical Sketch of the Spanish Theater," Moratín indicates his disapproval of this type of comedy, which he calls "tragi-comedy," while praising certain features of Jovellanos' play. *The Honorable Culprit*, he says, "although too far removed from the nature of good comedy, was admired for its expression of emotions, its good language, and the excellent prose of its dialogue."[31] Moratín seemed unaware of the fact that his own comedies at times bordered upon sentimental comedy. It is not surprising that this type of comedy should be accepted by all except the most dogmatic of the neo-classicists. This group had insisted from the time of Luzán that the justification of all drama lay primarily in its didactic potentialities. The theater should be "a school of manners." It should imitate life and must necessarily avoid affectation and extravagance.

The attitude of the *Regañón General*, the first number of which appeared in 1803, is one of the most striking examples of the effect produced by the pathetic genre within the ranks of the neo-classicists. On October 29 of that year, the *President* of that periodical published an article entitled "The Theater with Relation to Manners," in which he recognized that there were many vices that could not be made the object of ridicule, because "they are so odious that any humor is out of place in them. They are, therefore, not fit subjects for jesting; but they should not, for this reason, be left unpunished by public disapproval."[32] The task of ridiculing those vices that are only inconvenient or disagreeable should be left to humorous comedies, "but serious vices, particularly those that are harmful to society, and vices which, instead of being condemned by society, seem to be approved by it, and which cannot be suppressed by law, should also receive their punishment." The god-less man, the hypocrite, the boaster, the ingrate, the slanderer, the seducer and corrupter of innocence, and the false friend "would be treated too gently if we were content only to laugh at them." Such characters, he says, "should be exposed not to the laughter of the public, but to its indignation, and I see no reason why serious comedy should not undertake this task."[33] The *President* recognizes that this genre does not meet the approval of everyone and that many consider it "monstrous," but he wishes to know,

... What can there be monstrous in presenting vices that cause odium from their most reprehensible side; in showing moral turpitude in all situations of life; in pointing out their evil consequences, contrasting them with lovable virtues that contribute to the happiness and charm of society; and in giving instruction through example about duties that are difficult to discharge?[34]

In the present condition of the Spanish stage one must be content that the plays produced on the stage "not familiarize the public with vice, that vice not be treated as a joke, that new kinds of corruption not be introduced, that virtue not come to be scorned by exposing it to public laughter, and that the public not be entertained at the expense of its innocence."

It is evident that in the opinion of many neo-classicists *serious comedy* or *sentimental comedy* fulfilled the requirements of a regular theater. As long as the unities were observed and the so-called comedy had a moral purpose, they were willing to dispense with the comic element. The line between real comedy and that which many chose to call *serious comedy* rather than *lachrymose comedy* or *urbane tragedy* is sometimes rather difficult to draw. We find a very strong tendency among critics to excuse the absence of *vis cómica* even in works of such leaders as Moratín, and in those of his followers, Martínez de la Rosa and Gorostiza.

1. *Teatro Nuevo Español* (Madrid, 1800) I, xx.
2. *Ibid.*, p. xxi.
3. *El Memorial Literario*, February 4, 1801.
4. *Diario de Madrid*, February 15, 1800.
5. *Ibid.*, April 7, 1800.
6. Andrés Miñano, *El gusto del día*,

comedia original en dos actos, con un Discurso preliminar (Valencia, 1802).
7. "Discurso preliminar."
8. *El gusto del día*, Act II, Sc. 6.
9. *Ibid.*
10. "Discurso preliminar."
11. *Ibid.*
12. *Ibid.*

13. *Ibid.*
14. *El Memorial Literario,* 1803, IV, 245-53.
15. *Ibid.*
16. See p. 314 above.
17. *El Memorial Literario,* IV, 245-53.
18. *El Regañón General,* July 2, 1803.
19. *Ibid.,* July 9, 1803.
20. *Ibid.*
21. Antonio Alcalá Galiano, *Recuerdos de un anciano* (Madrid, 1878), p. 72.
22. *El Regañón General,* September 3, 1803.
23. *Ibid.*
24. *El Censor,* April 21, 1821.

25. Jovellanos, *Obras Escogidas (Clásicos Castellanos,* II, 28).
26. *Ibid.,* pp. 28-29. This is the article which, as we have seen, appeared in *La Espigadera,* No. I, 1790, and which was obviously written by Forner: it was included with little change in his *Exequias.*
27. *Ibid.*
28. *Ibid.,* pp. 29-30.
29. *Ibid.,* p. 30.
30. Menéndez y Pelayo, *op. cit.,* III, 399.
31. Moratín, *Obras,* p. 319.
32. *El Regañón General,* Oct. 29, 1803.
33. *Ibid.*
34. *Ibid.*

XV

Neo-classic Comedy after Moratín

AFTER the production of *The Consent of Young Maidens* and the storm of protest it aroused among nationalist critics, Moratín withdrew from the theater. The turbulent political condition of the country soon diverted the attention of those few writers who might have devoted their energies to drama and, in the words of Mesonero Romanos, "the modern Spanish theater was dying in its infancy from complete lack of support."[1] At the close of the war in 1814, however, the neo-classic movement received fresh impetus from the works of two dramatists of more than ordinary ability. The first of these, Martínez de la Rosa, had already composed a comedy, *The Power of a Position,* which was performed for the first time in Cádiz in 1810, but which did not reach the theater in Madrid until October 24, 1812. His next comedy, *The Daughter at Home and the Mother at the Masquerade,* was not produced until 1821, and his remaining contributions to neo-classic comedy: *Unfounded Jealousy* (1831?) and *The Wedding and the Duel* (1839), were not performed until after his brief and mild incursion into the field of romanticism.

Manuel Eduardo de Gorostiza, whose neo-classic comedies were all composed from 1818 to 1833, is sometimes considered as the outstanding leader of the Moratinists. It may be fairly said that, from the retirement of Moratín until the advent of romanticism, the history of neo-classic comedy in Spain is little more than a projection of the literary personality of that author. The forces which were to culminate in the romantic movement were very much in evidence by 1821, and the subsequent history of the Spanish stage is largely an account of the rivalry of these two groups, which ended in a temporary and uncertain victory for the romanticists, followed by a period of eclecticism which prevailed to the end of the century. Lista, in *El Censor,* gives a picture of the condition of the Spanish theater in 1821:

If any theater should attract the attention of a periodical that is both political and literary, it is without doubt the Spanish, which in its present condition is made up of the most discordant moral and literary elements. From the *Devil Turned Preacher* and *Saint Pascual Baylón* to *The Female Hypocrite* in the comic genre, and the translations of Voltaire and of Alfieri in the tragic, there is no gradation or degradation that is not welcomed on our stage. Comedies of Saints, those that deal with God and the Virgin, comedies of magic, comedies of heroic love affairs, *cloak and sword* plays, comedies that deal with Moors and Christians, comedies of caricatures in the manner of Cañizares, and lately comedies of manners follow each other in our theaters, mixed with innumerable translations that we have made from the French and Italian theaters. . . .[2]

From 1814 to 1833 many writers besides Martínez de la Rosa and Gorostiza composed original comedies, but only three deserve more than a passing mention: Javier de Burgos, Gil y Zárate, and Bretón de los Herreros.

Martínez de la Rosa

Although all of Martínez de la Rosa's comedies except *The Power of a Position* are subsequent to Gorostiza's period of greatest activity, he will be treated first since, in theory at least, he is the direct heir of the master, Moratín.

His first comedy, *The Power of a Position*, was given its initial performance in Cádiz in 1810 during the bombardment of that city by the English. Alcalá Galiano makes a brief mention of this first performance: "The theater was in a dangerous section, and I have already told in another place how a shell passed over us and fell very near while the audience was wildly applauding Martínez de la Rosa's *The Power of a Position*."[3] This play, a two-act comedy in prose in the Moratinian manner, was composed in the short space of one week. The comedy, indeed, reveals a certain lack of polish which may be attributed not only to its hasty composition, but to the inexperience of the author. In his "Foreword" to the first edition Martínez de la Rosa gives a statement of the moral lesson contained in the work and modestly recognizes its defects:

The keen desire to present upon the stage a certain type of hypocrite, who under the cover of religion opposed beneficial reforms, stimulated me to undertake as a mere pastime the composition of this comedy. Since it is my first attempt in such a difficult genre and since it was planned and finished in the short period of a week and has been neither corrected nor polished, I cannot flatter myself that it has literary merit.[4]

The plot of this comedy is simple enough to meet the approval of the most exigent neo-classicist. The entire play revolves around the love affairs of Don Teodoro, a liberal in politics, and Carlota, the daughter of the reactionary Don Fabián. The marriage of the lovers is threatened by the opposition of Don Melitón, who seeks to prejudice Don Fabián against Don Teodoro by declaiming against the dangers of liberalism. The father of the latter, Don Luis, also a liberal, aids the lovers and succeeds in unmasking the hypocritical Don Melitón, who is shown to be a despicable egoist, willing to betray the very principles he has so warmly defended in order to obtain a position within the liberal party. The title of the play, *The Power of a Position,* suggests the stratagem used in the solution of the comedy. The play ends with the reconciliation of Don Teodoro and Don Fabián and the betrothal of the lovers.

The character of Don Melitón is admirably portrayed. His baseness is brought into pronounced relief by contrast with Don Fabián, who, although imbued with the same opinions which Don Melitón pretends to hold, is sincere in his convictions. The author contrasts the patriot with the egoist, the man whose errors are due to prejudice with the hypocrite. Within the same party are found both honesty and immorality. Because of the political association of such contradictory elements, it is necessary to be both tolerant and severe in dealing with political problems. Lista states the lesson to be derived from this comedy:

> So that, in addition to the natural and direct moral lesson the plot presents in itself, this rule can be deduced indirectly, without which there is no salvation in periods of political turmoil: "Let us convince those who are deluded; let us unmask the hypocrites and let us punish only those who are delinquent.[5]

It would be difficult to crowd into one character more despicable qualities than those found in Don Melitón. He is cowardly, stupid, and egotistical, actuated only by self-interest, and ready to repay the kindness of his benefactor, Don Fabián, with the basest ingratitude. After his attempted treachery has failed he seeks to regain Don Fabián's esteem, and when he sees that Don Fabián can no longer be deceived, he threatens to denounce him to the authorities as a freemason.

Lista insists that this comedy is more than a "comedy of circumstances":

> This play should not be placed among those that are of purely transi-

tory interest. It has a very profound didactic purpose, which is indicated and developed with great skill. . . . It will remain in the repertoire of the theater and its performance will always be applauded, because men will always have reason to recognize "the power of a position."[6]

That the play did, indeed, meet the approval of the spectators for a number of years is evidenced by the fact that it was played twenty-three times from 1820 to 1822. On its first run in Madrid it lasted for five days in October, 1812, and was repeated on November 12, 13, and 22, 1814.

The language of the comedy is free from affectation and is suited to the characters, who conform entirely to the classical requirement of uniformity. Carlota thinks only of her love and her father only of the dangers of liberalism. The base Melitón is consistently portrayed and shows none of the belated repentance so often employed by classicists in their assumed role of correctors of public morals. The action of the play, because of its lack of complication, is easily brought within the unities.

Martínez de la Rosa's next comedy, *The Daughter at Home and the Mother at the Masquerade*, in three acts and in verse, was not composed until eleven years later (1821). This is distinctly a comedy of manners and follows closely the pattern set by Moratín. The object of the author, as Larra points out, is "to convince foolish mothers, who are at the same time frivolous old women, of the danger to which they expose their daughters when they neglect their education for the gay whirl of society, which neither their age nor their domestic and social responsibility can induce them to forego."[7] In order to accomplish this purpose it is necessary, according to Larra, to paint the consequences of violations of maternal duties in such a manner that the mother will be thoroughly ashamed of her conduct and will shed "bitter tears of repentance."[8] This is precisely the method used by Martínez de la Rosa in *The Daughter at Home*. In his "Foreword" to the comedy, he says: "I chose as the subject of this composition the censure of a vice, . . . common in the present condition of the world, of the bad example and neglect of mothers."[9]

In this play a mother who refuses to recognize the passage of years uses artificial adornments and a forced vivacity in a vain attempt to hide her age. She thinks only of pleasure and imagines that she still has all the charm necessary to insure the admiration and attention of young men. She even carries her coquetry to the extreme of trying to steal the suitor for her daughter's hand. This suitor is a heartless philanderer, who attempts to woo the mother and the daughter at the same time. The mother is finally brought to realize the serious consequences of her conduct and the danger to which she has allowed her daughter to be exposed. There is a convenient young man in the comedy, who, in spite of his knowledge of the passion of the girl for the philanderer and of her attempted elopement, is now quite willing to marry her.

On December 8, 1821, *El Universal* published an unsigned review of this comedy. The critic begins his remarks with the statement that "the composition of an original comedy is one of the most difficult works to which the human mind can apply itself, because, with the great number of writers who have devoted themselves, with more or less success, to dramatic poetry, little room remains for anything except copies or imitations."[10] The purpose of comedy, he says, is to describe manners in such a way as to encourage the imitation of virtue and the correction of contemporary vices. The poet may choose to ridicule the prejudices and defects peculiar to each generation. But in this type of play, when the circumstances that give rise to the motive for ridicule have passed, the effect is lost. The reviewer cites *The Café (The New Comedy)* by Moratín and *One Fool Makes a Hundred* by María Rosa Gálvez de Cabrera as examples of plays which were composed to meet temporary conditions and believes that "they will only serve in the future as documents for the history of our civilization and manners."[11] In order that a comedy may have a lasting appeal, it is necessary for it to combat vices common to all ages and to all countries. There have always been "hypocrites, misers, cheats, covetous people, etc," and these characters are always fit subjects for ridicule. The reviewer finds that *The Daughter at Home* possesses this universality because "the moral purpose of this play is to show the consequences of the bad conduct of certain old coquettes, who, neglecting the care of their families and the custody of their daughters, run incessantly from the theater to dances and from promenades to parties."[12]

The comedy is well constructed, the characters interesting and true to life, and the dialogue completely natural. The play is marred, however, by a too obvious moral purpose, reinforced with long speeches by the uncle. There are in the first act several of these sermons, typical of the school of Moratín, which become rather tiresome. The critic in *El Universal* regrets that Martínez de la Rosa did not follow Moratín in alternating comic and pathetic scenes. In the third act, he says,

... it would have been desirable for some slightly different comic scenes to have been interpolated between the sentimental passages as in *The Consent of Young Maidens*, where, in spite of the disillusionment of Don Diego and his sad sacrifice, the queer conduct of Doña Irene, and especially the contrast between the two old people, excite the laughter of the spectators and leave them with no feeling of sadness at the end of the comedy.[13]

Larra also calls attention to the dominance of the pathetic note in *The Daughter at Home* and to the similarity of Martínez de la Rosa's technique to Moratín's. He finds entirely excusable, however, the former's failure to interpolate comic scenes.

Since Larra's article is so entirely in line with the position taken in 1803 by the *Regañón General*,[14] it may not be out of order to give a somewhat detailed analysis of it. According to Larra, the writer of comedy has only one object: the correction of the vice which is proposed as the theme of the work. The means he chooses, however, may differ. He may choose to treat the vice in the manner of Molière, presenting its ridiculous side, or he may choose to follow writers like Kotzebue, who correct vice "by developing before our eyes the incidents of passion and drawing tears from our hearts."[15] It is only necessary that a dramatist always present truth and never compromise with verisimilitude. Larra declares that "this general principle, which is dictated by nature itself and sanctioned by common sense, can scarcely be challenged even by the most rigid neo-classicist."[16] This principle has been recognized by many recent authors, who have not hesitated to use both methods in the same play. The first, according to Larra, who made use of this novelty was Moratín. Among the later writers some have chosen to follow the school of Molière and others that of Moratín. Martínez de la Rosa has shown in *The Daughter at Home* as in his other plays that "comic force" is not his principal merit: "The works of this author usually reveal a depth of feeling that must have made him adopt this genre, which we would be glad to call mixed, if we thought we had a right to give names to things."[17]

Although Larra has only praise for the principal characters of this play, he finds that the minor characters are not so skilfully drawn. He objects particularly to the character of the uncle, "one of those old men found in some of Moratín's comedies, who are thrown in to form a contrast, not with their characters, but with their maxims."[18] The author should not put the moral of the comedy in the mouth of some character, but should allow it to be derived from the action: "The uncle serves no other purpose in *The Daughter at Home* than that of the exposition which, for this reason, is neither skilfully presented nor very new; and the solution, which could really have been effected without him."[19] Larra feels that the character of Luis is entirely unnecessary and even injurious to the comedy, because "he does nothing except things that no one should or could do."[20] It seems, in fact, that Martínez de la Rosa's only purpose in introducing him is that he may catch Inés on the rebound. The author thus follows the old tradition that comedies must end with marriages. Larra is enthusiastic in his praise of the language and versification of the play:

We shall say nothing about the language, because to praise it as an extraordinary merit in Martínez would be to suppose that it might not have been excellent; this would be an insult to this poet, who is one of our best scholars, and about whom we shall always speak and write with respect and envy. The versification could hardly be better; and the dialogue, which is generally animated and comic, is sprinkled with wit in the very best taste.[21]

Although *The Daughter at Home and the Mother at the Masquerade* is generally conceded to be the best of Martínez de la Rosa's comedies and is unquestionably superior to *The Power of a Position,* it does not seem to have met with as much public favor, since it was produced only fourteen times from 1821 to 1822 against twenty-one for the other play.

The counterrevolution of 1823 resulted in the exile of all those who were suspected of liberal ideas, and the neo-classic theater received another setback. Mesonero Romanos summarizes briefly the effect of this political upheaval upon the theater:

All these writers were caught in the second banishment which had its origin in the counterrevolution of 1823; their works and even their names were forbidden; and the theater and literature were again entrusted to the most implacable censure or abandoned to the most disdainful neglect. In the almost complete lack of authors, and even the impossibility of there being any for the above causes, the old repertoire of Tirso, Lope de Vega, and Moreto was the beneficent recourse of our actors.[22]

After the composition of *The Daughter at Home,* Martínez de la

Rosa abandoned the field of comedy for a time. His long sojourn in France as a more or less voluntary political exile afforded him an opportunity to come in direct contact with the literary current that was beginning to dominate Europe. As the result of this influence, he composed two dramas, *The Venice Conspiracy* (1830) and *Aben Humeya* (1830), the fame of which, as we shall see, eclipsed that of his neo-classic comedies and tragedies to such an extent that critics are wont to give pre-eminence to his role as a transitional dramatist. Although the connection of *The Venice Conspiracy* with Spanish romanticism is not to be denied, this one-sided evaluation of Martínez de la Rosa's dramatic production is misleading—at least, in so far as his literary creed is concerned. Despite some temporary, and very minor, concessions to the new school, and his own declaration of unwillingness to align himself with either of the warring parties, he must be considered as an inherent classicist. During his exile he composed his *Poetics* (1827), which is an uncompromising statement of neo-classic precepts; and after his return to Spain he gave to the theater a neo-classic tragedy, *Oedipus,* and two neo-classic comedies, *Unfounded Jealousy or the Husband in the Fireplace* (1831) and *The Wedding and the Duel,* which was not performed until 1839.

Martínez de la Rosa composed *Unfounded Jealousy* sometime before 1831. In the "Foreword" to the 1838 edition of his works, the author says that this play was composed during his exile "purely for pastime and for exercise in the difficult art of dialogue." Having returned to Spain he conceived the idea of presenting the work in the theater of Granada, "being encouraged to do so by my desire to contribute, in so far as I was able, to a benefit fund that was being raised to help some charitable institutions."[23] The success of the play in Granada moved him to send it to the Madrid stage, where it was presented on January 29, 1833, and repeated fourteen times that year. According to Larra, the play was received in Madrid with "the most flattering applause."[24] In the same year the comedy was performed on the Barcelona stage. The announcement in the *Diario de Barcelona* for July 1, 1833, shows the esteem in which the author was held in that city:

Antonio Valero, the first actor and stage director of the Spanish company, has chosen for today, a day set for his personal appearance, a performance made up of two modern plays, new to this theater, which have received general applause in the best theaters of Spain. The first on the program will be an original comedy by Martínez de la Rosa, whose name alone is sufficient to attest its merit. This play, which has been eagerly awaited by theatergoers in Barcelona, is *Unfounded Jealousy, or the Husband in the Fireplace,* written in two acts and in verse, and filled with that comic wit and gay and pleasant dialogue which stand out so brilliantly in all the plays of the estimable author of *The Daughter at Home and the Mother at the Masquerade.* This play will be followed by an interlude of dancing, and following that there will be presented another new comedy in two acts by Don Ventura de la Vega, entitled *To Win Love with a Wig.*[25]

Unfounded Jealousy was repeated in Barcelona on August 14 of the same year.

The play is thoroughly domestic in its setting and reveals the author's aversion for excess of any kind. The note of tolerance and moderation which he strikes in *The Power of a Position* and in this play, together with the unimpeachable moral tone of all his comedies, may be considered characteristic of the man.

The title indicates the theme of the comedy and the ridiculous position in which a jealous husband places himself in order to spy upon a supposed seducer. Don Anselmo, a model husband in all other respects, suffers from an overpowering jealousy which makes his wife most unhappy. Her brother, Eugenio, whom Don Anselmo has never seen, arrives with a cousin, Carlos. When Carlos learns the state of affairs, he offers to cure the husband of his jealousy, which is nourished by the gossip of a rascally servant. With difficulty Doña Francisca is persuaded to aid in the conspiracy in which the cousin and the brother change places. Carlos fans the flame of jealousy in the husband by representing Eugenio as a rake whose amorous conquests are legion.

In order to test the extent to which his unwelcome guest will carry his gallantries with Doña Francisca, the husband persuades her to receive him while he hides in the fireplace. This, the most comic scene in the play, suggests the scene in Molière's *Tartuffe* where the husband hides under the table, although in the French play the scene is prepared by the wife, while in this case it is the husband who takes the initiative. Don Eugenio, warned by a gesture from Doña Francisca that her husband is in the fireplace, plays his role of would-be seducer to perfection. After he leaves, the husband comes out covered with soot and determined to get rid of his guest. This he accomplishes by means of a note. A part of the plan of the conspirators is to convince Don Anselmo of the rascality of his servant. The pretended seducer, who has taken lodging elsewhere, bribes this servant to admit him to Doña Francisca's room during his master's absence. Of course, Carlos arranges to bring the husband back shortly after the servant has admitted Eugenio, who then takes refuge in a pantry, from which there soon comes a crashing sound caused by the breaking of dishes. Doña Francisca, fearing the consequences of the trick, throws herself at her husband's feet, proclaiming her innocence and insisting that Eugenio is her brother. Don Anselmo runs after the intruder and the scene threatens to turn into the Golden Age type, but at this moment Carlos enters and prevents the affair from having a serious outcome. The husband is informed of the trick, the faithless servant is dismissed, and the husband declares himself cured of his unreasonable jealousy.

Larra compares this comedy with Gorostiza's *Indulgence for Everybody* in the lack of verisimilitude of the plan:

These plans...do not seem to us the most dependable, because it necessarily follows from their nature that when the person who is supposed to be reformed learns that everything has been a trick, his conviction will be weakened and the result will be exactly opposite to that which is intended.[26]

He objects also to the ease with which the servant, who has been represented in the first act as so attached to his master, allows himself to be bribed. Among the merits of the comedy, Larra lists "a pure and skilfully handled language; a decorous style; an admirable dialogue, full of life and wit; a vigorous versification; a consummate knowledge of theatrical resources; and conviction achieved through ridicule."[27] He concludes that *Unfounded Jealousy*, even removed from the stage for which it was written, will always be "a beautiful monument of our literature and a model for those who wish to write comedies in Spanish."[28]

Needless to say, the comedy follows the rules faithfully, being written in octosyllabic *romance* and guarding the unities with room to spare. In the action there is no suggestion of subplot. The exposition is a model of naturalness; there are no long speeches; and the moral of the play derives almost entirely from the action with a minimum of preachment.

The "Foreword" to Martínez de la Rosa's last comedy, *The Wedding and the Duel* (1839),[29] is particularly interesting in that it reveals the author's dissatisfaction with romanticism and his aversion for excesses of any kind. The comedy, he tells us, was composed several years before, during his exile in France, "for a mere pastime during a bathing season and with no intention that it should be performed."[30] Nor did his reluctance to produce the play cease on his return to Spain. Not only had political controversies diverted his attention from the theater, but he also felt that his drama would not satisfy the taste that had recently come to prevail in Spain as a result of foreign influences:

> It was, therefore, to be feared that a favorable reception would not be given to a composition that is very simple, lacking in pomp and show, reduced to a purely domestic action between four walls, and which starts and ends in the space of a few hours; all of these being qualities which although they might have met with excessive favor at another epoch, have recently become the objects of disapproval and disdain.[31]

Martínez de la Rosa believes that it is a common failing of men to be violent in their opinions, especially when such opinions have been made fashionable by their novelty. He rejoices, however, that "the movement which was threatening to corrupt our theater not only in its literary aspect, but in another that is more important and transcendental, has begun to pass away."[32] This reaction he considers "another proof of the good judgment of Spaniards."

In the meantime, a dramatic section had been established in the Liceo of Madrid for the purpose of reviving the glories of the old Spanish theater and of encouraging the modern. Wishing to contribute to this laudable undertaking, "Martínez de la Rosa decided to offer one of his compositions to be performed for the first time in the Liceo. He was strengthened in this determination by seeing the complete success which had attended the performance there of Moratín's The New Comedy, in spite of the fact that times and ideas had undergone a notable change since that play was produced for the first time. He hoped, therefore, that a comedy of the school of Moratín might be well received, "even though it did not possess the singular qualities which recommend those of that master."[33] He expressed himself as entirely satisfied with the reception given to The Wedding and the Duel. A large part of the applause, however, he modestly attributed to the "urbanity and courtesy of such a select audience" and to the natural manner in which the play was performed.

In La Esperanza for October 20, 1839, there appeared a review of the comedy with the cast of characters. We find here a practical working out of a recommendation made as early as 1787 in the *Correo de Madrid*.[34] The quality of the acting of this group of amateurs is at least an indication that the unnatural performances of the regular actors sprang from histrionic traditions that were ill-suited to the simplicity of a neo-classic comedy. In the case of *The Wedding and the Duel* appears the name of Ventura de la Vega in the role of Carlos. This dramatist, who was later to compose a master-piece of neo-classic comedy, *The Man of the World* (1845), com-bined with his literary interests an unusual histrionic talent.

The Wedding and the Duel is another example of the type of comedy popularized by Moratín: the domestic comedy, which attacks the abuse of parental authority in arranging marriages. In its main plot this play parallels *The Consent of Young Maidens* more closely than any of those written in imitation of Moratín. There is the same selfish and loquacious mother, who attempts to gain finan-cial security for herself by marrying her daughter to a rich old man. The daughter, Luisa, is as submissive to the will of her mother as is Doña Francisca in *The Consent of Young Maidens*. She is in love with Carlos and is heartbroken but powerless to resist her mother. Like Francisca, she writes her lover informing him of her situation. Don Juan, the old man whom she is to marry, begins to suspect that the girl is being coerced by her mother. Although irascible, he is nevertheless frank and honest and is unwilling to marry the girl against her will. Like Don Diego, he interrogates Luisa in the pres-ence of her mother, who insists upon answering his questions herself without permitting her daughter to speak. A challenge to a duel which Don Juan receives from Carlos removes all doubt from his mind and he determines to arrange matters so that the mother will consent to the marriage of her daughter to the one whom she really loves. When all preparations have been made for the marriage between Luisa and the old man, Carlos rushes in to demand satis-faction of his rival, who not only does not oppose his desire to marry the girl, but reproves him for his rash words and insists that the mother give her consent to the marriage of the young couple. The comedy ends to the satisfaction of everyone.

There is a secondary action which is entirely unnecessary to the solution of the main plot. In giving its analysis of the play, *La Esperanza* omits this part entirely. A certain Countess, having been placed in a convent by her parents who desired to profit from her inheritance, had welcomed the opportunity to marry an old man to avoid taking the veil. Now a widow, she attempts to find the love which had been denied her. Joaquín, the nephew of Don Juan, pays her ardent court. She returns his affection until she discovers him in intimate conversation with another girl, Teresa. She flies into a rage and Teresa faints. In this scene there is a bit of farce, when Joaquín seeks to hide under a table at the approach of Luisa and turns it over. Apparently the author did not consider that the simple plot he had announced in his "Foreword" was sufficient to maintain interest and so sought to bolster up the play with this secondary action.

La Esperanza comments only very briefly upon the minor characters because "they have little to do with the principal action and are almost unnecessary to the plot."[35] Although the principal characters are well portrayed and sustained, the play lacks interest because the solution is evident from the beginning. The language and the versification are up to the author's usual standard and compensate in a measure for the defects of the play. It should be noted here that, following his custom, Martínez de la Rosa varies the assonance frequently within an act. As we have seen, the usual procedure of the neo-classicists was to change the assonance only with the act. This freedom in Martínez de la Rosa's comedies was effective in preventing monotony. La Esperanza praised the performance of this comedy enthusiastically, saying that it did not seem possible for a play to be performed by amateurs with such propriety, assurance, and intelligence.[36]

Two years after the performance of The Power of a Position and while Cádiz was still besieged by the English, Martínez de la Rosa composed a tragedy, Padilla's Widow, which was performed in July, 1812, in an improvised wooden building out of range of enemy fire. This tragedy might also be called a drama of circumstances, inasmuch as it was calculated to appeal to the patriotism of the inhabitants of a besieged city. In the preface to the 1814 edition of the play, the author freely confesses the extent of his indebtedness to the Italian dramatist, Alfieri:

When I undertook the composition of this play in the year 1812, I had just read Alfieri's tragedies and was so impressed by their merit that I took them as my model, proposing to write a drama with a single action, which would be brought to its conclusion without episodes, without confidants, with very few monologues, and with a limited number of interlocutors. I proposed to imitate the vigorous thoughts, the concise style, and the lively dialogue which, to a certain extent, compensate for lack of incidents and nakedness of plot in the works of this author.[37]

When he came to choose a subject, the desire that it should be orig- inal and taken from Spanish history and perhaps even more, he says, the extraordinary circumstances in which the city of Cádiz found itself at that time, closely besieged by a foreign army and engaged in carrying out domestic reforms, directed his attention and inclined him to give first choice to the revolt of the federated cities of Castile against the tyranny of Carlos V during the early years of his reign.

The story, for there is no real plot, deals with the attempt on the part of Padilla's widow to prevent the surrender of Toledo. Realizing the complete futility of further resistance, her father-in-law, Pedro López de Padilla, her friend, Mendoza, and her husband's onetime rival for leadership, Don Pedro Laso de la Vega, all counsel surrender. The widow, however, blinded by grief over her husband's death and motivated solely by a desire for vengeance, prolongs the resistance with the power of her personality and the fire of her oratory.

Although the tragedy, following the neo-classic pattern, is divided into five acts, it is exceedingly short, having only 1,373 verses. With its complete lack of action, this means 1,373 lines of almost consecutive dialogue. Menéndez y Pelayo is not too severe when he says:

> The plot is poor, or rather there is no plot at all, because from the first word the solution is obvious. This tragedy resembles one of those interminable roads in La Mancha, where one is always in sight of a town but never gets to it. Five acts of lamentation over lost liberty and of dis- putes between those who wish to give up and those who oppose surrender is all that the poet managed to derive from such a rich subject. These endless conversations take place in the Palace of Toledo, because the author says so, but they might just as well have taken place in Thebes.[38]

Martínez de la Rosa not only adopts the "uniformly solemn and high-sounding language of Alfierian tragedy," but also "excludes all local details and manners."[39] Menéndez y Pelayo calls the solution of the tragedy an anachronism. "What could be more improbable," he asks, "than to attribute suicide to a Spanish woman in the sixteenth century?"*

In its review of the tragedy upon its revival in 1820, the *Censor* says that, in spite of defects inherent in its theme, it was well ap-

---

*In the *Historical Sketch of the War of the Federated Cities,* which served as an introduction to the 1814 edition of the tragedy, Martínez de la Rosa states that, after imposing her will upon the people of Toledo for a long time and kindling the fire of their patriotism, Padilla's widow escaped in disguise and took refuge in Portugal when the city finally fell.

plauded because, "independent of the merit of a good language and lively dialogue, the author made use of the dramatic picture it presents in order to inspire hatred for tyranny and love for liberal institutions."[40] When the tragedy was presented at the Cruz on October 28, 1814, it lasted for five days; the next month it was repeated for two performances. It was not played during the next five or six years, but when political events once more aroused Spaniards to patriotic enthusiasm in 1820 and again in 1836, the play was revived along with Quintana's *Pelayo*, which was always popular at such periods. *Padilla's Widow*, like Quintana's tragedy, was much more effective as propaganda than interesting as drama.

Six years after the composition of *Padilla's Widow*, during his imprisonment in Peñon de la Gomera, Martínez de la Rosa composed another tragedy, *Morayma* (1818), which was published with his other dramatic works in Paris in 1827, but which was never staged. In this play, he says, he tried to choose a subject which "would offer fewer objections and would lend itself better to dramatic treatment" than his first tragedy. By chance a book that was well known in Spain, but that he had never read, *The History of the Civil Wars of Granada*, fell into his hands. This work appealed to him so much that he determined to seek in it a subject dealing with his native country which would be suitable for performance in the theater. In spite of the years that have passed since the composition of this work and the greater breadth of experience he has acquired, he confesses frankly "that the subject of this composition not only seems beautiful to me, but seems to possess all the qualities required by the masters of art."[41] The tragedy is written in hendecasyllabic *romance* meter and is divided into five acts. The first three acts take place in "a magnificent hall of Moorish architecture" in the palace of the Alhambra and the fourth in a room in Morayma's apartment. The setting for the fifth act is impressive:

It is night. The theater represents the famous Court of the Lions, with the fountain in the middle of the stage. Several streets of grouped columns form the contour, which is lost in the distance. From time to time the dull noise of the wind is heard and on the floor can be seen an iron hatch, which appears to cover the entrance to a subterranean passage.

Boabdil has ascended the throne of Granada after the overthrow of his father Hassam and the defeat and virtual extermination of the band of the Abencerrajes. Morayma, his half-sister from the union of his father with a slave girl, has married and now has a son by Albinhamad, leader of the Abencerrajes, and one of those who have been treacherously slain. She makes no attempt to conceal her hatred for her brother, whom she holds responsible for the death of her husband. Boabdil threatens her with dire punishment if she does not abandon her open hostility and refrain from insulting him. The king owes his victory and his throne to a large extent to the aid of Alí, the chief of the band of Zegríes, traditional enemies and rivals of the Abencerrajes, who has been in love with Morayma since childhood.

Counseled by his mother, Ayxa, who seeks revenge for the preference shown by her husband for a slave girl, and angered by his sister's attitude toward him, Boabdil decrees the death of all the surviving sons of Abencerrajes. Alí, who is represented as consistently noble and valorous throughout the play, seeks to dissuade the king from carrying out his decree and reminds him of his past services. Boabdil, who is weak and cowardly, is on the verge of relenting when Mahomad, a false friend of Alí, informs him that the latter is plotting to usurp the throne. Although the innate nobility of his character is sufficient in itself to make him oppose the edict of the king, Alí also hopes to win the love of Morayma by saving her son from death; and she, actuated only by her maternal love, leads him to believe that she will yield in the event he succeeds — confessing, however, to her close friend, Fatima, that she has no intention of being untrue to the memory of her husband. Alí confides all of his plans and his love for Morayma to his supposed friend, Mahomad, who immediately reveals them to Ayxa and then to Boabdil. Moved by her hatred for her brother, Morayma incites Alí to rebellion; but before the latter has time to act the king learns of the projected uprising, comes with his guards, takes Morayma's son from her, and delivers him to the custody of the African slave, Aliatar, informing his sister that he will hold the child as a hostage. Upon the advice of Mahomad, who pretends to aid him in his plans, Alí bribes the guard, and having secured the child, takes him to Morayma. He finally convinces her that no recourse remains except for him to take her son to safety through the subterranean passage that leads from the castle. After a heart-rending struggle between her love for her son and her fears for his safety, she delivers him to Alí's arms. When Alí enters the passage, he is met and killed by guards who have been posted there by the treacherous Mahomad.

In the last scene Boabdil's guards and henchmen rush upon the stage with drawn sabers and lighted torches, followed by the king, his mother, and Mahomad. Boabdil, unaware of what has happened, is urging his men to pursue and capture Alí. At this moment a leader of the guard comes up from the subterranean passage, carrying in his arms the bloody body of Morayma's son, and reports that Alí has been killed. When the mother sees her dead son she rushes to embrace him, but falls before she reaches him. Boabdil orders that she be taken to her room and that he be notified when she regains consciousness. After examining Morayma, however, Fatima announces that she is dead, the victim of her overpowering grief. Boabdil cries out, "Quickly, let us flee from this place of horror!" and when his mother tries to calm him, he cries out again: "Come, follow me all. . . . The earth is slipping from beneath my feet!" With these words of the king the tragedy comes to an end.

It is to be regretted that this play was never performed. Given the proper staging and competent actors, it might have been received with favor and even with enthusiasm by Madrid audiences in the 1830's. Although it lacks the patriotic appeal of *Padilla's Widow*, it is vastly superior to that work in plot structure and dramatic interest. The outstanding success of *Oedipus* in 1832 proved that the public was not as opposed to classic tragedy as it had been in the latter part of the preceding century, and that a play in that genre could succeed without an emotional appeal to Spanish nationalism. Of course, it would have had to be performed before the enthusiastic reception accorded *The Venice Conspiracy* in 1834 had linked Martínez de la Rosa, temporarily at least, with the romantic movement. *Morayma*, coming from the same author at that time, might have seemed uninspired and colorless.

The year following his return to his native land in 1831, Martínez de la Rosa presented at the Príncipe a classical tragedy, *Oedipus*, which occupies a unique position in the history of the neo-classic movement in Spain. Following the failure of Montiano's *Virginia* even to reach the theater, neo-classicists had limited themselves to national or biblical themes and to comments upon Greek tragedy. Their general attitude may be summed up in statements made in 1793 by Pedro Estala in the "Preliminary Discourse on Ancient and Modern Tragedy" which precedes his translation of Sophocles' *Oedipus the Tyrant*. After calling this tragedy "the most perfect model that Greece produced . . . the admiration of Aristotle . . . and of all centuries,"[42] he asserts that if it were presented in a Spanish theater, "it would bore the audience with its simplicity," this change in taste being due to differences in religion, government, and manners.[43] The following argument by Estala against Greek tragedy in a modern theater is cited by Martínez de la Rosa in his version of the *Oedipus* and may have influenced his choice of subject:

The clearest evidence that Greek tragedy is inadmissible in the modern theater is found in the two *Oedipuses* by Corneille and Voltaire. These two great writers tried to adapt this masterpiece of the Greek stage to the French theater; they varied the circumstances; they introduced different episodes and made many changes; but in spite of all their efforts, their imitations of such an excellent work turned out to be wretched.... And why? Because the basis of this tragedy is not a human passion, or its effects, but a blind fate, which means nothing to us; and as this fate and a hatred for monarchy make up its essential nature, no matter how many episodes are added, no matter how much genius is employed in arranging its plan in all possible ways, it can never interest our public. In a word, Greek themes the fatalism of which can be converted into a human passion are adaptable to our theater—that is, themes like those of Phedra, Iphigenia and others of that type; but the Oedipuses, the Medeas, and the Atreos will never be successful in our theater no matter how much they are altered.[44]

Martínez de la Rosa is confident that Estala was entirely wrong; that "the aforesaid theme is very suitable even today for a tragedy"; and that the very episodes and the efforts to which Estala refers are the reasons for its lack of success on the modern stage.[45] When Martínez de la Rosa wrote the "Annotations" to his *Poetics,* he chose to make an analysis of this tragedy "because it is perhaps the best example of the Greek theater, being cited repeatedly by Aristotle as a model."[46] In his preface to *Oedipus,* the Spanish dramatist traces the development of this theme from Sophocles to the present time, analyzing carefully the Latin version by Seneca; the French versions by Corneille, Voltaire, and La Motte; the English by Dryden and Lee; and the Italian by Forciroli; and concluding in each case by saying that the tragedy has suffered from attempts to bolster up the plot by the addition of episodes. The lack of success of such eminent authors convinces him, not, as it did Estala, that the story is unsuitable for the modern stage, but rather that all of these writers followed the wrong course. Having decided to use this story, he proposes "to see whether it is possible for him to pour the old metal, without alloy or foreign matter, into a modern mold."[47] He has, however, varied the plan and structure of the original because "my enthusiasm for such a beautiful composition does not extend to the point of believing that a

Greek tragedy can be transferred body and soul... to the Spanish theater."[48] He has attempted to correct the principal defects that critics have noted in the original plot, but he does not choose to follow them in their insistence that the choir and the crowd be suppressed:

> Persuaded that the presence of the people and of the choir can help modern tragedy in certain cases, I have not wished to renounce the aid they may lend to this composition; especially since, to say nothing of other advantages, they serve to give greater pomp to the spectacle and to prepare the minds of the spectators to receive more easily the impressions the author wishes to impart and also, in this case, to contribute to dramatic verisimilitude."[49]

The literary fame of the original work and the reputation of Martínez de la Rosa were sufficient to insure at least a fair attendance at the first performances of the new tragedy. Actually, its reception by the Madrid public must have exceeded all expectations. José María de Carnerero made no attempt to restrain his enthusiasm in his review of the play which appeared in *Cartas Españolas* on February 9, 1832. The eagerness of the public to buy tickets was such, he says, that it became necessary to erect barriers at the ticket booths to avoid disorder—a practice that, for a long time, had been observed almost exclusively with operas. "Now," he exclaims jubilantly, "it is not the opera alone that requires them; the Spanish theater is showing signs of life, and conceited Euterpe yields place, in her turn, to Thalia and Melpomene."[50] Carnerero speaks in glowing terms of the splendor of the stage setting, which surpassed anything that had ever been seen in Spanish theaters. As a matter of fact, his description has been lifted almost bodily from that given by the author in the edition of the tragedy published in Paris four years earlier:

> When the curtain was drawn the eyes of the spectators were agreeably surprised by a magnificent scene in a form previously unknown in our theaters; a scene which represented a great square in Thebes with the portico of the palace at the back; at one side the façade of the temple of Jupiter; and on the opposite side, the entrance to the Pantheon of the Kings. The groups of people with olive branches in their hands and garlands on their heads, kneeling in supplication before two altars placed at the door of the temple; the notes of sacred music and the songs of the choirs; the presence of the high priests; and the intelligent arrangement of the entire scene announced immediately that we were witnessing a classical performance, one that was worth more than it cost, and in

which everything combined to meet, in a worthy manner, the requirements of the palace of arts in a civilized capital. Not even in Paris has
any tragedy been performed with greater splendor.[51]

Carnerero comments with equal enthusiasm upon the unprecedented
success of the tragedy:

If Estala were alive and could attend the present performance of
Oedipus, he would see that he was mistaken, for the play is producing a
marvelous effect and attracting immense audiences that never tire of
admiring the beauties of a production which, based upon a story from
antiquity, has placed on the Spanish dramatic crown one of the most
beautiful jewels that could adorn it; thanks to the author who needs no
other titles than those his *Oedipus* gives him to occupy one of the most
distinguished and lofty seats on the tragic Parnassus.[52]

The reviewer can think of no tragedy in the Castilian language that
can rival this one and believes it would not be difficult to prove
that it will stand comparison with the best that have been written in
foreign languages. This account of the splendor of the performance
and the merit of the tragedy ends rather incongruously with a paragraph which leads one to suspect that the critic may have lost his
bearings in his enthusiasm and been sailing with the wind:

Let us conclude with a few words about the stage setting. It is good
on the whole; but it is marred horribly by that wretched palace in the
background, which although of Corinthian architecture, the most adorned
of all ancient styles, has been so overdone by the painter that it offends
Greek simplicity. Furthermore, the insistence upon presenting the entire
front of the palace in such a limited space causes it to be done in
miniature. By presenting a portico extending out on one side and supposing the main body of the building to be hidden from the spectators,
all this could have been avoided. The temple of Jupiter is well located,
the Pantheon produces a good effect. The equestrian statue can be considered useless and a hindrance on a reduced stage. Furthermore, I do not
know whether the Greeks cast statues in bronze.... Stone was the
material they consistently preferred.[53]

We may be sure that at the close Carnerero was telling the truth
and that much of the preceding description was pure oratory.
Unquestionably, *Oedipus* was comparatively well staged and well
received by the spectators upon its initial performance, and, it may
be assumed, at subsequent performances; but it certainly did not
start a vogue for classic tragedy modeled upon the Greek, for no one
was encouraged by its success to compose works in the same pattern.

It did prove, however, that audiences in Madrid had lost any prejudice they may have had in the past against classic tragedy as such. For some time, indeed, they had been quite tolerant, and were prepared to witness a romantic play one night, a neo-classic comedy the next, followed perhaps by a sentimental drama or a classic tragedy, with no distinction between original works and translations; always, of course, reserving their greatest acclaim for comedies of magic or comedies that dealt with sacred themes.

Martínez de la Rosa's greatest triumph on the Madrid stage, it is generally conceded, came in 1834 with the performance of his historical drama, *The Venice Conspiracy*, which, we are told, "inaugurated the romantic era in our theaters."[54] Although his biographer says in 1845 that "the man who, a short time before, had caused classic purity to be applauded with frenzy in his *Oedipus*, drew equal applause from the public with a composition that was essentially romantic,"[55] a witness closer to the event assures us that "what can be affirmed as a fact is that *The Venice Conspiracy* has been applauded in Madrid and in all Spain more than *Oedipus*."[56] This critic, Eugenio de Ochoa, who at that time was probably the most vigorous exponent of romanticism in Spain, declares that Martínez de la Rosa's *Oedipus*, "together with Quintana's *Pelayo*, make up the entire wealth of good tragedies written in conformity with Aristotle's precepts" and attributes its success to "the sustained perfection of the language, the scenic effect, and especially the newness of the spectacle; because the choir, the music, and the splendor of the decorations were novelties of considerable importance to us." On the contrary, he continues, "*The Venice Conspiracy* lacked the prestige of versification and music, being written in lowly prose, to use Voltaire's expression." In Ochoa's opinion, this drama is "surely the most beautiful flower in Martínez de la Rosa's poetic crown" and its author "has the added glory of having been the first to introduce the doctrines of romanticism into the modern Spanish theater." He expresses the devout hope that his example will find many imitators. Larra, however, in an almost equally enthusiastic review that appeared two days after the first performance, says merely that the play belongs to the same genre as Moreto's *The Grandee of Alcalá* and Rojas' *García del Castañar*, that is, to historical drama, "the faithful representation of life, in which kings and vassals, people of the upper and the lower classes, and public and private interests are mixed together as they are in actual life."[57] Martínez de la Rosa probably found somewhat uncomfortable the "new poetic crown" Ochoa had placed upon his brow. He certainly had no intention of enlisting in the ranks of romanticism when he published this drama in Paris in 1830. In the preface he says that for many years he had wanted to compose a dramatic work taken from the history of Venice, and that in this play he has tried to give an accurate presentation of the well-known conspiracy that took place there at the beginning of the fourteenth century, and at the same time to portray faithfully the characters and manners peculiar to that age and that nation. He is uncertain whether the simple plot of his drama will prove interesting on the stage. He is careful to affirm that in its composition he proposed to impart the greatest naturalness to sentiments, style, and language. None of these remarks bear any resemblance to a romantic manifesto.

In his "Notes on Historical Drama," which were published in the same year as *The Venice Conspiracy* and *Aben Humeya*, Martínez de la Rosa gives a clear statement of his conception of this type of play, which he insists fulfils the basic purpose of drama, "to combine utility and delight."[58] In their historical comedies, Spanish poets of the Golden Age, "who had more genius than judgment," were more inclined to present deeds that would awaken curiosity and carry the interest of the spectators along with the rapidity of the action "than to work carefully and persistently to probe the secrets of the human heart or to portray a character with all his shadows and shades."[59] These poets, "rather than to subject themselves to such an arduous task, preferred to dazzle with their facile inventiveness and to give free rein to their imagination."[60] Most of them lacked the necessary instruction and therefore fell into manifest errors, such as those "pointed out by the judicious Luzán."[61] In handling historical themes, truth is the first essential and the poet must take great care not to turn the reins loose and allow his imagination to run blindly. The unity of action is as necessary in historical drama as in comedy or tragedy. The only real concession that Martínez de la Rosa makes in the case of historical drama is in a slight relaxation of the unities of time and place. In order that events may follow each other without confusion, and that the appearance of truth may be preserved, it may be necessary to change the scene of the action. In his remarks on the unities, he is careful to disavow any intention of taking sides in the current conflict between classicists and romanticists:

In the midst of the fierce war between two opposing literary parties,

I believe that, on this point as well as many others, the truth lies in a strict middle course. A poet who sacrifices an extremely beautiful situation, or who falls into a manifest absurdity in order not to change occasionally the place of the action, has a very meager conception of his art; but one who makes his characters wander from place to place without judgment or moderation runs the risks of reminding the spectators of the very thing he is trying so hard to make them forget. Each act, as a distinct and separate part, can very well be supposed to occur in a different place, especially if they are not very far from each other; there are few dramatic plots that require any greater laxity for their convenient and easy development.[62]

With regard to the unity of time, Martínez de la Rosa, in the three years that intervened between the publication of the "Annotations" to his *Poetics* and the "Notes on Historical Drama," has modified his position somewhat, and is now willing to allow the action to last several days, rather than confine it to the narrow space of twenty-four hours, provided the intervals are distributed between the acts with such judgment and skill that the spectator is not made conscious of the passage of time. Again he is careful to make it clear that he is counseling moderation. He is very much afraid that the intelligence of the spectators will be offended and their interest will wane "if they should see incidents piled upon incidents, and see the characters travel post haste in order to represent in a few hours what transpires in many years."[63]

The Venice Conspiracy represents a practical application of these rules and concessions. Even a cursory examination of the work will suffice to show that there is a conspicuous lack of episodes and that the unity of action is rigidly observed; that the action is limited to a very few days; and that all the scenes are in the city of Venice, even though, as Larra notes, the audiences of Madrid were treated to the sight of "five new decorations at one performance."[64]

Allison Peers aptly calls attention to the romantic elements in the play: "the striking changes of scene and of atmosphere," the multiplication of characters, the "introduction of crowds and counter crowds," the "sharp contrast between the gloomy pantheon and the plaza illuminated for Carnival," and the creation of "the first romantic hero of Spanish nineteenth-century drama."[65] These points of contact with romanticism, however, do not prevent *The Venice Conspiracy* from being what its author called it and intended it to be: a historical drama, in which he proposed to "give the greatest naturalness to sentiments, style, and language."[66] What romanticism there is in

The Venice Conspiracy is certainly mild in comparison with that to be found in a drama like *Don Alvaro, or the Force of Fate*, with its mixture of prose and verse, its complete lack of verisimilitude, its frequent change of scenery within the acts, and its deliberate and wanton violation of the unity of time; a drama which the most enthusiastic of romantic critics, Eugenio de Ochoa, was moved to call immediately after its performance "the exact type of modern drama, a work of study and conscience, full of great beauties and of great defects, sublime, trivial, religious, impious, the terrible personification of the nineteenth century"; a work in which the "saintly prayers of the faithful mount to the throne of God amid blasphemies and cries of rage and despair; where one sees characters that range from the most ideal and fantastic to the rustic muleteer."[67]

During his residence in Paris, which lasted from 1823 to the latter part of 1831, Martínez de la Rosa, encouraged by the success on the Paris stage of a translation of his comedy, *The Daughter at Home and the Mother at the Masquerade*, composed in French a historical drama, *Aben Humeya, or the Revolt of the Moriscos Under Felipe II*, the performance of which was enthusiastically applauded in that city on July 19, 1830.[*]

Having decided to compose a historical drama, the author says, he determined to choose "a great event that would awaken attention and excite interest."[68] It was also necessary that this event should have in it something extraordinary that would distinguish it from all others. He is confident that the subject he has chosen "fulfils almost all the conditions which the masters of art can require." It is not easy, he says, "to find in history many events as extraordinary and as dramatic as the revolt of the Moriscos under Felipe II."[69]

The stage directions in *Aben Humeya* are very complete and call for realistic and rather elaborate settings. The first act takes place in a room of a Moorish country house on the outskirts of Cadiar in the mountains of Alpujarra, with a door at the back of the stage which opens upon a kind of terrace and affords a view of the countryside. Within this act the scene shifts to a vast cavern with an arched

---

[*]In the biography which precedes Martínez de la Rosa's *Poetical and Literary Works* (Paris, 1845), the favorable reception of this play is attributed in large measure to its timeliness. "When the author gave to the theater of Porte Saint Martin his drama, *Aben Humeya*, in 1830, the July revolution, which came shortly after, was a new as well as unexpected occasion of triumph for the author. We were witnesses to the ovation which in those moments of fervid enthusiasm the happy insurgents of Paris gave to the unfortunate insurgents of Alpujarra." (*Obras Completas*, I, v).

ceiling which is supported by large odd-shaped rocks, and from which hang groups of stalactites. The second act represents the square of the town of Cadiar with an old mosque that serves as a temple for the Christians; the scene of the third act is a large hall in an old Moorish castle. The doors leading to the bedrooms are covered with tapestry and through two windows can be seen a part of the town, illuminated by the moon. At the back of the hall, which terminates in arches supported by columns, there are two parallel stairways leading to a transverse gallery above the theater level. Under the gallery between the two stairways can be seen the entrance to the caves, protected by bronze gratings. A large lamp hanging from the arched ceiling illuminates a part of the room.

Such a setting was calculated to appeal to the imagination of romantics in the 1830's, as were also the melancholy tone that pervades the work and "the extremely effective scenes of the Morisco uprising, the burning and destruction of the town of Cadiar on Christmas night, and the cries of vengeance of the Morisco outlaws, interrupted by the prayers and songs of the Christians."[70] Menéndez y Pelayo cannot understand "the coldness with which the Madrid public received this drama and the lack of importance attached to it by some biographers of Martínez de la Rosa, perhaps because it seems to be more of a novel than a tragedy."[71] This critic insists upon classifying the drama as romantic and as belonging to the genre "consecrated by lofty examples from Shakespeare to Schiller and Manzoni." To him *Aben Humeya* is "one of the most truly historical dramas that have been written in Spain and one of the few that have true local color."[72]

In spite of its elaborate setting, the plot of *Aben Humeya* is simple and contrasts rather sharply with the romantic effect of the varied and picturesque crowd that furnishes local color to the drama: Morisco rebels, Castilian soldiers, villagers, shepherds and shepherdesses, Negro slaves, women and slave girls in the service of Zulema and Fatima. In the reign of Felipe II, the Moriscos, who live in the mountainous region of Alpujarra, have been subjected to severe persecution by the Spaniards who seek to erase all trace of their origin, prohibiting the use of their native language, religious practices, and customs, and even decreeing that the wearing of veils by Morisco women be discontinued. Angered by these repressive measures and fearing even greater persecution, the Moriscos rebel and elect as their chief Aben Humeya, the last descendant of the old dynasty.

They slaughter the Christians in the area, attacking them while they are in church singing hymns and Christmas carols, and set up an independent government. Muley-Carime, Aben Humeya's father-in-law, who abhors violence, seeks to restrain the Moriscos.

Aben Humeya is elected king by the rebels in a mass meeting in the picturesque setting of a vast cavern which has served as a home for their high priest, Alfaqui, who, in this secret hiding place, has been keeping alive the religious fervor of the Moriscos. Two of the leaders of the revolt, Aben Abo and Aben Farax, disapprove of the haste with which the people have chosen a king before a kingdom has been securely established. Aben Humeya's arrogance and immediate assumption of regal power and splendor irritate them to such an extent that they seek to discredit him in the eyes of his followers and to depose him.

Muley-Carime, realizing that the revolt has no chance of success, seeks to bring about peace between the Moriscos and the Spaniards, entering into secret negotiations with the enemy in order to accomplish this purpose. The Captain-General of Granada sends Larra to suggest terms to the rebels. He is assassinated and a letter is found on his body that proves Muley-Carime's connection with the Spaniards. Aben Humeya, faced with the alternative of sentencing his father-in-law to death or sharing his disgrace, summons the old man and, after severely reprimanding him for his treason, gives him the choice of taking poison by his own hand or being executed publicly. Aben Abo and Aben Farax, in the meantime, have succeeded in inciting the people to rebellion against their newly elected king. In a battle between the insurgents and a few followers who remain loyal to him, Aben Humeya is wounded and takes refuge in the palace. Aben Farax and Aben Abo enter in close pursuit and Aben Humeya dies at the hands of the latter, who is immediately proclaimed king by the conspirators. The tragedy ends with Aben Abo's declaration that he will put the crown on his head only after he has defeated the enemy.

Aben Humeya was performed four times in February, 1836, five times at the Príncipe in June, and once in November at the theater of the Sartén, making a total of ten performances that year. This was the same year that witnessed the first performance of *The Troubadour* by Garcia Gutiérrez, which was easily the most popular of all the romantic dramas produced in Spain, being given twenty-five times in its first year.

In his review of the play shortly after its performance in Madrid, Larra is extremely critical, not only of its plot, but also of its craftsmanship:

There is no interest, no dramatic resource, either old or new. It has only one effective scene, the one in which Aben Humeya reproaches Muley for his treason. No single passion dominates; no character stands out; no important deed is developed; and the style itself is generally inferior to the other works of the author. Where is the creative fire? ... An obscure historical personage cannot be a fit subject for the theater unless his deeds are responsible for the success or the ruin of a public cause. But, what is the public cause here? What is the moral or political lesson that the author has tried to give us with the death of Aben Humeya? If he had proved that the Moorish rebels lost their cause through the dissension which arose among them, that would have been a great and even opportune objective; but to do this he would have had to continue the drama; he would have had to give us the result of this discord. Because, once he has made it terminate with the death of Aben Humeya, the only lesson that can be derived is that if one wishes to be king he must not have a father-in-law who writes to a Christian.[73]

Allison Peers calls attention to the affiliation of *Aben Humeya* with what he calls "pseudo-classicism" in that, while the "unity of place is stretched slightly, that of time is adhered to so rigidly as to destroy every vestige of probability."[74]

In the prologue which preceded the French edition of the play, the author says:

In the midst of all the battles that are taking place in the field of literature, and the sort of revolution that reigns in the theatrical world, the first condition I imposed upon myself in undertaking the composition of this work was that of forgetting all systems and of following as my only rule those clear and unquestionable principles which make up the very essence of drama, and which will always form, as far as the theater is concerned, the code of good taste.[75]

Martínez de la Rosa, although he was making some concessions to the prevailing taste in France at the time he composed *Aben Humeya*, quite obviously did not believe that he was deviating to any appreciable degree from established neo-classic precepts. Indeed, if this author had not written *The Venice Conspiracy*, and if this play had been written in hendecasyllabic *romance* meter instead of in prose, it might have been accepted as just another neo-classic tragedy with a breach of the unity of place in the first act, and its failure might have been attributed even by such critics as Menéndez y Pelayo to faults inherent in the products of that school.

Dramatic Theory

As we have noted, Martínez de la Rosa's interest in the theater was not limited to the production of plays, but, like Moratín's, found expression in a detailed exposition of his literary creed. His *Poetics* (1827) is one of the most complete statements of neo-classic precepts since Luzán.

In discussing this work, Menéndez y Pelayo correctly maintains that it "does not go two fingers beyond that of Moratín and La Harpe."[76] It is true that Martínez de la Rosa added little to what had been said by neo-classicists since the days of Luzán, and from the numerous references to the French critic, La Harpe, found in the "Annotations" to his *Poetics* it is evident that he drew heavily from that source for any new material. Indeed, it seems that La Harpe was considered by Spanish neo-classicists generally, after the publication of his *Lyceum or Course in Literature* in the early years of the nineteenth century, as an authority on literary principles. At least, his was the most complete and most easily available work at the time that purported to discuss European literature in general and tried to reconcile existing literary theories. We find him frequently cited by the *Memorial Literario;* and Moratín, in his "Historical Sketch of the Spanish Theater," quotes a statement made by the Frenchman in 1797: "If in Spain they do not apply themselves to the portrayal of characters and eccentricities in society, it is because Spain has not changed in recent years and is still as it used to be."[77] We have already noted the indebtedness of Mor de Fuentes to the French critic.[78] Menéndez y Pelayo considers it almost incredible that a *Poetics* so narrow in its expression of dramatic principles should be written "after Wilhelm Schlegel's course or after Manzoni's indisputable and profound letter against the dramatic unities."[79]

Martínez de la Rosa starts his "Annotations" with a rather conventional definition of tragedy:

Tragedy does not relate, but imitates and represents a serious action, capable of exciting terror and pity in the hearts of the spectators. To achieve this purpose, it attempts to approach reality in so far as this is possible and convenient.[80]

Of course, tragedy must choose some serious misfortune which occurs to people of high rank, and not an everyday occurrence. The soul of tragedy, he says, "is the struggle and contrast of passions, without which it would seem a cold and lifeless body."[81]

He discusses at considerable length "the new rule some French legislators have tried to introduce as a fixed principle," that is, the precept of "not bloodying the stage."[82] He finds that the Greeks frequently presented corpses unnecessarily on the stage in order to add terror to the spectacle, and that the Romans, who took delight in witnessing actual bloodshed by gladiators in the arena, were not disposed to ban pretended bloodshed from the theater. The English tragedies of Shakespeare are characterized, he says, by excessive recourse to horror, and in Italy, "the cradle of modern tragedy," Alfieri has not been willing to subject himself to this precept. In France Racine, "the most sensitive and delicate of French tragedians," did not choose to conceal the sight of blood from the audience and presented Mithridates on the stage with blood pouring from his wound. While Corneille observed the rule more than did any of his contemporaries, preferring in *Horace* to have Camila die behind the wings and not following Sophocles in allowing Oedipus to appear with blood dripping from his empty eye sockets, he nevertheless refused to admit the precept as binding in all cases. Martínez de la Rosa concludes that "the only thing certain on this point is that spectacle which cause horror should be avoided; and that wounds, deaths, or such things, although they may be presented on the stage, should not be multiplied too much, because their terrible effect is thus diminished and they might reach the extreme of appearing ridiculous."[83]

In regard to verse forms suitable for tragedy, he states emphatically that "no nation possesses as many advantages as the Spanish," the French being condemned to the monotony of rhymed couplets and the English and the Italian to the single rhythm and cadence of blank verse. Instead of blank verse or couplets, which were employed by some writers in Spain at first, and which are as well adapted to the Spanish language as to the French, English, or Italian experience has shown conclusively that no metrical form suits that class of composition as well in the Spanish theater as that exclusive property of Castilian poetry, the hendecasyllabic *romance*, which possesses "to distinguish it from prose, the measure, the cadence and the harmony common to blank verse, and, in addition, the charm of a repeated echo, which never becomes monotonous because of the dissimilar ending of the odd numbered lines . . . combining in this way the charm of pure rhyme with greater freedom."[84]

Martínez de la Rosa's discussion of the unities follows rather closely the pattern set by Luzán and Moratín, both of whom stated rigid rules and then admitted certain modifications. After accepting the customary definition of the unity of action, he cites the opinion of various French critics and then gives his own interpretation of the unity of place:

> If I must state frankly my opinion on such a thorny matter, I shall say that I recognize as most perfect a drama in which there is no compromise at all and the action is limited to three and not twenty-four hours; but just as more freedom has been allowed the poet in this regard, I find no serious objection to changing the scene, providing two conditions are observed: first, that not only shall the scene not move from one town to another, but that the entire action take place in a reduced area, like a square, a temple, and the interior of an adjacent palace; and it will be still better if it is restricted to the various parts of the same building; second, that a change of scene never occur in the middle of an act, cutting the connection of the scenes and spoiling the effect of the drama, but during the intermissions.[85]

In regard to the difficult question of the unity of time, although he recognizes as most desirable a drama which observes this precept so closely that the spectator "feels that during the time he has been in the theater, the action he has seen imitated on the stage could actually have happened,"[86] he nevertheless tries to reconcile this extreme conception with the commonly accepted opinion which admits the space of twenty-four hours by allowing the excess time to be distributed between the intermissions. Like Luzán, he accepts Corneille's recommendation that "when the poet cannot observe the unity of time exactly, he should be careful not to put into his play anything that will indicate the duration of the action."[87]

The exposition, he says, should be clear, brief, and ingenious, that is, "so skilfully done that its purpose of acquainting the spectator with antecedent events will not be manifest, but will be concealed and be accomplished by indirect means."[88] As has been noted, one of the principal objections of the neo-classicists to the *comedia* was the long and unnatural exposition made with the obvious intention of informing the audience of what had happened before the play started, and sometimes giving a long historical background of the action. Like Luzán, Martínez de la Rosa objects to the use of monologues.

He is quite insistent upon the moral function of comedy, which, he says, "proposes, through an action skilfully imitated on the stage, to present vices and moral faults from their ridiculous side, in order to prevent the spectators from falling into similar vices and faults."[89] It follows from this statement that comedy should not represent criminal actions, but common vices of society that do not reach the point where they are punishable by law.

Comedy copies no particular individual, but observes the ridiculous defects in society, combines different features, and forms an ideal model, which it then holds up to ridicule:

> Let us suppose, for example, that a writer of comedies wishes to censure avarice. What must he do? Certainly not portray some usurer in the city with his particular characteristics, but form in his mind the perfect conception of a miser, combining in one imaginary person all the ridiculous qualities that may fit such a character, and then disgrace him publicly by presenting him in flesh on the stage.[90]

Martínez de la Rosa follows the traditional practice in poetics of giving in detail the rules which should govern tragedy, and then stating that the greater part of these rules are equally applicable to comedy. The unities, he says, should be observed as scrupulously as possible. The dramatic knot should be tied closely in order to awaken and maintain interest, and should be untied in an unexpected manner that will seem natural to the spectators. Only a simple style suits comedy, since it "imitates familiar conversation between enlightened people."[91] It should, therefore, avoid the two extremes of affectation and coarseness. Martínez de la Rosa recommends for comedy the octosyllabic *romance*, since in this genre the versification should be "smooth, simple, close to prose, swift enough to follow the animation of the dialogue, flexible enough to adapt itself to the various forms of conversation, and as free and unencumbered as thoughts themselves."[92] He says nothing about the use of prose in comedy, although his first comedy, *The Power of a Position*, was written in this medium, nor is he as liberal as other neo-classic critics in permitting the use of *redondillas*.

His attitude toward sentimental comedy may be inferred from the fact that there is a strong sentimental element in most of his plays:

> ... if I must express my opinion frankly, I believe the fact that it does not enter into Aristotle's classification is not sufficient reason to close the

door to that kind of composition, which may fulfil completely the purpose of drama, which is to give the people useful lessons and entertain them pleasantly.[93]

This does not mean, however, that he believes this genre equal in merit to true comedy. There is no doubt, he adds, that this hybrid type of drama, which affects to a certain extent the "vehement and passionate tone of tragedy, while it tries at the same time not to rise above the simplicity of comedy, offers in exchange for its few advantages a very serious danger to drama." This danger is that of confusing the two genres and corrupting both. As horrible examples of the perversion of art found in some sentimental comedies, he cites *The Prisons of Lamberg* and *The Mines of Poland,* in which there are "subterranean passages and caves, abductions and assassinations, melodramatic tyrants, and even vampires." But it would be unfair to compare these absurd compositions with Jovellanos' *The Honorable Culprit,* which "shows wisely the character this new class of drama should assume."[94]

Nearly a century after Luzán formulated his neo-classic precepts we find the same ideas restated by Martínez de la Rosa with minor alterations. Later preceptists like Javier de Burgos, Hartzenbusch, and Gil y Zárate, however, reveal a much greater liberalism. Martínez de la Rosa, as has been noted, later modified his dramatic creed to a certain extent under the influence of romanticism. Menéndez y Pelayo says: "In reality, Martínez de la Rosa's *Poetics* is the key that closes the period opened by Luzán's *Poetics.*"[95]

After the composition of his *Poetics,* Martínez de la Rosa seems to have wavered for a time in his staunch loyalty to the tenets of neo-classicism. But it was inevitable that his early training and his conservative nature should make him abhor the exaggerations, immorality, and impiousness of the romantic school and lead him back toward his former position. The result was, with him as with so many of his contemporaries, a compromise which produced an eclectic attitude toward dramatic principles. In the prologue to the 1833 edition of his poetry he indicates the change that has taken place in his ideas. In this prologue he reveals an eclectic taste, but even in his eclecticism he gives evidence of a profound respect for rules and expresses fear that his countrymen will carry literary freedom to excess. He is somewhat embarrassed to publish his poetry, since he has previously composed a work on poetics and is afraid that his poetry will be judged by his own rules. This leads him to a statement concerning the controversy between classicists and romanticists, similar to that which he had already made in his "Notes on Historical Drama."[96] Although he begins by saying that he feels little inclination to enlist under the banner of either party, the statement he gives of his literary creed still aligns him with the neo-classicists:

There is no doubt, in my opinion, that works of the imagination, like the fine arts, are subject to fixed and invariable rules that are based upon the principles of sound reason and, it can even be said, upon the very nature of man.[97]

Since the writing of his *Poetics*, however, his ideas have undergone sufficient change to impel him to add:

... but it should not be inferred from this that some of the rules prescribed by the masters of art are not subject to change in order to conform to the changing taste of ages and of people; for works of the imagination should not be measured by petty scales; nor should they be condemned lightly because they do not fit into Aristotle's molds; nor should it be said to the human mind, as God said to the waves: "Thus far shall ye go, and no farther."[98]

But liberty should not degenerate into license, and Martínez de la Rosa fears that Spanish poetry will revert to the exaggerated style of the seventeenth century if the new generation "through its eagerness to follow a new path, runs blindly without method or guidance and scorns the counsel of reason and good taste as useless shackles."[99] The statements contained in this prologue represent at best only a mild concession to romanticism and, taken with the "Foreword" to *The Wedding and the Duel*, his last dramatic work, indicate that in him the neo-classicist far outweighed the romanticist.

Gorostiza

In the "Appendix" to his *Selected Plays*,[100] Gorostiza declares himself to be an "enemy to every type of fanaticism, including literary fanaticism." This statement explains those deviations from the Moratinian mold found in his comedies—deviations which, to be sure, are not of sufficient importance to prevent his sharing with Martínez de la Rosa the honor of being the most worthy disciple of the master.

Of Gorostiza's dramatic works only five plays are known to be original: *Indulgence for Everybody, Customs of Yore, Tit for Tat or Men and Women, Don Dieguito,* and *Bread and Onions with You.*

His other plays are either translations and adaptations of French models or recasts of Golden Age comedies.

His first neo-classic comedy, *Indulgence for Everybody*, in five acts and in verse, was published in 1818. Lista, writing in *El Censor* in 1822, says that the germ of this comedy is found in the brilliant plays that deal with Memnon, who was guilty of all kinds of indiscretions on the very day he had determined to be completely wise and virtuous. He adds, however, that Gorostiza adds emphasis to the moral lesson contained in Voltaire's apologue.[101]

Don Severo, the protagonist of the comedy, who has all the qualities which should make a man esteemed in society, mars them by his lack of indulgence for the shortcomings of others. His marriage has been arranged with Tomasa, whom he has never seen. The action takes place in a small town in Navarra. In the opening scenes of the first act she, her father, Don Fermín, and her brother Carlos are awaiting the arrival of the groom from Castile. Carlos, who is a friend of Don Severo, is well aware of his uncompromising nature and expresses fear that the marriage will not be a happy one in view of the fact that his sister has lived in Madrid and is accustomed to the gaiety of the capital. He does not believe she will be satisfied with having such an inexorable censor pass upon all her actions. He suggests to his father that Don Severo be given a lesson that will make him more tolerant before the marriage takes place and before it is too late. Tomasa enters willingly into the plan, and when the prospective groom arrives he is told that his fiancée is out of town for a short time. Tomasa is then represented as a cousin, who is engaged to Carlos. In the short space of a day Don Severo is led into a declaration of love for the fiancée of his intended brother-in-law, accepts a challenge to a duel with the latter, loses by gambling money that does not belong to him, is guilty of deception and hypocrisy, and violates, in short, nearly all his vaunted code of morals. When he finds that he has been the victim of a joke, he does not become offended, but agrees with those who have caused his downfall that "it would be well for us to ask indulgence for everyone."[102]

Lista says that *Indulgence for Everybody* belongs to the type of comedy of manners in which the French writer Picard has so excelled, and that it closely approaches the style of Terence. Later in the same review he says that Gorostiza has imitated the style of Picard in manners and characters, and in the arrangement of the plot.[103] But in what he calls "the elocution," he believes Gorostiza's models are the Golden Age writers. Gorostiza imitates these writers, he says, in their freedom and facility of versification without falling into their lyrical *Gongorism* and affected style. He cites one passage in which he believes the imitation of Calderón is palpable. When Don Severo censures himself for his misconduct, Carlos asks him who will ever find out about it. Don Severo answers that his own conscience will know it, and when Carlos says that it will remain silent, Don Severo replies: "In this judge ever silent?" Lista compares this dialogue with one from Calderón where an attempt is made to persuade a noble young man to commit a misdeed. The question is asked: "Who, except you, will ever know about it?" and the young man answers: "What other witness is necessary? If I am vile, is it not enough that I should know it myself?"[104]

These statements by Lista should not be taken to mean that Gorostiza has embarked upon a new course, for *Indulgence for Everybody* violates none of the neo-classic precepts unless the slight liberty he takes with the versification be a violation, and this liberty has already found sanction in the writings of many neo-classicists. It will be remembered that even Moratín, although he preferred the octosyllabic *romance*, did not exclude the *redondilla*. Besides these two verse forms Gorostiza uses occasional *décimas* and short verses or *endechas*. But in these forms he avoids any suggestion of lyric flights, although there is an obvious attempt, in imitation of Golden Age writers, to vary the verse form to suit the moods and passions of the characters.

The language of the comedy is pure, graceful, and ingenious, although somewhat lacking in comic force. In the latter quality, however, it must be admitted that Gorostiza is superior in all of his comedies to other neo-classic dramatists.

One of the most conspicuous defects in the comedy is inherent in the intrigue. Larra notes the same defect in *Bread and Onions with You:* "The plan is defective in the same place as in other works by this author. We have already said upon another occasion that these plans in which several people invent an intrigue as a warning to another are incomplete and conspire against conviction, which should be the object of the trick."[105] It is, indeed, contrary to human nature to assume that Don Severo would accept in such a good-humored fashion the trick that had been played upon him. The same device is used by Gorostiza in *Customs of Yore*, as well as in *Bread and Onions with You*. Other defects in the comedy are the readiness with which Don Severo succumbs to the charms of the supposed

Flora, in violation of his code of honor which demands loyalty to his friend, Carlos; and the introduction in the solution of the plot of a servant whose previous minor roles does not justify her later activity. Lista comments upon this unnecessary use of the servant in terms which recall the statement made by Mor de Fuentes in the preface to *The Masculine Woman:*[106]

We should prefer that it not be the servant who informs Don Severo that everything that has happened to him is well known to everyone. In French comedy servants play a very important role, thanks to Molière. In our old theater they only took part as go-betweens; and this subordinate role can well be left to them without violating verisimilitude; but neither our manners nor our theater admit servants into the counsels and the affairs of the family. The intervention of Colasa, however, would not seem to us a defect, if this servant had taken a more active part in the play from the beginning.[107]

Another obvious defect arises from the conception of comedy as a vehicle for moral preachment. The characters frequently voice the author's own message to the public. The lesson is not allowed to derive from the action itself.

An attempt has been made by the Mexican critic Pimentel to give this comedy a deeper meaning than that which appears on the surface. He sees in Don Severo both the pagan and the Christian and suggests that a lesson for mankind can be derived from his spiritual fall.[108] There is, however, no real depth to the play, and any such attempt to read into it a profound moral lesson is to misinterpret entirely the purpose of the author.

Cotarelo y Mori believes with Larra that since Don Severo's fall is brought about by a conspiracy, the conclusion that general indulgence is necessary is only partially admissable. He says, however, that "in other respects and particularly in regard to art, the comedy is superior to anything that had been seen since Moratín, and posterity maintains it in this position."[109]

Indulgence for Everybody was performed for the first time at the Príncipe on September 14, 1818, with Máiquez in the role of Don Severo, and ran for seven days. It was repeated from the 11th to the 13th of November of the same year and was played twenty-three times from 1820 to 1833.

Gorostiza's next original comedy was *Customs of Yore* (1819), a pleasing one-act satire in verse against those who are always yearning for a return to the customs of a bygone age. The author explains in a "Note" his reason for writing the comedy and the cause of its failure to be played after its initial performance:

This comedy was written as a result of an order that came from on high and, for that reason, should be considered as a comedy of circumstances. It received unusual applause when it was presented, and the periodicals of the time spoke of it in the most flattering terms; but it has not been repeated since, because the author has not dared to rework it, as he could easily do and as he probably should do, in order that the Spanish stage might use a really original and not badly developed thought. Considerations of considerable weight, however, have removed the idea from his mind and he has preferred to leave *Customs of Yore* in its present form. What would have been said of it, if in the interest of dramatic art he had suppressed in this edition the allusions in the comedy to the marriage of the king? Poor Gorostiza![110]

The play was produced again, however, and ran for three days at the Príncipe in 1833, probably with the above allusions suppressed. They do not appear in the recast which Gorostiza made for the Teatro Principal of Mexico City.[111]

The plot of *Customs of Yore* is extremely simple, as is appropriate for a one-act play. Don Pedro is so convinced of the superiority of medieval life that he orders his household after the pattern of that time. Like a second Don Quijote he reads only old chronicles, and with him the imitation of old customs becomes a mania. Although he himself has arranged the marriage of the cousins Félix and Isabel, his nephew and his niece, he decides to postpone their marriage because they do not seem to love with the ardor of medieval lovers. To cure the old man of his mania the young couple engage the services of a troupe of actors and, taking advantage of a prolonged siesta of their uncle, set the stage so that when he awakens he imagines himself back in the Middle Ages. The old man, without much difficulty, is made to believe that he is the direct descendant of Pérez de Hita. Adventures follow similar to those Sancho Panza experienced in governing his island. The old man is forced to take part in a supposed defense of the city, for which he shows no more enthusiasm than did Don Quijote's squire when his castle was the object of attack. He faints at the moment of the supposed attack, thereby giving the conspirators an opportunity to restore the room to its original state. Upon regaining consciousness he believes what has happened has been a horrible nightmare; but he is, nevertheless, completely cured and withdraws his objections to the immediate marriage of the young couple.

Roa Bárcena believes this play is the one which best reveals the comic gifts of Gorostiza and says it might well have been written by Bretón de los Herreros, "because of its naturalness, intrigue, satire, and wit, and even because of the fluency and facility of its versification."[112]

In *Tit for Tat or Men and Women* (1819), another one-act comedy in verse, three women—a baroness, an elderly lady, and a coquette—are rivals for the hand of a marine officer. Assembled in the house of the baroness, the three ladies discuss their love, each unaware that the others are acquainted with the object of her affection. The officer has made each believe that he is coming to Madrid solely to see her. When he comes to the house of the baroness, he is very much disconcerted to find the three ladies together, but is forced to take part in the conversation, which is enlivened by the arrival of other guests. One of these, a would-be poet, has composed a poem on the "Judgment of Paris." The ladies decide to re-enact the scene and the officer is forced to play the role of Paris. He is induced by the wealth of the elderly lady to award the apple to her.

There is more than a suggestion in this play of Molière's *The Ridiculous Euphuists*. Don Juan, the poet, has composed a history of the crusades in *seguidillas*, has interpreted the most famous works of Greek authors without knowing a word of Greek, and has celebrated in sonnets, *sextillos*, and octaves every "spot, speck, feature, or mole" of all the Amarilises in his neighborhood. Although this play borders frequently upon farce, its humor is based upon human weaknesses and proceeds naturally from the action. Pimentel prefers *Customs of Yore* to *Tit for Tat* and censures the latter for its "lack of real interest" and for having a plot based upon "improbable coincidences."[113] The moral is contained in the two lines: "And only that sex is deceived—which thinks it is deceiving the other." The play was very popular on the stage, being performed no less than thirty-five times from 1827 to 1833 alone.

Don Dieguito (1820), a five-act comedy in verse, satirizes the contemporary society of Madrid with its *young roosters, dandies, dudes,* and *fops*. In this society move Don Cleto, Doña María, and their daughter, Adelaida. The parents have arranged the marriage of Adelaida to a simple rustic from the provinces, who is the only heir of his rich uncle, Anselmo. The latter arrives unexpectedly and, although a plain, uneducated countryman, he is sufficiently shrewd to see that the flattery the family showers upon Don Dieguito is

motivated by mercenary interest and that the girl has no love for
his nephew. He determines to thwart their plans. His first move is
to inform the girl's parents that he intends to marry and have direct
heirs, and suggests that he has not already put his plan into execution
because he has not been as successful as his nephew in finding a
young lady so virtuous and charming as Adelaida. The parents take
the bait and propose that he marry their daughter, declaring that
she has never been in love with Don Dieguito and has felt only contempt for him. When he sees that the girl is perfectly willing to
marry his uncle, Don Dieguito is disillusioned and declares his
intention of returning to his native province to seek a girl who will
marry him for love and not for his uncle's money. The uncle pretends financial reverses and returns with his nephew, leaving Adelaida and her parents in a helpless rage. Doña María turns upon Don
Simplicio, who has been their adviser in the whole matter, calling
him a false friend and blaming him for giving them such bad advice;
but he answers:

> ... it is not strange
> that such friends are found
> in a house where the master
> desires to receive only
> adulation and applause.
> If Don Cleto had not been so weak,
> and had not turned over to you
> the management of his house;
> if you, in the serious matter
> of arranging your daughter's
> future, had first consulted
> her heart; if Adelaida
> had a frank nature
> and a sensitive heart, then
> all of you would not have
> been deceived ... nor would
> my advice have been so selfish.[114]

Don Simplicio closes the play with the following lines:

> No, my friend;
> let us confess freely
> our error; and may Heaven grant
> that such a solemn shock
> serve to make us proceed
> with more caution in the future.

This comedy is typically neo-classic in the final injunction. The audience must be left with a moral lesson even if that lesson has to be dragged in by the hair.

Don Dieguito combines elements of the comedy of intrigue and the comedy of manners. Because of the complication of the action, Gorostiza experiences some difficulty in keeping the play within the bounds of the unity of time. Although not a complete innovation, *Don Dieguito* differs from most neo-classic comedies in that it does not terminate in a marriage. Moratín had avoided this traditional solution in his *The Old Man and the Girl,* but it cannot be said that neo-classic comedy differs greatly in this respect from the plays of Calderón, which "always end in marriage even though the subject may be the battles of Pentapolín with the rolled-up sleeves."[115]

María Esperanza Aguilar calls attention to the gallery of types which appear in *Don Dieguito:*

The genius of the author shines in that play more than in his other works. He makes less use of asides, and this increases the interest of the action, so that its varied situations excite the curiosity of one who reads the work or witnesses its performance. The unwary addlebrained fop, puffed up and entangled in the web of sordid interest; the old phlegmatic provincial, a keen observer, sagacious and sly, master of himself, with an expert knowledge of the human heart; and lastly the bold and hypocritical courtiers with their polished manners and base thoughts —all of these are portrayed with a masterly hand.[116]

Menéndez y Pelayo also notes the genre element in Gorostiza's comedies: "A period of our social history at the beginning of the nineteenth century is portrayed in Gorostiza's comedies, and we can only regret that these are so few in number."[117] Mesonero Romanos testifies to the continued popularity of this play and of *Indulgence for Everybody* when, in 1842, he writes that these two plays "were given unanimous applause, and even today they are performed to appreciative audiences."[118] *Don Dieguito* was performed twenty-nine times from 1820 to 1833.

Gorostiza's masterpiece, *Bread and Onions with You,* in four acts and in prose, which appeared in 1833, is the last of his original comedies. This play, which contains the merits and, to a lesser degree, the faults of his other comedies, departs somewhat from the traditional neo-classic rules in its infraction of the unities of time and place. But too much emphasis should not be placed upon this departure from the norm. The play is still a neo-classic comedy in its moral purpose, its contemporary setting, and its natural and unaffected style.

The theme of the play is well known. The satire is directed against a foolish and romantic young lady, Matilde, who, Quijote-like, has created for herself an unreal world, based upon the romantic and sentimental novels which she reads so avidly. She turns down the sensible Eduardo because he does not measure up to the standard of the heroes of fiction and because her father refuses to play the role of a cruel and unreasonable tyrant. The young man, who is deeply in love, realizes that to win her hand he must appear to her as a romantic hero. He pretends, therefore, that his uncle has disinherited him because he refuses to marry another girl and declares his intention to go away to some wild and distant land where he may drag out his wretched existence until death mercifully ends his suffering. The father, much against his will, is persuaded by the young man to refuse him admittance to the house.

Now that the marriage has the proper romantic setting, Matilde readily agrees to accept Eduardo, especially since he has planned that she elope with him, making her exit through a window in the accepted romantic style. After their marriage he takes her to a wretched one-room apartment, where she soon learns the inconvenience of poverty. Of course the stage has been set by Eduardo, and there are many comic incidents which accompany her disillusionment. The next day she is more than willing to return to her father's house to take up a pleasant if somewhat prosaic life with her resourceful husband.

Reviews of this play appeared in the *Revista Española* on July 9, 1833, in the *Correro Literario y Mercantil* on July 10, and in the *Correo de las Damas* on the same day. The review in the *Correo Literario* was written by Bretón de los Herreros and the other two reviews by Larra.

In his second article, Larra comments bitterly upon the difficulty which an ingenious Spanish comedy of manners experiences in competing with the "Hercules at the theater of the Cruz":

Two French giants, Mathevet and his pupil Triat, have made their appearance. The public has not shown itself unappreciative of their efforts. Our readers who have not seen the *horizontal column*, the *Siege of Mahoma*, the *rapid flight*, the *Roman chair*, etc., should run to the theater, and, without paying any attention to the titles, which have little relation to the acts, they will see great things, worthy, in a word, of the Olympic circus, because it appears that the Cruz, which until now has devoted itself to insignificant products of genius like comedies and tragedies, is rising to greater things.[119]

This is not the first time, he says, that genius has had to yield to strength. In spite of this competition, however, the new comedy by Gorostiza has been received "with much applause." Larra objects to the ill-sounding title and, although he admits that the comedy is filled with "pretty scenes, that are very comical," he objects also to a certain lack of refinement "which may shock the delicate feminine element of our readers, who will not like to see a matrimonial bed shown the day after a marriage, or hear onions mentioned, or see people eat raw chocolate, or . . . but let us pass lightly over the few defects of this composition."[120] This rather amusing bit of prudery does not seem to harmonize with the general liberalism of Larra's judgments. In his article in the *Revista Española* he questions the harm of reading novels: "It is a rather general error, in our opinion, to believe that novels are to blame for the foolish marriages and stupid connections that are being and have been made in the world."[121] He also shows an essentially romantic nature:

Although we believe that there is a great deal of truth in the object and substance of the comedy, we still do not believe that the character of Matilde is true to life; she is highly exaggerated. It has, as we see it, another defect, which is that of taking away from the spectator illusions that make up the happiness of life.[122]

These rather superficial observations, which are a reflection of the sentimental spirit of the age, are accompanied by the same objection Larra had voiced against Gorostiza's other comedies.

These articles provoked a heated answer in the form of a pamphlet by an admirer of Gorostiza, in which Larra was accused of "bad faith" and lack of intelligence. It was also suggested that Larra's criticism was a part of a *cabal* which had been formed against the comedy. This article was answered by Larra in the *Revista Española* for August 13, 1833. In the article he stands by his position, maintaining that Gorostiza's comedy has not been unduly censured in the periodicals but, on the contrary, "has probably been excessively praised."[123]

Critics generally have rejected Larra's evaluation of *Bread and Onions with You,* and the play is rightfully considered as Gorostiza's masterpiece. The Mexican critic Roa Bárcena says that it combines all the good qualities of Gorostiza's other comedies "and is probably the best of the three and one of the best in all the modern theaters."[124]

Gorostiza's interest in the Golden Age *comedia* is revealed not only in their influence upon his original comedies, but also in two recasts: *Women Can Also Keep a Secret* and *What Women Are*, which were the result, as he tells us in the "Foreword" to the edition of 1826, of "a simple argument between a group of friends, who were discussing the old Spanish repertoire, and although all agreed upon their intrinsic merit, differed on certain particulars."[125] The dispute evolved around this point: Were the defects attributed to these comedies the inherent consequence of the dramatic genre that was in vogue at that time? Gorostiza maintained that they were not and that, if Lope and Calderón had sinned against the rules of reason, they had not done so through ignorance or through necessity, but because of the haste with which they wrote. He added that Golden Age comedies "were all monuments of wit and grace; but that, in his opinion, they would have been better if they had been more regular."[126] The dispute became quite heated until one of the group suggested that Gorostiza prove his point by making two recasts of Golden Age plays, which would be performed and judged. Gorostiza accepted the challenge and reworked Calderón's *You Are Welcome but Unwelcome if You Come Alone* with the new title, *Women Can Also Keep a Secret;* and Rojas' *What Women Are*, without changing the title. The result of the experiment appears to have been satisfactory, for Gorostiza did, in fact, recast them and read them to the group. The "Foreword" to the printed edition adds: "They pleased; they were performed; they were applauded; and until now they have never been published."[127]

The author leaves the reader to decide whether the first of these two comedies has lost any of its movement or complicated intrigue, and whether the second has lost any of its originality and piquancy from having been subjected to the unities. Gorostiza's attitude toward the *comedia*, like that of Trigueros and Solís, was quite different from that of Sebastián y Latre. The latter, as we have seen, felt only contempt for them and believed firmly in the moral necessity of reworking them in order that the recasts might drive the originals from the boards. Gorostiza, on the contrary, admired these plays, but felt that, since times had changed, they should be reworked in order to make them conform more nearly to contemporary manners and tastes. There is no antagonism or fanaticism in his attitude.

He found it advisable to make certain changes in *What Women Are.* In this comedy, he says, "we have suppressed, in the interest of decency . . . many jokes which did not scandalize our grandparents, but which today would perhaps seem improper."[128] His attitude toward these comedies is similar to that of Moratín toward the comedies of Molière, although he does not allow himself as much freedom as did that author in reworking the originals.

Menéndez y Pelayo comments rather unenthusiastically upon the quality of Gorostiza's dramatic productions: "His genius, festive and agreeable, but somewhat superficial, shines most in his dialogue in verse, where he not only uses *redondillas, quintillas,* and *décimas,* but also occasional sonnets, and at times stanzas of *arte mayor.*"[129] To this critic, Gorostiza is a poet of second rank even within his genre and bears the same relation to Moratín that Regnard does to Molière. His principal merit is "in the briskness and movement of the dialogue, in the abundance of comic wit, and in a continuous movement that is innocent and kindly."[130] Gorostiza, however, easily slips into vulgarisms and buffoonery, which are a faithful copy of the language used in middle-class social gatherings in Madrid at that time. He is no model of good taste or good manners and lacks that "inexhaustible store of correct, familiar, and picaresque language with which Bretón de los Herreros heightens the interest of the most trivial matters."[131] Menéndez y Pelayo concedes, however, that Gorostiza "has one quality which is indispensable in a writer of comedies, that is, the ability to amuse," a quality, he says, that is lacking in the comedies of Burgos, Martínez de la Rosa, Tapia, Gil y Zárate, and the others who wrote at that time.[132]

Cejador y Frauca, who regards nationalism as a prime requisite to good writing, says that Gorostiza was the best writer of comedies from Moratín to Bretón and was more national than Moratín.[133]

Javier de Burgos

Two comedies by Javier de Burgos, *The Three Equals* and *The Masked Ball,* are frequently cited as the most successful attempts in the entire neo-classic period to harmonize the old comedy and the new. Ferrer del Río gives this interpretation of Javier de Burgos' dramatic creed:

A classicist par excellence and a connoisseur of our old theater, Burgos professes the doctrine that the regularity of Moratín's comedies and Calderón's elegance are not incompatible; without violating the unities the action can be animated, for the rules do not oppose a multiplication of incidents and a search for ways to interest the spectators.[134]

When *The Masked Ball* was republished in 1842 in the *Revista Andaluza*, mention was made in a "Foreword" of a number of other comedies composed by Burgos: "The present comedy is one of the fifteen which are reported to have been written by this author, and the publication of which, along with his *History of Spain* and other works no less important, we hope, both for the glory of his name and for that of this nation, will not be deferred any longer."[135] Ferrer del Río says that during Burgos' exile his early works were destroyed by his political enemies, and only mentions as extant *The Three Equals* and *The Masked Ball*, together with two other comedies, *The Optimist and the Pessimist*, which was read before the Liceo, and *Disillusionment for Everybody*, of which honorable mention is made in the minutes of that organization and which was probably played on the stage at the Liceo. An earlier play, *The Heir*,[136] a three-act comedy in prose, probably printed in 1804 or 1805, escaped the notice of Ferrer del Río. This play differs completely from Burgos' later comedies. Not only is it written in prose, but it shows the unmistakable influence of the sentimental comedy in its long speeches extolling virtue and in the sensibility of its heroine. The play is very careful in the observance of the unities and has nothing in common with the *comedia*.

The Three Equals (1818),[137] his next comedy, in three acts and in octosyllabic *romance*, is a free reworking of *Conventional Love* by Solís and of *I Love All I See*, by Calderón. In the "Foreword," Burgos gives an account of the purpose of the play and of the circumstances which led to its composition:

At the beginning of 1818 the following question was discussed at a meeting of writers: "Would it be possible to write comedies which, without violating rules of art, would possess the spirited action and the warmth of language which are characteristic of our old theater? Or, in other words, would it be possible, without violating verisimilitude and without multiplying incidents, to complicate the situations and to use a versification, perhaps smooth-flowing and facile, perhaps brilliant and rich, but always smooth and harmonious?" I maintained, against the opinion of one of those who attended the meeting, "that it was possible to write comedies which would possess the qualities that had been indicated," and to prove my assertion I wrote *The Three Equals*.[138]

Burgos calls attention to the fact that the general traits of his main character are to be found in certain Golden Age plays, but insists upon the fundamental originality of his work:

> Don Pedro Calderón de la Barca in *I Love All I See*, Don Antonio de Solís in *Conventional Love*, and others of our old dramatists, in works not so well known, have presented a protagonist more or less similar to the one in *The Three Equals*. This circumstance was not sufficient to deter me. The easiest thing in such cases is to trace well the character of a personage who suffers from a very general defect. . . . The difficult thing is to imagine a dramatic combination in which the development of a very common character will produce impressions that are different from those produced in an earlier combination. One who compares the two comedies by Calderón and Solís with mine will see how differently the resources at the disposal of a writer of comedies have been handled.[139]

Burgos denies any intention of rivaling Calderón or Solís and declares that he only wishes to point the way which future dramatists should follow. If his comedy shows more verisimilitude, more coherence, and more regularity than the earlier plays, these qualities are not to be credited to the author but to the age in which he lives, for if those two writers were living at the present time, "they would have handled the same story better than I."[140]

The Three Equals would have been performed by Máiquez, for whom it was written, if that actor had not left Madrid at the end of the summer of 1818. Burgos abandoned his intention of producing the play and did not think of it again until some nine years later, when he saw some good performances of old comedies at the Cruz. The acting in *The Three Equals,* when it was performed on November 17, 1827, was satisfactory on the whole, "taking into consideration the condition in which the theatrical companies find themselves today. . . . José García Luna, especially, performed the role of the protagonist with zeal and understanding."[141] The final speech of Pedro, one of the "three equals," with which the comedy closes indicated the theme and the solution of the play:

> My friends, we three are left,
> like heads of fresh lettuce,
> all alike, and in a way
> that is a consolation.
> Don Carlos, come here.
> You come too, and let us form
> such a group of jilted men
> that everyone who sees us
> will say, as if he were

reading it in our faces,
that Don Carlos loses Inés
because he is fickle and flighty;
for if these qualities
are accompanied by charm
and talent, they may dazzle
for a short while,
but sooner or later
the world in its justice
only gives consideration
and esteem to truth.
They will say that you lose
Doña Luisa because of boorish habits;
because you are vain, grumbling,
peevish, and silly, faults
that the integrity I respect
in you is insufficient to cover.
They will say that I lose Inés
through my indifference,
for indifferent people should
not count upon anyone, since
their character prevents
anyone from counting on them.
So then, my friends, from now on
let us mend our ways, if we can.

Such a sermon at the close would seem to be sufficient to kill any play, no matter how great its merit might be in other respects. Eugenio de Ochoa, however, is almost enthusiastic in his praise of Burgos' comedy, saying that "the whole work is so superior to the two compositions by Calderón and Solís that no reader or spectator can fail to feel and proclaim it."[142]

This play immediately involved its author in a polemic with José María de Carnerero. The latter's criticism and Javier's answer appeared in El Correo Literario y Mercantil, November 10 and 14, 1828, and is another typical example of the constant feuds that were waged within the ranks of neo-classicism.

Burgos' next play, The Masked Ball, is even more like the comedia in the variety of incident, movement, and spirit which characterized the old theater. In this play, as in The Three Equals, there is a servant who has many of the qualities of the gracioso. The Masked Ball was never produced in Madrid, because, according to Ochoa and to the Revista Andaluza, of the excessive modesty of its author. Although the comedy achieved a "marked triumph" when it was played in Granada in 1832, Burgos refused to allow it to be presented in the capital.[143]

Even though in 1818 Javier de Burgos quite evidently thought the neo-classic precepts were necessary for dramatic perfection, his attitude toward that school had undergone some change by 1841, the date of his "Discourse on the Theater, Pronounced in the Liceum of Granada."[144] In this discourse he lampoons the neo-classic movement for the barrenness of its production and attributes to it no small part in the decadence of the Spanish theater. Probably he was influenced by Duran's discourse on the influence of modern criticism upon the decadence of the old theater, which had provoked heated polemics in the periodicals.[145] Javier de Burgos deplores the wretched condition of the contemporary theater in Spain, attributing it to the introduction of French romanticism: "So the theater has become a school of perversity, of corruption, of skepticism, and of detestable literary taste in addition. . . . What manners are represented by the dramatic compositions which, seven or eight years ago, began to invade our theater, and afterward have taken it over completely?"[146] Until the Spanish stage returns to its task of depicting national manners faithfully, there is no hope of reform. But when order is re-established, it will not be necessary, in order to construct a new theater, "to seek precepts in Aristotle or in Horace, but to find inspiration in Moreto and Calderón."[147]

Aristipo Megareo

Many dramatists of the preromantic period composed neo-classic comedies which either did not reach the stage or else attracted little attention even at the time of their performance and have long since passed into oblivion. Among these authors Aristipo Megareo, the pseudonym of Fernando Cagigal, Marqués de Casa-Cagigal, is frequently mentioned. Mesonero Romanos, after a brief discussion of the plays of Gorostiza and Martínez de la Rosa, says:

In the years between 1814 and 1824 many others contended for Thalia's mask; but all were very inferior to the two mentioned, the Marqués of Cagigal (Aristipo Megareo), the author of several comedies, among which may be mentioned as notable *Matrimony Discussed* and *Society Unmasked*, standing out occasionally in comedy . . .[148]

Javier de Burgos declares that in the twelve years which followed the peace of 1814, the theatrical repertoire was increased only by

...one or two unknown works by the Marqués de Casa-Cagigal; with *Don Dieguito* and *Indulgence for Everybody* by Don Manuel Eduardo de Gorostiza; with one or two light compositions by Don José Joaquin de Mora and Don José María de Carnerero; and with a few translations of foreign plays and recasts of Golden Age comedies . . .[149]

The comedies of Aristipo Megareo are very rare today. From the scarcity of comment on his plays in the periodicals it is difficult to justify Mesonero Romanos' statement that they "do not fail to be noteworthy." The *Minerva o el Revisor general*, in its announcement of *Matrimony Discussed*, says that it was performed from the 19th to the 21st of May, 1818, and that in these three days it produced a total of 17,238 reals. It was repeated the following year on July 1, 8, and 9.

Aristipo Megareo's dramatic works seem to have been limited to a one-act translation of an Italian farce, *The Happy Deception*, and the original comedies: *Lazy People; Society Unmasked* (1818), in three acts and in verse; *Education*, a prose comedy in three acts; and *Matrimony Discussed* (1817), also in three acts and in prose. The printed editions of his plays are characterized by very extensive stage directions. The comedy, *Society Unmasked*,[150] is written in octosyllabic *romance* and carefully follows the unities. In the stage directions we are told that the action begins half an hour before nightfall and ends at midnight. The final verses of the last act give an adequate idea of the lesson the comedy is supposed to teach:

> Well, my dear friend, this
> is society without a mask.
> It must be followed as you see it,
> for no one changes the world;
> and so it has its advantages;
> but to live in this society
> and avoid its dangers
> one must know it well.

Education,[151] also printed in 1818, probably was never staged in Madrid. This edition, like that of *Society Unmasked*, contains a quotation from Horace on the flyleaf. *Matrimony Discussed* was printed in 1817, although it was not performed in Madrid until the following year. It does not seem to have attracted any comment or review in the periodicals. All of Aristipo Megareo's comedies obey the unities and have a didactic purpose. They are, however, almost devoid of merit and exercised no influence upon the theater.

Sporadic Comedies

Among those dramatists whose production seems to have been limited to one comedy may be mentioned Ascanio Florigero, the pseudonym of Estanislau de Cosea Vayo, whose *Amalia or Not All Girls Are Coquettes* was performed in Valencia in November, 1827, and published in the same year with a long preface in which the author's neo-classic creed is stated; and Noraci de Vesald (Nicanor Valdés), whose *The Generous Litigant* (1826), a three-act comedy in verse, was also published in Valencia and contained a quotation from Horace on the flyleaf. Many neo-classic comedies of this period contained quotations from the Latin author or from Iriarte's fables as a kind of trade-mark.

The Generous Litigant[152] is a satire against ignorant and unscrupulous lawyers and closes with a typical neo-classic injunction:

> Don't forget that your position
> requires many virtues
> and a great deal of knowledge,
> for a lawyer is a man
> assigned by heaven
> to defend the life,
> the property, and the rights
> of his fellow-citizens.
> If he lacks talent,
> knowledge, and virtue, he is
> no lawyer, he is a pervert,
> upon whom the curse
> of the people will fall.

This comedy is written in octosyllabic *romance* and carefully observes the rules. It was probably never performed in Madrid.

The *young dandies* fared badly at the hands of several neo-classic dramatists. These plays are of only historical interest. In 1826 there appeared a sermon in the form of a comedy with the title *Advice to Young Dandies or Wayward Youth* written by one who called himself "an ecclesiastic who loves his country."[153] In 1827 *The Pathetic Fashion Plate*,[154] a three-act comedy in prose, which seems to have been rather popular from 1827 to 1833 (it was performed fifteen times at the Cruz), made its appearance; and in the following year a one-act comedy in prose, by D. Flechilla, with the title *Dandies and Charlatans or Fools in a Trap*, was published in Barcelona.[155]

A woman, Francisca Navarro, was active in continuing the tradition of Moratín in Barcelona with a number of comedies in prose and in verse: *To Love or Not to Love* (1828), five acts, verse; *Inclined to Fall in Love* (1828), three acts, prose; *One Night at a Party* (1828), three acts, prose; *The Man Who Plays the Woman* (1829); *My Portrait and My Chum's* (1829), three acts, prose; *The Husband of Two Women* (1828), three acts, prose; *The Andalusian Girl in the Labyrinth* (1829), one act, prose; *The Foolish Girl or The Ridiculous Sweetheart of Two Sisters* (1828), one act, verse; and *The Defense of Coquettes,* one act, verse. It is uncertain whether these comedies were staged in Barcelona. No mention is made of them in any of the periodicals of Madrid, and the editions printed in Barcelona contain no reference to their having been performed.

All of these comedies are written either in prose or in octosyllabic *romance,* carefully observe the unities, and contain a moral which is enforced in the final scenes. There is little to recommend them in language, versification, dialogue, or plot structure. An evidence of the attitude of the author toward the unities may be found in her "Note" to *One Night at a Party:* "This comedy is new in its invention. It ends entirely in each act, so that each can be performed separately; the first and second without the third; the second and third without the first; and the three together form a single play, observing the three unities of action, time, and place."[156] It appears that Francisca Navarro regarded the unities as a kind of game.

1. Ramón de Mesonero Romanos, "Rápida ojeada sobre la historia del teatro español," *Semanario Pintoresco Español* (Madrid, 1842), p. 398.
2. *El Censor,* January 13, 1821.
3. Alcalá Galiano, *op. cit.,* p. 201.
4. Martínez de la Rosa, *Obras Completas* (Paris, 1845), II, 3.
5. *El Censor,* June 22, 1822.
6. *Ibid.*
7. Larra, "Representación de la Niña en Casa y la madre en la máscara," *Revista Española,* April 14, 1834.
8. *Ibid.*
9. Martínez de la Rosa, *op. cit.,* II, 75.
10. *El Universal,* December 8, 1821.
11. *Ibid.*
12. *Ibid.*
13. *Ibid.*
14. See p. 425 above.

15. Larra, *op. cit.,* pp. 154-55.
16. *Ibid.,* p. 155.
17. *Ibid.,* p. 157.
18. *Ibid.,* p. 158.
19. *Ibid.*
20. *Ibid.,* p. 159.
21. *Ibid.,* p. 162.
22. Mesonero Romanos, *op. cit.,* p. 398.
23. Martínez de la Rosa, *op. cit.,* II, 431.
24. Larra, "Primera representación de Los celos infundados o El Marido en la chimenea," *Revista Española,* February 1, 1833.
25. *Diario de Barcelona,* July 1, 1833.
26. Larra, *op. cit.*
27. *Ibid.*
28. *Ibid.*
29. Martínez de la Rosa, *op. cit.,* Vol. II.
30. *Ibid.,* "Advertencia."
31. *Ibid.*

32. *Ibid.*
33. *Ibid.*
34. See p. 324 above.
35. *La Esperanza*, October 20, 1839.
36. *Ibid.*
37. Martínez de la Rosa, *op. cit.*, II, 30.
38. Menéndez y Pelayo, "Don Francisco Martínez de la Rosa," *Autores Dramáticos Contemporáneos* (Madrid, 1882), p. 14.
39. *Ibid.*
40. *El Censor*, 1821, V, 319.
41. *Ibid.*, p. 191.
42. Pedro Estala, *Edipo Tirano, tragedia del griego en verso castellano, con un discurso preliminar sobre la tragedia antigua y moderna* (Madrid, 1793), p. 5.
43. *Ibid.*
44. *Ibid.*, p. 33.
45. Martínez de la Rosa, *op. cit.*, II, 250.
46. *Ibid.*, I, 234.
47. *Ibid.*, II, 250.
48. *Ibid.*, p. 252.
49. *Ibid.*
50. *Cartas Españolas*, February 9, 1832, IV, 178.
51. *Ibid.*, pp. 178-79.
52. *Ibid.*, pp. 180-81.
53. *Ibid.*, p. 186.
54. Martínez de la Rosa, "Biografía," *Obras Completas*, p. xiv.
55. *Ibid.*, p. xiv.
56. *El Artista*, I, 158.
57. *La Revista Española*, April 25, 1834.
58. Martínez de la Rosa, *op. cit.*, II, 424.
59. *Ibid.*
60. *Ibid.*, p. 425.
61. *Ibid.*
62. *Ibid.*, p. 426.
63. *Ibid.*
64. *La Revista Española*, April 25, 1834, p. 177.
65. E. Allison Peers, *The Romantic Movement in Spain* (Cambridge, 1940), I, 255.
66. Martínez de la Rosa, "Advertencia," *La Conjuración de Venecia*.
67. *El Artista*, I, 177.
68. Prologue to the edition of *Aben Humeya*, published separately in Paris, *Obras Completas*, II, 291.
69. *Ibid.*, p. 291.
70. Menéndez y Pelayo, "Don Francisco Martínez de la Rosa," *Autores Dramáticos Contemporáneos*, p. 20.
71. *Ibid.*
72. *Ibid.*
73. Larra, *Obras Completas de Fígaro* (Paris, n.d.), II, 104.

74. Allison Peers, *op. cit.*, I, 275.
75. Martínez de la Rosa, *op. cit.*, II, 291.
76. Menéndez y Pelayo, *Historia de las ideas estéticas*, III, 475.
77. Moratín, "Discurso Preliminar," *Obras (B.A.E.* II, 322).
78. See p. 406 above.
79. Menéndez y Pelayo, *op. cit.*, III, 475.
80. Martínez de la Rosa, *Obras Completas*, I, 217.
81. *Ibid.*, p. 221.
82. *Ibid.*, p. 229.
83. *Ibid.*, p. 231.
84. *Ibid.*, p. 245.
85. *Ibid.*, p. 227.
86. *Ibid.*, p. 223.
87. *Ibid.*
88. *Ibid.*, p. 231.
89. *Ibid.*, p. 245.
90. *Ibid.*, p. 246.
91. *Ibid.*, p. 250.
92. *Ibid.*, p. 251.
93. Martínez de la Rosa, "Apéndice sobre la comedia española," *Obras Completas*, I, 224.
94. *Ibid.*, pp. 224-25.
95. Menéndez y Pelayo, *op. cit.*, III, 477.
96. See p. 449 above.
97. Martínez de la Rosa, "Poesías," *Obras Completas*, I, 4.
98. *Ibid.*
99. *Ibid.*
100. Manuel Eduardo de Gorostiza, *Teatro escogido* (2 vols.; Paris, 1826).
101. *El Censor*, June 1, 1822.
102. Gorostiza, *Indulgencia para todos*, Act V, Sc. 6 (*Obras de D. Manuel E. de Gorostiza* [Mexico, 1899], Vol. I).
103. *El Censor*, June 1, 1822.
104. *Ibid.*
105. Larra, "Representación de la comedia nueva de D. Manuel Eduardo Gorostiza, titulada *Contigo pan y cebolla*," *Revista Española*, July 9, 1833.
106. See p. 406 above.
107. *El Censor*, June 1, 1822.
108. Francisco Pimentel, *Historia crítica de la literatura y de las ciencias en México* (México, 1885), p. 613.
109. Cotarelo y Mori, *Máiquez*, p. 451.
110. Gorotiza, *Las costumbres de antaño*, "Nota del autor" (*Obras de Gorostiza* [México, 1899]).
111. See María Esperanza Aguilar, *Estudio bio-bibliográfico de D. Manuel Eduardo de Gorostiza* (Mexico, 1932), p. 20.
112. Roa Bárcena, *Velada Literaria*, celebrada por el Liceo Hidalgo la noche del

17 de Enero de 1876, para honrar la memoria del Señor Manuel Eduardo de Gorostiza (Mexico, 1876).

113. Pimentel, *op. cit.*, p. 619.

114. Gorostiza, *Don Dieguito*, Act V, Sc. II.

115. *El Memorial Literario*, review of Bouilly's *El abate de l'Epee*, translated by Juan de Estrada (Madrid, 1801), I, 1.

116. María Esperanza Aguilar, *op. cit.*, p. 21.

117. Menéndez y Pelayo, *Historia de la poesía hispano-americana* (Madrid, 1911), I, 121.

118. Mesonero Romanos, "Rápida ojeada sobre la historia del teatro español, tercera época," *Semanario Pintoresco Español*, 1842, p. 398.

119. *Correo de las Damas*, July 10, 1833. (Reprinted in *Post-Fígaro* [Madrid, 1918], I, 198-201.)

120. *Ibid.*, p. 200.

121. *Revista Española*, July 9, 1833.

122. *Correo de las Damas* (Reprinted in *Post-Fígaro*, p. 100).

123. *Revista Española*, August 13, 1833.

124. Roa Bárcena, *op. cit.*, p. 34.

125. Gorostiza, "Advertencia" de la edición de 1826. (Reprinted in *Obras de D. Manuel E. de Gorostiza* [Mexico, 1899], III, 5-7.)

126. *Ibid.*, "Advertencia," p. 6.

127. *Ibid.*

128. *Ibid.*

129. Menéndez y Pelayo, *op. cit.*, I, 119.

130. *Ibid.*, p. 120.

131. *Ibid.*, pp. 120-21.

132. *Ibid.*, p. 121.

133. Cejador y Frauca, *Historia de la lengua y literatura castellana*, VI, 372.

134. Antonio Ferrer del Río, *Galería de la literatura española* (Madrid, 1846), p. 62.

135. *Revista Andaluza*, 1842, IV, 656-702.

136. Francisco Xavier de Burgos, *El heredero*, comedia en prosa, en tres actos (Granada, n.d.) Imp. de Don Francisco Gómez Espinosa de los Monteros.

137. Xavier de Burgos, *Los tres iguales*, comedia en tres actos y en verso, representada por primera vez en el coliseo de la Cruz el día 17 de noviembre de 1827 (Madrid, 1828).

138. *Ibid.*, "Advertencia."

139. *Ibid.*

140. *Ibid.*

141. *Ibid.*

142. Eugenio de Ochoa, *Apuntes para una biblioteca de autores españoles* (Paris, 1840), I, 192.

143. *Revista Andaluza*, 1842, IV, 656-702.

144. Javier de Burgos, "Discurso sobre el teatro español, pronunciado en el Liceo de Granada," *Panorama*, Tercera época, Vol. V.

145. See pp. 515-21 below.

146. Javier de Burgos, *op. cit.*, p. 182.

147. *Ibid.*, p. 185.

148. Mesonero Romanos, *op. cit.*, p. 398.

149. Javier de Burgos, *op. cit.*, p. 180.

150. Aristipo Megareo, *La sociedad sin máscara*, comedia en tres actos y en verso (Barcelona, 1818).

151. Aristipo Megareo, *La educación*, comedia en tres actos y en verso (Barcelona, 1818).

152. Noraci de Vesald, *El litigante generoso*, comedia en tres actos y en verso (Valencia, 1826).

153. *Aviso a los lechuguinos o sea La juventud extraviada*, comedia neuva de costumbres, en prosa, en dos actos; con varias advertencias sobre la misma, y un prospecto sobre los trajes, por un eclesiástico amante de su patria (Madrid, 1826).

154. *La lechuguina patética*, comedia en tres actos en prosa, escrita por . . . A copy of this comedy in the Buchanan collection at the University of Toronto has the name of Don Pedro Gorostiza, the brother of Don Manuel, inserted in longhand as the author.

155. D. Flechilla, *Lechuguinos y charlatanes o Los majaderos en el garlito* (Barcelona, 1828).

156. Francisca Navarro, *Una noche de tertulia, o el Coronel D. Raimundo*, original (Barcelona, 1828).

XVI

The Last Stage of Neo-classic Drama

Gil y Zárate

GIL Y ZÁRATE, like Martínez de la Rosa, is principally remembered today as the author of plays which depart from neo-classic precepts, and like that author, he abandoned the excesses of romanticism and turned in his later works either to eclecticism or to a modified neo-classicism.

His first attempt in the field of drama was made with *A Fanatic Over Comedies* (1816), a prose comedy in one act.[1] This play, which was presented in private theaters with the title, *A Mania for Comedies,* in 1816, exerted little or no influence upon the development of comedy. It is a humorous satire on amateur theatricals which were extremely popular at the time under the name of "domestic comedies."

Gil y Zárate's first success was achieved with *The Meddler* (1825), a comedy in three acts and in prose, which was given its initial performance on August 10, 1825.[2] For the principal butt of ridicule in this comedy he chooses a busybody who believes that his own family is incapable of the indiscretions he is so ready to criticize in others, although the mother, who puts her own selfish pleasure above duty to her family, comes in for her share of censure. This mother, like the mother in Martínez de la Rosa's *The Daughter at Home and the Mother at the Masquerade,* bends every effort to secure the attentions of young men and even attempts to rival her own daughter in the affections of Gabriel. *The Meddler,* however, is much more indebted to Moratín's *The Consent of Young Maidens,* from which it takes the theme that parents should not attempt to control the marriage of their children. There is, however, one noticeable difference between the plays. Gil y Zárate never uses the characters as mere spokesmen to voice his own ideas, but allows the lesson to be derived from the action. In the solution the father, Don Melchor, is cured of his meddling in other people's affairs and the mother receives a shock that brings her to her senses. The play has sufficient intrigue to maintain the interest of the spectators without becoming so involved as to endanger the unity of action. The unity of time is as closely observed as it is in the comedies of Moratín.

The Meddler was only moderately successful. The statement has frequently been made that in his early plays Gil y Zárate rivaled the success of Bretón. This seems to be true with regard to the latter's early comedies, which created no sensation. *The Meddler* was played seven times from 1825 to 1833, *Be Careful About Sweethearts* ten times, and *A Year After the Wedding* fifteen times, while Bretón's *Old Age Folly* was performed thirteen times and *The Two Nephews* fifteen.

Gil y Zárate's second comedy to be staged was *Be Careful About Sweethearts, or School for Young People* (1826), in five acts and in verse.[3] A manuscript in the National Library, bearing the subtitle, *The Obligation of Marriage,* states that it was imitated from the French; but since no printed version uses this subtitle, and since there is no suggestion in Gil y Zárate's private papers that the comedy had a French model, there seems to be no adequate reason to question its originality. It was accepted as original by all the critics of the time.

In this play Gil y Zárate does not confine his satire to one character. The three principal characters—the greedy, covetous woman; the simple, honest young man who, through lack of experience, becomes the easy prey of a crew of sharpers; and the parents who, through cupidity, seek to arrange the marriage of their daughter— are types not new in comedy, but in this play so naturally drawn that the effect is more convincing than usual. The comedy differs from *The Consent of Young Maidens* and bears more resemblance to Martínez de la Rosa's *Don Dieguito* in that the daughter, who seems at first to be an admirable young lady, soon reveals that she is a worthy copy of her mother and readily abandons her suitor, Silverio, in order to ensnare Cándido because of his wealth. There is no need for parental coercion. In this play Gil y Zárate follows his custom of introducing an innocent and beautiful heroine, who is the victim of a conspiracy. Inés, who is in love with Cándido, finally becomes convinced that he has forsaken her of his own free will, and, unwilling to continue living in the corrupted environment of her aunt's house, goes away with her brother. Cándido, although hopelessly in love with her, insists, through a mistaken conception of honor, on keeping his promise to Isabel, even after he realizes that this promise has been extracted by trickery. Of course, since this is a comedy, the spectators know full well that in the end the tricksters will be exposed and Cándido will win Inés.

Be Careful About Sweethearts reveals considerable technical skill. There is practically no exposition and the plot is allowed to form and develop on the stage. This necessitates a violation of the unity of time, for it would be unnatural to crowd into one day all the elements that make up the intrigue. The unities of action and of place are carefully observed. Because of the popularity of the carefully constructed plays of the French dramatist Eugene Scribe, and of the Italian opera, it had become increasingly difficult for an original Spanish comedy to gain recognition. Gil y Zárate, who was an opportunist, understood this difficulty and gave careful attention to technique. He also made some concession to the popular taste for melodrama by the introduction in *Be Careful About Sweethearts* of a typical melodramatic villain in the person of Don Melitón. On the whole, however, this play departs little from the neo-classic comedy of the school of Moratín. Probably the most significant change, and the one which has already been noted in *The Meddler*, is the abandonment of a too obvious didactic purpose which found expression in long sermons and which marred so many neo-classic comedies. In the versification no change is to be noted, for all of Gil y Zárate's comedies are written either in prose or in octosyllabic *romance*.

Despite the efforts of the author and the unquestionable merit of the play, *Be Careful About Sweethearts* was only moderately successful, being performed only ten times from 1826 to 1833.

A Year After the Wedding (1826), Gil y Zárate's next comedy, is one of the best of the day.[4] This play was highly praised by both Spanish and foreign critics. One of the latter, Xavier Durrieu, a French critic, proclaimed it worthy of Moreto or Tirso.[5]

A Year After the Wedding is a comedy of manners in which the satire is directed against vain ambition in the person of the Marqués de Rosa, who, in order to rise in social rank and political power, does not hesitate to allow his beautiful and faithful wife to be seen in public with other men while he himself becomes involved with a vampire who poses as a baroness. In the end the Marqués is brought to his senses and the false friends, the Count of Fuendorada and the baroness, are duly exposed. In this comedy Gil y Zárate does not entirely observe the injunction he gives in his *Manual of Literature*[6] that the characters should never become mouthpieces of the author. Don Gregorio is Gil y Zárate and expresses the latter's views on vanity, extravagance, and superficiality.

In this play, as in his other comedies, Gil y Zárate observes the utmost economy in the number of characters. This makes it easy for the audience to follow the situations and enables the author to devote more attention to characterization. The unities of action and place are rigorously observed, although the play departs from the traditional neo-classic type in its violation of the unity of time. This violation is skilfully handled, however, and in fact is too moderate to be significant.

In the opinion of Xavier Durrieu, Gil y Zárate shows in *A Year After the Wedding* a talent which might have elevated him to an eminent position in the field of comedy:

> If he had kept on, Gil y Zárate, in our opinion, would have become an excellent writer of comedies, and the proof is that he has written one comedy, a real masterpiece of cleverness and of wit, in which the ridiculous aspects of contemporary Spanish society are very exactly and very interestingly portrayed.[7]

Although almost unknown today, this comedy was fairly popular in its day, having been performed fifteen times from 1826 to 1833. Of course, its popularity cannot be compared with that of an opera like *The Barber of Seville* with 108 performances from 1821 to 1833, or with that of a comedy of magic like Grimaldi's *The Goat's Foot* with 125 performances from 1829 to 1833. These two types completely dominated the stage of that period and discouraged the production of original plays, which invariably had short runs.

Gil y Zárate is remembered today principally as the author of the historical drama, *Guzmán the Good,* and to a lesser degree as the author of the ultraromantic drama, *Carlos II.* The popularity of the latter play, however, was so distasteful to its fundamentally conservative author that he sought an injunction against its continued performance.[8] In his later plays, Gil y Zárate turned from violent romantic drama to modified neo-classic comedy, to sentimental comedy, and to historical drama, in all of which he observed a reasonable regularity.

Mesonero Romanos believes that Gil y Zárate's literary convictions were probably essentially classic, but that he realized that in order to achieve success it was necessary to follow the popular trend.[9]

Even at the beginning of his dramatic career Gil y Zárate gave evidence of a disinclination to limit himself to one genre. We find him, therefore, in the first period of his literary activity cultivating both neo-classic comedy and tragedy. His initial effort in the latter genre appears to have been a free translation of Arnaud's *Don Pedro*, which was performed at the Cruz in 1827 with the title *Don Pedro of Portugal*. The success of this work encouraged him to compose an original tragedy, *Rodrigo*,[10] which was accepted by the actors and approved by the political censor. All arrangements had been made to stage it with a competent cast and fitting decorations when the ecclesiastical censor, Father Carillo, refused to permit its perform-ance, saying that "although it is true that kings have frequently been fond of girls, it is not fitting that they should be represented as so enamored in the theaters."[11]

After the censors had rejected two tragedies he had trans-lated from the French, Gil y Zárate, still hopeful, composed another original tragedy, *Blanca de Borbón*, in 1829 and submitted it to the board for approval. This time it was the political censor who pro-nounced an adverse judgment. The author later admitted that the decision was understandable at the time in view of the fact that a Spanish king was publicly stigmatized in a work sprinkled with extremely liberal ideas.[12] Now thoroughly discouraged and disillu-sioned, Gil y Zárate abandoned all literary activity until, at the death of Fernando VII, a more liberal regime came into power in Spain. He felt bitter to the end of his life toward the insurmountable ob-stacles that had been placed in the path of his efforts during the years in which, he says, "the best part of my youth was spent when I might have written my best works."[13]

In 1835 Gil y Zárate again offered *Blanca de Borbón* to the theater, in spite of the fact that the recent swing in Spain toward romanticism seemed to offer little hope for its success. When the play was performed in June of that year it received favorable reviews in the periodicals; and even such an ardent romanticist as Eugenio de Ochoa took the opportunity to prove that he was far more open-minded than the neo-classicists, who had spurned "the beautiful drama *Alfredo*" merely because it was romantic, by giving the tragedy a qualified endorsement:

When we say that *Blanca de Borbón* is a classical tragedy, we have said that it is written in a genre we do not like. But we shall not for that reason try to ridicule it, even though ridicule seems to be in fashion now. The fact that some pseudo-classic periodicals have sacrificed the beautiful drama *Alfredo* to their unjust anger because it was romantic will not make us disdain *Blanca de Borbón* because it is classical. In spite of its genre this tragedy has many beauties, and heaven knows that we speak with all the sincerity of our hearts when we say we are convinced that it would be very good if it were not classical.[14]

Ochoa believes the author should be praised for having dared to face the dangers to which an altered public demand exposed the success of his tragedy. Even though the public seems to be in favor of neither of the warring literary factions, "it is certain that more courage is needed to present a classical than a romantic work because the latter offers with its changes of decoration and metrical diversity many more resources than the former to hold the attention of such an enlightened public as that which fills the orchestra chairs of our theaters every night."[15]

After the second performance of *Blanca de Borbón,* the *Diario de Avisos de Madrid* gave, under the heading "Boletín," a long review and criticism of the tragedy, prefaced by the following statement: "A new tragedy that is both original and good in the present sad condition of our literature is too much a novelty for us to let the occasion pass without a special article."[16] The reviewer praised the choice of subject: while other poets had treated the same theme, he said, Gil y Zárate was the first to present it upon the stage.*

The turbulent reign of Pedro of Castile, whose amorous misconduct was largely responsible for the atrocities that marred his life; the contrast of the virtue and lofty dignity of Blanca with the trickery and insolence of the seductive María de Padilla; the tyrannical weakness of character of the king who was moved alternately by fear of the angry people and by the force of a lewd passion; and the impetuous ardor of the Castilian Prince, Enrique of Trastamara, the avenger of the outrages committed against modesty and virtue, are elements too important not to have given our poets a desire to present them on the stage.[17]

*We have mentioned the fact that *Blanca de Borbón* was one of the three tragedies Quintana left unfinished when the French invasion and the political turmoil which followed put an end to his literary activity. The tragedy that the reviewer had particularly in mind, however, was probably by Dionisio Solís. Hartzenbusch tells us in his "Notes on the Life and Writings of Don Dionisio Solís" (*Revista de Madrid,* Segunda Serie, Vol. I, 1839) that "Don Antonio Gil y Zárate having read to him his *Blanca de Borbón,* written without knowledge of the work of our author, the latter judged that Gil's tragedy was preferable for the stage and urged him to have it performed."

Fortunately, he says, the subject fell into the hands of Gil y Zárate, who combines a profound knowledge of Spanish history with judgment and an intelligent appreciation of dramatic precepts, and who "has succeeded with this composition in adding a diamond to the poor crown of our Spanish Melpómene."[18] Although the reviewer admits that there are some defects in the tragedy, such as a certain languor in the first two acts, a bit of boldness in the interesting scene between Blanca and María, and some unnecessary lines at the close that mar the effect, he insists that the imperfections do not prevent the tragedy from standing comparison with the best that are being presented in foreign theaters. He particularly praises the versification, which is "beautiful, lofty, unaffected, sonorous, and appropriate for tragedy."[19] *Blanca de Borbón* was presented for the first time at the Príncipe on June 7, 1835, and was played seven times during the month. Unquestionably it must be considered one of the few good tragedies produced during the neo-classic period.

Two years later, as we have noted, Gil y Zárate temporarily abandoned neo-classicism to write an ultraromantic drama, *Carlos II.*[20] In the picture it presented of the wretched and pitifully weak Carlos II, "The Bewitched," with his servile obedience to the precepts of the Inquisition, and the king's monstrous and hypocritical confessor, Froilán, with his unholy passion for Inés, who proves to be the daughter of the king, this drama shocked even Salas y Quiroga, whose preface to his *Poems,* published in 1834, has been called "perhaps the boldest and clearest of all the romantic manifestos."[21] In *No me olvides,* a romantic periodical that lasted some ten months, Salas y Quiroga, who was both editor and principal contributor, speaks at length about the mission of the poet in an age "when the germ of incredulity and skepticism is creating such havoc." At such a time, he says, the poet should clothe himself with all his dignity to oppose the popular trend and, in his capacity as a priest of peace, should "preach a religion of brotherhood." On the contrary, "We see an edifice erected in the theater to impiety, an edifice of which many modern dramas are stones. In the theater a chain of dramatic works is being forged that will drag us without any doubt whatsoever to ignorance of history and to mockery of religious principles."[22] In view of Gil y Zárate's past literary practice, Salas y Quiroga thought that he would be the last to stoop to such a work, and that he would be one of those who would cry out loudest against the general corruption. Knowing that this author's works belonged to the classic school, when he learned that he had shifted his allegiance to romanticism he assumed that he would do so with the same dignity Bretón de los Herreros had manifested in translating Delavigne's *The Sons of Edward. Carlos II* seems to him "the most characteristically romantic play of this century," but it belongs for the most part to "that satanic school . . . which should be entirely abandoned in this century in which we know so well how to destroy and so little about how to build."[23] The work, he says, is a masterpiece, and for that reason has a greater potential for evil. He admits, however, that "the public, less severe than we, applauded this drama boisterously and filled the theater for several consecutive nights."[24]

Following this one incursion into the romantic field, Gil y Zárate returned in some of his later plays to a modified neo-classicism and in others combined romantic and neo-classic elements. His comedies, *Don Trifón or All for Money* (1841) and *A Friend in Office* (1842), may be called comedies of manners and conform reasonably well to neo-classic precepts. *Rosmunda* (1839), *Matilde* (1841), and *Cecilia, the Little Blind Girl* (1843) incline strongly toward sentimental comedy and are also fairly regular in their structure. Even his masterpiece, *Guzmán the Good,* is classical in its form. Indeed, if it had been written in hendecasyllabic *romance* instead of in a variety of meters, it would deserve to be called a neo-classic tragedy as much as the earlier work on the same subject by Nicolás Fernández de Moratín.

From 1839 to 1843, in addition to the plays already mentioned, Gil y Zárate published six dramas: *Don Alvaro de Luna* (1840), *A Monarch and His Favorite* (1841), *Masanielo* (1841), *William Tell* (1843), *The Great Captain* (1843), and *The Falkland Family* (1843), in all of which the author gave evidence of his conversion to eclecticism by combining romantic and neo-classic elements, although in only one, *Masanielo,* does he approach pure romanticism. In his *Manual of Literature,* as we shall see, Gil y Zárate seeks to justify the recognition of drama as a legitimate genre.

In 1841 Gil y Zárate published in the *Revista de Madrid* an article, entitled "The Old Theater and the Modern Theater," which is of particular value not only for an evaluation of the author's position with relation to Golden Age comedy, neo-classicism, romanticism, and eclecticism, but also for the light it casts upon the condition of the Spanish theater after romanticism had spent its force.

Few works of the human mind, Gil y Zárate says, have been

exposed to more vicissitudes than Golden Age comedies. Both in Spain and beyond her borders they have been the object either of unbounded praise or of pitiless criticism. Even today it is difficult to evaluate them "because they are an almost inseparable mixture of the good and the bad."[25] At present some people belittle them "to the point of believing that they were the product of a wild imagination or of the crassest ignorance." Others, on the contrary, laud them to the skies and scorn all subsequent plays. The former wish to abandon them completely to follow new models; the latter consider every foreign innovation a dangerous threat to Spanish nationalism. Gil y Zárate believes that both opinions are equally erroneous. It is true that at one time French classicism introduced its intolerance onto Spanish soil and attempted to annihilate everything that did not conform to its literary doctrines; but a century of combat has proven its impotence, whether because there was something false and contrary to nature in the system itself, or because it conflicted with Spanish taste and manners. It has been necessary, therefore, to abandon pure classicism in Spain, not, Gil y Zárate says, "because good tragedies and comedies in this genre have failed to please at times and may not still please when they are well performed; but because . . . the public will always prefer a spectacle with more animation and variety."[26] In his *Manual of Literature,* published two years later, Gil y Zárate asserts that the introduction of neo-classicism and the imitation of French literature in Spain were beneficial rather than detrimental to Spanish letters:

Was this change favorable or prejudicial to our literature? Did French influence destroy Spanish genius, curtailing its flights in order to drag it along the path of a humble prosiness? No; because what did not exist could not be destroyed. Spanish genius had disappeared, having died completely after raving so much in the last years of the seventeenth century; it needed to be reborn; and it was not possible for such a miracle to be performed with the same principles that had reduced it to the sepulcher. It had to be rejuvenated in the waters of good taste and sound criticism, and this was achieved by the imitation of French literature which excelled particularly in such qualities.[27]

It is necessary, according to Gil y Zárate, to combat vigorously the opinion of those who are still championing Golden Age drama and its imitation. "It is advisable," he says, "to point out that, no matter how much merit those comedies may have, they belong to a genre that has died; that they cannot satisfy our tastes or our intellectual needs; and that even though they offer much that is worth imitating, and can and should serve as a sacred flame to give renewed life to our poetic inspiration, the theater requires other qualities which must be derived either from the observation of society and nature or from the study of foreign drama."[28] Society in Spain has progressed so much since the Golden Age that the present century and that of Lope bear no resemblance to each other. Tastes are different and intellectual needs are more exacting. Drama has had to change its form and its essence because Spaniards are no longer satisfied with those compositions "which reveal only an excessive wealth of poetry, and which, if they please the imagination, seldom touch the heart."[29] More art, more study, and more depth are required today. Without excluding poetry, the use of imagery, and a variety of meters, "it is necessary to guard against the excesses that have so marred our old comedies in this respect, banishing euphuism, useless pomp, pedantic concepts, ridiculous affectation, and putting into the mouth of each character only those words that befit his position and character."[30]

The fact that classical literature has not been able to take root and grow in Spain does not mean that its influence has been of no consequence: "No matter how much is said against classical literature, its effect upon ours has been real and permanent. It has contributed to the correction of many of our errors, and in vain do we resist its precepts; some have remained and will be observed in spite of all the efforts of its enemies."[31] But just as neo-classicism has left its traces, so the influence of romanticism will endure. The latter has been beneficial in that it enabled Spaniards to break the ties of classicism, which seemed heavy but which could not be thrown off as long as the only alternative was a return to the old comedies. The new genre was welcomed because it allowed freer play for the imagination. Spaniards thought they saw in it a rich mine of plots and situations; and they were persuaded that, since romanticism was more suited to the Spanish spirit and in its forms approximated the Spanish *comedia,* the time had come to give a new impulse to the decadent theater and to rehabilitate the Spanish stage. In their enthusiasm the partisans of the new school went to extremes and committed serious mistakes. The reaction against classicism made them forget its precepts too often and also break them intentionally; but, Gil y Zárate says, "The first fervor has passed; sound reason is recovering its sway; taste is improving; good models are being read; instead of being despised, old models are being studied more than

ever; and, although there have been some exaggerated compositions, an activity has been attained which did not exist for more
than a century and a half and which should produce the happiest
results."[32]

There are three sources, Gil y Zárate declares, from which a
new national theater must be formed: Golden Age comedies, classical literature, and romantic drama. "The brilliant poetry of the
first, the regularity and good taste of the second, and the movement and passion of the third must all be harmonized in order
to produce a perfect composition."[33] In response to those who are
clamoring for the rejection of both neo-classicism and romanticism
and a return to Golden Age style, Gil y Zárate asks and answers a
number of questions:

What do those who are urging us to write again in the style of our
old poets wish? They want to reduce us to sterility, and take away from
us the very originality they are so strongly advocating; they want us
to be bad copiers of beautiful models. What shall we imitate in those
poets? Will it be their plots that degenerate at times into an incompre-
hensible confusion? Will it be their cold and trivial solutions? Will it be
their continual changes of scene? Will it be their hiding places, their
veiled ladies, their duels, and their disguises? Will it be their impertinent and shameless *graciosos?* Will it be their puns, concepts, and affected
language? Certainly not; all of these things would be regarded today
as insufferable defects. Some comedies where these defects were reproduced might pass in consideration of their object, but soon they would
cause displeasure and would be scorned. The old theater ended with
Calderón; a few years after his death the institutions, ideas, and customs
that furnished his themes and subject matter also began to receive their
death blow; it is, therefore, impossible to revive him, when they are
dead forever.[34]

If we analyze these statements, we shall be forced to the conclusion that Gil y Zárate's criticism of Golden Age comedy was as severe
as that of any of the eighteenth-century neo-classicists. The latter
had been saying the same thing for more than a century and because
of their censure of Lope and Calderón had been branded as enemies
to their nation. When Gil y Zárate adds that the old theater should
be studied carefully "in order to learn good versification, the happy
expression of all manner of concepts, the nobility of sentiments, the
urbanity and delicacy of language, the opportune use of different
meters, and sprightly dialogue,"[35] he is hardly going beyond the recommendations Luzán had made more than a century before.

In his *Manual of Literature*, written to serve as an elementary textbook on poetics and a history of Spanish literature and published in 1843 at the end of his literary career, Gil y Zárate expresses a dramatic creed which, although more liberal than the *Poetics* of Martínez de la Rosa, is still predominantly neo-classic in its spirit and basic provisions. The rules for drama which are given in this brief manual probably represent the thinking of most of the leading dramatists and critics in Spain after the smoke of the conflict between romanticism and neo-classicism had blown away. Neither Martínez de la Rosa, Bretón de los Herreros, Rodriguez Rubí, Patricio de la Escosura, Hartzenbusch, Alberto Lista, nor Mesonero Romanos could have found serious fault with the author's attitude toward the moral function of the theater or toward the general technical requirements of drama. Indeed, Martínez de la Rosa, Bretón, and Hartzenbusch had already expressed ideas that were quite similar, particularly with reference to the unities.

Even though he does not hold with the neo-classicists that the theater should be regarded as a school of manners, Gil y Zárate considers that it is an unpardonable defect "to break the precept of sound morality." The theater "is only a recreation, a diversion, but this diversion must never be converted into a school of vice."[36] The representation of any human action necessarily produces a moral effect, whether the author wills it or not, and if it does not strengthen innate sentiments of rectitude in the spectators, it is necessarily bad.[37] For aesthetic reasons, too, he is impelled to insist upon the moral beauty of a literary work, because "nothing can be beautiful unless it is moral."[38]

The principle of dramatic illusion is given logical treatment in this *Manual*. To be interesting and pleasing the action of a play must have the appearance of truth. Dramatic illusion, however, is only relative:

> The spectator always goes to the theater prepared to make certain concessions. . . . He is quite willing to concede that Greeks and Romans speak in Spanish verse; that wings and cloths represent buildings and trees; that the wounds and deaths he witnesses are feigned; all of this he concedes and tolerates because without it there would be no theater. But it must not be inferred from the fact that he tolerates these necessary improprieties that he will tolerate others that are unnecessary. . . . He tolerates, for example, the fact that the actors speak in verse, but he demands that the language be natural and in keeping with the position of the characters.[39]

Although he recognizes that unhappy endings in tragedy may at times be very effective, he nevertheless strongly recommends that the solution be made happy, if possible, even in this genre, because "the spectator, after having been strongly moved, seeks relief and his heart expands when virtue triumphs or the characters that have aroused his sympathy emerge victorious."[40]

His statement of the technical requirements of drama follows the conventional pattern. Happenings that the author cannot or does not choose to present before the eyes of the spectator must be supposed to occur between the acts and must be narrated. The scenes should be so linked that the stage will never be empty and all entrances and exits should be properly motivated. Monologues are justifiable only when "the character is stirred by a great passion and is beside himself."[41] Even then they should be very brief. No rule based upon reason exists for prescribing a fixed number of acts in a play. The number, on the contrary, should vary according to the requirements of the action; although a play with more than five acts is usually too long. The best exposition is "one which is woven so naturally into the action that as the latter develops it supplies the information required for the comprehension of the plot."[42]

Gil y Zárate recommends hendecasyllabic *romance* meter for tragedy because "it combines with its harmony the flexibility required by all the different tones of tragic style." He rejects entirely the use of prose in this "essentially poetic genre."[43] Comedy, however, being closer to real life and being a less poetic genre than tragedy, may well be written in prose. He himself prefers verse, especially in comedies of character, and designates octosyllabic *romance* as the most appropriate meter "because it is so flexible and so suited to all tones, particularly that of conversation."[44] He adds, however, that those who prescribe this meter as the only one admissible in this genre

do not take into consideration the poetic character of our nation and how sensitive we are to the attraction of harmony. . . . It is as unnatural to speak in octosyllabic *romance* as in a variety of meters, and if the latter affords us more pleasure, there is no reason to reject it. Furthermore, there are metrical combinations in our language that lend themselves better than others to the expressions of certain emotions and certain ideas. The *redondilla*, for example, has no equal for the epigrammatic language that comedy frequently requires.[45]

One of the principal defects we have noticed in neo-classic comedy has been its too obvious didactic purpose. Gil y Zárate makes it clear from the beginning that he considers the intrusion of the author a major defect in any play. The definition of drama, he says, carries with it the assumption that the characters will speak for themselves:

> By representation it is understood that only the characters who take part in the action are to appear, and never the poet himself. If he allows himself to be seen, whether by addressing the audience through the actors or by putting into their mouths a language which is obviously his own, the drama ceases to be a true representation and the illusion disappears.[46]

Gil y Zárate's attitude toward the unities shows a modified neo-classicism. Rigid preceptists, he says, have insisted that there be only one action that occurs in one place and within a period of twenty-four hours, while their adversaries have cried out against the narrowness of these laws, claiming that "they curtail the flights of genius."[47] On this point he disagrees sharply with the opponents of the rules:

> If there were no other reason than this to reject or modify the rules of the unities, we would be on the side of the preceptists. The rigidity of the rules does not seem to us ever a sufficient reason for breaking them, because they hamper only mediocre talents; a real genius, far from being discouraged, acquires new spirit and becomes greater through observing them.[48]

The question, he says, is whether the precept of the three unities produces better dramas, or whether there is something in the unities that is contrary to the essence of this class of literature and which opposes artistic perfection. There is no doubt, he declares, that the unities contribute to verisimilitude and to dramatic illusion; and if they are compatible with other conditions, they should be rigidly observed. Gil y Zárate leaves no doubt about his own position: "If the observance of the unities produces greater beauty, let them be kept; if, on the contrary, the beauties that result from their breach are preferable, let them be sacrificed, but only in so far as is absolutely necessary."[49] In regard to the duration of the action, Gil y Zárate sees no objection to extending the time beyond twenty-four hours. If one may suppose that in the two hours that the play lasts twenty-four hours have passed, "why not thirty, forty, sixty, or several days?"[50] The author must, however, distribute the lapses of time in the intervals between the acts. Just as he concedes that the time of the action may be extended, so also he allows the scene to change to different places provided the changes are made between acts and not before the eyes of the spectators, for "if they see houses fly away and trees and rocks come to replace them" the illusion is completely dispelled.[51] Gil y Zárate evidently has in mind here changes in decoration that have taken place in some recently performed romantic plays.

The author's remarks about the necessity for historical accuracy are particularly significant in view of the fact that so many of his own plays are historical dramas and of the popularity of this type during the period immediately following romanticism. The liberties taken by Golden Age dramatists would be intolerable now, he says, because the spectators are much more enlightened:

> We have said that a dramatic representation must be poetic. This means it is permissible for the poet to invent things that have never happened and take away or add what is necessary; but with all of this, it is necessary not to falsify history to such an extent that generally accepted facts are altered. Today particularly the audience is made up to a large extent of educated people, and the knowledge of this distinguished class opposes the boldness of the poet when he dares to depart completely and brazenly from historical truth. At an earlier time our dramatists were able to ignore this rule with impunity because they were dealing with a less enlightened and exacting public. Today such a fault would be intolerable, and for this very reason many of our old comedies have disappeared from the theater.[52]

Gil y Zárate does not advocate a mixing of comic and serious elements in tragedy or comedy. These two genres may continue to exist "as ideal types, as artistic entities";[53] but he gives his approval to a third genre, the drama, in which these elements may be skilfully combined. His definitions of tragedy and comedy are entirely conventional, but his definition of drama is broad enough to include Martínez de la Rosa's *The Venice Conspiracy*, his own *Guzmán the Good* and other dramas, and even romantic plays like *Don Alvaro*, *The Troubadour*, and *The Lovers of Teruel:* "Drama is the representation of an action sometimes extraordinary, sometimes commonplace, in which people of all classes and categories take part, and which is intended to produce in the spectators all kinds of emotions: terror, joy, compassion, and laughter."[54] Tragedy and comedy are opposite extremes; drama is an intermediate genre, which can assume either a more tragic or a more comic character in proportion as it approaches one of the other genres. Combining as it does elements of tragedy and comedy, drama is subject to the rules of the genre that it most closely resembles. Nevertheless, it has some characteristics of its own. "The dual nature of drama requires greater extension, greater amplitude, and its pictures must be broader and more complicated."[55] It requires more space, more time, and certain licenses that are not necessary in the other genres. Drama makes high personages speak at times in a more humble tone than is fitting in tragedy, and allows the characters of the lower class to use language that would be too elevated in comedy. Gil y Zárate makes it quite clear that he is not advocating a return to the tragi-comedy of the Golden Age. Transitions from sadness to laughter must be handled skilfully. "Sudden and unexpected variations always produce a bad effect, and we shall never approve that in a poetic situation a *gracioso* should come out with untimely buffoonery."[56]

While drama has the advantage of being able to present on the stage events and characters that would not be suitable in tragedy, "it is not for that reason permissible to present, as many modern dramatists have done, vices, crimes, and excesses that are repugnant to human nature and that should remain in perpetual oblivion."[57]

Even though Gil y Zárate's *Manual* shows no particular originality, it is a reasonable exposition of dramatic principles and modifies neo-classic precepts without falling into the excesses of romanticism. It could, indeed, have been adopted as a creed for a school of writers who had become weary of the struggle between classicism and romanticism and were inclined to embrace eclecticism as an easy and logical solution. Gil y Zárate comments in his article, "The Old Theater and the Modern Theater," upon the difficulty of writing dramas in an age of transition. Conditions have changed, revolutions have upset the social order, old institutions no longer exist, the slavery of thought has been replaced by unbridled liberty; and for these reasons "the spirit cannot be satisfied with mere flowers of the imagination; it demands a stronger diet."[58] The theater, therefore, has been forced to follow a new course and to adjust itself to circumstances in order to avoid being abandoned completely. Gil y Zárate does not believe that such drastic changes have been beneficial to theatrical art:

> On the contrary, we believe that this has been bad for the theater itself and even worse for the authors whose unfortunate lot it is to write in these times. Their compositions must inevitably share the character of uncertainty and exaggeration that marks the epoch; for, there being no fixed and dominant ideas, they cannot adjust themselves to a recognized

and generally accepted type, and for that reason cannot form a school.[59]

Gil y Zárate's remarks probably do much to explain the apathy of the public toward the theater during the romantic period itself and more markedly in the period that immediately followed. With no fixed ideas or goals, the authors could generate little enthusiasm within themselves; and as a result their plays could not stir the emotions or arouse the interest of the spectators.

Bretón de los Herreros

It is somewhat ironical that, after neo-classicism had produced a mere handful of successful comedies during almost a century of activity and when its opponents were pointing to this meager output as incontrovertible evidence that comedies written according to the rules could never please Spanish audiences, there should appear a writer who, following these precepts with little deviation, revealed a fecundity and achieved a popularity unequaled since the Golden Age. This dramatist, Bretón de los Herreros, wrote his first comedy, *Old Age Folly,*[60] in three acts and in prose in 1817 when he was barely twenty years of age and his last work, *The Bodily Senses,* which was also a comedy, exactly fifty years later, in 1867. Between these years his dramatic production reached the astonishing total of 103 original plays, which included 54 full-length comedies, five dramas, one tragedy, one comedy of magic, and four *zarzuelas,* the rest being one-act comedies. During this time he translated 62 plays, of which 29 were full-length tragedies, comedies, or dramas, and reworked some ten Golden Age plays.[61]

In 1835 the romantic critic Eugenio de Ochoa, who was unwilling to concede that anything good could come from neo-classicism, insisted that Bretón had created a new genre:

Whatever may be each individual's opinion about the literary merit of Bretón, it is undeniable and all will agree that this poet has been able to form a distinct genre, a genre of his own, which resembles neither that of the old dramatists nor that of Moratín, nor that of anyone else. This genre should be called, and is called by those who are familiar with contemporary literature, "Bretón's genre."[62]

This statement, which contains an element of truth but completely ignores the often repeated declarations by the author himself of his indebtedness to Moratín, has been taken up by subsequent critics, with the result that Bretón is credited with a far greater deviation from neo-classic precepts than an examination of his comedies reveals. Bretón's friend and biographer, the Marqués de Molíns, tells us that in 1817, when Bretón was twenty years of age,

The works of Moratín fell into his hands and, after reading them, he felt himself possessed with an almost superstitious admiration for this notable writer of comedies; his vocation was immediately determined and, being eager to embark upon it at once, he composed the comedy, *Old Age Folly*, which was performed for the first time with flattering success on October 14, 1824.[63]

Following the performance of his first comedy, *Old Age Folly*, and encouraged by Grimaldi, the author of the phenomenally popular comedy of magic, *The Goat's Foot*, whom Mesonero Romanos calls "the theatrical dictator,"[64] Bretón began to translate tragedies from the French theater, such as *Andromaque, Mithridates, Iphigénie and Orestes, Doña Inés de Castro, Dido, Antigone, Ariadne,* and *Mary Stuart*. In 1825 his original comedy, *The Two Nephews*, clearly written in imitation of the works of Moratín, was performed at the Príncipe, where it was well received. This play was followed by *The False Key; Valeria, or The Little Blind Girl of Olbruc;* and other translations from the French, together with five recasts of Golden Age comedies: Calderón's *It Is Worse Than It Was*, with the new title, *Her Own Jailer*, and *There Is Nothing Like Silence*, with the original title; Lope's *The Tellos of Meneses;* Moreto's *The Force of Nature*, with the new title, *The Prince and the Peasant;* and Coello's *The Engagements of Six Hours* with the title *What Difficulties in Three Hours!*

Bretón's first conspicuous success came in 1818 with a three-act comedy in octosyllabic *romance, I Am Going Back to Madrid*, in which, the Marqués de Molíns says, "imitating Moratín and surpassing in sprightliness and grace the *Barón* by the great master, he succeeded in adding a title to his well-known name, so that he was called for a long time *the author of I Am Going Back to Madrid.*"[65] In spite of the success of this play on the stage, Bretón turned his attention for the next two years almost entirely to translation. He himself explains why he produced so few original works during this first period:

Original compositions paid so little then that, to prove how wretched and precarious the condition of writers was, it is sufficient to say that *I Am Going Back to Madrid*, which had an uninterrupted initial run of almost a month, brought me only three hundred reals; and at a time when the theaters of the provinces contributed nothing, because no one respected or recognized the right of ownership in dramatic works. Translations paid almost as much, although they were much easier to write and the translator's reputation was not so much at stake. I devoted myself, therefore, to translating everything that was handed over to me, because, without any inheritance or employment, an honorable man needed some income; and I only composed an occasional comedy of my own in order to comply with what the public had a right to expect and in order to obey my own irresistible calling.[66]

Although Bretón had written his first comedy in prose and had confined himself to octosyllabic *romance* in his subsequent plays, he says that from the beginning he had felt a strong desire to use true rhyme. Yielding finally to this urge and encouraged by the example of other writers who were tending to abandon the exclusive use of *romance* meter, he produced *Marcela, or Which of the Three?* in three acts and in a variety of meters. In a note to this play in the complete edition of his works, published in 1850, Bretón explains the reasons for this innovation. Critics usually quote only the first part of this note as evidence of the author's dissatisfaction with the restrictions placed upon versification by neo-classicists and omit his closing remarks in which he expresses contrition over some of his metrical exuberance:

In this comedy the author opened a new and a freer course for his imagination. In his previous plays he had not dared to use any meter except the octosyllabic *romance,* because it was the one recommended by very respectable authorities, and because, in fact, it is best adapted to the liveliness and propriety of dialogue. He felt, in the meantime, a terrible itching to use rhyme; he was burning with the desire to allow his pen, which he felt had been too restrained, to gambol a little in the field of poetry. Studying Lope, Tirso, Calderón, Rojas, Moreto, and Alarcón, he envied in this respect their happy independence. . . . All of the contemporary poets were loosening, and some of them were beginning to shake off, the scholastic yoke. Constant in his literary faith, although not a blind follower of an exclusive school, he succeeded in avoiding the pitiful aberrations into which others were falling; but he had to take an inventory of himself and test his strength to see whether it was possible to reconcile the vigorous portrayal of emotions, the *vis comica* of the dialogue, and the naturalness of the language, with a more artful, varied, and pleasing versification, which would not, however, be too lyrical and picturesque.[67]

As he continued his experiment, he says, he found that the use of pure rhyme seemed to help, rather than hinder, his handling of dialogue because it made him formulate his thoughts more epigrammatically and stimulated his imagination. The extraordinary success of *Marcela*, he believes, was due in large measure to the appeal which this richer and more varied versification had for the public. He determined, therefore, to follow the same practice in his other plays; but, "in trying to avoid the simplicity of his former style, he frequently went to the other extreme." He wishes now that he had time to rework all his plays "and to purge them of the metrical exuberance which he had lavished upon them." He would like "to use a pruning hook mercilessly on a considerable number of labored and inappropriate stanzas" and upon entire pages of *esdrújulas* which he introduced for no other reason than to test his ability to handle such a difficult verse form. He hopes the public will pardon him for these as well as for his other sins.[68]

Only in the use of a variety of meters does *Marcela* deviate to any appreciable extent from neo-classic precepts. Even here there is no suggestion of the lyrical flights of Golden Age versification, for almost the entire play is written in octosyllabic *romance* and *redondillas*, with a limited number of *quintillas* and *décimas*, one sonnet, a forty-eight verse *letrilla*, and forty-six verses of *silvas* thrown in for seasoning. In spite of this concession to popular taste, extreme care was taken to make the language seem natural. So well did Bretón succeed in this respect that he was accused of taking his characters directly from life. The metrical variety introduced in the play seems to have been sufficient, however, to arouse the enthusiasm of the public and of the Marqués de Molíns himself, for the Marqués says:

> *Marcela, or Which of the Three?* marks the first and truly gigantic step taken by Bretón in his new and glorious path. *Marcela* is the formula of his dramatic genre, the abstract of his doctrine, the rebirth of that harmonious and varied versification with which our great poets of the nineteenth century adorned our theater, and the first, or at least the most popular, throwing-off of the yoke that French doctrinairism had imposed upon us; for that reason our author's title was changed so that from that time he was called *The Author of Marcela*.[69]

Nevertheless, two years after the composition of *Marcela* we find Bretón declaring in the *Correo Literario y Mercantil* that the best dramatic meter is that closest to prose and urging the avoidance of excessive rhyme.[70]

This comedy, which was given sixty-six performances during the author's lifetime, was the most popular of Bréton's plays. Next in order of popularity were *What People Will Say and What It Matters to Me* (1838), with fifty-nine performances; *An Arbitrator in Discord* (1833), with forty-five; *I Am Going Back to Madrid* (1828), with forty; and *The Man from the Country* (1840), with thirty-seven.

Bretón's one attempt to write an original classical tragedy was received so unfavorably by the public and by critics that he returned immediately to neo-classic comedy. His *Merope* (1835) was hardly calculated to stand the competition of the exciting and elaborately staged romantic dramas that were being introduced at the time. Eugenio de Ochoa comments in *El Artista* upon the reaction of the public: "*Merope* is in all respects a classic tragedy; this explains everything. If this tragedy has displeased in Madrid, it is not so much the fault of the author as of the genre in which it is written; even though it had been much better it would still have displeased."[71] Ochoa was evidently quite moderate in his criticism, for the play was performed only three times and was never revived. Bretón's talents obviously were in the field of comedy and not in tragedy or, as we shall see, in romantic drama.

Yielding to what seemed a preference on the part of the public for more spectacular plays, Bretón composed in 1834 a melodrama, *Elena,* in four acts. The author says on the title-page that with this drama he made "his first experiment in a genre quite different from that which he was accustomed to cultivate," and that he did so at the instigation of friends who urged him "to try his ability to create situations with keener interest and to depict emotions and characters that did not fit into the accepted mold of comedy." Modern romanticism, he says, was at its height and it was almost inevitable "that sooner or later he should carry an offering to the altar of the new idol." He tried, nevertheless, "not to convert his worship, which was probably not very voluntary, into fanatical superstition."[72] In this play, the Marqués de Molíns says, Bretón formed a plot that resembled those of Ducange and Bouchardi more than those of Victor Hugo and Dumas, "without the horrors of the first or the romantic beauties of the second."[73] *Elena* was performed from the 23rd to the 26th of October, 1834, and appears never to have been brought back to the stage.

The following year Bretón made an excellent translation of Casimir Delavigne's moderately romantic drama, *The Sons of Edward,* which was performed from the 4th to the 8th and again on the 14th and 15th of October, 1835, and was played a total of twenty-nine times during the author's lifetime. The success of this translation prompted him to compose another original drama, *Don Fernando the Summoned,* which was performed for the first time on November 30, 1837, and had a run of eight days. This drama was one of the few plays reviewed by Salas y Quiroga in *No me olvides.* This critic begins by saying that the author of the work is so well known in Spain by every person of taste that his name alone is sufficient to guarantee an interest in his productions. His success has been achieved, however, in only one genre in which he has no rival and, since *Don Fernando the Summoned* belongs to an entirely different type of drama, the question arises as to whether the author has an aptitude for the new genre. Salas y Quiroga concludes that it would be better for Bretón to return to his comedies and abandon drama, in which field he has little chance of success. *Don Fernando,* he says, shows no originality and holds no interest:

> The dramas of the day resemble each other so much that, bearing in mind the misfortune of the Carvajal brothers and the summons given to the king of Castile, we knew almost exactly the course Bretón's work would take. We supposed that it would be completely lacking in interest, that we would see the execution of the Carvajal brothers, that there would be a revolution, a jail, tyrannical princes, an oppressed people, etc., and we were entirely right. The first act is paved with those maxims that are introduced in all the dramas of the day to draw applause... which the author failed to arouse because the public is becoming satiated.[74]

These are strong words coming from one who had been and was still supposed to be a champion of romanticism. It seems obvious that the public, and Salas y Quiroga as well, were becoming weary of romantic dramas that were supposed to give evidence of originality and imaginative freedom, but which were becoming as stereotyped as any of the neo-classic tragedies or comedies.

Bretón's third drama, *Vellido Dolfos,* which was performed in December, 1839, was even less successful than *Don Fernando,* being given only six times. A fourth drama, *The Boatgirl,* in which the Marqués de Molíns sees a considerable similarity to Calderón's *The Alcalde of Zalamea,* had its first performance on January 13, 1842, and was played a total of thirteen times. This play marks the end of Bretón's connection with romanticism.

While Bretón was making moderate experiments in romanticism from 1834 to 1837, he gave no indication of abandoning his old school, but, on the contrary, composed three of his best and most popular comedies: *All Is Farce in This World* (1835), *I Am Leaving Madrid* (1835), and *Die and You Will See* (1837).

The Marqués de Molíns believes that in departing from the simplicity of neo-classic comedy Bretón was motivated in his translations and recasts by financial needs and in his dramas, *zarzuelas*, and comedies of magic by a desire to demonstrate his versatility and to exercise his tireless inspiration. Bretón himself declares in the prologue and notes to the complete edition of his works published in 1850 that, even though he wrote a few historical dramas and other types of plays, never for a moment did he cease to be "constant in his literary faith and in his almost superstitious admiration for Moratín, whom he rarely failed to follow as a model"; and never was there any "fickleness or hesitation" in his dramatic convictions.[75]

As late as 1841, an article in *El Iris* by Bermúdez de Castro definitely places Bretón among the followers of Moratín: "Many writers followed Moratín with good or bad fortune, observing his dramatic precepts and taking lessons in theatrical art from his example. In his footsteps came Martínez de la Rosa, Gorostiza, and Bretón de los Herreros."[76] Bermúdez de Castro insists that "the point of departure" of these three writers is the same:

Recognizing the principle established by Moratín, they seek their inspiration in the society that surrounds them; whether they portray characters that stand out strikingly or present manners in order to ridicule them, the source of their creations is always in the world in which they live and which they are analyzing.[77]

Although this article involved its author in a polemic with Hartzenbusch, who saw in it excessive praise of Moratín, it gives a far more accurate picture of the principles that underlie Bretón's dramatic compositions than did the statement made by Ochoa six years earlier.

Almost the only evidence of an eclectic attitude on Bretón's part in any of his critical writings is to be found in an article that appeared in the *Correo Literario y Mercantil* in April, 1831, which purports to reproduce a conversation between Don Fabricio, a romanticist; Don Timoteo, a classicist; Don Aurelio, enthusiastic over spectacular drama in the style of Cañizares; and Don Claudio, equally enraptured with sentimental comedy. After each has defended his particular system, Don Prudencio, representing Bretón, says:

Gentlemen, all extremes are vicious. Between following literally the precepts of Horace and rushing through the country in search of incidents with no other guide than caprice, there is a prudent middle road that the enlightened writer can tread with success. Those classical poets who have flourished since the restoration of good literature have had no scruples against giving a bit more latitude to the unities of time and place, although not to the unity of action, because that is inviolable in all poems. From the seventeenth century to our time tragedies and comedies have been written that are of such merit, even though they depart somewhat from the rules prescribed in the famous *Epistle to the Pisones*, that if the author of that work were alive he would not hesitate to approve them. Theatrical effect is the first thing a dramatic writer should seek; it is his supreme law, and he should not renounce an excellent story because it is impossible to subject the combination of the plot to the rules, if he can promise himself a glorious success by deviating from them without violating verisimilitude very much.[78]

Bretón's admiration for Moratín and the regular theater, however, has not diminished, for in July of the same year we find him, in discussing the unity of action, asserting the immense superiority of the works of Racine and Moratín over the contemporary romantic monstrosities which have recently made their way into Spain:

Let us allow the innovators beyond the Pyrenees to bewilder the multitude by bringing across the stage in a few hours, like a magic lantern, men, armies, seas, centuries. . . . Such dramatic storehouses can scarcely aspire even to a few months of existence, while *Phèdre* and *The Consent of Young Maidens* live and will live as long as there is a love for letters.[79]

In this article, Bretón justifies the simplicity of the comedies of Terence and of modern neo-classic dramatists and, incidentally, the extreme simplicity of his own compositions, declaring emphatically that "the simpler the plan and the less complicated the action, the better the poet can handle passions and other dramatic ornaments."[80]

In addition to the recasts of Golden Age plays we have already mentioned, Bretón reworked Lope de Vega's *If Women Didn't See*, Alarcón's *The Walls Have Ears*, Tirso's *From Toledo to Madrid*, and Calderón's *With Whom I Come, I Come* and *Confound Well-Wishers*. His attitude toward Golden Age comedies and the advisability of recasts is adequately expressed in a note to *If Women Didn't See*:

Of all the tasks a writer can take upon himself there is none so thankless and sterile as that of reworking old comedies; not, however, because it is a profanation or a crime, as some claim, to correct the plan of comedies composed by Lope, Calderón, Rojas, or Moreto. Those renowned poets were not perfect in all the qualities required by theatrical art, although in some they were certainly inimitable. One ordinarily notices great irregularity in their plans; little cohesion in the infinite number of incidents that form their plots; redundance and excessive euphuism in the dialogues and the narrations; carelessness and errors in style and versification; as well as expressions and turns of phrase that are no longer understood. There are few dramas of that time that can be performed today as they were originally written; and, therefore, to adapt them to the stage by giving them, without disfiguration, some of the qualities which they lack and which are required by good criticism is to do honor, not offense, to the memory of their famous authors.[81]

The recaster has all to lose and nothing to gain, for if he improves the original, he receives no credit; while he is held responsible "not only for the errors he makes in the recast, but also for the mistakes he has not been able or has not dared to correct in the original." The recasts he has made, Bretón says, have not been upon his own initiative, but at the insistence of the management of the theaters, "whose desires were necessarily respected by one who for many years had no way to earn his meager living except with his pen."[82]

Contemporary with Bretón are a number of writers who, in one or more comedies, show the influence of Moratín and his school. Among these may be cited Patricio de Escosura with *The Inexperienced Lover* (1830); Eugenio de Tapia, whose two comedies, *The Stepmother* (1830) and *The Suspicious Spinster* (1832), were reviewed at length in *Cartas Españolas* on January 5, 1832; Espronceda and Ros de Olano with *Neither the Uncle nor the Nephew* (1834); the Duque de Rivas with *You Are Worth as Much as You Have* (1834); Bancés e Hidalgo with *Don Crisanto or a Mania for Politics* (1835); Pedro Gorostiza (the brother of Manuel Eduardo) with *The Distrustful Man* (1837); Hartzenbusch with *The Visionary Girl* (1840) and *The Lame Girl and the Bashful Man* (1843); and Rodriguez Rubí with two comedies: *The Lesser of the Evils* (1840) and *Bulls and Reed Spears* (1840). These comedies are among the last echoes of neo-classicism. Their authors either abandoned the theater after one or two plays or yielded to what they believed was a popular demand for a type of drama with greater variety of interest or capable of arousing stronger emotions.

Flores y Arenas

In 1830 Flores y Arenas composed a three-act comedy in verse, *Coquetry and Presumption*,[83] which, after meeting an enthusiastic reception in the theaters of the provinces, was equally successful in

Madrid, where it was warmly discussed in the periodicals. Bretón de los Herreros published a very unflattering review in the *Correo Literario y Mercantil* on May 16, 1831, to which Carnerero replied in *Cartas Españolas* on May 24 of the same year, reminding Bretón that "criticism is easy, but art is difficult." Although admitting that the comedy contains many defects which spring from the inexperience of youth, Carnerero says that *Coquetry and Presumption* "is one of the few really good plays the Spanish stage has seen since the time of Moratín."[84] Flores y Arenas came to the defense of his comedy in a long article published in *Cartas Españolas* on June 25, 1831, which in its turn was answered by Bretón in the *Correo Literario y Mercantil* on July 1, 1831. There can be little doubt that Bretón was excessively severe in his censure, and the entire polemic does him little credit.

A recent history of Spanish literature says that Flores y Arenas' *Coquetry and Presumption* was composed in the same year as Bretón's *Marcela* and "seems like a rather faded copy of the same subject."[85] *Coquetry and Presumption* actually preceded Bretón's play on the stage in Madrid by seven months. An examination of these plays reveals their dissimilarity in plot, characterization, and moral purpose. In *Marcela,* a young widow is besieged by three suitors, weighs each in the balance and finds him wanting, and ends by marrying none of them. In *Coquetry and Presumption,* the marriage of Antonio and Adela has been arranged by their respective parents. The youth, while he holds the fair sex in little esteem, believes that all women find him irresistible and conceives the idea of coming to Cádiz to win the love of Adela under the assumed name of Fermín. Adela, who is a coquette, explains her attitude toward love to her servant, Inés. Although she pretends to be in love, she has never really experienced that emotion nor does she expect to do so. Adela carries her coquetry to the extreme of trying to hold the affections of the supposed Fermín while she declares herself to be deeply in love with his friend, Luis. The latter is not deceived and determines to teach both Adela and Fermín a much needed lesson. In the solution, Fermín is made to see the true character of Adela and realizes that his charm is not sufficient in itself to win and hold the affection of a woman. He breaks the engagement, leaving Adela in a most unhappy and embarrassing position.

It is certainly most unlikely that any similarity between this play and Bretón's *Marcela* would have escaped the attention of Carnerero and Bretón. The former, indeed, finds the model of Adela in Célimène, the coquette in Molière's *The Misanthrope,* a play cited by Flores y Arenas himself in his reply to Bretón. Carnerero praises the theme of *Coquetry and Presumption:*

This subject is very fitting for good comedy, and especially at a time when coquetry and presumption have taken such deep root in social communications. Both vices, which fuse into one, have been frequently attacked on the stage with more or less success, but the great, the first model of coquettes will always be Célimène in Molière's *The Misanthrope.*[86]

Flores y Arenas' comedy follows the example set by Gorostiza and Javier de Burgos and anticipates Bretón in the use of a variety of meters. Although the bulk of the play is written in octosyllabic *romance* or in *redondillas,* the author occasionally uses *décimas* and, in one scene, the six-syllable *romance* employed by Gorostiza. In every other respect the play is typically neo-classic. The principal defects in the comedy are the long speeches, the general verbosity of the dialogue, and the excessive simplicity of the intrigue. Carnerero praises the play for "the multitude of comic graces, well-delineated passages, dramatic facility, very beautiful verses, and a pure and harmonious language, which frequently recalls that of Lope and Calderón."[87]

Bretón's censure of *Coquetry and Presumption* is entirely unworthy of such an eminent dramatist. The first shafts of his criticism are directed against the use of the word *coquetismo,* or *coquetería,* which he says "is a foreign expression," and against certain "imprudent words" which offend the "most numerous and no less laudable part of society."[88] This criticism by Bretón reminds one of the prudery with which the romantics censured certain expressions in Molière's *The School for Wives.* His entire criticism is limited to details equally unimportant and is more indicative of malice than of a sincere desire to evaluate impartially Flores y Arenas' comedy. Carnerero lampoons those who "try to destroy the products of another's talent with a few damaging words,"[89] and expresses his regret that they should vent their literary spite upon a young man "who in the first steps of his career indicates how far he can go if he has the necessary encouragement."[90]

Flores y Arenas himself declares that such criticism as that made by Bretón, "instead of being the enlightened guide of inexperience, is the assassin of genius."[91] He disavows any intention of adopting the theater as a career and indeed goes on to declare that the composition of *Coquetry and Presumption* has been for him merely a pastime.

The success achieved by his comedy in its first year vindicated its author. From 1831 to 1833 the play was produced eighteen times against twenty-four for Bretón's *Marcela*. (Of course, the popularity of the latter play has been much greater through the years.) Flores y Arenas declared himself entirely satisfied with the reception given his work. His statement made in *Cartas Españolas* in June, 1831, that his play had been performed with applause during the preceding year in all the theaters of Spain except in Madrid and Seville is evidence that it was composed at least as early as 1830. It seems that the polemic his first play aroused may have discouraged him from entering upon a dramatic career, for this play and *To Reckon Without the Host* (1849)[92] and *To Be Conceited Over One's Appearance* (1851), both distinctly neo-classic, comprise his dramatic production. The latter of these plays does not seem to have been performed in Madrid, or, if it was, it attracted little attention. According to Hurtado and Palencia these plays and *The Man of the World*, by Ventura de la Vega, are "the last Moratinian comedies of merit."[93]

Ventura de la Vega

Even after romanticism had spent its force in Spain one dramatist, Ventura de la Vega, continued the Moratinian tradition. His comedy, *The Man of the World* (1845),[94] was called by one of his contemporaries, Antonio Ferrer del Río, "the most complete classical comedy in Spanish dramatic literature."[95] Ventura de la Vega had already distinguished himself as a translator of comedies from the French and as a dramatic critic. His friends constantly urged him to abandon a work which was unworthy of his talent. The above-mentioned critic characterizes the literary efforts of Ventura de la Vega before the composition of *The Man of the World* succinctly by saying that he "does everything with comedies; he reads them, studies them, criticizes them, translates them, rehearses them, performs them; all he fails to do is to write them."[96]

Finally yielding to the desires of his friends, he composed *The Man of the World*, which was staged in 1845 and which, according to contemporary critics, marked an epoch in the theater. In the first dramatic review published in the *Revista Literario de El Español*, on October 6, 1845, Manuel Cañete says of this play:

The Man of the World is one of the most beautiful jewels to embellish the literature of our epoch; and the general verdict of the public . . . has confirmed this fact in the most expressive way. Seldom have we seen an enthusiasm that was so sincere and so well deserved; seldom has opinion been so unanimous.[97]

Cañete compares Ventura de la Vega to Scribe and says that his play is in no way inferior to that author's *Slander* and *The Glass of Water*. Although this comparison may seem today doubtful praise, it must be remembered that Scribe was extremely popular on the Spanish stage at that time, and Bretón, Hartzenbusch, Carnerero, and Ventura de la Vega vied with each other in translating his numerous plays into Spanish.

Ventura de la Vega's comedy is particularly significant in that it reveals the current of neo-classicism which persists throughout the romantic era, constantly restraining the extravagance of that school, and which, even as late as 1845, is sufficiently vital to awaken the enthusiasm of spectators and critics. The success of this play proves rather conclusively that the numerous failures of neo-classic comedies were due more to lack of talent on the part of their authors than to the rigidity of the rules.

Cañete sees in Ventura de la Vega's comedy a perfect blending of those elements which constitute a good comedy:

The simplicity and regularity of the plan, which, nevertheless, holds the audience in constant suspense; the supreme skill with which the characters are not only drawn, but made to stand out in pronounced relief; the naturalness of the incidents; the denouement, which is accomplished without violence; the great number of stylistic beauties; and, above all, the moral thought which it contains, are qualities that suffice to make up a perfect comedy. If one considers the fact that the much vaunted unities are completely and easily observed, he cannot fail to grant that Ventura de la Vega's work is a product of genius and talent.[98]

It is also significant that this success was achieved without any notable concession to the prevailing taste for diversity in versification. Ventura de la Vega succeeds in avoiding monotony by a skilful alteration of octosyllabic *romance* and *redondillas*.

The influence of Moratín is palpable in this comedy, although many critics have chosen to regard it primarily as a prelude to *high comedy*, which was to be so successfully cultivated by López de Ayala and Tamayo y Baus. Ventura de la Vega's admiration for Moratín finds a practical outlet three years later in *The Critique of*

The Consent of Young Maidens (1848), written in imitation of Molière's *Critique de l'Ecole des femmes,* to accompany a special performance of Moratín's masterpiece.

1. Antonio Gil y Zárate, *El fanático por las comedias,* comedia en un acto (Madrid, 1844).

2. Gil y Zárate, *El entremetido,* comedia en tres actos en prosa, representada por la primera vez en Madrid en 1825 (*Obras dramáticas* [Paris, 1850]).

3. Gil y Zárate, *Cuidado con las novias o La escuela de los jóvenes,* comedia en cinco actos, en verso, representada por la primera vez en Madrid en 1826 (*Obras dramáticas).*

4. Gil y Zárate, *Un año después de la boda,* comedia en cinco actos en verso, representada por la primera vez en Madrid en el teatro de la Cruz el 30 de mayo de 1826 (Madrid, 1826).

5. Xavier Durrieu, "Théâtre Moderne de l'Espagne," *Revue des deux mondes,* 1844, VII, 601-33.

6. See p. 494 below.

7. Xavier Durrieu, *op. cit.,* p. 612.

8. Marqués de Valmar (Cueto), *op cit.,* II, 224.

9. Mesonero Romanos, *op. cit.,* p. 399.

10. Marqués de Valmar, "Don Antonio Gil y Zárate," *Autores Dramáticos Contemporáneos,* II, 222.

11. *Ibid.,* p. 223.

12. *Ibid.*

13. *Ibid.,* p. 224.

14. *El Artista,* I, 300.

15. *Ibid.*

16. *Diario de Avisos de Madrid,* June 11, 1835.

17. *Ibid.*

18. *Ibid.*

19. *Ibid.*

20. See p. 484 above.

21. Allison Peers, *op. cit.,* II, 55.

22. *No me olvides,* Núm. 28, November 12, 1837, p. 6.

23. *Ibid.*

24. *Ibid.*

25. Gil y Zárate, "Teatro Antiguo y Teatro Moderno," *Revista de Madrid,* Tercera Serie, 1841, I, 112.

26. *Ibid.,* p. 113.

27. Gil y Zárate, *Manual de Literatura,* Segunda Parte, *Resumen Histórico de la Literatura Española,* 1844, III, 306-7.*

28. *Revista de Madrid,* 1841, p. 114.

29. *Ibid.,* p. 117.

30. *Ibid.*

31. *Ibid.,* p. 119.

32. *Ibid.,* p. 120.

33. *Ibid.,* p. 122.

34. *Ibid.,* p. 123.

35. *Ibid.*

36. Gil y Zárate, "Principios Generales de Poética y Retórica," *Manual de Literatura,* Primera Parte (Madrid, 1844), p. 248.

37. *Ibid.,* p. 249.

38. *Ibid.*

39. *Ibid.,* p. 253.

40. *Ibid.,* p. 261.

41. *Ibid.,* p. 263.

42. *Ibid.,* p. 257.

43. *Ibid.,* p. 288.

44. *Ibid.,* p. 291.

45. *Ibid.,* p. 292.

46. *Ibid.,* p. 245.

47. *Ibid.,* p. 263.

48. *Ibid.,* p. 264.

49. *Ibid.,* p. 265.

50. *Ibid.,* p. 274.

51. *Ibid.,* p. 275.

52. *Ibid.,* p. 246.

53. *Ibid.,* p. 282.

54. *Ibid.,* p. 284.

55. *Ibid.,* p. 292.

56. *Ibid.*

57. *Ibid.*

58. Gil y Zárate, "Teatro Antiguo y Teatro Moderno," p. 121.

59. *Ibid.,* p. 122.

60. Manuel Bretón de los Herreros, *A la vejez viruelas,* comedia original en tres actos (Madrid, 1825).

61. These figures are a breakdown of the list of performances given in *Bretón de los Herreros, Recuerdos de su vida y sus obras, escritos por el Marqués de Molíns* (Madrid, 1883), pp. 546-55.

62. Eugenio de Ochoa, "Don Manuel Bretón de los Herreros," *El Artista,* 1835, II, 3.

63. El Marqués de Molíns, "Don Manuel Bretón de los Herreros," *Autores Drama-*

ticos Contemporáneos (Madrid, 1882), p. 149.

64. Mesonero Romanos, *Memorias de un Setentón*, Nueva Edición (Madrid, 1926), p. 66.

65. El Marqués de Molíns, *op. cit.*, II, 150.

66. Bretón de los Herreros, *Obras Escogidas* (Paris, n.d.) Tomo I, Preface, p. xxi.

67. *Ibid.*, I, 55-56.

68. *Ibid.*

69. *Autores Dramáticos Contemporáneos*, II, 151.

70. *Correo Literario y Mercantil*, August 7, 1833.

71. *El Artista*, I, 216.

72. Bretón de los Herreros, *Obras Escogidas*, p. 83.

73. Marqués de Molíns, *Bretón de los Herreros, Rescuerdos de su vida y sus obras*, p. 118.

74. *No me olvides*, December 10, 1837.

75. Bretón de los Herreros, *Obras* (Madrid, en la Imprenta Nacional, 1850).

76. *El Iris*, 1841, I, 98.

77. *Ibid.*

78. *Correo Literario y Mercantil*, April 13, 1831.

79. *Ibid.*, July 22, 1831.

80. *Ibid.*

81. Bretón de los Herreros, Note to *Si no vieran las mujeres*, refundición de la que escribió con el mismo título Lope de Vega

(*Obras de D. Manuel Bretón de los Herreros* [Madrid, 1850]).

82. *Ibid.*

83. Francisco de Flores y Arenas, *Coquetismo y presunción*, comedia original, en tres actos (Madrid, 1831).

84. *Cartas Españolas*, May 24, 1831.

85. Ernest Mérimée, *A History of Spanish Literature*, translated, revised and enlarged by S. Griswold Morley (New York: Henry Holt & Co., 1930).

86. *Cartas Españolas*, May 24, 1831.

87. *Ibid.*

88. *Correo Literario y Mercantil*, May 16, 1831.

89. *Cartas Españolas*, May 24, 1831.

90. *Ibid.*

91. *Ibid.*, June 25, 1831.

92. Flores y Arenas, *Hacer cuenta sin la huéspeda*, comedia en tres actos y en verso, original, primera obra estrenada en el Teatro Español (Madrid, 1849).

93. Juan Hurtado and Angel González Palencia, *Historia de la literatura española* (Madrid, 1932), p. 838.

94. Ventura de la Vega, *El hombre de mundo*. (Reprinted in *Autores Dramáticos Contemporáneos*, Tomo I.)

95. *El Laberinto, periódico universal*, Vol. II, núm. 33.

96. *Ibid.*

97. *Revista Literaria de El Español*, October 6, 1845.

98. *Ibid.*

XVII

The Rise and Fall of Romanticism

On february 6, 1828, an announcement appeared in the *Diario de Avisos de Madrid,* giving the inhabitants of that city notice that they would soon have an opportunity to witness a product of "a new literary system called romanticism":

> Preparations are being made to put on the stage as soon as possible, with great theatrical effects, a new drama translated from the French; but the Company believes it necessary to make this announcement longer than usual, not with the object of attracting the attention of the public and of arousing its curiosity by praising the work, but in order that the illustrious spectators may know that the actors seek only to please them, leaving to their impartiality the decision with respect to its merit. It is well known that there is in Europe a new system called romanticism, whose partisans maintain, against the opinion of the classicists, that there is only one rule to observe in dramas, and that one is reduced to moving the spirit and the imagination of the readers or spectators by exciting their interest to such an extent that they will be charmed and enraptured to the end of the composition, and the moral effect which the author proposes will be achieved in a vivid and indelible manner. This is clearly the principle followed by the famous writer, Victor Ducange, in the drama we are offering to this respectable public, the title of which is *Thirty Years or the Life of a Gambler,* divided, not into acts according to the customs of the modern theater, but into *jornadas,* following the practice of our old plays, and presenting an action that lasts the number of years indicated by its title.[1]

The enthusiastic reception of this play by the public is attested by an article that appeared seven months later in the *Correo Literario y Mercantil,* where the complaint is made that "the excellent comedy, the *Misanthrope* by Molière, perfectly performed, was abandoned by the public, while *Thirty Years or the Life of a Gambler* has filled the Coliseum, rivaling even the opera."[2] The success of this play is but another evidence that the public was as little concerned at this time with the fight critics were waging against translations of French drama and melodrama as it had been at the turn of the century with similar attacks against translations of sentimental comedy. The same general condition, which still existed in 1842, moved Hartzenbusch to remark bitterly: "There are today some compositions that are more favored by spectators than others and they are foreign plays, most of which have very little literary merit. Why are they preferred to original works? How do the French manage to please Spaniards better than Spaniards can please themselves?"[3]

Shortly after its performance Larra wrote in *El Duende Satírico del Día* a thoroughly neo-classic and violently antiromantic and anti-French review of Ducange's drama:

This melodramatic play belongs to a new kind of poetry that did not exist in the times of Horace, Terence, and Plautus, and much less in that of Menander and all of those outmoded classicists, who did not know how to compose anything except plays adjusted to reason, with many rules, as if rules were necessary in the composition of comedies; ... and who did not have genius enough to emancipate themselves from their slavery; this is romantic poetry, and there is a great dispute today on Parnassus over whether the irregular plays called "romantic" should be admitted or excluded.[4]

Of course this decision is being made without consulting Spaniards, who are too uncultured to have a vote on such matters. When Lope and his school were writing so many of these long and tedious comedies, "the French opposed them because it was still not time for *romanticism* to be discovered, the composition of this kind of nonsense being reserved for M. Ducange." At that time Spaniards were treated as barbarians, from which it can be seen that they always do everything backward; at that time, through the mouth of Boileau, the French said that their neighbors beyond the Pyrenees, "without running the danger of having their plays hissed, piled events of years into one day and the hero of their barbarous, rough, and unpolished spectacles was wont to appear as a child in the first act and as an old man in the last."[5]

Considering the condescension with which French critics during the classic period had regarded Spanish drama and all the contemptuous remarks they had made about it, Larra, and later Mesonero Romanos,[6] may be pardoned for reminding them that they had suddenly discovered, or invented, the very type of drama that had been the object of their scorn for a century and a half. Indeed, French romantic drama turned its back completely upon all the precepts that French critics had propagated throughout Europe during the better part of two centuries, and equaled or excelled the irregularity of the Spanish Golden Age *comedia*. Larra taunts them for their ideological inconsistency and for having composed such "amphibian and nonsensical" melodramas as *The Orphan Girl of Brussels, The Thieves of Marseille, The Little Blind Girl of Olbruch, The Two French Sergeants,* etc.

A beachhead having been established with Ducange's drama, the opponents of neo-classicism attempted to consolidate their gains. The very critics who had condemned Spanish imitation of French regularity found themselves now in the position of approving the imitation of French irregularity, for the type of romanticism that made its appearance in Spain in 1818 was not the result of a slow and logical development of Golden Age elements, or of nostalgia for the literary ideals of that period; nor was it the result of a pent-up resistance to the restrictions of neo-classic precepts. Larra points out the fundamental difference between the romantic movements in France and Spain. In his review of Dumas's *Catherine Howard,* when it was performed in Spain in 1834, he says:

> It must be confessed that in Spain the transition has been a little strong and rapid. France can count a half-century of political revolution while our revolts have not lasted half that long. . . . France has taken a half-century to accomplish her literary revolution and has brought it about gradually; poetic license has had to gain ground step by step, beginning with the *boulevard* theaters and with the melodramas of *Porte Saint-Martin* until they finally won a place in the *French Theater;* and in a single year we have passed in politics from Fernando VII to a constitutional government, and in literature from Moratín to Alexandre Dumas. It should also be taken into consideration that Aristotelian and Horacian classicism had had time to weary the French public from the time of Louis XIV to that of Napoleon, and that we have not yet exhausted the possibilities of the classic genre, since only twenty-odd years have passed from Comella to our time and during this period we have enjoyed some three or four comedies by Moratín, an equal number by Gorostiza, a few by another writer, and a number of translations, not all of which are good, of Molière and of second-rate French authors. In a word, we are taking coffee directly after the soup.[7]

This, Larra says, accounts to a large degree for the opposition to the innovations currently found both in politics and in literature. Instead of traveling by degrees, Spaniards have proceeded by leaps and bounds.[8]

The first and one of the closest approaches to a manifesto of romanticism in Spain was Agustín Durán's *Discourse Upon the Influence Which Modern Criticism Has Had in the Decadence of the Old Spanish Theater*, written and published in 1828. When the work was republished in the *Memorias de la Academia Española*, the editors called it "the true precursor of romanticism" and said that "it opened the way for the renaissance of genuinely Spanish form and taste."[9] Durán starts his discourse with a bitter indictment of neo-classicism:

> Truly lamentable for the glory of our country and of Spanish litera-ture has been the ruin of our old theater, prepared and consummated by Spanish critics of the past and present centuries, who, blindly prejudiced in favor of doctrines and principles inapplicable to the dramatic system of which we were the inventors, succeeded in extinguishing the splendid flame of national genius which illuminated all of civilized Europe.[10]

This highly oratorical and palpably false statement serves as an introduction for what is, on the whole, a reasonable analysis of the essential nature of Spanish Golden Age drama as distinguished from that of the Greeks and Romans. Although he affects neutrality in the incipient war between romanticists and classicists, saying "I do not belong to any party,"[11] Durán's sympathies at this time are so completely on the side of the new literary movement that he ex-hausts his vocabulary in a search for contemptuous terms to hurl at the neo-classicists.

At the end of his discourse he admits that he has assumed the role of spokesman for the romantic party:

> Our Spain abounds in translations and compilations of the elements of literature; but all have been written in the spirit of classicism. No one up until now has tried to give our youth an idea of what the romantic genre is, in spite of the fact that in Germany, France, and England the discussion on the subject is almost finished.[12]

He declares that he proposes to show in his discourse:

> first, that the old Spanish drama is, because of its origin and its way of considering man, different from drama written in imitation of the Greek; second, that this difference is produced by the fact that there are two distinct genres which do not admit exactly the same rules or forms in their expression; and third, that since Spanish drama is more eminently poetic than classic drama, it should be regulated by precepts and licenses farther removed from prosaic verisimilitude than those that have been established for the other genre.[13]

While the rest of Europe was still submerged in the darkness and ignorance of the Middle Ages, Spain "was making rapid progress not only in the arts of imagination, but also in the exact and the natural sciences." When the Moors were finally expelled from the peninsula, they left to their conquerors a great part of the knowledge, habits, and customs they had brought with them from the Orient. After the conquest of Granada "religious enthusiasm, the cult of love and beauty, and the worship of the glories of Mars . . . absorbed, so to speak, all the energy and activity which the Spanish knights had employed in shaking off the Mohammedan yoke."[14] In the sixteenth century Spanish poetry acquired its complete splendor with a combination of native and Italian metrical forms. Then, Durán says,

. . . our theater was created, forming the prodigious and admirable consolidation of all these sublime and poetical resources. From Lope de Vega to Calderón the brilliance of our drama was constantly perfected and increased. National glories, triumphs of her warriors and of her Christian heroes, delicate and chivalrous love, the concept of honor and jealousy, all this was related, sung, and performed on the national stage, which conserved all its beauty and superiority until the end of that century; when, abusing its own riches, it came to exaggerate and lavish them in such a manner that it converted them into defects, and the defects into intolerable vices.[15]

Later in his discourses Durán launches into a panegyric to the qualities of Golden Age dramatists. The youth of Spain, reading and believing this praise, must surely have felt that the salvation of the theater depended upon an abrogation of all the classical precepts that were being taught in the schools and the enthronement of everything that was represented by the theater of the seventeenth century. The merit of these authors, Durán says,

. . . does not consist, as some critics claim, only in producing good and harmonious verses, but also in being, perhaps, the best poets in the world, in spite of their defects. Who, for example, can compete with Lope in fecundity and invention? Who can deny Calderón primacy in the art of combining plans, in directing and making the most of situations, in the perfection of narrations, in his manner of presenting his eminently poetic ideas, and in the noble artistry with which he made the octosyllabic verse, or *romance*, worthy and capable of expressing the most sublime thoughts? Who can fail to admire in Tirso the harmonious wealth of rhymes, the elegance of language, the graces of elocution, and the comic wit that abound in his dramatic works? And what shall we say of the ingenious

Moreto, the first poet who was able to bring to the stage the true comedy of character and develop it with as much perfection as the famous Molière? Well, all of these illustrious writers were the disciples, imitators, and even at times copiers of Lope; and so in their works we see the type of his school, although at times in a corrected and chastened form. Moreto, in particular, appropriated and made his own many of the dramatic situations and combinations Lope had indicated or developed in his comedies.[16]

When that theater which had reached such a degree of perfection fell victim to the depraved taste of euphuism, it found no helping hand to lift it from chaos and degradation. At this stage "critics of the eighteenth century, more attentive to what it was than to what it had been, attributed to its essential nature all the defects that were foreign or accessory, and decided to destroy it and to substitute a theater imitated from the French."[17] Forgetting that a large proportion of the plays that had met the approval of Madrid audiences for the past fifty years had been translations of French and Italian plays, Durán adds that these critics "succeeded in reducing us from the glory of having created an original genre that was adjusted to our character and manners to the role of mere imitators of an exotic and foreign theater, which has never prospered and will never prosper in our soil as long as we are Spaniards and not Frenchmen."[18] For the next twenty years, however, the Spanish stage was to be invaded and almost dominated by French melodrama, French romantic drama, and the "well-made" plays of Scribe; and the constant complaint of authors and critics was to be that audiences seemed to prefer these plays rather than original works.

Thoroughly warmed up now, Durán goes into a diatribe against the ideas and activities of the neo-classicists:

The spirit of novelty and the servile admiration of everything that came to us from France formed a multitude of pedants, who, without understanding the Montianos and the Luzáns, and without the instruction or the sensibility necessary to discern the merit of the Corneilles and Racines, believed themselves worthy of the magistracy of Parnassus, for the sole reason that in the name of Aristotle and Boileau, whose works they perhaps had never read, they dared to abhor the dramas of Lope and Calderón. This plague of critics, justly called Gallicists, looking contemptuously upon the characteristic originality, the rich and harmonious language, and the sublime poetry of our old poets, overran the Spanish dramatic Parnassus and filled the theater with all those worthless plays, adjusted to the three unities, that have dominated it for almost a century. The stupid and unfeeling partisans of the new criticism, provided always with foreign rules and calipers, and fortified with a cold and indigestible erudition, made their way to the theaters, not to yield themselves to the sweet or terrible emotions which the creations of our writers were supposed to produce in their hearts, but only to see whether they conformed to the puny rules to which they were trying to subject them. In this way the famous names of Lope, Tirso, Moreto, etc., formerly so admired and so justly applauded, were finally banished from so-called good society. With these methods they achieved the shameful triumph of smothering the beauty of our drama; and they were so successful that since that time Spain has not produced again any of those sublime creations, previously so envied and admired by cultured nations.[19]

Durán attributes the dethronement of the Golden Age theater entirely to the unreasonable and relentless attacks of neo-classic critics and maintains that the general public never wavered in its loyalty and enthusiasm for the *comedia.*

The general public, guided by their own impressions and by their intimate feelings of pleasure, filled the theaters whenever they saw Lope, Tirso, Calderón, and Moreto on the stage; and perhaps their detractors left the theater as moved as they were ashamed at having participated in the general enthusiasm, against the rules of Aristotle and their party spirit.[20]

Durán is quite willing to agree with neo-classic critics that the Spanish *comedia* is not like the Greek, Roman, or French tragedy and comedy. He will also concede that Spanish plays are frequently nothing but novels put into action; but he will insist always "that they constitute in themselves a genre that is susceptible of the greatest perfection, and filled with charms that perhaps could never be equaled in the classic theater or produced by reducing the romantic spectacles of our dramas to the rules of Boileau and Aristotle."[21]

At two points in his discourse, Durán departs from his indictment of neo-classicism and his eulogy of Golden Age drama long enough to proclaim the emancipation of the intellect and the exaltation of the imagination, which perhaps form the essence of romanticism. After saying that the precepts have never produced and will never produce "the sublime creations of a Shakespeare, of a Calderón, or of a Schiller,"[22] he declares:

True enthusiasm proceeds from ecstasy and rapture of the soul, which, throwing off the shackles of the real or prosaic world, snatching, so to speak, from the celestial model a ray of divine light that does not lend itself to the exact calculations of human reason, rises to the ideal realms of human beauty. *Est Deus in nobis:* this is the emblem of all privileged talents, and especially that of great poets and orators whose inspirations are destined to direct the human heart, stirring the imagination and exciting emotions rather than demonstrating mathematically what cannot be subjected to calculation.[23]

And later, after comparing the beauty of a formal and carefully tended garden with that of a rough but magnificent landscape, he asks: "Will anyone claim still that we should renounce the feeling inspired by these sublime and magnificent pictures because it is not possible to understand their structure, and because we cannot reduce them to the limits of a gardener's art?" Then he answers his own question and again raises the standard of romanticism:

No! Let us enjoy the pleasures that art affords, but let us never give up the ineffable joys furnished by direct works of creation; let us open our soul to the emotions they inspire, even though we cannot analyze them; let us feel, even though rules contradict our feelings; since, after all, sensations are facts, and rules are abstractions or theories that may be badly applied or inaccurate.[24]

Neo-classicists may be excused to a certain extent, Durán says, for their attempt to introduce French regularity during the eighteenth century, in view of the debased condition of the Spanish theater at that time; but "after the Germans have treated the matter with such clarity, and experience has demonstrated how harmful exclusive systems are in literature, what excuse can they now have for their torpor? Have they not seen the effects of their bitter diatribes and the ruin they have brought upon our literature?"[25] In pointing out the errors committed by modern critics, it is not his intention, he declares, to deprive them of credit for the important services they have rendered to literature in general. By the end of the seventeenth century Spanish literature had become so corrupted that hardly a trace remained of its former brilliance. It was, therefore, very fitting that "the dike of a vigorous and severe criticism should strive to hold back the torrent of bad taste that was demolishing our Parnassus."[26] If Luzán and Montiano had been better acquainted with the true merit of Golden Age drama and had not been so offended by its defects, and instead of attempting to exterminate it had dedicated their efforts toward its correction, "who doubts that we would be indebted to them for having perfected it and would not have reason to attribute to them the complete loss of our originality and the overthrow of the dramatic genre of which we were the inventors?"[27]

Durán traces the origin of romanticism to the Middle Ages, at which time a chivalrous feudal organization produced new habits and manners and the Christian religion replaced paganism, "giving a new direction to thought and opening a broad field to the imagination for poetic creation based upon spirituality."[28] Man having been transformed from republican to monarchist, and from pagan to Christian, it was inevitable that "the expression of the spirit should replace symmetry and personified harmony."[29] In classic literature man is regarded objectively and his virtues and vices are considered in the abstract. For this reason he loses all individuality and is merged with all other men who share the same qualities. "So it is," Durán says, "that the miser, the misanthrope, and the hypocrite can be treated as if they were avarice, misanthropy, and hypocrisy personified," and the classicist, in his compositions, can set for himself a fixed and determined moral objective. The romanticist, on the contrary, "considers the moral purpose as purely accessory. He seeks to create and to portray individual characters, and the more or less vague morality that may be deduced from his works must be derived from the singular deeds performed by the characters."[30] For these reasons, Durán maintains, it is impossible to restrict romantic drama or comedy to the three unities, because the individual characters are not abstractions, and are the result not of a single passion, vice, or virtue, but of a combination of these qualities. It is likewise impossible "because the gradual development of the emotions of an individual cannot take place in the short space of twenty-four hours"; nor "can a portrait of the inner man be derived from a single act or circumstance in his life."[31]

The best defense that could be made of the Spanish dramatists of the seventeenth century, in Durán's opinion, would be to publish not only those works of theirs that have some analogy with classical drama, "but also those which because of their essence and purpose belong exclusively to national romantic drama," making available to the studious youth of the land in this manner "more resources, models, and instruction than can be found in all the patchwork of precepts that have been published so far."[32] It is to be hoped that the publication of the plays of Lope, Tirso, Calderón, Moreto, and other Golden Age dramatists

will revive the enthusiasm of Spanish youth, whose imagination has been withered by the excessive shackles placed upon it for more than a century, forcing it to abandon and even to despise the pleasing path of original creations, opened by the sublime geniuses of the times of Carlos V and of Felipe IV.[33]

Durán's attitude toward classical precepts, as revealed in the preceding *Discourse,* contrasts sharply with statements made by him eleven years later, after he had had an opportunity to witness the rise and rapid decline of romanticism, and after he had seen the effect his ideas had produced upon the young writers of the day. Nationalist critics refrain from quoting these statements, probably because they show a retreat on the part of Durán from his advocacy of complete freedom of the imagination and his insistence upon the deadening effect of the rules upon creative talent. His change of attitude must be considered a victory for neo-classicism, in spite of his declaration that he is merely trying to correct a widespread misinterpretation of the ideas he had expressed in his *Discourse:*

For the repose of my conscience this point needs a friendly clarification. Warned by the fact that when upon another occasion I attacked the intolerance of the classicists and demonstrated that the abandonment of their conventional rules did not prevent the production of beautiful and perfect works, not only did the enemies of my system treat me as a literary anarchist, but many who were friendly to my doctrines (and this grieved me no little) put them into practice in a very anarchical manner; I desire to protest and I do protest against any unfaithful interpretation that may be given to the ideas I express in this article.

I find myself so far from condemning the study of the classics that I rather believe them indispensable to form an essentially beautiful taste and to produce immortal masterpieces. This study, if it falls under the sway of good and philosophical criticism, serves to enable even mediocre talents to produce agreeable works; but if a great writer takes it and uses it, then it is the most powerful and effective way to exalt and to ennoble him; since far from beating down the flight of the imagination by subjecting it to exotic forms from other countries, the reading of the old classics teaches him to find new roads of invention; suggests to him new means of imitating nature; and is the best and safest remedy against slavery of the mind; because it is also a spur against laziness and the best and softest bit that can be used to restrain the anarchical boldness of the ignorant and the false learning of pedants.[34]

In a critical analysis of Tirso de Molina's *Condemned for Lack of Faith* which appeared in the *Revista de Madrid* in 1841, we find a somewhat chastened Durán decrying the logical application that had been made during the last decade of the very principles he had

advocated in his *Discourse*. We also find him admitting that much of
Golden Age drama in its original form is unsuitable for performance
before a contemporary audience. The moderation of the following
remarks on the precepts contrasts strikingly with the virulence of
those which formed the body of his *Discourse:*

> To judge the products of the imagination, it is not enough now to
> have read and studied the poetics of Aristotle, Horace, and Boileau,
> because philosophical criticism should not limit itself to applying those
> rules we call rules of good taste, but must in addition have as a founda-
> tion a profound knowledge of the physical and moral history of peoples,
> of their most intimate customs, and of the predominant ideas which at
> different times constituted their social state, and which motivated their
> successes and their mistakes.[35]

Spanish popular poetry and the Golden Age theater, which represents its essence, taken as the object of philosophical study and not
as a model for servile imitation, has, in Durán's opinion, been instrumental in preserving the national character of the Spanish theater
and in separating it "from the exaggerated and delirious system
which stains and darkens with savage and immoral creations the
literary glories of that nation which in better times produced a
Corneille, a Molière, and a Racine."[36]

He notes that some of the illustrious and youthful writers in
Spain have allowed themselves to be dazzled for a while "by bad
romanticism," but after studying national poetry have abandoned
it, and following the road marked by sound criticism have produced
works that honor the present generation. Others, however, "going
to the other extreme, thought that we were the same as we were
three hundred years ago, and that in order to please the public it
was sufficient to violate purposely all the rules of wisdom and
good taste, to introduce a variety of meters, and to change scenes
frequently."[37] Good criticism can make these also see the error of
their practices, by pointing out that, "because the present century
is less credulous, the modern theater must observe more material
verisimilitude than did the old, and finally that, since it is better
acquainted with history and past manners, it does not allow anachronisms of any kind." For instance, he says, "at the present time
an audience would not tolerate a theological drama like this one by
Tirso, which is divided into two almost distinct actions and filled
with supernatural recourses and disconnected situations."[38]

Durán's *Discourse*, as we have seen, makes adequate provision for the type of romantic protagonist found in such Spanish plays as the Duke of Rivas' *Don Alvaro*, Pacheco's *Alfredo*, García Gutiérrez' *The Troubadour*, Hartzenbusch's *The Lovers of Teruel*, and Gil y Zárate's *Carlos II*, as well as in such French dramas as Victor Hugo's *Hernani* and *Lucrecia Borgia* and Dumas's *Catherine Howard, Anthony, Thérèse, Richard Darlington*, and *The Tower of Nesle*, all of which were performed in Madrid from 1835 to 1837. Certainly none of these characters could be called abstractions or recognizable types, and probably for that very reason they could not maintain their popularity after their novelty had worn off. Dealing as they did with unusual and even abnormal characters and manners, such romantic dramas were necessarily produced in numbers too limited to meet the needs of the theater. We find, therefore, that except for the years from 1835 to 1837, romantic plays never constituted more than a small percentage of the performances on the Madrid stage. Allison Peers, in his recent work, *The Romantic Movement in Spain*, has backed up with incontrovertible evidence earlier findings by M. Le Gentil, and has exploded completely the myth of a triumph of romanticism in Spain. In so far as it represented a revolt against dramatic regularity, it was indeed a "flash in the pan."[39] According to M. Le Gentil,

The reign of French romanticism lasted no more than two years, from 1835 to 1837; Hugo, Dumas, Béranger, and Lamartine were still translated, but Spanish patriotism asserted itself anew. No people was converted with greater difficulty or was less faithful to the exaggerations of a school which liked to represent the country of *Hernani* and *Carmen* as the home of antithesis, enthusiasm, and chimera.[40]

If we take the term "romantic revival" to mean a renewed interest in the early history and legends of Spain, we may concede that in this respect romanticism made a substantial and permanent contribution to Spanish literature; but if we interpret it to mean a renewed enthusiasm for Golden Age drama, its failure in this regard was even more complete than the failure of its revolt against classic regularity. Critics have left no stone unturned in an attempt to prove that Spanish literature and Spanish drama in particular were essentially romantic from their inception. During the eighteenth century nationalist critics tried valiantly to make it appear that the only thing wrong with the theater was the war waged by neo-classicists against Lope, Calderón, Tirso, Moreto, and other Golden Age dramatists, the obvious inference being that, if this opposition could be silenced, the Spanish theater would again assume a pre-eminent place in European drama. The public, of course, was unconcerned with, and to a large extent unaware of, the heated polemics between the partisans of the two schools.

When all obstacles to the complete domination of nationalistic ideas were removed at the death of Fernando VII, those who had looked forward so eagerly to such a time must have been very much disappointed and disillusioned by the public's complete apathy toward Golden Age drama—an apathy that was, as we have observed, only the last stage of a growing lack of enthusiasm that dated at least from the last decade of the eighteenth century. Far from reviving the popularity of Golden Age comedies, the romantic movement was coincident with the almost complete cessation of their performance on the Madrid stage. During the decade from 1809 to 1818 there were 1,766 performances; from 1825 to 1834, 1,287; and from 1835 to 1844 the figure dropped to 434. In the year 1837, which is usually considered as the peak of romanticism, only nine Golden Age plays were given for a total of twenty performances.[41] More significant than the number of performances is contemporary testimony with regard to the attendance. In 1835 Eugenio Ochoa, who, as a romantic, would hardly be inclined to exaggerate the lack of popularity of these plays, says:

> This week we have had the pleasure (not without a mixture of bitterness, to be sure) of witnessing the performance of *Life Is a Dream,* one of the most justly praised productions of our immortal Calderón, which for a long time had not been seen on the stage. We have indicated that this pleasure was not unmixed with bitterness because, if we exclude a few dozen almost always loyal spectators who attended the performance, it was not easy for the harmonious verses of Calderón and the original and sublime raptures of Segismundo to find any echo in the hardened hearts of the benches that made up the most numerous and compact part of the audience.[42]

Later the same year *El Artista* reprints an announcement that had appeared in the *Diario de Avisos de Madrid* (July 16), which it calls "a profession of faith of the management of the theaters," upon the occasion of the performance of Dumas's *Lucrecia Borgia.* The management recognizes that the title of the play and the name of the author suffice to attract public attention without the necessity of any comment. Nevertheless, in presenting a work that is destined, whatever may be its success, to form an epoch in the Spanish theater, it wishes to explain its reasons for choosing the work. In making this explanation, the management comments upon the public's lack of interest in Golden Age drama:

It is unquestionable that public taste in dramatic literature has changed in the last few years. The productions of our old theater have progressively lost their prestige until they have come to be performed in these last years to such a reduced number of spectators that they could be counted at a glance, in spite of the fact that they have been presented by the same actors who earlier had acquired a just renown in their performance. In vain has an attempt been made to reanimate this genre in its death throes with recasts entrusted to the best writers, and by bringing back to the stage forgotten comedies by the best writers of the seventeenth century, performing them exactly as they were written and trying to select those in which they displayed best their spirited imagination. It has been necessary, therefore, to renounce almost completely a genre that formerly provided the basis of the repertoire of our theaters.[43]

This loss of popularity of Golden Age drama was not due to any war that was being waged upon it by neo-classicists. Indeed, members of this group and others who were generally considered as eclectics were responsible with their recasts for whatever lingering interest these plays might have had for the new generation. Every effort was made by such writers as Bretón, Hartzenbusch, Carnerero, and Mesonero Romanos to adapt the old plays to contemporary manners and taste. This they were doing not in accordance with any neo-classic program, but at the earnest request of the management of the theaters and with the hope that a revival of these plays might serve as a dike to hold back the flood of "bad" romantic plays that was threatening to engulf the theater. In 1834 it occurred to the management that probably the failure of the old comedies on the stage was due to the fact that only *cloak and sword* plays had been chosen for rehabilitation and that the public would show more interest in others that, in vehemence of passions and exuberance of imagination, more closely approximated the new plays that were being imported from France. The following announcement of the projected performance of Alarcon's *The Weaver of Segovia* indicates a sincere desire on the part of the management to restore interest in Golden Age drama:

The romantic drama in six *jornadas*, entitled *The Weaver of Segovia*, is being rehearsed for performance as soon as possible. The first and

second parts of the old comedy of the same title, written by D. Juan Ruiz
de Alarcón, have been combined to form the drama which we are
announcing. The suppression of a few scenes that might unnecessarily
hinder the progress of the action and some slight corrections that have
been made in several places in order to give it more unity and verisimilitude do not deprive *The Weaver of Segovia* of its originality as a drama.
The management, being convinced that the multitude of recasts that
have been made of seventeenth-century plays, few of which have been
well done, have contributed to a considerable extent to the discredit in
which our old theater lies, proposes to restore some of the renowned
productions which give best evidence of the pleasing exuberance and
the vigorous imagination of those rare dramatists, whom Molière and
Corneille did not disdain to imitate. Up until now only *cloak and sword*
plays have been taken from the dust of the archives to be rehabilitated
in a reworked form, doubtless because this class of comedies entered with
less violence into the narrow mold of the Aristotelian unities, which have
disfigured many of them. The present management recognizes no less
merit in a number of old dramas, which, like the one we are announcing,
operate in a more extended arena, and, therefore, allow room for more
incidents and a more complete development of passions. *The Weaver of
Segovia* belongs to this class; and, although it does not lack the defects
inherent in the literary freedom, at times carried to excess, with which
this author and his contemporaries wrote, it perhaps possesses for this
very reason a greater number of beauties harmonized with true talent.
The management has another object in performing this play, and that is
to show that our theater has abounded for more than two centuries in
romantic creations in no way inferior to those which have recently taken
possession of the French stage; and that, consequently, no one can deny
Spanish dramatists either priority in the romanticism which is so popular
today or the praiseworthy circumstance of having cultivated it without
detriment to morals.[44]

In spite of the good intentions of the management, we are told by
Eugenio Ochoa that the play was a complete failure and that it was
hissed by the audience.[45]

In 1837, as we have noticed, the Golden Age theater showed
almost no signs of life. In the year which represents the peak of
the success of romantic drama in Spain, Salas y Quiroga, in a
flowery eulogy of Calderón, laments the complete indifference of
his generation to this idol of the Golden Age and concludes with
these words:

> You are dead, O Calderón, and we are few
> Who go back to your tomb and to your plays;
> And in payment for this love we bear you
> The stupid, unfeeling crowd holds us fools.

> Fools we are if they be wise, for 'tis better
> To be held as fools in the world today
> Than to wallow in a mire so filthy
> That no madness could equal its infamy.

With all the enthusiasm generated in Spain over the new day that was supposed to have dawned for the theater with the coming of romanticism, the fruits of this movement proved disappointing from the beginning even to its most ardent supporters. *Don Alvaro, or The Force of Fate,* by the Duque de Rivas, was almost the alpha and the omega of the new romanticism in the Spanish theater, for it exceeded in irregularity and spectacular effects anything that followed. This drama had been much publicized and was being eagerly awaited by the partisans of the new school when the following announcement was made in *El Artista:*

> Tonight the first performance of *Don Alvaro, or The Force of Fate,* a drama in five acts, in prose and verse, will definitely be given. In our next number we shall speak to our readers about its success, making at the same time an analysis of the beauties and defects we find in it.[46]

After announcing the performance in the coming month of April of *Alen Ferrando or the Crusaders,* by Salas y Quiroga, the writer, unable to restrain his enthusiasm, continues:

> It is quite evident that we are in a holy and privileged epoch; only in that way can the unheard-of wealth of Spanish plays that are observed in our theaters be explained. Besides the two that have already been indicated, another, entitled *Alfredo,* which is highly praised, will soon make its appearance.[47]

In view of the almost complete lack of comment on *Don Alvaro* in the periodicals of the day and the myth of its phenomenal success, the account in *El Artista* of its disappointing reception on the stage is of particular interest, coming as it does from such a thoroughly romantic source:

> When we announced to our readers the coming performance of this drama, we did not doubt at all that it would meet with a vigorous resistance on the part of many writers, and even more, that the public, astonished by the novelty of its framework and the liberty its author has taken in violating many rules commonly considered laws of good taste, would receive with coolness and prejudice this new experiment in a genre which, in spite of what some people say, originated in this country. Our sus-

picions have not been unfounded, although the public has shown itself more benign and more just than we really expected. The first night there was uncertainty and evidence of agitation; but the storm that some people predicted did not break out; and the judgment pronounced in the five following performances has been entirely favorable to the author. We do not believe at all that the literary antecedents of the author and his social position have been the only things that have recommended *Don Alvaro* to the benevolence of the public. We are, on the other hand, quite persuaded that, even though this drama had been superior to the most perfect productions of our old authors, it would have been censured by many who condemn before they see; who think they are doing the author of a play a favor if they stay until the next to the last scene of the second act; who during the performance entertain themselves by noticing whether such and such an actress has rings under her eyes or whether her legs are well shaped; and who, after looking at the boxes, smoothing their hair and humming some passages from the opera *Norma*, make a show of their intelligence by announcing aloud what such and such an actor is going to do or say, bursting out laughing at the most sublime moments, and making fun of what is beyond their comprehension and what they have probably not even heard. These are the enlightened judges whom we have heard laughing at all the performances of this drama during the mysterious organ melody, when Don Alvaro faints for the second time, and in other situations that can only inspire laughter in men with hearts of oakum, in trivial men in whose mouths the word *poetry* is a sacrilege. . . . These critics, and not the public, hissed the most sublime scenes in *The Weaver of Segovia* by Alarcón; they are the ones who applaud the plays of Scribe (perhaps because anyone is capable of translating one of them and acquiring in that way with little effort the brilliant title of dramatic author).

But, if, unfortunately, these critics are all too numerous, it must be confessed, nevertheless, that there are conscientious men, filled with erudition and talent, who do not approve completely—or at all, perhaps—our literary doctrines, and who see in Calderón and Shakespeare only a chaos of horrors, monstrosities, and delirium, in which from time to time an occasional sublime beauty is found. With these men the weapons of reason should be employed.

Up until now the *Eco de Comercio* is the periodical which has come out most openly against the modern school, and consequently the one that has censured *Don Alvaro* most bitterly. . . .

The *Eco* is surprised that the Duque de Rivas has been able "to lower himself to the level of those who supply the theaters of the suburbs of Paris, presenting in ours a composition that is more monstrous than all those we have seen up until now on the Spanish stage."

The one who can really be given the title of purveyor is our adored Scribe, who employs in his factory a considerable number of young people, whose works he corrects after they are finished (and not always does he do this), putting his name on them to increase their value, just as a manufacturer of pomade prints his seal on the jars he offers to the public. No one who is at all aware of what is going on in the theaters of Paris is ignorant of this fact.[48]

Of the other two plays that had aroused the enthusiasm of *El Artista*, the composition by Salas y Quiroga for some unknown reason failed to make its appearance, and *Alfredo*, by Joaquín Pacheco, was performed from the 23rd to the 25th of May with extremely poor attendance and then abandoned, thereby justifying the opinion of contemporary critics who dealt harshly with it. Although Espronceda, writing in *El Artista*, makes every effort to find merit in the play, he is finally forced to admit that "*Alfredo* is only a beautiful dramatic thought," and that "the entire drama is lacking in good craftsmanship, which fact contributes to chill interest and make the play languid and at times annoying."[49]

The outstanding theatrical event of the year 1836 was García Gutiérrez' *The Troubadour*, which was given thirteen consecutive performances on its initial run and was repeated twelve times during the year. *Aben Humeya*, by Martínez de la Rosa, which also appeared this year, had ten performances. No other romantic drama worth mentioning appeared until the following year, when Harzenbusch's *The Lovers of Teruel* ran eight days consecutively in January and was repeated seven times later in the year. Two dramas by García Gutiérrez, *The Page* and *The King-Monk*, were given seven and six performances respectively, both of these plays being far inferior to *The Troubadour*. The other dramas performed in this banner year for romanticism were Escosura's *The Court of Buen Retiro* and *Bárbara Blomberg;* Bretón's *Don Fernando the Summoned;* Gil y Zárate's *Carlos II; Doña María de Molina*, by the Marqués de Molins; and *Fray Luis de Leon*, by José Castro y Orozco. They aroused little enthusiasm in the public.

As we look at the total production of romantic drama from 1835 to 1837, only three plays stand out: *Don Alvaro* (1835), *The Troubadour* (1836), and *The Lovers of Teruel* (1837); and of these only *The Troubadour* enjoyed any sustained popularity. It is significant that in each case the play represented the first attempt of its author in the field of romanticism, and none of the three ever produced another work in the same style that rose above the level of mediocrity. When Larra reviewed *The Troubadour* and *The Lovers of Teruel*, he found a number of defects but concluded that these could be overlooked in view of the inexperience of their authors. About *The Troubadour* he says:

> At this point, shall we state our opinion frankly? All the defects which can be noted in *The Troubadour* arise from the lack of experience of the author. This is not a reproof, because to require of him in his first work what comes only with time and practice would not be fair. He has conceived a vast plan, a plan better suited to a novel than to a drama, and he has composed a magnificent novel; but upon reducing such a broad conception to the limits of the theater, he has had to struggle with the narrowness of his mold. For that reason, he had not had time to prepare his characters properly.[50]

And in his review of *The Lovers of Teruel*, after calling attention to numerous merits and pointing out a few defects, he says; "In our humble opinion the beauties obscure the defects; we urge the poet to continue the career he has started so brilliantly."[51]

In its so-called "profession of faith" in 1835, contained in the announcement of the coming performance of Victor Hugo's *Lucrecia Borgia*, after recognizing the indifference of the public toward Golden Age comedy, classical comedy, sentimental drama, and the "improperly called" romantic drama in the style of Ducange's *The Life of a Gambler,* the management tries to explain this apathy and the increasing difficulty of satisfying public demand:

> It has been said, and probably not without reason, that this difficulty arises principally from the lack of stability in tastes and ideas which is the natural result of the epoch of transition in which we find ourselves; that a true literary revolution is now unavoidable; and that in the matter of theatrical spectacles nothing can be as much in keeping with the severe character of modern ideas as the grave, profound, and philosophical drama of the newest French school, the leaders of which are Victor Hugo and Alexandre Dumas.[52]

The management believes that it is time to make a test, "in order to determine the course the modern Spanish theater should take," by presenting the most celebrated work "of the first apostle of romanticism." It realizes the seriousness of the questions and problems which the performance of such a work will stir up, "for it is not only the drama itself that the public is going to judge, but also the genre to which it belongs."[53]

If the management was correct in its opinion that *Lucrecia Borgia* was a test case, then romantic drama failed in 1835 in Spain, for the public rejected the work and with it the genre it represented.

In his review of the drama in *El Artista*, Eugenio de Ochoa says, "Let no one say now that he does not know what romanticism is; for, if he does not, let him go to see *Lucrecia Borgia* and he will find out and can discuss later whether he likes the romantic genre or not."[54] *Lucrecia Borgia,* he says, with its great defects, "is the personification of that magnificent genre created by Calderón and Shakespeare, cultivated so brilliantly by Goethe, and raised so such a height by the two giants of the modern French theater, Victor Hugo and Alexandre Dumas."[55] The public, however, has been incapable of appreciating its true merit. Although some people are uncertain about the reaction of the spectators, Ochoa does not hesitate to declare that not only did it not please but that it was impossible for it to do so. This declaration, he says, coming from one "who will certainly not be accused of being a partisan of neo-classicism," needs an explanation:

Lucrecia Borgia has terrified our public; it has caught it unawares, and in spite of itself the public has been forced to applaud; therefore, in order not to expose itself to the shame of repeating that forced applause, *it has been very careful not to return to the following performances.* This drama, we repeat, has terrified; it has moved Spanish audiences to the bottom of their hearts; it has exercised a magic charm; but to say that it has pleased is inexact; that would be like saying that the light of the sun is pleasing when it first strikes the eyes of a captive who has been shut up from infancy in a dark dungeon.[56]

Ochoa is convinced, however, that when the public becomes familiar with the true beauty and the "magnificent poetry of the romantic genre," it will like all the works of Victor Hugo and will again appreciate Golden Age drama, and "instead of the theaters being empty when Golden Age plays are presented, the public will fill them and will applaud these plays with rapture."[57] When that day comes and *Lucrecia Borgia* is presented, "the applause will be universal; bursts of laughter will not be heard in the fifth act... nor will the theater be practically deserted at the fourth performance."[58] What disillusionment the following years must have brought to Ochoa, in view of the public's continued disapproval of romantic drama! His testimony of the reaction of the spectators in 1835 to *Lucrecia Borgia* is more significant than the fact that this play started on July 18 and had a run of eight days with an intermission of one day; that it was repeated on September 8, October 2, and December 29; and that it was revived in 1837 for two performances. After its first run, it is noteworthy that revivals lasted only one night. In the same year, Dumas's *Richard Darlington* was given only five performances upon its first appearance on the Spanish stage. In commenting upon Dumas's play, *El Artista* is bitter and sarcastic in its condemnation of the superficial and desultory taste that prevails in Madrid, where the public seems incapable of appreciating the beauties of romanticism:

What theatrical novelties we have witnessed in Madrid; two in a week: *Richard Darlington* and *The Change of Portici!* Fortunate Madrilenians! No one thinks of anything except amusing you and providing you with pastimes that will make you forget the bitterness of life; yesterday it was the new drama; tomorrow it will be the new opera; day after tomorrow, the exposition; then will come winter with its dances, its concerts, its aristocratic strolls in the Salón del Prado during the morning . . . ; truly, no man of taste can live outside of Madrid. Where else can one see what is seen in this great capital? Here Bellini enraptures and Mozart is heard with supreme indifference; here the halls of the museum are deserted and the Puerta del Sol is filled at all hours of the day; here people will scarcely attend the first performance of a new drama (unless it is translated), and they fight their way to get tickets to the opera; here *Richard Darlington* displeases and *The Goat's Foot* edifies. . . . How could the fine arts fail to prosper in such an atmosphere?[59]

In his review of Bretón's *Merope*, Ochoa comments upon the lack of stability in all phases of Spanish life and attributes the complete indifference of the public toward the theater in a large measure to this state of uncertainty:

The public in Madrid is decidedly not in favor of the classic genre. Shall we say then that it is in favor of the romantic? I believe it would be more accurate to say that it has no interest in either. It is true that we find ourselves in an epoch of transition in politics, in literature, and in everything; we feel that we are lacking in something but we do not know what; we are only certain that what we need is not what we have had so far. In the theater, we see examples of this truth continually; the public hisses indiscriminately the classic and the romantic, original works and translations; everything tires it; everything bores it. The public goes to the theater with the same indifference with which an English millionaire who has exhausted all gastronomic sensations goes to a banquet.[60]

The only really popular plays during the year 1835 were Bretón's *All Is Farce in This World* with fourteen performances; Belmonte's *The Devil Turned Preacher,* an old play that always seemed to have the same appeal to Spanish audiences as comedies of magic, with fifteen performances; and Larra's prose translation of Scribe's *The Art of Conspiracy* with no less than twenty-seven. It is somewhat puzzling that, when Spanish audiences were represented as so surfeited in 1832 with plays written entirely in assonance that they flocked to see Bretón's *Marcela* largely because of its metrical variety, they should in 1835 attend in equal numbers and at many more performances a prose translation of a French comedy, and that this same comedy should exceed in number of performances in one year even *The Troubadour*, the outstanding romantic drama that took Madrid "by storm" in 1836, and which Mesonero Romanos calls "a real theatrical event that placed the final seal of approval on that epoch of renaissance for the stage."[61]

At no time during the so-called triumph of romanticism were translated or original plays of this school popular enough to support the theater. It appears, indeed, that an all-time low in the prosperity of this institution may have been reached in 1837 after *Don Alvaro, The Troubadour,* and *The Lovers of Teruel,* the three important plays upon which the fame of romantic drama in Spain rests, had already been produced. In June of that year, Salas y Quiroga says: "Our theaters continue to be deserted."[62] In October he declares: "The theater is abandoned in such a scandalous manner that the management is losing money."[63] And in December, he repeats that "during the present season the management has lost a great deal of money."[64]

Declarations of eclecticism, or at least of an unwillingness to take sides in the conflict between classicists and romanticists, become increasingly common after 1836 and find expression particularly in the *Semanario Pintoresco Español* which was founded in that year by Mesonero Romanos, and which counted among its collaborators such eminent critics as Antonio Gil y Zárate, Eugenio de Ochoa, José de la Revilla, Antonio María Segovia, Mariano Roca de Togores (Marqués de Molíns), Enrique Gil y Carrasco, and Salvador Burmúdez de Castro.[65] In the first article on the theater that appeared in this review, José de la Revilla, speaking for the editors, declares that in their attempt to be entirely impartial and to point out defects and merits in the works of both schools they realize that they will run the risk of being accused by some of their readers of espousing the cause of the romanticists and by others of favoring classicism. They hasten, therefore, to make the following statement of their literary independence:

We protest sincerely that we belong exclusively to neither of the two schools. As staunch partisans of beauty, we enjoy with equal pleasure the charm of the works of Sophocles and of Victor Hugo; of Shakespeare and of Molière. Wherever we see beauty we shall admire it, for we have never applauded error or scorned ability because it came to us under the name of a particular school.

We have always believed that there is, in our humble opinion, no single way to imitate nature; although we have understood that all ways are not equally good in achieving that result. We have also considered it quite certain that to limit imagination to a single and exclusive form would be as harmful as to unchain it and leave it abandoned to delirium and frenzy. Both extremes are excluded from our literary creed, which is not, and should not be, blind like religious faith, for what is good in the latter would be in the former a very serious detriment to the progress of letters.[66]

The following year, however, in an unsigned review of Bretón's *Die and You Will See,* the *Semanario Pintoresco* takes the opportunity to condemn the immorality and extravagance it finds in the works of those whom it chooses to call "romantics of the French school," and to contrast them with the plays of Bretón, who, "as the heir of the dramatic laurels of the famous Inarco [Moratín], marches at the head of the chosen group of young writers who announce a new era of prosperity and glory for our theater."[67]

Faithful to the principles which he found established by the father of our classic theater, the productions of Bretón have been distinguished up until the present time by the regularity of their form, by their skilful portrayal of manners and characters, and by the grace and comic force of interesting and animated dialogue; and in this respect it must be confessed that the author of *Marcela, Old Age Folly, I Am Going Back to Madrid,* and *All Is Farce in This World* has acquired a just title to the sympathy and gratitude of the Spanish public.[68]

But the present generation, having been subjected to the most intense sensations and being thirsty for novelty of all kinds, is no longer satisfied with the simplicity of regular drama. This fact has given rise to a new literary sect, which resists all restraint and maintains that the imagination is free to fly as high as its wings will permit. The *Semanario Pintoresco* does not deny that this principle has certain merits, if it is not carried to excess, and believes that the romantic movement would probably have met with little opposition even from those who were most addicted to the old forms, if its followers had been guided by the same high moral and political ideals as the classicists.

But the so-called romanticists of the French school have unfortunately confused essence with form and, deviating in most of their productions from that political and religious moral objective which alone is capable of giving interest and permanence to works of literature, have fallen into an extravagance of ideas, into an abyss of horrors, into such an exaggerated and ridiculous coloring that the term "romantic" has almost become synonymous with the terms "false" and "immoral."[69]

The *Semanario* counsels dramatists to work to restore Spanish drama to its former splendor and vigor since "modern taste has freed them from certain restraints which were perhaps unjust because of their arbitrary nature," but warns them at the same time not to imitate the French "by hurling themselves headlong into the thorny field of materialism and immorality."[70]

Later in the same month, in a review of García Gutiérrez' *The Page*, the same critic, who now signs himself "M" and who was doubtless Mesonero Romanos himself, expresses almost identical reactions to the "poisonous" influence of French romanticism:

In other articles on modern dramas we have expressed our humble opinion about the criminal abuse which authors today, particularly the French, have made of that gift from heaven, converted in their hands into a poisonous weapon of seduction and evil, which lends to the new literary school an immoral character that bears no necessary relationship to a just relief from certain erudite rules with which the authority of the ancients attempted to hinder the free flight of the imagination. Regretting sincerely such a fatal mistake, we have fervently exhorted our young writers to avail themselves of what is favorable in the new school without falling into its errors; to give free rein to their imagination, without abandoning, however, true philosophy: the philosophy of virtue.[71]

The reviewer regrets to say that the author of *The Troubadour* has failed in his second drama to give proper attention to its moral content. In striving for effect he has presented a picture of society that is more horribly fantastic than real; and he has not even compensated for this gloomy picture by a contrast with interesting characters and noble sentiments as he did so skilfully in his first work. The characters in *The Page*, he says, "are all equally odious and voluntarily criminal."[72]

Also in 1837 there appeared in the *Semanario* a review of Patricio de la Escosura's *Bárbara Blomberg*, in which the critic, who signs himself "S. el E.," comments with some degree of annoyance, it seems, upon the disfavor into which all mention of laws, rules, and precepts has fallen. After declaring that historical dramas should conform to the essential facts of history and should avail themselves of art only in embellishing and adorning the principal theme, without disfiguring or altering it in any way, he continues:

> We do not dare even to indicate that this maxim of utility and convenience should be considered as a rule of art for fear that this word "rule" will cause a scandal in these days when, at the same time that great advances in enlightenment and progress in human understanding are being proclaimed, to mention "law" is annoying, to speak of "rules" is intolerable, and to refer to "precepts" is considered ridiculous. Since we are not romantic in the sense that the classicists consider the term, and since we are not classicists as the romanticists interpret the word, let us avoid disputes and party denominations; let us not run counter to those who insist upon maintaining that art can exist without rules; and, proclaiming the same eternal truth with different words, let us christen the rules and the precepts with the name we have indicated, calling them maxims of utility and convenience.[73]

Although the *Semanario Pintoresco*, in its first number, had avowed its intention to maintain strict neutrality in the conflict between classicists and romanticists, it almost immediately took a strong position, as we have seen, against so-called French romanticism—its attacks being directed, however, against the content rather than the form of the works of that school. In 1839 it declared itself satisfied with the agreement that had apparently been reached by the leaders of the classic and romantic schools in Spain with regard to the necessity for a liberalization of the rules, and noted also with satisfaction the friendly spirit that had prevailed during a series of discussions recently held in the Atheneum and the Lyceum on the relative merits of the two schools:

> By a singular coincidence debates have been held simultaneously during the last few days by our best writers and at different places over the interesting question of the classic and romantic schools, and we see with pleasure that, laying aside animosity and party spirit, all seem to be in accord in regard to the necessity for a rational broadening of certain forms which were advised, rather than given as precepts, by the great masters of poetic art. The interesting discussion held for four nights at the Atheneum, the opening of the professorships at the Lyceum, and finally, the series of articles on this subject published in the *Tiempo* of Cádiz, have brought to light the literary opinions of a select portion of our contemporary authors. In all these discussions and articles the participants and authors have not allowed themselves to be swayed by the prestige of authority, nor have they rebelled against reason in a desire to follow the impulse of fashion, but have considered the question seriously

and philosophically. The discourses pronounced in the Atheneum by Martínez de la Rosa, Alcalá Galiano, and others; those of Moreno, Escosura, and Espronceda in the Lyceum; and, finally, the excellent articles by Lista in the *Tiempo* of Cádiz, have in our opinion fulfilled their purpose completely and have made clear the uselessness of the barrier which ignorance or bad faith has tried to erect between the eminent writers of the two schools.[74]

The *Semanario* is still as insistent as ever upon the necessity for strict morality in all theatrical productions and attributes most of the opposition to the new movement to its failure to observe this basic principle:

Having agreed upon the justice of allowing greater freedom to flights of the imagination than that permitted by so-called rules which have been misunderstood or incorrectly applied, writers should have recognized, nevertheless, the necessity of giving prominence in every work to a sustained interest, a true coloring, and a moral or philosophical object or purpose. This question of morality, which has complicated that of liberty of literary forms, is the one thing that has made the so-called romantic banner odious to many people; but let it be understood that the false use many writers have made of it, especially the French, has nothing in common with this or that literary form; those writers, guided by more or less criminal impulses, have availed themselves of the literary form in vogue to spread their antisocial principles and, in so doing, have made odious that same literary freedom which seems so sublime and magnificent in Lope de Vega and Shakespeare.[75]

In support of the ideas it has just expressed, the *Semanario* reprints an article, entitled "What Is Called Romanticism Today," by Alberto Lista, that had appeared a short time before in the *Tiempo* of Cádiz. Lista begins his article with this assertion:

Nothing is more opposed to the spirit, sentiments, and manners of a monarchical and Christian society than what is now called romanticism, at least in so far as it concerns the theater. Modern drama is worthy of the times of primitive and barbarous Greece. It only describes physiological man, that is, man delivered over to the energy of his passions, with no restraint whatsoever of reason, justice, or religion. If he satisfies his love, his desire for vengeance, and his hatred, he is happy. If he encounters insurmountable obstacles to the realization of his criminal hopes, he takes refuge in suicide.[76]

He declares that, while he has never believed that the primary purpose of the theater should be the correction of manners, he does believe that it should be "an innocent diversion"; and inasmuch as it portrays man, it necessarily exercises a moral influence upon the spectators.[77] His quarrel with romanticism is particularly over its insistence upon discrediting the monarchy and the church:

> That determination to tarnish and vilify in the theater the splendor of the throne; especially that mania of presenting to the eyes of the spectators vices and crimes, true or invented, of which some ministers of religion have been guilty; that attempt to destroy all ideas of social order and of morality announce a calculated and widespread plan to revive in present-day Europe that hatred for kings, priests, and virtue, and that insanity which produced all the disasters of the French Revolution. The present age will not tolerate anarchy either in literature or in conversations; it has, therefore, taken refuge in the theater....[78]

But the vogue of this movement will pass and then it will be clearly seen that present-day romanticism, which is essentially "antimonarchical, antireligious, and antimoral," can never be accepted as an appropriate literary form by a people "who have been illuminated by the light of Christianity, who are intelligent and civilized, and who have become accustomed to entrusting their interests and their liberties to the protection of the throne."[79]

The most effective weapons against the new romanticism were probably satires published in various forms by writers who were fundamentally neo-classic, like Bretón de los Herreros and Eugenio de Tapia; and by eclectics who leaned toward classicism, like Santos López Pelegrín, who wrote under the pseudonym of Abenámar, and Mesonero Romanos. Eugenio de Tapia, who had written two neo-classic comedies, *The Stepmother* and *The Suspicious Spinster*, as early in 1832, and who composed *The Favorite Son or the Partiality of a Mother* and *A False Suitor and an Inexperienced Daughter*, both equally neo-classic, in 1839, published in the latter year his *Satirical Jests in Prose and Verse*,[80] in one of which he ridicules very effectively the extravagance of the romanticists and their fondness for ghosts, cemeteries, and dwarfs.

The most damaging of all the satires that heaped ridicule upon romanticism in Spain was entitled "Romanticism and Romantics" and was written in 1837 by Mesonero Romanos. The author himself, in a note placed at the end of the article when it was reprinted in 1862 in *Escenas Matritenses*, attributes the success of his satire particularly to its opportuneness and to his own boldness in publishing it at the very peak of popularity of the new school when the new sect of Hugolaters was in complete control of the republic of letters. The modest and philosophical comedies of Moratín, Gorostiza, and Bretón, he tells us, had been replaced by *The Troubadour, The Lovers of Teruel,* and *The Force of Fate;* "the precepts of Aristotle, Horace, Boileau, and Luzán had been buried; Shakespeare, Dante, and Calderón were the new poetic gods; and Victor Hugo was their high priest and prophet."[81] The author carried his daring to the extreme of reading his satire in the Lyceum of Madrid, which at that time was a meeting place for the leaders of the new movement as well as for its opponents. There, he says, it brought a smile to the lips even of those whom it censured; and although there were some individuals who accused him of directing his ridicule at the persons and writings of certain well-known romantic leaders, the genuine talent of the latter made them recognize not only the good intention of the author but also the correctness of his literary judgment. Some twenty-five years after the composition of his satire, Mesonero Romanos himself evaluates its effect upon the exaggerated form of romanticism in vogue at the time:

He believes that he contributed to the fixing of opinion in a middle ground between classical and romantic exaggerations; at least his satire coincided with the peak of the latter of these movements, and from that time romanticism yielded ground perceptibly to a point that was rational and admissible to men of conscience and of letters. Furthermore, his satire gave the signal for similar attacks in the theater and the press, which, undermining successively that ridiculous faction, finally put an end to it.[82]

Mesonero Romanos begins his satire with a discussion of the contradictory and varied opinions currently held about the nature of romanticism. No one seems to know exactly what it is or what it represents. This term, which is "so popular and so convenient that it is applied to persons as well as to things, to truths of science and to the illusions of fantasy, still lacks a precise definition."[83] Having come into possession of this pretended discovery, of this magic, indefinible, and fantastic talisman, the present generation has attempted to view everything through its seductive prism and, not content to limit it to literature and fine arts, has carried it to moral precepts, to historical events, and even to the sciences:

The bold writer who accuses society of being corrupt at the same time that he contributes to its further corruption with the immorality of his works; the politician who exaggerates all systems, distorts and contradicts them all, and attempts to combine feudalism and republicanism

in his doctrine; the historian who poetizes history; the poet who invents a
fantastic society and then complains that society does not recognize its
portrait; the artist who seeks to paint nature even more beautiful than
it is in its original; all of these manias, which must have existed in all
epochs and which doubtless in former times have passed as aberrations
of reason or weaknesses of the human race, are called "pure romanticism"
by the present age, which is more advanced and more perspicacious.[84]

The author claims that Victor Hugo, having as a youth spent some
years in Madrid, became familiar with Spanish romanticism in the
School for Noblemen's Sons, and then returned to Paris where, having taken out the customary inventor's patent and having provided
himself with material from Spain, he opened up shop, declaring himself to be "the Messiah of literature, who had come to free it from
the slavery of the rules." This new literary ideology, Mesonero
Romanos declares, was transmitted by poets to novelists, historians,
and politicians, and these, in turn, passed it along to the public;
and so, after traveling through all Europe, it finally made its way
in a perverted and exaggerated form back to Madrid. There this new
ideology, this virus, attacked the author's nephew, who first applied
his new acquisition to his own person, poetizing it by applying
romanticism to his attire, "because," he said, "the figure of a romantic
should be Gothic, ogival, pyramidal, and emblematic."[85] He soon
converted his person into a model of the Middle Ages, casting aside
all unnecessary apparel and adornments and limiting himself to
tight-fitting trousers that accentuated his muscular build, a short
frock coat buttoned up to his Adam's apple, a black handkerchief
carelessly tied around his neck, and an odd-shaped hat tilted over his
left brow. Having romanticized his person, he proceeded to roman-
ticize his ideas, his character, and his studies. Declining to follow
any of the careers his uncle proposed to him, he declared his
intention to become a poet, a profession that seemed in keeping
with his newly acquired temperament and which, according to him,
led directly to the temple of immortality.

Mesonero Romanos gives a description of the means by which
his nephew sought to prepare himself for his chosen career:

In search of sublime inspiration, and with the object of forming his
gloomy and sepulchral character, he frequented night and day cemeteries and anatomical schools; he entered into friendly relations with
gravediggers and physiologists; he learned the language of the horned
owl and the barn owl; he climbed sharp cliffs and lost himself in dense
woods; he investigated the ruins of monasteries and inns (which he took

for Gothic castles); he familiarized himself with the poisonous properties of plants and tested the blade of his knife on animals in order to watch their death throes. He exchanged books I had recommended to him, written by Cervantes, Solís, Quevedo, Saavedra, Moreto, Meléndez, and Moratín, for those of Hugo, Dumas, Balzac, Sand, and Soulié. He filled his head with all the charming fantasies of Lord Byron and the gloomy pictures of d'Arlincourt; he did not miss a single one of the theatrical monstrosities of Ducange or the fantastic dreams of Hoffman; and in periods when he felt less inclined to melancholy, he entertained himself with *Cranioscopy* by Doctor Gall and *Meditations* by Volney.[86]

Feeling that he was now qualified to embark upon his career, he scratched out a few dozen "fragments" in prose and finished some short stories in prosaic verse, all of which began with dots and ended with the word "Curses!"[87] His first serious project was the composition of a romantic drama, the title and contents of which Mesonero Romanos describes as follows:

SHE...!!! AND HE...!!!
Natural Romantic Drama

Emblematically Sublime, Anonymous, Synonymous,
Gloomy and Spasmodic;

Original, in Different Prose and Verse Forms,

In Six Acts and Fourteen Tableaux.

By....

Here there was a note that said: (When the public asks for the name of the author).

The Fourth and Fifth Centuries. — The scene is all Europe and the action lasts about a hundred years.

CHARACTERS

A wife, who represents all wives; a husband, who represents all husbands; a savage, who plays the role of lover; a duke; a tyrant; a youth; the Archduchess of Austria; a spy; a favorite; a hangman; an apothecary; the Quadruple Alliance; a night watchman; a choir of Carmelite nuns; a choir of Monks who attend dying persons; a man of the town; a town of men; a ghost who talks; another ghost who grabs; a messenger; a Jew; four gravediggers; musicians and dancers; a retinue of soldiers, witches, Gypsies, friars, and ordinary people.

The titles of the acts (because each bore its own title after the manner of a code) were, if I remember correctly, the following: 1. *A Crime.* — 2. *The Poison.*—3. *It Is Late.*—4. *The Pantheon.*—5. *She!*—6. *He!*; and the stage sets were the six that were required by all romantic dramas, that is: a dance hall; a forest; a chapel; a cave; a bedroom; and a cemetery.[88]

The rest of Mesonero Romanos' satire deals with his nephew's love affair with an equally romantic eighteen-year-old girl, which terminates abruptly when her parents discover a letter to her, in which he proposes that both die in order that they may be truly happy, saying that she must kill herself, and that, after her death, he will scatter flowers over her grave and then die himself so that they may be covered by the same stone. In order to prevent his nephew from indulging in further romantic excesses, his uncle sends him to the army. At the end of a year of military service, the youth returns to Madrid completely cured of his malady.

In addition to clever satires on romanticism, which appeared in *Nosotros* (1838-39), *El Correo Nacional* (1838-42), *El Porvenir* (1837), and in *Abenámar y el Estudiante* (1838-39), Abenámar (Santos López Pelegrín) published in the *Revista de Madrid* in 1840 a serious evaluation of the *comedia* and of neo-classic and romantic drama. The old Spanish theater, he says, is "the best and the worst in the world." He is far from recommending that the *cloak and sword* plays be revived "with their immoral and ridiculous duels, their veiled ladies, and their court mayors with bailiffs and lantern":[89]

It is necessary, although painful, when we turn our eyes to Calderón, to give him a look of admiration, accompanied by a smile of scorn; of scorn, yes, for nothing else would befit those aberrations of the intellect and those insults to reason, to manners, and to religion of which that poet was so prodigal, believing as he did that honor consisted in being in a constantly belligerent state like English cocks and in going around every corner looking for a fight over trifles. From this point of view, Calderón is an execrable and highly antisocial poet.[90]

Although he admires the structural simplicity of Moratín's comedies and believes that only in simple plots can the action be sufficiently unified and dramatic interest be maintained, he censures him and his school for carrying their desire for perfection to excess and their mania for philosophism to pedantry. "The three unities, ridiculous even in their name, became fashionable and rules were given for the composition of a comedy just as for cutting a waistcoat or preparing a dish of tomatoes and red pepper."[91] It is a pity, he declares, "that a man like Moratín should have enslaved his imagination by Gallicizing his intellect in such a manner." The only defect in Moratín's plays, he says, is that insistence upon the rules,

that voluntary abdication of the spirit, which forced him to enclose himself in such a narrow circle that, in order to emerge successfully from it, he had to avail himself of his great talent, of dialogues full of truth and beauty, and of that inimitable language which distinguishes him among all of our dramatic poets.[92]

Abenámar expresses even stronger opposition, however, to "that so-called modern school that has been smuggled into Spain from the other side of the Pyrenees," and aligns himself with the eclectics in advocating a middle course between classic narrowness and romantic license:

Between the exaggerations of this school and the rigid narrowness of Moratín, there is a middle ground that consists in giving free rein to the spirit, but at the same time in conforming to good sense, which excludes from the theater and from society everything that is monstrous, improbable, and patently immoral . . . , but which admits everything else.[93]

He accuses both schools of having committed literary crimes, the classic school the crime of intolerance and the romantic school that of immoral license. "The former," he says, "ties the wings of the imagination; the latter throws it into the air to fly with a bandage over its eyes." The solution is to take the theater where Calderón, Tirso, and Moreto left it and to dress it in modern clothes; or rather, "to link the old theater with the ideas, manners, and requirements of the present age," that is, "to write as those dramatists would write if they were alive today."[94]

Abenámar's solution, which was so popular at the time and which was accepted as a panacea for all theatrical ills, although couched in eloquent language, was too intangible to be of real service. Critics and writers at this time were, as we have seen, almost unanimous in their advocacy of a liberalization of classical rules; but they were coming to agree almost equally in recognizing the necessity for restraint. The unities of time and place were not to be discarded entirely, and, indeed, were to be observed in so far as was consistent with verisimilitude; but while there might still be grounds for dissension over interpretations of the rules, both classicists and former romanticists had united to oppose the new romanticism that had come from France. Since a return to the old romanticism of the Golden Age was recognized as inadvisable, impractical, and indeed impossible, nothing remained except to hold rather vaguely to the

spirit of romanticism in its opposition to unnecessarily rigid rules
and to reject almost everything in the new romanticism that had
seemed to hold so much promise only a few years before. In 1840,
Diego Coello y Quesada voices disillusionment over the results of
the movement and pessimism over the future of the theater:

> The theater is decaying by moments. The brilliant ray that once illum-
> inated Aeschylus and Euripides, Shakespeare and Calderón, Schiller and
> Corneille, is sending forth today its last reflections and perhaps will
> shortly be extinguished forever. Ten years ago a new day seemed to dawn
> for dramatic literature, a new and brilliant future; but that day has
> passed and hope for the future has disappeared.[95]

Romanticism, in so far as it pertained to the theater, was by its
very nature doomed to failure throughout Europe. Although a strict
interpretation of the theory of dramatic illusion is certainly un-
tenable, it must be conceded that any definition of drama should include the term verisimilitude or its equivalent; for it is inconceivable
that the theater should remove itself so far from reality as to have no
meaning or message for the spectators. Golden Age comedies themselves tended to, and usually did, reflect types and manners of their
period; and as types and manners changed drastically in the last part
of the eighteenth century and the first part of the nineteenth, these
comedies became progressively less acceptable to the public. It will
be remembered that Ramón de la Cruz's *sainetes* were popular with
the *vulgo* because that element of the population saw itself and its
life reflected in them. Even the heroic comedies of Comella and
Zavala y Zamora, in addition to their emphasis upon spectacle and
stage effects, purported to depict the life and manners of the strange
lands that served as scenes for the action. Spectators would surely
lose interest in a theater that always dealt with unusual happenings
or with characters that were extraordinary, antimoral, antisocial, and
antireligious. Romantic drama might serve to punctuate a dramatic
season, but it could not be counted on to fill a repertoire.

After the novelty of the new romanticism had worn off and the
first wave of enthusiasm had subsided, writers and critics alike
began, as we have seen, to take inventory of the situation. The partisans of the national school, who from force of habit or through a
rather vaguely understood feeling of patriotism had tenaciously
resisted all innovations, loudly asserting that classical precepts
"clipped the wings of genius" and longing for a return to the
freedom of literary expression that had characterized the Golden

Age, found now that they had been fighting for a cause they no longer really believed in; that when they had gotten what they wanted, they no longer wanted it. Upon sober thought they could not fail to realize that a return to the Golden Age in any material sense was impossible and, indeed, would be ridiculous. In their opposition to neo-classicism, these nationalists found they had enlisted in the ranks of an essentially foreign movement which represented, it is true, a renunciation of literary restraint and an enthronement of the imagination, but at the same time violated all Spanish concepts of morality and religion. We find, therefore, that these nationalists were soon making common cause with neo-classicists against what they called "bad romanticism" and "French romanticism." Their own differences were pushed into the background by this new enemy that seemed to threaten the very foundations of Spanish religious and social life. The terms *classicist* and *romanticist* having become distasteful to writers and critics alike, the name *eclectic* and the term *happy medium* were adopted by a generation that had grown weary of polemics to designate a new literary school in which everyone could do very much as he pleased. The elements of this new creed were predominantly classical and represented in many respects almost the antithesis of Golden Age drama.

1. *Diario de Avisos de Madrid*, February 6, 1828, p. 148.
2. *Correo Literario y Mercantil*, September 12, 1828, pp. 1-2.
3. Juan Eugenio Hartzenbusch, *Ensayos poéticos y artículos en prosa* (Madrid, 1843), p. 235.
4. *El Duende Satírico del Día*, March, 1828. (Reprinted in *Postfígaro*, Tomo I (Madrid, 1918).
5. *Ibid.*, p. 32.
6. Mesonero Romanos, "El Romanticismo y los Románticos," published in *Semanario Pintoresco*, September 17, 1837, II, 281-85. (Reprinted in *Escenas Matritenses*, 2a Serie [Madrid, 1862], pp. 115-33.)
7. Larra, *Obras Completas de Fígaro* (Paris, n.d.), II, 90-91.
8. *Ibid.*, p. 91.
9. Agustín Durán, *Discurso sobre el influjo que ha tenido la crítica moderna en la decadencia del teatro antiguo español, y sobre el modo con que debe ser consid-* erado para juzgar convenientemente de su mérito peculiar (Madrid, 1828). (Reprinted in *Memorias de la Academia Española*, II, 280-336.)
10. *Ibid.*, p. 280.
11. *Ibid.*, p. 298.
12. *Ibid.*, p. 321.
13. *Ibid.*, p. 282.
14. *Ibid.*, p. 285.
15. *Ibid.*
16. *Ibid.*, p. 319.
17. *Ibid.*, p. 287.
18. *Ibid.*
19. *Ibid.*, p. 288.
20. *Ibid.*, p. 291.
21. *Ibid.*, p. 316.
25. *Ibid.*, p. 296.
23. *Ibid.*
24. *Ibid.*, p. 294.
25. *Ibid.*, p. 296.
26. *Ibid.*, p. 305.
27. *Ibid.*
28. *Ibid.*, p. 307.
29. *Ibid.*, p. 311.

30. *Ibid.*, p. 313.
31. *Ibid.*, p. 315.
32. *Ibid.*, p. 318.
33. *Ibid.*
34. Agustín Durán, "Poesía Popular (Drama Novelesco), Lope de Vega." *Revista de Madrid*, 2ª Serie, Tomo II, 1839, pp. 62-75.
35. Agustín Durán, "Análisis crítica del drama de Tirso de Molina, intitulando *El Condenado por Desconfiado*," *Revista de Madrid*, 3ª Serie, Tomo II, 1841, p. 109.
36. *Ibid.*, p. 123.
37. *Ibid.*, p. 124.
38. *Ibid.*
39. E. Allison Peers, *A History of the Romantic Movement in Spain*, II, 15.
40. M. Le Gentil, *Les Revues littéraires de l'Espagne pendant la première moitié du xixe siècle* (Paris, 1909), XVII. See Allison Peers, *op. cit.*, I, 16.
41. This record of performances has been taken from Charlotte M. Lorenz, "Seventeenth Century Plays in Madrid from 1808-1816," *Hispanic Review*, VI (1938), 324-31; and from N. B. Adams, "Siglo de Oro Plays in Madrid, 1820-1850," *Hispanic Review*, IV (1936), 342-57.
42. *El Artista*, I, 48.
43. *Ibid.*, II, 34.
44. *Diario de Avisos de Madrid*, October 4, 1834, II, 426.
45. *El Artista*, II, 48.
46. *Ibid.*, I, 144.
47. *Ibid.*
48. *El Artista*, I, 153-54.
49. *El Artista*, I, 264.
50. Larra, "El trovador," *El Español*, March 5, 1836.
51. Larra, "Los amantes de Teruel," *El Español*, January 22, 1837.
52. *El Artista*, II, 34.
53. *Ibid.*
54. *Ibid.*, II, 47.
55. *Ibid.*
56. *Ibid.* The italics are mine.
57. *Ibid.*, II, 48.
58. *Ibid.*
59. *Ibid.*, II, 144.
60. *El Artista*, I, 216.
61. Mesonero Romanos, *Memorias de un Setentón* (Madrid, 1881). New edition (Madrid, 1926), VIII, 150.
62. *No me olvides*, June 25, 1837.
63. *Ibid.*

64. *Ibid.*, December 10, 1837.
65. Mesonero Romanos, *op. cit.*, VIII, 183-86.
66. J. de la R. (José de la Revilla), "Teatros," in *Semanario Pintoresco*, I (1836), 15-16.
67. "Muérete y verás!" *Semanario Pintoresco*, II (May 7, 1837), 141.
68. *Ibid.*
69. *Ibid.*
70. *Ibid.*
71. *Ibid.*, pp. 165-66.
72. *Ibid.*, p. 166.
73. S. el E., "Bárbara Blomberg," *Semanario Pintoresco*, II (December 10, 1837), 387-88.
74. *Semanario Pintoresco*, 1839, 2ª Serie, I, 102-3.
75. *Ibid.*, p. 103.
76. Lista, "De lo que hoy se llama el Romanticismo," *Semanario Pintoresco*, 2ª Serie, I (1839), 103.
77. *Ibid.*, p. 104.
78. *Ibid.*, p. 103.
79. *Ibid.*
80. Eugenio de Tapia, *Juguetes satíricos en prosa y verso* (Madrid, 1839), pp. 14-15.
81. Mesonero Romanos, "El Romanticismo y los Románticos," *Semanario Pintoresco*, September 17, 1837, II, 281-85. (Reprinted in *Escenas Matritenses*, 2ª Serie [Madrid, 1862].) My references are to a new edition of the *Escenas*, published in *Obras de D. Ramón de Mesonero Romanos* (Madrid, 1925), pp. 113-31.
82. *Ibid.*
83. *Ibid.*, p. 113.
84. *Ibid.*, pp. 114-15.
85. *Ibid.*, p. 116.
86. *Ibid.*, p. 118.
87. *Ibid.*, p. 119.
88. *Ibid.*, pp. 121-22.
89. Abenámar (Santos López Pelegrín), "Teatro," *Revista de Madrid*, 2ª Serie, III, 157-58.
90. *Ibid.*, p. 161.
91. *Ibid.*, p. 159.
92. *Ibid.*
93. *Ibid.*, p. 160.
94. *Ibid.*
95. Diego Coello y Quesada, "Consideraciones generales sobre el teatro y el influjo en él ejercido por el romanticismo," *Semanario Pintoresco*, 2ª Serie, II (1840), 198.

XVIII

Conclusion

THE NEO-CLASSIC MOVEMENT in Spain can be understood only by considering its dual nature. In the first place, it was a reaction against the bad taste and extravagance of the *comedia*. This is the negative side. The positive side is represented by an attempt to replace this theater with another based on good taste and subjected to the restraining influence of the classic rules, which were considered as the product of natural laws and not of the ingenuity of man. If the neo-classicists were too rigid in their application of these rules and too dogmatic in their attitude, their guilt finds a measure of palliation in the fact that only by drastic methods can a tradition of such long standing be uprooted. Revolutions are not characterized by mildness. And even though the neo-classicists might have preferred to proceed with greater moderation, such a course was rendered impossible by the virulence of the attack to which they were subjected by the partisans of the national school. Violence was met with violence, and the dispute degenerated into a series of bitter polemics. In such an atmosphere artistic creation and fair evaluation were all but impossible.

The neo-classic movement was forced to restrict its activity for half a century to the realm of theory. Much work of a purely educational nature was necessary before any drama of the new school could hope to gain recognition. Weeds had to be removed and the soil tilled before any seed could be planted. Added to this difficulty was the unquestionable lack of dramatic genius on the part of those who attempted to give a practical demonstration of the rules.

When, after almost a century, neo-classicists seemed on the point of making a positive contribution to the theater, a political upheaval engulfed the very men who might have carried out this work. In 1833 the author of an article in the *Boletín de Comercio,* who was probably Gil y Zárate, recognizes the lack of positive achievement on the part of neo-classicists, but adds: "The apprenticeship of this new system was long, and when we were finally reaching the time to harvest the fruit of so much earnest effort and were beginning to shine in the field of classic literature, the French invasion came to interrupt the course of this new era of glory."[1] Although "imagination has again mounted the throne," and although the majority of Spain's literary men will enlist in the ranks of the partisans of the new school "because its freedom is more in keeping with our temperament," the author does not believe that neo-classicists will yield without a struggle. "Those who held the scepter so long are defending it with tenacity and, although it is now somewhat broken, they certainly will not yield it until an honorable capitulation has been effected."[2]

To understand the short duration of the romantic movement in Spain in its extreme form, it is necessary to take into account not only the violent opposition which its antisocial and antimoral tendencies aroused in public and critics alike, but also the tenacity with which neo-classicists clung to their principles and constantly resisted the inroads of this new delirium just as in the previous century they had waged a militant campaign against the extravagances of the *comedia* and the works of the Calderonian decadents, and then against the monstrosities of the school of Comella and against French melodrama. The impression is too often left by critics that, in the struggle between romantics and neo-classicists, the former emerged victorious and the latter could offer little resistance. It was, however, "an honorable capitulation."

It must not be inferred from the above statements that the immediate result of the compromise effected between neo-classicism and romanticism was a new era of prosperity for the Spanish theater. The public still had to be reckoned with. That same public which in Lope's day refused to be satisfied "unless they saw on the stage in two hours everything from Genesis to the final Judgment";[3] that same public that took such delight in *autos sacramentales* and later in the monstrosities of Comella, Zavala y Zamora, and their crowd; that public which had never lost its enthusiasm for the comedies of magic and flocked to see the *Magician of Salerno, Pedro Bayalarde* in the time of Moratín, later receiving with even greater enthusiasm Grimaldi's *The Goat's Foot;* that public which in the early 1830's applauded such melodramas as *The Orphan Girl of Brussels* and *Thirty Years or the Life of a Gambler;* that public had been little changed by the ebb and flow of literary currents and still preferred spectacular or unliterary entertainment.

In 1839, at the peak of the supposed triumph of the romantic movement, Ventura de la Vega expresses his keen disappointment at the reception accorded to Eugenio de Ochoa's *Uncertainty and Love.* The public, he says, which refused to attend the first perform-ance of an original drama by a new author, while it constantly com-plained of the mass of translations from Scribe that swamped the Spanish theater, "flocked eagerly two days later to watch a juggler throw balls into the air with one hand and catch them with the other."[4]

We find critics returning in 1841 to the old complaint that the public is incapable of appreciating artistic creations and rejecting the idea that the decline of the Spanish theater is attributable to the scarcity of dramatic talent. In that year José de la Revilla writes in the *Semanario Pintoresco:*

> There have not been lacking those who have attributed the decline in attendance at the theater to the scarcity of authors. But it is most strange that precisely at the time when an increased number of original dramas of no slight merit have appeared on the stage, at that very time, it is shame-ful to say, ... there have been long periods when only a single theater has remained open in the capital of Spain! And bear in mind that we are not in the times of the Comellas and their crowd, ravenous patchers of insipid farces. Our present dramatic poets, to borrow an expression from the celebrated Moratín, are worth more when they rave than the above writers when they attempt to write rationally. The names of Bretón, Gil y Zárate, Hartzenbusch, Gutiérrez, Rubí, and many others, some of whom, subservient to a new school, left the path of good taste to return to it later with greater splendor, form one of the brilliant pages of our modern literature. ... Nevertheless, the theater has been and is deserted.[5]

This apathy of the public toward the theater, he says, cannot be attributed to a lack of original plays or competent actors; nor can it be attributed to a lack of variety, for "the same play is rarely per-formed more than three times in one year." Neither are the empty theaters due to poverty in all classes of society, for "if we turn our eyes to the bull ring and to the olympic circus and gymnastic per-formances that are given in the theaters themselves, we shall find that people of all classes attend these spectacles in great numbers."[6]

When a similar decline in attendance at the theaters occurred at the turn of the century, critics found an easier and much more con-venient explanation. It was only necessary at that time to lay upon the shoulders of neo-classic preceptists the blame for all the ills that beset the theater. The recurrence of the same situation after the neo-classicists had been silenced and when there was no governmental intervention of any kind either in the selection of plays or in the management of the theaters makes one wonder whether there may not have been some slight injustice in attributing the earlier condition entirely to the activities of Moratín and his school.

A certain liberalism in the application of the rules found champions, as we have seen, even among many of the earliest neo-classic preceptists and had been advocated to varying degrees by Javier de Burgos, Mesonero Romanos, Gil y Zárate, and Bretón de los Herreros. The theater was no longer regarded as a school of manners in which a moral lesson must be driven home in the speeches of some mouthpiece of the author. Any lesson a play might contain must be taught by a practical demonstration which proceeded naturally from the action.

Hartzenbusch, who certainly was not prejudiced in favor of neo-classicism, recognized the necessity of some restraining principles, and even conceded that masterpieces might be written in accordance with the unities.

If it is convenient, if it is often necessary to deviate from the three unities of action, place, and time, will it be useful, will it be necessary to do so always? Shall the infraction of the old rule be converted into a precept, so that it will be considered a literary crime to write in accordance with the revoked law? By no means. With the classic system and with the opposing system, writers have produced works of indisputable beauty, which will always be the object of admiration for all those who love literature. In *Phèdre*, in *Zaïre*, in Alfieri's *Orestes*, in *Cayo-Greco*, in *Oedipus*, in *The Hypocrite*, in *The Consent of Young Maidens*, in *Marcela*, no one misses anything; the narrowness of the rules is unnoticed; nothing is violent there; everything is natural, animated, and beautiful. It seems that if their authors had tried to leave the classic limits, their works would have lost a great part of their merit.[7]

This statement by Hartzenbusch is but another evidence of the spirit of eclecticism which followed the rise and almost immediate decline of romanticism. This movement did not triumph—it came; it hastened the liberalization of overrigid classic rules and then yielded before those very influences which it had so vigorously attacked.

In the article already mentioned, which was published as early as 1833 in the *Boletín de Comercio*, it was recognized that Spanish literature, which in the Golden Age was so highly imaginative, would have maintained its prestige

... if this quality alone had sufficed to establish it upon a solid and permanent foundation; but the soil upon which imagination builds is variable and will sustain nothing unless taste consolidates it. Spain became lacking in taste and this quality which she disdained became the patrimony of another nation that came behind her along the road of knowledge, and which, with fewer natural advantages, succeeded not only in passing her, but in sinking her into oblivion and even in making what was once the admiration of the world be held in scorn.[8]

With the plays of Bretón de los Herreros and *The Man of the World,* by Ventura de la Vega, neo-classicism as a literary movement may be said to have come to an end, although the so-called *high comedy* and modern comedies of manners have far more neo-classic than romantic or Golden Age ingredients. Times have changed and dramatists have concerned themselves with broad social problems rather than with individual eccentricities, but the handling is in general the same. The themes are taken from contemporary society and, whether in prose or in verse, these plays seek to approach the natural speech of everyday life. The strained metaphors and inflated language of the school of Calderón are conspicuously absent. Gone also are the *graciosos* and the eloquent descriptions of scenery which so aroused the ire of neo-classicists. All unnecessary complication of intrigue is avoided. The moral is unmistakable, and the unities, although not rigidly observed, are not wantonly violated. One has the feeling that such plays as *Materialism, The Snowball,* and *Honest Man,* by Tamayo y Baus, and *Consuelo* and *The Percentage,* by López de Ayala, would not only have met the approval of neo-classic critics of the age of Moratín, but would even have aroused their enthusiasm, although *Consuelo* might have been classed as a sentimental comedy, and as such might have precipitated another controversy over the mixing of the genres.

In 1871, long after neo-classicism and romanticism had taken their places in history and no longer existed as literary movements, at least one eminent critic credits the former with the subsequent regularity and moderation that prevailed in the theater. In an answer to a discourse pronounced by Manuel Silvela upon his entrance into the Royal Academy on "The Influence Exercised by the Classic School upon the Spanish Language and Theater," Cánovas del Castillo supports this critic in his contention that neo-classicists were not responsible for the decline of the Spanish theater in the eighteenth century and affirms that contemporary comedy and drama owe their form to the neo-classic school:

What has been criticized most in Moratín has been perhaps the severity of the rules upon which he based his dramatic system; nevertheless, it is a fact that after the critical period of romanticism had passed, most of those rules returned to control the disposition of comedies of manners, which were his almost exclusive favorites. It can be affirmed without hesitation that those comedies which are esteemed today differ little from the regular and moderate form introduced by Moratín. The modern chivalrous drama, the last offspring of our old theater, which was born in the heat of romanticism, has always used greater liberty because of its nature; but not even this type of drama makes a show of systematic license. The reform that Moratín carried out in the national theater, therefore, has not been sterile or transitory.[9]

In 1886 representative plays by the Duke of Rivas, García Gutiérrez, Zorilla, Ventura de la Vega, Narciso Serra, Hartzenbusch, Martínez de la Rosa, Rodriguez Rubí, Bretón de los Herreros, Gil y Zárate, Nuñez de Arce, López de Ayala, and José Echegaray were published in a work entitled *Contemporary Dramatic Authors, and Jewels of the Spanish Theater of the Nineteenth Century.* With the exception of *Don Alvaro, or the Force of Fate* by the Duke of Rivas and *The Lovers of Teruel* by Hartzenbusch all the plays selected were fairly regular in form and style and showed a much closer affiliation with neo-classicism than with the Spanish *comedia* or with French romanticism.

When he was chosen to write the "General Prologue" to this collection Cánovas del Castillo again gave credit to Moratín and his school for their regularizing influence on Spanish drama:

To the purified taste, moreover, of that excellent comic poet, and to the reasonable severity of modern criticism, our contemporary comedies, apart from the advantages mentioned above, owe the fact that they have, if not as spontaneous and rich, at least less bombastic, impertinent, and gongoristic versification than most of those of the seventeenth century.

Everyone knows, also, that the new dramas are much less irregular than the old ones in their action and changes of scene because of the influence of Moratín and the preceptists of his school, who educated most of the contemporary authors.[10]

1. *Boletín de Comercio,* February 8, 1833.
2. *Ibid.*
3. Lope de Vega, *Arte nuevo de hacer comedias.*
4. *El Artista,* 1839, I, 275-76.
5. José de la Revilla, "Revista teatral," *Semanario Pintoresco,* 1841, pp. 2-4.
6. *Ibid.*
7. Juan Eugenio Hartzenbusch, "Discurso sobre las unidades dramáticas,"

Panorama, 1839, segunda época, I, 229.
8. *Boletín de Comercio,* February 8, 1833.
9. Antonio Cánovas del Castillo, "Contestación al discurso anterior," *Memorias de la Academia Española,* 1871, III, 339.
10. Cánovas del Castillo, "Prólogo General," *Autores Dramáticos Contemporáneos* (Madrid, 1886), I, liii. (Reprinted in *Arte y Letras* [Madrid, 1887], pp. 228-29.)

Index of Plays

General Index